PRAISE FOR
EDWARD HUMES
AND
MEAN JUSTICE

"Fascinating reading. . . . *Mean Justice* unfolds like a good mystery, with gripping detail, surprising, not to say extraordinary revelation, superb background, a lucid style and solid, commanding conclusions."
—*Rocky Mountain News*

"The story is told like a movie. . . . Humes' nonfiction account reads like many of the courtroom novels so popular now—except Pat Dunn is real, a victim and in prison."
—*New York Daily News*

"Gripping. . . . We should read this book and weep for all who have lost their liberty or even their life because of a prosecutor who wanted to win too badly."
—*Christian Science Monitor*

"In *Mean Justice*, Humes describes in jolting detail how a society obsessed with punishing criminals has provided almost unlimited p......

......Press

MISSISSIPPI MUD

"A story almost too unbelievable to be true. But it is. . . . Terrific."

—Ann Rule

"Reminiscent of Truman Capote's *In Cold Blood.* . . . Read[s] as smoothly as a finely crafted suspense novel."

—*Chicago Tribune*

"*Mississippi Mud* reads like a well-constructed mystery novel, and Edward Humes' lucid and unadorned prose admirably suits this complex story of venality and betrayal."

—*New York Times Book Review*

NO MATTER HOW LOUD I SHOUT

"Passionate. . . . A sad, maddening, brilliant book."
—*Washington Post*

"A finely etched, powerfully upsetting portrait."
—*The New York Times*

"The book reads like a pilot for a Michael Crichton TV series. . . . Stories careen by in an *ER*-style blur but still manage to touch a nerve. . . . Humes has produced a thoughtful, nuanced work, set apart from the flood of wonkish policy books by his often beautiful prose."
—*Washington Monthly*

ALSO BY EDWARD HUMES

No Matter How Loud I Shout

Mississippi Mud

Buried Secrets

Murderer with a Badge

MEAN JUSTICE
★★★★★★★★★★★★★★★
EDWARD HUMES

POCKET STAR BOOKS
New York   London   Toronto   Sydney   Tokyo   Singapore

A Pocket Star Book published by
POCKET BOOKS, a division of Simon & Schuster Inc.
1230 Avenue of the Americas, New York, NY 10020

Copyright © 1999 by Edward Humes

Originally published in hardcover in 1999 by
Simon & Schuster Inc.

All rights reserved, including the right to reproduce
this book or portions thereof in any form whatsoever.
For information address Simon & Schuster Inc.,
1230 Avenue of the Americas, New York, NY 10020

ISBN: 0-671-03427-8

First Pocket Books printing October 1999

10 9 8 7 6 5 4 3 2 1

POCKET STAR BOOKS and colophon are registered trademarks
of Simon & Schuster Inc.

Front cover photo © Benjamin Shearn/FPG International/PNI

Printed in the U.S.A.

QB/

PREFACE

This book owes its origin to an off-hand remark made in 1994 by private investigator Laura Lawhon, whom I had come to know both professionally and socially: She suggested I might be interested in writing about the experiences of a client of hers recently convicted of murder in Kern County, California. I am usually skeptical of such suggestions, and Laura's was no exception; my experience as a newspaper reporter and author writing about the justice system taught me that claims of innocence from convicted criminals are often made, seldom proved, and usually refuted. But four boxes of documents and many trips to California's Great Central Valley later, I found I had discovered a tale worth telling about the *People of Kern County vs. Patrick O'Dale Dunn*. And I had found a much larger issue to ponder as well: how a town's—and, indeed, an entire nation's—fear of crime and desire to be safe has made the conviction of innocent men and women startlingly common.

Many individuals aided in the research and writing of *Mean Justice*. I wish in particular to thank Tamara Koehler, formerly of the *Bakersfield Californian*, for her invaluable assistance, generosity and insights, and Richard Beene, executive editor of the *Californian*, for his hospitality in making the considerable historical resources of his newspaper available. Also generous in their sharing of time and information were Stanley Simrin, H. A. Sala, Susan Penninger, Jim Fahey, Offord Rollins III, Offord Rollins IV, Denver Dunn, Pamela Kniffen, Eric Banducci, Jeff Niccoli, Vernon "Dusty" Kline, Kate Rosenlieb, Marie Gates, David Goldberg, Gary Pohlson, Georgia Herald, Jerry Mitchell, Rex Martin, Jennifer Dunn, the excellent staff of the Kern County Superior Court Clerk's criminal section and Pat Dunn. As always, my literary agent, Susan Ginsburg, and my editor, Laurie Bernstein, were unflagging in their support and assistance. And, as always, my wife, Donna, proved to be my best editor, best writing coach and best friend.

If little faults, proceeding on distemper,
Shall not be wink'd at, how shall we stretch
   our eye
When capital crimes, chew'd, swallow'd and
   digested,
Appear before us?
                    —WILLIAM SHAKESPEARE, *HENRY V*

The function of the prosecutor under the
Federal Constitution is not to tack as many
skins of victims as possible to the wall. His
function is to vindicate the right of people as
expressed in the laws and give those accused
of crime a fair trial.
                    —JUSTICE WILLIAM O. DOUGLAS

Innocent until proven guilty? Talk about legal
fiction.
                    —LAURA LAWHON,
                    PRIVATE INVESTIGATOR

MEAN
JUSTICE

BEGINNINGS AND ENDINGS

JULY 1, 1992

He postponed calling the sheriff for hours, seizing on any interruption that would let him avoid the moment he dreaded most. He paced. He drank beer. He called his son for advice. He drank more beer. He drove past the dusty corners of East Bakersfield, staring at pedestrians as they braved the glare and spongy asphalt of summer. He returned home and tidied the house, startled by every unexpected creak or rustle. And when a prospective tenant for the shopping plaza that he and his wife owned stopped by unexpectedly to discuss plans for a new pizza parlor, he welcomed the man into his home, spoke at length about the virtues of his College Center strip mall, and then even drove the visitor out to squint approvingly at his other properties in the area. Burned a good ninety minutes that way.

He just did not behave like a man worried about his missing wife, the prosecutor would later say. No way. He took that man out to the mall, and he acted like he hadn't a care in the world. He never once mentioned his wife. Not once.

Finally, late in the afternoon, he found himself alone again in the silent, empty house, out of excuses, out of hope. He picked up the phone and sighed, a pleasant, beefy man in his late fifties with blondish gray hair and pale blue eyes that puffed and drooped like a hound dog's. The hands holding the phone were rough and chapped, though he had given up physical labor years ago.

"Sheriff's department," a woman's voice answered on the third ring. "How can I help you?"

"Hi, sheriff's department," he answered, his tone forced and bright. Though he was Californian born and raised, he spoke in the flat midwestern accent of his Oklahoma forebears, in a deep, rumbling voice that slipped often and easily into a nervous chuckle. "Who am I speaking with? This is Pat Dunn."

"Valley," the dispatcher said.

"Valley? Like in San Joaquin?"

"Yeah," the woman answered warily.

"Oh, that's a neat name."

"Thank you," the dispatcher said, laughing obligingly.[1]

Listen to the tape of that call, the prosecutor would say. *He's laughing, joking. Do you laugh and joke because the woman you supposedly love has disappeared? Or because you think you just got away with murder?*

The dispatcher's name was Valentina Braddick, though she preferred Valley. Each day, she took dozens of calls from angry people, sad people, panicked, confused and distraught people. Pleasantries, much less compliments, were in short supply; Pat had immediately gotten on her good side. "Okay, Pat," Valley Braddick said. "What can I do for you?"

He took a deep breath, sounding unsure, groping for words. "Well, my wife went walking yesterday afternoon or evening, and, uh, she's fifty-six years old and, uh, she took the big black dog with her. And she didn't come home."

"Mmm-hmm," Valley murmured. It was one of several small sounds she habitually made, her way of prodding callers along without actually interrupting them.

The caller cleared his throat and continued. He and his wife normally went to bed early in the evening, he explained, often by seven o'clock. And most times Sandy got up by three in the morning to go walking. She'd bring one or two of their dogs along. Been doing it for years now, always at three or four in the morning, before the desert heat could blast the city into submission. She insisted it was the safest time to walk, even though she plowed through some of Bakersfield's worst neighborhoods.

But, last night, he had awakened with a start a little before ten to find Sandy and their big black Labrador gone—five, six hours before her usual walking time. He said he looked around the house, growing more and more uneasy at her absence. He and Sandy were creatures of habit, he said, and he knew this wasn't right; she would never go walking at this hour. Still, he decided to drive her usual route. He searched East Bakersfield until midnight—and found no sign of his wife anywhere. When he got back home, though, he found the Labrador in the yard where he belonged and Sandy's keys on the kitchen counter. He called out, he searched the house, but it was silent and dark: no Sandy, no note, nothing. He said he had been alternately waiting and searching their part of town ever since. Finally, though, he convinced himself to call the sheriff's department for help.[2]

He waited eighteen hours to report his wife missing. Eighteen hours. Is that what a husband who fears for his wife's safety would do? Is that what you'd do?

"She took some cash and, uh, she's gone," he finished. "I don't know where she is."

So, this was a routine missing-persons report, Valley thought to herself. Nothing she hadn't heard a hundred times before. Husbands and wives took off all the time without a word to their spouses. Nothing the sheriff's department could do—or would do—about it, unless there was something unusual about the case, some suggestion of endangerment or foul play.

"Okay," she said, another prod for the caller to continue.

"It's been less than twenty-four hours, but I'm—I'm worried," he said. Then he switched gears and volunteered something else. "Her mother died of Alzheimer's disease."

This got Valley's attention. A report that someone's wife grabbed cash and took a powder was not news at the sheriff's department, but a missing woman with mental problems was an entirely different matter. "Did your wife have Alzheimer's disease?" she asked.

Although it did not strike Valley as unusual at the time, his answer, like so many other parts of this conversation, would later seem ambiguous and odd to those scrutinizing his every word and action. He said, "Well, I don't know that. I'm not a doctor. I just know she forgets things." He said the problem was infrequent, slipping in and out of sight, and he gave one example: His wife might feed the dogs three times in a single evening, forgetting that she had done so each time.

"Yeah, she does have memory problems," the dispatcher agreed.[3]

The people who knew her best never saw any evidence of a failing memory in Alexandra Dunn. Only the defendant claimed she had Alzheimer's disease. And I submit to you that's nothing more than his cover story.

As they talked, the dispatcher occasionally had to place him on hold to attend to other calls and he was twice disconnected, forcing him to call back but giving him ample opportunity to gripe and chuckle about modern technology. Finally, Valley told him the sheriff's department would indeed log a formal missing-persons report on Sandy. Because of the memory problems he described, Sandy would be listed as a "dependent adult," which meant that, if the police found her, they would pick her up whether she wanted to come home or not. Valley then asked for Sandy's description—her looks, her clothing, her vital statistics. She also asked for the name of Sandy's dentist. Valley did not explain the need for this particular bit of information, so as not to distress her caller. She knew what he did not, that dental records can be used to identify the missing, but only when they turn up dead.

Later, when she asked for his full name, he sounded relieved not to be talking about his wife as he answered, "Patrick O. Dunn, 'O' for 'Outstanding.'" It was said in a self-deprecating, sarcastic way, and he and Valley laughed. Others, though, would not be amused. They would call his humor unseemly, as they would his response to the dispatcher's next query about his race. He joked: "How 'bout old and fat?"[4]

There's no other way to say it. He was flirting. It's right there on the tape. It simply is not the voice of a man desperate to find his wife.

Valley entered the information into the Kern County Sheriff's computer system, then told her caller to get a pencil and paper and to write down the case number, KC92-14851, so he could call back and have it canceled should his wife return home.

"I got it," he said. His voice, for the first time in their conversation, sounded weary and defeated.

After some words of encouragement and a suggestion that he check the hospitals and the jails in case Sandy had an accident or got arrested, Valley said good-bye and went on to her next call. He hung up and stared at the telephone for a long time, as if waiting to see what would happen next. Time passed—minutes, hours, he couldn't be sure anymore. The ice in his tall glass of whiskey made soft cracking sounds as it slowly melted. Outside, the relentless desert sun of Bakersfield's summer shriveled the lawn and made the air shimmer outside his kitchen window, but the man who reported his wife missing that day would later remember feeling colder than he had ever felt in his life.

When he made that call, I assure you of one thing: Alexandra Dunn was already dead. And he knew it. Because he killed her.

EIGHT MONTHS LATER: MARCH 24, 1993

The lawyer wept as he drove south on Highway 99, great heaving sobs that left the wheel unsteady in his hands. He struggled to keep his charcoal Mercedes between the lines and on the asphalt, but the tears occasionally blinded him. Mercifully, the highway was ruler-straight here, not a curve for miles, the rows of crops and irrigation pipes flashing by in a seventy-mile-per-hour blur. The Kern

County courthouse parking lot was twenty-five miles behind him now, the low sprawl of Bakersfield just a small blur in the rearview mirror, and still he couldn't stop crying. The jury's verdict kept drowning out everything else in his head, a vicious chant, a sucker punch.

Guilty. Guilty. Guilty.

The lawyer tugged on his tie, blinking hard. The black-leather interior of the car was littered with papers, transcripts, yellow legal pads. On top, mocking him now, were the notes he had scrawled for his closing argument. As he had delivered those words, he had told himself the stony looks and crossed arms in the jury box meant nothing—that's how sure he had been of this one. "Please do the right thing," he had said just before sitting down at the defense table for the last time, putting it in their twelve pairs of hands. "This guy's not guilty. Do the right thing." He had harbored no doubts they would heed his plea. The case was such a winner, he and his partner and one of their investigators literally had the champagne on ice. He had never done that before. Never. Nor had he ever said to a client, "Don't worry. There's no way they'll convict." Until this case.

And no matter what else happened in a case, he never, ever told *himself* that a client accused of murder was innocent. Not guilty, yes. Reasonable doubt, yes. In all the many other cases he had tried, he had always talked the good lawyer talk, even to himself, focusing on the paucity of the evidence, the holes in the testimony—the stuff of doubt and acquittal. Otherwise, you couldn't do the job; it would drive you crazy. Every good defense lawyer knows it. Only this time, in Bakersfield, far from his home turf and his comfortable practice and the judges he knew by first name, he had dared to say it—and, more to the point, to believe it: "My client is an innocent man. I know it. He is being framed for a murder he did not commit." After twenty-six years in the courtroom, with dozens of capital cases under his belt, he had never before allowed himself the luxury to believe wholeheartedly in a client's absolute innocence. He had always considered it irrelevant. Until now.

Guilty. Guilty. Guilty.

Laura Lawhon had watched the lawyer stagger to his car and drive off, shaking her head, feeling just as devastated as he did, but willing herself to stay strong, to meet the eyes of the gloating cops and jurors who had gathered together like conspirators after the trial. The defense lawyer could drive off and lick his wounds; Laura, the private investigator, had to stay on and continue with the case, to try to turn things around, to hunt down some forgotten clue that might pry the case back open and offer another chance to prove the client innocent. The odds of this were not good.

It wasn't really the lawyer's fault, Laura knew, yet she couldn't help feeling as if something had been missed, some words left unuttered, some proof left unoffered— some path she, as an investigator, had not taken. They were an out-of-town defense team new to Kern County and its ways, with only three months to prepare for trial. They had tried to take a crash course on the place—or so they had believed. Laura had carefully researched the local judges and they managed to get their case before a former public defender, figuring that he, at least, would give them a fair shake in a county known for its hanging jurists and merciless prosecutors. This judge, Laura learned, had distinguished himself during a dark episode in Bakersfield's recent past that many called the Witch

Hunt. Hysteria had swept the community then after the "discovery" of massive rings of child molesters, some of them suspected of devil worship and human sacrifice. The wave of arrests that followed sparked a national panic about satanic child abuse and spawned a torrent of similar prosecutions. That such a baneful national phenomenon began not in sin-addled Los Angeles, but right here in California's heartland, became a lasting source of shame for a community that considered itself a shrine to family values—the "All-America City," as Bakersfield billed itself. Much of the evidence turned out to be bogus, but dozens of people went to prison anyway, some with sentences of hundreds of years, as the authorities sought to purge the evil—and stepped over the line from prosecution to persecution. The Witch Hunt became so pervasive that innocent mothers and fathers grew afraid to discipline or touch their own children for fear they, too, would be accused. But Laura had learned that one judge in Kern County had stood up to the hysteria, accusing the sheriff and the district attorney of brainwashing children and breaking the law, and he insisted on reuniting families that the authorities had torn asunder. The judge was pilloried at the time, but now, six years later, as innocents falsely imprisoned during those terrible years were set free, he seemed a visionary. When Laura told the defense lawyer about him, the attorney excitedly announced, "This is the judge we want."

To their dismay, however, this same judge seemed to take every opportunity to rule against Laura's client. He skewered the defense regularly and vigorously, seeming to take offense at the slightest suggestion, real or imagined, that the big-city, out-of-town lawyers considered him a bumpkin. His rulings had greatly bolstered what on paper appeared to be a very shaky prosecution case.

Yet, even with a hostile judge and adverse rulings, Laura had given the defense attorney all the ammunition he should have needed to take apart the prosecutor's case and reveal it as a passel of unproved suspicions, outright lies and insinuations lacking evidence to back them up. So what if the defendant hadn't acted like the Hallmark greeting-card version of a devoted, grieving husband? So what if he laughed a little when he called the sheriff's department? So what if he waited a while before calling the cops? Maybe he kept hoping against hope she would return to him. Maybe he wanted to spare her the embarrassment of telling all her friends she was losing it. So what? Laura had fought such insinuations with hard evidence and testimony that, she felt certain, demonstrated her client's innocence. She had even marched into court with the brother of the state's star witness in tow, who explained how the key testimony in the prosecution's case had been concocted. What more could a jury ask for? The DA had been left reeling, Laura thought, and the defense lawyer, exhilarated.

The outcome seemed so obvious that, toward the end, the foreman of the jury, a country-and-western musician with long dark hair and an oversized wooden cross around his neck, had started flashing thumbs-up signs and small, sly grins at the defendant's family and the defense team when he'd walk by in the hall. It was totally improper, of course, but what were they supposed to do? Complain? God, Laura thought now, if only they had.

Guilty. Guilty. Guilty.

It was a setup, a cruel joke. They had come to Bakersfield and figured it would be like trying a case anywhere else, cocky big-city lawyers slumming in a small town. Instead, they had stumbled into the front lines of the nation's "war on crime," a buzz saw of a justice system manned by veteran, accomplished career prosecutors, juries that were inclined to convict more often than most, and a startling record of imprisoning more people per capita than most any other place in the country. Only later did Laura find out that, inside the jury room, the jury foreman with the smile and the thumbs-up gestures had been leading the charge to convict. It seemed unbelievable: A second lawyer on the defense team, a veteran former prosecutor who knew a good case when he saw one, had to excuse himself to throw up after the verdict was read. The head of the private investigation firm that employed Laura had sat slack-jawed in disbelief when the clerk unfolded the scrap of paper and read the verdict. Only Laura had seen hints of things to come. Before deliberations began, her boss had offered her double or nothing on her fee if the client was found innocent, but she had said no, she'd just take her hours, win or lose, and leave it at that. Somehow, Laura had known. She had looked at the jurors and had seen what everyone else on the defense team had missed, just as she had sensed something dark and troubling below the surface of this case—and this town—from the very beginning. She had even tried to warn the others, to tell them about some of the other cases she had come across here, convictions that seemed to materialize out of thin air. There had been suspects threatened, coerced and tricked into confessing to crimes that they did not necessarily commit. In some cases, remaining silent when accused had been considered evidence of guilt rather than a constitutional right dating back to the Founding Fathers. Blacks and Hispanics com-

plained of being excluded from jury service, as if this were
the 1950s instead of the 1990s. The same people responsible for imprisoning innocents during the Witch Hunt
days were still in power, as popular as ever, and prosecuting this case. The war on crime was out of control here,
Laura had warned. The local lawyers even had a saying for
it, rueful and sad, one she had heard over and over again
in this courthouse: "Only in Kern County."

The rest of the defense team hadn't taken it seriously.
The local lawyers were just whiners, it was suggested.
Other cases didn't matter. Their client was one of
Bakersfield's elite: Republican, white, a high school principal who married into wealth, yet still a country boy
through and through. Jurors would see him as one of
their own. The lawyers were sure of it: This one was a
winner, even in Kern County.

"But I'm innocent," Patrick O'Dale Dunn had whispered numbly after hearing the jury pronounce him
guilty of murdering his wife for her millions. The defense
lawyer had cried then, too, bawling like a baby right in the
middle of the courtroom, and the client had tried to
comfort him with a pat on the back, saying it would be all
right. Which only made it worse, because everyone on the
team knew that it would take something close to a miracle for it to be all right now. They'd have to scrape around
frantically for some new bit of evidence and then fight
like hell to justify a new trial. Even then, the satisfied look
on the judge's face and the burning in Laura's stomach
told her how it would likely end up. Unless she could
come up with that miracle, a man she felt certain was
innocent would spend the rest of his life in prison.

For now, the attorney who had been so sure of victory
just a few hours earlier couldn't do a damn thing about it

except cry, his face wet with angry, useless tears as his car climbed the Grapevine Pass and raced toward the Kern County line. Laura envied him his escape. It was up to her now, to knock on more doors, to ask more questions, to search for answers that she thought she already had found, but which twelve seemingly reasonable people had rejected. If there was to be a reversal of this verdict and a new trial for her client, she would have to start from scratch and unearth new answers, ponder once again who killed Alexandra Dunn and why—and what forces at work in this place might have led to her client's conviction. And, given the confidence-shattering verdict, she'd be a fool not to entertain another possibility: Could she have been all wrong about this evidence, this town, this client? Might it be that this irascible man with the stubborn streak and ill-timed quips—whom Laura nevertheless had come to care for deeply—had killed his wife after all?

"You're not gonna give up on this old man, are you, Laura?" he whispered to her as she gathered her files to leave the courtroom. His eyes were wide and glassy. Shock, Laura thought to herself, and she forced a smile, feeling guilty for the questions she had been silently asking. Yet part of her did wonder, even then: *Was it all an act?* Then Pat Dunn's papery voice called out to her again, sounding harsh and loud in the empty courtroom though still but a whisper. "You still believe in me, don't you?" he pleaded.

The room suddenly seemed musty and disused with the crowd departed. Laura stared at Pat a long time before she finally nodded and answered, a sad half smile on her lips: "Only in Kern County."[5]

PART I
Pat and Sandy

And then the dispossessed were drawn west—from Kansas, Oklahoma, Texas, New Mexico; from Nevada and Arkansas families, tribes, dusted out, tractored out. Carloads, caravans, homeless and hungry; twenty thousand and fifty thousand and a hundred thousand and two hundred thousand. They streamed over the mountains. . . . They were hungry, and they were fierce. And they had hoped to find a home, and they found only hatred. Okies.

—JOHN STEINBECK,
The Grapes of Wrath

1

BAKERSFIELD IS LESS THAN A TWO-HOUR DRIVE FROM downtown Los Angeles, yet it has always existed in happy isolation, kept separate from the smog and sprawl of its southern neighbor by the iron gray of the Tehachapi Mountains and the treacherous asphalt snake of the Grapevine Pass, its one connection to the urban centers of Southern California. To cross the Grapevine and its sparse brown brush and stony thumbs of granite jutting through thin soil is to enter a different world, the antithesis of the California of popular imagination.

On the northern side of the Grapevine lies the vast brown and green checkerboard of Kern County, a fertile flatland dominated by big farms and small towns and a people who take outsized pride in being *not* Los Angeles. It is a land not of glitter or oiled bodies on white-sand beaches or any of the other icons of the California Dream, but of crude oil and tractors, of black dirt under the fingernails and molten, breezeless summers, a place virtually unknown to tourists, though the fruits of its oil derricks and furrows can be found in most every American's gas tank and pantry.

The city of Bakersfield and its 221,700 citizens preside over an otherwise rural county larger than many states. Once a wonderland of lakes, streams and riparian forest,

it was blasted into desert seventy years ago by the vora-
cious faucets of Los Angeles, then irrigated just as voraciously into some of the most productive farmland on
earth. As a boy, Pat Dunn ran home from his summer job
through a dense, green jungle of trees and brush lining
the riverbed that divides the city. The chapped landscape
of Bakersfield today was known to its frontier settlers as
Kern Island, but the river that cut through and enveloped
it long ago became a dry and empty sandlot most years.
Gone, too, is the vast Tulare Lake, where fishermen once
caught giant terrapin for turtle soup served in San
Francisco restaurants, and where steam-driven paddle-
boats once traveled from the Bakersfield area to the San
Francisco Bay. Now the ghost of that lake rises only in
years of record snowfall, when spring comes to the
Sierras and snowmelt flows down to flood the farmland
now claiming the ancient lake bed. The rest of the time,
the water is given to the carrots, almonds, grapes, citrus
and vegetables of every shape and color—most of the
nation's table food comes from Kern and the neighboring
counties that make up California's Great Central Valley.

The place and the people north of the Grapevine
evoke the Great Plains more than Hollywood.
Immigrants fleeing the midwestern Dust Bowl of the
thirties—Pat Dunn's family among them—boosted Kern
County's population by more than half during the
depression. The newcomers' descendants, once derided
as "Okies" by the same folks who denounced Steinbeck
and banned *The Grapes of Wrath* (in large part set in a
mortified Kern County), now run the place. Theirs is the
heartland of California—the *real* California—conservative, law-and-order, the toughest jurisdiction in the
toughest state in the Union when it comes to cracking

down on crime, no small claim in a state with a prison system dwarfing that of every *nation* on earth save China. Here, the most powerful and feared politician in town is not the mayor or the local congressman. It's the district attorney.

The region clings to its frontier legacy, a rough-hewn place built by gold and oil fever, where gunfights and lynchings continued well into the twentieth century, and where a fierce desire for law and order still competes with an intense distaste for government, regulations and outside interference in local affairs. Homesteads are still sold by the acre here, not the square foot. Horse ownership is common, gun ownership more so. Huge banners along Highway 99 politick against conservation and in favor of subsidized water for farmers: "Food Grows Where Water Flows," they say. Smaller, hand-lettered signs dot the side roads with more iconoclastic messages: "IRS stands for In Range Shooting." The American Civil Liberties Union may have closed down its Bakersfield office, citing lack of interest, but the tax-protest and militia movements have flourished here. Indeed, a flamboyant local state senator suffered no loss of popularity for associating with white separatists or for rising in the Capitol rotunda in Sacramento to inveigh against the "one-world government" conspiracy so popular with his militiamen admirers. Around the same time Pat Dunn's legal travails began, this senator tried to avoid paying the IRS $150,000 in back taxes by renouncing his U.S. citizenship in favor of something he claimed took precedence: "white man's citizenship."[1] The senator served eighteen years representing Kern County in the California state legislature before term limits—not the voters—forced him to retire in 1997.

While the politics of water, taxes and fear of one-world governments may be a factor behind the scenes, out front, on the stump and in the headlines, it is crime that most often concerns this community. Crime is a concern that, though shared with the rest of the nation, seems a special obsession here, part of a long and vivid history that has repeatedly drawn the nation's eyes toward Kern County in ways both dramatic and bizarre. The pursuit of wild criminal conspiracies are a recurring theme, with widespread belief in them rarely hindered by a lack of evidence: satanists, poisoned watermelons, killer bees and a sinister shadow government dubbed the "Lords of Bakersfield" all have aroused fears and demands for harsh punishment in recent years.

Even a century ago, journalists passing through remarked on the extremes of frontier justice in Bakersfield. One trial in particular drew headlines in 1877, a sensational case of horse thievery that ended in the summary execution of five rustlers. The fate of the accused was not so remarkable for the era, perhaps, but the courtroom argument that led to their sentence was quite extraordinary, setting the standard for justice in Kern County for years to come: "If it please the court, and the gentlemen of the jury, of all the low, miserable, depraved scoundrels that I have ever come in contact with, these defendants, without any grounds for defense, are the most ornery rascals that I have ever met, and I think the best thing we could do is take them out and hang them as soon as possible."

This passionate argument, which preceded the lynch mob's handiwork by a matter of minutes, was made by the *defense* attorney appointed in the case.[2]

Yet this same town that could be so ruthless in its war

on crime was at the same time also gripped by a breath-taking municipal corruption far more costly than any stolen horse. Beginning early in the century, open partnerships existed for years among police chiefs, elected officials, houses of prostitution, illegal casinos and the protection rackets that sustained them all. The civic corruption in Bakersfield became so institutionalized that, on certain downtown streets, one sidewalk would be reserved for "proper" citizens, while across the street the promenade belonged to hookers, gamblers and drug dealers operating in plain sight. The situation continued for much of this century, surviving even a 1950s threat of occupation and martial law from the commander of a nearby Army base. The essential contradiction here—of a community fanatically intolerant of crime, yet curiously accepting of official misconduct—would become another recurring theme in Kern County history.

This civic schizophrenia revealed itself again when a different and far more malevolent brand of corruption came to light in the 1920s, when the county grappled with a wave of terrorism, beatings and arsons sponsored by the Ku Klux Klan. The white-hooded riders of the KKK had taken over the county by night—and many government offices by day, as one after another elected official swore allegiance to the Klan. KKK violence in California, particularly in Kern County, rivaled that of the Deep South in this era, though the West Coast version was aimed at whites as well as at black and brown citizens. Doctors, dentists, detectives and businessmen were beaten, threatened and driven from town for opposing the KKK's "invisible empire." One evening in the Kern County city of Taft, an oil-laden desert town just west of Bakersfield where beer was cheaper than water, most of the police department and civic leaders turned out to watch the Klan torture several people in a local ballpark. They gathered as if viewing a spectator sport; refreshments were served. (In 1975, Taft again made national headlines when thirteen black athletes were run out of town by a white mob, while neighboring Oildale became infamous for its "No Niggers Allowed" road signs.)

By 1922, avowed Klan members controlled the Bakersfield mayor's office, various police departments throughout the county, much of the sheriff's force of deputies, several judgeships, the city school district, and the county board of supervisors, whose powerful chairman, once exposed, unabashedly wrote that he was proud of "the good work" of the KKK, adding in a front-page newspaper column, "I make no apology for the Klan. It needs none." He would serve a total of six terms and twenty-four years in office—most of it after his Klan affiliation was made public.

The Klan's allure in Kern County and other parts of Southern California lay as much in clever marketing as in its traditional message of racial hatred. The group pitched itself as a Christian fraternity that could combat the frontier corruption plaguing Bakersfield and other cities of the era. As such, it was able to attract not only avowed racists, but also ordinary members of the community who had tired of the open culture of vice—and who were willing to tolerate the Klan's brutality if it meant cleaning up the streets, trading one form of crime for another. The KKK in Kern County billed itself as the scourge of immorality, but it simply recruited the corrupt, rather than combat them, then launched its own brand of terrorism and thuggery on dissenters of every race.

Yet the Klan's infiltration of Kern County government

and law enforcement and its brazen attacks on ordinary citizens also led to one of the county's finest moments in its long war on crime. A courageous District Attorney named Jess Dorsey, aided by a crusading local press, revealed the organization's long reach and corrupting influence. The DA showed how members were required, among other things, to take an oath that superseded any vows of office or citizenship—police chiefs and sheriff's deputies literally swore to protect the Klan before enforcing the law. Numerous police chiefs and officers, judges, and city and county officials had taken this oath and had attended meetings in which fellow Klansmen planned and described lynchings, beatings, kidnappings and arsons— yet none of these officials interceded or reported the crimes. Some took part in the offenses, while others used their official standing to cover for Klan members.[3]

"Here the most brutal atrocities on the coast have been committed," the *Bakersfield Californian* editorialized on May 19, 1922, in the wake of a scathing grand jury report on the KKK's growing presence in Kern County. "Here the Klan has gained its greatest headway in official circles. And here lies the greatest danger for the future, unless the organization is destroyed while public sentiment demands its destruction."

For a brief time, it seemed that District Attorney Dorsey might succeed in bringing about that destruction. Blistered by headlines and public protests after years of acting with impunity, most of the Klan members in public office resigned or were ousted. But others, Kern County Board of Supervisors Chairman Stanley Abel among them, simply grew a bit more discreet—clinging to their positions by razor-thin election margins, though their closets still held white capes and hoods.

The furor ended anticlimactically, with Dorsey's vaunted grand jury charging a mere three Klan members with assault. At the trial, a line of one hundred fifty prominent citizens snaked out of the courthouse, each man eager to testify to the defendants' good character. The three offenders, though convicted, walked out of court on probation. In the aftermath, a newspaper called the *Kern County Klansman* smugly wrote, "Listen, Mr. Dorsey, there are more Klansmen in Kern County today than there were thirty days ago . . . If you think that you have put the Klan out of business in this county you are badly mistaken."

The controversy soon died, and District Attorney Dorsey found himself voted out of office. A decade later, not long before Pat Dunn was born in a farm camp north of Bakersfield, the luster came off the county's war on crime, when another wave of beatings, false imprisonments and suspicious deaths hit Kern County. But this time, the justice system did little to combat the crimes and much to protect the perpetrators. For in this case, the target of the violence had shifted from local victims to outsiders who commanded far less sympathy—the Dust Bowl refugees and other impoverished migrant workers who arrived in Kern County in the mid-to-late 1930s from throughout the Southwest, desperate for work and easily preyed upon. It was a time of goon squads, red-baiting, labor riots and disease-ridden shantytowns built of cardboard and hunger.

The Klan members still in government found new favor in this era, for now the local press and a new DA joined them in supporting "stern treatment"—a euphemism for beatings and union-busting—as justifiable and necessary to protect farm profits and ward off the communist menace that the immigrants supposedly represented. Farm workers from Oklahoma, Arkansas and other drought-plagued states came to be reviled as shiftless lowlifes who would overrun the good citizens of Kern County—then numbering only 30,000—with their burgeoning numbers. Signs sprang up in Bakersfield restaurants and other public places, proclaiming, "No Niggers or Okies." In 1939, Kern County—still led by Klansman Stanley Abel—banned *The Grapes of Wrath* from schools and libraries in protest of its fictionalized portrayal of the farm workers' plight, inadvertently putting John Steinbeck on the national map and exposing Bakersfield to national ridicule. (While Steinbeck has long since returned to the local library shelves, even to this day, Kern County remains home to some of the richest farms and the poorest farm workers in America.)

Among the desperate and poor legions flocking to Central California during this era of Great Depression and Dust Bowl drought was the Dunn family. Leaving behind a ruined farm and a foreclosed house, they arrived three years before Pat Dunn was born. Toward the end of the Dunns' time in Oklahoma, the dust-laden winds sweeping across the devastated land had become so thick and pervasive that they would swallow the sun for days at a time. Birds dropped from trees, suffocated. The Dunns had to sleep with wet rags covering their mouths and noses, lest they suffer a similar fate. When there was nothing left but debts and death and the sifting sound of dust, they packed up what belongings their aging car could hold, and headed toward the promised land they had heard so much about: California.

Their first home in paradise was a tent.

2

LILLIAN DUNN HAD TWO PASSIONS IN LIFE: HER FUN-damentalist religious beliefs (all her lady friends back home were "sisters") and labor unions. Before Pat was born, she worked the fields with her husband and three older children by day and helped organize Okie laborers by night. Inevitably, as was customary for the times, Lillian was denounced as a communist for her union activities and was briefly imprisoned for participating in a farm-worker protest that erupted into a riot and a shooting. When the judge in the case asked Lillian Dunn if she was a communist, she said that she did not know exactly what that was, but if a communist was someone that wanted to be paid enough to feed her children, then she must be one. Lillian had a blunt, tart way with words—a trait she passed on to Pat, and one which did not always serve her (or him) well. Even Lillian's friends described her as "difficult," while others seemed to feel far less charitable, her children among them.

Despite her unrepentant response to the judge, charges were eventually dismissed against Lillian Dunn. Still, it remains unclear whether she was being disingenuous about her knowledge of communism or if his question merely piqued her interest in the subject. Either way, when Pat was born in 1936, she was intimate enough with the philosophy of Marx and Lenin to name her new baby after a communist labor organizer she had met in Kern County.

By the time Pat was born, the Dunns had left their tent in favor of a small house in the Little Oklahoma neighborhood of Delano, an impoverished farm community where, three decades later, César Chávez would form the National Farm Workers Association, soon to become the United Farm Workers of America. Pat's mother and father separated when Pat was still a small child; he grew up under his older brothers' sporadic attempts at paternal attention. During World War II, Pat helped support the family by picking cotton and grapes and caring for the family garden, chickens and cow. As he recalls it, his first day in the first grade marked the first occasion on which he ever held a pencil in his hand. "Needless to say," Pat would joke many years later, after he had become a teacher and school counselor, "I was behind my classmates and may never catch up."

After the war, the Dunns moved to Bakersfield where, at age twelve, Pat landed a job with the Bakersfield Indians, a minor-league farm club for the Cleveland baseball team. Tall for his age, graceful and athletic, Pat chased foul balls, ran errands for doughnuts, shined the players' shoes, and—this was the magical part, something Pat would have done whether they paid him or not—occasionally even pitched batting practice. He'd float lazy knuckleballs over home plate, hearing the bat crack into each pitch, watching the ball arc overhead into the outfield. Once he threw to future Hall of Famer Hank Greenberg, a thrill he still describes a half century later with childlike wonder and reverence. For a kid in that era—before the arrival of exorbitant player salaries and season-busting strikes and the nomadic movement of players from one high-bidding club to the next—this was a dream job. The team manager called him "The Indispensable Mr. Dunn," a title that puffed up the boy far more than his first paycheck—ninety-nine cents for four days' work. (The crestfallen look on his face that first payday must have left an impression; his boss immediately upped his salary to one dollar per night.) Pat Dunn would never hold a job that paid him less or made him happier.

In high school, he needed steadier employment for lunch money and to buy clothes—his mother offered him no money for such luxuries. As a freshman, Pat would walk home every day and stop at each store along the way to ask if they had any work. After several weeks of this, the manager at the Barker Brothers furniture warehouse finally threw up his hands and said yes, he had work, especially for such a persistent kid. This steam-roller approach to getting what he wanted would become a regular pattern in Pat's life, sometimes to his benefit, when people found his forcefulness admirable or even charming, and sometimes to his detriment, when his insistent refusal to alter course led him astray. When he vanquished the Barker Brothers manager, he was only fourteen but easily passed for older. No one asked his age so long as he could pick up the tables and couches and haul them around as needed.

Years later, after high school and a brief, unmemorable tour in the air force, Pat enrolled in Bakersfield Community College and began studying to become a teacher—something of a surprise to those who knew him in high school as more interested in cutting classes than passing them. It was in college that he met and married a fellow teaching student, Nancy Leonetti, who was as warm and open as Pat was boisterous and prickly. Around the same time, he took back his old part-time job at the furniture warehouse to pay the bills while he finished college. And it was there that he first met Alexandra.

The year was 1960. Kennedy was running against Nixon, the economy was booming, Detroit made the best cars in the world, and Kern County, with a population one-tenth its current size, was pumping more oil than any other *nation* in the world. And a Bakersfield native by the name of Earl Warren—who had left the California governor's mansion to become chief justice of the United States Supreme Court—was about to enrage his law-and-order hometown with a then-novel legal principle: that cops and prosecutors gathering evidence of crimes should have to obey the law like everyone else, or pay a heavy price. Out of this commonsense yet revolutionary notion, the Warren Court crafted the "exclusionary rule," which bars prosecutors from using illegally obtained evidence in court—a rule that Kern County officials have occasionally flouted, regularly railed against, and repeatedly attempted to overturn ever since.

In 1960, Pat's new mother-in-law ran an upscale women's clothing store next to Barker Brothers, and she occasionally invited him over for his lunch break. One day, she introduced Pat to a new sales clerk, a thin and pretty young woman who had just moved to Bakersfield from the East Coast: Alexandra Hoey. "Call me Sandy," she had said in a strong New York accent, all flat vowels and long *R*s. To Pat's Okie sensibilities, she sounded as exotic as a Parisian.

After that casual meeting, Pat would see Sandy after

work from time to time waiting for the bus and he would stop his car to offer her a ride home. She almost always accepted. During these drives, she told him about growing up on Park Avenue in Manhattan, and how her mother was an expert in Asian artifacts, having inventoried a huge shipment of plundered artwork and pottery seized from the Japanese during the war years. "She wrote the book on jade," Sandy proudly announced whenever the story came up, and Pat would always marvel at this as if he had never heard it before. That was the limit of their relationship then—Sandy never even met Nancy Dunn. Pat's older brother Jay believes that Pat was smitten with Sandy even back then, but Pat shrugs off the suggestion, saying that he was married at the time and never had any such thoughts—none that he acted upon, anyway. In any case, within the year, Sandy was gone from the clothing store and from Pat Dunn's life.

A wealthy Bakersfield developer and real estate speculator named Patrick Paola, who built a respectable fraction of modern Bakersfield, had become a regular customer at the clothing store. He wanted only Sandy to attend to him as he personally selected his wife's wardrobe. Mrs. Paola would either stand mutely by his side, or not even come into the store. "He's very old school," Sandy told Pat during one of their rides home. "He doesn't let his wife do anything." Pat remembers thinking that sounded pretty odd to him—he couldn't imagine picking out Nancy's brassieres, or her letting him do so even if he wanted to. But he made no comment, as he clearly heard in Sandy's voice that she thought Mr. Paola quite charming and sophisticated, Old World ways and all. Being taken care of, it seemed, even in such a heavy-handed fashion, strongly appealed to her.

Not long after that conversation, Sandy left her job at the clothing store and Pat stopped seeing her waiting for buses. The next thing he heard, Patrick Paola—nearly thirty years Sandy's senior—had left the wife he so jealously cared for and had begun courting the twenty-six-year-old sales clerk from Manhattan. They married a short time later, in 1961. Sandy told friends of how she tried to resist Paola's advances, fretting that everyone would think that she was some kind of gold digger interested only in Old Man Paola's money. But while Sandy tended to be intensely concerned about what others thought of her, proud and acutely conscious of what she considered to be her lofty station in life, her new husband cared little about what people thought of him. He was, according to one contemporary, a fast-talking deal maker with huge ambitions and a modestly proportioned conscience. "That's okay, honey," he had told Sandy with a laugh when she mentioned her fears about being seen as a gold digger. "Tell them, hell, yes, you're after the money. That'll shut them up." From that moment on, this anecdote became her lifelong foil—she would tell it as a kind of preamble to describing her years with Pat Paola, just in case someone really did think she was a fortune hunter.

Pat Dunn lost touch with Sandy after her marriage to Patrick Paola, though he would occasionally hear reports from his mother-in-law about the courtship and marriage, and how Mr. Paola had begun doing everything for Sandy just as he had for his first wife, right down to selecting her shoes and underwear. Pat's in-laws knew the Paolas—in fact, Pat and Nancy Dunn held their wedding reception at his restaurant, gratis. But the Dunn family did not move in the same circles as the Paolas, who went about building a number of Bakersfield landmarks, from housing developments to bowling alleys to shopping malls, and accumulating several million dollars in cash and real estate in the process.

Twenty-five years passed without them crossing paths again, except for one time when Pat helped his father-in-law—then a Paola employee—measure the square footage of the Paolas' home for an appraisal. In those twenty-five years, Pat and Nancy Dunn raised three children, Patrick Jr., Danny and Jennifer. Pat taught elementary school and junior high math classes in the Bakersfield school system, later becoming a counselor, then taking a job as principal for a tiny school district at the windswept top of the Grapevine Pass, in a historic community called Tejon Ranch. He eventually left that position on an early retirement in 1981 after taking the losing side in a heated political battle with the school board over the size of the faculty at the district's two schools.

Seizing on California's sky-high real estate market at the time—and the record number of defaults that the high prices were causing—Pat entered the mortgage-foreclosure business the following year. He cleaned, repaired and boarded homes that had been repossessed—sometimes, he did the evicting and repossessing, too—so that the properties could be resold by the banks or federal housing agencies that held the notes on them. The homes of the dispossessed were rarely left in pristine condition, and Pat soon had more offers for work than he could handle. His company quickly grew from two trucks and crews into nine and handled business throughout the broad valleys and boom towns of Central California. It was a dirty, sad business, and Pat took pity on some of the people whose houses he seized, particularly the wives and mothers who had been abandoned and left holding a bad mortgage and a mailbox full of bills. He would help them pack up, take their possessions to storage and drive them wherever they needed to go—the one part of this thankless work Pat enjoyed. "It takes some of the sting out," he'd say when a less charitable colleague would ask him why he bothered. Of course, not every soon-to-be-homeless person was so easily mollified, and some were unwilling to simply hand over their house keys to this bluff, big man with his sheaf of legal papers. But when trouble arose, Pat's standing instruction to his crews was to avoid any altercation and simply call the police. "You can always depend on the man in blue," Pat would preach. "He's on our side."

Pat also worked on the side with the city and county fire departments, clearing overgrown lots that had become fire hazards. Altogether, this sort of slapdash work on houses and empty lots proved to be quite a lucrative business, and Pat began making more money than he had ever before known. The *Bakersfield Californian* even profiled him in an article that depicted him and his foreclosure work admiringly, even quoting his philosophical musings on why so many homeowners ran afoul of their mortgages: "Demon rum and failed marriages," he said sagely.

His observations, however facile, were bitterly applicable to his own life.

Pat's marriage to Nancy had deteriorated over the years as his drinking increased. His decline had started during his flap with the school board, a career change that he claimed to take in stride, never admitting even to himself that his abrupt departure from education left him disappointed and depressed. As his foreclosure business expanded, Pat let his crews do the field work while he conducted most of his business from home—making it easier to start drinking earlier and earlier in the day. His consumption became prodigious; he could gulp down a six-pack in one sitting with little effort. This reliance on booze only intensified when two of his three children began having problems of their own.

His oldest, Patrick Jr., had always been an easy kid, a quiet and respectful young man who effortlessly earned A's in school and gained admission to Stanford University. Jennifer and Danny, however, were quite the opposite, providing continual sources of heartbreak for the family. Jennifer not only became an unwed teenaged mother, but she lost her infant son, Jordan, to crib death. Despite his anger at Jennifer over the pregnancy, Pat had loved his little grandson dearly, and the baby's death marked the only occasion Jennifer ever saw her father cry—until Sandy disappeared.

Danny, the middle child, was another matter. As a teenager and young adult, he had constant scrapes with the law—drug problems, thievery—and he had a quick temper. Fed up, Pat finally ordered Danny out of the house, and they had a fistfight that night—the only time that Nancy and the two other children say they can remember him striking anyone, no matter how much he had to drink. Pat and Danny never spoke again after that night. "I have only one son now," he would later tell Jennifer. Danny, it seemed, remained furious at his father, accusing him of all sorts of abusive behavior.

By the mid-eighties, whenever Pat Dunn was at home, he had a can of Coors glued to his right hand, or a tall whiskey and soda in front of him. In the Dunn household, there was a standing, if unspoken, rule that no one

got in the car with Dad after three o'clock in the afternoon. Pat, however, stubbornly refused to acknowledge
any problem and would grow irate at the mere suggestion
that he drank too much, vociferously arguing that he
never missed work or failed to provide for his family—all
true, if beside the point. Pat's model of manly virtue was
drawn strictly from the Hollywood idols of his youth—
the silent stoicism of Wayne, Cooper, Bogart. A man who
provides for his family, who makes a home, who puts
meals on the table, who builds a better life for his kids
than the one he enjoyed by definition shows he loves his
family. You didn't actually have to say it aloud—your
daily life said it all, Pat believed. By those standards, Pat
thought his drinking irrelevant, and he couldn't see that,
to his family, he checked out every time he emptied a bot-
tle. He really did love his family, deeply, but he didn't see
the need—and, in any case, couldn't find it in himself—
to actually utter those three words, *I love you*, unaware of
just how much they would have meant to his wife and
children. Speaking of such things was far more difficult
for Pat than taking a heavy sledgehammer to a ruined
house—or, for that matter, showing kindness to an evicted
stranger.

Pat could be a warm and witty companion, and his
family and friends knew him to be a well-meaning man,
but he also seemed arrogant at times, particularly when
he "had a few," the family's term for heavy drinking. Then
he became something of a know-it-all, sitting back in his
chair and dispensing lofty opinions and advice, usually
preceded by the words, "When I was a principal . . . " The
way he said it at times, he might as well have been a member of the Cabinet, and it became clear, then, just how
much he missed his former career. In time, Pat's drinking

left him with few close friends and a world that extended beyond his armchair with increasing rarity. Always a big man, he grew overweight and sedentary, his beer belly hanging low over his waistline, the slightest exertion leaving him breathless.

Predictably, Pat's drinking gradually tore the family apart.[4] As the kids neared and reached adulthood, Nancy professed a desire to go back to college, to take up hobbies, to widen her horizons. Pat, meanwhile, wanted to sit home and drink, maybe shoot the occasional game of pool. He never wanted to go out; the last movie he left the house for was *The Guns of Navarone*. Twenty-five years together and Nancy, who had always been the glue of the family, the one who planned the events and forged the friendships, increasingly felt like a stranger to her husband. It's not that she stopped loving him—there was just something about Pat, she would insist, that shone through even in his darkest moments, something kind and good—but it was no longer enough. In a decision that was a long time coming, but which still seemed to take Pat by surprise, Nancy filed for divorce in 1985. She moved out of the house, taking with her Jennifer, the only one of the couple's children still living at home.

Without really thinking about it, Pat gave everything but his business to Nancy and wished her well. He harbored no ill will toward her, no bitterness, though he was bewildered and hurt and wished she would change her mind. Yet he couldn't find the words to ask her to stay. He thought them, heard them in his head, but just couldn't make them come out. He didn't know how. He rented an apartment and lived alone.

A year or so later, his foreclosure business still thriving (even as the California real estate market was crashing), the fire department called and told him about some acreage in East Bakersfield choked with weeds and trash. The landowner being cited for the violation was a difficult middle-aged widow who had been totally uncooperative, distrustful of all the contractors the fire department suggested, yet unwilling to do the work herself. "How about you give her a try?" Pat was asked.

"Sure," he said. "What's the lady's name?"

"Paola," the fire official told him. "Alexandra Paola."

3

T HAT SAME AFTERNOON, PAT WENT TO THE PAOLA
Development Company office at the College
Center mall in East Bakersfield. The sixties-era
strip mall had begun to look a bit ragged by then, he
noticed, with several vacant storefronts and an air more
gritty than prosperous. Pat Paola's big dreams hadn't
quite panned out: Decades earlier, he had snapped up
property all over East Bakersfield, betting heavily that
development in the city would move in his direction and
make his land worth far more than what he paid for it.
Instead, most of the upscale shopping and higher-end
neighborhoods went the opposite way, to the northwest,
and many of the Paola properties remained vacant after
twenty years, his visions for that part of town unrealized
and now in the hands of his widow.

The College Center had aged poorly in the process.
The proprietor's office was dingy and dark, with battered
metal desks and stained carpeting on the floor. The surroundings shocked Pat. An older man sat playing solitaire
at a scarred table stacked high with old papers. He
ignored Pat, flicking cards and frowning at his hand, not
bothering to respond to Pat's greeting. And then
Alexandra Paola stood up from behind another desk. She
looked radiant in a blue sundress with lace around the

collar, her short hair silver now. Pat hadn't seen her in twenty-five years, but he thought she looked more lovely than he remembered, the only note of brightness in that shabby little office. Whenever he told the story of their meeting that day, he would always remember thinking Sandy didn't look like she belonged there. The place and the woman simply did not fit. The dismal office's gray pallor could not touch her.

Alexandra immediately remembered Pat from those long-ago rides home from the dress shop, and they spent nearly an hour catching up, first in the office while the old man continued playing solitaire with a sour look on his face, then while driving out to see the acreage that the fire department wanted cleared. Pat Paola, Sandy explained quietly, had been sick since 1975, first with heart disease, then cancer, and finally senility. Sandy had taken care of him throughout, finally having to dress and feed the man who had once done everything for her. At the end of his life, he would either sit in his easy chair, recognizing no one, or he would be seized by sudden bursts of energy that saw him stripping his clothes off and running outside, cackling madly, then telling neighbors his wife had locked him outside with no clothes. To Pat's surprise, Sandy described these incidents with the ghost of a smile on her lips. "You must miss him a lot," Pat said, and Sandy nodded silently.

When he finally died three years earlier, in 1983, Alexandra had tried to keep his businesses and real estate dealings going. But Paola had maintained a complex web of interlocking companies and transactions, and after so many years of being so sheltered by her husband, Sandy confessed, "I did a pretty poor job of it." Her woes had esca-

lated recently when she learned that a trusted bookkeeper—
a woman who had worked for Paola Enterprises since 1961
and who had seemed like a member of the family—had
been embezzling from them for years. Seventy thousand
was gone at minimum, perhaps as much as a quarter million, Sandy whispered, shaking her head, nearly trembling
at the thought. "Maybe more," she said. "The police don't
know, the accountants don't know. I don't know."

The turmoil brought by this betrayal had been compounded by Sandy's impulsive, almost desperate decision
to remarry a year after Paola's death. As Sandy told it, her
new husband, Leon—the older man playing solitaire at the
mall—had misrepresented his own wealth and holdings
and had run up all sorts of debts against Sandy's money.
She called him a smooth-talking charmer who loved only
the Paola fortune. In her loneliness, the woman who
always feared that she would be thought of as a gold digger had ended up being preyed upon by one, she told Pat
with a bitter smile. They had separated within a year, amid
a nasty battle over property he had hauled off and tried to
sell through the classifieds. Pat wondered to himself why
Leon was still hanging out at the mall, but he bit his
tongue, not wanting to pry, letting Sandy tell him what she
wanted to tell him. Now, she continued, all sorts of other
people were coming out of the woodwork to offer impossibly good investments and real estate deals, if only she
would give them a piece of the Paola holdings. Her late
husband's real estate on the east side had finally jumped in
value as Bakersfield relentlessly grew from a town into a
major city and open space fetched an increasing premium.
"I know just enough to say no," Sandy said ruefully.

Pat spoke little of himself during the drive, saying only
that his own troubles seemed small indeed compared to

Sandy's. But he had an engaging, supportive way of listening, of not seeming to judge, and Sandy would later say he seemed at that moment one of the kindest and most understanding men she had ever met.

They drove on to the weed-choked property cited by the fire inspector, and Pat said he would take care of it, then call her back. In a few days, he had removed the weeds and trash from the lot, as well as cleared the grounds of a neighboring apartment building that Sandy owned, too. He refused to charge her, and Sandy, who had remained extremely thrifty despite her wealth, seemed particularly delighted by this gesture. When Pat mentioned that he and Nancy were separated, Sandy invited him to her house on Crestmont Drive, where she had lived for a quarter century with Pat Paola—the same house Pat Dunn had helped measure years before. Pat remembered admiring the big ranch-style house, with its pool and cabana and rich tile work.

Arriving for his visit in 1986, however, he barely recognized the place. Sun and heat had etched and faded the paint. There were cracks in the plaster. Green plastic garbage bags stuffed with old clothes sat on the porch and in the side yard, a rusty old bicycle propped against them.

When Sandy opened the front door for Pat, a wave of heat washed over him. It was July and quite hot outside, but the interior of the house was well over ninety degrees. The house had air conditioning—a matter of survival in desert summer—but Sandy would not run it. Instead, she would turn on several floor fans in the living room and aim them at whatever chairs were occupied. Pat sat down gingerly, the hot stream of air from the fan washing over him like jet exhaust. He felt like he had climbed into a kiln.

Like the porch, the interior of the house—living room, dining room, halls—was piled high with debris. Cardboard boxes of all sizes had been stacked one on top of the other like child's blocks, with pathways through their rows—a shut-in's maze. Nothing was dirty; the house was just impossibly cluttered, as if Sandy had not thrown anything away in twenty years. Pat later learned this was exactly the case: Sandy never tossed out a newspaper, a magazine or a worn-out article of clothing. Even the plastic bags from the produce section of the supermarket were kept. Sandy had an enormous roll of them in her kitchen cabinet, washed, dried and ready for reuse so she wouldn't have to spend money on sandwich bags. She had kept in the house all of her late husband's clothes and possessions, as well as some of her second husband's things, and everything left behind by her mother, who had recently died after a long struggle with Alzheimer's disease—an entire second household of furniture, clothes and bric-a-brac crammed into this one home. Pat imagined he had entered some dark and crowded curio shop, where one table might hold beautiful jade sculpture, clearly valuable, while another was piled high with yellowing copies of *Ladies' Home Journal* or chipped jelly-jar glasses. Once again, it struck him that this handsome, gracious woman who welcomed him into a labyrinth of junk did not seem to fit her surroundings. He figured that when her first husband died, Sandy had started bleeding money to embezzlement and an unscrupulous new spouse, and ended up broke, forced to live like a bag lady. No wonder she wouldn't clear the weeds from those lots, he told himself. He remembers thinking, *Here's someone who really needs me.*

He suggested they go out for lunch, and they decided

to drive to a place up in the canyons outside Bakersfield called Balanced Rock, where Pat knew of a restaurant famous for its home-style coleslaw—their first date. It was July 4, 1986, a brilliant, sunny day so hot the sky seemed burned clean of color. Within the year, as soon as each of their divorces became final, Pat and Sandy married.

Exactly six years after that first date, on July 4, 1992, the murder case against Pat Dunn began in earnest.

4

I N AUTUMN 1986, AFTER PAT AND SANDY HAD BEEN LIV-
ing together in the old Paola house on Crestmont
Drive for two or three months, she got up one morning and said, "Let's take a ride. I need to see the lawyer."

Pat said sure, and, once in the downtown law office, he
sat in the waiting area watching the secretaries while
Sandy met with her attorney privately. It was a law firm
that specialized in family law, real estate matters and other
kinds of civil litigation, and Pat assumed that the meeting
had to do with Sandy's imminent divorce from her second
husband. But when they left the office an hour later and
settled into the car, Sandy tossed a thick brown envelope
onto his lap and said, "Here, put this away somewhere."

He looked at her and raised an eyebrow, and she said,
"It's my will. I'm leaving you everything."

Pat thought she was joking at first, but, sure enough,
inside the envelope was a simple four-page will prepared
by Sandy's lawyer just that morning. The will named Pat
as Sandy's sole heir and appointed him estate executor. It
left nothing to the Paola family and omitted Sandy's only
sister, Nanette, with whom Sandy had been feuding for
years since their mother died and left everything to
Sandy. The new will also specifically bequeathed just one
dollar to any potential heir who contested the will.

Touched and surprised, Pat wasn't sure what to say. Speaking aloud about such emotionally charged subjects still made him uncomfortable. He chuckled to cover the mixture of warmth and embarrassment he felt, then breezily asked, "So, what are you worth?"

He figured Sandy had little left at that point, just whatever the house might bring in, perhaps a bit more. He had seen the way she was living before they began dating, and he had taken it upon himself to clean out the pack-rat clutter, the rooms crammed with boxes and the trash bags on the porch. He had heard her talk of Leon misrepresenting his own wealth, then trying to dive with open arms into the Paola fortune. So he almost veered the car off the road when Sandy nonchalantly answered, "About three million, give or take a couple hundred thousand."

Pat shook his head in wonder. Apparently, Sandy had been a lot smarter with her money than she let on—something Pat would come to understand firsthand as he watched her over the years deal confidently, sometimes ruthlessly, with various accountants, brokers and businessmen.

When they got home from the law office, Pat stuck the will in a desk drawer, where it remained for six years. It was September 16, 1986, the day, prosecutors would later claim, Sandy became worth more to Pat Dunn dead than alive.

Though that last will and testament would one day become a dagger-like piece of evidence against Pat—part of his motive to murder, police and prosecutors would say—there had been no pressure on Sandy to write it that day.[5] Pat hadn't asked for it, and Sandy offered him no explanation as to why she suddenly found it necessary to craft a new will leaving him everything before they had even married. Pat shrugged it off. Perhaps she just wanted to make sure her second husband got nothing should she die before their divorce became final. It did seem that the will and the divorce were linked in Sandy's mind; she signed papers the very next day at the same law office to put formal marriage dissolution proceedings into motion against Leon.

The will changed little in Sandy and Pat's relationship: It was not as if Sandy, while living, was turning over responsibility for her finances to Pat. Most of the money and real estate holdings she had inherited from Pat Paola remained her sole property, even after she married Pat, and she continued to use her first married name on checks and bank accounts—"Alexandra Paola Dunn," she'd sign, and when she spoke her full name, it was with emphasis on the *Paola*, a symbol of status in Bakersfield, at least in her mind. "That's the good Paola," she'd always say with a nervous laugh, "not the bad *payola*."

In time, she and Pat developed some of the Paola properties together, they held joint accounts, and Pat had access to Sandy's money whenever he asked for it. The pair even opened a line of credit for two hundred thousand dollars at one bank, with either to draw, though it was backed by Sandy's assets alone. Neither of them ever touched it. Still, it remained clear that Sandy's money was hers alone. And though Pat might be present for meetings with business partners and investment counselors, dispensing opinions and advice, he also usually concluded by saying to Sandy, "Whatever you want is fine with me." For most of their time together—until a year or so before Sandy vanished, when Pat began taking a much more dominant role in their various real estate projects—it was clear to all that Sandy had the final say.

As far as anyone who knew them could tell, this arrangement never bothered Pat. Nor did Sandy's attachment to her Paola name and identity. If it did trouble him, he never complained to anyone about it. Sandy must not have been overly concerned about Pat having designs on her money, either; when the divorce from Leon came through in March 1987, she sought no prenuptial agreement or any other protection for her assets. She and Pat just piled into the car and drove off for a quiet, private marriage ceremony—in Las Vegas, the one and only flamboyant gesture they made as a couple.

After a weekend in Sin City, as Pat insisted on calling it, they settled back into the same old house in East Bakersfield, where, with very few exceptions, they led quiet and uneventful lives. Sandy was the much more active of the two, with her daily predawn power walks and her penchant for collecting jade sculpture. Pat ran his foreclosure business out of the house and, in fits and starts, collected antique guns as a hobby. They were known to be creatures of habit who had many casual friends but few close ones, who went to bed by seven or eight o'clock most nights, who preferred backyard barbecues with neighbors and friends to going out on the town, and who both drank prodigious amounts of alcohol daily, which in part explained their early bedtimes. Pat was quite open about his round-the-clock drinking, while Sandy tried, often successfully, to conceal hers. Many friends were under the impression that she didn't drink at all. Together, however, the two of them could easily polish off a fifth of hard liquor in a day, and those who did business with the couple quickly learned to schedule meetings in the morning.

Even with the drinking, their friends and most of their neighbors considered the Dunns charmingly eccentric—people who genuinely seemed to like and love one another in their own, occasionally crabby way. Pat prided himself on his abilities as a host, never allowing a guest's glass to stand empty, always putting steak, not hamburger, on the grill. Sandy would sit back and smile at her husband's fussing over visitors—the kitchen was more his domain than hers. But, in all other matters, she always took care of Pat, catering to him in every way, doing things for him without being asked, making sure he always had fresh stores of shaving cream, enough of his favorite beer, the week's *TV Guide*. They were little things, really, but things no one had ever done for Pat, a man still stung by childhood memories of having to work just to get new clothes for school. He regularly marveled to friends and family about how Sandy seemed to know just what he needed when he needed it. "And *poof*, just as something's about to run out, there's a new one sitting there, a fresh toothpaste or a new razor," Pat told one friend, as if he were describing an act of magic rather than Sandy's well-timed trip to the grocery store. This solicitous care would move Pat in ways no extravagant gesture ever could. To Pat's way of thinking, such small kindnesses were the best way of all to say I love you, and he had finally found a partner in life who felt the same way. As Pat told it, Sandy took care of him in a way his first wife, even his own mother, never would or could, which is why early in their marriage he began calling Sandy "Mom."

Given their odd hours and other eccentricities, the Dunns were by no means universally beloved. Some acquaintances felt their relationship seemed to be based as much on bickering as on love, and there was some truth to this. Both could be stubborn and opinionated people at times, and Sandy in particular was known as much for the staying power of her grudges as for her genteel manner. Their detractors, and there were several right in the neighborhood, saw only this negative side of the Dunns. These people tended to describe Sandy as a flighty snob who at times affected an ostentatious manner reminiscent of Zsa Zsa Gabor. They considered Pat a gold digger who had risen above his station in life. (Still, even their critics had to admit that the Dunns' humble clothes, home and habits suggested that the couple had little interest in flaunting their wealth—to Pat and Sandy, money was a tool, not something to be displayed.) Those in the neighborhood who had known and liked the legendary Pat Paola seemed particularly unkind about "the new husband," as they called Pat Dunn. They never really forgave Sandy for marrying a mere schoolteacher, and they were particularly scandalized when Pat drove Paola's vintage tail-finned Cadillac in the Bakersfield Christmas parade, something Paola traditionally had done before senility left him incapable of carrying out the annual ritual. "As if Dunn could take Mr. Paola's place," sniffed one angry neighbor. "He has no right to drive that car."

Pat and Sandy seemed oblivious to much of this, though Pat was known to play the occasional practical joke on neighbors who disliked him. He continually feuded with one next-door neighbor in particular, a retired plumber named Otis Coppock, whose partial deafness exacerbated his and Pat's regular misunderstandings. In one of their more memorable bouts, Coppock's daughter, a former schoolmate of Pat's daughter, yelled over the fence at Pat one day during a Dunn family barbecue, and Coppock later telephoned with a follow-up complaint. Apparently, the Coppocks felt the Dunns were being too noisy. "Listen, Coppock," Pat snarled into the phone, shouting so his neighbor would hear every word, as his daughter, Jennifer, and son Patrick listened. "Meet me outside and bring your dog. And I'll kick your ass and my dog will kick your dog's ass and go ahead and bring your daughter, too, and my daughter will kick her ass to boot."

Pat could barely keep from laughing during this mock tirade. To him and his kids, who were giggling in the background, it was all an absurd joke. But Coppock took it as a serious threat and slammed the phone down. He never spoke to Pat after that day, and made no secret of his animosity toward his neighbors. Though Sandy wasn't there on the day of the barbecue, she battled with Coppock as well, and he once accused her of mistreating the ailing Pat Paola, whom he idolized. Coppock had occasionally seen the naked Paola in the backyard, and believed the ailing financier when he ranted about Sandy taking his clothes and locking him out. The plumber would later say Sandy struck and abused her elderly first husband, thereby contributing to his death, though he also once claimed Sandy drove her second husband to death as well, despite the fact Leon was very much alive.

Still, most people who knew the Dunns seemed willing to accept their eccentricities—his practical jokes, her unshakable habit of hoarding everything from plastic bags to old clothes. They were known as loyal friends willing to help those close to them when trouble struck. Pat and Sandy helped one financially strapped couple start a business of their own, and Pat gave work and one of his trucks to a troubled young man—an old friend of his son Danny—when no one else would hire him.

Mostly, every day seemed the same at the Dunn household. Sandy would rise before dawn to go for her early morning walk, and Pat would have the coffee ready by the time she returned two hours later. As he kept the cups full, Sandy sat at the kitchen table and read the newspaper aloud for Pat. They liked keeping informed about doings in their city, particularly about city politics, as they began laying plans to develop some of the vacant land Sandy had inherited from Pat Paola, still trying to fulfill his visions for East Bakersfield. In the last year of Sandy's life, Pat became much more active in her financial affairs as they worked on two large developments, a housing tract and a movie-theater complex. The theater project had run afoul of certain city officials, and so Pat began to read voraciously about city politics. The city council, the planning commission, the county government—all had to be understood, massaged and placated if the plans were to go through, he told Sandy.

The Dunns also obsessively read about crime in Bakersfield, their main concern and fear, something they shared with many of their neighbors. Their interest was particularly keen because the College Center mall Sandy had inherited—where she took her daily walks—was now in a high-crime area. They also followed the increasing power and prestige of Kern County's tough, law-and-order district attorney, whom they both supported in his uncompromising approach to law enforcement. Pat and Sandy felt Bakersfield needed someone like this DA in control, for the city seemed increasingly prey to the most bizarre and frightening crimes—escalating violence, serial killers, a Dungeons and Dragons murder ring that claimed the life of the district attorney's own barber, a disturbing number of corrupt cops, judges and other officials, and, of course, the devil-worshiping child molesters who had made national news in recent years. "I was one of the first principals to bring counselors into the school to talk about child abuse and abductions," Pat said every time one of the big molestation cases hit the papers. "I saw it coming."

Like most of their neighbors and peers, Pat and Sandy had been horrified when, one by one, these molesters began walking out of prison after appealing their convictions. Now, the newspapers said, the molesters were supposed to be the victims—of tainted evidence, of prosecutorial misconduct, of mass hysteria. But the Dunns, along with nearly everyone they knew in Bakersfield, didn't buy any of it. They believed their district attorney when he declared that the appeals judges were wrong, that these jurists were misguided liberals who cared more about criminals' rights than crime victims. "It's those damn judges," Pat agreed heartily when Sandy read him the latest news about convicts appealing their way out of prison. "They won't let the police do their job."

It never seems to end, Pat often said when Sandy finished reading the crime news. Just a few months before Sandy disappeared, the Dunns had followed the case of a high school track star named Offord Rollins, convicted of murdering his former girlfriend to clear the way for a new girl. It was an ugly case that, because of its racial overtones, tore an enormous rift in the community. Rollins was black, the murdered girl Latina, the judge and jury all white. The prosecutor pointed to violent rap lyrics penned by the young athlete as evidence of his viciousness; the defense lawyer complained that official racism and misconduct, not hard evidence, put his client in prison. Even an archconservative like Sandy had wondered aloud one morning over her newspaper whether the defense lawyer might be right. "That case just doesn't make sense" she had started to say.

"They wouldn't have arrested him if he hadn't done it," Pat interrupted reflexively, adamantly—a true believer. "He *must* be guilty." To Pat's way of thinking, no innocent man could ever be prosecuted in America without the truth sooner or later coming out. "There'd be no reason to do it," he told Sandy, applying free-market reasoning to the justice system. "What would the cops and the DA get out of framing that kid? It's not like they get paid by the arrest. There's nothing in it for them."

Pat's law-and-order attitude, his trust in "the men in blue," never seemed to waver, not even after he and Sandy had their own brush with the legal system three years after moving in together—the one documented instance of marital discord in the Dunn household.

On October 19, 1989, shortly before nine in the evening, Sandy dialed 911 on her bedroom telephone. When the dispatcher answered, Sandy said, "He hit me. My husband hit me. And I want him arrested." She reported that the assault had happened five minutes before she placed the call to the authorities. The dispatcher promised help would be there quickly.

When sheriff's deputies arrived exactly six minutes after Sandy placed the call, they found Pat sitting calmly in the den of the Crestmont house. He was chatting with one of his best friends, Kate Rosenlieb, a former student who, at Pat's urging, had gone on to take a seat on the Bakersfield City Planning Commission, which reviewed every proposed real estate project in the city. The two

were sitting and drinking beer, and Rosenlieb clearly had
arrived before Sandy called the police and had been
there for some time. Pat had telephoned her earlier in
the evening and asked her to come over for a visit. She
would later say she had seen nothing untoward happen,
and hadn't even set eyes on Sandy until the deputies
arrived.[6]

Once the police walked in, Sandy emerged from the
back of the house. She had a small cut behind her right
ear that had left a touch of blood on her earlobe and in
her hair, though she refused any medical treatment. "He
was angry with me, I don't know why," Sandy told the
deputies. "He was drinking and yelling. I came in the
bedroom and pulled back the covers to go to bed, and
that's when he hit me. Twice, with his fist."

The deputies arrested Pat on the spot for misdemeanor spousal abuse. They asked him no questions, but
he volunteered, "No, I did not hit her." Later, they took
him to the county jail, where he asked for a lawyer,
though he never actually saw one or hired one.[7]

Kate Rosenlieb, meanwhile, offered to stay at the
house to help, but Sandy said, "No, I want you out of
here." Sandy looked dazed, but Rosenlieb still left—without the deputies asking her a single question, not even
taking her name. She left feeling deeply disturbed, certain
that her friend Pat, someone she long admired, had
indeed struck Sandy. The incident would leave a long-
lasting impression on the young city official, one that
would return to haunt her and Pat Dunn. No one—not
Pat, not Rosenlieb and not the sheriff's department—
realized Kate actually could have provided an alibi of
sorts for Pat, as she was sitting talking with him over
beers when Sandy claimed to have been beaten.

Something was wrong with Sandy's account, though no one knew it at the time.

As Pat would later tell it, this incident marked the first time that he noticed Sandy display a memory or mental problem. He didn't recognize it at the time, but he would later come to see this episode as a first symptom, perhaps, of the early onset of Alzheimer's disease. According to Pat, there had been no fight and no hitting that night—Sandy simply went rigid, her face blank as she stood in the bedroom. Then she lost her balance, slipped and struck her head on a bench at the foot of the bed. As Pat bent to help her up, she looked up at him with a dazed expression and said, "You hit me." She then refused to listen to his denials, refused his offers of help, and insisted she just wanted to be left alone. So he left the room and called Kate Rosenlieb, who came over a short time later. He didn't realize Sandy had called the police until they walked through the door and arrested him.

After that night, Sandy rarely talked of this incident, so only Pat Dunn's account survives. What is known is that Sandy immediately went down to the jail and posted Pat's five-thousand-dollar bail, and he returned home with her. They continued living together, and most of their neighbors remained unaware that anything had happened. Even Otis Coppock, who watched every move at the Dunn house, was unaware that Pat had been arrested. The case against Pat was eventually dismissed after Sandy told prosecutors that nothing had happened, that she had made a mistake, and that she would not press charges. Legally, this meant Pat was innocent of spousal abuse, just as he had claimed all along. Given that Sandy initially claimed Pat struck her at a time when he apparently was sitting having a beer with a friend, there is every reason to accept her recantation at face value. It is also true, however, that many wives lie to protect abusive husbands. Though she never let him know it, Pat's good friend Kate Rosenlieb secretly suspected this was exactly what Sandy did: She lied to protect him. It was an assumption that would later have grave implications for Pat Dunn.

Whatever happened between the Dunns that night— accident or violence or the beginning of a long, slow mental decline for Sandy—their marriage and their daily rituals continued as if nothing had happened. If anything, the couple seemed to grow closer. They searched for retirement homes in Hawaii and Cabo San Lucas, putting bids in on several properties, but in the end deciding to stay in their comfortable home in Bakersfield, at least for the time being. And when Pat grew ill with a ruptured appendix in January 1992, Sandy withdrew twenty thousand dollars from one of the Paola accounts and paid cash for the surgery, as neither of them had medical insurance. Then Sandy nursed Pat back to health at home, caring for him constantly for nearly a month. Several of their friends remarked on how solicitous Sandy seemed throughout Pat's convalescence, and how grateful he was for all the care and attention she lavished upon him. He repeated his now familiar boast: "Nobody takes care of me like Mom."

During this time, however, Pat's business began to falter for lack of attention. Normally, he aggressively telephoned banks and mortgage lenders daily, pursuing their business and seeking new homes in foreclosure. But since falling ill, he had let things go. "Why don't you just close it down?" Sandy finally asked. "We don't need the money. Let's play with what we've got."

Pat felt hesitant at first, but Sandy got their accountant

to pull together some figures to show that the business was now costing more than it brought in, and Pat finally said, "Good idea. Let's play with what we've got."

A short time later, Sandy made an appointment with Kevin Knutson, a financial planner, to discuss forming a living trust. Knutson lived with Teri Bjorn, the Dunns' real estate attorney, and the couples occasionally socialized. At a barbecue at the Dunns' house, Knutson and Sandy began chatting about investments, and she mentioned her desire that Pat have greater access to her finances and the Paola properties, particularly if she were to slip mentally, from Alzheimer's disease or any other cause. When Knutson remarked on how trusts could be used to shield assets and avoid inheritance taxes far better than a simple will would, Sandy seemed very interested. She invited Knutson over to discuss the details of setting up such a trust for her and Pat. The meeting was set for the morning of June 30, a Tuesday. "Come at lunch time," Sandy said. "We'll feed you." It would be the very day Sandy disappeared.[8]

By this time, the night that Sandy had Pat arrested for spousal abuse seemed a part of the distant past, almost forgotten and never discussed. There had been no recurrences—if anything, the incident had served only to strengthen Pat's faith in the hard-as-nails justice system of Kern County. Indeed, he considered the experience a demonstration of how well the system worked. "The police had to err on the side of protecting her," he would later say. "I understand that, and I think it's right. The truth came out in the end. That's the way the system works."

To almost everyone's astonishment, it was a faith Pat Dunn seemed to retain right up to the day he was convicted of first-degree murder.

5

TRACING SANDY'S MOVEMENTS AFTER SHE VANISHED on the night of June 30, 1992, should have been child's play, for her habits were utterly predictable. Indeed, even the police who came to believe wholeheartedly that Pat Dunn was the culprit would concede that anyone could have stalked Sandy with ease. Each day was the same: Sometime between 3 and 4 A.M., she would rise in the darkness and change in the laundry room, where she would not disturb Pat. She'd layer T-shirts against the desert's morning chill, but she always wore shorts—she was very proud of her trim, smooth legs. Then she'd run a comb through her short, silver hair, grab the dog leash, and head out the door.

A brisk walker, Sandy covered nearly six miles of East Bakersfield every day, winding through the College Center strip mall that she and Pat still owned and managed. Sandy would let her dogs, J.D. and Buddy, run in a field next to the Mervyn's department store, then head back home, all before sunrise. Her route rarely varied.

"I like to walk then," she would say whenever Pat or anyone else expressed concerns for her safety at that hour. "That's when the good people are out." By that she meant her companions in wakefulness at that hour were policemen, security guards, farmers, bakers, milkmen—the people whose work is preparing the world for each new day. Pat eventually stopped objecting, figuring this actually made some sense, though he persisted in complaining about her jewelry—the twenty-five thousand dollars' worth of diamonds and gold she habitually wore. "Leave the damn baubles and bangles off when you're walking," Pat exhorted her. Sandy ignored his warnings. Only after her jeweler added a cautionary warning to Pat's did she reluctantly remove her rings, necklaces and other adornments during her predawn power walks. "You just don't know who you might run into," the jeweler said, and Sandy finally acquiesced, six months or so before her disappearance.

Jewelry was the one indulgence of an otherwise frugal person who spent little on clothes and whose idea of dining out during her and Pat's courtship was finding some office party or business opening from which she could filch a free meal of hors d'oeuvres. When Pat started dating her, she was eating dinners of microwaved cabbage four nights a week—not for lack of money, but because she just didn't care much about food. Gold and gems, however, particularly interested her. "I like to put my money in jewelry," she once told Pat. "That way, no matter what happens, we'll never be broke."

From time to time, Sandy walked with other women, but her early hours and fast pace soon wore out would-be walking partners. At first, Pat used to try to keep up with her on her morning expeditions, but too much booze and belly made that a losing proposition. Sandy ate next to nothing and, in her fifties, still played in tennis and soccer leagues with college students. Pat used to say Sandy wore the pads off the paws of their poor old Labrador, J.D., which is why he bought a German shepherd and named him Buddy—to be her new walking buddy, so the aging J.D. could rest up. But the old Lab couldn't bear being left out, and both dogs usually ended up joining her. Except on the day she disappeared.

Pat had initially reported to the sheriff that Sandy took Buddy with her on her last walk. He told the dispatcher who took his missing-person's report that Sandy must have returned while he was out searching, left the dog in the yard and her keys in the kitchen, then departed again and vanished. But as the days passed, Pat became less and less sure about these events. He didn't really know for certain that she had come back while he made that first search of East Bakersfield, he would later tell detectives. Perhaps, in a fog of sleepiness and worry that first night, he simply overlooked the keys and the big dog when he got up. Buddy could have been sleeping in the shadows out in the yard when Pat first looked around. The keys could have been there on the counter all along. He just didn't know.

Pat kept going over it all in his head: His and Sandy's last full day together had begun like every other. By the time Sandy had completed her walk, Pat was up, with coffee made and poured—as always. They had settled in and she read him the newspaper while they sat in the kitchen, the light growing warmer and brighter as the sun rose above the rooftops. Pat listened and kept the cups brimming. As usual, no matter how thick or thin the paper, Sandy had finished reading at 6 A.M. sharp with a dramatic rendition of their horoscopes. "Make a fresh start," the stars told Sandy that day. Pat was advised to be serious concerning home and marriage. "Intuition works overtime," his horoscope warned.

At six, their morning ritual had them climbing into Pat's white Chevy Blazer to go "ride fence"—their term for an hour-long drive around town to view the twenty-one properties that Sandy had inherited, several million dollars' worth of mostly vacant real estate left behind by Pat Paola, waiting to be built up. They particularly liked stopping at their Morning Star housing development, where bulldozers had begun moving earth in preparation for home construction, and at their eleven acres on Columbus Avenue, where they were planning to build a twelve-screen movie-theater complex—if the city would just stop reneging on promises made years earlier.

"I could watch those big yellow machines all day," Sandy had said outside the Morning Star project. It was what she always said. "We're really building something, aren't we?"

Pat remembers the pride in her voice. The long-vacant land, a scraped and dead eyesore on the east side, was finally going to become something useful and attractive, a place for families and children—the realization of a dream that had begun with her late first husband. "It's going to be beautiful," Pat agreed.

They chose not to linger that last morning at the inactive Columbus Avenue site, however. Neither of them wanted to talk about their movie-theater project. They had just completed an ugly battle with the Bakersfield planning commission and the city council, and now might be headed toward an even uglier lawsuit over the city's decision to deny a vital zoning change that would allow the complex to be built. The decision had been a stunner. The same council members who had just said no to their project had two years earlier asked Pat and Sandy to create a detailed and costly plan for the area and led them to believe the eighty thousand dollars they were investing in the planning and engineering would be rewarded with approval. But a small and vocal group of angry residents had come to the council meeting on June 3 and complained about the project. None had seen the plans, but it seemed to Pat and Sandy they would have opposed any design other than keeping the land vacant. The councilwoman who represented their ward, despite allowing the Dunns to believe otherwise, backed their objections, arguing that this was "her" ward, and that the rest of the council should fall in line with her wishes. That was the way the council worked, each ward a mini-fiefdom, and a majority of the other members went along with her, previous promises to the Dunns—tape-record-ed ones, made in open meetings—notwithstanding. It was a stressful, difficult time for Pat and Sandy. The loss of eighty thousand dollars, while substantial and difficult to stomach, would not break them. But the sense of out-rage at being outfoxed and, as far as they were concerned, misled in the political arena left them boiling and bitter.

"It was predestined to be voted down," Pat had com-plained, nearly shouting at the podium during the June 3 meeting. "Tell me that's fair. Tell me it's legal." He even tried to question some law students whose class hap-pened to be observing in the audience that day to see if they thought the proceedings were legal.

"Wait a minute, just let yourself rest, Mr. Dunn," the mayor finally interrupted, alarmed and angry. "We don't want to poll the audience."

A few minutes later, the Dunns' project died. Pat and Sandy were left standing open-mouthed and humiliated.

In the weeks that followed, Sandy at times seemed beside herself over the council's decision. She felt espe-cially betrayed by two friends in city government who had been in a position to assure the project's future, but who had instead doomed it. The first of these was Kate Rosenlieb, who, as a member of the planning commission, could have supported her friends' movie-theater development. Sandy had confided in Kate how much she wanted the project to succeed, and had even threatened to kill herself if the city rejected the Dunns' latest plan for the vacant property. Kate could not tell if this suicidal talk was mere histrionics or a genuine threat. In any case, she declined to do Sandy's bidding when the planning commission next met. Instead, citing her friendship with the Dunns as a conflict of interest, Kate abstained from consideration of the project, leading to a narrow vote rejecting the plan. Sandy had always assumed Kate would be an ally, one reason why she had joined Pat in pushing their young friend to run for the commission in the first place. After the vote, Sandy stopped talking to Kate. (Pat, on the other hand, told Kate he had no problem with the abstention—he said he wanted her to do what she thought was right.)

Sandy grew even more angry at another friend, City Councilwoman Pat DeMond. Sandy believed DeMond stabbed her in the back by voting against the project once it got before the city council, which had the power to override the planning commission's decision. As Pat and Sandy saw it, DeMond had previously hinted she would support the movie-theater development, and her one extra vote was all they needed for passage. Since the vote to reject the project, Sandy refused to speak to the councilwoman and had even snubbed her at the supermarket, leaving DeMond uttering greetings to her retreating back. "I want nothing to do with that woman," Sandy later told Pat.

A few days after that awful council meeting, the

Dunns had lunch at their home with a longtime friend, Jim Marino, a thirty-year-old engineer and another member of the city planning commission. Marino, a veteran of several of the Dunns' projects, had supported their theater proposal and, unlike Rosenlieb, chose not to abstain from the vote. At lunch, he noticed how stressed Sandy seemed by the whole ordeal with the city, and he was happy when she turned the subject toward lighter topics. "How are your kids doing?" she asked as she moved in and out of the kitchen preparing the meal and setting the table. Marino gave a rundown of everything his three children were doing—school, summer activities, birthday plans. Pat stood at the bar making drinks, listening. Then, about five minutes or so later, Sandy emerged once again from the kitchen, smiled at Marino and asked, "So, how are the kids?"

It was an eerie moment, Marino would later recall, and he glanced over at Pat, who was looking down, still apparently busy pouring and mixing—but noticeably avoiding the younger man's eye. Sandy looked at her guest expectantly, so he again told her all about his kids, repeating the story virtually word for word, waiting for her to say, Oh, you just told me all that. But she never did. She just nodded and smiled and then returned to the kitchen.

A few minutes later, she popped out again and asked in a bright, happy voice, "So, how are your kids?"

This time, Marino caught Pat's eye. His friend just shrugged and smiled helplessly. And Marino repeated the story again, with Sandy oohing and ahhing as if she had never heard any of it. Now the other occasions in recent months when Sandy had somehow forgotten his preferred beverage with lunch—for ten years, it had always been the same, black coffee—began to make sense. Though still in her fifties, Sandy, whom he liked and respected, was having memory problems, Marino realized. And through her husband's smiles and shrugs and gentle prods, Marino saw Pat was well aware of it—and doing everything he could to cover it and spare Sandy embarrassment. Marino left the Dunns' house that afternoon feeling helpless and sad. He genuinely cared for Sandy and Pat, but his affection for them did not cloud his judgment that Sandy's mental state had begun a slow yet perceptible decline.[9]

Three and a half weeks later, on the morning of June 30, Sandy seemed fine to Pat as they rode fence. Still, anxious to avoid reliving the stress of the council debate, Pat had studiously avoided mentioning the Columbus project or lingering near the site. Things actually were looking up for the project. Just a day earlier, he and Sandy had spoken with the architect—himself a former planning commissioner and a city hall insider—who said he would make clear to the Bakersfield city attorney that the Dunns had been victimized unjustly. The mere threat of a lawsuit might be enough to change the decision, given the council's flip-flops with the Dunns, the architect said, for the city had just had to pay out a whopping settlement to another developer for similar broken promises. "I'm very optimistic," he told them, and Sandy's mood had visibly brightened after the conversation. Still, the project and everything connected to it remained a sore subject, and Pat just drove on by.

Later that last morning, around 11:30, Kevin Knutson, the insurance agent and financial planner, came by for lunch and to discuss the living trust he and Sandy had spoken of at the barbecue a few weeks earlier.

Knutson, a tall, glib former college baseball player, settled into the Dunns' den, where a sandwich from Pat's favorite deli already awaited him. While he ate, he played a videotape for the Dunns that explained how an irrevocable trust worked, how it allowed the transfer of an estate to an heir without necessitating probate or incurring hefty estate taxes, because it accomplished this transfer without a will. The video also described how a living trust could be set up to direct decisions about finances and medical care to a spouse or other family member if an individual were to become ill or unable to manage his or her own affairs. The example used in the video was of a woman who became incompetent due to Alzheimer's disease.

As far as Knutson was concerned, this living trust was academic at this point—he had never noticed any mental or memory problems in Sandy or Pat. "But you have to plan for contingencies, to prepare for the future. That's the essence of financial security," he explained.

Knutson questioned the Dunns about their assets, and Pat readily admitted that, with his business shut down, he really had no assets to speak of. Nor did he have a will. Sandy said most of their money was in her name—her cash, bonds and real estate were by this time valued at about five million dollars. In place of her existing will leaving everything to Pat, she said she would like most of their wealth transferred to an irrevocable trust in her and Pat's names—meaning that each would have access to the funds, and one would retain control if the other grew ill or died. "I want Pat taken care of if anything ever happens to me," she told Knutson. "And I don't want it all bleeding away in taxes."

When Pat left the room, Sandy quietly asserted that

she wanted to make sure that none of Pat's children inherited anything. She didn't care for any of them, particularly the youngest, Jennifer, who had become pregnant with a second child out of wedlock, much to Sandy's embarrassment and outrage. Sandy suspected Jennifer stayed close to her father only to get at the Paola fortune, and she didn't think much more of the two Dunn boys. "I don't want them to get a penny," she said coldly. "And the same goes for my sister. I don't want her to get one penny. Nothing."

She also told Knutson that, if she ever were to develop Alzheimer's disease, she wanted Pat to be able to take over without problems. Knutson said all of these stipulations could be written into the trust. Sandy nodded with satisfaction.

After a few hours of lunch and discussion, Pat suggested he and Knutson take a ride so the planner could see some of the real estate that would be placed in the trust. So they went out riding fence, as Pat and Sandy had earlier that day, and Pat pointed out each property. At one point while they were alone together, he told Knutson, "You know, I really am worried about Mom. I think she's having some memory problems, maybe Alzheimer's. It's little things, but I'm worried."

Knutson turned to Pat in surprise. "I don't really see it, Pat. My mother had Alzheimer's, and I don't see any of those symptoms in Sandy. I really don't."

Pat grew quiet for a moment, then said, "You really wouldn't notice it unless you were around all the time. But I hope you're right."

By the time they got back to the house, it was somewhere between four and five in the afternoon. As Knutson walked to his car to go home, Sandy came out of the house and gave him a hug. "Thanks for all your help," she said. Both Pat and Sandy seemed relaxed and happy, he would later say.

"I'll put together a proposal and I'll call you Thursday or Friday to set up a time to go over it."

"Great," Sandy replied.

It would be the last time Kevin Knutson would see Sandy alive.[10]

After Knutson left, Pat cooked two thick steaks on the barbecue. Sandy fried some rice. She seemed quiet and even a bit depressed, perhaps by Knutson's video and its discussion of Alzheimer's, Pat would later say. She went to bed early in the evening, as usual, with Pat following an hour later. By ten that night, she was gone. She had left their bed hours before her habitual walking time and never returned. Something happened to her, Pat Dunn told the authorities. I'm sure of it.

The authorities thought so, too. And they had some very firm beliefs about where to start looking for answers.

6

THIRTEEN YEARS BEFORE ALEXANDRA PAOLA DUNN disappeared and Pat Dunn became a target for prosecution, a combination of events both spontaneous and conspired catapulted into power and prominence a little-known, baby-faced prosecutor with a hunger for authority and a belief that the nation's justice system had drifted dangerously leftward in favor of criminals. As the new district attorney for Kern County, Edward R. Jagels would transform Bakersfield from an ordinary farm community and oil town into the toughest town on crime in America—in the process, sealing the fate of his ardent supporter Pat Dunn, along with many others like him.

The pivotal moment in this region's modern war on crime came on April 12, 1979, a time when Sandy still lived with Pat Paola, and Pat Dunn still lived with his first wife and worked as an elementary school principal. It was the day they and the rest of Bakersfield came to know, all too briefly, a girl named Dana Butler.

It was not so much Dana Butler's murder itself, or even the identity of the prime suspect, who turned out to be a man of power and prominence. It was not even the fact that this case, more than any other, marked the day that Bakersfield's small-town complacency finally died and just about everyone seemed to realize that nothing—

not distance, not time, not even the mighty Grapevine—could keep the twentieth century's most fearsome scourge, random violence, from taking root. In the end, what really made this case so important to Kern County's future came down to what the authorities did about it. Or, rather, didn't do.

Dana Butler was a fourteen-year-old honors student who vanished on her way home from her church one afternoon. Three days after her mother reported her missing, her corpse appeared on a highway shoulder just outside the Bakersfield city limits. She'd been stabbed forty times, perhaps tortured. There were no witnesses. The murderer had bathed and dressed the body before dumping it by the side of the road. When the police arrived, Dana was still damp, cleansed—or so the killer thought—of trace evidence, the tiny hairs, fibers and fluids so crucial in such cases. Detectives learned in short order from Dana's friends that she had been one of a number of high school students who had been the underage houseguests of a fifty-six-year-old retiree named Glenn Fitts. Fitts had been throwing parties at his home, where he'd ply teenagers with drugs and booze, then ask some for sex in return. Dana had been to his house shortly before her disappearance, her friends said, and had spoken of plans to party there the very day she died.

With this information in hand shortly after Dana's body was found, Fitts became an obvious suspect in the murder. Yet the Kern County Sheriff's Department was reluctant to pursue him, for an equally obvious reason: Until his retirement a year earlier due to a heart ailment, Glenn Fitts had been chairman of the law-enforcement program at Bakersfield Community College, director of the Kern County Police Academy, and a member of the Bakersfield Police Commission. He had personally instructed most of the cops and sheriff's deputies in Kern County. Then, as a city police commissioner, he oversaw many of them.

Given his exalted status among many Kern County cops, the investigation of Fitts seemed halting at best. Weeks passed before detectives mustered the nerve to request a search warrant for their mentor's home, something that would have been done long before in virtually any other murder case. Even with that delay, and the opportunity it offered for evidence to be destroyed, a powerful case against the former police commissioner emerged once the search finally was performed. Traces of blood matching Dana's rare blood type were found in Fitts' house on carpeting that had been steam cleaned just after the murder—but not cleaned quite thoroughly enough to eliminate all trace evidence. Fitts told police the blood was his, but testing proved that to be a lie. Further testing linked carpet fibers and human hairs found on Dana's body to his house and car. Pubic hairs consistent with those of Fitts were found clinging to Dana's head. This was the sort of cold, hard, clinical evidence detectives dream of finding when they must build a circumstantial case in the absence of eyewitnesses to the crime. In many respects, such evidence can be more convincing and reliable than eyewitnesses. Any hesitation detectives felt about going after the ex-commissioner faded in the face of the physical evidence against him.

However, when the sheriff's investigators brought their case to the district attorney's office, they were told no, there would be no prosecution. The DA himself, a veteran prosecutor named Al Leddy, and his top three deputies made the call, overruling a lower-level trial deputy who had said, sure, of course there's enough evidence to prosecute Fitts.

To the sheriff and his detectives on the case—as well as to other prosecutors in the Kern County DA's office—the decision looked extraordinarily timid at best and, at worst, smacked of a cover-up and of favoritism of the worst kind. It enraged cops and deputies throughout Bakersfield, creating an instant divide between normally natural allies, the cops in the street and the prosecutors in the courtrooms. Fitts, it seemed, was untouchable. He blithely put his house up for sale and made plans to leave town for good.

But the sheriff made sure that word leaked out about the evidence against Fitts—and about the DA's unwillingness to prosecute the suspected killer of Dana Butler. The local press picked up the story, and the protests began. A grassroots organization called Mothers of Bakersfield began picketing the courthouse, Al Leddy's home and Glenn Fitts' house, demanding justice in the Butler case—an extraordinary sight in a conservative community where protesters generally were reviled. The group begged the California Attorney General to investigate, a request that was summarily denied. Unwilling to relent, the sheriff, despite Leddy's and the state's decision to do nothing, placed Fitts under round-the-clock surveillance. Meanwhile, Dana's parents filed lawsuits against Fitts, putting his name into the public record. Then, after a long refusal to name him as a suspect despite his involvement in the case being an open secret among reporters, the local news media finally published Fitts' name in connection with Dana's murder.

Under this mounting pressure, the DA finally agreed

to bring the case before the grand jury. Even then, senior prosecutors withheld key evidence from the panel and ultimately closed the investigation without asking for an indictment. But if this was intended to provide political cover, the tactic failed: District Attorney Leddy finally had to charge Fitts or face a near insurrection in his town. The charge he settled on was not murder, however—it was contributing to the delinquency of minors, for passing out drugs to kids. Even then, prosecutors and a compliant judge tried to shield Fitts by sealing files that normally were open to the public, but the howls of protest that resulted led to the unsealing of the records a day later. The police commissioner's dalliances with children became instant fodder for public court files and television news shows. In the midst of the ensuing uproar, Fitts was found in his yard shot in the head, a death officially ruled a suicide, though a neighbor reported hearing two shots, and the gun found next to Fitts had been fired only once.

The case, abruptly ended with so many questions unanswered, had a profound and lasting effect on Kern County. District Attorney Al Leddy decided not to run for reelection, and his top prosecutors, who had harbored ambitions to succeed him, also bowed out. Winning the DA's election in Kern County without support from the cops irate over the Fitts case would have been tough. The police had in the past taken to the streets and banged on doors for candidates with great success. They literally got DAs elected—or defeated. Prosecutors involved with the Dana Butler–Glen Fitts fiasco would have faced long odds indeed if they had run. The race, then, was open to a new candidate, one who could garner support from law enforcement as well as the grassroots Mothers of

Bakersfield organization that had risen to prominence in the wake of Dana Butler's murder.

And so, an obscure but extremely aggressive young prosecutor named Ed Jagels, with an infusion of family money and the law enforcement support denied his predecessor, stepped into the vacuum left by the Butler case. At the time, he was known chiefly around the courthouse for a combative attitude toward judges, most of whom he openly despised, and for the extreme, almost vicious approach he took to trying cases—he attacked defendants, witnesses and defense attorneys with gleeful vigor, always seeking to take control of the courtroom and the case. He had a habit of accusing anyone who disagreed with his ultraconservative views of being in league with criminals and of "perverting" the law—particularly if the disagreement emanated from a trial judge or appeals court. The local bench suspected that Jagels was the source for some extremely unflattering articles about Kern County judges that appeared in a statewide legal publication, in which one supposedly cowardly judge's courtroom was derogatorily labeled "Foster Farms," the name of a popular purveyor of chicken parts. (Jagels denied being the anonymous source but did not disavow the sentiments expressed.)[11] Later in his career, after he became DA, Jagels' public tirade over the California Supreme Court's exclusion of a coerced confession in a murder case left his critics sputtering and even some of his supporters uneasy.

"If a couple of victims of these homicides wore black robes, appellate black robes, instead of being gas station attendants and ranchers and jewelry store clerks, we'd start getting a little bit different decisions," District Attorney Jagels told reporters in one of his most notorious press conferences. "I guarantee that."[12]

When Jagels announced his candidacy for district attorney, he surprised most everyone but the cadre of similarly minded young prosecutors he led, a new generation of prosecuting attorneys who were less interested in the cushy private practices sought by their predecessors, and more concerned with remaking the justice system in their own image. As DA, Jagels promised to crack down on child abusers like no one else before him. Never again would a criminal like Glenn Fitts be allowed to roam free. His would be the most aggressive DA's office in the state, Jagels promised, an office that would push the envelope on the streets and in the courtrooms, doing whatever it took to put crooks away. He would draw the line against elevating "criminals'" rights over victims' rights, he vowed. His campaign slogan: "Ask a cop." His most ardent supporters: the Mothers of Bakersfield and their leader, a self-styled child-abuse expert named Jill Haddad, who later would play a pivotal role in the DA's office and the then-nascent Witch Hunt cases.

Together, they wanted to transform the justice system of Kern County into the nation's toughest, a virtual criminal-conviction machine.

All they had to do was win.

Ed Jagels stood perfectly still, watching the moment—his moment—play out in the crowded debate hall. For many of those present, it seemed the 1982 election was being decided right in front of them, just weeks before the vote. And the best part was, all Jagels had to do was sit back and enjoy it as his opponent, one of the hated judges, crashed and burned right next to him. It was almost like prosecuting some scumbag defendant and watching him self-destruct on the witness stand, the lies unraveling like cheap socks.

"I can't really respond to that," the judge sputtered to the implacable woman in the audience, the one with the tightly curled hair and the file of legal papers held overhead like a bludgeon. "I don't really recall the case you're referring to."

But the woman kept waving those papers, legal files from an awful case of abusive parents and a murdered child, a bad ruling pulled out of the judge's past, one that demanded an explanation not even Learned Hand could have conjured.

Jagels supporters in the audience thrilled at the unexpected confrontation. There was one of Kern County's best-known and most powerful jurists, Judge Marvin Ferguson, the cigar-chomping courthouse insider, double chin quivering, vainly searching the faces in front of him for some clue as to what to say to this woman who would not sit down. Until this moment, Ferguson had been the easy favorite to win the district attorney's race, the candidate with all the support from the legal community, the one with the political connections and the campaign war chest. He had dismissed the upstart Jagels with a wave of his stubby hand, refusing to call him by name, referring to him instead simply as "that young guy." He mocked Jagels for his inexperience, saying the young guy had tried a mere eight cases before a jury in his brief career—and had been harshly criticized by an appeals court in one of them. Ferguson considered Jagels impertinent and dangerous, and he had vowed to crush him. And for a long time, it had looked like he would do just that. Now everything was about to change. The room seemed filled with crossed arms and stony stares, all of them directed at Judge Ferguson—and all because a community activist named Jill Haddad had a question.

Why was it, Haddad wanted to know, that five years ago, Judge Ferguson had sent a four-year-old girl named Mary Ann Azevedo home to abusive parents after county welfare workers asked the judge to put the child into protective custody? "I think that shows a pretty cavalier attitude," Haddad suggested, "with overwhelming evidence of child abuse."

The judge looked blankly at the small, intense woman with the thick sheaf of paper. He vaguely recognized her as someone the newspaper occasionally wrote about, identifying her most often with the ambiguous title of "child-abuse crusader." He didn't know what she was getting at now, but he sensed that whatever was in that folder wasn't going to be pretty. "I resent the implication that I'm soft on child abuse," he finally huffed. His inquisitor continued as if he hadn't spoken.

When the case came to you, Haddad said, Mary Ann had been beaten by her stepfather. The girl was left with a broken collarbone, a burned hand and a possible concussion and skull fracture. Mary Ann's mother did nothing, waiting all day to bring the girl to the hospital, then refusing to report the beating to police. The emergency room had to do that. "Yet you sent Mary Ann back home with her."

Haddad paused as the audience listened raptly. Everyone knew what was coming, yet dreaded it, too. Ed Jagels still just stood there and nodded slightly, lean, silver-haired, a grim smile on his face—a cool and calm contrast to the flustered judge next to him. For Jagels, it didn't get any better than this: First the old DA had been pushed out of the way after mishandling Dana Butler and Glenn Fitts, and now he had Ferguson on the ropes. Haddad reached the inevitable end of her story: As soon as the stepfather got out of jail a few months later, he and the mother moved with Mary Ann to Mississippi, where he promptly beat the girl to death. "Thanks to your order," Haddad concluded.

Ferguson stood stammering at the front of the room. Somehow, Haddad had gotten hold of confidential child-welfare files that were never supposed to see the light of day. They came to her anonymously in the mail, she would later say. The files revealed one of the most unfortunate rulings of Ferguson's career. He knew, as every judge knew, that one bad decision could erase a thousand good rulings so far as the public was concerned. Unable to recall any details of the case—the blur of plaintiffs and defendants make it impossible for any busy judge to remember cases by name—he finally offered a thread-bare response: "Since it is against the law to divulge juvenile matters, it's difficult to defend myself."

The audience seemed almost as shocked by the judge's reliance on rules of secrecy as it was by the awful story itself. Thanks to Dana Butler, violence against children had become a hot-button issue in Bakersfield even as a national movement was taking root as well to end what had been a tendency to treat child abuse as a mere "family problem." Ferguson, thanks to Haddad, was being cast as part of the old guard, and Ed Jagels, recognizing a devastating blow when he saw one, knew how to finish it off—just as he would finish up a summation in the courtroom.

"We have some very good judges in Kern County, and I'm happy with them," Jagels told the audience. Then he turned to look at Ferguson, voice heavy with trademark sarcasm. "We also have some very bad judges who worry too much about being reversed."

There was only one thing to do about it, Jagels continued: They had to put the bad judges out of office, the ones who were more concerned with protecting criminals than the rights of crime victims. Jagels promised, as he had throughout his campaign, to make the task of removing bad judges part of his job description as DA. He'd start with the chief justice of the California Supreme Court, the wildly unpopular Rose Bird, and work his way down, he vowed.

The one hundred fifty members of the audience applauded loudly. Suddenly the race for DA was not about experience or standing in the community or courtroom smarts, the issues Ferguson wanted to argue. It was about vigor and youth and new ideas versus the old, corrupt system that got us where we are now. It was about Ed Jagels versus the baby-killing judge.

This contrast in images became an enduring theme for the rest of the campaign. Ferguson never recovered from Jill Haddad's seemingly spontaneous surprise, and Jagels never looked back. The death of one child, Dana Butler, had made it possible for Jagels to run for district attorney. And the death of another, Mary Ann Azevedo, made it possible for Jagels to win.

What no one knew at the time was how Jill Haddad, the head of Mothers of Bakersfield and a member of Jagels' campaign committee, had obtained those confidential records on the murdered little girl. Later it was revealed that another supporter of Jagels' candidacy—a prosecutor colleague of his named Colleen Ryan—had gone to the courthouse while on maternity leave and, with a group of other supporters and DA employees that included a good friend of Jill Haddad's, obtained the records. The clerk who handed over the confidential files was unaware that Ryan was on leave and assumed the prosecutor sought the records for official business of the district attorney's office. But there was no official business—just political dirty work. Ryan turned the records over to Jagels' political consultant and, two weeks later, Jill Haddad was waving them during that fateful campaign debate. What had seemed at the time to be a spontaneous confrontation between a citizen and a candidate—a pivotal moment in the election—had in reality been a campaign ploy.

Had it come to light then, such a revelation might have altered the outcome of the election. But word of this escapade remained hidden until long after Jagels had won by a comfortable margin and sat securely in office. A county grand jury investigating a citizen complaint finally uncovered the ploy, however, and recommended that Colleen Ryan be reprimanded for her misconduct. During the grand jury investigation, Ryan steadfastly denied that Jagels himself had anything to do with the plot, and Jagels, just as steadfastly, refused to discipline her, no matter what the grand jury said. He defended her throughout, and later backed her bid for a judgeship, which she won and still holds in Kern County. The *Bakersfield Californian* editorialized against Jagels for a time, accusing him of tolerating prosecutorial misconduct and calling him the new "law and no order" district attorney, but the controversy soon died down, Jagels' indignant denials winning out in the end.

What everyone seemed to miss in the furor was the fact that the confidential documents raided on Jagels' behalf really told a very different story than the one put forth at that debate. Jagels' opponent did make the fateful order to send the girl home; that much was true. But it turns out the district attorney's office, through inaction, had left the judge no other choice—no prosecutor even appeared at the hearing. Furthermore, it was Jagels' own office that plea-bargained the murderous stepfather out of jail after only a few months, not the judge. In the end, not only had a prosecutor's misconduct helped get Ed Jagels elected. It had also allowed blame for a child's murder to be heaped on the wrong man—and the wrong part of the justice system.[13]

Few outside the clubbish world of the Kern County courthouse even knew who Ed Jagels was back when he announced his candidacy for district attorney. Many who did know him found Jagels a cold and distant man, excruciatingly formal—though he took pains to overcome this side of his personality during his campaign, carefully posing with jacket slung over a shoulder, his tie loosened, as he knocked on doors with groups of cops and deputies. He was a consummate politician, always, and he looked the part, with his helmet of straight, silver hair that somehow could not add a day to his smooth, boyish face. His lips seemed perennially pursed, as if he were on the verge of a smirk. Only his eyes seemed old, pale blue and heavy-lidded, with purplish circles beneath them, almost like bruises—"a zealot's eyes," the local newspaper wrote during the campaign. Jagels liked that.

A college student during the Vietnam War, he is said to have provoked several fistfights with war protesters and to have been shot at once for his trouble—though these experiences apparently did not spark in him any particular interest in law enforcement as a career. As Jagels has told it, he simply drifted into law school, deciding to earn his degree for lack of any more compelling interests. It was just something to do. He ended up in Bakersfield on a whim, pulling off the highway while driving from Los Angeles to a job interview in San Francisco. On impulse, he interviewed at the Kern County DA's office on a Friday. There was a deputy DA spot open. He started work the following Monday.

By the time he wrested control of that office seven years later, there was nothing indifferent or whimsical about Jagels' approach to his job. His fervent desire to attack crime—and to control the machinery of justice in Kern County—had become increasingly obvious to those close to him, as he came to refer to the halls of justice as *"my* courthouse."

Still, the speed with which Jagels rose to prominence astonished his opponents. Before announcing that he would seek the DA's office, Jagels had been barely visible, at least as far as his cases went. He did not make headlines and, within the legal community, was known around the courthouse principally for his skirmishes with judges.

The most dramatic of these came shortly before he announced his candidacy, in the form of an appeals-court opinion on a simple armed-robbery case he had prosecuted two years earlier. It seems Jagels had a virtually airtight case against a stickup artist named Tony Perez. Two eyewitnesses had identified the defendant, including a clerk who had waited on Perez several times at the Circle K convenience store he later robbed. There was really no doubt about the outcome of the case—it was what prosecutors like to call a slam dunk.

Yet Jagels still managed to create controversy, earning the distinction of being upbraided by the California Court of Appeal for blatant misconduct in the court-room, where he was accused of infecting an entire trial with racist appeals and contemptuous and insulting behavior. During the Perez trial, the judge on the case repeatedly had to order Jagels to calm down, lecturing him as if speaking to a tantrum-prone child, and at one point unfavorably comparing the prosecutor's behavior to his teenage son's. "There cannot be any doubt that the district attorney, in this case, exceeded the bounds of good taste and proper courtroom decorum," the Fresno-based Fifth District panel of the state appeals court later wrote. "The instances of misconduct are legion: Jagels' rantings, ravings, constant apologies, characterizations of defense counsel and defense counsel's objections, personal attacks, allegations of impropriety, attacks on defense witnesses, improper questions, defiance of rulings, and the need for the court to continually admonish counsel. . . . He should have been severely reprimanded."[14]

This was not simply a matter of a wayward prosecutor failing to follow some dry legal principles or niggling technicalities. Appellate opinions going back sixty years have warned that when district attorneys don't play by the rules, the safeguards built into the justice system begin to crumble. Misconduct by any player in the justice system is serious—jurors, judge, a defense lawyer. But the consequences can be most devastating when the culprit is the prosecutor, now the single most powerful figure in the justice system, or in all of government, for that matter.[15] Even presidents must bend to the will of prosecutors, special and otherwise, who are accountable to none, operate largely in secret, and who are themselves immune from prosecution or lawsuits even when responsible for gross or deliberate miscarriages of justice. Most justice system participants and observers agree that the majority of professional prosecutors behave honorably and adhere to the rules (which, in any case, more often than not favor their cause over their defense attorney opponent's anyway). But the temptation to bend or break the rules to gain additional advantage can be enormous, given the lack of any meaningful supervision or sanctions for prosecutorial misbehavior. The courts have long recognized this imbalance of power and the enormous stakes involved, for prosecutorial misconduct not only serves the intended goal of making convictions more likely for the guilty, it also increases the possibility that the innocent will be convicted as well.[16]

Had it been a close case, Tony Perez could have had his conviction overturned because of the prosecutor's actions. Instead, the appeals court decided that Jagels' misconduct made no difference in this case—it was, to use a catchall legal principle that appeals courts frequently employ when they find problems but don't wish to set a criminal free, "harmless error." In other words, the evidence against Perez was so overwhelming that he would have been convicted regardless of Jagels' behavior. The prosecutor had gone over the line for no good reason, according to the appellate justices, and risked the loss of a conviction that should have been a cakewalk.

Far from being contrite about his performance, Jagels later seemed quite proud of the opinion railing against him, saying he would do the same thing again.[17] He explained his conduct in the Perez case by saying he had to take control of the courtroom because the judge was letting the defense lawyer run amok. Indeed, in touting his qualifications to be the next district attorney, Jagels expressed disappointment to one newspaper reporter that he had not been criticized or reversed by appellate courts more often. If the criminal-coddling judges criticized him, Jagels reasoned, he must be doing his job. His opponent in the DA's race, Judge Ferguson, tried to make a campaign issue out of the Perez case, citing it as an example of Jagels' inexperience and ethical lapses. But with typical rhetorical skill, Jagels managed to turn his own bad behavior into an example of his going the extra mile for public safety—in contrast to judges who liked to stand by and carp about technicalities.

"It is not enough for a district attorney simply to go to the office and put in eight hours," he told reporters during the campaign, voice thick with indignation. "The district attorney . . . is the only person who understands the system and has the victim's and public's perspective."

Jagels' protectiveness of this turf he had staked out as his and his alone would eventually become legendary. One day after he became DA, he chased a news photographer up a stairwell, trading insults and profanities with him after the photographer had taken a picture of a murder victim's family crying in a courthouse hallway. The photographer had every right to take pictures in a public area of a public building, but Jagels appeared incensed. "You're not going to do this in *my* courthouse," he is said to have shouted. The DA had previously tried to prosecute the same photographer for shooting the scene of a child's drowning—a case thrown out of court after the judge lambasted Jagels for overstepping his authority. "What are you going to do, Ed? Arrest me?" the photographer taunted back. "You already tried that, and it didn't work."

The dig infuriated Jagels. According to the photographer, a red-faced and shaking Jagels hissed "Fuck you" in response just as they emerged from a stairwell into a lobby where more news reporters, including a TV crew, were milling about. The camera swung toward the tight-lipped DA, and the photographer recalls smirking, "Would you like to repeat that, Ed?"

"You heard me," was all Jagels replied, then stalked off.[18]

The story gets told and retold by reporters in the Kern County courthouse as an example of Ed Jagels' zealousness. But what it really shows—beyond sheer arrogance, a common enough trait among successful DAs and other high-powered lawyers—is Jagels' political acumen. He knew he didn't need the law on his side on this one. Sure, the photographer might have the constitutional right to take snapshots of tearful parents of a murdered child, or to record for posterity the image of an eight-year-old boy's sodden, limp body being pulled from a canal. That didn't matter. Jagels knew the public would be on his side for trying to stop it, for trying to spare victims from pain and the insensitivity of newsmen. (It also didn't hurt that journalists are even less popular with the public these days than lawyers, and that there are no actual sanctions written into the law for prosecutors who exceed their authority in this way.) That sort of approach—putting victims first—became a Jagels trademark. It is one reason why no one has even bothered to mount a serious campaign against Jagels in subsequent elections.

Not that anyone envisioned such electoral invulnerability back in 1982, when Jagels first sought the DA's office. Most observers at the time considered him an unlikely choice for the job, young and inexperienced, an unknown to the general public, lacking support from the Republican good ol' boys who ran the county. Many of the senior prosecutors in his office threw their support to his opponent, as did most of the Bakersfield legal community. Jagels had no hallowed Okie bloodlines (over the years, the Oklahoma immigrants had risen to power out of sheer numbers; even the term *Okie* gradually lost its bite, becoming instead a source of folksy pride). He wasn't even a native of Kern County. He had come over the Grapevine from the old-money Los Angeles enclave of San Marino, a wealthy second-generation lawyer whose mother frequently appeared in the society columns, and whose father had ties to Washington power brokers like Attorney General William French Smith, as well as ample cash to support his son's campaign. Jagels' campaign-donor list was like no one else's in Kern County. It read like a who's who of corporate California, with the president and vice president of Occidental Petroleum kicking in, along with a host of corporate, society and legal luminaries from Los Angeles—friends and contacts of the family back in San Marino.

Such a pedigree might have been deadly to other would-be office-holders in Kern County, where out-of-town job applicants at the district attorney's office were routinely warned they were about to enter "redneck country," and where loathing of carpetbaggers from the "big city" can be palpable. But Jagels had something better than local roots or experience or political chits or even that greatest currency of public life, name recognition. He had timing, incredible timing.

Ed Jagels had sensed something new on the horizon in the first years of the eighties, a powerful undercurrent roiling through his community and ready to crest: a profound change in the way people looked at their justice system. He had seen, far more clearly than his contemporaries and competitors, that a new and cynical public perception of the courts was taking hold, one that made professional experience in the justice system a negative, not a positive. Jagels' message, then, became as simple as it was compelling: The system had been perverted by the judges and the defense attorneys. It had been turned into something that served the bad guys instead of the good guys. And that, in turn, enabled Jagels to ask, So what if the insiders, the lawyers and the judges, were against him? They defend criminals for a living, he would say in his stump speeches. If they are against me, what does that say about the kind of district attorney I'll be?

Jagels quickly saw he had struck a cord with this pitch—supporters began flocking to him. Once in office, he became particularly adept at bashing Rose Bird, the California Supreme Court chief justice and civil libertarian who had become the bull's-eye on every conservative's target after she repeatedly overturned death sentences. The "Bye, Bye Birdie" bumper stickers he and his political organization put together were immensely popular—they couldn't print them fast enough—as was his characterization of her rulings as "pro-defense fanaticism." His campaign to oust the chief justice spread far beyond the boundaries of Kern County, bringing him headlines and stature throughout California, and when his campaign succeeded and Rose Bird was voted out of office, Jagels' name was bandied about as a likely candidate for state attorney general. From the moment he launched his first election campaign, law enforcement fell in behind Jagels in droves. Every police agency, association and union in Kern County, the largest and smallest departments alike, endorsed him, convinced this newcomer would never have let Dana Butler's murderer roam free. Jagels knew, then, that he had tapped into something big—indeed, he began building his whole career on it, feeding the outrage, the notion that the justice system was broken and needed radical surgery to restore common sense to the courtroom and safety to the streets.

It was an unassailable position in so many ways, and a relatively novel one for the time. Frustrations were just beginning to build back then, not just in Bakersfield, but all over the nation—over repeat offenders, escalating violence and criminals who seemed to walk out of prison just days after getting there. And Jagels found a natural constituency who shared these views: Long before he chased a news photographer up a courthouse staircase, he became one of the first prosecutors in the country to ally himself with the then-nascent crime-victims' movement. He sensed early on the enormous political clout that movement would one day attain. He championed a Crime Victims Bill of Rights that has since become law in California (though portions of it were later found to be unconstitutional), and he has been rewarded with the undying support of crime-victims' groups, which themselves have risen from obscurity to become potent lobbying forces in state legislatures around the country.

In forging this alliance, Jagels redefined the job of district attorney. No longer would he be merely a prosecutor of criminals, an upholder of the law. Kern County's DA, in Jagels' view, would also be an advocate for the *victims*. He would be *their* lawyer, their avenging angel. And his enemies were the judges, the black-robed symbols of everything wrong with the justice system—splitting hairs, defying common sense, perverting the law to benefit criminals, he'd say in speech after speech.

His prescription for fixing the system was also groundbreaking for the times, and always the same: Change the law to shift legal discretion—the code word for power in the justice system—away from the dreaded judges and toward prosecutors. Despite the fact that prosecutors already were the most powerful figures in the justice system, Jagels continually portrayed himself as a crime-busting underdog, bereft of the laws and powers he needed to do his job right. To remedy this supposed handicap, Jagels has throughout his career pushed for laws that not only would stiffen punishments for criminals, but that would also limit judges' choices as they made rulings on evidence and passed sentences. That way, it would be prosecutors, in choosing what charges to file and what evidence to use, who would decide a criminal's sentence. Jagels also helped pioneer the ultimate weapon in this approach, California's "Three Strikes and You're Out" law, which puts three-time offenders—even nonviolent ones—in prison for life, whether a judge wants it that way or not.

This prescription has taken hold across the United States: Jagels' time as district attorney has paralleled a quantum expansion in the powers of prosecutors throughout the nation, as Three Strikes laws and other limitations on judicial discretion have spread. As an eloquent spokesman for his cause and a power to be reckoned with throughout California, Jagels' influence has ranged far beyond his fiefdom in Kern County.

The take-no-prisoners, judge-bashing posture Jagels adopted to achieve his goals turned off the veterans in his office, but it made him a natural leader to most of the younger assistant DAs, who also had come to the conclusion that judges were as much the enemy as criminals. Here was a guy who publicly announced that he wanted to recall most of the California Supreme Court, who thought illegally obtained evidence ought to be permissi-

ble in trials, and who considered it a badge of honor to be
reversed by an appellate judge. He proclaimed the
requirement that police should have to take thirty seconds to advise a suspect of his constitutional rights—the
famous Miranda warnings created by Bakersfield native
Earl Warren—an outrage that should be ignored whenever possible. No wonder the deputies and patrol officers
were knocking on doors for Ed Jagels by the dozen. He
was their dream DA.

Once he took office, Jagels quickly reorganized his
staff, removing the senior prosecutors who had opposed
his candidacy from high-profile and supervisory jobs
they once held. In their place, he installed the young,
aggressive, like-minded prosecutors who had put their
careers on the line to support him. And, almost immediately, the office Jagels had built in his own image began
performing just as he promised it would: The Kern
County District Attorney's Office began accumulating
the toughest record in California, sending more people to
prison per capita than any other county, filing a higher
percentage of cases brought to them by police than any
other county, and garnering longer sentences than any
other county. Jagels boasted that he had the most aggressive, law enforcement–oriented DA's office in the state,
and few argued otherwise. Because California was often
ranked at or near the top nationally in terms of punishing criminals, Jagels legitimately could lay claim to being
one of the toughest prosecutors in the United States.

The tough new approach had its price, however. The
office, led by a man once upbraided by the court of
appeals for a "legion" of misconduct, began taking
increasing, sometimes withering, criticism for the conduct of several of its prosecutors as they put together

their unparalleled record. By Jagels' second term in office, complaints of prosecutorial misconduct in Kern County had tripled compared to when his predecessor was in office.[19] Many local lawyers concluded that Jagels' no-holds-barred brand of prosecuting encouraged—perhaps even rewarded—such transgressions.

"They have apparently got a DA down there who's playing this thing close to the line every time," one disgusted appellate justice complained in the midst of a hearing in 1989, in which Jagels' office was accused of hiding key information about a jailhouse informant's credibility. "That fellow down there that's the DA is just outlandish . . . And his deputies all have the same philosophy. Whether they violate certain rules or principles or not, they depend on harmless error and so forth to get them out of it."[20]

The appeals justices expressed concern that a victory-at-any-cost culture had taken root in the district attorney's office under Ed Jagels, a Wild West approach that sometimes put winning the case above following the rules. But such criticism had no effect on how Jagels ran his office or on his enormous popularity with his Kern County constituency, whose concern was crime and punishment, not the technical niceties of courtroom behavior. They wanted Jagels to put the bad guys away, and all they knew was that he was good at it. Many concluded he had come just in time, as his arrival in office seemed to coincide with an explosion of huge and sensational cases—big drug cases, big child-molestation cases, big murder cases. And always, there was Ed Jagels, on the TV screen, smooth and steely, righteous and sure of himself, promising to put an end to it all whenever a new crisis loomed, the solution always being the same:

tougher laws, tougher judges, more power to police and prosecutors.

His message resonated. Even as schools and parks and clinics suffered, Kern County bolstered the budgets of the sheriff, police and prosecutors. It built a new, bigger jail far out in the desert, doing everything it could to crack down on crime, hard and sure, stretching every nickel to keep the darkness at bay. None of this was unique, of course. In an age of rising crime and anxiety, many communities have made similar efforts. But unlike other communities that made like sacrifices only to see the plague come knocking anyway—the teenagers who killed, the crack houses spreading like cancer, the random violence that could strike anyone, anytime—in Kern County, the sacrifices seemed to pay off. If there was to be a war on crime, Kern County intended to play to win.

By the time a silver-haired woman named Sandy Dunn disappeared in 1992, local law enforcement had assembled an impressive record of solving crimes. The district attorney had put together an all-star staff that rarely lost a big trial. The county became known nationally for its massive, ground-breaking and largely successful investigations of child sex crimes, helping abate a terror that had gripped the community for years. No matter how horrible the crime or how intricate the mystery, a solution almost always seemed at hand in Bakersfield. So it would be with Pat Dunn.

7

MAXJUSTICE

BY INDEPENDENCE DAY, SANDY HAD BEEN GONE FOR three days. For three days, Pat had searched along the looping route Sandy liked to walk every morning long before dawn. He found no sign of her. No one else saw her, either—no one who spoke up, anyway.

Pat would later say he felt paralyzed by his fears. He was afraid to tell people Sandy was missing, knowing if she came back, she'd be angry with him for saying anything that made her look silly or sick. Yet he was afraid of keeping silent, fearing that the only way to save Sandy might be to spread the word she had vanished. The problem was, with Sandy gone, he felt aimless, ineffectual, a broken clock stuck in place, motor grinding. He didn't know how to fill his mornings anymore—none of the rituals were possible. There was no one to listen to his bad jokes or to ride fence with or to make sure the toothpaste didn't run out. Mom had always taken care of him. Now he had to fend for himself. Pat swore to himself he'd never take Sandy for granted again if she could only come back to him. Her absence tore at him as he berated himself for not doing more, for not foreseeing this crisis, for not being there when Sandy needed him most. Alone in the big, empty house, he'd pace through the rooms, whispering over and over, "Where are you now? Where are you now?"

When he wasn't out searching, Pat filled the time by drinking, more than ever. He started downing beers and whiskey together, beginning early in the morning, then leaving to drive Sandy's walking route. If she was mentally confused but otherwise okay, he would later explain, he figured she might return to familiar places and patterns. This had happened before, Pat would tell the police: She once got lost while driving in a familiar neighborhood and had to call Pat from a phone booth to ask him to come get her.[21]

Pat kept telling himself he was charting a sensible course: He continued to search; he had called the authorities, who presumably were searching as well; and he otherwise kept up appearances, telling almost no one else what was going on, hoping for Sandy to return to him. He talked to a store owner at College Center, he rescheduled an appointment with the housecleaner, he spoke with several other friends and acquaintances, going on with his daily routines and conducting business as usual, all without mentioning Sandy's disappearance and, in some cases, sounding normal, untroubled, even upbeat to some people he encountered. "Everything's great," he told the housekeeper over the phone on July 1. "I had two meetings today, and both went well."

In those early days of Sandy's disappearance, Pat revealed the crisis to only a handful of people. He told his son Patrick Jr. and his daughter, Jennifer. He reported Sandy missing to the sheriff's department. And he spoke to his real estate attorneys, Teri Bjorn and Jim Weins, trying to arrange the payment of some large bills—several hundred thousand dollars' worth—that were coming due on the Morning Star housing project. This was a ticklish matter because the money was still mostly in Sandy's name. Kevin Knutson hadn't set up the trusts yet—if he had, Pat could have gotten the money himself. To pay the Morning Star debt, Sandy had started cashing in some of her municipal bonds and transferring the two hundred thousand in proceeds to a joint account, but the process had not been completed before Sandy vanished. She still had to sign for the transfer. Pat faced a quandary: He couldn't touch that money on his own, but paying the bills was vital to keeping their project alive. "If we don't get these bills paid," Pat told his lawyers, "Mom'll kick our butts when she gets home." The lawyers assured him that some sort of arrangement could be worked out, since Sandy's intentions were clear. And, after all, they asked, she leaves everything to you in her will, doesn't she?

"Yes," Pat had answered. "She does."[22]

Finally, Pat told one other person about Sandy's disappearance: Kate Rosenlieb, the city planning commissioner, his former student and current friend, perhaps his closest friend. Sandy might have stopped talking to Kate after the disastrous vote on the Dunns' movie-theater project, but Pat had continued seeing her on the sly. He tried to be careful about these visits, straining to keep Kate and Sandy apart without seeming to be doing so, arranging for drives and lunches away from the house. "Shuttle diplomacy," he had called it. Now he needed to talk to his young friend. He wanted to confide.

"I can't find Mom," Pat told Kate. It was July 3, and Pat was exhausted, his fingers numb as he grasped the telephone. "I've been looking all over for her and I can't find her anywhere. I'm afraid something terrible has happened. I fear the worst."

He would later remember trying to stay calm, trying to

keep his fears in check so they could have a rational conversation, willing his voice to remain a strong monotone even though he was beside himself with fear. Kate would remember him sounding as if he didn't care. "I just fear the worst," he repeated.

As Kate listened quietly, he told her the whole story, how he had reported Sandy missing to the sheriff's department, how he had searched for her every day during her normal walking hours, how he thought she had suffered some sort of memory lapse. And he explained something he hadn't really told anyone else before—what made him think that Sandy might have taken the large sum of money he had mentioned in his missing-persons report. In her typical hoarder's fashion, Sandy kept thousands in cash stashed around the house, usually in rolls of ten one-hundred-dollar bills bound with a rubber band and hidden in the pockets of clothes in her closets. In looking around for a clue to Sandy's whereabouts, Pat said, he had found six rubber bands in a pocket where there should have been cash. Though he couldn't be sure—the rubber bands could have been there for weeks or months—he reasoned she could have taken six thousand dollars with her.

"But why?" Pat asked in a tired, toneless voice. "I just don't know what's going on."

Kate Rosenlieb didn't know what to say. Something about the story Pat told her, and the way he told it, did not sit well with her. She asked some pointed questions, though Pat didn't seem to notice their implication as he answered dutifully. Kate asked about Sandy's jewelry and wallet, and Pat said she had left behind her purse, her identification, her jewelry—everything, even her house keys and her dogs. Kate decided that didn't sound right.

The Sandy she knew would never leave without her wallet and her keys. On the verge of panic as she listened to Pat, Kate, too, began to fear the worst—but those fears were of Pat, not for Sandy. Maybe it was her memory of that night three years earlier when the police arrested Pat for spousal abuse, and Sandy had stood there in the living room looking dazed, blood on her ear. Or maybe it was the dead-calm voice she heard from Pat's end of the phone. Or maybe it was the fact that he had been trying to convince Kate for the last six months that Sandy was developing Alzheimer's disease, forgetting things, losing it. "Bullshit," she had said then. Sandy could be childish and eccentric, she believed, but not senile. Was it all a cover story? Kate wondered now. Had he been setting up an alibi for months?

Despite these inner doubts, Kate kept her voice as calm and even as Pat's, feeling almost as if someone else were talking when she asked, "What was Sandy wearing when she disappeared?"

"I don't know," Pat replied, after a pause that Kate found suspicious. "I was asleep when she left." He had told the same thing to the sheriff's department. He could only guess what she was wearing, based on what she usually put on for her walks. "A couple T-shirts," he ventured. "A blue jogging jacket, shorts. I just don't know."

Still sounding calm and emotionless to Kate, Pat said he wanted to see her. Kate told him she couldn't at the moment, but she agreed to meet him for breakfast the following morning to talk some more. She would later say she didn't want to do anything until she had seen Pat in person and heard him out, looking into his eyes as he spoke. But after hanging up the phone, she kept thinking about the conversation. To her, Pat had sounded more than calm and unruffled. It wasn't so much what he said as how he said it: As if he hadn't just given up hope, but that he *knew* Sandy was dead. She had no evidence that Pat had done anything wrong, just a feeling. But it was a powerful one. Kate picked up the phone again and called her friend Pat DeMond, the city councilwoman who had helped torpedo the Dunns' movie-theater project, and who now faced a possible lawsuit because of it. The councilwoman had no use at all for Pat and had not spoken with Sandy for almost a month, but the first words out of DeMond's mouth, once Kate had told her Sandy was missing, were, "He killed her."

That's when Kate really started to panic.

A thinly attractive, often acerbic employee of a Bakersfield real estate developer, Kate Rosenlieb was known around town for her angelic smile, quick temper and controversial stands on growth and the environment, for which she had been criticized as being too liberal. This was the ultimate insult in a county dominated by two parties: the conservative Republicans and the ultraconservative Republicans. She relished the controversy, however, delighting in making headlines—and in being a source for reporters, the insider who could stir the pot with behind-the-scenes dirt and the occasional conspiracy theory.

She had known Pat Dunn for years, ever since he had taught her in sixth grade. She remembered him as an affable teacher who used wincingly bad jokes and his six-foot-three bulk to keep the kids interested and in line. Years later, they met again by chance and became fast friends. She often told Pat that he was one of the few people in her life who made her feel she could accomplish worthwhile things—that he had given her support she had never found at home, not with her own father or in her short-lived marriage. Her father, she would say, always seemed dissatisfied with her grades, her career, her appearance. It was Pat Dunn who praised her, flattered her, encouraged her to go for the planning-commission job, then suggested she run for city council as well. She had rebuffed the notion, but was immensely flattered that he thought of her that way. He teased her by calling Kate his little John Wayne, a nod to her willingness to wade into a fight, guns blazing, but you could see the admiration in his eyes when he said it. Just as Pat had become like a second father to her, it seemed to Kate that she helped make up for his own stormy relationship with his daughter, Jennifer, who never really forgave him for the divorce from Nancy and whose relationship with Sandy had been poisonous at best.

Kate had been a regular visitor to the Dunn household for years, coming over for drinks or dinner or just to shoot pool. That was Pat's game—she could never best him on the billiard table. "Christ, I'm a drunk old fat man with no eyes, and you still can't beat me," he'd taunt, squinting over his thick glasses. Sandy she found to be a bit prickly, rigid and hard to get along with, an odd spendthrift who, despite her millions, lived like she was one step from the soup kitchen. She and Kate never really clicked. But Pat and Kate would spend time together effortlessly. He was never an outwardly affectionate man, but Kate would sometimes throw her arms around him and tell him, "I love you," which pleased and embarrassed Pat, invariably evoking some sort of gruff response. "How could you resist?" he'd say with a laugh, sucking in his gut a bit. Though he'd never admit it Pat would do just about anything for one of those hugs.

Yet now, on the basis of one phone call, Kate had decided Pat Dunn was a killer. She would never be able to adequately explain why. There certainly was no evidence. It was more a feeling, a premonition, she'd later say, a reading between the lines of things Pat had told her. "I think he confessed to me, without actually saying it," she'd later say. "That's how well I knew him. In his own way, he was confessing."

Kate Rosenlieb may have thought she heard a confession that day, and therefore was justified in what she did next, but others who knew her and Pat later questioned both Kate's judgment and her motives. Pat's friends came to see her as a woman who, perhaps only unconsciously, sought the limelight and now imagined herself cracking a sensational murder mystery, even if it came at the expense of a close friend. They also were suspicious of the fact that Kate was part of a Bakersfield city government suddenly at odds with the Dunns, and that she was an even closer friend to city officials embarrassed and angered by Pat's bald criticism in a public meeting, with its accompanying threat of unpleasant and costly litigation.

Whatever the motivation for her snap decision, Kate Rosenlieb decided that same night that she could not sit by idly while Pat got away with murder. She wouldn't wait to see him after all before taking action, she decided. Instead, within a few hours of hearing from Pat that Sandy was missing, and after conferring with City Councilwoman Pat DeMond, Rosenlieb picked up the phone and called the police.

"I want to report a murder," she began.

• • • •

By the time Kate Rosenlieb made that call, the missing-persons report that Pat Dunn had phoned in to the sheriff's department had been entered into Kern County's local law-enforcement computer system. In theory, this meant the police would be on alert about Sandy's disappearance, but in practice, it meant nothing more would be done. No one other than Pat had been looking for Sandy for the past three days. No bulletins had been sent. The file containing Pat's report had been dumped on the desk of a detective who was away on vacation through the Fourth of July weekend and, in any case, even if he had been in the office, he wouldn't have done anything. Police agencies adhere to the general rule that, by and large, most missing adults are missing by choice, usually because of disagreements or other tensions at home. Most such reports are resolved when the "missing" person calls or returns (or files for divorce). Such reports are routinely taken by police agencies and just as routinely ignored. The benign neglect is disturbed only if the missing person is a child, or if evidence of foul play surfaces.

As the case stood, there were no such suspicions initially, and in the normal course of events, the report could have languished for days or weeks before anything at all was done. But then Kate Rosenlieb and Pat DeMond got busy. Kate repeatedly called the Bakersfield Police Department, only to learn the Kern County Sheriff had jurisdiction over the Dunns' neighborhood. So she called the sheriff's department, trying to report her suspicions, but she could find no one of consequence to listen to her. Frustrated, she finally drove to sheriff's headquarters in person. She found a building emptied by the national holiday as she wandered through the unlocked offices, marveling at the unoccupied desks and wide-open file room, as if crime, or at least the machinery for dealing with it, had suddenly come to a standstill. At last, she stumbled across someone sitting at a desk shuffling papers, who directed her down a hall to a room with radios and the day's official watch commander. "My friend's been murdered," she blurted, "and no one is even here to deal with it."

As opening lines go, it was a grabber, but once it was established that Kate had not actually witnessed a murder, the ensuing heated discussion went nowhere. Kate announced that she knew that Sandy Dunn had been killed in her home, but as she could not say how she knew this, nor provide one bit of evidence to support such an allegation, the watch commander apparently saw no reason to take Kate seriously. She left the sheriff's office more frustrated than ever, feeling desperate and frightened.

But Rosenlieb had set into motion more than she realized. City Councilwoman DeMond used her clout to get in touch with Carl Sparks, the sheriff of Kern County, and to personally voice her suspicions and desires in the matter. Sheriff Sparks listened deferentially, then called the watch commander who had dismissed Rosenlieb. And the Dunn case abruptly took on a newfound urgency.

On the morning of Saturday, July 4, the same sheriff's watch commander telephoned a redheaded, easygoing detective named Vernon Kline—"Dusty" to most everyone who knew him. It was Kline's day off, but the watch commander instructed him to postpone his Independence Day barbecue plans so he could interview someone about the disappearance of one Alexandra Paola Dunn. It was supposed to be another detective's case, the watch commander said, but Dusty would have to fill in because of the holiday. Kline was in the sheriff's sex-crimes unit—which handles missing-persons cases as a sideline—and the watch commander told him he would have to take the report.

In a missing-persons case, the source of the report is almost always the first witness to be interviewed—the detective will seek out the spouse, the parent, whoever first noted and reported the disappearance. But in this case, Dusty Kline did not immediately seek out Pat Dunn. Instead, in accordance with the wishes of two politicians—a city councilwoman who disliked Pat and the county sheriff whose ear she had—the first person interviewed about Sandy's disappearance was Kate Rosenlieb. It would be Pat's dear friend Kate who provided authorities with their critical first impressions of the case, and whose opinions indelibly shaped the police investigation that followed.

When Dusty Kline met her for the first time, Rosenlieb had just returned from her breakfast appointment with Pat Dunn. By then, she had become so riled by her discussions with Pat DeMond and the watch commander, and so convinced Pat had killed his missing wife, that she left hidden at her home a tape recording of her theories about the murder—just in case she, too, met Sandy's fate, whatever that was. She also stuck a pistol in her handbag, ready to blow a hole in her second father's head if need be.

Though they had planned to stop at a diner that morning, Kate and Pat skipped eating—Pat said he wasn't hungry and would rather drive and talk. "Let's go up in the mountains," he suggested. Kate said no, she had a work-related appointment later in the morning and had to stay close to town. This was a lie, but Pat was too preoccupied to question why she would be working on July 4. He simply drove them around town, each of them drinking canned beers from a six-pack on the seat next to them, though it was still early morning. They returned without exchanging gunfire (and without Pat having any idea what Kate suspected).

During the drive, Pat told her much the same story he had related on the phone, with Kate believing him even less than before. Pat would recall feeling exhausted from sleepless nights and worry, drained of emotion, but Kate saw next to her a man who seemed not in the least bit upset. "I just don't know what happened to her," he said, and then added, once more, "I fear the worst." Later, he would say, "She's dead, Kate." When she asked why he seemed so pessimistic, Pat hesitated a few seconds, then pointed at the car keys dangling from the ignition. "These are her keys. If she was alive, she'd have them."

Kate would later recall begging Pat to go to the sheriff's department with her, but Pat shook his head. She thought that was very significant. When they parted, Pat felt a little better having unburdened himself to a friend. Kate left to tell Detective Kline that there was no way Sandy Dunn could be missing.

"She's dead," Rosenlieb told him with an angry certainty, without offering any evidence beyond her gut feeling. "You don't have a missing-persons case here, you've got a murder. I know it."

And though it pained her to say so—she assured Kline she loved Patrick Dunn like a father—Rosenlieb told the detective she was quite certain of one thing: Pat Dunn was the killer.

She then gave Kline a long list of reasons to justify her suspicions. She said Sandy never left home without a quarter of a million dollars' worth of jewelry on—yet Pat claimed none of her jewelry was missing. "That's impossible," Kate swore. "Unless he killed her himself."

She next told Detective Kline that Pat had refused to drive with her to the sheriff's department to report Sandy missing, an obvious indication of guilt, as Kate saw it. "He said he didn't want anyone to know."

Then she explained how Pat had been trying for months to build a cover story for this moment by trying to convince her that Sandy was showing signs of Alzheimer's disease. But Kate said neither she nor anyone else who knew Sandy would believe him. "She was sharp as a tack—childlike at times, but totally together," Kate told Kline. "He's been talking about this for six months, but it's crap."

Kate told Kline that Pat's whole story of Sandy's disappearance reeked—because, she said, there was no reason for him to have gone searching for Sandy. It was normal for Sandy to go walking at night. "Why would he search when nothing was out of the ordinary?"

Then she told Kline to check his department's files for past crimes by Pat Dunn. "He was arrested for beating her before, you know. Your reports won't show it, but I was there."

Finally, she told Detective Kline that the Dunns had been drinking excessively and arguing terribly for months. They were under terrific stress, battling over their development projects, and were losing a fortune, she said. It was so bad, she half expected to go over there one day and find one had killed the other, then followed in suicide. "Obviously," she said, "I was half right."

In all, it was a startlingly harsh indictment, particularly as Kate also described Pat as a dear friend and someone about whom she cared deeply. Kline took it all in, then said he would go talk to Pat.

"Don't go alone," Kate warned. "He could be dangerous."[23]

Promising to be careful, Kline excused himself and drove over to the Dunns' house. He wasn't yet sure what to make of Kate Rosenlieb, but she seemed believable to him—her status as a city official, and her friendship with Pat, certainly enhanced her credibility as an accuser. He had no way of knowing then that Kate had been wrong about most everything she had just told him. She was wrong about Sandy wearing jewelry on her walks (and she inflated its value tenfold besides). She was wrong about Sandy's walking habits—Sandy never walked in the evening, only early in the morning. And she was wrong when she said no one else believed Sandy might be developing Alzheimer's. As for constant and vicious arguments, Kate seemed to be the only one who had observed them. No one else who knew the Dunns had noticed any unusual fights. Kline could not have known any of this; he didn't even know then that Pat had reported Sandy's disappearance to the sheriff's department days before talking to Kate. Kline had not yet checked the files or the missing-persons log, and so Kate's claims about Pat being reluctant to go to the sheriff's department sounded quite serious. Indeed, Kate's account, as reflected in Detective Kline's written report, shows she even got the basic time frame wrong, telling the detective that Sandy disappeared on July 2, when the true date was June 30. Again, Kline had no way of knowing the truth.

Primed, then, to be suspicious, when he got to the Dunns' house, Kline did indeed find Pat's behavior odd, not at all what the detective expected from a man whose wife was missing. Pat had been drinking and seemed out of sorts, though he readily invited the detective in to have a look around. Too readily, almost anxiously, Kline thought, as if Pat were making a show of cooperating, rather than showing actual concern. Kline was so ready to believe the worst at this point, even Pat's cooperation seemed suspect. Pat, once again, told the story of Sandy's disappearance, with the details closely matching Rosenlieb's account, only without her incriminating interpretations and without any of the changes and inconsistencies that police expect to find in cover stories and lies.

When Pat finished, Detective Kline asked him about Sandy's keys. Rosenlieb had told Kline about Pat's previous remarks about the keys, but Pat hadn't brought them up in this latest rendition. Now, a look of confusion passed across Pat's face as if, Kline later would remember thinking, he were a child who had just been confronted with a lie. Pat stumbled over his words, then finally pointed to his wife's keys on the kitchen counter, right in front of them, and said, "Well, there they are. Right there."

Kline watched the older man standing there, and Pat looked away, breaking eye contact. *He's lying,* Kline thought. *Rosenlieb's right.*

"It was almost as if he had forgotten about those keys—like he had made up a story about Sandy going out, but forgot to hide the keys that she would have taken with her," Kline would later recall, years after the case had ended. "It was pretty boneheaded, really. But it was one of the main reasons I started feeling he was lying."[24]

Kline didn't know then—and apparently never realized—that there was nothing suspicious about Pat's response. Pat had already told sheriff's dispatcher Valley Braddick about the keys in the kitchen, and he had assumed Detective Kline already possessed all of that information. Pat also assumed, incorrectly, that Kline had come to his house in the first place after reading the missing-persons report—why else would the detective even be there? But Kline didn't even know such a report existed. He was at Dunn's house because of Kate Rosenlieb. If Pat appeared confused by Kline's question, it wasn't because he had been caught in a lie or an incomplete cover story—it was, Pat would later say, because he was surprised at the detective's ignorance. If he looked away, it wasn't out of fear of the detective, but out of embarrassment *for* the detective.

Dusty Kline would later say he went to see Pat Dunn that day with an open mind. However, in the report he later wrote, it is clear that Kate Rosenlieb's perspective on the case left a powerful impression on him. The observations—and the misinformation—relayed by Rosenlieb in her initial meeting with Kline would forever color the investigation of Alexandra Dunn's disappearance and death. Almost everything Rosenlieb said was accepted at face value. Almost everything Pat Dunn said was dismissed or interpreted as incriminating.

From that moment on, the search for Sandy virtually ended—before it had really begun. The case became a search not for a missing woman, but for evidence—evidence that Pat Dunn had murdered his wife.

And so the homicide investigation began, based on

misinformation that led to suspicion. Now the sheriff's department needed a body, a murder weapon, blood, a confession—any or all would do. Best of all, though, would be a witness. An eyewitness. The sheriff's detectives who began working the case as a murder knew, sooner or later, something would turn up. In Kern County, it almost always did.

8

"I WANT A DEAL," JERRY LEE COBLE REPEATED, EYES DARTING around the small, antiseptic interrogation room. Blunt as a bullet, Coble looked older than his thirty-four years. He smelled of sweat and stale beer, his eyes rimmed red. He cleared his throat, the dry sound of an engine that wouldn't catch, then added, "I'll tell you whatever you want to know. But you gotta cut me a deal."

Eric Banducci leaned back in the interrogator's chair and regarded Coble without expression. By the detective's count, it was the fifth, maybe sixth time this skinny little hype had used the word *deal* in the space of fifteen minutes. By this, Sheriff's Detective Banducci understood Coble, an ex-convict, desperately wanted what every ex-con wanted—not to go back to prison. Of course, Coble hadn't wanted it badly enough to stop committing crimes. But now that he had been caught stealing sixty grand in brass fixtures and copper wire from the irrigation company that had been generous enough (or, as Banducci figured it, stupid enough) to hire him, Coble was willing to sell out whoever he could in order to stay free.

The thing is, Banducci knew Coble. And he knew heroin addicts. He expected this man would give up his best friend, his brother, even his mother if that's what it took to walk out that door free and clear. Or, to be more specific, he'd do anything to stay free long enough to score his next fix. That he would lie in the process, Banducci believed, was axiomatic. That's what addicts do. The only heroin junkies who don't lie through their teeth, Banducci would tell junior cops with dreams of nailing Mr. Big through the likes of Jerry Coble, are in the graveyard. "And they just lie still," he'd say with a grim laugh.

"Why should I cut a deal with you, Jerry Lee?" Banducci asked after a long pause. The detective had a narrow smile on his craggy face. "I've already got you, and I don't have to cut any deals with you or anyone else to put you away. So why should I trade steak for hamburger?"

Jerry Lee Coble hung his head, then said, once again, "Man, I got to make a deal. I can't go back."

Coble's scam had been sweet while it lasted. On parole from prison for a long string of felonies, Coble had hired on as an electrician for a Bakersfield pump company. He was, to be fair to the company's hiring officer, a more than capable electrician, having been trained by the Marine Corps a lifetime ago to install instruments on jet aircraft. But his heroin habit was far stronger than his work ethic, and within weeks, he began to systematically divest his employers of brass fittings, copper cable—anything he could get his hands on. He'd strip the wire of its insulation at his parents' trailer or his brother's place on the ragged southern edge of Bakersfield, a farming center called Weedpatch, one of many crossroads communities adrift in the sea of farmland and oilfield that is California's vast Central Valley. Weedpatch had once been home to one of the dreaded Okie labor camps that John Steinbeck had scathingly portrayed in *The Grapes of Wrath.* Now it was a quiet, perfect place for Coble to dispose of his stolen goods. His brother or his teenaged nephew would sell the stripped metal at scrap yards. They got only pennies to the dollar, but when you're moving tons of the stuff, it still brings in thousands. Plenty of money for Jerry to score all the dope he needed.

But the thing about heroin is, you always need more. As his need for drugs grew more insatiable, Jerry's thefts grew increasingly reckless until he was finally placing orders for new electrical cable, expensive braids of copper thick as a man's wrist that his company didn't even use. It came straight off the spool and went right to the scrap yard, gleaming and new. Once the thefts became that oafish and obvious, it was only a matter of time before Coble found himself staring at Eric Banducci's scuffed cowboy boots propped up on the table between them.

As it happened, Jerry's nephew got busted first. The first thing out of the kid's mouth when the deputies burst through the door told Banducci all he needed to know about Jerry Coble's integrity: "That fucking bastard," the kid blurted, "That goddamn Jerry set me up." Not even his own family trusted Jerry Lee Coble.

Jerry Lee had tried to escape when the cops came for him, driving his El Camino past the orchards and cattle farms of Weedpatch with deputies in pursuit, at first refusing to pull over, then leaping from his pickup and trying to dash on foot through backyards and over fences. When he finally was brought down, heaving and exhausted, a gun to his head, Jerry Lee started right in with his negotiations. Before his interrogation had begun, before he had even caught his breath, he told one cop, "I don't want to go back. I'll do whatever it takes."

It's a sad, hard truth, Banducci would later say, that dealing with people like Jerry Coble is a way of life in the justice system. Whether it was in a major city like Los Angeles or a farm town like Bakersfield, there wasn't much difference, the detective knew: Deals make the wheels of justice turn, and we'd hardly ever put crooks away if not for their blabbing about themselves or their colleagues. But Coble was a three-time loser from a family that produced several career criminals. He had no credibility, in Banducci's estimation, even though he had been an informer in the past. Some cops might have tried to use Coble on that day in April 1991, when he was so desperate to stay out of jail he would say or do practically anything a detective might want. But not Banducci. He told Coble there would be no deals with the likes of him.

"C'mon, just tell me what you want," Coble pleaded.

"What do I want?" Banducci said, exasperated by the tenacity of this thief. "I want you to be a man for once in your life and take responsibility for your actions. Why don't you just come clean? Just once in your life?"

Coble stared at Banducci as if the detective had lost his mind. Then he said, "Man, get me a dope cop in here. I can do a dealer who never touches anything less than quarters."

Instead, Banducci brought Coble to the county jail to book him. Once in the jail, the ex-con suddenly doubled over, a pained look on his dark, lined face, and pronounced himself an epileptic in need of treatment, and suffering from heroin withdrawal to boot. Coble knew jail policies better than the detention officers who ran the place—his declaration triggered an automatic transfer out of the jail to a secure ward at the county hospital.

Softer time, free drugs, nurses: Now it was Banducci's turn to stare at Coble with grudging admiration. The thief had indeed found a way to avoid jail. For now.

"But you'll have to do better than that to *stay* out," Banducci muttered to himself. Many months later, the detective would be surprised to learn that Jerry Coble had done just that.[25]

9

FOR THREE WEEKS, PAT DUNN SEARCHED AND WAITED, alternately paralyzed by depression, then frantically active. He spoke repeatedly with the family lawyers, brokers and accountants, hoping to find some way to keep their real estate ventures going without Sandy's signature on the checks. That's what Mom would want, he kept saying. They tried to help, asking to see Sandy's bank accounts, her will, her important papers. In the end, though, they told Pat there was nothing that would allow Sandy's separate accounts to be touched. The one thing that would have empowered Pat to write the checks—the living trust Sandy had asked their financial planner to draw up—had not been completed. And so Pat finally gave up. Morning Star and the theater project ground to a halt. There would be no more riding fence. His and Sandy's dreams for their vacant properties died.

After that, Pat found himself just sitting in his kitchen, staring blankly at the newspaper, dirty cups piled in the sink, his hands shaking. The worst moments were the brief flares of false hope, when someone would call and claim to have seen Sandy in a restaurant or out walking or sitting by the curb. Pat and a friend checked out many of these calls themselves, and passed all of them on to the sheriff. None panned out. Either the person who was supposed to be Sandy had vanished by the time the tip could be checked out, or it was the wrong person. Several of the calls were prompted by the wanderings of a mentally disturbed homeless woman bearing a passing resemblance to a disheveled and grimy Sandy. Each call was as crushingly disappointing as the first.

No one, it seemed, could find Sandy or tell Pat what had happened to her—not friends, not neighbors, not strangers on the streets she used to walk, and certainly not the sheriff's department. Pat's relations with the detectives investigating her disappearance had deteriorated over the weeks, as their questions became more pointed and Pat's frustration mounted. "You're not doing anything," he exploded at one detective. "Why aren't you out looking for my wife?"

They *were* looking, of course, but not for Sandy. They were looking for evidence against Pat. Every witness they located, every friend of the family they talked to, every neighbor interviewed, every accountant, financial advisor and secretary—all were questioned about Pat and his relationship with Sandy. There was no physical search for a missing woman, nor any comprehensive follow-up on the reported sightings of her. The detectives instead wanted to hear about fights, about plans for divorce, about any attempts by Sandy to cut Pat out of her will. When they asked about Sandy's habits, it was more to debunk Pat's account rather than to find clues to her disappearance. Yet Pat, friend to the police to the end, could or would not see the full implications of all this.

Three weeks after Sandy Dunn disappeared, however, the reality of Pat's situation hit home—literally. Just before half past nine in the evening, a loud knocking at the front door and his dogs' frantic barking awakened Pat from a deep sleep. Disheveled and out of sorts, Pat told the dogs to be quiet and pulled the door open, blinking. Fourteen members of the Kern County Sheriff's Department stood waiting outside on his doorstep. After a moment, he let them in, a look of resignation on his face as the crowd pushed its way through the door.

"We have a warrant to search your house," one of the detectives said, thrusting some papers in Pat's face. "And we want to ask you a few more questions."

They didn't say so just then, but they also wanted to *tell* Pat something. There had been a big break in the case, but they wanted to reveal it at the right moment, so they could gauge his reaction. Would he be surprised, they wondered, or did he already know? That was the question they wanted answered, not with words, but with expressions, body language, eye contact. These are the subtle clues in which police interrogators place great stock. Entire courses are taught on the subject—along with methods of psychological warfare designed to wrest confessions from suspects while dissuading them from uttering the four words cops hate most: *I want a lawyer.* Pat was about to experience this brand of interrogation firsthand.

This confrontation had been building for weeks. There had been several previous visits by detectives, and many conversations, none of which satisfied either Pat or the detectives. A week earlier, they had even called Pat down to the station, kept him cooling his heels for more than an hour in a meeting room, then told him the detective who wanted to see him had left. They capped this with a surprise request that he take a lie-detector test, then and there—the examiner was standing by. It was all a calculated ploy to throw Pat off guard, and it worked. He finally lost his temper.

"You're just jerking me around," he had yelled, storming out, refusing the test—and raising even more suspicions.[26] He had already angered the detectives by bitterly complaining about the picture of Sandy used by the sheriff's department for a missing-persons poster—they had dug up the old police photo taken when Pat was arrested for domestic abuse. No injury was apparent in it, but the picture was very unflattering, showing a confused frown on Sandy's face, her heavy glasses dominating the image. Pat hated it. "Mom would be horrified if she saw it," he had told Detective Kline. "You never asked my permission to use that photo."

"We've been asking you for days to give us a picture, and you never did," Kline had shot back. "So we used the only one we had. And we don't need your permission."

"I told you, I couldn't find one," Pat replied miserably. He had looked around the house, but he and Sandy just weren't picture takers, he said.

Kline, however, had not believed him, though he never could figure out what Pat's problem was. It didn't make sense, Kline reasoned, whether Pat was guilty or not: If innocent of murder and sincere in his belief that Sandy was wandering and missing, Pat should have been glad the sheriff found a photo to use. And even if Pat *had* killed his wife, Kline thought, he would want at least to *appear* to cooperate. Why not provide a snapshot? At this point, what could it hurt? "Mom would just be devastated by this," was all Pat would say, through gritted teeth.

The flap over the photo, followed by the polygraph refusal, had been the last straw for the detectives. Any lingering doubts they might have had about Pat's involvement evaporated when he passed up this supposed opportunity to clear himself once and for all with a lie detector. "If it were me, I'd demand it myself," Detective Kline would later say. "But not Pat."

Pat, however, felt he had tolerated enough official insinuations. He had no intention of entrusting his life and liberty to a box of wires. He didn't trust technology, nor did he trust its operator, a sheriff's department that seemed more interested in pursuing him than his missing wife. "No thanks," he had said as he stalked out of the department. To Pat's way of thinking, he had showed guts, character and righteous indignation, the hallmarks of an innocent man. To the sheriff's detectives, he was showing his fear of being found out.

The simple fact was, Pat could do no right in their eyes. Kate Rosenlieb's view of the case had prevailed. Her passionate, detailed allegations won out over the irascible and distracted Pat Dunn. By July 6—a mere five days after Pat reported his wife missing—the sheriff's department had decided Sandy was dead. There was no body, no blood, no evidence of foul play. Yet the sheriff had placed a homicide detective named John Soliz in charge of the case, with Kline, the missing-persons specialist, assisting. Together, they tried to find support for their belief that the Dunns' marriage had been falling apart and that Sandy's millions, along with an impending divorce, gave Pat a motive for murder. Several witnesses, Kate Rosenlieb among them, had fueled this speculation, though such a theory meant disregarding what many other witnesses had to say. To the detectives, a room-by-room search of the Dunn house was the next logical step in their quest.

So now, three weeks into their homicide investigation, the detectives had a search warrant in hand, issued by a Kern County judge who had found probable cause that

Pat had committed a felony—although the papers filed by the sheriff in support of this finding seem curiously devoid of evidence that Pat broke any laws.[27] Nevertheless, the compliant judge had granted almost unlimited authority to the team of fourteen detectives, deputies and technicians to search every inch of the Dunns' home on Crestmont Drive and their three cars for any evidence of a violent death.

A week earlier, Pat had let another team search the house without a warrant. They found nothing incriminating, but detectives later groused that they were hampered in this examination. They said Pat was "hostile" and kept hovering over them. The detective in charge later admitted he had been allowed to linger in the home as long as he wished and that the out-of-shape Pat could not, in truth, intimidate a phalanx of cops. But the homicide detective, John Soliz, still wanted to come back, in part because certain laboratory tests had to be done in complete darkness, and the voluntary search had been done by day.

The warrant handed to Pat was thick, twenty-three pages, but something on the cover page caught Pat's eye right away: the sheriff's team was authorized to search for "blood stains and/or blood splatters which are consistent with a significant injury resulting in the loss of blood." Pat had to read it over several times before he realized what it meant.

They think I killed her right here.

"While the criminalists do their job, Mr. Dunn, why don't we go in the den to talk," Detective Soliz suggested. "We're still investigating the case and we were wondering if you had any new information."

But Pat was mesmerized. Another line in the warrant

grabbed his attention: Among the property that could be seized under the warrant was "the person of Alexandra Jeanette Dunn, a.k.a. Alexandra Jeanette Paola."

My God, they think I've got her body here.

It took an effort for Pat to tear his eyes away from the legal papers and to focus on what was being said to him. They were all staring at him curiously. The homicide detective was flanked by Dusty Kline and his boss, Sergeant Glenn Johnson, the head of the homicide unit. But Detective Soliz was clearly calling the shots. It was his name on the search warrant application, and he was doing the talking. He had an air of authority about him, deliberate in his movements, a man with impenetrable eyes and a clipped way of speaking that, when he wanted it to, could make the most polite utterances sound blunt, even rude.

Pat vaguely waved the thick sheaf of papers in his hand and ushered the detectives, Sergeant Johnson and a fourth officer, a member of the sheriff's department brass, into his den. In the past, he had treated them like guests even when their insinuations grated on him, telling himself they were just doing their jobs and assuming—incorrectly—they at least were actively searching for Sandy as well. This time, however, Pat pointedly failed to offer them anything to drink. As the technicians and deputies began rooting through his house, he perched on a bar stool and watched.

"So, do you have anything new to tell us?" Soliz asked again. All four of the sheriff's people were still staring at him. Kline had his arms crossed.

Pat cleared his throat, his head still ringing with the words he had read on the search warrant. Knowing they suspected him was one thing, but to see it in black and white, that changed everything. He decided to try one more time to point them in another direction. "Well, I got a call from a man named Rutledge who said he saw Mom around town," he finally said. "We're still putting up fliers." Pat had also been getting calls from a self-described psychic named Louise, who refused to give her last name or number. "She called again," Pat told the cops. "She says Sandy is by some water and by some rocks. Maybe Santa Barbara."

Soliz took no notes, nor did he use a tape recorder,[28] and Pat felt the detective seemed uninterested in what he was saying. Whether this was really the case or simply an interrogation tactic eluded him—Pat simply couldn't read Soliz. The detective abruptly changed the subject and asked, "Why did you take Rex Martin on a drive out to Caliente and Paris-Lorraine?"

Pat seemed taken aback by the unexpected question. "I needed someone to talk to," he answered after a pause.

"Why Rex Martin, though?" Soliz persisted. "He told us you really weren't that close."

Pat nodded at this: Soliz was right, he and Rex Martin had never been close—at least, not until Sandy vanished. Rex Martin was a business partner of the Dunns. He was the builder on their Morning Star housing development and he owned a one-third share in the project. Pat had known Rex since kindergarten, but the two had been little more than acquaintances over the years and had rarely socialized. Martin just happened to call on July 5, a day when Pat needed someone to talk to. On impulse, Pat had asked Rex to take a ride with him. They ended up at a distant hamburger stand Sandy always liked, far outside the Bakersfield city limits in the mountainous area near the small Kern County towns of Caliente and Paris-Lorraine.

"You can get the best hamburgers here," Pat had explained to Rex. "With Mom and me, it was always a search for the best of something—the best pie, the best coleslaw, whatever." During the drive, Pat had told Rex all about Sandy's disappearance, his search for his wife, his fears about her mental state and what might become of her. Pat had wanted Rex to know because Sandy's money was fueling Morning Star, and he felt the builder should know that the project might not go forward were she not found. Yet they ended up hardly speaking at all about the project. Mostly, Pat talked about how much he missed Sandy and how worried he was for her, fearful that she had been hurt or worse. Rex responded by offering to help in any way he could, and the two men had seen one another or spoken almost daily ever since.[29]

But Pat found it difficult to put any of this into words for the detectives, and he merely told Soliz, "I don't know why I chose Rex. I just wanted to talk to someone."

Then Soliz seemed to switch gears again. "When you went driving with Kate Rosenlieb, why did you want to go into the mountains?" he asked. "What's so special that you keep wanting to go out that way?"

Again, Pat said he needed someone to talk to, and he had suggested a drive to the mountains—which Kate refused—because he and Sandy often took the same drive to see wildflowers.

As he gave this answer, Pat began to see that the detective was getting at something, that he saw some connection here, some theme that tied in with the investigation of Sandy's disappearance. Pat puzzled over this, squinting at the detective. Soliz, in turn, would later report perceiving a slight sign of nervousness in his suspect when the subject of the mountain drive with

Kate Rosenlieb came up. Pat got up from his bar stool and went into the kitchen, where he got some ice and poured whiskey over it.

Did you and Mom argue a lot? Soliz asked, following his quarry with dark eyes. *Did she ever hit you? Why did you refuse to give us a picture of Sandy, so we had to use the old one taken when you were arrested for hitting her? And why did that make you so mad? And why did you tell Kate Rosenlieb you "knew" Sandy was dead when you talked to her on July Fourth?* The questions bombarded Pat, and he answered without elaboration: *No. No. I don't know.*

They talked for twenty minutes before Soliz decided it was time to spring his surprise.

"A woman's body was found in the Kelso Valley two weeks ago," the detective said in his blunt way. "Just a few hours ago, we identified that body. It was your wife."

Pat stared, shocked into silence not so much by the news—after three weeks, he really wasn't surprised to hear Sandy was dead—but by the hard, almost cruel way in which the news was delivered. It seemed to him as if Soliz's words were weapons and the detective was trying to batter him with them, to force him into submission. The other men in that room did not even make a pretense of trying to comfort Pat. And then the detective pulled out the photos.

They were black-and-white glossies, shot by the coroner's office, a dark and grainy horror show. They depicted a wizened, blackened corpse. The body had been found half buried and half mummified in a barren canyon sixty miles east of Bakersfield ten days after Pat had reported her missing. The burial site was not all that far from the hamburger stand where Pat had taken Rex— up in the mountains, where Pat wanted to take Kate. That was why Soliz had asked Pat about those drives and why he found Pat's nervousness so telling. To the detectives, it seemed obvious: Pat Dunn had been driven to return to the scene of his crime, perhaps looking for the nerve to confess to his friends, but in the end keeping his secret.

Pat couldn't tear his eyes off those pictures. He vaguely heard Soliz explain what happened. A German tourist hiking in the desert spotted a large flock of birds on the ground and thought the scene might make a good photograph. But as the hiker approached, the startled scavengers took off in a sullen black cloud, revealing what had attracted them: Sandy's body. She lay naked, her head and shoulders exposed, her blackened hands rising up from the rocky soil as if clawing toward the sky. She had been stabbed to death somewhere else, then carted to this shallow grave of pebbles and dust. Soliz kept the cause of death from Pat, standard procedure in such a police interrogation, to see if the subject knows more than he should.

"Why did it take so long to identify her?" Pat croaked.

"The body was badly decomposed when it was found, and we were unable to get fingerprints. We ended up using dental charts." This last was said bitingly—Soliz had previously asked for the name of Sandy's dentist, and Pat had said she had none. But the detective nevertheless found a dentist who had treated Sandy—yet another reason for Soliz to suspect Pat. Soliz didn't notice, it seems, that the dental records predated the Dunns' marriage. Pat hadn't lied—he simply hadn't been around when Sandy saw that dentist.

Unspoken also was Kate Rosenlieb's role in all this. Soliz didn't mention it, but the only reason the Kern County Sheriff's Department had even tried to identify the desiccated, fifty-three-pound corpse as Sandy's was because Kate Rosenlieb had spotted a tiny article in the newspaper about the chance discovery of an unidentified body in the desert. Once again, it was Rosenlieb's excited call to the sheriff's department that set things in motion, when she insisted to Dusty Kline, "That's her, that's her. That body in the desert was Sandy." Dusty Kline's reply had been, "What body?"[30]

Kline checked into it, though, and then he called Rosenlieb back to say that there was no way that this "Jane Doe" could be Sandy. The body was too small, the hair was blonde, the weight was way off. It had been murder, all right, but some sicko had done it. Stripped her, stabbed her, mutilated the body by cutting tissue out of her rectum, then half buried her in a strange sitting position, almost like you'd bury someone in the sand during an outing to the beach. Pat Dunn might be a killer, Kline figured, but he wouldn't do that to his wife's body.

But Kate, amazed and furious that the authorities were not trying to identify Bakersfield's most prominent missing person—and probable murder victim—had insisted it must be Sandy. There was no logic to this, just Kate's instincts again. If Kline didn't listen to her, she said, she would lobby the sheriff and the DA: she would get Pat DeMond and her other friends on the city council involved, she'd go to the press—Kate was continually threatening reprisals and lobbying efforts if the detectives failed to aggressively investigate Sandy's disappearance and Pat's involvement. So Kline and Soliz finally relented. They went ahead and had the tiny body of Jane Doe checked, had examiners cut off the withered fingers with tin snips and soak them in dish detergent to raise the ruined fingerprint ridges. ("It really does soften hands,

Madge," one of the other detectives joked, parroting the old TV commercial for Palmolive dish soap.)

In the end, though, the old dental records did the trick, proving Kate right after all. There was no question, then, that the unrecognizable corpse was Sandy's, something the police might never have determined without Rosenlieb's pushy insistence that they make a comparison. After that, Kate's credibility was never questioned by the sheriff's department. She became, at times, an unofficial part of the investigation. No one questioned how she could have known that the unidentified body was Sandy's, though had Pat displayed similar intuition, detectives immediately would have assumed it was based on inside—and guilty—knowledge. Through it all, Pat knew nothing of Kate's role in the investigation. He thought Kate was still his best friend, the one ally he could count upon.

"Was Mom molested?" Pat asked after handing back the pictures.

"Why would you ask that?" Soliz responded, eyes narrowed.

"Because it was one of her greatest fears."

Soliz made it clear he found this hard to believe. "Why would she go out walking at three in the morning without any type of protection other than her dog if this was her greatest fear?"

Pat knew the answer to this, as did many of Sandy's friends: her firm belief that such times were inherently safe because only "the good people" were out working then. But, for some reason, the answer eluded him. He had just been confronted with the discovery of his wife's body, by the terrible allegations suggested by the search warrant, and, worst of all, by those grisly photos. He didn't know what to think anymore, and so he just slumped on his stool and muttered, "I don't know."

Things went downhill from there. The search of the Dunn house lasted through the night, a total of fifteen hours, as the technicians and criminalists tromped through every room, spraying, sweeping, scooping up records and papers. Soliz, Kline and Sergeant Johnson spelled one another as they interrogated Pat the entire time, virtually nonstop, accusing him, pleading with him, even reducing him to tears. They made him repeat his story of Sandy's disappearance over and over, looking for the merest inconsistencies in times and dates, letting him pour himself tumblers of liquor between sessions. They accused him of knowing Sandy was dead all along, that he had said as much to Kate Rosenlieb, that he had never acted like a truly concerned husband. They said they knew he had murdered Sandy, and they berated him for leaving her body half buried in the desert like so much discarded trash.

"I can't believe you wouldn't even take care of your own wife's body," Dusty Kline said at one point during the long interrogation, as Pat sat gaping. "I had told everyone, sure, you had done it, but I knew you would at least show some respect for the dead, that when we found Sandy, she would be taken care of. But you didn't even do that. What kind of piece of shit are you?"[31]

Pat had wept at this, big, silent tears rolling down his pale cheeks, and Soliz and Kline had leaned forward, their faces expressionless, waiting for the admission that so often comes when you push a crook to the edge like this. The air was charged. This was what they had been working for through the night.

The moment was a classic of modern policing—the

use of intimidation, official lies, apparently damning knowledge, and other psychologically dominating tactics to interrogate criminal suspects. These methods have proven extremely effective since the brutality of the "third degree" was outlawed in the forties and fifties—more effective, in fact, than physical abuse ever was. Modern interrogation methods are so potent they not only solve many crimes, they also have elicited a surprising number of documented *false* confessions by innocent men and women.[32] Even so, the courts have given police wide latitude in how they persuade suspects to talk, and there was absolutely nothing illegal about the marathon questioning of Pat Dunn that night, particularly because Soliz chose to conduct the session at his suspect's home. In that setting, Pat was not under arrest and theoretically remained free to leave at any time. Practically speaking, however, everyone present knew Pat was a captive in his own home, unlikely to abandon everything he owned to fourteen members of the sheriff's department. By not arresting Pat, Soliz also circumvented the famous Miranda warnings, though even if he had recited them, it is doubtful Pat would have remained silent or demanded a lawyer. Pat, like most suspects (except, ironically, for career criminals well schooled in the system), believed that invoking his rights would be tantamount to an admission of guilt, and that continuing to talk might still allow him to explain things and extricate himself. The police count on this popular misconception that turns the Constitution on its head: Talking, unlike silence, almost always leads to contradictions sooner or later, which can be used as evidence of guilt. With Pat, the detectives had fifteen hours to try to rattle him into slipping and incriminating himself.

But that moment never came. Pat did not contradict himself in any meaningful way, nor did he utter any telling inconsistencies, not even as the night sky turned gray and bloody with a grim new dawn. Pat told the same story so many times that the detectives did not even bother putting it all down when they wrote up their reports days later. Pat continued to insist the investigators had it all wrong, that they were looking in the wrong places, that now that Sandy's body had been found, they needed to pursue the *real* killer.

As Pat would later recall it, one of the sheriff's officials present responded to these exhortations by cocking his finger like a gun, then looking Pat right in the eye and saying, "We already are."

"Mr. Soliz, you will reach a point where you will quit looking at me and start looking for whoever hurt Mom," Pat said. Pat considered this his definitive protestation of innocence, but Detective Soliz saw it another way. In his official report, Soliz wrote, "He never admitted to killing his wife but he also never denied killing her."

Even Pat's willingness to keep talking, to cooperate and endure fifteen hours of sometimes abusive interrogation, was deemed suspicious. "If it were me," Dusty Kline later said, "if I was innocent and some detective talked to me about my wife that way, I would have said, 'Arrest me, or get the hell out.' But he never did, like he thought he could convince us if he just kept talking."[33] Pat would later laugh bitterly at this, noting that he just couldn't win, for when he refused to talk to the detectives on another occasion, they said his lack of cooperation was suspicious as well.

Even so, after all the questions and the long night's search, the detectives left empty-handed but for the

Dunns' three cars, which were towed from Pat's driveway to a county lot for examination. Left stranded, exhausted and humiliated, Pat had to ask Rex Martin for a ride to a car-rental agency, where he leased a white Ford Tempo.

To the detectives' dismay, Pat had admitted nothing during the long interrogation. And their exhaustive search of the house produced even less: They had found nothing to link Pat Dunn to the murder of his wife, no blood, no sign that evidence had been removed or cleansed, nothing. Only their suspicions remained, stronger than ever.[34]

In the morning, as the detectives were leaving, Kate Rosenlieb came by the house to see Pat. He met her in the driveway. "They think I did it," he told her, shaky and hoarse from his sleepless night. "I can't wait until they get past me and start looking for who really did it."

He looked old, beaten down. His now familiar claim of innocence sounded sincere, but Rosenlieb cautioned herself not to accept that at face value. She started crying, though, and threw her arms around him. "I love you," she said. "And I'm so sorry this is happening to you."

"Oh, don't you worry, I'll get through this," Pat said gruffly, touched by Kate's heartfelt embrace. He assumed Kate meant she was sorry about him being falsely accused, as opposed to the darker import of her words—that she was sorry that this man she loved was a murderer about to be caught. "Now you better go," he told his friend. "Those detectives'll see you and the next thing you know, they'll be calling you my girlfriend."

After that day, Pat finally realized he had become the sheriff's prime suspect in his wife's death. He assumed he was under surveillance. On several occasions, he saw a car cruising slowly up and down Crestmount Drive, a shadowy figure inside peering at his house. He told this to Rex Martin and to another old friend, a retired sheriff's deputy named Jerry Mitchell, who had been helping Pat search for Sandy during the weeks before the body was found and identified. Pat wondered if the car might be an undercover police vehicle.

"I'd be surprised if they weren't watching you," Mitchell had told Pat. "As far as they're concerned, you're guilty."

A few days after the big search and interrogation, Pat called Mitchell to say the same car was cruising by his house again. Now, though, he felt even more troubled. It didn't look like a police car—or a policeman inside, he said. "Maybe whoever hurt Mom is coming back to finish the job with me," Pat said.

Just then, seeing Rex Martin pull into the driveway, Pat hung up with Mitchell. When his friend came inside, Pat told him about seeing the suspicious car cruising by—and, as they were standing there in front of the living-room window talking, the car returned. "There it is," Pat shouted.

"I'm gonna follow that sonofabitch," Martin answered, "and get his license number." Pat grabbed a scrap of paper and a pencil and handed it to Martin, who ran outside and jumped into his white Chevy Suburban. Martin pulled out of the driveway and sped to the corner, catching sight of the car, a small green Pontiac Sunbird, a few blocks off. He followed it to a nearby shopping center, where the driver, short and thin with a ponytail, got out and walked into a photo shop. Martin wrote down the license plate number and the man's description, then returned to Pat's house.

Pat called Jerry Mitchell back and gave the retired deputy the information to check out. "I can't run license numbers anymore, now that I'm out of the department, but I'll tell you what," Mitchell told Pat. "I'll give it to Soliz and ask him to check it out."

Some days later, Mitchell informed Pat that he had telephoned the information to Detective Soliz, but that he never heard anything back. "Probably nothing to it," Mitchell suggested.

Pat didn't see the green car after that, and soon forgot all about it. For a time.

10

A MONTH AFTER THAT NIGHTLONG SEARCH AND interrogation at Pat Dunn's house, the sheriff's department still had no case against its prime (and only) suspect in the murder of Alexandra Paola Dunn. They had no murder weapon, no witnesses, no evidence. They had sprayed every room in the house with Luminol, a substance that, under ultraviolet light, reveals minute and hidden blood stains, even on surfaces that have been scrubbed clean to the naked eye. That was why they had showed up late at night to search Pat's house, so they could conduct the Luminol tests in darkness. A similarly extensive examination had turned up evidence in the Dana Butler murder case years before, even after Police Commissioner Glenn Fitts had commercially steam cleaned the rug on which Dana bled. Yet the Luminol had revealed not a drop of blood anywhere in the Dunn house, not in the bedroom, where they figured Pat had stabbed Sandy, not even in the plumbing, parts of which they dismantled and tested for evidence that he had washed off bloody hands or clothes. And it had been a bloody murder, no doubt about that: The coroner said Sandy would have bled profusely from her abdominal wound.

The search had come up empty everywhere else as well: There were no telltale plants, fibers or traces in the

home or in any of the Dunns' three cars that might link
Pat to the place where Sandy was buried. Two of the cars,
the old fin-backed boat of a Cadillac that had been Pat
Paola's and Sandy's old Chrysler Cordoba, had been
under canvas covers and likely had not been moved in
months, if not years. Still, the criminalists had vacuumed
and sprayed and printed them right along with Pat's
white Chevy Blazer. They had scraped dirt from the axles
and wheels, combed foxtails and seeds from the carpets
and upholstery. But nothing in the cars matched the burial site. If anything, the search of the cars had suggested
none of them had ever been to the place where Sandy's
body was found. Soliz had even gone to the gravesite and,
though weeks had passed since the body was found and a
previous search had turned up nothing, he still reported
finding several gray carpet fibers there. He excitedly
brought them to Dunn's house for yet another search,
expecting a match. But there was no gray carpeting anywhere in the house or in the cars—the fibers had to have
come from someone or somewhere else. Pat Dunn's was
exactly the opposite of the Dana Butler case, in which the
physical evidence seemed so overwhelming while the suspect was given every benefit of the doubt.

These setbacks aside, John Soliz remained more certain than ever that Dunn was guilty: Pat's seemingly odd
behavior, his drinking, his failure to tell friends and associates about Sandy's disappearance for days, his failure to
produce a photo of Sandy or to take a lie detector test, the
fact that he stood to inherit all of his wife's considerable
wealth—all reeked of guilt to the veteran homicide detective. Everyone who looked at the case from this perspective said the same thing: Pat must have done it.

And it wasn't *all* just hunches and perceptions—there

really was some damning testimony out there, Soliz knew. There was the secretary for the Dunns' accountant, for one, an earnest young woman with a firm, clear memory and a set of office calendars to back her up. The secretary, Ann Kidder, had contradicted Pat's story in a big way when she recalled Sandy telephoning her on July 1 to reschedule an appointment. Nothing unusual about that—except that this phone call came twelve hours *after* Pat Dunn swore Sandy had disappeared. This discrepancy was one of the main reasons the case had become a homicide investigation long before the body turned up. Such a glaring inconsistency could not be easily explained away. Soliz considered the secretary a great witness, and she was absolutely certain that she had spoken to Sandy at the critical time. Which meant, as far as Soliz was concerned, Pat Dunn had to be a liar. Maybe he reported Sandy missing first, to set up an alibi, then killed her, Soliz theorized. Was that why Pat had not wanted anyone to know she was missing? Because he hadn't done it yet?[35]

Another big hole in Pat's story, Soliz believed, was this whole Alzheimer's business. Friends of Sandy, particularly Kate Rosenlieb and Pat DeMond, were emphatic that Alexandra Dunn had no memory problems—Pat had to be lying about that, too. A few people had supported Dunn on this, but many others said no way, Sandy was bright and alert. Soliz had even asked Pat why so many people contradicted him on the Alzheimer's question, and all he would say was, "They don't know Mom like I do." Rosenlieb had insisted this was a cover story, and Soliz tended to agree with her.

Finally, there were friends of the Dunns—Rosenlieb especially—who described the couple's marriage as a battleground. One friend said she was certain Sandy planned to get a divorce—plans a tearful Sandy supposedly had announced just weeks before her demise. That was the key, Soliz figured. Because of Sandy's will, Pat had a lot to gain if his marriage outlived his wife, and a lot to lose if the marriage died first. Pat had five million reasons to kill, Soliz knew. But odd behavior and a possible motive, as suspicious as they might be, did not amount to hard evidence. If he was going to nail Pat Dunn, the detective needed more.

John Soliz had a reputation as a dogged investigator, a Texas transplant who had been with the Kern County Sheriff since 1975, first as a patrol deputy, then in narcotics, and now in the most prestigious assignment for a detective in any police department, robbery homicide. He trusted his instincts in a case—which is why, after observing Pat Dunn, hearing him talk, seeing him refuse the lie-detector test, he felt confident that Dunn was guilty, a lack of hard evidence notwithstanding. In Soliz's estimation, Pat was smart enough and wily enough to clean up a crime scene. Enough time had passed, perhaps, to account for the fact that even microscopic evidence was missing from Dunn's home and cars. He felt Pat had been trying to divert him toward fruitless avenues of investigation—spurious sightings of his wife, tales of Alzheimer's—and he observed Pat getting defensive and resistant as he pressured and provoked him, another sign of guilt in Soliz's opinion.

Soliz saw himself working hard and diligently on this case, interviewing far more witnesses than in many other murder investigations. Throughout, he would later reflect, he tried to keep an open mind, to look at other possibilities. But everything kept pointing at the husband. No surprise there, really: It has long been a truism that a majority of homicides are committed by family members or lovers, rather than by strangers (though this balance has in recent years shifted somewhat). Every indication in the Dunn case suggested to Soliz that the old pattern applied here.

And so it had galled the veteran detective that, after their long interrogation, they had to leave Dunn's house empty-handed, their handcuffs still clipped to their belts instead of on Dunn's wrists. Soliz *knew* what happened. And there's nothing worse for a cop than knowing what happened—and not being able to prove it. What they needed, he knew, was a witness, someone who could finger Dunn as the killer. The vain searches, Pat's denials, none of it would matter if they had a witness. And for a long time, Soliz had felt certain something would pop up: The case had been all over the papers and television, with increasing hints that the authorities suspected Pat Dunn. Soliz's boss had even made an on-air appeal for information. But nothing came of it.

Then, on August 19, a month and a half into the case and just as it was drifting to the bottom of the pile of human misery accumulating on Soliz's desk, the call came in that would change everything. Anonymous. A gruff, male voice who asked the secretary for Soliz by name and claimed to have information on the Dunn case. As the secretary transferred the call, Soliz wondered: Would it be another worthless tip, like the dozen other calls they had gotten reporting Sandy, dazed and dirty, supposedly roaming around a Bakersfield slum—a week after the body was found in the desert. Or would it be something of value? The detective grabbed the phone and barked one word, as he always did: "Soliz."

Silence. Then the voice. "I don't want to get involved. I don't want to identify myself. But I have some information for you . . . "

"I'm listening," Soliz said. And he did.

After the caller and the cop chatted for a while, and Soliz heard enough to conclude that there might be something of value here, the caller abruptly abandoned his desire to remain anonymous. He would get involved after all, and agreed to meet the detective for lunch at a Denny's restaurant off the freeway, so he could pass on his information in person.

Once they were together and the waitress had filled their coffee cups, Soliz's new informant had quite a story to tell. A month and a half ago, he told the detective, he drove to a market on the east side of Bakersfield for a rendezvous with a drug dealer named Ray. It was after midnight, the parking lot deserted and quiet, perfect for scoring a fix. But upon arrival, Ray lamented that he had lost his dope. A police cruiser had started tailing him and he panicked, tossing out the window his bindle of heroin wrapped inside a crumpled cigarette pack. The cop car had moved on, but the dope was gone, Ray said. He wasn't sure exactly where this happened—he had no street names—but he described the intersection. Faced with a gnawing need for heroin, Soliz's new informant decided to try to find it himself, and he began trolling the area at one in the morning in search of an old Marlboro box with a precious, dirty secret inside.

While cruising through an east-side neighborhood of spacious homes with broad green lawns, the informant spotted an intersection that looked like it might be the right one. He stopped his car so he could search for Ray's lost drugs. Then, while poking around in the middle of the street, he heard a strange noise. It sounded like furniture moving inside one of the houses.

"I got scared. So I hid behind some trash cans," he told Soliz. That's when he saw a man dragging something out of a house across the street, about thirty feet away, a large, heavy bundle wrapped in a sheet and a blanket. The man loaded his bundle into a white Chevy pickup truck with a camper shell, which was parked in the driveway next to a white Ford Tempo or Taurus. Then, just as the bundle was sliding out of sight, the informant saw something else. "A human hand flopped out of one end—a woman's left hand."

The man was Pat Dunn, the informant told Soliz, and the hand had to have been his wife Sandy's. The witness was so shaken by what he saw that he hightailed it out of there and fled in his mother's green Pontiac Sunbird, borrowed for the evening drug buy.

It was a wild story, Detective Soliz knew. But he saw no reason to doubt the tale, which confirmed all of his suspicions about his prime suspect. And if it checked out, the detective had his witness—just what he needed to nail Pat Dunn.

There was a catch, though. The informant had some legal troubles of his own. For him to cooperate with the police and testify in court against Pat Dunn, he would need a break on his own grand-theft charges. He was out on bail, but his sentencing hearing, after many delays, was coming up soon.

"I need a deal," Jerry Lee Coble told the homicide detective, shaking his ponytailed head. "I can't do any more time."

Soliz nodded. He could have put in a call to his department then, so he could talk to the man who had busted Jerry Coble for grand theft. Detective Eric Banducci, after all, occupied a desk close to Soliz's. Soliz might have asked his colleague about Coble's background, his credibility, his penchant for truthfulness or lies, his fervent desire to snitch his way out of going to prison for his many thefts and frauds. But Soliz saw no need to do that: He believed Jerry Lee Coble. He *needed* Jerry Coble, to complete his quest for justice in the murder of Sandy Dunn.

"Let's talk to the DA," Soliz told his new witness. "See what we can work out."[36]

PART II
Laura

It becomes inescapably clear that the prosecutor, for good or ill, is the most powerful figure in the criminal justice system.
—BENNETT GERSHMAN,
Prosecutorial Misconduct

FEBRUARY 1993

1

FEBRUARY 1993

THE LONG CLIMB OUT OF THE LOS ANGELES BASIN into the Kern Valley is a twenty-mile uphill trek of singular scenic monotony, a steady rise through the stony Grapevine Pass, where gusting summer winds can topple a mobile home as if snuffing a candle, and where a December rain mild at sea level can glaze the Grapevine summit with sheets of black ice even tire chains cannot bite. On the best of days, lines of tractor-trailers inch up the steep incline like a march of garden slugs, great black clouds of diesel grit trailing from their stacks, staining the procession of yellow signs urging summer drivers to turn off their air conditioners lest they overheat their engines. Despite these sensible warnings, a few northbound motorists, unable to relinquish the Los Angeles custom of exceeding all speed limits by at least twenty miles an hour with air conditioner on full blast, daily push their cars beyond the tolerance point as they climb the grade. Now and then these unfortunates can be seen trudging the highway shoulder or speaking into cellular phones from inside their expired cars, provoking slight, smug smiles from passing locals who would just as soon see the road to LA closed down entirely.

The Grapevine was meant to be a lifeline to Bakersfield and Kern County, carved out in one form or another a century ago to allow riders and stagecoaches to make easier passage from San Francisco. But in truth the residents of the Kern Valley have come to view the Grapevine as their Great Wall, limiting both entrance and flight. The locals have always taken comfort in the knowledge that no amount of urban development, no matter how feverish or sprawling, will ever climb the Grapevine and envelop the oil wells and carrot fields to link the evils of Los Angeles with their town. The gangs and the crime and the misery of LA could stay on its side of the mountain. Downtown Bakersfield's wide, empty Main Street with its big, empty stores—standing where pioneer land baron Thomas Baker's alfalfa once grew around a sign inviting travelers to graze free in Baker's Field—would stay safe from the worst excesses of Southern California. Kern County would remain a family town, a sanctuary amid the madness. Or so it seemed for a very long time.

Wild West. Frontier law. Hanging judges. The half-serious words of warning about Kern County dished out as a kind of *bon voyage* to Laura Lawhon from various lawyers she knew kept coming to mind as she began the steep descent from the top of the Grapevine to the floor of the valley. Her view was as if from an airplane, squares of brown tilled earth tiled in with the faded yellow of aging hay and the drab green of orchard and vineyard, stretched out in a neat geometric grid, orderly, precise, the random contours and ragged edges of the once wild land wiped clean by man. It was a familiar sight to her now; she had made this tedious drive far too often in recent weeks. Not for the first time she thought, if only the loose ends of her case could be fit together in such an orderly pattern as the one arcing across her windshield, her life would be far easier.

Murder had brought Laura Lawhon to Kern County— a client charged with murder. Patrick O'Dale Dunn faced the death penalty, accused of killing his millionaire wife, Alexandra, after she threatened to throw him out and leave him penniless—or so the prosecution claimed and the local news had dutifully reported. Laura had other theories in mind. She just needed the time to develop them. The state's case seemed weak to her, hinging, as she saw it, on one key witness, a heroin addict who just happened to be in the right place at the right time. Jerry Lee Coble's account of his fortuitous predawn visit to Crestmont Drive not only brought a sudden solution to a case that had stymied the authorities for months, but it also guaranteed the convicted career criminal[1] the one commodity he craved more than anything—freedom. His payment as star witness in *People vs. Patrick Dunn* had come in the form of a generous plea bargain from the Kern County District Attorney, a deal that allowed Coble to elude what had been an impending six-year prison sentence for grand theft. It was all far too convenient for Laura's liking. She believed Coble to be an opportunistic liar. Now it was her job to prove it.

But Pat Dunn's trial would begin in less than two months, giving Laura very little time to pick apart a case that the police and the prosecution had had nearly a year to construct. She had to dismantle their investigation like so many jigsaw pieces, then try to force it back together into a new pattern—one that would exonerate Pat or, at the least, let a defense attorney raise reasonable doubt about his guilt.

Rednecks. Gun nuts. Cowboy cops. The words of warning kept coming to mind, though, to be sure, Laura knew stereotypes when she heard them. They were unfair, the easy shorthand city dwellers employed to describe places where farms and livestock and scuffed cowboy boots dominate. She knew they weren't right, not entirely, anyway. After all, people looked at the expensive jewelry and clothing she wore, the Rolex on her wrist, the Louis Vuitton handbag she lugged when visiting clients at the county jail, and sometimes they drew sweeping and unfair conclusions about her, too: rich girl, spoiled, shallow—the usual crap. Laura's colleagues—and courtroom opponents—all came to understand that you underestimated her at your own peril. Well, all right, maybe she was rich and spoiled, Laura would concede, an unlikely private eye who had come to the business late, after graduating college at twenty-nine and falling in love with detective work during a semester's internship. But there were reasons she was prized by the defense attorneys who paid for her services: her insights, her intelligent analyses of complex criminal cases, her ability to get people to talk in a way most lawyers and police officers, who too often attempted to dominate their subjects, never could.

Getting people to talk was Laura's forte: Somehow, the crooks, cops and ordinary citizens who inevitably get caught together in the complex web that surrounds any big criminal case would look at Laura, the smile lines on her freckled face, the hazel eyes that met theirs without flinching, and they would trust her. They would talk, and they would say the most amazing things. Some would want to mother her, others to flirt with her, still others figured her for a pushover they could lie to. Didn't matter to Laura—the important thing was they were talking. Truth, lies or a mixture of both, all were welcome, all were fodder for the case, for all could be used to enhance or undermine credibility as needed during a trial. Some people would spend twenty minutes talking to Laura on the doorstep, explaining why it was they didn't want to talk—and in the process give up a complete interview without even knowing it. That's why Laura never called ahead of time—people could hang up on her that way and that would be the end of it. Instead, she just knocked on doors cold, her invulnerable smile and gleaming white teeth at the ready. Very few doors slammed in her face. These were the qualities that got Laura the Dunn job in Kern County, far from her usual turf.

So Laura knew better than to accept at face value the warnings she received about Kern County. Contrary to the clichés she had heard, she found Bakersfield very much like other cities around the country—diverse, growing and complex. She saw from the start that it was a much bigger town than she had anticipated, that it was full of hardworking, honest people like any other city, that most of the cops and prosecutors she met seemed honest, even helpful. This was not the nightmare town she had been warned about. And yet . . . Those warnings kept coming to mind as she drove down the Grapevine. Because there was something to them, too.

You want to know what Kern County's like? one lawyer had told her. *Imagine Mayberry, except Andy Griffith's got a big ol' shotgun he likes to mow people down with, and Barney Fife likes to frame people, and Aunt Bea is a John Bircher, and old Floyd down at the barbershop, well, he got a bug up his ass one day and blew up the family-planning clinic, which all the other good citizens of Mayberry thought was just swell. They'd just as soon pin a medal on him.*

Bakersfield *did* make her think of a big, sprawling

Mayberry, old-fashioned and quaint, with its dimly lit steakhouses with the green leather booths unchanged since the fifties, and street signs that proudly pronounced the community an "All-America City." High school athletes were local heroes here. People measured the passage of time by harvests and plantings. The most celebrated favorite sons were Buck Owens and Merle Haggard, the country-music legends who gave Bakersfield a reputation as a kind of West Coast Nashville. Big, goofy billboards inexplicably promoting water sports stood tall out on the highway, welcoming visitors to this city in the desert. There was a wholesomeness to the place, to the fields of grazing cattle and the farmers on their tractors, a celebration of small-town virtues and the value of hard work and common sense, even as the city of Bakersfield grew quite large.

But the dark side was there, too, the "anti-Mayberry," Laura called it. The sheriff's department in Kern County *did* seem to shoot more people than most police agencies in the state.[2] Kern County once *was* a West Coast haven for the Ku Klux Klan—just as in the 1990s it became a stronghold for armed militias. The only clinic in town that performed abortions *was* torched that year, an arson widely celebrated and never solved. (Kern County earned the distinction that same year of having the second highest rate of teen pregnancy in California—and the highest birthrate of all among girls fourteen or younger, children having babies on an almost daily basis here.) And some of the judges *were* right out of the Wild West, it seemed. One infamous judge, now dead, kept a noose hanging in his chambers and liked to be referred to as the "Judge Roy Bean of the San Joaquin" (though he belied this hanging-judge image by once dismissing charges against a courtroom filled with accused criminals, simply to teach a lesson to a police chief whom he disliked).[3] Another Kern County judge was censured for playing practical jokes on defendants—sending a rattlesnake head to one man who was phobic about snakes, and a phony signed message and photo from Connie Chung to another defendant obsessed with the celebrity newswoman, nearly provoking a nervous breakdown.[4] There was the "Bubble Judge," who sealed off the air vents to his courtroom, more concerned about dust and "spores" than the stifling atmosphere he created. And then there was the judge who invited a stripper on trial in his court to perform a private dance in his chambers. Not that he would allow that to influence his decisions in the case, of course.[5]

But as far as police officers framing people, accidentally or otherwise, well, Laura wasn't ready to go that far. At the courthouse, she had begun to hear from local sources stories about cover-ups and conspiracies, of innocent men and women imprisoned for crimes they did not commit, of a law-enforcement zealousness that sometimes crossed the line. But she wasn't certain what, if any, credence could be given these sometimes apocryphal stories. She knew the vast majority of men and women in law enforcement were honorable professionals who sincerely desired to help others, to do their duty. But even good intentions could sometimes lead to injustice, she knew. For an outsider like Laura, telling the difference would take time—more time, probably, than she had to solve the case of the *People vs. Patrick Dunn*. In the end, she sensed Kern County would always be foreign terrain to her. Laura normally worked in urban Orange County, two hundred miles to the south, as did the lawyer who had hired her. The Dunn family had not wanted local legal talent to try the case. Pat had originally retained Stan Simrin, reputed to be the best defense attorney in town, a former local bar association president with an excellent record of winning tough cases—and for taking on the powerful district attorney. But Simrin had been replaced abruptly just before Christmas, after a falling-out with Pat's brother Mike. Mike Dunn, a well-off Orange County businessman, was footing the bills for Pat's defense, as Sandy's accounts and will were all frozen in the wake of the murder charges, and Pat's own money had been spent in a vain attempt to keep their real estate ventures afloat. So it had been Mike who chose the new lawyer, someone he knew from Orange County.

Though it got her this job, privately, Laura wondered at the wisdom of hiring an out-of-town legal team. Here she was, a tourist, with a jumble of fold-out road maps and a collection of fast-food wrappers on the floor of her Mercedes. She had no sources in Kern County, no insider knowledge of the courthouse scene, no clear idea of what she was up against. Pat's defense seemed to be going well, the case against him teetering under Laura's scrutiny, but her unfamiliarity with Bakersfield and its justice system left her unwilling to relax. The defense case could easily turn into a disaster, no matter how good things might look for Pat at the moment.

Laura felt ill prepared for this place, having grown up and lived in worlds much different from this one. Her hometown of Westport, Connecticut, was a place of wealth and privilege where she had shared neighborhoods with the likes of Martha Stewart and Paul Newman. She grew up with cotillions and ski vacations and thinking every teenager automatically received her own car at sixteen. At eighteen, she had left this life behind in an act of rebellion that stunned her parents, leaving home to marry a country boy, Wayne Lawhon, a working man as far from her world as Bakersfield. Wayne was determined to create his own wealth to support Laura, rather than rely on his new wife's family money. And so he did, moving to prosperous Orange County, California, to open a mobile-home-parts company. Plainspoken and blunt, Wayne was utterly devoted to his wife, denying her nothing, treating her like some rare and exotic creature who might fade from view at any moment. Laura kept the books for the business and raised their three children until, at age twenty-nine, she announced, as Wayne always feared, that she wanted more.

She promptly divorced Wayne, though they later remarried. In the meantime, she went to college and studied sociology, planning on a career in law, only to fall in love with being a private eye during an internship that was supposed to end in a few months but which she could not let go. Sandberg Investigations opened for Laura a window into a world of mystery and jeopardy that she had never before glimpsed from her pampered childhood or her cocooned life with Wayne. That she could be someone's last best hope for justice—and the justice system's tool for finding the human truth behind the facts of a crime—intoxicated her. After barely a week at the investigations firm, she knew that this was what she wanted to do in life. In a field filled with cynical ex-cops, burned out by their careers on the streets and the terrible things that they had seen there, Laura brought a vivacious idealism to her work, a big-hearted approach that let her see the best in all her clients, even the clearly guilty ones. She was not naive—she knew many, if not most, of her clients had done terrible things. But she still found herself liking all but a few—lost souls she would, against her better judgment, end up giving her home phone number, so they could reach her whenever they felt desperate or sad. On vacations, even in far-off Hong Kong, she talked incessantly about her cases and penned lively postcards to her jailed clients. She particularly agonized over those special few she believed innocent. "Can you imagine the terror of being innocent and in prison?" she asked Wayne once—but only once. Her husband, a law-and-order conservative mostly sympathetic to Bakersfield's desire for order, rolled his eyes at his wife and quipped, "Aren't all those poor guys in prison innocent?"

Wayne warned Laura that her usual approach to cases might not fly in Bakersfield, and she took seriously one word of caution he offered. He said he knew country people, the suspicions they harbored toward anyone who smacked of "city slicker," the resentment they felt when good, hardworking folks were treated like hicks, particularly when they were proud of their city and knew its explosive growth of late had given them size but little stature. So, going in, Laura understood she might be perceived as the carpetbagging city girl come to show the bumpkins how it was done, with the resentment and the resistance palpable. Wayne had steeled her for this, for slammed doors and silent stares in response to her questions.

Instead, as she began to knock on the doors of witnesses and friends of the victim, she found herself greeted not with hostility, but with small-town hospitality—even after confessing that she worked for the accused in one of Bakersfield's juiciest murder cases. She had never

seen anything quite like it. "It really is Mayberry," she told
Wayne in one of her first nightly phone calls home. And
yet, even as she was invited in for coffee and offered plates
of cookies on doilies, something nagged at her. For in the
fictional Mayberry—and in every other place Laura had
ever worked—she felt certain that, given the meager evidence, Pat Dunn would be home grieving his wife and
getting on with life right now. But in Bakersfield, Pat
Dunn faced a possible trip to death row.

"I didn't kill Momma."

Pat Dunn spoke to Laura in a measured voice. No
phony displays of emotion here, Laura thought, evaluating the potential witness even as she seemed to be chatting casually. No genuine displays of emotion either, for
that matter. Right away, in this first jailhouse meeting,
she sensed why the detectives took an immediate dislike
to Pat—they didn't see what they expected to see. No
extravagant displays of grief, no outraged protests of
innocence. The detectives found this suspicious. But to
Laura, this showed Pat wasn't posturing, he wasn't playing a role. He was just being Pat.

"I didn't kill her," he continued. "Not for money, not
for anything. I loved her."

Laura nodded sympathetically at the big man with the
short graying hair and owlish glasses. He looked morose
and out of place in the jail visiting room, clad in ill-fitting
regulation blue denims. Such comments had no real
effect on Laura's opinions—every client delivered a similar recitation. Laura would let them get this ritual out of
the way, then try to shift focus to more useful points: his
wife's habits, his habits, his activities and conversations
on the day Sandy died, who he had talked to about the

case—the stuff of alibis and legal argument. At the same time, she would try to get a sense of who the client was and how he could best be presented to a jury.

"They're going to try to suggest you were not sufficiently concerned about Sandy's disappearance," she said, as gently as possible. "That you didn't act like a worried husband, that you delayed reporting her missing for too long."

Laura paused. She, like Pat's lawyer, was concerned about the call Pat made to report Sandy missing. The tape of that conversation showed a jokey, folksy manner during what should have been a very serious moment for Pat. People reacted strongly to that tape, particularly women, who tended to come away with very negative impressions of Pat after listening to it. He had flattered and bantered with the sheriff's dispatcher on the phone, and while this proved nothing in itself, Pat's defense team had to acknowledge and respond to the effect it likely would have on a jury. "Tell me about the phone call to missing persons," she asked. Laura groped for a neutral word. "It sounded . . . strange."

"I wasn't flirting, Laura, if that's what you mean," Dunn replied. Laura thought she heard irritation in his voice. His first lawyer had raised the same point, Pat explained, after playing the tape for his wife and observing her very disapproving reaction to Pat's conversation with the female sheriff's dispatcher. "Hell, I'm just a fat, old man, Laura. I just had heard that you can't report someone missing for three days. And all I knew was that I wanted them to take the report. So I was doing everything I could to keep her on the phone, to get on her good side, so to speak. That's all."

"Okay," Laura said. She'd accept that for the time

being, as much because of the easy, convincing way he said it as for the logic of his reasoning. But what about his vagueness on the tape when reporting Sandy's memory lapses? "Why did you back off that? Why didn't you push harder for them to begin searching right away?"

Pat looked down at his hands, shaking his head. Then he shrugged. "It's the same reason I put off calling the sheriff right away: I was afraid I'd embarrass Mom," he said miserably. "It seems stupid now, I know, now that we know she's gone. But back then I figured she would come back to me. I was worried, and I wanted to do something, but I knew she be madder'n hell if I did anything to humiliate her. She was forgetting things, I knew it, she knew it. But we didn't really talk about it. And she sure as hell didn't want it advertised. She was so proud. She didn't want anyone else to know. They say why didn't I tell the housecleaner and the pesticide man and the guy at the pizza parlor and everyone else. Well, Mom could never have faced those people again if I had told them. She had this idea we were in some higher social station. You know, that's the New Yorker in her, growing up on Park Avenue and all. Anyway, that's the reason. I did it for Mom."

Laura watched as Pat took a deep breath, trying to compose himself. "You know, I still can't believe she's gone," he said with a sigh. "I don't know how I can live without her. She took care of me, really took care of me, like no one else ever has." He told his favorite story then, the one about how Sandy always magically anticipated his needs, replacing his shaving cream or razor blade just as he needed them. Laura heard the wonder in his voice and found herself wondering about the Dunns' relationship—and how Pat managed to survive before he was married, if fetching toiletries from the corner market seemed so awesome an accomplishment to him.

"She really, really took care of me," Pat repeated, but now his eyes, pale blue and searching for belief and understanding, were raised up and drilling into Laura's. "She always put me first. You don't know what a wonderful feeling that can be. Or at least, I never did—before Mom. I never had that before. That's why I always called her Mom, because she took such good care of me. And why I never could have killed her."

Laura listened intently. She knew from reading the police reports that these same words, almost verbatim, had been relayed to police by Kate Rosenlieb—how Pat was concerned about being alone with Sandy gone, worried about not being cared for, about the little things Sandy always attended to. But when filtered through Rosenlieb and the cold language of police reports, these words sounded unfeeling and selfish. Even with his wife missing, all he thought about was himself, they suggested. But here, spoken by Pat, the connotation seemed entirely different to Laura. These were words of loss and sorrow—and love. Why, Laura wondered, had the police—and his friend Kate—been so eager to read the worst possible interpretation into Pat's distress?

Pat had fallen silent. After a moment, Laura gently prompted him to continue. "Why don't you tell me how you met, how you ended up together?"

"Well, those are two different stories," Pat answered, relieved by the change in directions. "We met a long, long time ago, before this town changed so much. You know, back when it used to be a good place to live. Back when I still thought the police could do no wrong and that everyone they arrested had to be guilty." He laughed, a short, sad bark.

"You don't think that now?" Laura said. She meant it as a joke, but Pat took the question seriously.

"I never thought twice about it before I was locked up in this place. Now I think it's more than just a mistake with me. It's not just my case you should be investigating. It's the history of this whole damn county. Now there's a story."

2

APRIL 1982

THERE IS A SPECIAL INTERVIEW ROOM IN THE KERN
County District Attorney's Office. It has a toy
box and dishes of candy and crayoned pictures
adorning the walls, though none of these accessories can
make this room a happy space. Decidedly unhappy stories are told here, pulled like decayed teeth from the
mouths of the small and the vulnerable.

On this day, the room reeks of pain. A six-year-old boy
cries mournfully. Between sobs he says, "I miss my
mommy." A prosecutor and a sheriff's detective try to
calm him, shutting the tape recorder on and off as they
alternate between the questions and answers of an official
interview, and comforting whispers that everything will
be okay, everything will be okay. The two men in the
room would have preferred to leave this little boy alone,
but they had to have the truth.

This was a very different sort of interrogation than the
normal exchange between cop and suspect. This was delicate, tough, grueling, a prying of secrets not from a
crook but from a victim, and a child victim at that, in a
case that was tearing a town apart.

Unfolding in this room like some twisted stage play was
Bakersfield's crime of the century, or so the cops and the
prosecutors kept telling one another in excited asides.

What had started out as an investigation of one father accused of molesting one daughter—originally thought to be a misdemeanor—had mushroomed into an enormous case, a hideous case, an unthinkable ring of child molesters. Members of prominent families were implicated, even a county social worker who handled adoptions. It seemed these monsters were selling their own kids for sex out of sleazy motels, shooting kiddie porn, maybe even snuff films, staging orgies, drugging and defiling children, then threatening them with death if they talked. The grandmother of one of the kids had coaxed and teased the story to the surface, then called the cops. Now the scandal of it—the terror of it—had just begun to reverberate throughout Bakersfield, where most people believed themselves immunized by distance and determination from the big-city horrors two freeway hours to the south. This case had crashed into the city like a force of nature, like one of the floods that transforms a dry sandlot in the middle of town—the dusty bed of this once-mighty branch of the Kern River—back into the raging torrent it used to be before the boom of houses and farms sucked it dry.

This new, terrible flood had to be understood, contained, defeated. Bakersfield wanted its children safe and the monsters put away. The problem was, some of the kids, like this boy in the interview room, had said nothing had happened. This boy maintained he had never been molested. But the prosecutor and sheriff's deputy do not believe this, and so they question the six-year-old insistently, even mercilessly, prodding, leading, urging him to tell it all. When he denies that certain events happened—as he keeps trying to do—they press him until he says otherwise. *Well, your brother told us about the men in motel rooms doing things to your butts with their penises. You know the word* penis, *don't you? Your brother wouldn't tell us a lie, would he?* In fact, the brother had told them no such thing.

When there is hesitation still, the inquisitors say to this little boy who desperately misses his parents, who has been swept from his mother's arms by men with guns and uniforms, that the only way they can *help* his mommy and daddy is if he tells the truth. And they make it abundantly clear that the truth, so far as they are concerned, is a tale of gruesome molestation. Anything else has to be a lie. So, after a while, the boy starts saying yes to their questions. Anything to get it over with.

Even then, the inquisitors cannot get everything they want. They keep zeroing in on the motels, places where kids have supposedly been sold for sex—the heart of their case if they are to make the sex-slavery charges stick. The grandmother had told the police about the motels and the money, and they want the kids to confirm it.

"Okay. While you were there, did you see any money?" the prosecutor asks.

The boy shakes his head. "No."

The prosecutor repeats the question, as if the boy had not answered. "Did you see any money in the room?"

"Uh-uh."

"You see your mom and dad have any money?"

"No."

This goes on for a time, until the boy finally is pushed into saying yes, there was money. But he then describes the implausible scenario of seeing six naked strangers running from a motel-room orgy with wads of cash in their fists. To the interrogators' frustration, the boy still insists these people gave no money to his parents. They just ran naked into a public parking lot with it.

Later, the tape of this interview is filed away and kept secret. The official report on the interview—the one given to the dreaded defense attorneys—is written the next day and says nothing about money or the boy's initial denials.

The boy is questioned in this manner dozens of times over a period of months, but never again on tape. He is not allowed to see his family. After a while, he stops denying that "the bad things" happened, and his story, at least as it is told in the official reports, slowly evolves until it corroborates everything the police suspect, and more. The same progression occurs with his brother and two other child victims.[6]

After eighteen months in a foster home, without once seeing his parents but with regular question-and-answer sessions with his official inquisitors, who pry ever more salacious details from him, the boy marches into court, where his mother, father and their two friends are on trial. Now seven years old, the boy sits stiffly, as if drained of emotion. For a year-and-a-half, his entire life has consisted of cops and attorneys and social workers and, most of all, questions, over and over, about "the bad things." Now the prosecutor hones in on the money issue that so frustrated the interrogators at the outset. "What word was it that you used to call the strangers?" he asks the boy.

"Customers," the boy answers without hesitation.

"Customers," the district attorney repeats, emphasizing a word that the boy hadn't used or even seemed to know during the long-ago taped interrogation. "Did I tell you that word?" the prosecutor asks for the benefit of the jury. "Or did you tell me?"

"I told you that word." The boy then describes how the "customers" in the motel would molest him and the other kids, then give money to his parents. As he speaks, he rarely looks at his mother or father. He has somehow come to believe they hate him and wish he would die.

When the defense attorney's turn comes, he asks if the prosecutor had helped the boy "remember" that customers had given his parents money.

Again, the boy answers without hesitation. "Yes."[7]

It doesn't matter, though. The jurors are certain—just as the detectives and the prosecutors are certain—that no child could ever be convinced to lie about such horrendous things, especially when it involves the kid's own parents. They might lie to *cover up* a molestation, to protect their parents from arrest or themselves from embarrassment, but they would never lie the other way. Couldn't happen. You couldn't make it happen if you wanted to. That's why they know subjecting the kids to high-pressure interrogations is okay. That's how you get the truth, the tortuous, slow, unpleasant work of breaking down a child's insistence that nothing happened. You had to lead kids, explain that you already knew the truth, ignore the denials until they start agreeing with you. Then, all they have to do is answer "yes." It's easier for them that way. That's how you save a kid—and a community—from monsters.

The boy's young parents, a machinist and a Sunday-school teacher, are convicted of many counts of child molestation. Together with the other couple on trial with them, they receive sentences of over one thousand years in prison. Putting them away is, Kern County District Attorney Ed Jagels proclaims, one of Bakersfield's finest moments.

It was also just the beginning.

• • • •

What would later be called the Bakersfield Witch Hunt began one sunless April morning in 1982, when a detachment of sheriff's deputies led Brenda Kniffen from her home, pale and blinking, hands manacled behind her, neighbors dropping their garden hoses and newspapers to stare open-mouthed at the spectacle as her young son wailed in grief, "Mommieeeeeeeeee." Brenda's husband, Scott, was picked up at work a short time later. The local shock wave only deepened when word spread that the previously law-abiding Kniffen couple had been accused of accepting $150 to allow their two young sons to be molested in a roadside motel. Seven accomplices were also arrested. The teams of sheriff's deputies, prosecutors and social workers who fanned out across the county to pick up the malefactors took the extraordinary step of inviting news crews along to document the amazing roundup of nine monsters—and the rescue of their children.

In the close-knit community of Bakersfield, where wholesome family values were considered a birthright along with fishing holes, shotgun racks and country music on both ends of the radio dial, there could be few more horrifying notions than the idea of two seemingly normal parents selling their children for sex. Except for one thing: The dawning realization that the Kniffens and their partners were not alone.

The Kniffens' capture was followed by a procession of similar arrests in the coming months and years. As the cases generated ever more headlines and the story spread beyond the city limits, it became clear that the original case was not the aberration the citizens of Bakersfield wanted it to be. It seemed that, on the contrary, the first arrests were part of something much bigger, a long-invisible iceberg that had been bearing down on the town from some dark place for years, unseen and evil, and now threatening to destroy the entire community. Bakersfield suddenly found itself preparing for war—a war for the soul of its children.

The hunt had begun.

Over the next three years, local authorities came to believe they had discovered eight large child-molestation rings, each part of an interlocking underground of abuse, child pornography and exploitation of the young. More than seventy people were arrested. Hundreds more were implicated and put under investigation. Dozens of children were taken from their parents after social workers, sheriff's deputies and investigators from the district attorney's office decided that they had been used and abused in the most hideous ways imaginable for years, virtually in the open. In time, a task force was formed to investigate even more terrifying testimonials from the child victims: allegations of murder, Satanism, cannibalism and ritual human sacrifice. It was said there were women in this city who allowed themselves to be impregnated for the sole purpose of producing infants to be killed on Satan's altar. The same awful story was told by victim after victim: Children were drugged, hung from hooks, violated and sometimes beheaded. Blood was guzzled like sacramental wine. Photographs and movies were taken of the molestations. The children didn't want to tell any of this at first—during initial interviews, virtually every one of them denied much, if anything, had happened to them. But in the end, after many question-and-answer sessions as well as group therapy with other victimized children, it all came out.

The horrendous allegations soon placed the community under a national media spotlight that it would have preferred to avoid but, once turned on, could not be so easily doused. In those days, barely a week went by without some seemingly outstanding and caring parent being torn from his or her family in handcuffs, their children deposited in a special clinic set up to help heal the victims of abuse. Empty lots and backyards all over Kern County were dug up by sheriff's deputies hunting for the tiny bones of sacrificed babies. Everywhere, there was a feeling that anyone could be involved, that no one could be trusted—and that no one was above suspicion. Aunts and uncles stopped cuddling their nieces and nephews, afraid of how it might look. Lifelong friends stopped talking because one or the other knew someone who had been implicated. Parents grew afraid of disciplining their children for fear they'd be reported for abuse. Some even hired video crews to film them as, one by one, each child and adult in the family spoke to the camera and attested to the fact that there had never been any molestation in the home—just a precaution to ward off a false accusation down the road. The tapes were then hidden in attorneys' safes and bank deposit boxes. One gardener hid his high up in a palm tree. It's not that these folks thought innocent people were being arrested. Quite the contrary: There was no chink in the community's armored certainty of the suspects' guilt. This was a more self-centered concern, a matter of self-preservation. The city had to be purged, everyone knew that. You just had to be careful.

It is difficult now, with the clarity of hindsight, to fully understand the devastating fear that gripped this city in the 1980s—and continues to plague other communities to this day. The stories of atrocities have a familiar, well-worn ring to them now, but back then the horror was fresh and the belief in the infallibility of law enforcement in such matters was complete. At the time, the sheer unbelievability of the allegations had the perverse effect of making them seem more credible: Who could—or would—make up such things? It helped that the pump had been primed by a wildly popular book, *Michelle Remembers*, which purported to be the recovered memories of an adult who, through counseling, recalled a childhood filled with human sacrifices and ritual abuse by satan worshipers in Canada. The patient and her therapist, who left their respective spouses to marry one another after coauthoring the 1980 bestseller, began appearing on nationally televised talk-shows, lecturing police and social workers, and consulting on criminal cases around the country regarding ritual abuse and recovered memory. Suddenly, other victims began making similar claims of abuse, usually after reading the book or being in contact with a therapist or investigator who agreed with the authors' premise: that there exists throughout the world a large-scale and powerful underground of devil worshipers who use and abuse children in their rituals, and that memories of this ritual abuse can be suppressed for many years, then recovered through therapy. Years later, many of the "facts" in the book were revealed to be fictitious,[8] but the fever had already spread. And in Kern County, for the first time, the allegations were not the hazy, recovered recollections of distant childhood abuse. They were immediate, in real time, with real offenders named and thrown in irons. Seldom since the Salem Witch Hunt three hundred years ago—or Bakersfield's embrace of the Ku Klux Klan as savior rather than hatemonger in the 1920s—have police, prosecutors, press and public engaged in such a mass suspension of disbelief and critical thinking. The most incredible allegations were accepted and promoted as fact, while any contradictory evidence was disregarded. Naysayers faced the distinct possibility of being accused themselves. Bakersfield dreaded the evil in its midst, and yet embraced without question belief in its existence.

Gripped by a form of hysteria that robbed the community of its tradition of neighborly trust, the people of Bakersfield and surrounding Kern County soon found themselves at the forefront of a national phenomenon. Throughout the 1980s, cities across the country, following Bakersfield's lead, suddenly found in their dark corners case after case of organized, large-scale child-molestation rings, many of them linked to devil worship, murder and human sacrifice where nothing had been suspected before. Overnight, a virtual industry was born to deal with these cases. A new lexicon found its way into the public consciousness, words like *McMartin, Amirault, Little Rascals. Repressed memories, ritual abuse, satanic conspiracy.* And there appeared investigators who specialized in such matters, social workers who could help reluctant children recall their chilling experiences, group therapists who could bring victims together to heal—and to help them withstand the witness stand once the molesters were brought to trial. All of this began in Bakersfield. With the Witch Hunt.

And no place did it better. The McMartin Preschool prosecutions in Los Angeles got more press—similarly vile and spectacular (but ultimately unproved) allegations that ended in the stunning acquittal of all accused. But the suspects in the big Bakersfield cases would not be so lucky. They were almost all convicted, the most egregious among them receiving prison terms as long as four hundred years—virtual life sentences, longest in

California history, and exactly the stern sort of message the community demanded.

No, there would be no McMartins here, even as that benighted case became a cautionary emblem of the nation's flirtation with satanic hysteria. This wasn't Los Angeles. Here, the authorities were trusted, not suspected, their reputation now legendary, proven by fire. They had exorcised an unspeakable evil no one had even suspected existed. When the last of the molesters was put away and the hysteria had passed, the sheriff's deputies and the prosecutors found they were heroes. Investigators at the sheriff's department embraced the aggressive, proactive posture adopted in battling the molestation rings and began employing it in all their big cases—Pat Dunn's included. District Attorney Ed Jagels, meanwhile, had become the most popular man in Kern County, and the most powerful—his influence reaching as far as the state Capitol in Sacramento, his name dropped as a future candidate for California Attorney General, perhaps even governor. As for the rest of Bakersfield, it slowly returned to its old, familiar rhythms, the demons gone, the city once again safe for its children.

Then, an attorney named Stan Simrin picked up the phone and dialed another lawyer, a young and idealistic fellow who had been appointed to represent the interests of two young children who were among the first to reveal that child molesters and devil worshipers had joined forces in Bakersfield. Nothing about these cases, or this town's view of them, would be the same after that one simple phone call.

"I want you to come over and listen to something," Simrin told the other attorney, in his mild, understated way. "It will give you a . . . "—he paused as if searching for words—" . . . A new perspective on this case."

The man on the other end of that call, Jay Smith, was reluctant to accept Simrin's invitation. A stout, curly-haired lawyer with an infectious smile and a calm, easy way with kids, Smith had been appointed by the juvenile court to represent nine-year-old Kevin Nokes and his seven-year-old sister, Tanya,[9] two of seven children allegedly molested by various members of the Nokes family and their friends. The Nokes name in 1984 became synonymous in Kern County with child abuse, child pornography and unspeakable rituals. Simrin represented Brad and Mary Nokes, parents of Kevin and Tanya, who were star witnesses in Kern County's terrifying and still-expanding satanic conspiracy case. The parents denied harming their children, but, from Jay Smith's point of view as the kids' court-appointed protector, Simrin's clients were as dangerous as rabid dogs.

Now Smith pondered the request. He wasn't personally acquainted with Simrin, but he had, of course, heard of Bakersfield's most prominent criminal defense attorney. Simrin had a stellar reputation, not only for his work in the courtroom, but for his tireless volunteer work at his synagogue, for the mock trial classes he taught every year in the local public schools, for his long-standing leadership in the county bar association. But this reputation counted for little with the people who believed Kern County was besieged by devil worshipers—a group that included many of the deputies, social workers, prosecutors and judges in charge of the Nokes case. These officials expected Jay Smith's backing; it was seen as a tacit part of his duties as legal representative of the Nokes children. And though no one had stated it aloud, Smith knew he was expected to have nothing to do with Stan Simrin. The defense attorney was, as one social worker put it, voice dripping with contempt, "the enemy," someone who was thought not to care a whit for a child's welfare.

Nevertheless, Smith felt he had an obligation to listen to all sides: Despite the unspoken politics of his appointment, officially, he was charged with being an advocate for the children, not a mindless ally of the state. Though the interests of the police and prosecutors did seem to match his own in this case, he still had a duty to make certain, to listen to all sides. And, so far, he had heard only one side.

He didn't have any real doubts that his two young charges had been terribly abused. All you had to do was meet them, listen to them. He had seen from the moment he met them that these kids were destroyed. Their glassy stares, their flat monotone speech when describing horrendous scenes of brutal rape and abuse, their intimate knowledge of sexual practices no child should imagine, much less experience—all of it showed just what monsters these poor kids had for parents. Clearly, the Nokeses were guilty of unimaginably cruel and heinous child abuse, and Smith felt nothing Simrin could say would change his mind. He knew what he knew: Those kids had to be protected from their parents. They broke his heart every time he saw them. And he wanted those responsible to pay for it. Big-time.

Still, he finally told Simrin, yes, I'll come over. He walked down the street, then rode up to Simrin's office in one of the mahogany-lined elevators inside the glass and steel of the Bank of America building. It was Bakersfield's tallest, just across the street from the courthouse, and home to many of the area's largest and best-known law firms. Inside one of the more modest offices on a lower floor, Smith found the two-lawyer firm of Simrin and Moloughney.

"Come on in, come on in," Simrin greeted him, steering him toward one of the client chairs in front of his utilitarian steel-and-wood desk. It was a no frills law office, just books and plaques lining the walls, papers strewn everywhere. Smith regarded Simrin warily, his eyes moving between the lawyer and the small, clear spot on Simrin's desk, where a tape recorder sat, turned toward the client chairs. He wondered what he was in for.

A former pharmacist, Simrin, at age forty, had decided to earn his law degree from a correspondence school, and then quickly built his reputation in Bakersfield and throughout the state. He was a short, sallow man with a crooked smile, a closetful of bad ties and a habit of putting his leg up on the edge of his desk when lost in conversation, so that one scrawny shin stuck out, a shiny, pale beacon. In the courtroom, his ability to take apart witnesses—and prosecutors—was admired and feared, and he earned the ultimate compliment the justice business has to offer: The cops all hate him. Except when they're in trouble—then they hire him.

Now he propped his foot up on the desk and, without further explanation, turned on the tape player.

On the tape, Smith heard the calm, reassuring voice of Susan Penninger, a former probation officer who had become a private investigator. Smith knew her, liked her, trusted her. He glanced up at Simrin, whose face was inscrutable, giving nothing away. Penninger's voice stated the time and date, and announced that this tape would be an interview with one of Jay Smith's young clients, Kevin Nokes.

He listened as Penninger began to ask simple, open-ended questions. Smith heard no pressure, no coercion, no attempt to suggest an answer with a leading question. Just good, solid, kind interviewing. In response, the boy began to speak. His name was Kevin Nokes, he said. He was nine years old. He named his school, his parents, his sister, the aunt he was staying with after the arrest of his parents. And, in question after question, calmly and clearly, he denied being molested, denied that his parents ever hurt him, denied knowing anything about the terrible things the police kept asking about and insisted had occurred.

But it wasn't the denials that got to Jay Smith. It was the tone of voice, the way Kevin sounded: He sounded like a normal kid. A kid who showed no signs of being traumatized. Smith recognized the voice—there was no doubt it was Kevin on the tape. But Smith had never seen or heard the boy sound so normal. He had always known the children, both Kevin and his younger sister, Tanya, as basket cases, more like concentration camp survivors than children.

The tape had been made less than a month after the Nokes children were removed from their parents and placed with an aunt. When the DA's office learned that Kevin's aunt had allowed a defense investigator to talk to the boy, the county swooped in and took both children away—though the aunt had every legal right to allow Susan Penninger to speak with Kevin, and the DA had no legal authority to remove the children. Nevertheless, the Nokes children were taken to foster care and group therapy and separated from all family members from that day on. The official reaction to what Kevin Nokes told Susan Penninger was not to question the validity of the case against his parents but to encircle the children with an impenetrable barrier. From that day on, the Kern County District Attorney barred defense lawyers and investigators from talking to other suspected victims of molestation rings—not only in the Nokes case, but in *all* molestation-ring cases. Only sheriff's deputies, prosecutors, social workers and their allies in the investigation could get access. Any foster parent or relative of a victim who defied this directive would lose custody, no questions asked. The stated motive was to protect the children from further abuse, but there was a secondary effect: One side—the prosecution—held all the cards.

Jay Smith had met the Nokes children for the first time two months after Susan Penninger made her tape. At that time, he decided they were the most traumatized, dysfunctional abuse victims he had ever encountered. Yet now, as Simrin's tape recorder played on, Smith sat in the attorney's small office stricken, his face pale. He felt dizzy. He had always assumed the Nokes family was responsible for the kids' thousand-yard stares, their robot-like answers to questions, their numbed, emotionless manner. But this tape . . . This tape was of a normal boy, a happy boy, a boy totally confused and upset about what was happening to his family—but who had not been traumatized in any noticeable way. Jay Smith had never met the boy on the tape. He only knew the child whose life had been taken over by Kern County, and who, after two months of the county's ministrations, appeared profoundly damaged and would never be the same. Smith had walked into Simrin's office believing certain things, things the social workers and detectives had told him: that children couldn't lie about being molested, that there was no way these kids could be induced to make false allegations against their own parents. Now the ground had shifted beneath his feet. He realized everything he had believed to be bedrock truth was wrong. Kern County's sheriff and district attorney were on a crusade, Smith saw. It wasn't about justice or truth. They wanted monsters to hang. And if they couldn't find any monsters, Smith decided, then they'd create some.

Jay Smith wanted to cry out, *My God, what have they done? What have we done?* But he had no voice, no words. All he could do, as the tape spun to an end, was place his face in his hands and weep. As Stan Simrin searched through the clutter of his office for a box of tissues, Smith sat and cried for the families, for the children, for his town, for himself. Something had happened. The impulse that had started it all had been good and decent—a desire to protect children, to make the community safe for everyone, to hold wrongdoers accountable. But something had happened to this impulse, something twisted and dark, and no one had thought to question it, not even a good and decent man like Jay Smith. Which is how witch hunts are born, Smith realized in one searing instant—not through the designs of evil people, but within the hearts of the good.

There were indeed monsters in the world, Smith now realized with a terrible certainty. And, without knowing it, he had been one of them.[10]

3

did not. Out of arrogance, or ignorance or a combination of
both, Pat Dunn felt certain the authorities would come
around to his way of seeing things, and he kept talking to
them and trying to answer all of their questions, sometimes sober, sometimes not. He even gave an interview to
the Bakersfield Californian, which covered the case extensively and quoted Pat as saying that he was the prime suspect, though an innocent one.

A DECADE LATER, AT THE BEGINNING OF HIS OWN
ordeal, Pat Dunn would also turn to Stan
Simrin for help. At first, Pat hadn't thought he'd
need a lawyer, but once it became clear the police considered him more suspect than grieving husband, Jim
Wiens, one of the Dunns' real estate attorneys, had
passed on Simrin's name and number. "Call him," Wiens
advised. "Listen to him. He's the best."

Pat did talk to Simrin, but opted not to retain him at
the outset, certain that the authorities sooner or later
would accept his protestations of innocence and look to
other explanations for Sandy's disappearance. Simrin
cautioned Pat to be as cooperative as he could in helping
the police find his missing wife. "Of course I'll cooperate," Pat had started to answer, but Simrin interrupted
him with the second half of his warning: When it came to
questions that pertained not to Sandy but to Pat—questions about his movements and motives, alibis and feelings—it would best if he declined to answer. When
viewed through the prism of a suspicious mind, Simrin
explained, anything a person says about such matters can
sound like the words of a guilty man.

"Thank you very much," Pat had said heartily. He may
have intended to take Simrin's advice, but in the end, he

did not. Out of arrogance, ignorance or a combination of both, Pat Dunn felt certain the authorities would come around to his way of seeing things, and he kept talking to them and trying to answer all of their questions, sometimes sober, sometimes not. He even gave an interview to the *Bakersfield Californian*, which covered the case extensively and quoted Pat as saying that he was the prime suspect, though an innocent one.

And then the addict-turned-star-witness Jerry Lee Coble came along. He, too, spoke to police many times, refining his story, adding new details. Unlike Pat Dunn, who police never tape recorded, one of Coble's statements was taped—but only after he had told his story several other times and Detective Soliz drove him out to view the Dunn house and neighborhood to "refresh" his memory. Still, even with Coble as a star witness, two more months elapsed before the district attorney's office—lobbied by Kate Rosenlieb and other prominent citizens, including various members of the Bakersfield City Council—finally charged Pat with the murder of Alexandra Paola Dunn.

Held without bail, Pat was cut off from the estate by the accusations of murder and by objections to Sandy's will filed by her sister, Nanette Petrillo, who appeared far less estranged from Sandy in death than she had been in life. Pat had spent most of his personal savings, about one hundred thousand dollars, to prop up the real estate ventures, leaving him with no money for a legal defense once he realized he needed one. So he had turned to his brother Mike to finance Stan Simrin's hefty retainer.

One of the first things Simrin did was put an investigator on Jerry Lee Coble, guessing that the state's star witness might also be its weakest link. It wasn't long, then, before Simrin saw the significance of the ponytailed man in the green Pontiac who had been lurking outside Pat's house in late July, the man that Rex Martin had pursued. The piece of brown paper on which Rex had scribbled the mysterious car's license plate number was still in Pat's house, saved, ironically, because it had a phone number for Sandy's sister penned on the other side. Simrin checked it against motor-vehicle records and found a match: The car belonged to Coble's mother. Coble had been to Pat's house, all right—but he was there three weeks *after* the murder. No doubt, Simrin told Pat pointedly, Coble had constructed his account from observations and news reports, and from scouting out the Dunn household while driving by long after the fact.

The clincher to this theory, what made it so powerful, was that it did not rely solely on testimony from friends of Pat Dunn, who conceivably could have looked up Coble's license number, then concocted their story. No, it was backed by Coble's own words. Simrin noticed that in his tape-recorded interview with Detective Soliz, Coble recounted seeing two cars outside Pat Dunn's house on the night of the murder: a white, full-sized, newer-model Chevy pickup truck with camper shell, into which the body was allegedly loaded, and a white Ford Tempo or Taurus. Coble never mentioned an ancient twenty-three-foot Cadillac covered with enough blue canvas to outfit a clipper ship, or another covered car, the old Chrysler Cordoba, both parked and never moved from Pat's driveway until police took them away days later. Everyone else who went to the house around the time of Sandy's disappearance had seen those cars, along with Pat's white Chevy Blazer. Kevin Knutson, the financial planner, saw them. So did the exterminator who came to the house on the afternoon of Sandy's disappearance. So did all the neighbors. It was all in the police reports: Even Detective Dusty Kline saw the three cars there on July 4, when he first chatted with Pat. But not Coble. Instead, Coble described two vehicles that sounded just like the ones that were parked in the driveway on the day—three weeks after Sandy's disappearance—that Rex Martin chased a ponytailed man in a green Pontiac: the rented Ford Tempo and Martin's Suburban, a model that has the same grille and body design as a full-sized Chevy pickup. Simrin, scrutinizing the tape-recorded interview Coble gave at the sheriff's department, believed that Detective Soliz had also spotted this discrepancy, as the detective asked not once but twice about any other *cars* Coble might have seen in the driveway that night. But Coble had not caught the hint and had stuck with his story. "Now he's trapped," Simrin said with a predatory smile during a jailhouse meeting with Pat. "We've got him."

Pat's response was immediate: "Well, we've got to tell the DA and the sheriff that Coble's a liar, so they'll know they made a mistake and they'll drop the charges."

Simrin stared at his client, shaking his head. "Absolutely not. We won't say a word."

Pat, anxious to be out of jail and out of trouble, could not comprehend Simrin's reasoning. He started to argue, but Simrin cut him off. The authorities have decided you're guilty, Simrin told Pat. Anything you tell them, they will try to twist against you or disprove. They will consider our attack on Coble's credibility to be a trial tactic, a defense trick. They will say that your friend Rex Martin would do anything to cover for you, even fabricate this story—and it will not bother them at all that they previously found it to their advantage to argue that he was not a close friend, when they insinuated it was somehow odd for you to talk to him about Sandy. "In any case," Simrin warned, "they will not drop the charges. You will only be hurting yourself and helping them."

Pat still couldn't understand this. He did not know, as Simrin did, how things worked in Kern County, how the district attorney's office had accumulated a long history of pursuing charges with unrivaled aggression, winning at all costs, even if the evidence was tainted or the informants were lying. Simrin knew, and he had proven it in case after case, though nothing ever seemed to change. Prosecutors here, as in many places, did not readily admit to being in error. They assumed any defense must be a lie or a trick.

"But don't they want the truth?" Pat asked.

"Yes," Simrin said, "and they are convinced they have found it. They believe the truth is you are guilty. And now they will do whatever it takes to convict you."

He again tried to explain how they were long past the point of convincing the sheriff's department or the Kern County District Attorney that Pat was innocent. That point had been reached and passed within a week of Sandy's disappearance, before, even, the discovery of her body. The only ones to convince now were the twelve people who would be sitting on his jury. And toward that end, they had to keep the information they had learned about Jerry Coble secret, reserved for trial, where they could spring it on the prosecution when Coble took the stand. "That way, he'll have three seconds to think of a response, instead of three months to cook up some new lie."

Despite such dire warnings, persuading Pat to remain silent proved an arduous and ongoing task. As the weeks went by, Pat would periodically suggest going to the

authorities with "the truth." But Simrin, with help from
Pat's daughter, Jennifer, managed to keep Pat silent. They
would have a preliminary hearing in December, Simrin
said, where they would get a chance to question Coble on
the stand without tipping their hand and thus lock him
into a story. Then, at trial, they would expose him as a
liar. "It's exactly the position we want to be in," the lawyer
told Pat at one meeting. "Knowing more about their witness than they do."

Simrin left, thinking he still had Pat under control. But
Mike Dunn, who was footing the bills, disagreed with the
attorney after Pat brought him up to speed. Mike, like his
brother, had little experience with the justice system,
though that didn't stop him from writing lengthy cri-
tiques of Simrin's work and shooting his own amateur-
video reenactment of Jerry Coble's story of seeing Pat
dispose of Sandy's body, in which he illustrated how
some of the things that Coble described were physical
impossibilities. Mike Dunn assured Pat that the police,
once they realized Coble had lied, would back off the
case. He also was concerned that the $50,000 up-front fee
demanded by Simrin did not begin to cover actual trial
costs. So he advised Pat to go against Simrin's advice. "I
think we should tell them everything," Mike said, and
Pat, envisioning a quick release and a return home for
Christmas, said okay, big brother. Let's do it.

On the eve of Pat's preliminary hearing, a formulaic
proceeding in which the prosecution presents the bare
minimum of evidence necessary to hold a suspect for
trial, Mike Dunn called Detective Soliz. After complaining to the detective about Simrin's fees and insistence that
they keep quiet about their evidence against Coble, Mike
Dunn told Soliz all about Rex Martin following Jerry Lee

Coble, and how the cops had it all wrong about his brother Pat. He garbled the story, though, saying Coble had been spotted by Rex on the night before Sandy disappeared. In Mike Dunn's flawed rendition, Coble wasn't just a liar looking to skate on his own legal troubles. "Coble," Mike Dunn announced, "was the *murderer.*"

Mike Dunn then asked if, given this new information, his brother might get released from jail on his own recognizance until the DA dropped the charges. "I'll get back to you," Soliz replied.

The official response to this information, however, was just as Simrin had predicted. Soliz immediately conferred with the prosecutor assigned to the case, and they decided the defense was lying. They then set out to undermine Rex Martin's story, calling him at his office, catching him off guard, hoping to build some contradictions into his story. Jerry Lee Coble was questioned at length about the cars in the driveway, so he could prepare for the witness stand. Later, the prosecutor would show him pictures of the vehicles, to help sort things out for him.

Meanwhile, someone in law enforcement told Jerry Coble that the Dunn defense team was trying to pin Sandy's murder on him, making Coble all the more anxious to testify against Pat, and hardening his and his whole family's attitude and resolve when previously it had wavered. Now it was personal—the Dunn forces were trying to get *him.* (For years after the trial, Coble believed that the heart of Pat Dunn's defense strategy was to accuse him of murder, when, in fact, no one other than a mistaken Mike Dunn had ever espoused that theory in or out of court. Indeed, it was crucial to Pat's defense to prove Coble was nowhere near the house until weeks after Sandy vanished.)

Jennifer Dunn called Simrin in a panic that night before the preliminary hearing. "They told the police everything," she wailed. "Uncle Mike told them everything."

The next morning, Simrin confirmed what Jennifer had told him. He arrived at the courthouse furious, his careful preparations wasted. He always tried to use preliminary hearings as tools to hone his defense in a case, not as a forum for educating the government. It was the one and only time in a criminal prosecution that the defense holds a true advantage—the prosecution has to show its cards, while the defense doesn't (a procedure few states other than California mandate, and one that prosecutors have long opposed).[11] Now Simrin's hand was exposed.

"You don't know the damage you've done," he told Mike and Pat Dunn. "Don't you know that you are facing the rest of your life in prison? Or worse. They can still seek the death penalty if they choose."

Mike Dunn remained unapologetic. Pat claimed he had no part in the communication with Soliz, though now that it was done, he wanted to mount a full defense, including taking the witness stand himself. "We can end it right here," he and Mike Dunn predicted.

They still didn't get it, Simrin realized. Pat still believed there were some magic words that could be uttered to make it all go away, that he could say just the right thing and he would walk out of the hearing a free man. He simply didn't understand the process, how the justice system even now was marshaling its considerable forces with one purpose in mind: not to listen to him, not to consider his point of view, but to put him away. Simrin argued and pleaded with Pat to stay silent, to minimize the damage already done, but when the client insists on invoking his right to testify, the lawyer, in the end, has no choice but to comply. Simrin threw up his hands and let Pat try to talk his way to freedom.

It didn't happen, of course. As Simrin predicted, Pat was bound over for trial, an outcome never in doubt. The prosecution did everything it could to bolster Jerry Coble's testimony and to undermine Pat's defense—a "free shot," Simrin called it. Worst of all for Pat was his utter lack of preparation for the rigors and intimidation of testifying in open court. In the end, he blundered badly on a key point—his testimony about the day Rex Martin wrote down Jerry Lee Coble's license plate number.

This was the heart of his defense. Rex had been very clear about the fact that he didn't remember the exact date of this incident, saying only that it was a few days after he had given Pat a lift to a car-rental agency following the search and seizure of Pat's three cars. Given that months had passed, this vagueness was reasonable, even expected. But Pat was adamant about giving a specific date.

The problem was, he gave the wrong date. The run-in with Coble could not have happened on the day he swore to, for a variety of reasons, the most compelling of which was the fact that there was no way for Jerry Coble to have even heard of Pat or Sandy Dunn at that time, much less set him up. The first major news article on the case was not published until a day *later*. The district attorney now had a powerful weapon in his arsenal to use to diffuse Pat's defense: a glaring inconsistency.

Dignified and understated, Simrin was not the type to raise his voice or make a scene, but neither was he the sort to cede control of a case. He quietly threatened to

quit if Pat did not heed his advice in the future, or if Mike
Dunn had anything more to do with the case other than
paying the bills. Pat wavered, but in the end, shortly after
the preliminary hearing, Mike prevailed upon his brother to fire Simrin and hire a well-regarded criminal attorney he knew out of Orange County, Gary Pohlson.[12]

    Which is how Laura Lawhon came to be in Kern
County with just a few short months to prepare a defense
before Pat Dunn began the trial of his life.

4

AS THE GRAPEVINE SLOWLY FADED INTO THE DIS-tance behind her, Laura took the Highway 99 branch off the Golden State Freeway, twenty-five flat, straight miles to Bakersfield. Looking north down Highway 99 was like sighting down a gun barrel at a distant target, now a dirty brown smudge on the horizon in front of her. The smoggy pall hanging over the city, as gritty and thick as anything surrounding Los Angeles, always looked out of place to Laura in this wide-open land, an incongruous haven for some of the dirtiest air in California.

Gradually, the communities of Pumpkin Center, Greenfield and Weedpatch drifted by amid the groves and fields. The occasional crop-dusting plane riding low atop white plumes of spray, the smell of smoke, manure and chemicals rich in the air. Reddish iron clusters of valves and pipe rose from the soil on either side of the highway every half mile or so, massive knots of irrigation pump and line, feeding the long, muddy trenches that kept the crops from withering in their shadeless land-scape. The few arthritic trees planted along the shoulders and median were gray with dust, their branches twisted by constant thirst. There was nothing natural about this blasted landscape, and the sight of it left Laura feeling adrift and alone each time she passed through.

After a half hour on the curveless road, the city slowly began to take form around her car, bits and pieces of Bakersfield rising out of the farmland like scouts of an advancing army, first a gas station by a highway exit, then a concrete shopping center, then the inevitable strips of convenience stores and fast-food drive-throughs and cut-rate nail salons that were gobbling up America's most productive farmland at a phenomenal pace. This paving over of cropland promised an uncertain future for Kern County, and represented a continual source of friction between the city dwellers, the farmers, the environmentalists, the developers and the elected representatives who wished to offend no one with a checkbook. Each trip up, Laura noticed the tentacles of development extending a bit farther, just one more burger joint, another field bulldozed and covered with asphalt.

She had returned to Bakersfield to resume interviewing the witnesses against Pat Dunn, her third trip in as many weeks. She was going through the government's witness list one by one, revisiting each step in the sheriff's investigation, looking for new information and old contradictions. Experience had taught her that the police reports never told the whole story, and that what wasn't there could be just as important as what was. Law-enforcement agencies prefer to produce reports that tell a certain story—a story of guilt. Inconvenient details that fail to contribute to the desired story line, Laura knew, often got left out, like unwanted scenes on the floor of a Hollywood cutting room. In Laura's experience, there was nothing impartial about most police investigations. There was always an agenda. And so every witness in the Dunn case had to be reinterviewed, so Laura could learn what the police reports failed to say. Today's assignment was a woman named Marie Gates.

Laura took a freeway exit near downtown and drove to a block of single-story homes with small, exhausted lawns. The pulse of heat that enveloped her as she opened her car door felt tangible, like the surge of a crowd. She felt perspiration bead her forehead even before she could shut her door and squint through the glare for the correct address.

"Come on in, dear, excuse the house. I've been having a terrible time getting my kitchen cabinets done," Marie said brightly after answering Laura's first knock. Inside, past the pale woman with the long white hair and brilliant turquoise nylon jogging suit, Laura could see a house in shambles, the rugs rolled up and standing in a corner, the kitchen ripped apart, as if a remodeling job had been halted midway. A dog and several cats roamed amid the debris. Marie continued to fuss and apologize as she ushered Laura to a seat inside the cool, dark living room.

"Oh, that's all right," Laura said diplomatically. "You can see how nice it will look when everything's done."

"Oh, I just love you to pieces. I feel like you're my own daughter," the woman told Laura warmly as they walked inside, basking in the compliment. It was a somewhat odd thing to say, given that they had met only once before, and then for a mere half hour, but Marie was the sort who put great stock in first impressions. Laura settled in and Marie brought over tea and cookies, occasionally cooing to her pets in baby talk. Then, her hostess duties complete, she sat down and asked, "Now, what can I tell you, dear?"

Laura hesitated for a beat, looking at the older

woman's kind smile and clear blue eyes. Marie Gates was an old friend of Pat's mother, Lillian, and one of the witnesses Laura most needed to pursue. She had provided the only unequivocal testimony that the Kern County authorities could find suggesting Pat Dunn might have had an unambiguous motive for murder. The informant, Jerry Lee Coble, had given the sheriff the who, what and when of Sandy's demise. But Marie Gates put it all together for them. She gave them the *why* of Sandy's murder: She had sworn Sandy planned to leave Pat—and to leave him penniless.

Marie Gates was also the first witness to give Laura that odd feeling that haunted her during this case, the one that made the hair on the back of her neck stand up, the one that had her glancing in the rearview mirror just a bit more often than traffic safety dictated. Maybe it was the eager way in which this sweet, kindly older woman pulled Laura aside during their chat a few days earlier, when Laura went to speak with Pat's mother and found Marie there, too. Maybe it was the smile on her face that never quit, even as she pulled Laura out of earshot of Lillian Dunn so she could say the most terrible things about Pat, how he was a drunk and a wife beater and a murderer. "Everyone knows it," Marie had said earnestly. "I don't know a single person who thinks he's innocent. Really."

As she spoke, her voice had been suffused with such jovial certainty that Laura did not know how to reply. All she could think of was how convincing this woman would sound to a jury: Unchallenged, Marie Gates could destroy Pat. So Laura had asked for a more detailed talk, on tape. She left unstated the reason for her request—to see if Marie would hold up while testifying for the prosecution, or if her credibility could be undermined, as

Laura hoped. Prosecution witnesses often are told they
do not have to talk to the defense if they don't want to,
and many are wary, but not Marie. To Laura's surprise,
she had readily—even excitedly—agreed to today's taped
interview and invited the out-of-town private investigator to her home.

"So," Marie asked again, eager for questions. "What
can I tell you?"

"Well, I wanted to talk to you about the last time you
saw Sandy," Laura began, and that was all it took to get
started. Marie brushed her white hair from the sides of
her face, almost as if drawing curtains, as she leaned forward in her chair and began narrating a story she had
already told the sheriff's detectives, as well as her neighbors, friends and just about anyone else interested in
Sandy's murder—the story of a last, fateful conversation
with Alexandra Dunn.

The story had changed over time, but it always started
the same way, with Marie behind the wheel of her old,
finned Chrysler, spotting the figure of her friend Sandy.
In this rendition, Marie's first sight was of Sandy shaking
and sobbing at the curb not far from the Dunns' home. It
had been a few weeks before the disappearance, Marie
asserted, though she could not give an exact date. She
was, however, exacting in her description of her despondent friend.

"All that day she was crying in the street," Marie said,
shaking her head. "She had her hands up like this"—
Marie demonstrated the gesture, covering her face as if in
despair—"And I pulled over and said, 'What's the matter,
darlin'?'"

Laura nodded, taking notes in addition to recording
the conversation.

"Sandy was crying," Marie continued, animated, reliving the moment, unconsciously mimicking Sandy's voice as she recounted the dialogue. "And she says, 'Oh, Marie, I've made a mistake, I've made a terrible mistake.'"

When Marie asked what she was talking about, Sandy explained that her marriage had been a mistake, her husband was a terrible man, and she wanted out. She'd pay for the divorce herself if she had to, Marie recalled Sandy saying. She just wanted him out of her life, away from her money, away from her house. Immediately.

"And she says, 'He's hitting me, or hitting *on* me,'" Marie went on. Laura looked up, frustrated. The two phrases held very different, even contradictory, meanings, but Marie was unsure which it had been. The conversation with Sandy, it seemed, had been hurried, and it was hard to remember exact phrases. "She was talking so fast and I was on my way to pick up children," Marie said, and then lapsed into a characteristic digression, this time to explain how she baby-sat various kids in the neighborhood, walking them to and from school at times, except school was out for the summer when this encounter with Sandy supposedly occurred. However, before Laura had a chance to question the point, Marie had returned to her main narrative about Sandy.

"She says, 'I'm afraid, I'm afraid,'" Marie recalled, again mimicking Sandy in a wistful, forlorn little voice.

Marie looked at Laura then, and speaking in her own voice heavy with foreboding, told of how she wanted Sandy to get in her car, to come home with her only to have Sandy say no, she'd be okay, she could handle the divorce—and her husband—on her own.

"And she walked home, it's just around the corner,"

Marie finished with a mournful flourish, as if delivering a eulogy. "And I never saw her again."[13]

Laura scribbled furiously, sensing she was onto something: Marie's story had changed from the one she had told the sheriff's detectives, in ways both subtle and dramatic. Laura knew this because she had spent days poring over Marie's past statements to the authorities, as recorded in sheriff's department reports on the case. The reports, by law, had been turned over to the defense once criminal charges had been filed against Pat, and they revealed some startling inconsistencies in Marie's various accounts.

For one, in her many conversations with the authorities, Marie had claimed to be an old friend of Sandy's who saw her regularly. They had been "the best of friends," Marie said. Yet Pat told Laura he and Sandy barely knew Marie Gates, that she had never once set foot in their house. To Laura, Pat's version seemed to make more sense, for no one else close to the Dunns knew anything about Marie Gates. Marie herself said that she had never even known that Pat and Sandy were married until a year before Sandy's disappearance—well after the Dunns' fifth anniversary. How close, then, could Marie and Sandy have been? This startling admission was right in the police reports, but the sheriff's detectives hadn't confronted Gates with this inconsistency. And Marie hadn't even known about Leon, Sandy's second husband. Laura had to tell her about Leon.

"Oh, I guess I was living out of state then, dear," Marie explained, dismissing the contradiction with a wave of her hand. But Laura had established something crucial: Marie Gates was not as close to Sandy as she claimed, and certainly couldn't be classified a confidante.

Then there was Marie's shifting story. She had first come to the attention of the sheriff's department by making several anonymous phone calls to the authorities, offering nothing more than a little speculation each time. Initially, it seemed, she was regarded at the sheriff's department more as the neighborhood busybody than as someone with hard information. Unwilling to identify herself at first, she had been randomly assigned a code name as a matter of routine under the sheriff's "Secret Witness" program. She was known as "Taylor 1."

In appropriately hushed whispers, Taylor 1 had called first to accuse Pat of murder, pointing out that he hadn't reported Sandy missing right away, and therefore must be guilty. Then she called back, changing her story to suggest that Pat's daughter, not Pat himself, was responsible for the murder. Taylor 1 also upbraided the sheriff's department for failing to search Pat Dunn's "Bronco"—she apparently meant his Blazer, a somewhat similar four-wheel-drive utility vehicle—but this, too, was incorrect. All of Pat's cars, the Blazer included, had been seized and searched inch by inch. Throughout these anonymous calls, Marie Gates offered no evidence to back up her assertions, no real details and no indication of whether she was passing on firsthand information or simple gossip. In those first calls, she never mentioned anything about Sandy seeking a divorce, either, nor did she say anything about seeing Sandy walking around crying and proclaiming her marriage a mistake—though these points would later form the centerpiece of her story.[14]

The first time Marie Gates spoke to a sheriff's detective without the comfort of anonymity was in a phone conversation with Detective Dusty Kline, who happened to pick up her Taylor 1 call that day. By then it was August

18. More than six weeks had passed since Sandy disappeared, with Marie never mentioning her last encounter with Sandy to anyone. (Coincidentally, August 18 was the day before Detective John Soliz and Jerry Lee Coble found one another.) Nevertheless, when Taylor 1 called the sheriff's department this time, she received a very different reception from the usual perfunctory humoring: For the first time, someone showed interest in what she had to say, with Kline questioning her at length, then cajoling her into identifying herself.

"We really need some help, and you sound like someone who knows something important," Kline pleaded. This new enthusiasm for what she might have to say apparently appealed to Marie, and she agreed to speak on the record. Then, warming to her story, Marie gave Kline her first account of seeing Sandy out walking about two weeks before the disappearance, sometime in mid-June, as Marie drove home. Marie told Kline she pulled over to chat with her friend. Kline's report detailing this interview shows she mentioned nothing about seeing Sandy crying or appearing upset. She told Kline that Sandy came over to the car and announced, "I made a terrible mistake. I want my husband out of my house and out of my life."

In an aside, Marie confided to Kline that she never had cared much for Pat Dunn——"a con man and a womanizer," as far as she was concerned. She had much preferred Sandy's first husband, Pat Paola, who she described as one of the finest men she had ever known. "I would have told Sandy never to marry Pat Dunn if I had known she was planning on it," Marie proclaimed with an air of satisfaction. "I knew he was no good."

She went on to explain how Sandy had given her husband until the end of the month to get out—which would have been June 30, the very day Sandy disappeared. The authorities loved that, as it fit perfectly with their theory of the case, a perfect trigger for murder.

"She said she wanted his girl out, too," Marie added. At the time, Marie thought Sandy meant that Pat had a girlfriend living in the house. Now, she told the detective, she realized Sandy had been talking about Pat's daughter, Jennifer. She did not explain how she knew this, or why she had been mistaken in the first place, and, at least as far as Laura could tell from the police reports, Detective Kline didn't ask. (In any case, Laura knew Jennifer, then five months pregnant, was living with her mother, not Pat, at the time.) Marie also claimed Sandy was upset because her husband and his daughter had hit her. This alarmed Marie enough that she begged Sandy to get in the car and come home with her.

"No, I'll be okay," Marie recalled Sandy saying in an uncertain—and unconvincing—voice.

Gates concluded this first conversation with Detective Kline by contradicting one of her earlier Taylor 1 statements, in which she had said she suspected Pat of murder because he failed to report Sandy missing without delay. Her new version asserted that she began suspecting Pat Dunn of murder when she learned he had never mentioned Sandy's disappearance to his mother, Lillian. "She found out from the television news," Marie said. "Isn't that awful?"[15]

Marie also thought it highly suspicious that Pat had Sandy quietly cremated without religious services, choosing instead to spread her ashes over the Morning Star project site that she loved so much. "She was a devout Catholic and should have had a service," Marie said

indignantly. A few other witnesses, Councilwoman Pat
DeMond among them, had voiced similar sentiments,
and sheriff's detectives considered the cremation another reason to doubt Pat, evidence that he hated his wife
and sought not only to murder her physically, but to
harm her in death as well.

But Marie Gates was wrong on all of these points.
Laura knew—as did the sheriff's detectives—that Pat had
told Lillian Dunn about Sandy within three or four days
of her disappearance, right around the July Fourth holiday weekend and well before any television coverage of
the case. Lillian herself had told this to the sheriff's investigators. Nor did Marie Gates seem to know that Sandy
had left the Catholic Church in anger in the mid-1980s,
after a disagreement over a charitable contribution.
Sandy had donated a large sum of money to the diocese
with what she thought was an understanding that a facility under construction would be dedicated to the memory of Pat Paola—a promise church officials denied making and never fulfilled, though they kept the money.
Sandy was extremely bitter about this, and had even filed
suit against the church. All her close friends knew this,
that she had vowed never to go to church again—but not
Marie Gates.

Once again, detectives did not press Marie on these
issues, Laura could see from the reports. They wanted to
believe her. Nor did anyone ask Marie why she waited six
weeks to tell her story to the authorities, why she never
mentioned this last encounter with Sandy during her
Taylor 1 calls, or why Pat's supposed failure to tell Lillian
about the disappearance, rather than this far more damning conversation on the street with Sandy, triggered
Marie's suspicions. To Laura, it made no sense.

When police interview a suspect—or a hostile witness—they try to lock him or her into an initial, detailed
story, Laura knew. Then, any deviations from that original story line can be labeled lies and used as evidence of
a guilty state of mind. But the standards are very different for witnesses favorable to law enforcement, whose
changing stories may be welcomed and given the innocuous label "refreshed recollections"—so long as the
changes benefit the prosecution's case. In subsequent
renditions, Marie's story kept evolving, always to the
detriment of Pat Dunn. In the next telling after the initial
interview with Kline, Marie recalled Sandy looking nervous as she walked that day, something she never mentioned before. Now Marie was not simply stopping for a
pleasant chat, but had pulled over to ask what was wrong.
In later renditions, Sandy was walking along sobbing,
tears streaming down her face, when Marie pulled over to
ask what was wrong. In this more dramatic version, while
Marie tried to talk Sandy into getting into her car and
coming home with her, someone drove up and yelled at
Sandy to go home. Marie said at first that she wasn't sure
who this was, but she thought it might have been Pat
Dunn. In subsequent versions, she became sure the man
was, in fact, Pat Dunn. Still later Marie said Sandy had
told her she had made a terrible mistake in marriage, but
that she didn't believe in divorce.[16]

With many witnesses, such inconsistency and outright
mistakes—coupled with a virulent and admitted dislike
of the defendant—would be fatal to their credibility.
Certainly the sheriff's investigators seized on every
inconsistency in Pat's story, no matter how minor, to
brand him a liar and a murderer. The problem was, Marie
Gates was the sort of lovely older widow that every neigh-

borhood seems to have, the one with no children of her own, but who is always baking for the neighbors and watching their kids. She was in her seventies but still vigorous, with that perfect, long white hair and clear blue eyes and a melodious, soothing voice. She told a tragic tale of how all seven of her children had died at birth or in infancy, and how, now that her husband had died, she had no one left—except for the children in her neighborhood, whom she cherished as her own, walking them to school and showering them with treats.

Marie, then, was clearly a sympathetic witness, so when it came time for her to tell her story in court, it wouldn't matter that all of the Dunns' other friends agreed that there never was any talk of divorce. It wouldn't matter that Sandy told her financial planner just hours before her disappearance that she wanted Pat to have *more* control over her finances—hardly the words of a woman intent on divorce, or who had given her husband until the end of the month to get out (particularly when the meeting with the financial planner was on the last day of the month). And it wouldn't matter, in the end, that Marie Gates was wrong on so many points, or that her story never seemed to come out the same way twice. Laura knew jurors would look at her serene face and hear that angelic voice with the slight quaver in it, and believe anything she said on the witness stand. And, after all, they would hear her tell her story only once, and it would sound good. Like the authorities, they would *want* to believe her. Any defense lawyer who tried to attack her would come off as an ogre, unless he was very, very careful—and, even then, only if Laura provided the proper ammunition to support an all-out attack.

And, she just might find it, Laura realized. Here was

Marie, telling the story yet again, kindly and patient and sounding utterly believable—and, once more, scrambling it into a new version. This time, Sandy wasn't just walking along and crying. Now she had her face buried in her hands and had been walking around town sobbing all day. Then Marie told Laura something else she claimed to know, but that she had never mentioned before in conversations with sheriff's detectives—that she knew for a fact Sandy took her daily walks during daylight hours, not in the dark. This provided further evidence of Pat's perfidy, she said.

"He keeps saying she used to walk after midnight and stuff," Marie scoffed, adamant and sure of herself. "That's a lie."

Laura just nodded, knowing that Sandy's nocturnal walks were well documented and not just based on Pat's word. She, and the sheriff's detectives, had interviewed neighbors, one of Sandy's walking partners, her jeweler, and all backed up Pat's description of the odd hours Sandy kept. Even the cops conceded that much. Yet again, this "dear friend" of Sandy's seemed to know very little about her.

Marie also told Laura that Sandy had met with an attorney the day before she disappeared, apparently to talk about a divorce. Marie had heard about this supposed legal consultation from a woman who knew Sandy, but didn't want to get involved. "I can't give you the name," Marie whispered. "I promised to keep her out of it. She's afraid of the Dunns." Laura had heard about this alleged meeting before, too, and knew it never happened. The rumor mill had confused Kevin Knutson, the financial planner who met the Dunns on Sandy's last day, with a lawyer.

As Marie continued to pass on other such revelations, it gradually became clear to Laura that she was incorporating into her story all sorts of things that other witnesses in the case had said. One minute, she parroted a neighbor of the Dunns who claimed to have heard a loud argument between Sandy and Pat, from which Sandy drove off in an angry, erratic fashion, two days before she disappeared. Marie and this neighbor had apparently compared notes at length. Then Marie quoted something Kate Rosenlieb had said, about seeing a small cut on one of Sandy's shins several months before she disappeared, which Sandy supposedly blamed on Pat.[17] Moments later, she repeated something that Pat DeMond had told sheriff's detectives about Sandy's sister Nanette, who was challenging Sandy's will and trying to leave Pat Dunn penniless by taking over the estate. (DeMond was a paralegal by trade; she worked for the sister's attorney even as she lobbied law-enforcement officials from her city council position to prosecute Pat Dunn.) As Marie spoke, it suddenly dawned on Laura that the prosecution's witnesses might all be talking to one another, sharing information and recollections. And Marie—consciously or unconsciously—was beginning to repeat other witnesses' information as if it were her own. Could that be how this story of seeing Sandy in the street evolved? Was it a gradual merging of the events Marie had actually witnessed with other stories she had heard over a period of months, until Marie herself couldn't be sure which was which?

Laura asked Marie to go over once again her last conversation with Sandy, and Marie happily obliged. "Sandy was crying . . . and she says, 'Oh, Marie, I've made a mistake, I've made a terrible mistake.'" This much Laura had heard before—the mistake in marriage Marie had previ-

ously mentioned. But then came the inevitable new revelation: "Because when she met Pat, Sandy had told me,
'Oh, I met a guy, he's in real estate, he has holdings out of
town, la-di-da. And, you know, he wouldn't be after my
money.'"

Laura put her teacup down and listened intently.
Marie, she felt certain, was about to disclose something
crucial.

"And she said, 'I made a mistake. He told me he had
money, he told me he had holdings out of town. But he
doesn't. He lied.'"

There it is, Laura thought to herself. *Gotcha.*

Marie continued speaking, reliving the moment,
oblivious to Laura's intent gaze. "And she said, 'He's after
me all the time, let's do this, let's do that . . . . He says he
don't like tightwads and pennypinchers.'"[18]

Laura and Marie talked a good half hour more after
that, but Laura had everything she needed, relaxing,
putting her notepad down, just chatting. The subject
changed, with Marie reminiscing about how she met her
husband, how happy they had been until the day he died,
and how she later dumped a would-be second mate for
cheating on her even as he proposed marriage. Laura
nodded and smiled, and Marie rambled, a lonely woman
happy for the company of someone who actually listened. She even offered to take Laura out to dinner, but
Laura only half heard, for she kept thinking about
Marie's account of Sandy's last words, this image of a
doomed woman talking so fast she could hardly be
understood, describing a husband who lied about his
own riches while coveting his wife's money and real
estate, who couldn't wait to get his hands on Sandy's
wealth and spend it.

Marie Gates had never said any of this to the authorities—or at least if she had, they weren't admitting it. For that man Marie described couldn't possibly be Patrick O. Dunn, Laura knew. Pat had never claimed to have any wealth when he met Sandy. He was a retired school principal with a marginal foreclosure business. And, at Sandy's urging, he had even shut down that business while recovering from appendicitis. Sandy had paid for the operation, twenty thousand in cash. Later, during discussions with their financial planner, Pat candidly announced, "I don't have any assets of my own," at which Sandy had shown no surprise, no anger, no reaction at all. Clearly, then, Sandy had no illusions about Pat's net worth. She well knew who had the money in the Dunn family, and had known it all along.

Yet Marie wasn't totally wrong, either, Laura knew: Sandy once *did* have a husband whom she accused of misrepresenting his financial worth and of wanting to spend her money on luxuries and get-rich schemes. She once *did* have a marriage that she often described as a mistake—and a husband she considered a con man. But it was her *second* husband, Leon, she had always described in this way. Not Pat.

Somehow, Marie had gotten the two confused, Laura decided. She saw no other explanation. The statements Marie remembered Sandy uttering made no sense unless applied to Leon rather than Pat. They clearly matched up with a husband Sandy had dumped in a hurry after finding out he was not what he claimed be—not Pat, to whom she had been married for five years. Even the way Marie quoted Sandy—talking about "my husband" and "his girl," rather than naming them as Pat and Jennifer— fit perfectly. Placed in this light, all the contradictions made sense. Laura never really believed Marie would simply fabricate this encounter with Sandy, no matter how much Marie might have hated Pat Dunn. It was much easier to believe that, over the past several months, Marie, in her desire to help and see justice done, might simply have confused some earlier conversation with Sandy about the failings of her second husband. Because Marie never knew about Leon, she could easily have thought Sandy was talking about Pat. Laura couldn't wait to get back to her motel room to dash off a memo to Pat's lawyer.

She quickly wrapped up the interview, stowing her tape recorder and her notebook, and gently begged off Marie's invitation to dinner, saying, "Oh, I didn't realize how late it was." As Marie walked her to the door, she again declared that she loved Laura like a daughter. "I can see the goodness in you, dear," she said.

Laura started to smile at this endearment, but then her expression froze in place as she saw the older woman's eyes go cold and her mouth become a thin, white line. "But that man you're working for is as guilty as sin, and I hope he fries," Marie spat. "And I'll do anything I can to see that he does."[19]

Laura felt her stomach lurch, for it seemed like another person had replaced the kindly old lady. Some might argue Laura had simply witnessed the reaction of a woman who, understandably, hated the killer of a friend and wanted justice done. But to Laura, something else had peeked out from behind Marie's saintly mask, just for a moment, and caused her to wonder anew about all of the inconsistencies and evolutions in the woman's story she had been ready to dismiss as honest errors or the haze of old age. And, even beyond that, there was something else, something less obvious and more fundamental, that ran through everything this woman had said about Pat and Sandy and her knowledge of them. Laura couldn't put her finger on it, but she knew it would be vital to the case. She shivered, though it was still very hot outside.

Then the moment passed. The warm smile was back in place on Marie Gates' face. The plate of sugar cookies was being waved under Laura's nose and the kindly grandmother to every kid on the block was asking, "Would you like to take some with you, darlin'?" Laura shook her head, forcing a smile, resisting the urge to bolt. This interview would haunt her for the rest of her time in Bakersfield, as would the fear that nothing she encountered in this case was what it appeared to be on the surface.

This was truer of Marie Gates than Laura ever realized. She had made an important discovery—but the full significance of what Marie told her that day would continue to elude her.

5

For THE POLICE, A MURDER CASE INEVITABLY BEGINS
with a body. Even the Dunn case started that
way—though in Sandy's case, it started with a
missing body. For private investigators, however, the
process begins very differently, starting where the police
work ends: with the "Murder Book."

The Murder Book is the compendium of all the police
reports assembled over the course of a homicide case. It
can run several inches thick, providing a detailed road
map of how the police assembled their case, charting the
path taken from suspicion to evidence to arrest. Murder
Books can be dry or compelling, depending on the
authors, and though they use jargon and official terms to
evoke an air of objectivity, they are anything but unbiased. They often begin with a suspect, and the separate
reports that make up its chapters reflect the slow accu-
mulation of evidence and witnesses in support of the
detective's theories about that suspect. Witnesses like
Marie Gates, who help the case, are given prominent
roles. Witnesses who tend to disprove the detective's suspicions are often minimized or disregarded as irrelevant,
mistaken or liars. They often are barely mentioned in the
police reports, if at all, and of course these unexplored
avenues, deemed fruitless by the authorities, are gold

mines for people like Laura Lawhon. In them lie the seeds
of a defense.

The murder book Laura picked up detailing the disappearance and death of Alexandra Paola Dunn read with the
usual air of inevitability, as if a veritable evidentiary jugger-
naut had led police to lay this terrible crime at Pat Dunn's
door. That is, they read that way once she had pieced
together the jumbled stack of reports and files retrieved
from the DA's office, more than a thousand pages handed
over out of order and in disarray. Laura felt certain they had
been shuffled purposely. The laws of legal discovery require
the government to turn over all pertinent information to
the defense before trial (there are no Perry Mason
moments in today's courtrooms, at least when the attorneys are behaving ethically), but those laws do not require
the information to be given in any particular order. Indeed,
some appeals courts have sanctioned the tactic of burying
evidence valuable for the defense inside tens of thousands
of pages of useless material, where it might never be found
or recognized. The mess was not so big in the Dunn case,
however, and Laura didn't really mind anyway: She enjoyed
the process of assembling the raw reports herself, putting
them into large, white plastic binders, in chronological
order and cross-referenced with a master witness list,
almost like a cast of characters at the beginning of a play-
bill. There was no point in getting upset about the jumble—the defense handed over its own disclosures in just as
messy a fashion. It was all part of the game.

Before interviewing any witnesses or even the client
himself, Laura had read and reread the Murder Book. She
had never seen anything quite like the Dunn investigation—a missing-persons case in which no one looked for

the missing person and everyone seemed to assume the husband was a murderer long before any evidence of a murder actually surfaced. Even reports that Sandy had been spotted roaming around various parts of Kern County, looking disheveled and disoriented, had been largely ignored—dutifully recorded in the police reports, but seldom pursued in any meaningful way by detectives on the case, who already had decided Sandy was dead long before her body had been identified. One of these sightings was made just three days after Sandy disappeared—a time when the coroner who later performed the autopsy on her shriveled corpse conceded she might still have been alive. But the sheriff never followed up on it.

Now Laura was racing the calendar, with a mere six weeks remaining to match and counter the accusations leveled in the Murder Book. Marie Gates offered some promising, if confusing, avenues to explore. But there were so many other leads that Laura wasn't sure where to begin. She had come to the case late and she feared that she might not be able to do it justice. Everything took time, too much of it: To thoroughly discredit a single, seemingly convincing witness like Marie Gates would require days of work and interviews with at least a half dozen people who could gainsay various bits and pieces of her story—one person to say Sandy did in fact walk at night, another to describe her marriage to Leon and to authenticate the divorce papers, yet another to say no, Sandy and Marie Gates weren't close friends at all. And assembling all that didn't begin to address the strategic problem of packaging the resulting jigsaw of witnesses and information into a palatable, easy-to-understand presentation for jurors who would want very much to believe Marie Gates. And Marie was only one witness.

The same complex recipe would have to be assembled to combat each and every major prosecution witness.

Even assuming she succeeded in amassing all that information, Laura did not feel confident. She kept hearing things around the courthouse, from a local private investigator she had run into and who had briefly worked on the Dunn case. "He may be innocent," the other PI, Susan Penninger, had said. "But in Kern County, that's not always enough."

Penninger possessed a wealth of experience with Bakersfield's justice system and some of its most controversial cases, including working with Stan Simrin to unravel the Nokes molestation-ring case. "You know, I still write letters to a guy doing life in prison, and I know he's innocent," she said. "I *know* it. And I can't do a damn thing about it."

It was another of those Bakersfield moments for Laura. Almost eighty degrees, and Penninger's words made her shiver.

And this only intensified another problem Laura had to deal with in this case. Contrary to the bulk of her cases, in which the evidence proving her clients' guilt left little room for doubt, she had come to the decision that Pat Dunn was an innocent man. Which wasn't to say she thought he was a terrific guy. In fact, he was a very odd man, quirky and difficult one moment, self-effacing and kind the next, then just as likely to turn selfish, arrogant and overconfident. He had screwed himself royally, him and his brother Mike, by tipping his first lawyer's hand to Detective Soliz. It had blown up in their faces, Laura knew—Jerry Coble was still the prosecution's star witness, and now he was ready for them. Meanwhile, Pat was beside himself, writing endless notes and commentaries and letters about the case, deluging both his lawyers and the investigators, making collect calls whenever his jailers would permit it, driving everyone nuts. He had to be counseled repeatedly not to tell his story to fellow inmates, any one of whom could gladly turn state's evidence and get in line behind Coble as a prosecution informant given the chance. "Sometimes, I just have to talk to someone, and I don't care anymore," Pat had lamented. Yet, despite it all, Laura had come to like Pat Dunn, to appreciate his sense of humor and his own brand of cranky toughness.

After studying the Murder Book, after concluding that the police selectively chose who and what to believe, and after talking with Marie Gates, Laura felt certain that whatever else he might be, Pat Dunn was no killer. This no doubt would make Pat happy, but not so his private investigator. She knew, just as every good defense lawyer knows, that believing in the innocence of a client makes things harder, ratcheting up the pressure and the stress, interfering with the cold and rational assessments necessary to win a case. By believing in Dunn's innocence, Laura *had* to find a way to win. Nothing else would be acceptable.

"Problem is," her husband, Wayne, had reminded her in his eternally blunt way just before she left for Bakersfield, "your side usually loses."

Laura returned to her motel room and began thumbing through the police reports, drawn once again back to the Murder Book and to the question of why the sheriff, and now the district attorney, so single-mindedly pursued Pat Dunn as the one and only suspect. Not even the complete absence of any physical evidence deterred those suspi-

cions. When search after search of the Dunn home and
cars came up empty, it slowed the authorities down, of
course—they couldn't arrest him without any evidence.
But they never turned their suspicions elsewhere. It puzzled Laura, convinced her something more was at work in
this case. Here was a woman reported missing, with a documented history of walking at three and four in the
morning through a rough area of town, sometimes wearing expensive jewelry, whose habits were utterly predictable and who easily could have been stalked and kidnapped by anyone hanging around the shopping center at
night. Here was a woman who had not just been stabbed,
but carved up, with tissue excised from her rectum—a
gruesome touch the police had not even attempted to
explain. Here was a woman whose own court testimony
had put her first husband's embezzling bookkeeper
behind bars—a bookkeeper who reasonably could be
expected to harbor bitterness toward Sandy, and who was
now out of prison. And here was a woman who had just
told her financial planner she not only wanted her husband to have more control over their money, but she also
wanted to cut off from any inheritance her own sister and
all of Pat Dunn's children. Furthermore, Laura had
learned that several workmen making repairs on offices at
Sandy's College Center mall late at night and early in the
morning were drug abusers with criminal records—and
friends of Danny Dunn, Pat's troubled middle child.
Sandy would have walked right by them on the night she
disappeared if she stuck to her normal route.

In Laura's view, it should not have required much
imagination for the sheriff's department to figure out an
alternative and just as likely solution for their case: Take
one middle-aged woman, walking alone at night in a

high-crime area. Add her unwavering habits over a period of months. Then factor in the possibility she was slipping mentally. She might as well have had a target
mounted on her back, as far as Laura was concerned: She
was ripe for robbery, abduction or worse at the hands of
the unsavory characters working in the mall, or someone
else with an old grudge, or any passing stranger with a
hunger for money or violence who spied an easy victim.

No one could say any of these alternative theories was
accurate, but to Laura that was the point. Each of these
potential avenues of suspicion—any one of which could
have pointed to possible motives and killers having nothing to do with Pat Dunn—had been ignored by sheriff's
detectives from the start. Such alternatives had not
received even cursory attention. They might all be blind
alleys, certainly, but no one had bothered to check them
out. From the moment the case began, thanks to Kate
Rosenlieb's passionate complaints about Pat and the
sheriff's own initial theories on the case, the focus had
been in one direction only.

They wanted Pat Dunn. Period.

Detective Soliz made no bones about it. There had
never been any other suspects, he would later explain. He
had never felt a need to find any. As far as he and his
department were concerned, everything pointed to husband murdering wife. It had been obvious within a matter of days. Had Soliz learned anything that pointed his
investigation of Sandy's death toward another theory, he
would have pursued it happily. But that, the detective
would say, never happened.[20]

Laura Lawhon had another view. She knew some,
though certainly not all, police investigators formulate
their theory of a case early on, then pursue only the leads

that support that theory. Once the path is chosen, the case takes on a momentum all its own. There have been instances where evidence, and even confessions, have been ignored because they implicated the "wrong" suspect.[21] Erroneous convictions in Kern County as well as elsewhere have resulted from just such a predetermined investigative path. Laura felt certain that the Dunn case fit this model perfectly.

A prime example of this tunnel vision, Laura decided, lay in the treatment of another key witness, a young woman named Ann Kidder. Kidder worked for a Bakersfield accountant, Rick Williams, who handled a number of Sandy's accounts and businesses. Kidder, an experienced secretary, took pride in her job, in her ability to run an office and, especially, in her ability to remember the names of clients, both in person and on the phone. "I'm a people person," she said. "And I feel like I have a particular gift for recognizing faces and voices."

Kidder never met Sandy in person, just spoke to her on the phone a number of times, primarily in June 1992, scheduling appointments or putting her through to Rick Williams so she could speak directly with her accountant. On most occasions, Kidder recalled, Sandy had a confident, professional-sounding voice, distinctive and slightly accented from her New York origins. As Kidder explained to the authorities early on in the case, Sandy had called on June 29 to cancel an appointment that same day—the day before she disappeared. The appointment was rescheduled for July 1, the day after she vanished. Sandy even gave directions to her house, so Williams could go there for the appointment, rather than conduct it in his office.

On July 1, Sandy called again, around half past nine in

the morning, Kidder recalled. She wanted to reschedule the appointment once more, this time for July 6. Ann Kidder immediately recognized the voice as Sandy's, but its normal tone of businesslike confidence was gone. Sandy seemed stressed out, upset, even babbling, as Kidder remembered it. "The Indians are coming down out of the mountains and my husband needs to talk with them," Sandy gibbered. Then she complained, "My husband doesn't like to wear clothes."

As Kidder recalled, Sandy rambled on for a time about these two subjects, the Indians and her husband's dislike of clothing, but Kidder eventually managed to get the appointment rescheduled and to bid Sandy farewell. The secretary then told her boss about the call, and she logged the change in each of their appointment calendars.

Laura knew Detectives Kline and Soliz had interviewed Kidder several times. They had her show them the appointment books, including the pages where she had erased and replaced the meeting times. Ann Kidder was absolutely certain she had spoken to Sandy that day, and both she and her boss were sure of the date—Sandy had called on the morning of July 1, the day of the appointment.

But that call would have been made twelve hours *after* Pat had woken up and found his wife missing. In the early stages of the sheriff's investigation, this conflict in times and dates was deemed one of the most glaring discrepancies in Pat's story, creating a "cloud of suspicion which indicated foul play," as Detective Soliz wrote in his first report on the case. The detectives sensed immediately that Ann Kidder would be an important witness against Pat Dunn, even though it was Pat who first led police to her doorstep. The detectives never would have talked to Kidder but for Pat's suggestion. It seems Rick Williams had arrived as scheduled for his July 6 meeting with Sandy, which Pat seemed to know nothing about. When Williams found out Sandy was missing, he told Pat what Kidder had said about the odd, babbling call on July 1. Pat immediately called Detective Kline to pass on the new information. "I just don't know what to think anymore," Pat said at the time. But Kline and Soliz knew what to think: that they had just unearthed some good dirt on Pat Dunn.

Yet a month later, Laura saw, everything changed. That's when Jerry Coble came forward and described seeing a body hauled out of the Dunn home at one in the morning on July 1, eight hours *before* Ann Kidder's conversation with Sandy. Suddenly, a witness the detectives initially found so credible when she seemed to incriminate Pat couldn't be believed anymore. After Coble's entrance in the case, detectives returned to interview Kidder again, but this time to ask her questions never posed during previous interviews: How she could be so sure it was Sandy she talked to? Couldn't she be mistaken? Maybe she was distracted when the call came in, confused about who it was from? Could the caller have been an impersonator?

To Kidder, it seemed clear that the sheriff's department no longer believed her.[22] Laura knew the secretary was right: For now, Kidder provided an alibi for Pat Dunn rather than a nail in the case against him. She swore that she spoke to a murder victim long after the murder supposedly occurred, which would mean Coble lied and Pat was innocent. Nothing had changed to cause detectives to doubt her, other than the sudden revelations from Coble. Which meant the sheriff's department was confronted with two choices: Believe Ann Kidder, who had no criminal record, no ax to grind, no reason to lie, and who had office calendars and her boss to back up her recollections; or believe Jerry Coble, a career criminal facing six years behind bars, who had begged to cut a deal so he could incriminate someone else, and who offered nothing but his good word to support his story—unable to provide even a last name or phone number for his drug connection "Ray," whom he had supposedly met just before glimpsing Pat cart off Sandy's corpse.

In short, it came down to believing in Ann Kidder and Pat Dunn's innocence or Jerry Coble and Pat Dunn's guilt. The sheriff's department chose Jerry Coble.

Laura found it hard to understand how such a choice could be made, even in the most aggressive of sheriff's departments and DA's offices. At the courthouse one day, she ran into her fellow private investigator Susan Penninger and told her about Coble, Kidder and the sheriff department's single-minded pursuit of Pat as their suspect. "Is it just Pat Dunn?" she wondered. "Or is there something else going on here?"

Laura had not really expected an answer to her musings, but Penninger gave one, returning to a subject she had hinted at in previous conversations. "It's definitely not just Dunn," she said. "I've had two innocent men in prison right now. One I can't help. The other, I'm still working on. This is Bakersfield, after all."

Laura looked at the other investigator, raising her eyebrows in question at the bitterness in Penninger's voice. She was surprised to hear a Bakersfield native voice such thoughts. Penninger, a short, slim woman with a round face that looked youthful from a distance but careworn up close, went on to tell Laura that she had lived all but a few years of her life in Kern County. She had worked for years as a probation officer—she was law enforcement then—before moving to the public defender's office and, after that, private investigating. Penninger had seen the Witch Hunt play itself out, at first believing the monstrous charges, then gradually concluding that innocent families had been sacrificed to appease public hysteria and an investigation run wild. She knew Bakersfield's justice system from all sides, and she described it as one that had devolved into isolated camps, with each faction regarding the other as the enemy in a way that seemed unique in its extremity. Unlike the San Francisco Bay area and other places she had worked, the boundary between personal and professional had evaporated in Bakersfield. Since she had become a defense investigator, the social workers and cops she had known and worked with as a probation officer had not only become her professional adversaries, they stopped talking to her entirely. Friends of ten years, people she had gone on cruises with, vacationed with, looked right through her without a word, passing her in the courthouse hallway as if she wasn't there. She had lost all credibility with them—simply because she dared to question the authorities of Kern County, to raise the possibility that their every utterance in a police report or courtroom might not be 100 percent accurate.

"Let me tell you about my heartbreak case." Penninger looked at Laura. Every private investigator had such a case if they've been at it long enough—the man or woman they believed to be innocent, but still couldn't save. Penninger's was named Carl Hogan. She had worked his case five years earlier, but it still haunted her. Hogan, a soft-spoken man, seemingly gentle and shy, had ended up with a life sentence for a fatal sledgehammer attack on a seven-year-old boy and his mother, a savage, senseless crime. Hogan had been the obvious suspect from the start, found standing over the bodies, the bloody hammer in his hand. He swore he had simply stumbled on the victims, the wife and son of a friend he had gone to visit, and had slipped into shock at the sight. But the police did not believe this. They felt sure Hogan was the killer.

Penninger believed otherwise, certain that the authorities, in their zeal to nail Hogan, had overlooked evidence contradicting their theory, while manufacturing major pieces of evidence against him. Even the California Supreme Court seemed to agree: Hogan's initial conviction and death sentence had been reversed after it was revealed that sheriff's investigators, in marathon interrogations, had convinced their dazed and frightened suspect that he was mentally ill, that witnesses had seen him commit the murders (a lie designed to encourage his belief that he was losing his mind), and that they would get him psychiatric help if only he would confess. It was the sort of bare-knuckled interrogation detectives had tried on Pat Dunn, but with Hogan, it worked. He finally broke down and confessed, saying if witnesses saw him do it, then he really must have done it. This confession, of course, was not used to get him "help"; it was used by prosecutors to secure his death sentence. But the state supreme court found his tearful confession both coerced and unbelievable, and ordered a new trial even as Ed Jagels railed about liberal judges frustrating justice.[23]

For his retrial, Penninger helped build a defense that accounted for Hogan's every movement on the day of the murders, showing, she believed, that he could not possibly have had the time to kill anyone. Hogan could have been in the house only a few seconds before his friend walked in and found him standing over the bodies, she told Laura. But that was not enough: She had not been able to persuade judge and jury of Hogan's innocence. It was one of Susan Penninger's greatest sorrows.

"So he's still in prison?" Laura asked, fascinated yet chilled by the story. She couldn't know if Hogan was guilty or innocent, but she did know jailhouse snitches were notorious for their embellishments.

Penninger shook her head. She had stayed in touch with Hogan and his family over the years, and had just gotten a nationally renowned minister and private investigator, James McCloskey, interested in the case. McCloskey's Centurion Ministries had become famous for proving convicted murderers innocent and winning their releases. But before the minister could get started, Carl Hogan died in prison of heart disease.

"And now I've got another one, just as bad, just as innocent," Penninger said, eyes closed. "Except this one's not over yet—the appeals are just starting. But if you really want a preview of Pat Dunn's case, take a look at this one. Take a look at Offord Rollins."

6

LAURA DID TAKE A LOOK AT THE CASE OF *The People of Kern County vs. Offord Rollins*, and what she saw left her stricken. It convinced her that Pat Dunn's case was not at all unique in Bakersfield, for it seemed Rollins had been pursued with the same single-minded focus that made Pat a homicide suspect from day one, that same settling on a theory of the case from the outset, with facts forced to fit theory rather than the reverse. To Laura's thinking, if Offord Rollins, a good student, high school president and Olympic-caliber athlete, could be convicted on the paltry and contradictory evidence assembled against him, then Pat Dunn's chances might not be nearly as good as she and his lawyers had hoped.

The Rollins case had been another victory for the same Kern County Sheriff's Department homicide unit that secured Pat's arrest. It began on a smoky August evening eleven months before Alexandra Dunn vanished, when a teenager named Sandy Ornelas came charging up a scrubby embankment near the interstate, arms wind-milling crazily, fear plowing such deep furrows into his sixteen-year-old face that his friends could see with perfect clarity, even through their haze of six-packs and wine coolers, just what he would look like at age forty.

Ornelas had been searching for fallen branches to heap

on a bonfire. He and ten other high school students had spent the evening busily getting stoned near a weedy drainage ditch outside Bakersfield, a godforsaken chunk of grit and rock surrounded by farms midway between the small Kern County towns of Shafter and Wasco. The spot had no name, but it had long been a popular place for teenage partying, handed down over generations of high school students. It was isolated yet convenient, tucked behind a convergence of highways and bathed in the dim amber afterglow of freeway light standards, littered with bottles, cans and condoms, the mummified remains of a thousand similar beer busts and trysts. The white noise of high-speed traffic on Interstate 5 provided a constant background, a dull hiss almost like rushing water. There was a clear area suitable for parking and drinking, then a winding path down an embankment to a dark drainage slough, where there was plenty of old growth and loose wood for fueling fires. It was there that Sandy Ornelas made his find.

He and another boy had walked the path gingerly, lighting their way with a makeshift torch fashioned from a beer carton. As the boys walked, they kept noticing dark spots of what looked like motor oil dotting the path. Ornelas' buddy tried several times to ignite these spots with the tip of his torch, but they wouldn't catch fire.

"You hold the light and I'll go down and grab some wood," Ornelas said when they reached the scrubby area at the bottom. He picked his way down through the darkness, grabbing a branch here, a stick there, moving fast, trying to get out of the claustrophobic space as quickly as possible. Then, as he stooped to pick up one last nicely sized piece of wood, the flickering orange light of the torch revealed that the gnarled-looking branch he was about to grasp had fingers on it. And the fingers were attached to an outstretched arm and, beyond that, a body, motionless and in shadow, reclining with its other arm flung across its forehead, as if in repose. The blood-stained figure didn't move.

Ornelas started yelling a heartbeat later, dashing toward his friend with the guttering torch, then running right over the boy, bowling him over as he careened up the path to the parking area, to the comfort of a crowd, to the older boys who hooted at his terror for a moment, then saw his face and realized something must be very wrong. It was left to them to trudge through the darkness step-ping over the spots of oil that were really blood, so they could see for themselves what had frightened their friend.

They found a teenage girl, shot through the back and the head, an inexplicable act of violence, a senseless crime, a—there's really no other word for it—*big-city* crime. For all the wrong reasons, this community had finally earned the slogan it plastered on its street signs and letterheads and welcome-to-town placards. In a nation where violent crime had become the great com-mon ground in small towns and large, Bakersfield was, at last, the "All-America City" it had so long claimed to be.

On the surface, the execution-style murder of Maria Madera Rodriguez couldn't have been more different from Sandy Dunn's disappearance and fatal stabbing, beyond the fact that both bodies were found in the desert. Maria was a petite and pretty Hispanic high school girl with an active, sometimes-risky sex life well hidden from her mother. She had been found within hours of her mur-der. There was a known crime scene, physical evidence, blood, witnesses, footprints. Everything missing in the

Dunn case could be found in the investigation of Maria's death. Yet Laura saw many parallels—too many, for her comfort—as Susan Penninger told her about the case.

By the time homicide investigators had cordoned off the area, much of the evidence—footprints, tire tracks, blood, plants and fibers—had been trampled over and thoroughly compromised by the boys, by paramedics, by coroner's investigators and patrol deputies who wanted to see and examine the body. Before racing off to get help at a nearby fire station, all the kids had traipsed down to gawk at the body, including one boy whose wheelchair slid and skittered along the path, obliterating untold amounts of evidence in the dirt while leaving behind narrow tracks of its own.

Not all the evidence had been trampled, however. One of the deputies trained his flashlight on the parking area and found that the kids' cars, and some of the official vehicles as well, were parked next to and on top of old tire tracks, footprints and, most important, puddles of blood that the partyers hadn't even noticed when they pulled up in the darkness. The parked cars had preserved the evidence like lids on a jar, preventing anyone from walking over these areas in the rush to see the body. Some of the sheriff's investigators and other witnesses would initially report that the blood under the cars appeared fresh and still damp when first discovered,[24] which meant, in that hot desert climate, that the murder almost certainly had to have occurred after sundown. Otherwise, the heat of day would have left the blood dried and caked long before the body had been discovered. A print from a running shoe with a distinctive tread was found in one large, still-damp puddle of mud and blood—evidence investigators hoped to match up with a killer's shoe.

Later, though, despite what was initially observed and reported, the authorities would claim all of the blood puddles were hard and dry when first found—they only *looked* wet because they had appeared shiny in the beams of deputies' flashlights. This change was crucial, because it meant the murder could have occurred earlier in the day, a convenient revision, since the prime suspect had an airtight alibi for the late afternoon and evening. It was here, Laura decided, that the Rollins case began to resemble Pat's, and Carl Hogan's, for that matter. Each exhibited the same tendency of Kern County authorities to interpret and reinterpret evidence until it fit a desired theory. To the prosecution's way of thinking, declaring the blood dry instead of wet was just correcting a misstatement, nothing more. But Laura had to wonder: If wet blood had been consistent with the prosecution theories in the case, would the blood still be wet in the police reports? If the secretary Ann Kidder had not contradicted Jerry Coble's story, would she still be an officially credible person and a witness against Pat Dunn?

Susan Penninger had found another interesting fact that kept cropping up in the police reports in the Rollins case: The girl's body, and everyone who went near it, came away covered with sticky brambles from a dry desert weed, the tamarisk pentandra, whose distinctive clinging burrs under a microscope resemble nothing more than a dark-winged angel with halo. The lowly tamarisk weed would become crucial in the case much later, because the killer should have been covered with the burrs. This would mark another point where evidence and theory in the case did not match up.

No identification was found on the girl, and the sheriff's department cleared the crime scene with the body classified as a Jane Doe—identity unknown. Tracks and shell casings from a variety of firearms found on the ground suggested she had fought with one or two assailants, then had been felled by a shot, dragged, and shot again. Rape appeared unlikely, as her black stretch pants were still on. But her blood-soaked white blouse and bra had been pulled up as her body was dragged, and her bared chest was deeply abraded by the rough terrain. When the coroner's technicians turned her body over, investigators spotted a smear of lipstick on her back, apparently from a dropped or discarded lipstick container found on the trail a few feet away. It remained unclear whether the body had simply been dragged over the lipstick inadvertently, leaving an unintended smear, or if the marks represented some kind of a message from the killer. The lead detective on the case seemed to choose the latter, writing in his initial report that the markings appeared to be evidence of a ritual killing. This belief would soon be discarded, but not because ritual murder had been disproved by actual evidence. Rather, it did not fit the emerging theory of the case.

Within forty-eight hours of the murder, two breaks turned the case firmly in one direction. First, a Bakersfield businessman named Dale Knox read in the newspaper about the unidentified body found in the desert and called the sheriff's department. Knox said he had been driving near that very spot early on the afternoon before the body was found and had seen an older-model maroon Buick or Oldsmobile speeding from the area, kicking up dust and driving in an erratic manner, even cutting him off after tailgating him. "It was some dumb Mexican," Knox told Deputy Paul Hussey, an old friend.[25] This information was passed on to Detective

Randy Raymond, the homicide investigator in charge of the case.

A few hours later, Detective Raymond received a missing-persons report that had been filed with the police in Shafter, a small town a few miles from Bakersfield. A seventeen-year-old girl had disappeared from her home on Friday. She was supposed to have gone to a park to meet her boyfriend that morning, but she never returned home. The family had called all her friends and looked all over town, waiting overnight in hopes of hearing from her, then filed a missing-persons report Saturday morning. Raymond took one look at the accompanying photograph of a smiling Maria Madera Rodriguez and knew he had identified his Jane Doe.

Still, he had to make absolutely sure—and he had to know more. So he drove to Maria's home and spoke to her distraught mother, Miriam, who knew nothing of the body in the desert. She greeted Raymond warily at her door and explained that she spoke little English. Raymond hadn't thought to bring an interpreter, but a wiry man with a beard and an ample collection of tattoos on his arm approached and introduced himself. Don't worry, Victor Perez offered, he could translate. Miriam gestured to him and said to Raymond, "My son-in-law," and the detective nodded.

Raymond wanted the whole story before breaking the bad news, so he did not mention the dead girl in the desert at first. He only explained that he needed more information about Maria's disappearance, and they talked for nearly half an hour, Victor acting as principal translator. Once he got what he needed, the detective informed Miriam, as gently as possible, that Maria was dead. The news of her child's murder caused Miriam

Rodriguez to collapse. The last thing Raymond did before leaving was summon an ambulance for her.

But he had his information. And he had a prime suspect. The story he extracted from Miriam via Victor Perez boiled down to this: Maria and her teenage boyfriend, Offord Rollins IV, had been going steady for the past six months. They had been arguing recently because Maria was seeing someone else. On Friday morning, the day she disappeared and died, Offord had called the house and spoke to one of Maria's sisters, then to Maria, and arranged to meet her in a park across the street at 11 A.M. Finally, Victor translated this startling piece of information: Maria's Aunt Lucy had seen Maria and Offord together Friday night in a maroon car—just like the one Dale Knox had seen speeding from the murder scene. That would mean Offord almost certainly had been the last person to see Maria alive.

When Raymond learned that Offord had been driving his father's Oldsmobile that weekend—and that it was an older car, maroon in color—the detective knew he had just solved a murder. Within hours, he had a seventeen-year-old high school track star and class president named Offord Rollins behind bars, accused of first-degree murder and facing life in prison. Only the fact that he was underage saved him from a potential death sentence.[26]

So far as Laura was concerned, as soon as the sheriff's department seized on Offord Rollins as the one and only suspect in the murder of Maria Rodriguez, the investigation's resemblance to Pat's became absolutely eerie. As with Pat, official pronouncements and press reports suggested a mountain of proof against the young athlete, but, in truth, there was little hard evidence linking him to the crime. There had been multiple searches of his home, with nothing to show for them, just like Pat's case. No murder weapon had been recovered. There was no evidence Offord ever possessed a gun at all. (After initially reporting that Maria had been shot by two different weapons—a finding that would have contradicted the official theory of Offord Rollins as lone gunman—the authorities revised their opinion and asserted that only one twenty-two-caliber rifle had been used.) Nothing in Offord's house or room matched the soil or plant material around Maria's body, and no one who ran into Offord that day saw any signs of tamarisk burrs clinging to his clothing or car. None of Offord's many athletic shoes—and as a football player and competitive long jumper, he had a closetful—matched any of the prints at the murder scene, including the one in the puddle of blood. The authorities could not even find anyone who actually saw their prime suspect and the victim together on the day of the murder, notwithstanding what Victor Perez had claimed.

There were, however, three pieces of evidence that supported the prosecution's case: Authorities found Maria's palm print on the outside (but not inside) of the maroon Oldsmobile that Offord drove that weekend, as if she had leaned against the car while waiting or talking. There were seventeen nylon fibers on Maria's clothes that seemed to match fibers from the Oldsmobile's seats—though the most that could be said of these is that they came from a *similar* car seat, as opposed to that specific car. And, finally, there was a single, tiny bit of tamarisk plant found clinging to the backseat of the Oldsmobile.

These were disturbing bits of evidence, Susan Penninger told Laura, but far from conclusive. Clearly,

Maria had been around and possibly inside the car. But Offord said he met Maria at a store and she leaned against his car the day *before* she disappeared, which could provide an innocuous explanation for the prints and the fibers. Unfortunately, he didn't tell the police this right away, and even led them to believe he hadn't seen Maria at all, which not only increased official suspicions, but added a troubling building block to the case against him—an apparent lie. Offord's account also required believing Maria had worn the same clothes two days in a row, something her family insisted had not happened.[27]

As for the bit of plant found in the car, tamarisk grew in many areas outside Bakersfield, and could have come from any one of numerous locations other than the murder scene. Furthermore, the significance of the burr was in question because of problems at the Kern County crime lab itself, a former dog kennel renowned for its contamination problems, which included ventilators that spewed soot into the examining rooms and a shortage of sterile, clean work areas.[28] Controls in the lab were so loose that the technician who examined Maria's tamarisk-covered body later conceded she may well have worn the same lab coat, uncleaned, the next day to examine Offord's car, raising the possibility that she inadvertently deposited that quarter-inch bit of weed on the backseat where it was found. Another technician, who checked the car for fingerprints inside and out, had probed the interior first and saw no plant material on the seat. Besides, if Offord had really been the killer, the car—which had a dusty, cluttered interior that clearly had not been cleaned or vacuumed before police seized it—should have contained many more pieces of the clingy plant, not to mention blood and soil from the murder scene. But it did not, not even the microscopic amounts that resist cleaning and can persist for weeks. Nor were any strands of Maria's long hair found anywhere inside the car.

Laura knew strange things sometimes happened in criminal cases, subtle changes in testimony and evidence that occurred, usually early on and almost always to the detriment of whoever the police suspected. Neither Pat Dunn nor Offord Rollins were unique in this regard. Witnesses' memories often grew more specific with time, although common sense suggests the opposite should occur. Police officers would come to court to testify and recall crucial observations they had made months earlier, though they had somehow forgotten to note those telling details in their reports at the time—reports that were supposed to be all-inclusive. Detectives would tape-record lengthy interviews with suspects, then report key, incriminating statements were made when the recorder was switched off—through sheer happenstance, of course. These sorts of things happened everywhere, but Susan Penninger told Laura they seemed to come up in every case she worked in Kern County, leading her to name the phenomenon "The Bakersfield Effect."

The testimony of Dale Knox, the man who had seen a maroon car like Offord's speeding from the vicinity of the murder scene, provided a perfect example, she told Laura. Knox had originally given his report on the day after Maria's murder, speaking at length about the maroon car and the "dumb Mexican" he had seen driving it with his friend Deputy Hussey, who also had been one of the first patrol deputies called to the crime scene. Hussey had taken notes on the conversation, but after relaying the information to Detective Raymond,

Hussey was told not to bother writing a report. Instead, he destroyed his notes, contrary to common police practice.[29]

When Raymond conducted his own interview of Knox the next day, he reported Knox had seen a black or Hispanic male driving the maroon car.[30] This change was crucial to the case, because Offord Rollins was black. His very dark complexion and facial features made mistaking his ethnicity an unlikely proposition. Here was a case in which a witness's uncertainty was more useful than a definite (and incorrect) opinion. And so, like magic, Penninger saw, the report of a Mexican driving a maroon car changed—right after Offord was identified as the prime suspect. Many months later, when the case came to trial and Knox took the witness stand, he couldn't say it had been Offord in the car, but he wouldn't rule him out, either.

This ambiguity could have been fatal to the prosecution, except that Detective Raymond remembered Knox describing the car as having some damage on its left side. The car Offord had driven that day also had damage on its left fender. Again, this was crucial, since it seemed to buttress the notion that it was Offord whom Knox saw fleeing the scene, not someone else in a similar vehicle. Yet Detective Raymond had not put this key piece of information in his police report at the time, nor did he ever mention it while testifying at pretrial hearings when asked to summarize what Knox had told him. It only came to light at Rollins' trial. Prosecutors saw nothing nefarious here, just the innocent omission of one small detail in an enormous and complex case. To Penninger, it was another example of the Bakersfield Effect.

This paled, however, next to the detective's interview

of Maria's mother, Miriam, which had been accomplished with the translating help of her "son-in-law," Victor Perez. First, it turned out Victor was not Miriam's son-in-law, but her eldest daughter, Marisol's, former live-in boyfriend. He had been arrested and jailed repeatedly for beating Marisol, as well as for a variety of other crimes. Marisol had eventually dumped Victor and moved in with one of the Shafter policemen who had investigated him for domestic abuse. Victor, meanwhile, stayed on living with Miriam, a curious arrangement made all the stranger by the fact that Maria had told several friends and one teacher that she despised and feared the man, and that she kept a heavy stick under her bed to fend off his unwanted advances. That the Kern County Sheriff's homicide detectives would press such a man into service as a translator of key information was unfortunate enough, but still more surprising was the fact that they seemingly never considered him a potential suspect in Maria's murder, even after learning of his background and history of violence. Once they had focused on Offord as their suspect, investigators appeared reluctant to do anything that might undermine their case—such as suggest there might be an alternative suspect.

Moreover, beyond questions about Victor's character, was the simple fact that virtually all of the information Detective Raymond gleaned that first crucial day from Victor's supposed translation was wrong. Raymond had come away from that interview with an image of Offord as a jealous suitor angry at Maria's relationship with another boy. In fact, Offord and Maria were not "going steady," as Victor claimed, nor were they quarreling over her other boyfriends. The truth was, they had not seen each other for several months. And it was Offord, not

Maria, who had another girlfriend and wanted to distance himself from the relationship. If anyone was obsessed, it had been Maria, who pursued Offord whenever possible, doodled his name and "I love you Offord" all over her schoolbooks and calendars, and who had page after page written out with variations of her own name were she to marry Offord, along with a list of prospective names for their children. She had other boyfriends and lovers, but Offord was her first choice. Victor revealed none of this to the police.

Victor had also told police that Offord called that last morning and arranged to meet Maria in a park across the street. The only completely accurate part of this statement was that Maria did receive a phone call in the morning from someone, and she did, in fact, go to the park, saying she was meeting Offord. But this was something she often claimed, sometimes falsely, to get permission to go out, because her mother trusted Offord more than any of her other friends.[31] No one actually heard Offord on the phone that day or saw Maria with him that morning at the park. (One member of the Rodriguez household said the caller identified himself as "Dre," short for Andre, a friend of Offord's.) A friend of Maria's who was walking by at the time saw her sitting on a bench in the park—talking to a woman. Later, as the friend returned from the store, he saw that Maria was sitting by herself. She got up and announced that she was going to walk to someone's house, turning down an offer of a ride from the friend, who then watched Maria walk off alone.[32] She had not met Offord in the park, as Victor had said: Whoever Maria saw between ten that morning and the time of her death was unknown.

But the biggest whopper by far was the statement by

Victor that Maria's Aunt Lucy had seen the girl with
Offord in a maroon car on the night of her disappearance. When contacted, Aunt Lucy said she saw no such
thing, and she didn't know what Victor was talking
about. Not that this mattered—a host of witnesses had
accounted for Offord's whereabouts that day, and had
done so for all but a two-and-a-half-hour period between
noon and 2:30 that afternoon (which is why it was so
important to the prosecution case that the fresh, wet
blood some people observed at the scene suddenly
became hard, dry blood in police reports—the murder,
originally thought to have occurred at night, must have
happened in the drying heat of day if Offord had done
it). Offord could prove he was more than one hundred
miles away in Los Angeles when Victor said he was riding
around with Maria.

The parallels to the Dunn case were obvious to
Laura—the misinformation Kate Rosenlieb provided at
the outset that made Pat Dunn a prime suspect bore a
striking resemblance to Victor Perez's role in the Rollins
case. Like Rosenlieb, Victor was the first witness to raise
suspicions about Offord Rollins by suggesting he had
both motive and opportunity to kill. And, as with
Rosenlieb, virtually everything of significance Victor told
the police that first crucial day was wrong. Maria's mother eventually denied saying any of what Victor attributed
to her. Whether it was bad translation, unintended error,
or outright lying by Victor, no one could say. All Laura
knew for sure was that bad information from Victor
Perez, who might otherwise have been considered a
potential suspect, had made it a certainty that the sheriff's department would go after Offord Rollins. And, as
with Pat Dunn, they never looked back.

• • •

That the investigative shortcomings of the Offord Rollins case might mirror those in Pat Dunn's did not concern Laura so much. Indeed, they served only to confirm that she was on the right track in her own investigation. It was the Rollins *trial* that terrified her, for it seemed there was nothing the young man's defenders could do in the face of the relentless prosecutor intent on putting him away, or the jury and judge seemingly willing, even eager, to help achieve that goal.

No doubt the prosecutor felt she had to be ruthless, Laura thought, for the problems facing her in the Rollins case appeared considerable. The evidence against Rollins was far from overwhelming, which would not be such a problem if the defendant were some disreputable career criminal, but which did pose difficulties with Offord, with his sterling reputation as a student, athlete and churchgoer in his small Kern County town of Wasco. The eldest son of a respiratory therapist and a utility-company executive, Rollins was a star high school football player and track champion in the triple jump, an event in which he ranked third in the nation and had a realistic shot at making the United States Olympic team. He was more than just well liked around town—the school superintendent let him date his daughter, and he had a long line of school administrators, teachers, coaches and ministers lined up to attest to his good character. He was the kind of kid who was profiled in heartwarming stories in the Wasco weekly newspaper, a class president who had overcome dyslexia to earn passable-to-good grades, who had tempered his legs into iron rods capable of immense jumps, who had never been in trouble with the law in his life.

He was not the perfect teenager, by any means—he somewhat cynically used Maria Rodriguez for sex while going steady with another girl he liked much better but didn't sleep with. And he wrote some truly bad, amateurish rap lyrics with his friend Andre Harrison, creating a notebook full of crude, sexist and violent images that emulated the misogynous music popular with so many of his friends, and which he hoped might earn him a little money someday. But none of this made him all that different from other teenagers at Wasco High School, where sex often became a contest and where rap music blared from boom boxes in the school yard.

In a case with ambiguous physical evidence, no witnesses and no apparent motive, the accolades Offord received, coupled with his reputation, might have tilted matters in his favor at trial. But the assistant DA on the case, a successful and aggressive career prosecutor named Lisa Green, had something extra to work with when the case came to trial: she had a defendant who was black and a victim who was not—and she had an all-white Kern County jury in the box, having systematically excluded the already disproportionately small number of blacks summoned that day for jury service.[33]

As Rollins' defenders saw it, long before pundits commenting on the O.J. Simpson murder trial popularized the term, Green expertly played the "race card," thereby tipping the scales in her favor. Through the course of a month-long trial held just two months before Sandy Dunn vanished, Green portrayed Rollins as a sexual savage who got his kicks from exhibitionism, sodomy, extreme promiscuity and copulating on his own mother's bed—though there was no evidence to support any of this beyond the prosecutor's own loaded questions to

Rollins and other witnesses in the case.[34] Isn't it true, Green asked a friend of Rollins, that he let you watch him have sex with the victim? That he did it where his mother slept? She asked such questions knowing the answers would be no—as they had been at pretrial hearings—yet equally aware that the mere asking would leave an indelible impression on the jury.[35] The audacity of the tactic spoke volumes to Laura about what the defense might be up against in Pat's trial.

Indeed, the DA's office had attacked Offord's character and sexual proclivities from the start, long before the trial in this highly publicized case. It started even as Offord, still seventeen, began his case in juvenile court. To buttress the case for moving him into adult court, the assistant DA on the case—a prosecutor who preceded Green—argued that Rollins' crime was particularly sophisticated and heinous because he raped and sodomized Maria before murdering her. Rape was the motive for murder, it was argued, probably because Offord got angry when Maria refused his request to have anal sex. The judge happily moved the teenager into adult court. Problem was, the DA's office at that time had in hand an autopsy report showing Maria had *not* been raped. Furthermore, the autopsy revealed she had regularly engaged in anal sex for months, if not years, but that she had not done so for at least twenty-four hours prior to her murder. The DA's office revealed this information and dismissed the rape and sodomy charges only after winning Offord's transfer to adult court—and after the incendiary allegations had been thoroughly reported in the news media.[36]

Once Rollins' trial started, the prosecution came up with a new theory. It was suggested that Maria, obsessed with rekindling a failed relationship, bothered Offord too much. So he decided to eliminate her. There was absolutely no evidence to support this—indeed, Maria's own journals and writings indicated that, while she still loved Offord, she also pursued sexual relationships with a number of other men in the weeks and months before she died. There was not a shred of evidence or testimony that Offord had ever exhibited or expressed any anger toward Maria.

Although the prosecution's theory of motive in the case had totally changed, Deputy DA Green kept asking witnesses at trial if Rollins liked having anal sex, hammering on a point no longer relevant to the case. Many of the jurors undoubtedly considered sodomy both distasteful and immoral, and repeated allusions to it allowed Green to score points as Offord squirmed in embarrassment. Even the judge got in on the act, asking a lascivious question of his own about what sorts of acts of "penetration" Offord and his new girlfriend enjoyed together.[37]

Green also used to similar effect some of the crude rap lyrics Rollins had written. Even though the judge had previously ruled most of them inadmissible, the jury was exposed to a broad selection of his songs. Green argued that one particular verse ("She wouldn't let me go, so I slapped the ho") out of more than a hundred pages of drivel, proved that Offord wanted to get rid of a clinging Maria. Nowhere in any of the raps is there any mention of Maria specifically, or any girl who resembles her, but the judge allowed this lyric to be used by the prosecution as evidence of motive. Other rap songs, however, were not supposed to be introduced, yet Green repeatedly recited some of Offord's most obnoxious lyrics to the jury, including one proclaiming, "I'm the nigga of the 'hood. Damn, this is feeling good . . . I'm reaching my gold, direct a bullet to your sold." The defense watched helplessly as the mostly white, middle-aged jurors recoiled.

The rap lyrics had made for potent ammunition from the start of the case, long before trial. A local newspaper obtained copies of Offord's rap lyrics, apparently leaked by sheriff's department sources. The paper described the raps as "sadistic scribblings," "evil poetry," and "fiendish jottings," writing that "glorifies drug dealers, degrades women, and promotes violence."[38] (Leaks of negative— and even false—information about Pat Dunn would later emanate from the sheriff's department as well once his case was pending.) Detective Randy Raymond was quoted at length in the article, which went on to explain how Offord's writings gave "a look inside his head." Green portrayed the writings in a similar way, as revolting revelations of a sick mind, as opposed to what Offord's friends and defenders claimed them to be— childish attempts to imitate a phenomenally successful and popular form of music that no more revealed a propensity for violence in Rollins than a Stephen King horror novel betrayed a murderous nature in that author.

Green underscored her portrait of Offord as a violent sexual predator by eliciting inadmissible hearsay testimony from one witness, who recalled "someone" had said that Rollins might have had a gun at his house in the months before the murder—a statement the judge on the case never should have allowed.[39]

At the same time, Green successfully argued that the jury should not hear about other potential suspects in the case whom the defense wished to accuse, namely, Victor Perez. Perez's incorrect information to police, his past violence against Maria's sister, and the witnesses prepared to testify that Maria feared and hated Victor were not enough, Green reasoned: In addition to a possible motive and a propensity for violence, there had to be some evidence that Victor actually might have committed the murder as well. And that couldn't be shown, Green said, because Victor had an airtight alibi. Miriam Rodriguez, Maria's mother, said she was with Victor the entire day that Maria disappeared, the prosecutor asserted. The judge agreed: No mother would lie to cover for her daughter's killer. So the jury never heard about Victor Perez.

There was just one problem. Long after the trial, it would become clear that Lisa Green had been mistaken: There was no such alibi. Miriam would swear that she went out alone to search for Maria when the girl failed to come home from the park that day, walking the streets for hours—without Victor. But Offord's jury would never know that.

Finally, in closing arguments, the prosecutor employed a tried-and-true, yet devastating tactic: likening the defendant to infamous criminals. Green tried to seal the case against Rollins by casting his lot with child molesters, Charles Manson, Judas Iscariot ("On the night of the last supper, Judas would have had twelve of the best character witnesses in the world," Green intoned), and, finally, the most notorious and threatening black athlete of the day, boxer Mike Tyson, who had recently been disgraced and sent to prison for rape (though he had not yet committed his most infamous act, trying to bite off the ear of an opponent during a prizefight). The analogy seemed clear: Rollins was just another black athlete out of control, a walking stereotype of rage, violence and promiscuity, committing unspeakable crimes with seeming impunity. Unable to offer evidence of a coherent motive for Rollins to have murdered Maria, the prosecutor turned him into a beast instead.

In an attempt to overcome these hardball tactics, Rollins' attorney brought in several scientific experts, including David Faulkner, a nationally recognized pioneer in the new field of forensic entomology—the study of insect activity at crime scenes. The experts testified there was no way Maria could have died before sunset, a crucial contention of the prosecution, given that Green conceded Offord's alibi for the late afternoon and evening. Her bloody body would have shown evidence of fly eggs and larvae if it had been left in the desert in the daytime, Faulkner told the jury. He even performed an experiment with the body of a dead pig at the murder scene that supported his conclusions—flies appeared in great numbers during the day, but not at all at night, because flies cannot see or navigate in darkness. The prosecution tried to rebut this testimony with its own expert, but the scientist brought in by the DA turned out to be an expert in mosquitoes, not flies, and even he ended up admitting that Maria's body should have had fly eggs on it had she died when the prosecution claimed. Laura, like Susan Penninger before her, thought the defense presented an overwhelming case, offering the jury tangible evidence to weigh against what she regarded as mostly innuendo, speculation and personal attacks. Even if the jurors were concerned by the fiber, plant and fingerprint evidence from the car and therefore were not convinced of Offord's outright innocence, Laura figured, surely there were too many doubts to sustain a conviction.

But the jury felt otherwise. As his father wept and whispered, "This town is evil," Offord was pronounced guilty of first-degree murder. The verdict left Laura wondering just what was needed to win an acquittal in Kern County. Could she do any better for Pat Dunn?

In the end, it seemed to Laura that the deck must have been stacked against Rollins, that there was a reason why an absence of flies just couldn't compete with the fiendish jottings of a sodomizing Mike Tyson clone. And she was right. Unbeknownst to anyone outside the jury room, a juror named Gregory Piceno told his colleagues he was well acquainted with the crime scene, having worked on a nearby farm for fifty years. In violation of his sworn oath to consider only evidence presented in trial, Piceno told the other jurors that there could have been pesticides sprayed near the body, thereby explaining the absence of flies. The defense testimony—which included assurances that no pesticides had been sprayed near the murder scene—was all "a damn lie," one fellow juror recalled Piceno saying during the trial.[40] This other juror, an alternate who did not participate in deliberations, would later claim several other members of the jury busily violated their oaths throughout the trial as well, by discussing the evidence and pronouncing Offord guilty in private conversations long before all the evidence was in—despite the judge's daily admonitions not to do so.

These allegations of jury misconduct came to light only after the trial had ended, and then, only because the alternate juror, aghast at the verdict, spoke up. Susan Penninger helped uncover this information and more—including new witnesses, one of whom had heard another man confess to killing Maria—but Judge Len

McGillivray declared that the proceedings had been fair and just. The alternate juror could not be believed, McGillivray decided, while accepting the other jurors' denials of any misconduct.[41] In a courtroom with eleven armed guards posted inside because Kern County officials were alarmed about protesters—mostly black—converging on the courthouse, Judge McGillivray announced that Offord Rollins' conviction would stand.

The only comfort Laura could take from the Rollins case was the unexpectedly merciful sentence imposed by Judge McGillivray. Over the DA's protests, the judge invoked a little-used law that let him return Offord to the juvenile justice system, where the case began. Offord's age, exemplary past and otherwise clean record justified this sentence, the judge ruled, which meant instead of serving the life term District Attorney Ed Jagels sought, Offord would go free at age twenty-five, after enduring a maximum of eight years of incarceration with the California Youth Authority. It was the only flaw Jagels found in what he considered to be an otherwise remarkable victory for his office.[42]

As Susan Penninger told it, questions about the performance of police and prosecution—not to mention judge and jury—in the Rollins case seemed obvious and legion, and she believed they should have led to much soul-searching, if not formal inquiries, within the Kern County justice system. Instead, there were only accolades for those responsible and this, more than anything, left Laura afraid for Pat Dunn and unsure of her own case, which had seemed rather powerful before she heard of Offord Rollins. You reward what you want to see more of, she knew.

A few months after Offord Rollins' sentence, Jagels

named Lisa Green his office's prosecutor of the year, the first such award he ever bestowed. Responding to claims that the Rollins trial was tainted by racism and official misconduct, Jagels told a reporter such attacks were "an utterly unwarranted and vicious smear offered up by bad losers."

"Not only did she try the case extraordinarily well," Jagels said of Green, "but she exhibited a level of class and professionalism which was an example to us all."

7

THE MOBILE HOME SAGGED IN THE MORNING SUN-
light, its metal sides rippling and dirt-streaked,
the yard around it strewn with blackened parts
from dismantled cars and machinery. Laura Lawhon, for
the third time, had driven from the Marriott in
Bakersfield to this lonely outpost on a rural road in
Weedpatch, surrounded by farms and the thick smells of
manure and pesticide. She watched the home, watched
the cars, took license-plate numbers. She waited. Coble
patrol, she called it: Looking for Jerry Lee Coble, his family, his associates—and information that would unravel
his critical eyewitness testimony about Pat Dunn dumping his wife's body into the back of a pickup truck.

She took a deep breath and walked to the rickety
wooden fence enclosing the rectangle of grassless yard. A
weathered man, looking at least sixty years old, with a cap
bearing a tractor logo on the front, peered out of the
screen door, then slowly walked toward Laura, careful to
keep several feet between himself and the fence. It
occurred to Laura that he might be afraid she would thrust
a subpoena at him, and he wanted to stay out of reach.

"Mr. Coble?" she said brightly, putting as much
wattage into her smile as she could muster.

The old man said nothing, just looked her up and

down, shaking his head slightly, making her acutely aware of just how out of place her light business suit and gold jewelry looked in this barren stretch of blacktop and scrubby fields. She knew this man was Elvin Coble, Jerry Lee's father, a thirty-year employee of a cement company—a gruff man and a hard drinker, but, unlike his four boys, someone who had never been in trouble with the law. His company thought so highly of his long service and loyalty to two generations of owners that it presented him with a shiny red pickup truck as an honorarium. Gleaming and new in front of that tired yard and weathered house, it appeared to be his most prized possession.

"Mr. Coble, my name is Laura Lawhon," she announced, sensing that, with this man, short and to the point was the only way to go. "I'm a private investigator. I work for—"

"I know who you work for," the elder Coble cut her off. "You work for that Dunn fellow. The one that killed his wife."

Laura flashed another smile at him and shrugged. She could have protested this pronouncement of guilt, said that nothing had been proven against Pat, that he remained innocent under the law, the usual rap. But she knew it would be a waste of time, knew this man wasn't going to help, knew the Cobles would stand behind Jerry Lee no matter what. Jerry was family. He was blood. And without his deal to testify, he was looking at six years in the slammer. Pat Dunn, on the other hand, was a stranger. Who else could the elder Coble support, other than his own blood? Who else could he choose to believe? Elvin's bulbous nose, red and thickly veined, bobbed in front of Laura. She could smell alcohol on his breath and his clothes, but his eyes were unclouded and, even though he had to know her job was to attack his son, she saw no malice in his stare, only a weary resignation, the look of a man who had been down this path one too many times with his wayward boys. Laura found to her surprise that she felt sorry for this man, knowing, thirty-odd years ago, he had held a baby son in his arms, had felt the wonder and possibilities of new life, and had never imagined that his boy would become a hype and a convict and a snitch. Elvin Coble could never have envisioned the day that cops and private investigators and attorneys would visit his home more frequently than neighbors and friends. She could see the pain etched in the lines of his broad, open face. But she had to push on, had to do the job, had to try.

"I just wanted to ask you a few questions about your son Jerry," she said.

Elvin Coble started to say something, but a voice called from inside, a younger man's—maybe one of Jerry's brothers. Maybe Jerry himself, for all Laura knew. She couldn't see more than a movement of shadows within the darkened trailer. "Tell her to go away," the voice said. "Tell her we don't want her around here."

"I can't help you," Elvin Coble said, neither angry nor sad—just tired. He turned away and returned to his home. Then he looked over his shoulder. "But I can tell you, every word my boy said is true. He wouldn't lie about something like that. He's not built that way. I sat there with him and that detective in that restaurant and listened to every word—and I know it's true. I heard the truth in my son's voice. That man Dunn killed his wife, sure as I'm standin' here."

Then he was gone, the screen door thumping shut behind him. Laura stared for a moment, hoping someone else would emerge, even if only to berate her. But no one did, though she felt sure that eyes were peering at her from inside. She turned and left, thinking about what Elvin Coble had said, how he had been there in the Denny's Restaurant when Detective Soliz interviewed Jerry Coble that first time. It was an interesting revelation—especially since the detective had somehow neglected to mention in his report that Elvin Coble was present.

The Cobles were the key, the heart of the case—at least, that's what Laura and the rest of the defense team hoped. Pat's lawyers felt sure that the prosecution would live or die by Jerry Lee Coble. Though Laura had other concerns, given what had happened to Offord Rollins, she agreed that the defense team's first and most important task had to be discrediting Coble as a witness. They already had accomplished a great deal toward this end: Thanks to Stan Simrin's work at the preliminary hearing, they had Jerry Coble on record swearing he had been to the Dunn neighborhood only once—on the night of the murder—then had not returned until Detective Soliz brought him there many months later.

In response, the defense had a witness to contradict Coble on this: Rex Martin, who said he saw Jerry Coble cruising by the house weeks after the murder. In addition, the defense had Coble's erroneous description of the cars in the Dunn driveway, which matched the scene weeks after Sandy disappeared and included the car Pat rented after his own were seized by the police—further corroboration for Rex's version of events, and a major hole in Coble's story. Even so, the defense team felt this might not be enough: in his ill-advised testimony at his preliminary hearing Pat had undermined this defense by misstating the date Rex followed Coble. So Pat's lawyer wanted to be able to flay Coble on the witness stand, which is why Laura and the other investigators from her firm pursued every member of the Coble family, looking for more ammunition, contradictions, anything—so far without luck. Either they couldn't find the family members, or when they did, they were told to get lost.

Hours had been spent combing the voluminous court records on the four adult Coble boys, Perry, Terry, Jerry and Gary, a group long known throughout Bakersfield law enforcement. The files stood two feet high when stacked one on top of the other, a record of thefts, assaults, robberies, drug crimes and burglaries. There were also hints that Jerry Coble had been an informant in the past, something that the DA, when queried by the Dunn team, reluctantly conceded had happened once before. In that case, Coble had not testified and his identity had not been revealed to those he accused, though his information had led to arrests and convictions. The authorities refused to release any other details to Pat Dunn's lawyers, saying that to do so would put Coble's life in jeopardy. Laura and the other investigators from her firm had tried hard to dig out more on Coble's informant activities, but they came up empty.

And Jerry Lee wouldn't talk to the defense, of course. Unbeknownst to Laura and the rest of the defense team, Coble still thought the Dunn defense team was trying to pin the murder on him, thanks to the comments Pat's brother Mike had made to Detective Soliz. Any momentary wavering in his resolve to testify against Pat—and he did waver at one point—vanished when he learned he might be considered an alternative suspect.

So that left Jerry Lee's family. One by one, they had refused to help the defense. Coble's mother hung up on them. Perry had nothing to say. Terry Coble, who had been arrested with Jerry for stealing brass and copper, would not help, either. He was ashamed of his brother—not because Jerry might be lying, but for cooperating with the police at all. In the Coble family, he explained in a brief phone conversation with Detective Soliz, it is a greater shame to cooperate with the authorities than it is to commit a crime. "We don't rat," he said.

That left the oldest, Gary Coble, the only one of the boys who no longer lived in Kern County. Ten years older than Jerry, he had an even longer criminal record. The Dunn team searched throughout Southern California for him, hoping he might somehow help their defense, but had been unable to locate him. Then, as they were about to give up, Pat's attorney, Gary Pohlson, received an unexpected telephone call.

"This is Gary Coble, Jerry's brother," the caller said. He spoke slowly, as if still debating the wisdom of placing this call, even after dialing it. "I don't want to be a witness. I can't testify. But I just want you to know, Jerry's lying."

At first Pohlson couldn't believe his ears. They had hoped one of Jerry Coble's relatives might have some information to contradict a piece or two of Jerry's story, perhaps offering differing stories on where he was that night, what he was doing the next day, that sort of thing. They had talked to his father-in-law, for instance, because Jerry had said he remembered which day he had seen Sandy's body because the next morning, he had to get up early to work for his father-in-law, who installed and repaired mobile homes. The father-in-law, however, making no attempt to hide his distaste for Coble, told Laura that Jerry Coble was wrong. "He didn't work for me that day. That's a lie." Those were the small contradictions that, if they found enough of them, could bit by bit render Coble unbelievable to even the most proprosecution juror. But now, here was Gary Coble, the star witness's own brother, providing not just some niggling contradiction, but the whole ball of wax: It was all a lie, just as Pat Dunn had insisted all along.

"What do you mean, he's lying?" Pohlson asked in reply.

"I mean, he made up the whole story so he wouldn't have to go to prison. He read about the case in the paper, he heard it on the news, he even pretended to be a delivery man with a package so he could knock on the door and get a look at the guy."

"He told you this?" Pohlson could barely contain himself.

"Yeah," Gary said after a moment. "He told me this."

Pohlson did a quick mental calculation: That last "yeah" meant Gary had heard a direct statement from his brother about lying. This was not hearsay, not supposition, not interpretation. Gary's story would be absolutely admissible in court, classic impeachment testimony, as evidence challenging a witness's veracity is known. Pohlson knew Gary Coble could be used to devastating effect in court—if the lawyer could get him there. Pohlson said, "We have to get together."

"No way," the star witness's brother replied. "I told you what I know. That's it."

Still, as final as his refusal sounded, Gary Coble didn't hang up. He listened as Pohlson wheedled and begged. Gary had to come forward, the lawyer pleaded; he had to

testify, had to save an innocent man from life in prison—
or from death row, a very real possibility. Gary kept saying no, no, no. But instead of hanging up and dissolving
back into the woodwork, he agreed, in the end, to talk
some more, to check back in to see if he could provide
any more information. And he kept his promise: After
two more long conversations, Gary left a phone number.
Pohlson immediately looked it up in a reverse index,
found the address in the San Fernando Valley area of Los
Angeles and drove out on a Sunday afternoon with one of
his law partners, arriving unannounced. They cruised by
the small tract house with its tiny yard, seeing cars in the
driveway and movement behind the windows, then
ducked around the corner and called on a cellular phone.
"We can be there in five minutes," Pohlson said when
Gary answered the call.

The man started to object, then sighed and said simply, "Come on."

Gary Coble turned out to be a virtual opposite of his
small, wiry, quick-witted brother Jerry. Gary was big and
meaty, built like a professional wrestler, a slow talker and, by
his own admission, no deep thinker. They sat down over
coffee and talked about Jerry, about the Coble family, about
how Gary believed he was not the only relative who knew
Jerry had lied. "They'll cover for him," Gary said. "And
they're gonna be mad as hell at me for talking to you."

Pohlson laid out a simple choice for Gary: Without his
testimony, Pat Dunn could easily end up going down for
a murder he didn't commit. There was no other evidence
of any import, Pohlson said. "Can you live with that?"

Gary closed his eyes and, after a moment, slowly
shook his head.

Three hours later, the two lawyers left the Valley with

a star witness of their own—Jerry Coble's own brother, who had no motive to lie and every reason to have just kept his mouth shut. Indeed, by coming forward, he not only risked ostracism from his family, he put himself at odds with the police and the DA at a time in his life when he apparently was trying to go straight. Pohlson felt Gary Coble's testimony all but cinched the case for the defense. Only Laura still felt uneasy.

"I don't like doing it," the new defense witness told her when they met later, "but I can't let an innocent man go down for murder. There's some things even I won't do."

"I only hope it's enough," she said.[43]

"Sometimes I get so keyed up, I just have to talk to someone," Pat told Laura a few days later. It was late afternoon, and the jail visiting room smelled of sweat and disinfectant, the telltale aroma of too many bodies jammed into too little space with too little hope. Pat perched on a chair, those big hands clasped in front of him, watery eyes moving nervously behind his glasses. "If I can't get the lawyers on the phone, then I turn to the inmates. I just have to talk about the case, about what they're doing to me."

"Pat, under no circumstances can you talk to inmates about your case," Laura admonished firmly, quietly— though in the confines of the small room, it seemed she nearly shouted at him. That was all they needed—Pat blabbing to some inmate, who then might decide to twist the conversation into a "confession," providing another nail in the prosecutorial coffin. Susan Penninger's client Carl Hogan had gone down the same way. "Half the guys in the place would love to be able to sell you out to the DA, Pat. You know you can't talk to anyone. You can't trust anyone. Look what happened when your brother talked to the cops."

Pat looked down at his hands and shook his head. He was angry, he said, going crazy in jail, unable to understand why this was happening to him. He expressed his helplessness by peppering the lawyers with phone calls and letters and endless jottings filled with his comments on the evidence, the witnesses, the police reports. Most of all, he kept insisting he had to take the stand at trial and set the record straight. Laura feared letting him testify, feared he might lose it, leaving such a bad impression the jury would miss his kind and caring and funny side and feel no compunction about convicting him. The five months behind bars since his arrest in October had taken a profound toll on him, Laura knew. Anyone, friend or foe, could see it. Some clients barely seemed to react to confinement, Laura had observed. To many, it was like coming home. Pat was not one of these. He looked older to Laura, diminished somehow, the confidence and belief in the justice system bled out of him day by day, his face pale and lined. He looked desperate, sounded desperate.

"I know, you're right," he sighed at last. "But you don't know what it's like, to be in here when you didn't do anything. It's killing me. You've got to get me out."

Laura didn't—couldn't—answer this plea. Instead, she tried to occupy him with helping her, returning to the questions that still stymied her investigation. She wanted to know more about his relationship with Kate Rosenlieb, what he knew of Marie Gates, the names of people who could support his contention that Sandy's memory had been failing. Pat gamely tried to help, but he was finding it hard to focus. After an hour, she left, feeling sad and helpless.

Anywhere else, Laura thought, the evidence in Pat's favor would probably be more than enough to carry the day. But what she had learned about the Offord Rollins conviction had shaken her. It didn't shock her that jurors and prosecutors might misbehave in a criminal trial—that happened, and far more often than anyone liked to admit. What horrified Laura was that when the misconduct was revealed, the Kern County justice system ignored it, dismissed it, said it didn't matter, even rewarded it. If there had been errors, they had been harmless errors, judges ruled after extensive hearings. The end, it seemed to Laura, justified the means.

Of course, Laura kept telling herself, there had been at least some tangible evidence in the Rollins case: fibers, plants, a car seen leaving the scene. You could touch them, hold them, argue over their significance—bits and pieces, however ambiguous, that a reasonable person could rely upon in declaring Offord Rollins a murderer. You didn't have to agree with that conclusion to understand it.

There was no such tangible evidence against Pat. It just wasn't there. Yet here they were, with trial fast approaching, and Laura couldn't shake the feeling that it was going to get worse, not better, even as the rest of the defense team brimmed with confidence.

She could understand why they felt confident. For reasons large and small, it appeared they were in good shape. There was more than just Gary Coble's willingness to testify, more, even, than the witnesses who swore Jerry Coble had cased Pat Dunn's house weeks after Sandy disappeared. Laura had found reasons to challenge the veracity of the whole investigation into Sandy's murder. Several witnesses she had contacted complained that homicide Detective John Soliz's memory was faulty, that he had gotten times, dates and facts wrong in his reports, and that damning conclusions about Pat had been drawn from this erroneous information.

As Laura saw it, such mistakes always seemed to be to Pat's detriment. Typical was one of the detective's reports concerning his interview with Sandy's investment counselor, Roger Norwood. According to Soliz's report on Norwood, "Alexandra Dunn told him she did not wish for anyone else, in particular Pat Dunn, to know what her investments were and what they were worth." This fit nicely into the prosecution's theory of motive: If Sandy had put a wall between Pat and her fortune, then the only way he could get to that money was to kill her.

It fit—but it was untrue. "It's absurd. Not only did I never say that," the graying, sixty-three-year-old Norwood told Laura when she showed him the report, "it's absolutely not true. Pat would sit in on meetings, he'd have input on the accounts, he even selected the fund manager for one account. There were no secrets." Norwood, who remembered Sandy fondly and said he would never do anything to protect her killer, even if it was Pat, insisted Sandy never expressed any such desire. "She was charming. She had that New York accent, never lost it, and always called me 'Rajah dahling,'" he said, mimicking the actress Zsa Zsa Gabor. "But that detective is trying to put words in my mouth. I have nothing bad to say about Pat Dunn."[44]

Soliz, Laura found, had gotten it wrong. With a few scratches of his pen, he had made it appear that Sandy wanted Pat kept away from her money right up to the time of her death, when in fact, the opposite was true. Another investment broker—Norwood's predecessor in handling Sandy's accounts at Merrill Lynch—had told Soliz Sandy had wanted Pat kept in the dark about her finances. But that counselor had stopped handling Sandy's accounts in 1988, about a year after Pat and Sandy got married, at a time when Sandy was still reeling from her difficult experiences with her second husband, Leon. The secrecy, if it existed at all, ended years ago, yet Soliz seemed to be putting the old broker's words in Norwood's mouth.[45]

The detective also attributed to Norwood an even more damning remark. According to Soliz's report, a few days after Sandy's disappearance, Pat tried to get the investment counselor to send him a quarter of a million dollars from Sandy's bond account—without ever mentioning the fact that Sandy had vanished.

This made Pat out to be a looter of Sandy's accounts, but the truth was, as Norwood explained it to Laura, that Pat *and* Sandy had asked him to sell off some of her bonds to pay bills on the Dunns' Morning Star housing project. Norwood did just that. But Sandy disappeared before a check could be cut. As for the phone conversation, it was Norwood who called Pat—to express his condolences over Sandy's disappearance. There was no attempt by Pat to hide the news about Sandy, Norwood recalled. To him, Pat sounded extremely upset about his wife. During the conversation, Norwood explained to Pat that he had liquidated the bonds, but that he couldn't release the funds without a signature from Sandy. Pat, Norwood told Laura, said he understood. There was no wheedling, no anger.

"He was in agony over 'Momma's' disappearance," Norwood stated. "Just devastated." Yet Soliz wrote in his report that Norwood "got the impression Pat Dunn was more concerned about the progress of the Morning Star project than he was about the disappearance of his wife."

"That's nonsense," Norwood responded when Laura asked him about it. If Pat truly were interested only in getting his hands on that quarter of a million dollars, he could have waited a few days until Sandy signed for the check and deposited it in their joint account. Then he really would have had access to the money—and a motive for murder. But not *before* the check came in.

Likewise, Detective Soliz apparently misquoted Kevin Knutson, the financial planner who met with the Dunns on the afternoon of Sandy's disappearance to discuss a living trust that would grant Pat more control over the couple's finances. According to Soliz's report, Pat Dunn told Knutson that he had zero assets—meaning he was entirely dependent on Sandy's money at the time of her death. But according to the defense team's interview with Knutson, what Pat really said was that, after his divorce from his first wife, he brought zero assets to his marriage with Sandy—five years earlier. Since then, Pat had made plenty of money through his mortgage-foreclosure business. Soliz also wrote in his report that Knutson recalled a surprised look on Pat's face when Sandy announced he was the sole heir named in her will, as if Pat had just learned of it for the first time. In the prosecution's theory of the case, this could have become the triggering event for murder. But Knutson later said the detective once more was mistaken: Knutson said he told Soliz that he had no idea if Pat was surprised by the will or not. Again, a witness had claimed the detective twisted information to make Pat look bad, and then used that incorrect information to obtain search warrants from the court and, ultimately, an indictment from the DA.

Then there was the matter of Sandy's mental state. Throughout the investigation, Detective Soliz and his colleagues at the sheriff's department insisted that no one who knew Sandy well had seen her exhibit any symptoms of Alzheimer's disease or memory loss. Pat's talk of memory impairment was a lie, a cover story, they believed. The district attorney adopted this theory, but its architect was Detective Soliz. His initial report on the case stated that a main "cloud of suspicion" over Dunn was the fact that everyone contacted, other than Pat, proclaimed Sandy sharp as a tack, with no memory problems. Soliz repeated this contention in a sworn affidavit filed in court to obtain the search warrant for Pat Dunn's home.

But in reading the reports, Laura saw immediately that Soliz was misstating the evidence in this instance, too. While it was true that most of Sandy's acquaintances said they noticed no memory or mental problems, the sheriff's own Murder Book quoted others suggesting that Pat might be right, that Sandy had become extremely forgetful and at times acted erratically. Pat's daughter, Jennifer, and a friend whose husband worked for the Dunns both attested to this. A banker recalled Sandy once forgot how to sign her name correctly. Then there was the accountant's secretary, Ann Kidder, who recounted the phone conversation with Sandy on the morning after she disappeared, in which Sandy babbled and ranted about the Indians coming down from the hills and how her husband hated to wear clothes. All of this information had been in hand when Soliz claimed in his reports and affidavits that no one had seen any memory or mental problems in Sandy Dunn. And on top of those statements, Laura had found at least three other witnesses who saw

Sandy experiencing mental or memory problems at times—people readily available to the detective, including a local television reporter, City Planning Commissioner Jim Marino, and the wife of the Dunns' handyman.

It went on and on, it seemed. The Dunns' architect, a city council member and other witnesses contacted by the police all said they had been misquoted when Laura showed them what they supposedly said to Detective Soliz. Even Kate Rosenlieb would later say the detectives had incorrectly attributed statements to her.

Then there was Cynthia Montes, the Dunns' house-keeper, who spent one full day per week cleaning for Pat and Sandy. She, too, appeared to be a key witness for the prosecution—in Soliz's reports. Those reports had Montes telephoning the Dunns at 5 A.M. on Wednesday, July 1, just hours after Sandy disappeared, to confirm a cleaning appointment early that same morning. Pat answered the phone, sounding out of breath; Montes heard the shower running in the background. He told her not to come because of an appointment they had that day. Montes said this exchange was most unusual, because every other time she called, Sandy or the answering machine picked up. Never Pat. And even more suspicious than that, Montes said, was that Pat never mentioned Sandy being missing when he rescheduled the cleaning time.

What Soliz and the prosecution made of all this was clear: They attributed Pat's being out of breath to his having just returned from carting a body, digging a grave and making the one-hundred-twenty-mile round trip to Sandy's burial site. The water was running in the background because he had been cleaning up the bloody mess his deed had left behind.

It sounded impressive, except, once more, there were indications that the witness's account and Soliz's report might not quite match up. Montes told Laura's boss, the investigator David Sandberg, that there had indeed been a change in the regular cleaning schedule around the time of Sandy's disappearance—that much, at least, was correct. Montes said she usually went to the Dunns' on Tuesdays or Wednesdays, but that week Sandy asked her specifically to come on Tuesday, June 30, at 5 A.M., a much earlier hour in the morning than usual. Montes would have to work around "a very important appointment" the Dunns had at about eleven that morning, she recalled. She was to start in the den, where the meeting was to occur, then clean other parts of the house after the Dunns' appointment had begun. This rescheduling had been discussed with Montes at least a week in advance, she said; either Soliz reported this incorrectly, or Montes had simply forgotten it during her interview with the homicide detective. In any case, Laura felt sure the "important appointment" had to be a reference to Kevin Knutson's visit—which took place on Tuesday, June 30, *before* Sandy disappeared. So the fact that Pat answered the phone out of breath and with the water running that Tuesday morning, and that he canceled Montes' house-cleaning visit, meant nothing: Sandy was quite alive at the time. It only became significant if the day of this call was moved forward to Wednesday, July 1—as it was in Soliz's report.

When this discrepancy was pointed out to Montes, she amended her story and told Sandberg the day must have been Wednesday after all, the morning after Sandy vanished. This must be so, Montes said, because she and "John," as she referred to Detective Soliz, had talked things over and decided her recollections were crucial to the case. In other words, Laura thought, Montes would adjust her recollections to fit the prosecution's theories.[46]

Though such discoveries were victories for the defense, they left Laura all the more uneasy. The Kern County District Attorney's Office had formed its theory of Pat's motives based on such misinformation. But as had happened with Victor Perez and Offord Rollins, even with the errors exposed, the DA was sticking with the original theory, no matter how much Laura might discredit it. They were going with Detective Soliz's version, even if their own witnesses later disputed it.

There had been roadblocks thrown up as well, and Laura remained frustrated and in the dark about some aspects of the case. A few key witnesses refused to talk to her, Jerry Coble chief among them. Pat DeMond, the city councilwoman, reacted similarly. This was doubly troubling to the defense because DeMond, in her day job as a paralegal, was assisting Sandy's sister in an attempt to wrest the estate away from Pat. DeMond left a terse message after Laura tried to contact her to arrange an interview: "I have nothing to say to you." And Roger McIntosh, a well-connected Bakersfield engineer hired to work on the Dunns' failed movie-theater development, would not talk to the defense team either. He had told Soliz that, during a meeting with the theater-project team, Pat ordered Sandy to shut up and sit down—a nasty confrontation that bolstered the prosecution's contention that there were bad feelings between the Dunns. Laura badly wanted to ask him about it, and why, somehow, no one else at the meeting could recall this outburst by Pat.

Most disappointing, though, was Kate Rosenlieb, Pat's

supposed closest friend. She would have nothing to do
with his defense, even slammed the door in the face of
one of Laura's colleagues. She remained a troubling
cipher to Laura, who wanted to understand why such a
good friend had turned on Pat so completely, so quickly.
But Pat couldn't help. He still thought the world of her,
and had no idea of the role she had played in his legal
woes.

As Pat's trial approached, Laura's inability to speak to
these key prosecution witnesses increasingly gnawed at
her. She knew she was missing something. She feared
these witnesses might take the stand and reveal some terrible surprise for which the defense was not prepared,
cinching the prosecution's case and sending Pat Dunn
reeling toward prison despite all the work done to unravel Jerry Lee Coble's testimony and the credibility of the
sheriff's investigation.

As it turned out, Laura's instincts were correct—
almost. But it wasn't new revelations from these witnesses that, in the end, decided the case.

It was what some of them were hiding.

MEAN JUSTICE

8

A S LAURA LAWHON TRIED TO PIECE TOGETHER THE why behind *The People of Kern County vs. Patrick O. Dunn*, the entire justice system of Kern County was about to be shaken to its core. A series of very different, very high-profile cases was about to come unglued, cases far more troubled—and troubling—than Dunn's, or Offord Rollins', or any other single prosecution in and of itself. A legal earthquake was building silently in Kern County, still invisible and unfelt, another mystery just beyond Laura's reach. She had heard hints of it, of course, but for the most part, the scandal that lay buried in Bakersfield's past was still ripening for the future.

When she finally learned of it, long after her work was done in Kern County, all the missing pieces seemed to fall into place for her. The Dunn case had not been one of a few isolated examples, Laura decided, but part of an avalanche. It turned out there had been dozens, even hundreds, of innocent people harmed by blind investigative and prosecutorial zeal in Kern County. The examples were legion: On an almost unimaginable scale, evidence had been manufactured, witnesses coerced, facts twisted beyond recognition to fit government theories, evidence of innocence kept hidden from those accused and tried. Cops, prosecutors and social workers had taken as gospel truth the most outra-

geous—and easily disproven—allegations of child molestation conspiracies, devil worship, human sacrifice and ritual
murder, ruining untold lives in the process of their extraordinary, misguided investigation. The acts of official misconduct ended up filling hundreds of pages of judicial
opinion, with the largest criminal investigation in Kern
County history thoroughly discredited.

As far as the courts were concerned, however, none of
this had anything to do with Pat's case, and yet to Laura,
it had everything to do with it. Understanding the justice
system in this place—and the injustice it could produce
and condone—was not possible without acknowledging
these revelations. For they pointed to an official mind-set
that, Laura would decide, in the end made Pat's conviction as inevitable as the tides. Everything that troubled
Laura about the Dunn case—and much, much worse—
had already been endured, many times over, in the Witch
Hunt cases. And for the longest time—fourteen years—it
seemed no one cared a whit.

The events that triggered the Bakersfield Witch Hunt
occurred in January 1980, when Pat Dunn was still a
school principal and Sandy was still Pat Paola's trophy
wife. It started in a neighboring county, where the
authorities eventually dropped the case for lack of evidence—a telling detail all but forgotten in the maelstrom
of events that followed.

It started small, as such things often do, with a little
girl named Jenny McCuan, and an obsessed woman
named Mary Ann Barbour.

Jenny was six then, a precocious and bright child, as
was her three-year-old sister, Jane.[47] They were the seem-

ingly normal kids of seemingly normal parents living in a nondescript Bakersfield tract home. Alvin McCuan was a railroad worker. His wife, Debbie, fifteen when she married Alvin shortly before Jenny's birth, ran a day-care center at her home. It was licensed and regularly inspected by the Kern County welfare department, and nothing untoward was ever observed by authorities, parents or children who attended. The McCuan children played with the other neighborhood boys and girls; Jenny did well in school, where her teachers noticed nothing unusual about her at all.

But after a visit to her grandparents' home in San Luis Obispo County on the Central California coast, Jenny complained that her Granddad Rod Phelps—Debbie McCuan's stepfather—had fondled her sexually. She made this complaint not to her own parents, but during a visit with her "stepgrandmother," a troubled thirty-seven-year-old woman named Mary Ann Barbour. Mary Ann was the wife of Gene Barbour, Debbie McCuan's second stepfather, and though she was not actually related by marriage or blood, Jenny and Jane considered Mary Ann a grandparent. The girls often visited and stayed overnight at the Barbour house.

For years, Mary Ann Barbour had been concerned about Jenny and Jane being molested, and she made a habit of closely inspecting their vaginas for signs of bruising or redness during visits. She also questioned them about molestation. Now, finally, after two years of amateur gynecological examinations and pointed sexual questioning, Jenny said her Grandfather Rod had molested her, just as Mary Ann had always feared. She immediately took the girl to a doctor, who found bruising and swelling and concluded Jenny had, indeed, been molest-

ed.[48] Mary Ann then told Jenny's parents and reported
the matter to the authorities in Bakersfield.

A Kern County Sheriff's detective and a social worker
interviewed Alvin and Debbie, found them completely
cooperative, and secured their promise to keep the girls
away from Rod Phelps. Then they interrogated their suspect. Sobbing, Phelps admitted to molesting Debbie
McCuan when she was a teenager, but denied doing anything to Jenny. Jenny, for her part, when interviewed by
Kern County authorities, denied that anything had happened, but after lengthy questioning by a social worker
named Velda Murillo—who began the interview by
telling Jenny that she *knew* the girl had been molested—
Jenny finally agreed that Phelps had fondled her. Later,
after more questioning, Murillo reported that Jenny
described other sex acts with Phelps, including inter-
course.

Velda Murillo, who would soon become a central figure in the Witch Hunt cases, shared with a small but
influential cadre of Kern County colleagues the belief
that the use of leading and suggestive questions was not
only acceptable, but essential as the best way to overcome
a child's natural tendency to deny being molested. Fear,
embarrassment and a desire to protect their relatives,
even abusive ones, would lead child victims to deny that
anything happened—unless they were pushed, Murillo
believed. This approach, coupled with the credo that
"children never lie" about molestation when they claim it
occurred, became the hallmark of child sexual abuse
cases in Kern County. When officials suspected a child
had been abused, the approach in Kern County boiled
down to this: Questioners simply wouldn't take no for an
answer.

The problem was, the social workers, sheriff's investigators and prosecutors who believed this were dead wrong. This strategy has since been revealed to be the absolute worst way of questioning children. Study after study has shown that such aggressive, leading questioning often generates false statements by children, not only when it comes to allegations of molestation, but on any subject.[49] Young children may try to be truthful, but once subjected to suggestive questioning by adults in authority, they can have difficulty separating genuine recollections from suggested ones. Children have a tendency to say what they think adults want to hear, and Murillo left no doubts about what she wanted her interviewees to say. Because her sessions alone with Jenny and other children she spoke with during the Witch Hunt were never recorded, and she seldom wrote reports herself detailing who said what during these interviews, no one knew exactly how she got kids to level their accusations until many years later, when she was subpoenaed and required to testify about her practices. It turned out the common practice in use during the Witch Hunt went like this: Murillo would lock herself in a room with a child thought to have been molested and "help" him or her recount the abuse by graphically describing an act of molestation, after which she would urge the child to agree that it had occurred. Once this process was completed, Murillo would next brief a sheriff's investigator, relaying the "disclosures" she had just obtained from the child. Then that investigator would question the child again for the record and file a report on the results, or simply rely on Murillo's "filtered" account. In either case, the report would be written in such a way that a reader would be led to believe that it was the *child* who first described the acts of sexual abuse, not the social worker. If during a follow-up interview a child failed to repeat the explicit and often sensational allegations Murillo reported, the investigator would remind the child of "the truth" they had previously "told" Murillo, so that they would not waver from the initial story. A child who subsequently denied being molested simply would not be believed. In such cases, it would be assumed that a molester or other relative had pressured or threatened the child into withdrawing the allegations; it never occurred to the authorities that it might be the investigators themselves applying the pressure on children to level accusations in the first place.[50]

Although Kern County investigated the case, San Luis Obispo County authorities ultimately prosecuted Rod Phelps, as the molestation was alleged to have occurred in their jurisdiction. The case later was dropped when Jenny refused to testify and again denied anything had happened. While Kern County authorities still believed Phelps to be a child molester, they were satisfied at the time that Debbie and Alvin McCuan would protect their daughters from future abuse. Jenny had clearly stated only her grandfather had harmed her, no one else.

Mary Ann Barbour, however, was not satisfied. She insisted to the sheriff and welfare authorities that the children had to be removed from the McCuan home for their own safety. The detective on the case considered her claims irrational, and perhaps he was right: Barbour was soon involuntarily admitted to a county mental hospital after threatening to stab her husband, and complaining of being unable to eat or sleep, obsessed with molestation and profoundly depressed. Doctors initially diagnosed her as delusional, but after a week, she was sent home with nothing more than sleeping pills.[51]

Mary Ann came home in January 1980 still obsessed and convinced that Jenny and Jane were at risk and that their parents were part of the problem. When the Kern County Sheriff's Department and social workers wouldn't do anything more, she called Betty Palko, a county adoptions worker she knew, and asked her to close down Debbie McCuan's day-care center. Palko arranged an unannounced inspection by another social worker, but nothing amiss could be found. When the matter was not pursued further, Mary Ann decided Palko must be part of a criminal plot as well. When she found out that Palko's boyfriend, Larry Walker, worked at the railroad yard with Alvin McCuan, and that the two couples sometimes played cards together, she became convinced that there was indeed a conspiracy at work.

Eighteen uneasy months passed, with Mary Ann continuing to question and examine Jenny and Jane during every visit, their parents unaware of the weekly inquisitions. Then, shortly after making contact with a child-abuse crusader who had close ties to the Kern County DA and a firm belief in the existence of large-scale molestation conspiracies, Mary Ann made a new, far more dramatic report to the authorities.[52] This time, Jenny and Jane, ages eight and five, both were victims. And this time, their father, Alvin McCuan, was accused along with Grandfather Phelps, putting the case squarely in the hands of Kern County authorities for the first time. Velda Murillo again questioned the girls in her usual way, and emerged from the interview with descriptions of terrible sexual abuse by their father, something Jenny had previously denied. The girls were taken into protective custody and placed in a county-run shelter for abused children, while Alvin McCuan was promptly arrested. When

Debbie McCuan—who had not been accused as yet—referred sheriff's investigators to her lawyer instead of coming in for an interview, the district attorney responded by seeking a court order removing Jane and Jenny from her custody. Then, despite her history of mental problems, Mary Ann Barbour received custody of the girls.

During Jenny and Jane's first interviews with Velda Murillo, the only molesters mentioned were the father and grandfather. Jane in particular was quite specific in saying only her father and grandfather had molested her and her sister. "Nobody else ever tried to do those things," she said. It was a statement that the authorities would soon ignore.

For after Jenny and Jane moved into the Barbour home, it seemed just about everyone Mary Ann Barbour feared, blamed or resented was eventually accused of molesting the girls: Debbie McCuan, whose continued visitation rights with the girls rankled Mary Ann; the social worker Betty Palko, who had not closed down Debbie's day-care center, and her boyfriend; and the girls' uncles Larry and Tom McCuan. The sheriff's department held off making any more arrests while they investigated, wondering just how big the case might get, hoping to lull their suspects into a false sense of security.

Mary Ann, meanwhile, again unable to sleep, kept the girls up all night with her several times, and then breathlessly called social workers and sheriff's detectives with new revelations from predawn question-and-answer sessions. She began claiming she was being followed and threatened. She said Betty Palko appeared in a Halloween costume, threatening to "wipe out" the girls. Over time, she made many more revelations—that the girls had been involved in child pornography, bestiality and orgies; that they had been sold as sex slaves at motels by their own parents; that they had been shown snuff films in which children were murdered, with a narrator pronouncing, "This is what happens to little girls who talk." She also said that Palko, in another threatening conversation, had called the girls "sow sluts," a supposed devil worshiper's term, and an ominous hint of the satanic allegations that were soon to blossom in Kern County.[53]

When questioned by a sheriff's investigator, the girls at first denied these new and sometimes patently absurd statements—in other words, Mary Ann said it, but the girls didn't. After spending more time alone with Velda Murillo, however, the girls started repeating the allegations and adding to them. The pornography, snuff films and orgies were all true, the girls finally agreed, their stories growing increasingly grotesque, with detectives and prosecutors assuming every word to be true and to have originated with the girls, not with Mary Ann Barbour. Any official who expressed doubts about the case was silenced by subtle intimidation and veiled threats that they, too, could fall under suspicion.[54]

On April 2, 1982, long after their father was arrested and charged, Jenny and Jane accused Scott Kniffen, an inventory manager for a diesel company, and his wife, Brenda, a Sunday-school teacher, of being involved in the orgies and molestations as well. The Kniffen name had never come up before, though the girls had been interviewed countless times by then. Indeed, just six months earlier, the girls had firmly stated that their father and grandfather were the only ones who had ever molested them. Now, though, the girls said not only were the Kniffens child abusers, but their two young sons,

Brandon and Brian, who the girls knew and had played with, were victims as well.

These new accusations came shortly after Alvin McCuan, the only person who had been arrested and charged so far in the case, asked his friend Scott Kniffen to be a character witness for him.

In short order, the accusations grew even worse. The girls started claiming they had been strung up from hooks in the Kniffens' living room and raped while dangling in the air. The girls had been filmed having sex with adults and other children, and the movies and camera equipment were stored at the Kniffen household, they said. Each new revelation was promptly rewarded with ice cream and other treats.

By this time, the molestation "ring" included at least ten adults, and the investigation had reached a frenzied pace, unlike anything ever seen before in Kern County. A young deputy DA, Medalyian Grady, who had yet to prosecute a felony in her brief career, had inherited the case—an assignment she first received when Alvin McCuan was still the only suspect, with no hint of the massive allegations to come. The assignment of a neophyte to prosecute a molester was not unusual for the time—in that era, cases such as the initial child abuse prosecution of Alvin McCuan would have been handled as a misdemeanor, for sex crimes against children were considered "family problems." But when Grady first reviewed the original McCuan case, she decided the traditional approach would be wrong, and she pushed her office for a precedent-setting felony prosecution.[55] Hearing the little girls relate graphic sexual scenes most adults couldn't imagine left her physically ill, and convinced her they were telling a terrible truth. "No five-year-old child could know those things without having experienced them," she would say after interviewing the girls, unaware that Velda Murillo had described the sex acts to Jane and Jenny, not the reverse. "How else could they know more about sex than I know?"[56]

Grady's decision to handle the original case as a felony proved prophetic—and convenient, once the additional eight defendants were added. And so, the novice prosecutor, with the best of intentions and an admirable dedication to saving abused children, launched the first of the big "ring" cases to be pursued in Bakersfield—or anywhere, for that matter. It was the biggest criminal case to hit Kern County since Dana Butler was murdered and Police Commissioner Glen Fitts killed himself over it, dominating the news for weeks, and breaking in a particularly sensational manner. Over Grady's principled objections, the DA and the sheriff invited newspaper reporters, photographers and news crews to accompany the six law-enforcement teams fanning out in Kern County as they made nine dramatic arrests early on the morning of April 8, 1982. Predictably, the resulting reports were blasted across front pages and on the evening news, sparking protests at the courthouse, widespread public revulsion, and demands that the authorities get tougher on child molesters.

Brenda Kniffen, her long blonde hair uncombed, her eyes still bleary from sleep behind her thick glasses, was standing in the kitchen, staring out the window while waiting for the morning coffee to brew when she saw the uniformed men with shotguns storm her house shortly after seven that morning. News photographers immortalized the moment. She still remembers young Brian wailing for her as she was sped away in handcuffs. The two young boys were brought to the district attorney's sex-abuse coordinator, Carol Darling, and her colleague Velda Murillo, who awaited them with cookies and milk and questions. Then the boys were interrogated by a detective and a deputy DA. Brian and Brandon were subjected to lengthy and suggestive questioning during this process. Their repeated denials that they had been molested were ignored until they agreed, under pressure, that they were abused.[57]

Placed in the care of Kern County and kept apart from their families—not just their mom and dad, but their aunts, uncles and grandparents, who had never been accused of doing anything wrong—Brandon and Brian came to believe their family had forsaken them and hated them. They became creatures of the government after that, their story changing over time in accordance with what prosecutors needed to prove. If prosecutors needed them to say they were brought to motels—something they had previously denied—then they were brought to motels. If money had to have changed hands, or pictures had to have been taken, then those elements, too, appeared in their stories despite previous denials. No one in law enforcement questioned these inconsistencies—so long as the accusations grew worse and more numerous. Only if the children backed off an accusation did the authorities begin to question their veracity, assuming that someone in their family had gotten to them. "If anybody is brainwashing children, it's the family of the defendants," Deputy DA Grady told reporters after one member of the Kniffen family complained about police tactics in the case. "They are lying about law enforcement."

Even when the older McCuan girl, Jenny, told Grady flat out that Mary Ann Barbour had pressured her into

falsely accusing one of her uncles, the push to prosecute
did not slack off. Jenny's revelation came after she and
her sister were placed in out-of-town foster homes for
their safety, in the wake of Barbour's constant claims that
she and the girls were being followed and threatened with
death. As soon as the girls were away from Mary Ann's
influence, Jenny began recanting. But when that happened, both girls were whisked right back to Mary Ann
Barbour, and the recantations stopped—along with the
talk of threats. Eventually, the DA grudgingly withdrew
charges against the falsely accused uncle, though the fact
that charges against one alleged molester had been manufactured seemed to cause no official concern.

"You just made a mistake, right?" Grady asked the little girl, who sat on the prosecutor's lap as they spoke.

"It was just a mistake," Jenny agreed.

"And that's the only mistake you made, right?" Grady
prodded further.

The child nodded, telling the prosecutor what she
wanted to hear.[58] It was a perfect illustration of a prosecutor's tendency to view his or her own witnesses' contradictions as honest and isolated mistakes with no over-
arching significance, while condemning a suspect like Pat
Dunn's inconsistencies as evidence of overall untrustworthiness and guilt. Despite the naked admission that
Mary Ann Barbour had coerced a key witness into fabricating allegations that put an innocent man in jail and his
children into custody, no questions were raised about the
remaining charges. The case continued unabated against
the others as if nothing had happened.[59]

Not even a total lack of corroboration of the girls' stories—reminiscent of the lack of physical evidence in the
Dunn case years later—slowed down the investigation.

The children described in detail where the pornographic films were kept, where the police could find the camera equipment used to photograph the orgies, where the sex toys were stored, and even where the hooks in the ceiling were supposed to be located in the Kniffens' house; Jenny in particular had been quite specific about where these items could be found, pointing out rooms, closets and cupboards. But none of it was true—not a shred of physical evidence could be found where the girls said it would be. Nothing was ever found, even though the arrests had been secretly planned and carried out in order to preserve all this "evidence" the girls had described.[60] Undeterred when it was proven there had never been hooks in the Kniffens' home capable of supporting a child, the sheriff's department responded by having Jenny stand in the living room with her hands extended over her head, as if suspended from the hookless ceiling, so a police photographer could capture the moment. The resulting photo, gripping and sad, was then entered into evidence by the DA, a powerful image for the jury to consider, though it illustrated something that could not have happened. Prosecutors later went to a local porn shop and bought several dildos to wave around as courtroom props—even though no such sexual devices ever turned up in any of the defendants' homes.[61]

In an attempt to counter the dearth of corroborating evidence, Jenny, Jane and the two Kniffen boys were taken to a physician hired by the district attorney. Dr. Bruce Woodling, who then practiced in the coastal California town of Ventura, presented himself as an expert in determining if children had been sexually abused. Among the tests he used was one pioneered in Great Britain which he called the "Wink Test," in which the examiner would lightly rub a cotton swab against the patient's anus. If the anus reflexively dilated (as opposed to constricting), Woodling claimed, it proved that child had been chronically sodomized. He also asserted that he saw scarring from molestation in the children—something other experts who would later look at his photos and reports could not see. As it turned out, in a case that would otherwise have pitted the word of four small children against their respectable and credible parents, Dr. Woodling's seemingly irreproachable findings became the decisive evidence for prosecutors.[62]

What no one grasped at the time (or, rather, what no one among the defendants, judge and jury seemed to realize) was that there were no scientific studies to support Woodling's interpretation of these tests.[63] One of Britain's foremost experts on the wink response in children has since testified that Woodling misused and misinterpreted the test, and subsequent studies have shown decisively that it is useless in determining whether children were molested—abused children and nonabused children alike often display the same "wink" responses. But at the time, when the science of child abuse was in its fledgling stage and new experts in the field were just starting to stake out their reputations, Woodling's test was taken as gospel by police, prosecutors, judges and juries.

The problem was compounded because the DA's office—which had essentially taken over control of the children's custody and care from the county welfare department workers who normally handled such matters—adamantly refused to allow any non-prosecution doctors to examine the children, arguing that additional exams would be too traumatizing for the young victims.

By the time the case came to trial, the DA not only was prosecuting the case, but also deciding where the children lived, who could visit them, and who could examine them. No one appeared to be concerned that there might be a conflict of interest in allowing one adversary in a court case to act as parent, judge, therapist and social worker in deciding what was best for a key child witness's welfare while also trying to hold together a very difficult prosecution.[64]

In 1983, when Ed Jagels took office as district attorney for Kern County, the Kniffens and McCuans already had been charged, but not yet brought to trial. By then, the constant flow of new and fantastic allegations had bloated the case to include an indictment of several hundred counts aganst the eight remaining defendants. Jagels replaced the novice Grady with a veteran sex-crimes prosecutor named Andrew Gindes, a brilliant but brittle attorney known for his zealousness and courtroom fireworks.

Gaunt, dark-haired and hollow-eyed, Gindes had moved to Bakersfield from neighboring Tulare County, where he had been embroiled in some controversy over the years, including the conviction of a young man for a murder he was later cleared of committing.[65] As Jagels knew he would, Gindes made Kern County's first molestation-ring case a personal crusade. Over the course of a marathon trial, the longest in Kern County history at the time, Gindes was repeatedly accused of withholding evidence from defense attorneys. He also fought successfully to keep the defendants from having their own medical expert examine the McCuan and Kniffen children. But then, without court permission or legal authority to do so, the DA's office had the children examined a second time by their own expert, Dr. Woodling, contradicting Gindes' passionate arguments that any more of the embarrassing anal and genital examinations would traumatize the kids. Gindes later worked this incident to his advantage, asserting to the jury that the medical experts offered up by the defense ought not be believed, because they had not personally examined the victims—conveniently failing to mention he was the one who prevented such examinations in the first place.

Throughout the trial, Gindes displayed a ruthless streak that soon made him one of the most feared prosecutors in Kern County. In the midst of trial, for example, an aunt of the Kniffen boys innocently questioned one of them at a playground, asking, "Is it true?" (The boy answered, "No.") Gindes responded by having the aunt criminally charged with obstruction of justice. Years later, when Brandon and Brian Kniffen recanted their accusations and said interrogators had coerced and confused them, they bitterly complained most about Gindes. They said he had bullied and manipulated them into testifying falsely against their parents and the others throughout the long trial. "He would slam books down, yell when we wouldn't cooperate," Brian Kniffen would recall years later. "He was demanding and scared us and wouldn't take no for an answer . . . I wish I could talk to him now and ask him . . . why, why did he do that to me?"[66]

Perhaps most important for his case, Gindes persuaded a judge to keep jurors from hearing anything about Mary Ann Barbour's mental problems, freeing him to make an astonishing argument to jurors. "Mary Ann Barbour, if anything, acted reasonably and rationally," he declared of a woman who had been hospitalized for being obsessed with molestation and for making death threats against her husband. "[She] never overreacted to anything."[67]

That evidence of Mary Ann Barbour's mental state could have a powerful impact in court became clear a short time later, when social worker Betty Palko and her boyfriend, Larry Walker, came to trial separately from the Kniffens and McCuans on the same charges. They succeeded in having the case moved from Kern County on account of overwhelming and negative publicity that presupposed their guilt, and a different judge ordered Barbour's psychiatric records turned over to the defense as clearly relevant. Three days later, Kern County DA Ed Jagels stunned news reporters covering the case and its "overwhelming" evidence by announcing he was dismissing the charges against Palko, Walker and two remaining defendants because, he said solemnly, "These children have been through enough."

Jagels made no mention of Mary Ann Barbour or the events that immediately preceded the dismissal. His office had already insisted that Barbour's psychiatric history be kept secret and the records sealed in exchange for the dismissal of charges—thereby making sure that the Kniffens and McCuans could not get hold of them to use in their own defense during appeals.

"We have no doubt of the defendants' guilt," Jagels maintained when he announced the dismissal—a curious position, given that, legally, Palko and Walker were innocent.[68] "But we have a moral and statutory obligation to prevent undue psychological damage to child victims."

It sounded reasonable—the kids had to come first, even if it meant some members of the "ring" went free. What Jagels didn't say was that sheriff's detectives and

DA investigators, unconcerned about forcing the children to relive their molestations or to submit to unwanted medical examinations when it suited the prosecution's purposes, continued to interview them in connection with other cases and in official attempts to keep them from being reunited with other family members.

The Kniffens and McCuans, meanwhile, were convicted and sentenced to a collective thousand years in prison—a sentence that prosecutors had promised to seek from the very beginning. Brenda Kniffen fainted in the courtroom when the guilty verdicts came in. Gindes' presentation and the judge's rulings so swayed the jury that the ten-month trial was decided in just a day and a half of deliberation.

Afterward, District Attorney Ed Jagels pronounced Andrew Gindes brilliant. His office gave glowing reviews to the sex abuse coordinator Carol Darling, who was said to be outstanding in her ability to persuade kids to disclose accusations against their own parents, then testify about them in court. At the same time, the DA assured the citizens of Kern County that his office was interested only in fair prosecution, not persecution of innocents.

"A person who is convicted of child molestation here," Jagels vowed, "you can be very certain is a person who committed the crime."

By the time Ed Jagels made this confident but ultimately incorrect pronouncement, Kern County appeared to be awash with massive rings of child molesters. The cases had multiplied quickly as the same techniques employed in the McCuan and Kniffen cases were used to "discover" a shocking number of similar conspiracies. Children questioned by county authorities were coaxed and prodded into accusing several adults each and naming various child friends and relatives as fellow victims. Soon children were driven around and asked simply to point out the "bad people." The newly named "victims" then would be scooped up for the same high-pressure interviews. Then the cycle would repeat with each round producing more allegations, more victims, more depths for the ever-widening investigation to plumb. Soon, hundreds of people with no prior criminal records came under scrutiny; dozens of children were removed from their homes and placed together in the same shelters and therapy groups. At least eight separate molestation rings, involving at least seventy-five adult suspects and approximately forty children, were uncovered in the space of a few months' time in 1984.

The county placed the children in group therapy, where they would be encouraged to share their stories of abuse with one another—after which investigators, prosecutors and judges would marvel at the similarities in their stories. All seemed to talk of being drugged, hung from hooks, photographed and filmed having sex, and forced to watch movies of children being murdered. As in the Kniffen-McCuan case, though, no movies, pictures, books or other evidence was found where the children said it would be, or anywhere else for that matter. Attempts to stage orgy scenes recounted by some of the kids were comical—the equipment and numbers of people simply couldn't fit in the rooms as described. After a while, the DA and the sheriff's department stopped even trying to find evidence to corroborate what the children were saying (just as, years later, there would be no documented attempt to corroborate Jerry Coble's statements about Pat Dunn).[69]

Yet despite the many shortcomings of these ring cases, the district attorney's conviction record was stellar, the nation's envy. Elsewhere around the country, such cases often ended in embarrassing dismissals, acquittals or protracted appeals. In Kern County, sentences exceeding fifty and one hundred years were the norm, with Ed Jagels and his hand-picked prosecutor, Andy Gindes, notching victory after victory with the twin mantras designed to overcome any doubts about the evidence: "We're doing this for the children" and "Children don't lie." (The record remained untarnished for years, but after winning the first rounds of many appeals, the district attorney would experience some profound reversals of fortune in the ensuing decade.)

As the arrests multiplied, and more and more children were whisked away in the night without explanaton, hysteria slowly gripped the community. It was not just a fear of these rings of molesters preying on the young people of Kern County, but of the investigation itself, which seemed ever more sweeping in scope and power. Jobs were lost, lives and families ruined, futures destroyed, all by mere suspicion, regardless of whether charges were ever filed or not. Children were separated from parents for months, barraged by talk of sexual abuse by counselors, cops and other children, then returned home because authorities, try as they might, found no evidence—some kids just wouldn't accuse, not matter how fervent the efforts to "help" them. Talk of false accusations slowly began to spread. Parents spoke of being afraid to hug or touch or punish their children. One woman was prosecuted for assault for trying to stop representatives of the district attorney's office from physically abducting her daughter in a courthouse hallway—a ploy they carried out so they could re-interview the child about her molestation at the hands of her mother's ex-boyfriend. The mother had fully cooperated with the police investigation, allowing her daughter to be questioned at length, but she had also been warned by the child's therapist to avoid forcing the girl to relive the trauma of her molestation over and over through repeated interviews. In Kern County, however, the DA wanted the kids to tell it over and over, no matter what parents might want or doctors might recommend, and though prosecutors had no legal right to seize and question this girl against her mother's wishes, they did so anyway, dragging the screaming child onto a courthouse elevator while a deputy DA tried to distract the mother. This was no ring case—just a sadly simple one-adult, one-child molest—yet the authorities still jailed the mother for daring to interfere with their wishes. Only defense attorney Stan Simrin's threat to file a kidnapping complaint with the FBI led to an abrupt dismissal of charges against the woman.[70] Such excesses were seldom if ever made public at the time, and if they were, the news was drowned out by the overwhelming belief that child-molestation conspiracies were rife in Bakersfield.

As the rings one by one were brought to trial, a circus atmosphere prevailed, the courtrooms packed, the press coverage intense. Deputy DA Gindes turned one trial—the Pitts case, so named for one of its nine defendants, Ricky Pitts—into a virtual textbook of prosecutorial excess and misconduct. Throughout, he made continual and improper references to the Bible, arguing at one point that Jesus Christ himself would believe the children in this case rather than their parents. He repeatedly introduced inadmissible and erroneous evidence, then blamed defense attorneys for the lapses. The judge on the case, Gary T. Friedman, joined in Gindes' crusade, belittling defendants and their witnesses in front of the jury, mocking several of them for having tattoos. He sided with Gindes on virtually every legal point, even when Gindes was clearly in the wrong. Friedman, later censured for playing cruel jokes on defendants, overlooked Gindes' frequent and sometimes blatant misconduct—letting the prosecutor berate and belittle defense lawyers before the jury, letting him imply the defendants had threatened the lives of witnesses when there was no such evidence, letting him bully children who claimed the allegations of molestation were false. At the same time, Judge Friedman skewered defense lawyers who had the temerity to object to Gindes' behavior. The judge wept openly during one girl's testimony for the prosecution, then later admonished a defense lawyer for not displaying proper decorum in court.

Later, after all of the Pitts defendants were convicted and each sentenced to as many as four hundred years in prison, three of the six child victims recanted. One specifically blamed Gindes and others in the DA's office for forcing them to testify falsely that they had been molested, just as so many other ring "victims" were beginning to claim. The district attorney's office coldly responded that the victims they had formerly championed must now be liars. Judge Friedman refused to overturn any of the convictions. The long sentences were richly deserved, he said, because of the unspeakable acts committed against children by the Pitts defendants. He had seen photographs of it—"Every perversion imaginable," he said.

Bakersfield applauded the tough sentences. There was

just one problem: The photographs cited by Friedman did not exist.

Phantom photographs, phantom medical evidence, phantom conspiracies: The justice system of Kern County seemed so intent on convicting the monsters in its midst that anything seemed possible. And then, a year after the first ring trial, in March 1985, the impossible seemed to happen: The devil showed up in Kern County.

Suddenly, an explosion of allegations surfaced that wrapped Satan worshipers, human sacrifice and child molestation into one massive, terrible conspiracy. A "Satanic Abuse Task Force" was created by the sheriff's department to deal with the problem—and to keep it secret, in order to avoid tipping off the devil worshipers, whose influence was said to extend to the highest corridors of power. A separate office in downtown Bakersfield was rented for the satanic investigators and their DA liaisons, a move both Sheriff Larry Kleier and District Attorney Ed Jagels agreed was necessary. Maps were put up with clusters of pushpins specifying suspected cult locations, burial sites, satanic churches and the like—though actual proof that such places existed had yet to be found. The absence of physical evidence did not deter the task force; its members were true believers, seasoned by their work against the molestation rings. Now Kern County was not only a haven for organized rings of child molesters, but also a hotbed of baby sacrifices, ritual murder, cannibalism and bizarre rituals of sex and degradation in "a bad church," as the child victims all began to call it at their interrogators' persistent urging.

The satanic investigation began with one child—a Nokes ring "victim" who had been interviewed many times before between June 1984 and March 1985 without ever mentioning anything about ritual abuse or "bad churches."[71] But shortly after several Kern County social workers returned from a training seminar that hyped devil worship as a major element in child molestation (the discredited "true" story of satanic abuse, *Michelle Remembers*, was offered up as training material), this girl began speaking of it during the now-familiar suggestive interviews that were standard practice at the time.[72] In short order, other victims began spouting similar stories, never mentioned in earlier interviews. The kids were all placed in the same county shelter for abused children, where they were seen by the same therapist, who firmly believed a huge satanic conspiracy was afoot in Kern County—and who did her best to encourage the children to confirm it. The resulting stories were remarkably similar: Children had been forced to drink blood, to eat human flesh, to submit sexually to monstrous characters in dark robes wielding inverted crucifixes and uttering terrible chants. One child stabbed "little bears, little wolves and little birds." Women gave birth to babies solely for the purpose of human sacrifice, their infant chests torn open, their hearts ripped out, their broken bodies disposed of in fire pits. Twenty-nine babies had been murdered that way, investigators calculated from the children's accounts. One child recalled how thirty-nine adults were present in a Bakersfield church, with a satanic minister presiding, when sixteen infants were murdered and cannibalized in just one night.

Eighty-five more adults were ultimately implicated, and more than sixty children came to be identified as victims, with many taken from their families. Dozens of baby murders were suspected, and the sheriff was intent on prosecuting them even if no bodies were ever found in the furtive excavations of suspected ritual sites. The task force began to examine the older ring cases, including those already tried, for ties to the newly discovered conspiracy. With that, the investigation into Bakersfield's satanic heart went full circle, returning to the children who launched the first molestation ring case: Jenny and Jane McCuan, and their guardian Mary Ann Barbour.

Soon after seeing the county therapist who tended to all of the other satanic victims, the McCuan girls began making similar accusations as well—something they had never before done in four years of interviews, testimony and promises that they had told everything. Based on their new revelations, the satanic task force began digging up a field outside the girls' grandparents' home in San Luis Obispo County, looking for victims of human sacrifice that the children promised were there. Secrecy was abandoned and the dig became a media spectacle, fueling new public hysteria as the residents of Kern County prepared for a battle for their very souls.

Nothing was found. Teams of forensics experts made similar excavations at homes and businesses throughout Bakersfield. Bones were triumphantly unearthed behind one house, creating a sensation—until it was ascertained the remains belonged to a family dog that had died of old age. There were no fire pits, no bad churches, no films or videos, no secret graveyards of ritual victims. A half million dollars in manpower and machinery failed, for the third time, to turn up any of the evidence the children described. At the same time, concrete proof that the new charges were utter fantasy surfaced time and again. In groundbreaking stories, the *Fresno Bee* reported that babies named by the children as victims of human sacrifice were found alive, safely at home. Other supposed victims, it turned out, had been stillborn in hospitals. Suspects were described incorrectly, addresses proved fictional—the children's, and thus official, accounts were riddled with obvious fabrications.

Yet, even then, there was no letup—just an increase in paranoia, a belief among task force members that the satanists were so numerous, so powerful and smart that they could cover up anything. When the attorney appointed to represent the interests of two of the children, Jay Smith, expressed doubts about the investigation and asked a judge to appoint an independent psychologist to determine whether the kids truly had been molested, the district attorney's office reacted with reflexive suspicion and intolerance. Smith had listened to the tape of one of his young clients at Stan Simrin's office, and he believed he knew a terrible truth at the root of the investigation. The district attorney, however, publicly attacked Smith and sued to remove him from the case. Smith was later warned by a former prosecutor that he had been placed under investigation himself.

At the same time, Sheriff's Sergeant Brad Darling, head of the Satanic Abuse Task Force and husband of Carol Darling, the DA's point person on molestation rings and ritual abuse, met in Los Angeles with investigators in the notorious McMartin Preschool case. Darling described for the LA cops' benefit the satanic murders and molestation rituals that were being disclosed by children in Kern County, and how best to combat such crimes. By then, he told his rapt audience, the suspects included lawyers, doctors, deputy sheriffs, coroner's staff members, a mortuary owner, a cemetery owner, two ministers—all supposedly tied to a cult with tentacles throughout the world. Darling said he believed there was a massive cover-up being engineered, a conspiracy of money-grubbing defense lawyers, cowardly judges, lying news reporters, publicity-shy civic leaders and all-powerful, massively wealthy molesters.

"If you make enough stinkeroo in the newspaper and the other media, if you file enough writs, if you make enough mailed threats to the judges, it's going to have an impact," Darling asserted at a subsequent seminar for child-abuse workers. "Many times we've found the courts backing away from what should have been their responsibility to handle things."

Some months later, Darling was compelled to take the witness stand in one case and admit that much of what he had said at the seminar was exaggerated or inaccurate. There had been no threats, no corrupt judges and lawyers, no wealthy defendants. Indeed, if the defendants prosecuted in the Kern County ring cases had anything in common, it was their blue-collar ordinariness—and the fact that they seldom had the money or clout to hire the best attorneys in town or mount a serious challenge to prosecutors and their "scientific" evidence. And, contrary to his claim that judges backed away from their "duty," Darling had to admit—with the judiciary of Kern County bristling and listening to every word—that thousands of years in prison sentences had been dished out to molestation-ring defendants, breaking all records in the state and the nation.[73]

But paranoia had infected the entire investigation by then, and the inevitable soon happened. The children began accusing even the men and women of the task force.

A detective who had busted a half dozen ring members, a senior deputy district attorney who prosecuted them, a social worker who worked with the first girl who supposedly revealed the existence of satanic abuse—each was accused of molestation and of worshiping the devil. The young boy whom Susan Penninger and Stan Simrin had captured on tape a year earlier sounding normal and denying being molested was now a virtual automaton, spewing allegations in all directions: The social worker and the prosecutor on his case had gone to the "bad churches" and killed babies and burned the bodies, he swore. For this boy, the bad people were everywhere he looked. And he finally turned on those who had created him.

These new allegations marked a turning point. In the past, every adult accused by the children became a suspect, no questions asked. If the kids said it, it must be true. But that unflagging principle changed when the detective, the prosecutor and the social worker were fingered. In their cases, the authorities, District Attorney Jagels chief among them, simply decided the children could not be believed—though no substantive attempts to investigate the allegations were made, a double standard Kern County officials have never explained.[74] Some of those involved in the satanic investigation believed the new allegations, and concluded their task force had been infiltrated and corrupted.

A curious thing happened then. The technique of aggressive and leading questioning of children had just led to a number of provably false charges—dead babies who were alive, bodies that didn't exist, evidence that couldn't be found, suspects who could not have done what the children said they had done—along with a number of other extremely uncomfortable charges against

officials few wanted to investigate. Until that moment, in
the spring of 1985, the Witch Hunt, though incompre-
hensible in hindsight, could have been chalked up to well-
meaning but poorly trained and misinformed investigators and prosecutors caught up in something beyond their
experience—overzealous, perhaps, but not corrupt.

Now, though, law-enforcement officials in Kern
County were on notice that mistakes had been made—
grievous ones that had ripped families asunder, destroyed
lives, held people out to unbearable public shame and
put others in jail. They knew, then, that their witnesses—
and their methods—could not be completely trusted.

Yet Kern County authorities did not begin to question
their investigative methods, nor did they begin to wonder
how many innocent people could have been accused by
the children. They continued instead to press forward on
their molestation-ring cases and, to accomplish this, the
sheriff's department and the district attorney's office
made a fateful—and unlawful—decision. As individual
cases came to court, prosecutors decided to keep any
satanic aspects secret.

To accomplish this, they created a file on a single fictional suspect—nothing more than a "John Doe" folder
into which all satanic allegations against all defendants
were placed—whose case never came to trial, who had no
attorney, and who therefore had no rights. (The
McMartin detectives and prosecutors in Los Angeles, in a
case that received much more publicity, used the same
tactic to hide claims by the children that accused child
molesters could fly, change shape and become invisible.)
The paperwork dodge allowed the sheriff and prosecutors to bring to trial a variety of defendants as if they were
handling straight cases of molestation free of the incred-

ible or provably false ritual allegations. Keeping the satanic elements of cases secret preserved the credibility of the remaining ring cases. This practice, carried out by the sheriff's department with the acquiescence of the district attorney, appears to have violated laws requiring disclosure of relevant information to the defense—but it allowed them to continue to imprison men and women for victimizing children whom the authorities knew had made false accusations.[75]

In the end, out of the hundreds of suspects investigated as ring molesters or satanic abusers or both in Kern County, fifty-five were formally charged. Another dozen, though not criminally prosecuted, were accused as unfit parents under the State Welfare and Institutions Code so that their children could be taken from them. Many more were arrested or referred by the sheriff for prosecution, but ultimately were not formally charged—though many faced public ruin anyway. Combined, these cases constituted the largest prosecution effort to target child-molestation conspiracies in the nation. And they helped ignite similar cases against as many as a thousand other "ring" members throughout the country, as Kern County investigators and social workers fanned out to spread the word of their winning techniques.[76] The Bakersfield ring cases also produced their own body of literature, including a book called *Satan's Underground,* which encouraged the hysteria and made national headlines as the account of a supposed survivor of ritual abuse. Written by a Bakersfield woman under the pseudonym Lauren Stratford, the book was subsequently discredited; the author's only provable connection to devil worship was revealed to be her work as a piano teacher for one of the Satanic Abuse Task Force detectives.[77]

But the word spread, and similar cases soon appeared coast to coast. Names like Little Rascals, Wenatchee and, of course, McMartin, quickly entered the national lexicon. Still, to this day, out of all the many communities that generated such cases, and out of all the many allegations of official improprieties that have followed in their wake, no single place has discovered more molestation rings or imprisoned more people for joining them. Kern County remains the national capital of child-molestation conspiracies, the place where a modern-day witch hunt began.

Years later, Laura Lawhon would learn of this history and feel a measure of the futility that must have overwhelmed those falsely accused during the Witch Hunt. To Laura, it was all ominously instructive. Although the questions, recriminations, outside investigations and revelations of official misconduct began almost immediately in the Kern County ring cases, many of the falsely accused still languished in prison through the eighties and well into the nineties. Some waited sixteen years for the truth to set them free, far longer than their counterparts in discredited ring cases elsewhere in the nation, as the Kern County authorities fought hard and long to sustain their flawed convictions. Some are waiting still.

And so Laura had to wonder: If it has taken so long to correct such flagrant injustices against so many innocents in Kern County, what chance did a lone Pat Dunn have to win his freedom?

9

But the word spread, and similar cases soon appeared
coast to coast. Names like Little Rascals, Wenatchee and,
of course, McMartin squarely entered the national lexicon. Still, to this day out of all the many communities
that generated such cases, and out of all the many allegations of official improprieties that have followed in their
wake, no single place has discovered more molestation
rings or imprisoned more people for joining them, Kern

I'LL BET HE WAS TERRIBLE," LAURA LAWHON SAID.
"Wasn't he?" The lawyers had just put Pat Dunn
through a bout of mock cross-examination, to see
how he would bear up under the pressure. His trial was
just weeks away, and the defense strategy and witness list
had to be locked down.

"The worst," a weary Gary Pohlson answered. "He was
absolutely awful. There's no way I can put that man on
the stand."

Laura really couldn't say she was surprised by the
lawyer's comment. She knew from her long visits with
Pat that he was a good storyteller, a man who felt considerable empathy for others—but who also, quite
understandably, felt sorry for himself and resented his
predicament. Pat had to tell things his way, slow and
roundabout, with plenty of digressions and colorful
detail. The rigid question and answer ritual of cross-
examination was not a good forum for him. He did not
like to be cut off or interrupted or stopped from saying what he wanted to say, which is what good cross-
examination is all about. It rattled him. The old principal
in him liked to take charge, something opposing lawyers
like to see—anything that can make a witness seem more
overbearing than an attorney is a victory in itself. Pat

started out fine on direct examination, but he just couldn't handle the cross.

The disappointing mock-trial session capped a difficult final month before *The People vs. Pat Dunn* came to trial, a time of lost opportunities and intense pressure. Now any thought of putting Pat up as a witness was out the window. That meant they could not address certain things only Pat could explain—like why he seemed so amiable on the tape of his missing-persons call to the sheriff. No one else could tell the jury how he had thought it necessary to coax and cajole the authorities to take a report before seventy-two hours had elapsed, a common fallacy. And it meant they had to live with his unfortunate, and inaccurate, testimony from his preliminary hearing, in which he misstated the date that Jerry Lee Coble cased his home. Inconsistencies might be overlooked in prosecution witnesses, but Pat, as the defendant, would be held to a higher standard. To the Kern County District Attorney and Sheriff, the slightest deviation meant Pat Dunn was a killer.

The thing was, Pat still wanted to testify, badly. He begged Laura and Pohlson, just as he had begged Stan Simrin months before.

"If I just get up there and tell them the truth, they'll understand I could never hurt Mom," Pat said over and over. "I've got to testify. The jury'll expect me to."

"Maybe so, Pat. But if you're not honest with them, they'll sense that, too," Laura warned. She was referring to Pat's continued insistence that he and Sandy had never quarreled or fought, that their marriage had been uneventful, merrily dull. Perhaps it was not the constant war zone Kate Rosenlieb had painted it to be, Laura knew, but too many people had seen spats—normal spats—

between them for Pat to be believed. They had arguments, like any normal couple. Why deny it? She counseled her client just to be honest, to admit to being human.

The prosecution wouldn't be allowed to use Pat's domestic-violence arrest against him in the trial, because the charge had never been proven and was ultimately dismissed. But the fact that Sandy called the police about Pat was a different matter. Regardless of whether Pat ever struck Sandy or not, the mere fact that she dialed 911 and claimed that it happened implied some sort of discord in the house, even if Sandy initiated it with a false report. The prosecutor would hold information about the call in reserve. And if Pat took the stand and denied the existence of any marital discord, the prosecutor could then introduce evidence that Pat was a liar by proving Sandy had once called the police to have him arrested. The judge would say Sandy's report to the police could be used only to challenge Pat's credibility on the subject of marital discord in the Dunn household, not that Pat was actually a wife beater, but Laura knew this legal distinction would almost certainly be lost on the jury. The result of even mentioning Sandy's call to 911 would be disastrous. Yet Pat remained stubborn on the subject, insistent that they never fought—just as he insisted neither he nor Sandy had drinking problems, which Laura believed to be patently false as well. People had talked of the smell of alcohol practically oozing from their pores at times, as if the Dunns had been pickled in it. There really was no doubt, yet Pat denied it, another of his odd blind spots.

In the grand scheme of a murder case, these were minor points, seemingly insignificant. In truth, however, they were crucial, for if Pat were to take the stand and be caught in any lie, no matter how innocuous, Laura knew the jury could easily decide to believe nothing he had to say. Were he sitting at home reminiscing with a friend, Laura thought, this fervent desire to portray his life with Sandy in the best possible light would have been endearing. Every husband should be so dedicated to a wife's memory—to Laura, this blind spot provided further evidence that Pat really loved his wife. But in the crucible of the courtroom, where the prosecutor would leap on everything he could to dispute Pat's version of things (just as the defense would do with Jerry Coble), what sounded to Laura like well-intentioned, rose-tinted memories might sound to jurors like cover-up, denial, a sham. If he lied about ordinary arguments, the prosecutor would thunder, what else might he lie about?

Still, Pat had a point. Juries are routinely instructed that it is a defendant's absolute right to choose not to testify, and that jurors must not hold a decision to remain silent against him or her. But everyone involved with Pat's defense knew juries still wanted to hear from the accused, and that this would be particularly true with a husband accused of murdering his wife. *What is he hiding?* they would ask themselves, no matter what the law or the judge instructed. Which is why the defense team had staged the mock cross-examination.

Gary Pohlson had almost been persuaded to put Pat on as a witness without a mock session. But one of his law partners, a former prosecutor whose instincts told him that Pat would be easy game on the stand, persuaded Pohlson such a gamble could be disastrous. "Let me have a go at him," the partner, Thomas Goethals, said. "I'll pull him apart, and you'll see. He'll self-destruct."

Held in a cramped jail visiting room, with Pat in his blue jailhouse coveralls, it turned out to be worse than even the former prosecutor imagined. Defensive and contradictory, arrogant one moment and at a loss for words the next, Pat withered under the harsh and accusatory questioning. He stammered, he hesitated, he looked uncertain—all the qualities you never want a jury to see in a client if you're a defense lawyer. Mostly, it was a question of Pat's delivery, not the substance of his answers, but to a jury trying to decide whom to believe and whom to doubt, demeanor counts a great deal. It became clear to Pohlson that Pat could never be allowed to take the stand. He just wasn't up to it. It would be out-and-out malpractice to allow it.

"Don't worry, Pat," Pohlson assured his client, who was as shaken by the mock cross-examination as the lawyers had been, reduced to a subdued silence by the ease with which his words had been twisted and used against him. "We've got the evidence on our side. We're going to do far worse to Jerry Coble, and the rest will take care of itself. We don't need to roll the dice by putting you on the stand."

But with Laura, Pohlson was not so sanguine. He knew about the disaster with Stan Simrin and the last-minute phone call to Detective Soliz, and he worried that Pat might again do something foolish in his desperation. "You've got to help me keep him under control," Pohlson told Laura. "If anyone can lose this case for us, it's Pat Dunn himself."

Laura did not see Pat's poor performance as a witness as evidence of his guilt. On the contrary, it reassured her in an odd way: She told herself there was no way this man could also be the clever, meticulous killer prosecutors made him out to be, capable of eliminating every bit of physical evidence from a violent, bloody murder. She knew the pressure on Pat to be enormous: The deputy district attorney assigned to the case, John Somers, one of Kern County's top prosecutors, kept waffling on the question of the death penalty for Pat, a subject known to weigh heavily on the calmest of men. It was not until February 23—with the trial scheduled to begin March 10—that Somers finally announced he would not ask the jury to execute Pat Dunn. Life in prison, without possibility of parole, would be the worst Pat could get.

Pat had not borne up well under this pressure. His letters and calls to Laura and Pohlson remained a constant barrage, increasingly shrill, a continual distraction for the defense team and a source of additional frustration for Pat, as no one had the time to deal with his innumerable requests, suggestions and demands. Jailhouse lawyers were giving him advice, suggesting legal motions to file. He had become his own worst enemy, it seemed, stewing in his helplessness and only adding to his predicament. He was never nasty about it, just desperate. Laura had given him her phone number and told him to call anytime, particularly if the urge to talk was leading him to speak to fellow inmates, one of the defense team's greatest fears. He was soon on a first-name basis with Wayne Lawhon, who did not have the heart to turn down the constant collect calls. It was Laura's job to baby-sit Pat through these tough times.

The "Pat Problem," as Laura came to refer to it, had started soon after he was arrested and taken into custody. At that point, he already had become embroiled in a dispute with Nanette Petrillo, Sandy's estranged sister, who had flown to Bakersfield for the first time in years after Detective Soliz called her with the news that Sandy's body had been identified. Nanette had visited briefly with Pat, accompanied him when Sandy's ashes were cast over the Morning Star project site, and then sent him a cordial, if cold, letter thanking him for his kindness and expressing an interest in obtaining only the possessions Sandy had inherited from their late mother. She particularly wanted her mother's jewelry and crystal. During her visit, Pat had given Nanette a jeweled dragon pin that had been her mother's and promised she could have the other jewelry as well. But Pat had been angered by Nanette's letter. It suggested Sandy had somehow acted improperly or taken advantage of their mother in moving her to California and becoming her sole heir. Sandy had always told Pat she had all but rescued her mother and that Nanette had been the problem, but the letter disputed this. All Pat knew for sure was that he could only recall one telephone conversation between Sandy and Nanette in the past six years, and it did not go well. "She made Mom cry," he told Laura. "I didn't like that." Still, he had tried to be civil, and Nanette's letter seemed to reflect that as well by expressing hope that Pat would allow "my Mother's original wishes [to] come to fruition," so that Nanette and her children would receive the jewelry and crystal.

"I wish you peace," Nanette wrote in closing, "and thank you again."

Despite such sentiments, and unbeknownst to Pat, Nanette Petrillo by that time had already hired a private investigator and had expressed her suspicions of Pat to Detective Soliz—whom she had gone to see immediately after visiting Pat. "He was totally abnormal," Nanette told the detective, showing no "remorse," though he was calm and polite as could be. She and her husband also told Soliz that they thought Alexandra had been an alcoholic, although in a previous phone conversation, Nanette had told the detective Sandy didn't drink and that she found it suspicious that Pat recalled Sandy having two glasses of wine before disappearing. If nothing else, the contradiction showed the siblings did not know each other very well. Still, Nanette did not hesitate to criticize her late sister, informing the detective that Sandy had been jealous of her, and physically and verbally abusive of their mother and probably abused Pat Paola as well.[78]

Soon after speaking to Soliz Nanette retained a Bakersfield attorney, David Goldberg, who put his own private investigator on the case, looking for evidence to attack Sandy's will and Pat's control of the estate. Even without such evidence in hand. Nanette promptly filed suit to block Pat from inheriting anything and to remove him as executor. Nanette asked to be appointed executor instead, and she claimed entitlement to Sandy's entire estate—not just her mother's possessions. In her suit, Nanette claimed Pat had coerced Sandy into leaving everything to him. He supposedly insisted she write him into her will during an emotionally vulnerable time in her life—her pending divorce from her second husband. The allegation, coming from a woman who had barely spoken to Sandy in years and now sought to inherit her fortune, was provably false, as the attorney who had drawn up Sandy's will knew there had been no coercion. The will's language had been in place for seven years without Sandy once expressing any interest in changing it, not to mention the fact that, on the last day of her life, she told a financial planner she wanted to make it easier for Pat to inherit everything should she die. Everyone who knew Sandy and Pat— particularly during the early part of their marriage— saw quite clearly that Sandy was fully in command of her financial matters, with Pat providing input, but not the final say. There was no coercion.

Still, the suit, combined with Pat's arrest, served a purpose: It prevented Pat from paying his legal bills (or anything else) with money from Sandy's estate. Even some of the assets that they jointly owned, like his antique-gun collection, were in limbo while he sat in jail. In effect, Pat was left nearly penniless. The *Bakersfield Californian* learned of Nanette Petrillo's suit and ran a lengthy story about it, quoting the allegations that Pat was a gold-digging cad, but without checking with the attorney who had prepared the will to see if the allegations were true.[79] Pat was apoplectic over the story, and then was floored a short time later when the same newspaper linked him to a woman named Diane Dunn-Gonzalez. This woman had been accused in probate court of using a position of trust to become the beneficiary of a mentally confused woman's million-dollar trust fund. The newspaper informed all of Bakersfield that these were "allegations strikingly similar to ones brought against Dunn-Gonzalez's brother, Patrick Dunn."[80]

Now Pat was not only a gold digger and murderer, he came from a family without scruples when it came to co-opting other people's hard-earned money. There was only one problem: Pat Dunn and Diane Gonzalez were not related. They had never even met. However, a high-ranking source at the Kern County Sheriff's Department had told a *Californian* reporter that the woman was Pat's sister and that their two "schemes" were clearly identical. In so doing, investigators used the media against Pat, just as they had used it to disseminate negative and erroneous information about Offord Rollins and the molestation-ring defendants, a tried and true method of getting innuendo and damaging facts to potential jurors that would never be admissible in a courtroom. The sheriff's investigators were happy to believe the false allegations about Sandy's will—they, too, never bothered to check with Sandy's probate lawyer or to verify the supposed sister-brother connection between Pat and Dunn-Gonzalez—as these tidbits provided more building blocks for their theory that Pat Dunn killed his wife for her money. Although the *Californian* ran a tiny correction about Pat's relationship to Diane Gonzalez a few days later, the net effect of the sheriff's department's bogus tip was to paint an extremely negative public portrait of Pat through the press as the money-grubbing member of a money-grubbing, dishonest family. That this whole element of the prosecution's case was shown to be untrue did nothing to subvert the official theory that Pat had been after Sandy's money, an accusation Kern County authorities tried in the press long before bringing it to court.[81]

Meanwhile, Pat, desperate to find money for his defense and hoping to make bail so that he could escape the oppressive environment of jail, did something he shouldn't have. From his cell, shortly after his arrest, he wrote two massive checks totaling several hundred thousand dollars to his daughter, Jennifer, hoping that she would be able to cash them before he was removed as executor of Sandy's estate. Instead, the checks were seized and entered into evidence against him. To Pat, he was just taking what belonged to him. But to the DA, those checks were tangible evidence of Pat Dunn's avarice.

Pat ended up raising money by selling Sandy's jewelry, which he had hidden from authorities in a secret cache in the ceiling of the Dunns' house before his arrest. His family retrieved it, and the fifty thousand dollars earned from the sales helped pay for Pat's defense. It was a desperate violation of the law that he justified by asserting that, once his innocence was proven, the entire estate would be his anyway. The sale was eventually uncovered by Nanette Petrillo's Bakersfield attorney and private investigator, but too late to do anything about it other than damage Pat's already worn image.

Pat, in fact, had been forthright with sheriff's detectives about hiding the jewelry, though he refused to reveal the hiding place. The irony of this, Laura later realized, was that by telling the truth about still having the jewelry in his possession with none of it missing Pat had made himself seem more guilty in the eyes of the authorities, since Kate Rosenlieb assured them that Sandy never went out without scads of jewels. Therefore, they reasoned, if Pat's story of his wife's disappearance were true, he would not have all the jewelry in hand. Had Pat lied at the outset and said that some or all of Sandy's jewelry was gone, his story would have agreed with Kate Rosenlieb's extravagant claims about Sandy's jewelry-wearing habits and bolstered the notion she had been the victim of robbery, kidnapping and murder at the hands of a stranger. A lie about the jewelry might have changed the whole tenor of the initial investigation by making Pat's story of Sandy's disappearance jibe with Rosenlieb's and thereby sound all the more likely. Instead, Pat had told the truth about having all the jewelry at home—and about withholding it from the investigators—and he was pilloried for it. But if Pat were the killer, Laura wondered, wouldn't he have claimed that the jewelry was missing so he could sell it with impunity? Didn't his honesty really suggest his innocence?

"No," Gary Pohlson had told her when she brought up the subject. "It suggests just one thing: A suspect in a criminal case should keep his mouth shut. That's the only thing that could have saved Pat, saying nothing at all. Truth or lies, it didn't matter what Pat had to say once he became a suspect. His words were going to be used against him no matter what."

33   AS THE MARCH 1993 TRIAL DATE APPROACHED, LAURA found herself on the phone almost daily with Pat, trying to keep him from despair while continuing to prepare him for courtroom battle. She had to stave off any repeats of the disastrous tip-off to Detective Soliz that had so undermined his defense at the preliminary hearing in December—a real possibility, she feared, because Pat still did not grasp the fundamental nature of his situation. In his heart, he still seemed to believe that if he just would be allowed to tell his story his way, everything would be fine, the authorities would see the light, and he could go home. With the sting of the mock-trial session fading with time, he had even started talking about wanting to testify again. Laura's response was to keep Pat occupied, putting him to work analyzing police reports and transcripts. It was busywork that, nevertheless, left Pat feeling like he was doing something constructive—and kept him from doing anything destructive.

10

AS THE MARCH 1993 TRIAL DATE APPROACHED, Laura
found herself on the phone almost daily with
Pat, trying to keep him from despair while continuing to prepare him for courtroom battle. She had to
stave off any repeats of the disastrous tip-off to Detective
Soliz that had so undermined his defense at the preliminary hearing in December—a real possibility, she feared,
because Pat still did not grasp the fundamental nature of
his situation. In his heart, he still seemed to believe that if
he just would be allowed to tell his story his way, everything would be fine, the authorities would see the light,
and he could go home. With the sting of the mock-trial
session fading with time, he had even started talking
about wanting to testify again. Laura's response was to
keep Pat occupied, putting him to work analyzing police
reports and transcripts. It was busywork that, nevertheless, left Pat feeling like he was doing something constructive—and kept him from doing anything destructive.

Pat's family, though, was another matter. Laura found
herself helpless to stop Mike Dunn, who contacted at least
three prosecution witnesses on his own—Jerry Lee Coble,
Coble's father, and Marie Gates among them. The defense
team only learned of this after the fact. The three witnesses
would all later claim that Mike tried to bribe them in some

fashion or another so that they would not testify against Pat. Coble would later say he almost took the offer. Marie Gates' allegations, meanwhile, soon spun to wild extremes, as she declared Mike Dunn an evil, powerful man who hired a hit man to accost her and cut off her hair.[82]

When questioned by Pohlson, the Dunns denied any attempt at bribery, saying it was Jerry Coble who extorted money from Mike. Coble, they said, promised to produce evidence that would clear Pat if he was paid off. But he simply took several hundred dollars without delivering, and threatened Mike Dunn with a knife.[83] No one on the defense team knew what to believe.

Then, just before trial, Mike Dunn whisked his mother, Lillian, to his home two hundred miles away in Orange County, where a doctor reported to the court that she would be medically incapable of testifying—despite the fact that, to Laura, she had seemed lucid and fit prior to her departure. This seemed a strange development: Though listed as a prosecution witness, Lillian might have helped Pat's case more because her previous statements to police contradicted some of Marie Gates' most incriminating recollections about Pat's behavior. But it was clear the rest of the family viewed Lillian Dunn as a loose cannon—she did not hesitate, for one thing, to accuse Jennifer Dunn of wrongdoing—and they were relieved that she would not be called as a witness.

All of these various setbacks to Pat's case could have been taken in stride, Laura believed, if not for the other shortcomings she saw arising in the defense case. For one thing, they had been unable to penetrate the shield the DA had erected around Jerry Coble. Laura knew Coble had been an informant in the past, but neither she nor her team could learn anything more. No help came from Soliz, either, who, despite his previous work in narcotics, where Coble was well known, claimed never to have heard of Coble before meeting him at Denny's to discuss Pat Dunn. There were tantalizing but ultimately unprovable hints from one former cop turned private investigator that Coble was a "pocket snitch," a euphemism for an informant who the police kept in reserve—in their pocket, so to speak—ready to be put into action in troublesome cases, just like Pat Dunn's. But that would mean Coble had been instructed by someone in law enforcement to target Pat, and neither Laura nor any of her partners could find the slightest proof to substantiate this tip. She had spent days at the little photo shop where Rex Martin recalled following Coble's green Pontiac. Laura had gone through every receipt and cash-register tape for the month after Sandy disappeared, searching for a transaction that might correspond to Coble's casing of Pat's house, but she came up empty. Laura also searched for "Ray," Coble's drug dealer—someone the police had not even bothered attempting to find—but came up empty there as well. Laura believed Ray did not actually exist, that he had been made up by Coble to pad out his story. If heroin addicts know anything, it's how to contact their dealers. Coble's statement to Soliz that he had no idea how to reach "Ray" was patently implausible, Laura knew, but she could not *prove* it was a lie. And only proof, not hunches, would serve Pat in court.

Frustration also mounted when, three weeks before trial, the district attorney sent Pohlson a packet of typewritten notes from Kate Rosenlieb, the defense's first preview of her story in her own words. The notes presented a radically different—and far more incriminating—ver-

sion of events than what Laura had learned from the
police reports on Rosenlieb. These late revelations
renewed Laura's curiosity about why one of Pat Dunn's
best friends would turn on him so thoroughly and so
vehemently. Pat still was no help on this subject, even
after seeing the notes, and Rosenlieb still would not speak
with Laura or anyone else associated with Pat Dunn's
defense.

It was clear Rosenlieb had become a far more important witness for the prosecution than anticipated—
someone who seemed infinitely more credible than Jerry
Coble. Rosenlieb was a political appointee, smart and
presentable, and had apparently nothing to gain from
lying—a claim Coble could never make. As one of Pat's
dearest friends, Rosenlieb seemingly possessed every reason to give him the benefit of every doubt, and jurors
would inevitably assume that, if she were biased in any
way, it would have to be in Pat's favor. And that made her
a most powerful witness for the prosecution. Her recollections of violent arguments between Sandy and Pat
before the disappearance would sound credible, as would
her portrayal of a less-than-worried Pat unnervingly certain of his wife's death long before her body turned up.
Others would contradict her, of course, and Laura was
sure that Rosenlieb was wrong on some of these very sub-
jective points, given her poor accuracy in other statements to police about Sandy's habits. But in Kate's dramatic retelling, the words she attributed to Pat sounded
like a virtual confession. Indeed, Rosenlieb had come to
believe that Pat had been trying to confess to her in their
conversations all along, and lacked only the nerve to say
it outright.

Now, as told in the newly arrived notes, her emotion-laden story had become far more damaging to Pat than anything the defense had anticipated. (And even then, Pat and his defense team had only part of the story—crucial elements that might have greatly aided them at trial remained missing from the packet sent by the DA.)

Throughout the long investigation of Sandy's murder, and in multiple police interviews, Kate had consistently told Detectives Kline and Soliz the same story of how she learned Sandy was missing: Pat called her on July 3, two days after the disappearance, and told her about it. She hadn't heard anything about it before then, she repeatedly told detectives. It was this July 3 conversation with Pat, along with their meeting the next day, that left Kate so suspicious of her former teacher and dear friend that she reported him to the authorities. His supposedly calm demeanor, his lack of concern, his pronouncement that he feared the worst, his reluctance to go to the sheriff's department with her to report Sandy missing (never mind that he had already done so days before)—all convinced Rosenlieb that the man she loved like a second father was a killer.

It was this rendition that the defense had prepared for. But eight months after Sandy died, on the verge of Pat's trial, Rosenlieb went to Deputy DA John Somers and told him a new, more damning story: She had really learned about Sandy's disappearance a day earlier, on July 2, and not from Pat Dunn, but through a phone call from Bakersfield attorney Teri Bjorn. Somers knew Bjorn was Pat and Sandy Dunn's real estate lawyer, as well as a good friend of Kate, with whom she served on the city planning commission.

According to the revamped story Rosenlieb told the prosecutor, she learned about Sandy's disappearance when Bjorn somewhat breathlessly broke the news. According to Kate, Bjorn had received a call from Pat a day earlier—July 1—*before* he had reported Sandy missing to the sheriff's department. In that call, Pat is supposed to have told Teri about the disappearance, then asked if he could somehow get power of attorney in Sandy's name and thus access to her money.[84]

In other words, Rosenlieb said, Pat had been trying to loot Sandy's accounts, just hours after she supposedly walked off and vanished. Undoubtedly, Kate told the astonished prosecutor, this was because Pat knew Sandy was already dead. Because he killed her.

In this new version, Pat never did call Kate to tell her about Sandy. It was Kate who called Pat the day after hearing from Teri Bjorn, to ask what he was up to. This is when, Rosenlieb now claimed, Pat told her he wasn't doing so good, because, "I can't find Mom." According to her new account, Rosenlieb knew that Pat was a killer before they ever had this conversation. This contradicted her earlier statements to detectives, in which she minutely detailed all the things Pat said and did to first arouse her suspicions. Months later, though, she recalled things differently: "I knew what he had done right away. I didn't have to talk to him."

When the prosecutor asked why she had kept silent for so many months, Kate apologized for deceiving the sheriff's detectives in her earlier statements, but explained that she had been caught in the middle by desperate pleas from Bjorn for her to keep quiet. Attorneys who blab about private communications with clients can be censured or worse, Rosenlieb said, and even if nothing official happened to Bjorn, Kate believed her friend's reputation in the legal community could be ruined.

"This was a big thing over my head. I wanted to tell the police everything, but I couldn't. Teri begged me not to say anything. She said she should never have told me, that it was privileged, that she could be disbarred . . . When I said I wanted to tell everything, she went to her baby, took him out of his crib, held him to her and said, 'He is all I have in the world. You will take my ability to make a living away. And then what about my baby?' "[85]

So Kate had sat on the information for months, she said, and lied to the detectives. (She never explained why, in her original story, she found it necessary to repeatedly insist that Pat called her with the news about Sandy's disappearance, then later change her story to say she called him.) In the end, as the trial approached and she feared Pat might get off, she told the DA she had to reveal the whole story. Almost in tears, she went to Somers' office and confessed everything, apologizing profusely and, knowing that she had probably just ended yet another friendship, asking if there were any way Bjorn could be spared.

Somers, however, was not angry, as she had expected. He was jubilant. Kate Rosenlieb had handed him precisely the evidence he needed to slam Pat Dunn—and his defense team—down hard. If what Rosenlieb was saying was true, it meant the first person Pat called about his missing wife was not the sheriff but his own lawyer—so he could get his hands on Sandy's money. Such a scenario would reveal Pat Dunn as a cold-hearted monster and bolster the prosecutor's argument that the killing was for financial gain—the "special circumstance" that could earn Pat Dunn the longest possible sentence, life without parole. All the prosecutor had to do was find a way to force Teri Bjorn to testify, attorney-client privilege notwithstanding. He began flipping through a law book, then stopped and peered at a page.

"You did the right thing," he told Rosenlieb, his boyish face solemn, though he must have felt like dishing out a high five. "Your friend will be all right. There's a loophole in the law. There's no privilege if the client is trying to commit a fraud or a crime. She can testify about it. If he was asking for a power of attorney—which only Sandy could legally grant—that's a fraud. He was asking his lawyer to help him commit a crime, and that's not privileged."[86]

"That's what he asked for," Rosenlieb excitedly agreed. "Power of attorney."

Kate next handed over seven pages of typewritten notes she had prepared on her views of the murder case, detailing her new story, her contacts with Pat, the way she believed she had spurred the detectives on when they seemed lackadaisical, and how she personally had led them to identify Sandy's body when she read about a corpse found in the desert. Dramatic and breathless, placing their author at the center of much of the action in the case, the notes were assembled many months after the disappearance, penned with the help of tape recordings and a few things Rosenlieb had jotted down over time. Even these original tapes and notes on her conversations with Pat were begun two weeks after Sandy disappeared, rather than immediately after, when her memory remained fresh. Moreover, she destroyed those original notes and recordings, making it impossible to check the accuracy of her newly typed notes.

Somers duly turned over to the defense those new notes, along with his intention to call Teri Bjorn as a prosecution witness, two weeks before trial. This came as a complete surprise to the defense, and all the more difficult to deal with, given Rosenlieb's refusal to speak with Pat's lawyers and investigators.

In a criminal case, late disclosure of information can sometimes lead to sanctions against prosecutors, but in this case, because Somers did not gain this new material until late in the case himself, he did nothing wrong. The problem is, the notes did not tell the whole story. They do not mention that Kate Rosenlieb deceived the police initially, nor do they explain the supposed reason for it: her desire to protect her friend Teri Bjorn.

More importantly, the notes passed on to the defense, written in the form of a journal, stop on August 1, weeks before Jerry Coble came forward, and three months before Pat was arrested and charged. The last entry Kate made in the notes given to the defense concerned her surreptitious surveillance of Pat's house. In it, she explained that she had decided to watch the house without contacting Pat just to make sure that he had not killed himself and that the dogs were fed. "This was the last time I checked," she wrote. "I finally came to grips with the fact that I could not take care of Patrick and that in reality, I had lost them both and I had to let go."

The clear implication of this final journal entry was that Kate, after this point, ceased being involved in the case and in Pat's life. But nothing could be further from the truth. There were more journal entries after that, ones that seemed to display a marked bias against Pat, though they were never given to the defense.[87] Kate, it seems, took a continued, active role in the case, a role that the district attorney knew about yet never revealed.

We're missing something, Laura kept saying, mostly to herself, as she watched the trial date approach and the rest of the defense team's confidence grow. The lawyers had decided they could best counter Kate Rosenlieb simply by keeping Teri Bjorn from testifying, something they felt reasonably sure they could accomplish, given the rigorous confidentiality surrounding communications between clients and lawyers. As for Rosenlieb herself, the defense could take a page from the prosecution's book and argue that her story had changed so radically that it could not be trusted. It all sounded good, but Laura sensed some terrible surprise, some new and unexpected testimony, looming just over the horizon.

As it turned out, Laura's instincts were on the mark: The defense team was missing even more crucial information before the trial of Pat Dunn began—information about witnesses, about evidence, about the police and the prosecution, all of it far more important than anything Kate Rosenlieb had to say. As happened in many other Kern County cases, from the molestation rings to the Offord Rollins prosecution, information that could only have helped Pat's defense and hurt the prosecution was kept secret.

Judge, jury and defense were all kept in the dark. With predictable results.

PART III
Trial and Error

But O the truth, the truth! The many eyes
That look on it! the diverse things they see.
     —GEORGE MEREDITH

All sides in a trial want to hide at least some
of the truth.
     —ALAN M. DERSHOWITZ

1

A S FAR AS LAURA LAWHON WAS CONCERNED, THE trial started slipping downhill before even a single witness was called. The disastrous slide began with Pat's new suit.

When she saw what Pat Dunn wore on the first day of trial, that shiny shapeless suit of brown polyester dug out from some forgotten rack in back of Montgomery Ward, she thought to herself, *We're going to lose. Right or wrong, it's the little things that make or break your case, and they're gonna look at him and say he looks like a used car salesman. A really shifty used car salesman.*

Pat rarely wore suits, and when Laura had gone by his house before the trial to see if anything in the closet would do for trial, she found nothing of any use. But she saw this as an opportunity. She found a local store that specialized in Western wear and picked out a subtly styled sport coat, slacks and boots, an outfit that would give Pat the prosperous look of a rancher, which she felt would go over well in this country-and-western town. Her boss, David Sandberg, however, said no way, take it back. He wanted a tweed jacket with elbow patches, the retired-schoolteacher look, which Laura didn't like, but could have lived with. Instead, Mike Dunn had settled the wardrobe debate for his brother with a quick trip to

Ward's. Pat now sat in court encased in a cheap and ill-fitting coat and open-necked shirt that made him look like someone who otherwise never wore suits—in other words, like a person pretending to be someone he was not. It was exactly the wrong subliminal message to be sending to the jury, Laura told herself. And there was nothing she could do about it.

She couldn't even complain to Pat's lawyer, Gary Pohlson, because over the course of the investigation, her relationship with Sandberg had soured and now she was prohibited from speaking directly with defense attorneys. Sandberg had not wanted Laura on the case in the first place. Early on, he had allowed her to believe that the firm wasn't even going to get the Dunn case, and let her leave on a vacation trip, only to be forced to bring her back because Pohlson wanted Laura involved. Then, during the investigation, he had parceled out assignments to her, but saved witnesses he deemed important for himself. She could not, for instance, interview Pat and Sandy's housekeeper, Cindy Montes, or Ann Kidder, the accountant's secretary who had spoken to Sandy after her disappearance—Sandberg wanted them. Such restrictions created problems, though, as Laura had questions of these witnesses that remained unanswered. Worse still, from Laura's point of view, was the order not to speak directly with Pohlson and the other defense lawyers. She had to report to Sandberg, who would then pass on her information. Laura chafed under these restrictions, but tried to live within them most of the time—something she would later regret.

On that first day of trial, after blanching at the sight of Pat's wardrobe, she sat in a hallway of the Kern County Courthouse, watching prospective jurors emerge after being questioned in court about their backgrounds and biases. Two of them stood near enough for Laura to over-hear them chat and get to know each other. One of them, a man with dark hair and a large wooden cross close around his neck, mentioned that he played in a band.

"Oh, what kind of music do you play?" the other man asked.

"Country-western," the man with the cross said. Then, Laura watched as the musician's mouth drew back in a sneer and his head nodded toward the courtroom doors. "You know, the kind of music those *defense* lawyers would hate." The word *defense* was pronounced with par-ticular disdain.

The men moved off then, headed for the basement cafeteria for coffee and snacks. Laura was horrified. She had worried that the out-of-town attorneys in their expensive suits would be viewed as outsiders, but even she had not expected this sort of hostility. Her first instinct was to run to Pohlson to tell him to make sure to strike the man with the cross from the jury. But she restrained herself, instead telling her boss David Sandberg what she had heard, so that he could pass it on. She followed the chain of command, just as he had asked.

A few hours later, the jury-selection process was com-pleted. Sixteen men and women—twelve jurors and four alternates—had been chosen to decide Pat Dunn's fate. When Laura saw them file out of the courtroom, the man with the cross walked among them. Laura was surprised to see him still on the panel, but figured Pohlson must have had a very good reason for keeping him. She shud-dered, though, when the time came for the members of Pat Dunn's jury to elect a foreman: They chose the man with the cross.

When she saw the suit Pat Dunn wore, and the man

who would serve as foreman of the jury seated in judgment, Laura had a premonition of what no one else on the defense team even guessed at that point: Pat was going to be convicted. Her head told her otherwise, she would later say, for the facts seemed overwhelmingly on Pat's side. But her heart was already breaking.

The rest of the defense team, and Pat Dunn himself, walked into court still brimming with confidence. In his opening statement to the jury, Gary Pohlson launched the promising strategy that he and his colleagues had plotted out months before, announcing that the case was about Jerry Coble and nothing else. The government had but one significant witness, the defense lawyer said, and if you believe him, go ahead and send Pat Dunn to prison. But that wouldn't happen, Pohlson predicted, looking into the eyes of the jurors, who seemed attentive and receptive at this early stage of the case. Coble would be revealed as a liar, a cheat and a con man. His claim that he saw Pat Dunn dispose of his wife's body was a concoction, the lawyer promised to prove, a frame job handed to police detectives willing to accept just about anything if it allowed them to make an arrest. Without Jerry Coble, Pohlson asserted, all of the other prosecution witnesses will prove just one thing: that the sheriff and the DA built the case on bias, misplaced suspicion and investigative incompetence, without a shred of hard evidence to back it up.

Pohlson paced a bit as he spoke, a comforting figure in the courtroom, stocky and middle-aged, his voice never raised. He had handled many tough murder cases in his regular practice in Orange County, and he had a good reputation on his home turf—though here in Kern

County, that didn't count for much. But he was earnest in his presentation, straightforward and plainspoken, never slick, never sounding like he was hiding something or talking down to his audience. Laura thought he got off to a good start.

"This case is about Jerry Coble, pure and simple," the defense lawyer said, supremely confident in his ability to skewer Coble as a witness, and that nothing else in the case mattered.

But Pohlson's opponent at the prosecution table, Deputy DA John Somers, had already decided that his star witness might also be his greatest liability. So, in his opening statement, and throughout his long presentation of witnesses, Somers all but ignored Jerry Lee Coble. Instead, he focused on ostensibly minor witnesses, people who talked about Pat's demeanor, Sandy's mental state and the couple's finances. Somers was going for a portrait of Pat as a cold, unfeeling man fully capable of murder, who coveted his wife's money and who could not be trusted to tell the truth. He didn't need Coble for that. It was a bold, risky and somewhat unexpected strategy, and it delighted Gary Pohlson.

"He can't win that way. We've got an answer for all of it and none of it proves a thing," Pohlson told Pat, who had sat stiff and morose throughout Somers' opening remarks. "He's talking smoke and suspicion—it's like he's ashamed of the meat of his case. Jurors can sense that."

And, for a time, it appeared that Pohlson was right, for Somers' strategy fared poorly at the outset and the early breaks clearly cut Pat's way. News reporters and court-room observers began, like the defense team, predicting an acquittal, as prosecution witnesses began saying things John Somers did not want to hear. As he had talked about

Pat's behavior, his alleged fights with Sandy and his motive to kill, the prosecutor had made a number of promises to the jury—promises he could not keep.

He said, for one thing, that his witnesses would clearly reveal Pat's motive for murder: Sandy controlled the purse strings in the family and had instructed her investment brokers to keep Pat in the dark about her money. This enraged Pat, Somers asserted, setting the stage for vicious arguments, then fatal violence, between the Dunns.

Somers next promised evidence to show that the Dunns' marriage had been crumbling for some time, and that the couple was overheard by a neighbor quarreling bitterly just one day before Sandy disappeared.

The catalyst for the murder, Somers vowed to prove, was the Dunns' meeting with financial advisor Kevin Knutson, on the very day Sandy vanished, in which Pat Dunn seemed stunned to learn that he was the sole beneficiary of Sandy's will. This was the moment Pat decided to kill his wife, the prosecutor suggested, the knowledge that he could finally get his hands on Sandy's money being the trigger that set his deadly plans into motion.

Finally, Somers promised the jury would hear of an exterminator who stopped by the Dunns' house to do monthly spraying after Knutson had left. Pat, the prosecutor asserted, gave the bug man a wink and a nod and said he could spare himself a little time and effort by skipping the office, a separate room detached from the house and out by the swimming pool. Somers did not spell out the significance of this, but his implication was clear: He wanted jurors to conclude Pat had killed Sandy late in the afternoon, after Knutson left but before the exterminator arrived, stashed her body in the office, then waited until 1 A.M. to dispose of the corpse, when he would be spotted by Jerry Coble.

An important point of corroboration here, Somers told the jury, was the fact that the Dunns' cleaning lady, Cindy Montes, had telephoned at five the following morning to confirm her appointment, with Pat Dunn answering out of breath and with the sound of water running in the background. The timing of all this left just enough time for Pat to have driven the sixty miles to Sandy's mountainous burial site, where he dug a hasty grave, then returned for a quick cleaning of the bloody mess he had left behind.

"It all fits together," Somers said. "The evidence points to only one possible conclusion: Pat Dunn is guilty."

In opening statements, this scenario did indeed sound compelling, even to Laura. But it soon fell apart for the prosecutor, who had been relying upon Detective Soliz's reports on the case, rather than his own firsthand interviews, for most of these facts. And as Laura knew they would, witness after witness took the stand and said the detective had misquoted or misunderstood them, leaving Somers' far-reaching promises largely unfulfilled.

First, Kevin Knutson remembered Pat as not at all surprised by Sandy's will during their meeting that last day of Sandy's life. Detective Soliz had gotten that wrong, Knutson said. Nor was the Dunns' marriage in trouble, he went on; Sandy had told him that she wanted Knutson to arrange things to allow Pat more access to her money, and to make sure he would be well taken care of if anything happened to her.

Then the exterminator took the witness stand and said he had done his work at the Dunns' house *before* the time Knutson left, which meant Sandy could not have

been dead in the office when the exterminator arrived—
she had hugged Knutson good-bye more than an hour
later. John Somers and Detective Soliz had gotten that
wrong, too.

Then the man who had been Sandy's investment broker since 1988, Roger Norwood, also complained that
Detective Soliz's report on their interview was inaccurate. The report—and Somers' representations of it to
the jury—starkly contradicted the actual state of affairs.
Norwood swore Sandy had never wanted Pat kept in the
dark about her investments—in fact, Pat participated in
most every decision made regarding Sandy's money, he
said.[1] The whole theory of motive laid out by Somers
for the jury—that Pat deeply resented Sandy's control of
the purse strings and seized an opportunity to kill her
for profit upon learning of the will—had been shot
down.

Then there was the testimony of Cindy Montes, the
housecleaner. Under Somers' straightforward questioning, Montes first explained how her normal cleaning day
for the Dunns fell on Wednesday, but that she did not go
to the house on Wednesday, July 1, the day Pat reported
Sandy missing. Now, here was something Somers had
expected to hear. He anticipated that Montes next would
explain this failure to clean on Wednesday by describing
how she had called to confirm that morning, but an out-
of-breath Pat picked up the phone and canceled. Again,
though, Somers was taken by surprise by his own witness: Montes began telling jurors a completely different
story.

The housecleaner explained that Pat and Sandy had
instructed her days earlier not to come that Wednesday.
"They had an appointment that week, and I had made

prior arrangements to go in on the Tuesday before, and I was to show up at five in the morning. And I called that morning to just let them know I was heading over. And Mr. Dunn answered the phone, and at that time he said that he wanted to cancel and that we should reschedule."

This testimony eroded the prosecution's case even more. Montes had just repeated the same thing she had said months ago to David Sandberg, but then later retracted: that she had called the Dunns at five in the morning on Tuesday, June 30, sixteen hours *before* Sandy vanished. In other words, the fact that Cindy recalled the notoriously out-of-shape Pat being out of breath, that she heard water running in the background, and that he canceled cleaning on June 30, meant nothing. Sandy was alive and well at the time—maybe it was her in the shower when Montes heard the water running. So, just as Knutson and Norwood undermined his theory of motive, Montes shot Somers' whole timetable for the crime. If Cindy Montes had gone on to explain how Detective Soliz had told her that her information about the case was "significant," and that therefore she figured her cancellation from Pat Dunn must have happened on Wednesday, July 1, after all, the entire prosecution case might have died then and there.

But John Somers could not allow this to stand, and he didn't. Remaining cool and outwardly unconcerned, he simply asked a leading question that contradicted what Montes had just said—and seemed to lead her to change her testimony more to suit Somers' theory of the case.

"You indicated it was five that you called," the prosecutor said. "Was that five A.M. on *Wednesday,* July 1?"

Montes looked at him. She and Detective Soliz had discussed in detail how important her testimony was to the case, that it *must* have been the day Sandy disappeared when she called. To stick with her initial answer that she had called on Tuesday would mean her observations really added nothing to the prosecution's case, that she had nothing "worthwhile" to contribute. After a moment, she answered, "Yes, correct."

The prosecution of Pat Dunn was back on track.[2] This time, for good.

2

FOR A WHILE, IT SEEMED THAT PAT DUNN MIGHT BE
marching toward acquittal and the district attorney headed for an embarrassing defeat. But after
that pivotal moment with the housecleaner, the breaks
began going John Somers' way.

When the Dunns' least favorite neighbor, Otis
Coppock, took the stand, he, too, told a story that differed from the account in Detective Soliz's report. But
this time, the contradictions helped Somers, giving him a
new theory to argue, one even better than the flagging
one with which he started. Soliz had written in his report
that Coppock heard Sandy and Pat arguing around five
or five thirty in the afternoon on June 29, more than
twenty-four hours before Sandy vanished. Coppock was
too hard of hearing to know what the argument was
about—in fact, he had heard only Sandy's voice, not
Pat's—but he claimed to have seen her drive away in the
Dunns' Chevy Blazer, looking very angry. He recalled that
he had heard loud fights between the Dunns in the past
as well. Since this happened a day before Kevin Knutson's
meeting to discuss Sandy's living trust, the defense considered Otis' testimony marginal at best.

However, on the stand, Coppock joined the long line
of witnesses claiming that Detective Soliz had gotten the

facts wrong. Now Coppock testified that he had overheard Sandy yelling and angrily driving off on June 30—
not a day before Sandy vanished, but just a few *hours*
before. By his recollection of the time, this would have
been an hour after Kevin Knutson hugged Sandy good-
bye. Before Coppock said this, Knutson had been the last
person other than Pat to see Sandy alive, and he had said
the Dunns seemed happy and content when he left. That
was bad testimony for Somers, good for Pat.

Now, even though it contradicted his opening statement, Somers could argue that Otis Coppock was the last
person to see Sandy alive, and that the Dunns had fought
furiously enough that evening for Sandy to storm off in a
rage, driving fast and erratically as she tore out of the
driveway. And as Pat Dunn had denied to the police that
there had been any argument at all between him and
Sandy that day, Otis' new story provided the added bonus
of making Pat out to be a liar.

And why lie, Somers asked, unless he killed his wife?
The prosecutor immediately dropped his theory about
the exterminator and the body hidden in the office as
Otis' unexpected testimony made that an impossible scenario anyway. Now he claimed that the Dunns had
argued so viciously and irreconcilably that last night that
Pat saw himself with no choice but to kill Sandy or be left
homeless and penniless by divorce. It was a stunning
example of just how fluid the "truth" is in a trial, how not
only the defense can shift its story to accommodate the
ebb and flow of evidence, but how the prosecution can
alter its key positions as well, and without ever questioning the underlying, bedrock premise that a defendant is
guilty. In this case, Somers made such a shift, even
though it meant conceding that the lead detective on the

case had erred in his reports. Altering the "theory of the case"—the *interpretation* of the evidence, as opposed to the evidence itself—is perfectly legal. Indeed, the United States Supreme Court has found nothing amiss when a Texas prosecutor, in successive trials, accused two different people of being the lone triggerman in the same murder. Using two utterly contradictory theories, a prosecutor won the death penalty for one man, then repudiated his own evidence from that case to go after another defendant for the same crime.[3]

Gary Pohlson, of course, went after Otis Coppock. First the defense lawyer argued that the contradiction in times—June 29 or June 30—made it impossible to know what the truth was. Second, he complained that Otis really didn't know what Sandy said during the argument, and got him to admit he couldn't hear Pat at all. For all Otis knew, Sandy could have been yelling at the dogs for barking too loudly, rather than shouting at Pat. (Pat later claimed that Sandy was actually yelling at Otis, whom she despised—but without Pat taking the stand, there was no way to tell this to the jury.) Coppock's enmity toward Pat also was offered as a source of bias, but the damage had been done. Somers' negative portrait of Pat had begun to take shape. None of this made him a murderer, not yet, but it did set the stage, with images of angry tirades and careening cars. And this gave the DA his first clear victory in the trial.

At this point, Laura began to see just how badly the defense had underestimated Deputy District Attorney John Somers. It had been easy to do, she realized, particularly for those who didn't live and work in Kern County. Somers was small and boyish in appearance, seeming both younger and more inexperienced than he really was. With rumpled, inexpensive suits and tousled brown hair, he had an air about him that all but begged to be under-estimated—a misjudgment he had used to his advantage time and again. He did not traffic in the hard-line rhetoric that had made his boss, Ed Jagels, a legend, nor was he ever tarred by the allegations of misconduct that sometimes plagued other prosecutors in the Kern County District Attorney's Office—though more than once he has been called upon to defend their work and to save it from reversal.

For the most part, Somers was known on both sides of the Bakersfield legal community as a man of reason and integrity. He avoided flash and drama in the courtroom; his style was to remain quiet, exceedingly polite and def-erential. He seldom attacked witnesses with aggressive cross-examination unless he absolutely had to—but when he did, he could be startlingly effective. He didn't live for the "Perry Mason moment," that mostly mythical, cathar-tic revelation that so often turns the tide of a television court case and even, on occasion, figures into a real-life trial, as when a former football star tried on a pair of blood-caked gloves in a Los Angeles courtroom. Somers preferred to slowly build a fortress of a case, a gradual, almost imperceptible assembling of small blocks that in the end crushed the defense under its sheer weight—less a knockout punch than the slow squeeze of a boa con-strictor. He believed wholeheartedly in the maxim that, as children, prosecutors loved to build things, while future defense lawyers enjoyed kicking things down. And so he always tried to build cases too strong to be uprooted by even the toughest courtroom bully. Attorneys often thought they were beating John Somers right up to the end of the case, only to sit mesmerized as he assembled all those little pieces into one coherent mosaic in his closing argument. And then they'd watch, palms suddenly gone sweaty, as one by one, the jurors began to nod in agreement while Somers spoke, as if to say, *Yeah, it was there all the time.* More than one lawyer in Bakersfield had experienced this moment, when they would turn to look at John Somers with new respect—and vow never to underestimate him again.

There was a reason, after all, that Somers ranked as one of his office's top prosecutors, no small accomplishment in a DA's operation that tried more felonies and sent more people to prison per capita than any other California county. Juries loved his homespun charm; he liked to throw in a mention here or there of his humble origins in Missouri, and he could be seen during the Dunn trial piously crossing himself as jurors entered the courtroom. But as good as he was with juries, his legal acumen carried just as high a value in the Kern County District Attorney's office: Somers was the lawyer Ed Jagels sought out to shore up the molestation-ring prosecutions when they began crumbling on appeal. Somers waded through the tens of thousands of pages accumulated in those cases, an entire room filled with materials, and found ways to fend off successful appeals and *habeas corpus* writs for years. He seemed to genuinely believe in the righteousness of his cause—one of the qualities that made him so formidable in court—but the net effect of his dedication was to keep men and women in prison for many years longer than they otherwise might have stayed behind bars until finally, in the end, they were cleared and set free.

In the trial of Pat Dunn, Somers slowly assembled, witness by witness, his puzzle-piece portrait of Pat as someone who had acted in a completely bizarre fashion and who was entirely capable of killing. Laura could feel the momentum building in the prosecutor's favor, though the rest of the defense team still felt certain that the prosecution couldn't win that way, especially after they finished with Jerry Coble.

Somers' evidence of marital discord between Sandy and Pat revolved around a few acquaintances' recollections of Pat growing angry at Sandy, usually during discussions of the movie-theater development that had been rejected by the city council. One of them, Roger McIntosh, the engineer on the project, described again how, during a project meeting, Pat told Sandy to shut up, then made a move toward his wife, causing her to retreat. (Others present at the meeting later recalled no such incident, with one pointing out that they were all seated around a large conference table, making the notion of Pat lunging at Sandy, and her backing off, an impossibility.)

Somers also turned to Ken Peterson, then a city council member (later he became a member of the Kern County Board of Supervisors), who spoke of a conference call with the Dunns during which Pat and Sandy argued about the development project, then hung up on him. Peterson also remembered another conversation in which Pat proclaimed himself "finished financially" if the project fell through, adding to the prosecution's notion that Pat was somehow desperate for money at the time of Sandy's death. (Pohlson disputed Peterson on this, pointing out that Detective Soliz's initial interview report on the councilman stated only that Pat would be "finished," which could be interpreted to mean he simply would give up attempts to develop that particular piece of land. Peterson, however, joined the chorus of witnesses who said Soliz wrote the statement down wrong. In any case, the substance of Peterson's statement simply was not true, Pohlson argued: The demise of the project would not have finished Pat financially. Though the eighty to one hundred thousand dollars the Dunns had spent readying the property for construction would represent a substantial loss for them, the Dunns possessed assets of over a million dollars in cash and millions more in real estate at the time of Sandy's death. Besides, the money was Sandy's to lose, not Pat's. Why, Pohlson reminded jurors, would he be desperate?)

Then there was Kate Rosenlieb, brought in by Somers to swear that the Dunns fought constantly and with increasing ferocity toward the end. Her testimony, surprisingly brief, was delivered with typical dramatic flair, as she seemed intent upon saying what she wanted to say—most of it to Pat's detriment—regardless of what the lawyers asked. To Laura, her responses seemed pitched in a way that made them as harmful to Pat's case as possible. For instance, when asked by a prosecutor if she saw Pat drink alcohol, instead of a simple yes, she responded, "I don't think I ever saw Mr. Dunn that he wasn't drinking." When asked if the Dunns argued, Pat's dear friend answered not yes or no, but, "There were tremendous fights, tremendous fights." When asked if Pat had been crying or upset by Sandy's disappearance, Kate didn't say no, not so far as she could see. She said, "Not in the least." Twice. Her choice of phrase said as much as the words themselves.

Kate also recalled that, when she asked Pat to go to the sheriff's department to report Sandy missing—something he had already done—his response terrified her: He had said it was too late, that he feared the worst, that Sandy already was dead, and that he didn't want anyone to know. There were charitable interpretations to all of these statements, but neither Kate nor Somers could give Pat the benefit of the doubt. Laura looked over at Pat to see how he was reacting to all this, but he looked dazed. He seemed to be shrinking before her eyes, as if he, too, saw what was coming.

Kate went on to provide Somers with some other key bits for his growing puzzle. She said Pat had once complained that Sandy wore too much jewelry on her early morning walks, and from that statement Rosenlieb and Somers then implied, incorrectly, that this remained Sandy's practice until the day she died. One of the first things Kate recalled asking Pat after Sandy vanished was whether her jewelry was gone, too. Pat told her no, it wasn't—all the jewelry was at the house, causing Kate to wonder how that could be, if Sandy always wore it— unless Pat's story was a lie. Now Somers had something else with which to attack Pat's defense.

When Somers was through with Rosenlieb, Gary Pohlson decided not to attack her credibility for changing her story and lying to the police. If he went after her hard, Pohlson feared she might blurt out something even worse, perhaps about the attorney Teri Bjorn. At that stage in the trial, the judge had not yet ruled on whether Bjorn could testify about her conversation with Pat about Sandy's disappearance, money and power of attorney, and Rosenlieb had not mentioned her during her direct testimony. Pohlson wanted to keep it that way. Kate left the stand blinking in surprise, astonished that she hadn't been roasted alive.

Pohlson took the same hands-off approach with Marie Gates, even though her testimony ended up doing much more damage to Pat than Kate Rosenlieb's had.

Gates repeated her story about running into a distraught and weeping Sandy one day in mid-June, two weeks or so before the disappearance (which Somers continually characterized as a "few days" before). Marie recalled for the jury how she heard Sandy announce her plans to divorce her husband because she had made a "terrible mistake" in marriage. And she recalled how Pat grew coldly angry after Sandy disappeared and ordered both his mother and Marie to stop talking about Sandy and to "Keep your dang mouths shut" because it would all "blow over." Laura and the defense team listened to this, frustrated, as they knew from interviewing Lillian Dunn that Pat's mother could refute this last claim. But Lillian was unavailable, thanks to Pat's brother Mike spiriting her off to Orange County.

Instead of grilling Gates, Pohlson tried to counter her emotional testimony by recalling to the stand Kevin Knutson, who said Sandy's last words to him were instructions to set up a trust that would give Pat greater control over their finances, so that, as she explained, "If anything happened to me, Pat would be taken care of." These were not the words of a woman about to divorce a husband, Knutson suggested.

But Pohlson did not go after Marie Gates directly, a tactical decision that left Laura uneasy, though she conceded it appeared to make sense at the time. Pointing out each of Marie's inconsistencies would have been a time-consuming exercise that could easily confuse the jury as well as introduce extraneous allegations that Marie had spouted in the past. It should have been clear from Knutson's testimony that Marie was just plain wrong, Pohlson reasoned, and Laura tended to agree. Why risk alienating the jury by attacking the grandmotherly woman? Even if the jury believed her, and Kate Rosenlieb, for that matter, Pohlson felt little damage was done. So what if the Dunns had arguments? So what if Sandy threatened him with divorce two weeks earlier, a threat she never acted on? If that proved murder, then half of the men in America could be on trial here, Pohlson said. Pat wasn't on trial for being a bad husband, nor was it a crime to be happy your spouse died, as Somers seemed to be suggesting. The prosecutor had to link Pat Dunn to the crime of murder itself, and for that, he needed Jerry Coble. And Gary Pohlson just knew he'd burn the chair out from under that witness. Eager to get to the meat of the case, he let Marie Gates go after just a few minutes of cross-examination, seemingly unconcerned by her testimony.

But if Pohlson's logic was so sound, Laura found herself thinking, why, then, did John Somers look so remarkably content? Sure, the prosecutor had just established at least some evidence of a motive, and he had a timetable for the killings, thanks to changing details in the stories of a neighbor and housecleaner. But if he was worried about an approaching courtroom land mine named Jerry Lee Coble, Laura couldn't see it. Instead, as he approached the heart of his case—something he had to know the defense was well prepared to attack—he looked positively delighted with the course of the trial. And that worried Laura.

The reason for Somers' contentment would soon become clear. The prosecutor had indeed reached the heart of this case. But to everyone's surprise, he did not use the words of Jerry Coble to get there.

He used the words of Pat Dunn.

3

JOHN SOMERS HAD DECIDED TO MAKE PAT DUNN, NOT Jerry Coble, his best witness. Pat didn't have to take the stand for this. In fact, the strategy worked better with the defendant sitting mute, looking befuddled and angry on the sidelines—a posture Pat seemed to be adopting with increasing regularity as the trial progressed.

No, the prosecutor didn't need Pat on the stand to use his own words against him. Instead, Somers pulled out sheriff's reports, transcripts and a host of witnesses to chronicle every utterance Pat had made about Sandy's disappearance over the course of months. Every minor detail, every niggling discrepancy, every inconsistency— what Somers called "the lies"—became fodder for a full-scale assault on Pat's credibility and character.

The prosecutor knew, as did Gary Pohlson, that there were no smoking guns in this case, no hard evidence that fingered Pat as a murderer—just Coble. But he also knew that the law allowed juries to decide that a defendant's lies about important facts in a case could prove "consciousness of guilt," the theory being that innocent people tell one consistent and truthful story, while the guilty weave a web of falsehoods to cover their tracks. Keeping track of the lies can be difficult, the theory goes, which leads to inconsistencies. A classic prosecution axiom is that the truth never changes, only lies do—at least when the words are the defendant's.

To demonstrate this principle, Somers brought in a procession of witnesses who purported to prove that Pat could not keep the story of Sandy's disappearance straight. The fact that Pat was so cooperative, talking to the detectives many times for many hours—and drinking copiously before and sometimes during these interrogations—ended up being used against him in this regard. Every inconsistency, real or imagined, arising during these many conversations became evidence of guilt in Somers' carefully crafted presentation. There were no big whoppers to be found in Pat's many statements about Sandy's disappearance, no inconsistency that could be proved an outright lie in the traditional sense. So Somers went for quantity, knowing that while one or two minor deviations in Pat's story would seem like niggling details, ten or twelve might have a far different impact on the jury. Somers even produced a huge chart of the "lies" for the jury's benefit, a virtual road map of deceit he said proved Pat Dunn could not tell the truth about the simplest matters.

First in this lineup came Valley Braddick, the dispatcher at the sheriff's department who took Pat's missing-persons report late in the afternoon following Sandy's disappearance. On the tape of the call, jurors heard Pat giving his first rendition of what happened to Sandy. He was somewhat vague on details, saying at various junctures that he woke up to find his wife missing at nine, nine-thirty, or ten o'clock at night. It was clear he hadn't been keeping track of exact times, and thus expressed uncertainty. Then, he said, at nine thirty or ten he started driving around looking for his wife and asking everyone he encountered if they had seen her. He returned home around midnight, then spotted the black dog in the yard and Sandy's keys on the counter—both of which he thought had previously been missing. He immediately resumed his search in the wake of this discovery, first around the house, then back out on the streets. He returned around two, went to sleep for a couple hours, then recommenced the search at four thirty.

Point by point, this first account matched the statements he would next make to sheriff's detectives. But Somers, anxious to build in as many contradictions in Pat's story as he could find, misquoted the tape, telling jurors in argument and on his big chart that Pat informed the dispatcher he "got up and drove around from nine to twelve." This was incorrect—Pat had given a range of possible times, from nine to ten for his discovery that Sandy was gone. Even the prosecutor, who was so critical of Pat's inconsistencies and so certain that they revealed a guilty state of mind, apparently could not keep all the times straight, either.

Pat Dunn explained this sequence of events next to Kate Rosenlieb, who then recounted it to Detective Dusty Kline. Kline, in turn, recorded Rosenlieb's story in an official report. According to this thirdhand account, Sandy went to bed at 6 P.M. on July 2. Rosenlieb made a mistake here, one of greater magnitude than any Pat could be accused of making, as the true date in question was June 30. Somers carefully avoided mentioning the July 2 error—he even told the jury that Rosenlieb had said it was June 30 all along. Otherwise, this account exactly mirrors what Pat told the dispatcher—in fact, he told the same consistent story to Rosenlieb twice, on July 3 and July 4.

Yet Somers still argued that Pat was being deceitful, on account of his supposedly telling Rosenlieb that he did not want to report Sandy missing because, as Kate put it, "he didn't want anyone to know." The obvious conclusion to be made here—since Pat already had filed a missing-persons report days before this conversation with Kate—was that Rosenlieb was the incorrect or inconsistent one, not Pat. Instead, the prosecutor listed this statement about not wanting anyone to know as another of Pat's "lies." The sheriff's department already did know, the prosecutor said, yet Pat concealed this fact from Kate—a lie. Why a murderer would lie to a friend to make himself look *more* suspicious was never explained, yet that was Somers' curious argument to the jury.

After his talks with Kate Rosenlieb, Pat next gave an account of the disappearance to Detective Kline directly. Again, what Kline heard mirrored all the other renditions, except Kline wrote in his report that Pat returned home from his second bout of searching at 4 A.M. and slept until 6—a two-hour discrepancy from the statement to Valley Braddick, which Somers seized upon as another "lie." This is the first genuine inconsistency in the prosecutor's litany. Kline, however, did not write notes or tape-record as he interviewed Pat, instead crafting his report a full day later. The defense argued that it was just as likely the detective made the mistake in chronology as it was Pat, given the poor record of accuracy in other sheriff's reports in the Dunn case.

But Somers wanted to show a pattern of deceit and he kept at it, with no detail too small to earn a place on his chart of lies. He brought in the engineer, Roger McIntosh, who, seven weeks after the fact, had told detectives about a conversation in which Pat supposedly gave

yet another time for Sandy's last, fatal walk. McIntosh put
the time at two-thirty or three in the morning, instead of
the nine to ten o'clock range that Pat had told everyone
else. Somers pronounced this "the biggest and most
major conflict in his statements," though the prosecutor
expressed no such concern when McIntosh could not
remember other details of this long-ago conversation—
the one incriminating fact was enough. Laura, for her
part, reckoned that the engineer simply confused Sandy's
normal waking and walking hour with the time of her
disappearance.

Another witness, Judith Paola Penney, the late Pat
Paola's niece, was summoned to provide proof of Pat's
supposed lies, but she ended up being the one with
inconsistent recollections. She testified that Pat had told
her of noticing Sandy missing at one o'clock in the morning—which would be a discrepancy—except that Penney
had previously told detectives that Pat said three o'clock.
On the stand, she admitted that her memory on the subject was vague. Yet despite this, Somers put only one set
of times on his chart where it referred to Penney, making
her appear far more reliable in her recollections than was
warranted.

Pat gave another statement to Detectives Soliz and
Kline on July 9, nine days after Sandy vanished.
According to Soliz's report on this interview, Pat reiterated the same basic story and times he had given in all of
his other statements to police. Every detail was consistent
except for one small point: Soliz reported Pat arrived
home at 10:30 P.M. to find the dog in the yard and the car
keys on the counter, when earlier statements placed this
at midnight. Neither detective seemed to notice this discrepancy at the time, although they immediately

pounced on and demanded explanation for any inconsistencies arising in other areas of questioning. As was his practice, Soliz used no tape recorder and took few notes during this interview with Pat, and he waited three weeks to document it. The defense pointed out this delay, arguing that it was just as likely that Soliz had made this minor mistake as Pat.

Finally, Somers turned to the marathon interrogation of July 23, when a team of three investigators questioned Pat nonstop all night while others searched the house for clues to link him to the murder. Again, no notes and no tape recordings were made, while the three detectives took turns interrogating Pat. Their quarry was apparently so consistent in his statements that night that the detectives did not bother to submit separate reports detailing what he said to each of them. Instead, Soliz summarized for his colleagues by simply writing: "Dunn kept giving the same answers or he would say he had already answered those questions and for us to ask new questions."

However, out of that fifteen hours of search and interrogation, Somers still managed to find one alleged inconsistency from the police report: At one point, Somers stated, Pat told Detective Soliz that Sandy went to bed at 3:30 or 4:00 in the afternoon, though previously he had always said she went to bed at 5:30 or 6:00—another glaring example, Somers argued, of how "it was getting tough to keep his story straight."

The problem with this point was that it, too, was as questionable as most of the others. On the witness stand, Somers asked Soliz about the July 23 interrogation, wanting to know when Pat said Sandy went to bed that last night. Detective Soliz immediately responded, "To the best of my recollection, it was about 5:30 or 6:00 P.M."—completely consistent with Pat's other statements, and contrary to the prosecutor's big chart. Only after a perturbed Somers suggested that Soliz take another look at his report—this one was written seven days after the interrogation—did the detective change his testimony to say Pat had said 3:30 or 4:00.

The jury had no way of knowing it, but even after looking at his report, Soliz didn't quote it quite accurately in his testimony. The report did not say 3:30 or 4:00, as he claimed. It says Sandy went to bed at 15:30 or 16:00, using the twenty-four-hour "military" time equivalent of 3:30 or 4:00 P.M. It is also one simple typographical error away from 5:30 or 6:00—the times Soliz initially remembered when questioned on the matter.

In short, a majority of the discrepancies cited by Somers can be disproved, explained or dismissed as the recollections of witnesses who were at least as inconsistent as Pat Dunn was made out to be. And even if there were a few small inconsistencies here and there, the defense argued, they meant little. Did saying four in the morning instead of two in the morning make Pat a murderer? Or just a confused, stressed-out husband who had a habit of drowning his grief in alcohol?

Still, Somers knew that the simple visual presentation of all of those entries on his chart would leave an indelible impression on the jury. Never mind that many of them were reaching, highly questionable or just plain wrong. When the arguing was over and the lawyers sat down, the prosecutor knew that big chart of "lies" would still be there, helping the jury decide what to think about Pat Dunn.

•   •   •

Still avoiding Jerry Lee Coble, Somers next turned to another important element of his case: attempting to prove only Pat had the *opportunity* to kill Sandy. As in all of Somers' cases, there were several components to this theory that fit together like puzzle pieces into a neat whole. First, Pat told detectives that Sandy slept in the nude, and her body was found naked rather than in her normal walking clothes. From this, Somers asked jurors to conclude she must have been killed in bed. Next, there was the fact that a pair of Sandy's glasses and her jewelry remained in the house—a grave discrepancy in Pat Dunn's story, Somers argued, because Sandy *always* wore her glasses and jewelry on her walks. Finally, the prosecutor accused Pat of telling an unintentionally revealing lie, one that only a man who committed the murder would tell: Pat, according to Somers, had claimed that Sandy was wearing a blue jogging jacket when she disappeared—yet that jacket later turned up in the Dunn home.

"The defendant told the police and others that she was wearing that garment when she left the house. . . . The fact of the matter is that that jacket was still at the house because Sandy Dunn didn't leave the house wearing it. She left the house wrapped in sheets and a blanket or something similar—because she was dead."

Again, the prosecutor had formulated a persuasive argument, weaving together a pastiche of small bits of circumstantial evidence that, alone, proved little, but that together might amount to something—were they true.

But the fact that Sandy's body was found nude really proved very little. The bodies of people kidnapped, molested and murdered by strangers outside the home have on occasion turned up unclothed, even in Kern County. Dana Butler, for instance, was found only par-

tially clad, with the rest of her clothing never recovered—
but no one suggested this meant she had to have been
killed while home in bed. And there were signs that Sandy
could have been attacked by some sort of sexual predator,
as her body had been mutilated in the rectal-genital area.
For the killer to have done that to her, she would have had
to be stripped. (Rape could not be proven or ruled out,
due to the advanced state of decomposition.)

As for the jogging jacket that Somers found so devastating, the truth was that Pat Dunn never said he *knew*
Sandy had worn it that night. Contrary to the prosecutor's argument, Pat initially said he had no way of knowing what Sandy was wearing, because he was asleep when
she left. It's right on the tape-recorded call of Pat reporting Sandy missing: "I don't know, because she has a ton
of clothes." He merely described the blue jacket as part of
her general walking ensemble, along with a variety of
T-shirts, blue jeans, shorts and white tennis shoes she
favored. Later, he told detectives he had looked in the
laundry room where Sandy normally changed for her
early-morning walks to avoid waking him, and because
he did not see the jacket or other walking clothes in there,
he surmised she had worn them that last night. In subsequent reports, the detectives simply wrote those were the
clothes Sandy wore, despite Pat's expressed uncertainty.
But it is clear that, at the outset, Pat simply guessed at
what Sandy had worn for her walk when she disappeared.

Sometime after Sandy's disappearance, the housecleaner, Cindy Montes, found a woman's blue jogging
jacket hanging with other clothing in a hall closet—a different location than the one Pat searched. The discovery
of the blue jacket, Somers said, showed Pat had been
lying. But contrary to the prosecutor's argument, there

was nothing inconsistent, inaccurate or even vaguely suspicious about this—the most Pat could be guilty of was not looking thoroughly through every closet in the house for Sandy's jogging jacket.

Then there was the matter of Sandy's glasses. Most people who knew her did say, as Somers argued, that Sandy almost always wore her glasses, even though her eye doctor had explained to Laura Lawhon that Sandy only needed them for reading. Cindy Montes, in particular, testified that when she would get to the Dunns' house early in the morning to clean, Sandy still would be in her walking clothes—and always had her glasses on. So when Sandy's glasses were found at home, Somers said, that again showed she never left the house that last night, at least not alive. Only Pat, then, had the opportunity to kill her. Somers failed to mention, however, that the police had established that Sandy owned multiple pairs of glasses, some of them prescription, some bought at the drugstore, which meant she could have been wearing any one of a number of pairs that night, just as she could have been wearing clothes other than the blue jacket. (There was also the possibility that, if Pat were being truthful about Sandy's deteriorating mental state, she could have simply forgotten the glasses.)

Then there was the jewelry. Much was made of Pat's admission that he had all of the jewelry at home and that none of it was missing. Had the jewelry been missing, it would have supported the notion that Sandy had been robbed or murdered during a walk, Somers said. But that was not the case. Relying on Kate Rosenlieb's testimony (though Kate had never seen Sandy in her walking attire and had exaggerated the value of her jewelry by a factor of ten), Somers argued that Sandy *always* went walking with her jewelry on. So the fact that Pat said she didn't wear it and that all her jewelry was at home showed that she had died nude in bed and that Pat Dunn had lied to cover his tracks, Somers declared.

But this scenario couldn't hold up, either. During her testimony, Cindy Montes hadn't just remembered Sandy's glasses. The housecleaner also recalled when she would see Sandy early in the morning after her walk, Sandy *never* wore jewelry—just a wristwatch and her glasses. With this statement, the only witness in the case who could attest firsthand to Sandy's walking attire shot down a major portion of the prosecutor's "opportunity to kill" theory. However, by coincidence, Montes made this point from the witness stand in a very low voice—so low that the defense team didn't catch what she said. When Montes was asked to repeat her answer, she only mentioned the glasses, neglecting to repeat the part about Sandy never walking with her jewelry on. Somers didn't correct her.

Even before the trial, Montes had told John Somers and sheriff's investigators that Sandy never wore her jewelry on her walks, just as Pat had always claimed. Yet this information was not put into any police reports, and therefore was never disclosed to the defense.[4] As a result, in his closing argument in the Dunn trial, Somers was able to say without challenge, "She *did* wear her jewelry when she walked and the defendant was well aware of it. . . . This is consistent with the theory she was killed while nude in bed . . . but not consistent with the theory that she was killed while out walking."

The argument sounded powerful and sure. But it was based on a premise John Somers had been told was false.

The prosecutor rounded out this portion of his case with a series of witnesses to rebut Pat's account of a memory-impaired Sandy wandering off and falling victim to some predator in the night. To refute the notion that Sandy might have been suffering from the early onset of Alzheimer's disease, Somers asked eight of the thirty-two prosecution witnesses about Sandy's mental state. Each one of them denied she had memory problems, and doubted that Sandy would ever just walk out in an Alzheimer's-induced haze, as Pat had suggested.

In number, these witnesses appeared impressive, but it turned out that not one of the eight was a close friend of Sandy's. Most were business associates who saw her just a handful of times during the year. One was the investment broker who hadn't seen her since 1988, and another was her former dentist, who hadn't seen her since she stopped coming to him in 1986—six years before she died. One was a secretary who talked to her on the phone twice a month about her investment accounts. One was the city councilwoman, Pat DeMond, who had sought to have Pat prosecuted from the outset, and who had not spoken with Sandy for almost a month before the disappearance. None of these witnesses saw Sandy more than once a month, on average—if they saw her at all. They all could easily have missed the sort of brief, episodic bouts of confusion and memory loss Pat had described.

The only really close friend of the Dunns to testify for the prosecution—Kate Rosenlieb—was never asked whether she had observed memory problems in Sandy.[5]

The defense responded to this part of the prosecution's case by calling just one witness, a man who was close to the Dunns and saw Sandy regularly—Rosenlieb's fellow city-planning commissioner, Jim Marino. Marino told the jury Sandy had displayed memory problems several times in his presence, and he described the time he visited the Dunns for lunch and Sandy kept asking over and over how his kids were doing, forgetting the most basic comments from one moment to the next. At other times, he said, she seemed perfectly fine.[6] (Marino also countered Kate Rosenlieb's description of the Dunns' marriage as a battlefield, saying he had never noticed any "tremendous fights." Though he admitted the Dunns could get "testy" with one another at times, he characterized their relationship as sound and built on love and respect.)

The fact that Sandy's mother died of Alzheimer's disease could have bolstered Pat's defense that Sandy might have been facing a similar fate, as there is considerable evidence of a genetic component to the disease—particularly with early-onset Alzheimer's, which would have been the type afflicting Sandy. Once Sandy's body was cremated, however, there was no way to know for sure: The only definitive test for diagnosing Alzheimer's disease—dissection of the brain after death—was not conducted. The defense did not pursue this point during the trial, however.

Although the medical examiner who performed the autopsy was not asked about the failure to perform this Alzheimer's test, Deputy DA Somers did make a point of posing a series of odd questions on a very different scientific topic, one that had been a key element in another recent murder trial: *The People vs. Offord Rollins*. He brought up the subject of flies.

Weren't there maggots and fly eggs, Somers asked, found on portions of Sandy's badly decomposed body? The medical examiner said yes—and not only on parts of the body found exposed to the elements, but also in areas that had been buried when the body was discovered.

Somers wanted to know how that could be. Did flies lay eggs underground?

No, the medical examiner answered, flies could not do that. The entire body had to have been exposed to the elements for some length of time before it was buried. Otherwise, there would be no flies or maggots where he had found them.

With that answer, Somers moved on to other subjects, ending an odd, brief interlude few people in the courtroom understood. But with his questions about the flies, the prosecutor had just proven that Sandy's body lay outside for an extended period of time before it was buried. It was not clear to anyone else involved with the trial just why Somers had elicited this grisly testimony, so similar to the pivotal evidence in the Rollins trial, where the absence of fly eggs had been cited as evidence of innocence. Whatever the reason, it seemed Somers did not like the answer he got, for he never brought up the subject again. Pat's defense team had no interest in flies, either, and the whole matter was soon forgotten in the heat and rancor of Jerry Coble's appearance on the stand.

And so, no one outside the Kern County District Attorney's office realized just how significant such testimony about maggots could be—or that those lowly flies could, just possibly, have proven Pat Dunn's innocence.

4

BY THE TIME JERRY LEE COBLE TOOK THE STAND, TWO radically different views of how the trial was going had emerged. Normally, both sides in a criminal case share a reasonably similar sense of where things are headed (which is to say that, in most cases, the defense knows it is getting creamed). But in the Dunn trial, it was as if the prosecution and defense were watching two different cases unfold.

Pat's defense team, impatient to bring out their big guns against Coble, had viewed the preceding witnesses primarily as a drawn-out waste of time and energy. Somers had, at most, used them to arouse some suspicion about Pat's behavior, point out his supposed inconsistencies and expose his supposed motive. But Pohlson felt sure the jury would look past the prosecution's insinuations and demand hard evidence. They would understand that Pat had kept quiet early on about the disappearance simply to avoid embarrassing his wife. Later, Pat clearly had been grief-stricken—the defense had the witnesses who could say so. Likewise, the defense felt certain the jury would see through Somers' inaccurate chart, the prosecution witnesses who couldn't keep their own stories straight, the fact that promise after promise made in the DA's opening statement had been broken by his own witnesses.

"All he has left is Coble," Pohlson said. "We get him, and everything else is just window dressing."

Laura remained troubled, but even she felt encouraged at this point. The prosecutor, so far as she could see, had delivered no knockout blows, though she wondered if they were underestimating the impact of Somers' little puzzle pieces, particularly the missing-persons call to the sheriff—with its the nervous joking and laughter that could easily be misinterpreted by people who didn't know Pat.

The other view of the trial—John Somers' view—was that he had made Jerry Coble's story almost beside the point. The chain of events, theory of motive, and circumstantial evidence pieced together through many witnesses, each of whom held a small part of the puzzle, had created a powerful case without Coble's eyewitness account, Somers believed.

"This testimony shows motive," he would argue. "It shows the opportunity Patrick Dunn had, Patrick Dunn and Patrick Dunn alone, who was alone with Alexandra Dunn during the last hours of her life. . . . It is about the conduct of the defendant, which, ladies and gentleman . . . defies reason if, in fact, she did wander off with Alzheimer's and disappear. But it's perfectly consistent with a man who has murdered his wife and knows it."

In laying the groundwork for that statement, Somers wanted to persuade jurors that his theory of motive to kill, the opportunity to kill, and the inconsistencies he charted in Pat's story were enough to pronounce the defendant guilty—or, at least, almost enough. If his strategy was working, the jurors would already believe the worst of Pat Dunn before they met Jerry Lee Coble, and they would need only an excuse to put them over the edge to convict. They might not like Jerry Lee Coble, Somers knew, but Coble could well prove all they would need to give the prosecutor the guilty verdict he sought.

Certainly it seemed clear to Laura Lawhon that the jury did not care one bit for the thin, ponytailed Jerry Coble. Their stony expressions and crossed arms said it all, particularly as he described his long criminal record and his decision to cut a deal so that he could elude six years in prison. But would dislike amount to disbelief?

Under Somers' gentle prodding, Coble told his now-familiar story about looking for a lost bindle of heroin at one in the morning, hearing a noise, hiding behind a trash can, and gazing across the street at Pat's driveway, brightly illuminated by a sodium-vapor light on the side of the house, which Pat conveniently left turned on while committing a capital offense. That's when, Coble claimed, he saw Pat Dunn drag a large bundle wrapped in a sheet and a dark blue blanket out his front door. Pat put the bundle into the back of a white pickup truck with a camper shell. The punch line remained the same as before.

"When he turned," Coble swore, "that's when I could see there was a hand sticking out of it. . . . It looked like a left hand."

Coble's would be the only testimony in the trial to directly link Pat Dunn to murder.

Even as he provided this pivotal evidence, Coble told the jury he really did not want to be in court testifying against Pat Dunn or anyone else, that it was not something he had sought out with any particular vigor, and that he hadn't really needed or wanted a deal on the theft case pending against him when he came forward with his information. He claimed that, despite his previous record, he would have gotten quick parole anyway, rather than the six years in prison he faced under the law—a claim belied by court records. In any case, Coble said that he had decided to come forward because he was trying to turn his life around by doing the right thing, so he could start over fresh. He had been crime-free ever since, he swore.

To Laura's surprise, Coble initially came across as far more pleasant and easygoing a man than she had expected—or hoped. But after that first impression was made, it went downhill for Somers and his informant, and it was here that all of Laura's research and groundwork began to pay off. First, Coble reluctantly had to admit that, in addition to describing a pickup truck that Pat didn't own, he also had originally told Detective Soliz that he had seen a white Ford Tempo or Taurus in the driveway that fateful night, and that he never saw the huge and unmistakable old Cadillac that the Dunns kept in the carport. Pohlson, with car-rental documents and witnesses, then showed that vehicles like those Coble described seeing on the night Sandy disappeared were not actually in the Dunns' driveway until weeks later, after Pat's cars were seized by the sheriff as evidence and he had to rent a replacement—a white Ford Tempo.

Under pressure, Coble tried to back off his statements to Soliz about the cars—and it was here that the defense nearly was hurt by Pat and Mike Dunn's early tip to the prosecution during the preliminary hearing. Coble was ready: He had gone over photos of Ford Tempos, and when Somers showed him one in court, he firmly denied that it depicted the car he saw outside the Dunn house. But he was undone by the firm and sure descriptions of the cars he gave to Detective Soliz at the time. Coble's only explanation for the change was that he had been "stressed" and hadn't really paid attention to the cars after all. All his attention was on the wrapped-up body, he said. Coble, of course, also denied casing the house or framing Pat. Still, even with his being tipped off and his attempts to parry the challenge to his story, it seemed the defense had scored big on cross-examination, just as Pohlson had promised. Coble's explanations did not appear to convince the jury, Laura observed.

Pohlson furthered his attack by forcing Coble to admit that he had previously claimed he could precisely remember the day all this happened because he was working for his girlfriend's father the next morning. Under questioning—and aware that the father was sitting outside in the courthouse hallway waiting to brand him a liar—Coble had to admit that was untrue.

Next, Pohlson had Coble tell the jury how he and Detective Soliz had driven through the Dunns' neighborhood and visited the house—before Coble gave a detailed, taped statement, thereby contaminating Coble's whole account.

"Soliz . . . doesn't test his recollection of the thing," Pohlson later lamented to the jury. "He doesn't test it so the defense can look at it, at an honestly taped statement. He goes out and shows him the house and shows him the light, the whole thing, then asks him the question, 'What did the house look like?' . . . That's rot!"

As for Coble's professed lack of interest in making a deal to testify, Pohlson elicited a grudging admission that the first words out of his mouth when he called Detective Soliz—even before he gave his name—concerned whether he could cut a deal on his own charges. If Coble was so disinterested in testifying and didn't really need a deal to get probation, Pohlson wanted to know, why was the prospect of a deal for leniency the first thing he talked about?

Even Coble's claims about seeing the body wrapped in a blue blanket were subject to attack, thanks to the work of the prosecution's own criminalist, who analyzed the handful of fibers found clinging to Sandy's body. First, none of them could have come from a white bedsheet. And, second, although there were some dark blue fibers collected, these were from a synthetic fabric with the trade name Olefin—which is used primarily for carpeting, and never in the sort of bedroom blanket Coble described, because of its flammability. Neither Pat's house nor his cars had Olefin carpeting in them.

Finally, the defense lawyer forced Coble to reveal his recidivist tendencies by making him admit that he had continued buying and using heroin for at least four months *after* cutting his deal to testify in the Dunn case, even though he had promised to stop using and knew that getting caught could have canceled his plea bargain and put him back in prison. Coble tried to minimize the sting of this, by saying that he used only five or six times a month, not much at all—his habit being limited by his lack of income at the time.

"I wasn't working," he explained. "I didn't have any money and I wasn't doing any crime."

And so the star witness left the stand a short time later, his credibility severely eroded. Pohlson felt he had just about won the case then and there, and Laura started feeling things might come out all right, after all. But she looked over at John Somers, too. He didn't look happy, but neither did he look devastated, and that worried her anew.

She did not know—as no one on the defense team *could* know—that Jerry Lee Coble had actually gotten off easy. He was damaged, certainly, but not destroyed, though he could have been. For there was a great deal of additional information available on his crimes and his lack of credibility, much of it known to the district attorney's office. Had it been presented to the jury, it could have severely eroded whatever remained of Coble's viability as a witness, and it could have dealt a serious blow to the credibility of the sheriff and district attorney as well. But that information was not used in the trial, and for one reason: The defense never saw it.

As in so many other cases in Kern County, and despite laws requiring full disclosure, key information about Coble was never given to Pat Dunn's lawyers. And, as a result, Gary Pohlson's victory over Jerry Coble remained a hollow one—for it would not last.

Whatever success Pat Dunn's defense team enjoyed with Jerry Coble, was soon upstaged by the painful appearance on the witness stand of someone close to Pat. The real estate attorney Teri Bjorn would be the prosecution's last witness, and its most devastating.

A month before trial, Kate Rosenlieb had told Somers about a supposed conversation between Bjorn and Pat within hours of Sandy's disappearance, and the prosecutor was anxious for the jury to hear about it—just as the defense badly wanted it kept out of court. Teri Bjorn certainly did not want to testify, and both she and Pat asserted that their conversation was protected by the rigid rules of attorney-client privilege, rendering it confidential and out of bounds to the prosecution. Somers, however, argued there was no right of confidentiality. Basing his argument on Kate Rosenlieb's secondhand recollections, he asserted Pat had sought Bjorn's help in gaining an illegal power of attorney over Sandy's money, a criminal act that would not be protected by the privilege.

With the two sides unable to agree on this crucial issue, the judge presiding over the case, Robert Baca, had reserved judgment on what role, if any, Bjorn would play in the trial until he had heard the rest of the prosecution's case. Pat's defense team had been pleased. They had wanted Baca on the case from the outset, for he was known to be prickly and independent, with a history of taking on the district attorney's office. Because Baca had been a public defender early in his career, Pohlson figured he would be particularly protective of attorney-client communications. Pohlson's enthusiasm for the judge faded quickly—the out-of-town lawyers simply did not get along with Baca—but even so, when the judge accepted Somers' suggestion that the court hold an *in camera* session on the Bjorn matter, the defense team was aghast. They had expected to prevail on argument alone.

Instead, Baca decided he should meet in chambers alone with Bjorn and a court reporter to determine if Somers was right. If there was at least some evidence that Pat had sought Bjorn's help in committing a crime, Baca said, the privilege would evaporate and conversation would be admitted as evidence in the trial.

In chambers, Teri Bjorn explained to the judge that she was not just a lawyer to the Dunns, but their friend as well. She said Pat had called her one morning to say Sandy was missing, describing to her how he had awakened to find his wife gone and how he had searched for her through the night. Bjorn couldn't remember all the details of this long-ago conversation or the exact words used, but what she did recall jibed with what Pat had said on other occasions to other people.

From Sandy's disappearance, the conversation next turned to the Morning Star housing project. Bjorn could not remember if she had brought the subject up, or if Pat had; she did recall she had been trying to reach the Dunns for about a week in order to talk to them about the project, so she may well have instigated the discussion. Both she and Pat were concerned that bills were coming due on Morning Star, and that the money Sandy had lined up for that purpose through sales of some municipal bonds had not been released yet. Pat, according to Bjorn, then said if Sandy came back and found the project shut down because the bills had not been paid, she would be very concerned. It was at this point that Pat asked whether some mechanism might be put into place to get the bills paid. "Could I use a power of attorney?" Bjorn recounted him asking.

As she explained to Judge Baca, she then responded no, because Sandy would have to sign such an authorization in advance, and as far as Bjorn knew, Sandy had not done so. It seemed clear to Bjorn that Pat did not know what a power of attorney was, she told Baca. Bjorn then recalled suggesting to Pat that she would talk to another lawyer in her firm about what else might be done to pay the bills until Sandy came home. And that was the end of any discussion about money or power of attorney, Bjorn said.

She added one more detail: "I believe he told me he had either filed or was going to file a missing-persons report."

This ambiguous point would be pivotal, because it could help determine an important point: when this call took place. If Pat had already filed the report, the conversation with Bjorn must have occurred on July 2, the morning after Sandy was reported missing. If so, there was nothing really strange going on. But if he hadn't yet reported Sandy missing, the conversation must have occurred on July 1, well before the missing-persons call. That would make Pat look very, very bad. He would have put Sandy's money before Sandy herself.

From his *in camera* session, Judge Baca ruled there was sufficient evidence to believe that Pat had sought Bjorn's services to commit a crime or fraud, which meant the attorney-client privilege didn't apply, and Bjorn would have to testify before the jury. The judge decided that Pat had been trying to gain control of *all* of Sandy's assets, even though Bjorn had testified that Pat's inquiry was strictly limited to paying bills that Sandy had previously expressed her intention to pay. In coming to this conclusion, it seemed the judge had listened less to Bjorn's actual testimony than to Somers' argument, which was based on Kate Rosenlieb's version of what Teri Bjorn had said (Somers had handed Baca a copy of Rosenlieb's notes to use as a guide). Indeed, Bjorn told Baca that Pat had only asked if a power of attorney were possible; he hadn't told Bjorn he wanted one put in place, as Somers and Rosenlieb had stated. The difference here is small but crucial: The former could be likened to asking an accountant if a certain tax deduction is legal; the latter would be akin to ordering the accountant to take the deduction whether it's legal or not. The defense might have objected to this leap in logic by the judge, but they were not allowed to be present for the *in camera* hearing and no transcript of the secret proceeding was made available until later.

So Teri Bjorn returned to the courtroom, where she was ordered to repeat her story. Her testimony before the jury mirrored what she had told Baca in chambers in most respects. Despite Somers' best efforts, she never actually testified that Pat had asked her for power of attorney over Sandy's funds. The DA twice asked if Pat requested a power of attorney, but Bjorn never gave him a yes or no answer. All she would say was what she had told the judge: that Pat was searching for a mechanism to pay the Morning Star bills, and that he didn't actually know what a power of attorney was—hardly the evidence Somers was looking for. Yet, from that, the prosecutor would later argue that Pat Dunn *asked for* power of attorney, and Judge Baca never corrected him. Neither did the defense: It seems everyone else in the courtroom remembered Teri Bjorn saying something she never actually said on the witness stand.

There was one crucial point on which Bjorn's courtroom testimony differed from her *in camera* version. The second time around, in front of the lawyers and jurors, Bjorn did not mention being unsure about whether she had spoken to Pat before or after he reported Sandy missing. Instead, she simply said, *to the best of her recollection,* the conversation occurred during the morning of July 1—which everyone in the courtroom knew would have been *before* Pat reported Sandy missing. Baca did not say anything about this discrepancy, and neither did Bjorn, so the defense remained in the dark. John Somers had hit the jackpot. In the end, the most devastating part of Teri Bjorn's testimony was not that Pat had sought her advice, but *when* he sought it.

The defense had witnesses and evidence available to suggest that the call described by Bjorn had been made later in the week than she recalled,[7] but their proof would have been complicated and hard for the jury to follow. Gary Pohlson decided not to make an issue out of it, instead arguing that it didn't matter what day the call was made because Pat's question to Bjorn was an innocent one. Pat had called to tell a friend about his missing wife, and that friend—who happened also to be a real estate attorney—brought up the subject of the Morning Star project and the outstanding bills. And in response, Pohlson said, Pat had simply expressed a desire to carry out Sandy's wishes in her absence, the actions of a man just trying to go on with life. If Pat's friends were unanimous about anything, it was that he was the type of person who would try to go on with his normal routines, no matter what—and that Sandy would have wanted it that way.

Pohlson's argument sounded reasonable as he delivered it, but it gave Somers an opening as well. With the July 1 date unchallenged and Bjorn's uncertainty in chambers never passed on to the jury, the prosecutor countered with a powerful and damning argument: The only person Pat Dunn called that morning, the prosecutor said, was his lawyer. He wanted to get hold of Sandy's money, he wanted to get power of attorney, he wanted to probate his wife's will right away. "I'm sorry, but that is not the first thing on your mind when your wife has disappeared. . . . But if you know that your wife is dead, ladies and gentlemen, then it's very important."

With that, Somers' portrait of Pat Dunn as cold-blooded killer was complete. He had already played that awful tape recording of Pat reporting Sandy missing, the jokes and laughter sounding loud and tinny in the hushed courtroom. The jury had already heard Kate Rosenlieb tell of how Pat had showed no emotion over his wife's disappearance—other than seeming happy at times. First his own words were used against him, then his best friend's and now his own lawyer's. As hard proof, Bjorn's testimony had little weight. But its emotional impact on the case seemed incalculable: It just didn't sound right. The mere fact that Pat's own lawyer was testifying against him was devastating. If the jury had known their conversation might have taken place a day after Pat reported Sandy missing, Bjorn's testimony might have had little force. As it was, when Teri Bjorn left the courtroom, the prosecutor rested his case, certain he had convinced the jury that Pat Dunn was guilty beyond a reasonable doubt.

5

B Y THE TIME THE TRIAL REACHED THIS POINT, PAT Dunn sat numb and barely able to follow the proceedings. He had been active and participating fully at the start, writing notes, whispering to his lawyers, savoring early victories and any look of chagrin on the prosecutor's face. But his enthusiasm had faded with time and, even now, with his moment finally arrived—the start of the defense case—he had become so intimidated and fearful of being on trial for his life that he found it hard to concentrate. He would later say he could remember little of what was said or done. He stopped expressing a desire to take the witness stand and instead kept saying to Laura, "I just wish it was over." She bit her lip and stopped herself from replying, "Be careful what you wish for." Because if it ended then and there, she feared, he'd lose.

The defense had been wounded by Judge Baca's decision to compel Teri Bjorn to testify, but though Laura was uneasy, the team by no means considered it a fatal blow. Gary Pohlson mounted Pat's defense as planned, presenting witnesses to speak of the good relations between the Dunns, to deny there were any serious fights, money problems or plans for divorce, and to confirm that Pat had confided in a select few early on about Sandy's disappearance. In addition to these, there was Jim Marino, who could testify about his own experiences with Sandy's memory problems, bolstering Pat's statements to police. Together, these witnesses provided a different mosaic than the prosecution's, a portrait of a man who had no reason to want his wife dead and who acted reasonably after her disappearance, and of a woman whose mental state left her at risk to wander off—making her easy prey for street criminals or worse.

The financial planner, Kevin Knutson, returned to the stand a second time, now a defense witness key to building this alternate assemblage of the puzzle pieces—Laura Lawhon's version. Knutson all but destroyed the prosecution's theory that a desire to get Sandy's money provided Pat's motive for murder. Knutson swore that during their June 30 meeting, one of the things Sandy said that she wanted was a living trust to allow all of her money to go to Pat without a will, without inheritance taxes, and without the ability of relatives such as her sister to interfere. There was no way Sandy wanted a divorce, Knutson added. The Dunns were getting along well, loving and at ease with one another when he left them on Sandy's last day alive.

Knutson went on to say that he would have had the papers drawn up in a week or two, and that Pat's financial position would have been infinitely better once Sandy signed them. Citing Knutson's testimony, Tom Goethals, one of Pat's lawyers, would argue, "There is no evidence Pat Dunn killed his wife to get her money. He didn't need to. . . . On June 30, he had every reason to let her live."

As important as the defense regarded this meeting on the day before Sandy disappeared, something that happened on the day *after* she vanished was equally critical.

Somers had tried to portray Pat's behavior that day as inappropriate for a worried husband with a missing wife, wanting jurors to see Pat as greedy, insensitive and, ultimately, very aware that the wife he claimed as missing was actually dead. But the defense wanted jurors to hear about *Sandy's* activities on the day after she disappeared—as told by Rick Williams' secretary, Ann Kidder.

Kidder reiterated the story she had told the sheriff's department, recounting how Sandy had called the accountant's office that morning of July 1, canceling her appointment for later that day with Williams. Kidder knew Sandy's distinctive voice from a dozen phone conversations, and had no doubt it was her calling.

Her testimony mirrored her previous statements: "She seemed to be upset, mumbling, going on. . . . She said her husband had scheduled an appointment with some Indians, and the Indians were coming down out of the hills and he didn't let her know about scheduling this appointment, and so she was real upset about that. . . . She said . . . 'my husband doesn't like to wear any clothes.'"

Ann Kidder was a godsend for Pat Dunn, or so it seemed to Gary Pohlson and Laura Lawhon. Attractive, soft-spoken, competent and professional—and lacking any reason to lie either for or against Pat Dunn's interests—Kidder seemed irreproachable. Which is exactly what the Kern County Sheriff and District Attorney thought when they considered her a prosecution witness, before they realized her story exonerated Pat rather than hanged him. For Ann Kidder had marked dates and times on her office calendars, providing her with documentary evidence to support her recollections about the exact time and date of this babbling phone call: Sandy Dunn talked to Ann Kidder eight hours after Jerry Coble swore her dead body had been hauled out of Pat Dunn's house.

Kidder provided the added bonus of making Sandy sound addled and bizarre, consistent with a woman suffering an episode of mental impairment and out wandering, perhaps placing her call from a phone booth somewhere en route to her encounter with a killer.

It was powerful testimony for the defense, though there was more to it than anyone appeared to notice during the trial. No one attributed any particularly significance to the content of Sandy's babbling—at the time, it seemed enough to the defense that she babbled at all.

Somers, like the detectives had before him, tried to confuse Kidder by throwing a passel of dates at her rapid-fire, hoping she would get some details wrong and give him some inconsistency with which to assail her credibility. He did find a few—for instance, Kidder recalled in her testimony that one earlier appointment made by Sandy was for 1:30, when the calendar said 2:00—but such minor niggling did not affect Kidder's core story, which had been consistent from the start. Somers also suggested the caller could have been someone imitating Sandy, but Kidder made it clear that this had not been the case. The prosecutor's attempts to suggest Kidder might be wrong about the July 1 date were countered by her boss, Rick Williams, who remembered it exactly the same as Kidder.

"Ann Kidder alone gets us an acquittal," Pohlson declared after she was through. And Laura had to admit that, in a swearing contest, she couldn't imagine the jury choosing Jerry Coble over Ann Kidder. Yet, Laura knew, that's exactly what happened at the sheriff's department and the district attorney's office when they chose to prosecute Pat.

As good a witness as Ann Kidder was, the heart of the defense lay in proving Jerry Lee Coble had actively plotted to frame Pat Dunn with lies. The groundwork had already been laid by Coble's erroneous description of the cars in Pat's driveway. The defense hoped to make the case against Coble overwhelming with the testimony of Rex Martin, who said that he saw Coble casing Pat's house weeks after the murder—when the white Tempo Coble described was in the driveway.

To Laura, Rex Martin was everything in a witness that Jerry Coble was not. A respected real estate developer and builder, Rex Martin projected an outwardly appealing image on the witness stand, silver haired and square jawed, a plain-talking former military pilot, as outgoing and open as Pat Dunn could be closed and prickly. Martin had served on the Kern County Parole Board and was as anti-crime as any Bakersfield bedrock conservative. Though he had known Pat for fifty years, Martin avowed he would not lie for Pat or help him get away with murdering Sandy, whom he had liked and respected. Laura watched with satisfaction as Martin repeated his story just as he had told it to her months earlier—no inconsistencies, no changes, nothing that would let John Somers say, see, it must be a lie, because the truth never changes.

Martin explained to the jury how, nearly a month after Sandy disappeared, he had tailed a man in a green Pontiac Sunbird who had been lurking outside Pat's house. He followed the man to a nearby photo shop,

where he got a good look at the man's face. Martin then
identified Coble as that man, identified a photo of
Coble's mother's green car as the one he had followed,
and identified a piece of brown paper on which he had
written the Pontiac's license plate number. Martin could
not give an exact date for when this occurred; he knew
only that he had taken Pat to rent the white Ford Tempo
on July 24, when Pat's own cars were seized, and that his
pursuit of Coble had occurred a few days later. He did
recall returning to work after the encounter with Coble
and mentioning the adventure to his secretary, so he
could say with certainty that it had been a weekday. That
would make it either Monday, July 27, or Tuesday, July 28,
a few days after a major article on the Dunn case
appeared in the local paper—an article that would have
given Coble all the information he would have needed to
begin constructing a frame. Even Martin's ambiguity
about the date was consistent, as he had expressed a similar uncertainty in earlier statements. Recalling precise
dates was difficult, he explained: By the time Pat was
arrested and he realized that the green Pontiac might be
significant, many months had passed, dulling memories.
At the time, following the stranger in the green car had
been a lark, an attempt to make Pat feel better, something
Martin never dreamed would have such a monumental
bearing on the case.

The exact date was unimportant, however, because
Jerry Coble already had sworn he had gone to Pat's house
but twice in his life—once on the night of the murder
and once when Soliz took him there to refresh his memory. Laura knew that believing Martin meant disbelieving
Coble's entire story.

Rex Martin's testimony was in part corroborated by

Jerry Mitchell, the retired sheriff's deputy and friend of Pat's, who confirmed getting a license number from Pat and Martin sometime during the summer, then passing it on to Detective Soliz. Mitchell was unequivocal in his testimony: He didn't have an exact date, nor could he find the piece of paper on which he had written the number, but he knew it happened. Since neither Pat, Rex Martin nor Jerry Mitchell had ever heard of Jerry Coble at that point—Pat was not arrested until October 28—there was no way any of them could have picked his license number out of thin air in order to construct a phony defense. Soliz's testimony, meanwhile, seemed less than solid on the subject. Rather than firmly denying Mitchell's story, he simply told the jury, "I don't have a recollection of Mr. Mitchell giving me a license-plate number." Out of court, Mitchell accused Soliz of lying to preserve his case, for had the detective admitted receiving the license number, it would almost certainly have ended the trial in Pat's favor.

But given Soliz's equivocal testimony in the matter, Somers was free to suggest that Martin and Pat had cooked up the story of the green car to get Pat off the hook, and that they had duped Jerry Mitchell. Somers also suggested a motive for Rex to lie: If Pat were acquitted, he could then get hold of Sandy's money and restart the now-defunct real estate projects the Dunns had going with Martin. To back this up, the prosecutor asserted that Martin had been caught in a lie by Detective Soliz: The sheriff's detective had written a report months earlier, quoting a telephone conversation in which Martin supposedly denied the handwriting was his on the scrap of brown paper on which Coble's license number was scrawled. If true, such a statement would directly contra-

dict Martin's sworn testimony at trial and undermine
Pat's entire defense.

Martin grew angry at this, retorting that he had said
no such thing. What Martin had told Soliz was that he
wouldn't identify any piece of paper for the detective over
the telephone or anywhere else. Martin had come to distrust Soliz, he said, after concluding the detective had
badly misquoted him in an earlier report—echoing a
complaint jurors had heard repeatedly from other trial
witnesses. "I didn't want to talk to him without a tape
recorder," Martin said. "I wanted what I told him put
down the way I told it."

The rest of the defense team seemed unconcerned by
this interlude, but Laura's doubts began to rise again. If
the jury had turned against Pat, if they wanted to convict,
she knew that Soliz's report on Rex's "lie"—a report she
knew to be inaccurate from her own investigation—
would give them all the excuse they needed.

Still, Martin struck her as a powerful witness as he
described how Pat seemed genuinely worried about
Sandy's disappearance and grieved her death, despite
what some people implied or thought. If Pat appeared
unaffected, Martin testified, it was only because Pat could
be a bit odd, a loner who hid his feelings well, sometimes
too well.

"I have never known Pat to be very demonstrative of
his feelings," Martin said. "It was obvious to me that he
was concerned and upset, but you know, as far as breaking out crying or anything, no." That, according to
Martin, wouldn't be Pat. If Pat had broken down
and wept excessively, then Martin might have gotten
suspicious.

When Rex Martin was through, the final attack on

Jerry Coble and the prosecution's case was delivered by Jerry's own brother, Gary. The defense hoped that, even if the jury worried about Martin and Mitchell possibly coloring their accounts out of loyalty to Pat, Gary Coble had no such potential for bias. Why would he tell lies to help a stranger and hurt his brother?

Hesitant and ill at ease on the witness stand—and joking about being more accustomed to the defendant's chair—Gary Coble recounted that Jerry, before even contacting Detective Soliz, first told him of witnessing a murder. The heavyset ex-con, looking far older than his forty years, shrugged and shook his head. He didn't believe Jerry's story from the beginning, he said, "Because I know my brother . . . He's pretty smart. . . . Sometimes he's too smart."

Months after that conversation, and after Jerry had testified at Pat's preliminary hearing, Jerry had gone to stay with Gary in Los Angeles, where he tried, unsuccessfully, to kick his heroin habit. It was during this difficult time that the truth came out, Gary Coble testified, reconstructing the conversation for the jury:

"I made a mistake. I messed up," Jerry told his brother.

"What do you mean?" Gary asked.

"That case. I didn't see what I told them I seen. I didn't see it."

Gary recalled getting angry at this revelation and berating his younger brother. This wasn't something minor, like a forgery or a bad-check case—this was murder. "You don't do stuff like that," he recalled telling his brother.

Jerry seemed to agree, Gary said in court, but he felt he no longer had any choice but to stick with his story implicating Pat Dunn in murder: "I'm so far in now, I can't back out. The cops told me if they caught me in a lie, they'll have my ass." And, more than anything, Jerry Coble did not want to go back to prison, his brother said.

Then Gary told the jury how Jerry set up his scam. While looking for a case in which he could manufacture testimony (and thereby cut a deal to stay out of jail) Jerry spotted a news article about Sandy Dunn's murder and found his opportunity. He then sat out in front of the Dunns' house for days, checking out the place and waiting to get a look at Pat so he'd be able to identify him in a lineup. When he saw someone leave a package on the front steps, he ran up, grabbed it and rang the bell. When someone answered the door, Coble handed over the package as if he were the delivery man, getting a good look at the man of the house.

After Jerry left Gary's home and returned to Kern County, Gary wrestled with his conscience, then called Pat's original attorney, Stan Simrin. Simrin gave him Gary Pohlson's number, and after many conversations with Pohlson, Gary finally agreed to testify, though he had fervently hoped to avoid it. Gary swore he had never met Pat Dunn or any member of the Dunn family, that he had not been paid off in any way, and that the only pressure on him came from those who wished he would not testify—namely, his family, who accused him of turning against his own blood. "I just don't understand why they're mad at me, but Jerry's got them," Gary said. "I'm just trying to do the right thing. I done wrong all my life and I know it's the right thing."

Even under Gary Pohlson's slow, careful and gentle questions, Gary Coble would never be confused with the best of witnesses, Laura clearly saw. He was nervous and

halting, and vague on some details. But, in his favor, he
made no attempt to minimize his lengthy criminal
record, which included burglaries, robberies, forgery and
other property crimes, or the fact that he had spent nearly half his life behind bars. And Gary Coble seemed genuinely perplexed at the notion someone might think he
was lying about Jerry, for he had nothing to gain but
ostracism from his family, who had rallied around the
younger brother. He knew also that testifying for the
defense in the case could make him an inviting target for
the sheriff's department and district attorney's office.
Indeed, the DA already had gone after him, filing a court
claim against him for back child-support payments
allegedly owed to an ex-wife, and attaching his paycheck
just days before he was to testify. The easiest thing for
Gary Coble to have done was to have kept silent.

Pohlson suggested the DA's action against Gary Coble
was the prosecutor's way of making life hard on a troublesome witness, but Somers tried to turn this around. He
suggested, in his tough and lengthy cross-examination,
that Gary had an axe to grind because he was angry at the
DA over the child-support claim. The prosecutor's theory
was that Gary Coble was so angry at the DA, he would lie
to set a murderer free, risk sending his own brother to
prison, and alienate his entire family—just to get even with
prosecutors over his ex-wife. "That's ridiculous," Pohlson
scoffed, but no one in the courtroom was laughing.

The normally civil and reserved Somers abandoned
his placid manner and tore into Gary Coble, leaving the
witness flustered and confused, muttering "Jesus Christ"
and "I can't believe this" from time to time. The prosecutor peppered Gary with questions about when Jerry came
to visit, when Jerry admitted to lying, when Jerry first tes-

tified in the case. Gary maintained that he didn't know, but Somers finally got him to confirm that Jerry's visit and their key conversation occurred in summer, "Because I remember it was still hot out." Later, Gary amended this to say it might have been October or November. Earlier in his testimony, however, he had said that the visit and conversation came after Pat's preliminary hearing— which had been in December. Somers had found an inconsistency to pounce upon, and asserted that this problem with chronology made Gary Coble's entire story unbelievable.

Then Somers asked a series of questions insinuating that the prosecutor had inside knowledge that Gary, not Jerry, was the lying witness in the Coble family. *Didn't you tell your brother Terry that you disliked the fact that Jerry was cooperating with the police? Didn't you tell your father the same thing? Didn't you tell your father that Jerry never really admitted fabricating his testimony?*

The questions suggested Gary's family knew his testimony about Jerry was a tissue of lies, and that they had told Somers so. Gary denied ever saying any such things, but Somers' questions planted the notion with the jury that there was a reason Gary had been ostracized by his family—and that it wasn't for telling the truth. The questions implied the existence of facts for which Somers offered no evidence. Somers never called the father, the brother or anyone else to the witness stand to support his bare insinuations. But neither could the defense challenge them.

John Somers called no witnesses to rebut any part of the defense case. Instead, once again, he used Pat Dunn's own words against him.

The prosecutor had already played the tape of Pat's missing-persons call, taking great pains to point out every laugh, every bad joke, every supposedly flirtatious remark, hoping the jury would see Pat as cold, hateful and unconcerned about his wife. Now Somers had Pat's preliminary-hearing testimony—in which Pat had shot holes in his own defense, against the advice of his first lawyer, Stan Simrin—read to the jury. Laura could only stew in frustration. If Pat had just heeded Simrin, if he had just kept his mouth shut, or if he had at least prepared for the rigors of the witness stand, he might have avoided this moment. But, as it was, he had provided Somers with a potent weapon.

In these transcripts, Somers had Pat Dunn, under oath, swearing that he clearly recalled the specific date in which Rex Martin followed Jerry Coble as Friday, July 24, the same day Rex took Pat to get his rental car. Rex had said the two events were several days apart. Pat would later say he made a simple mistake, that the days had blurred together, that he hadn't meant to sound so sure in his testimony—but during the preliminary hearing he had been so angry at John Soliz and John Somers and the notion that he could be charged with murdering his wife that he had just wanted to set the record straight, and he had wanted to sound as clear and sure as could be.

But he had not set the record straight.

He had given Somers an opening. For the news article that the defense argued could have tipped off Jerry Coble about the Dunn case, which provided the Dunns' address and strongly implied that Pat was a suspect and therefore an ideal candidate for a frame-up, had appeared in the *Bakersfield Californian* on Saturday, July 25. It seemed Pat had been wrong about the date. And though Rex Martin had always been consistent in his account, Somers would argue forcefully that "the story changed."

"That's the first sign of a phony story," the prosecutor told the jury. "It changes under pressure."

The last testimony jurors would hear in the case would be Pat Dunn's fateful error.

6

W HEN IT WAS TIME FOR THE ATTORNEYS TO DELIVER
their closing arguments to the jury, the prosecution and defense were still quite divided in
their perceptions, with each side believing it had built a
winning case. It was only while watching John Somers
deliver his masterful final speech to the jurors—and seeing their eager reaction to it, the grim smiles, the nodding
of heads—that first Laura, then the rest of the defense
team, and finally Gary Pohlson began to see things in a
different light. What they thought was a strong case for
Pat's acquittal might not be headed that way after all. The
shock and disbelief—the *unwillingness* to believe—was
palpable, and almost crippling at times, especially for a
defense team that had champagne chilling in the cooler.
Reduced to the role of spectators at a tennis match, they
alternately watched Somers and the jurors, suddenly feeling helpless—like every other lawyer who had ever
underestimated this skilled and ruthless prosecutor.

John Somers set about doing what he did best:
Assembling all the little pieces of the puzzle into a single,
imposing and seemingly irrefutable monolith. He
brought out his big chart of Pat's supposed lies, with all its
many niggling or questionable points, and made it seem
that Pat Dunn couldn't tell the truth about anything. He

revisited the testimony of Marie Gates and Kate Rosenlieb, and depicted Pat as the angriest, most desperate estranged husband on earth—yet one who had the audacity to tell detectives that he and Sandy never fought. Then Somers went over the finances, and by the time he was done with that recitation, he had Pat broke and without prospects, with murdering his wealthy wife the only way out. Interpreting Pat's every action or omission in the most negative light possible, the prosecutor reminded jurors of how Pat had failed to tell some friends and acquaintances about Sandy being missing or did not ask for their help in finding her (He didn't need their help because he knew she was dead, Somers said), how he failed to show grief at her loss (He wasn't sad—he was happy, because he thought he was getting away with murder), and how he seemed more interested in Sandy's money than her well-being (He tried to grab her accounts long before her body turned up—again, because he knew she was dead). The day after Sandy disappeared, Pat took his car in to be serviced and had the tires replaced—no doubt, Somers suggested, to hide the fact that he had been to the desert burial site a day earlier. (Though not asked about it during the trial, the mechanic later said changing the tires was his idea, not Pat's, because of severe and uneven wear.) Somers knew if he could make jurors dislike Pat Dunn, they would want to convict Pat Dunn.

"This case is not about Jerry Coble," Somers assured them. "It's about the collapse of the Dunns' marriage and the financial necessity—or the financial desire, I should say—for Patrick Dunn to obtain Sandy Dunn's money. . . . It's about the conduct of the defendant. . . . Perhaps most importantly of all, this trial is about the statements made to person after person by Patrick Dunn after the crime: false statements, statements which are inconsistent with each other . . . statements which show that Pat Dunn was covering up, that he was telling a falsehood."

Somers exhorted the jurors to go to the jury room and replay the tape of Pat calling to report Sandy missing, if they really wanted to know what the case was about.

"In some ways, that phone call tells you more emotional truth about what happened here than any other piece of evidence in this case. . . . It is less what he said in that phone call than the way that he said it. . . . He's happy in that phone call, or he certainly sounds happy. He is cheerful, he is joking, he doesn't sound upset. . . . Is that the state of mind, is that what you're going to hear from a man who is panicked because his wife has been missing for eighteen hours? No. It's what you're going to hear from a man who murdered his wife the night before and is starting to think that, maybe, he can get away with it."

Laura Lawhon listened to that closing argument, glanced at the jury, and decided that Somers had just won them over to his camp for good. When Gary Pohlson got up and took his best shot, arguing that there was so much evidence for the defense that the case wasn't even close, Laura knew she was right: the jurors weren't even listening. They sat stone-faced, polite, but not buying any of it. Laura found it hard to believe they could sit through this trial and hear the defense evidence and still come down on the prosecution's side, but one look at their body language told her that was what lay in store.

Gary Pohlson, finally, saw it too. Midway through his closing argument, his voice grew shaky and he began apologizing to the jury for being nervous. He said he

wanted them to understand just how clear it was that Pat
had no motive for murder, that the police had been hor-
ribly biased against him from the start, that Somers' big
chart was riddled with errors, that the secretary Ann
Kidder proved Sandy was alive when Jerry Coble said she
was dead. It went on and on, Pohlson said, an answer for
every prosecution salvo, as good a case for acquittal as
any he's ever seen.

"I really am scared, I am scared to sit down," Pohlson
admitted. "Please, keep saying to yourself, what did they
prove, what did they really prove?"

At last, though, Pohlson did stop, with one last plea.
"Please, do the right thing," he all but begged the jurors.
"Do the right thing."

As far as the jurors were concerned, that's exactly what
they did.

The day and a half awaiting the verdict was a strange
one, with everyone on the defense team but Laura again
convincing themselves that Pat would be acquitted after
all. That juror with the heavy wooden cross—the foreman—kept shooting them smiles and thumbs-up gestures in the hall. What else were they to think? Laura,
though, kept remembering some of the other Kern
County cases she had heard about, how confident
Offord Rollins' lawyers and family were that he, too,
would be acquitted—only to see him receive a life sentence instead. And she recalled listening in the hallway to
that same jury foreman at the beginning of the case,
hearing him describe to a fellow juror the kind of music
he played: Country. You know, the kind of music those
defense lawyers wouldn't like.

Pat told Laura he was unable to eat or sleep as he

awaited the news. He had developed a terrible rash from the stress, a constant itching. Yet when he was brought up from the holding cell to hear the verdict, Laura saw him walking straight and holding his head up, suddenly calm and dignified.

Then the verdict was delivered. Pat was pronounced guilty of first-degree murder, leaving Gary Pohlson stunned and in tears, a still-calm Pat gently patting his lawyer's back. There had never really been that much debate among the jurors, as it turned out, just a few who expressed some uncertainty, then quickly caved to the majority. Somers' argument that Pat Dunn and everyone who testified on his behalf were liars had carried the day. Gary Coble, Rex Martin, Ann Kidder—all were disregarded. And the smiling foreman with the cross had led the charge to convict from the start.

"Why did you leave him on the jury?" Laura would later ask Gary Pohlson. "After what he said about the defense lawyers and country music."

Pohlson looked at her blankly—he had never heard about that. Laura's boss had never passed on the information. The attorney appeared stricken when Laura explained it to him. "I never would have left that man on the jury if I had known that," he said.

As the stunned defense team waited for the judge to schedule a sentencing date, then fled the courtroom, they had no idea that there was a great deal more information they had not been told, and that it went far beyond the musical prejudices of the jury foreman.

The Kern County District Attorney had won a conviction in *The People vs. Patrick O. Dunn*. It had done so with a brilliant performance by John Somers, though his case did depend in part on errors and misstatements of fact. But, beyond that stellar performance, the conviction was won only after key, and damaging, information about some of the government's most important witnesses, evidence and theories was withheld from the defense. This phantom information was so explosive it could have made all the difference in the trial's outcome—if the defense and, more importantly, the jury, had known about it.

But neither did. And Pat Dunn's fate was sealed.

7

LAURA LAWHON SPENT THE REST OF THE SPRING OF 1993 alternately consoling a despondent client and hunting for evidence that might allow the guilty verdict against Pat Dunn to be overturned. She needed witnesses who could further corroborate Pat's story, or some missing or forgotten pieces of the puzzle— anything that might undermine the startlingly effective road map to conviction John Somers had drawn.

The first task facing her was interviewing the jurors. One by one, she appeared at their doors a week after the trial. "Cold calls," she called her modus operandi: Just show up without warning, knock on the door, and hope for the best. Those willing to talk to her revealed a jury that had, for the most part, accepted the prosecutor's arguments about the bits and pieces of evidence, and rejected virtually all the defense had to offer.

Their first vote had been ten to two for conviction, Laura learned, a tally that quickly became eleven to one. The one holdout clung to his not-guilty vote until after lunch on the second day, then caved in to the majority. He told Laura he had been concerned by the lack of physical evidence linking Pat to the murder, and by the phone call Ann Kidder spoke of receiving from Sandy after the murder was supposed to have taken place. But, in the end, the defense's lone advocate during jury deliberations decided Pat had been too inconsistent—at least on Somers' chart—and that the rest of the circumstantial evidence pointed unerringly toward guilt. Laura got the impression the holdout had finally given in less out of firm belief than to just get the case over with, for he also admitted that he did not believe the prosecutor's suggestion of motive in the case.

"I didn't think he did this for financial gain," the holdout juror said of Pat. "He had more to lose by having her die."

This statement floored Laura, because this same juror had voted with the others to find—beyond a reasonable doubt—that Pat killed Sandy for financial gain. He had joined the unanimous vote for this "special circumstance," a separate enhancement to the charge of first-degree murder in California, which qualified Pat for life in prison without parole (and could have sent him to death row had the DA asked for it). Murder for financial gain is one of a list of such special circumstances that must be found by the jury to allow a sentence of death or life without parole. When Laura asked the juror why he would vote that way if he didn't believe Pat had killed for money, the juror replied, "Oh, was that the second count? I guess I did go with that, even though I didn't think so." Laura left this cheerful man's home feeling sick to her stomach.

Most of the other jurors who talked to Laura told her that they had not believed Jerry Coble, or his brother Gary either. The only testimony that they had asked to have read back to them during their deliberations was Jerry's, and only that portion concerning the cars he saw in the Dunns' driveway, the part of his story the defense pointed to as proof he had framed Pat. (Several other jurors who would talk only to John Somers after the trial told him they had believed Jerry Coble's story.) Two of the jurors Laura contacted were critical of John Soliz, who they felt had been less than honest in his testimony, and others had doubts about Kate Rosenlieb. If she was such a good friend of Pat's, one juror asked, why was she writing notes about her conversations right from the beginning? It was an unanswered question that still bothered Laura, too. Marie Gates, in contrast, was particularly impressive to most of the jurors, Laura learned. Gates' sworn testimony that Sandy wanted a divorce tied everything together for the jury, and made it very clear why Pat committed the crime, several said.[8]

Still, the idea that some members of the jury disregarded Coble's testimony and yet still convicted Pat baffled Laura. What did the prosecution have if you disbelieved Coble's eyewitness testimony? To the private investigator, all that remained—even if you accepted at face value everything the DA claimed—was a marriage on the rocks; a wife who disappeared *before* she could carry out plans to give her husband more financial control; a husband unconcerned, even happy to see his wife gone; a man who immediately tried (unsuccessfully) to raid his vanished wife's accounts; and a hard-drinking husband who was inconsistent in his various descriptions of his wife's disappearance.

How, Laura kept asking the jurors, could that prove that Pat Dunn committed murder? It might make you suspicious of him, she conceded. It might make you wonder. But how did that prove beyond a reasonable doubt that he picked up a knife and stabbed the life out of his wife? And furthermore, if Pat really hated Sandy, as John

Somers suggested, then his being happy at her disappearance was not evidence that he killed her—it only verified that he hated her. If one truly believed the Dunns despised one another, one could just as well decide any displays of grief by Pat had to be phony and suspicious. Somers had cleverly constructed a portrait in which Pat, no matter what he did, always appeared guilty.

When Laura tried to nail the jurors down on the specific pieces of evidence and testimony that convinced them Pat was a killer and sealed their verdict, they grew increasingly vague. One said, "He just didn't act right." Another juror, shifting the burden of proof from the prosecution to the defense, said Pat's lawyer spent too much time trying to contradict the DA "instead of proving Pat didn't commit the crime"—standing the principle of presumption of innocence on its head. Another thought the testimony from the mechanic who said Pat had brought his Blazer in for service the day after Sandy disappeared, and that the two front tires were replaced, showed Pat was covering something. Yet another juror apparently entered the case looking for ways to convict. As she told Laura, this juror spent most of the trial fretting over the lack of physical evidence and repeatedly asking herself, "How are we going to find this man guilty?"[9]

One juror who would not speak with Laura was the foreman, the man with the cross whom she had overheard deriding the defense lawyers during jury selection (and who, in notes sent out from the jury room, identified himself as the "floor person"). According to another juror, he had been elected foreman because he told everyone that he was "happy" to be on the case, while everyone else grumbled about the vicissitudes of jury duty. When Laura went to see him after the trial, his mother came to the door to inform her that he wasn't home, but that she doubted he would talk to anyone associated with "the murderer" in any case. She explained that her son was very religious and that he felt he had to "do his part to fight the evil that is so predominant now in the United States." As an example of this evil, she cited the furor that erupted when a Los Angeles jury acquitted the policemen who had been videotaped beating black motorist Rodney King in 1992. Of the case that set off riots in Los Angeles and a scandal within the Los Angeles Police Department, which admitted that King had been brutalized by officers, she added, "Everyone knows King is guilty."

The unanimity of the sitting jury was sharply contrasted by two alternate jurors. From them, Laura got a completely different response to the case. As standby jurors, they, too, sat through the entire trial, ready to step in if one of the twelve voting jurors became sick or had to depart for some other reason. Their comments couldn't have been more at odds with what the others had told Laura.

Expecting a quick acquittal and hoping to hug and console Pat during postverdict celebrations, these two alternates had lingered in the courtroom after the deliberations began. One, a corrections officer, told Laura she found the verdict inexplicable and shocking. This woman thought the evidence quite clearly showed that Jerry Coble had cased Pat's home in order to frame him. Pat's behavior after Sandy's disappearance meant nothing to her, she said. "How can anyone have the right to decide how another person should act under such extraordinary circumstances?" she asked, a look of disgust on her face.

The second alternate told Laura she thought the sheriff's department had been terribly unprofessional. She couldn't believe detectives would interrogate a man all night and not record anything. "Mr. Somers gave a convincing argument, but when you went back to the evidence, it just wasn't there," she asserted. "Something had to have gone wrong in that jury room . . . I don't feel this man is guilty. And I can't stop praying for him."[10]

It was just luck of the draw that these two women were seated as alternates rather than placed on the main jury panel. Each was adamant that she would not have convicted Pat no matter what, a heartbreaking but meaningless footnote to the case as far as Laura was concerned. While these insights were interesting, they didn't give Laura what she needed. The jurors and alternates were quite clear on one critical point: They had obeyed all the judge's orders and restrictions, steering clear of news reports, avoiding discussions of the case outside of court, focusing only on the evidence and not on extraneous issues. Laura had hoped one among them would reveal some overt misconduct, some violation of the jurors' oaths—that might win Pat a new trial. Such juror misconduct had recently been revealed in the Offord Rollins case, where defense attorneys still were fighting hard for a new trial. But nothing of the sort had happened in Pat's case: His jurors had behaved exactly as they were instructed and sworn to behave.

"Then how could they find me guilty?" Pat asked during his next jailhouse meeting with Laura. Deep circles were etched beneath his eyes; he had dropped forty pounds since his arrest. Haggard and despondent, he kept shaking his head, seemingly unaware of the gesture, as if he were silently and reflexively chanting no, no, no all the time. "If they believed Jerry Coble, if they believed the lies, I could at least understand it. But this . . . Where's the sense of it?"

Laura nodded at him. He didn't expect an answer, knowing that she had none. Still, there *were* answers, hidden from them both.

First there was the story of how Jerry Lee Coble came to make the deal that made him the star witness against Pat Dunn. It was a story the defense never heard.

Laura knew there had been a meeting at a Denny's restaurant between Detective Soliz and Coble, at which Coble first told his story and asked for a deal to elude his own legal troubles. But neither Laura nor any other member of the defense team knew about an earlier meeting bringing Coble together with Kern County law enforcement—the one in a sheriff's interrogation room a year before Sandy's murder, when Jerry Lee Coble first begged to be allowed to make a deal. At that time, Coble promised to testify against—and to help set up—virtually anyone the sheriff's department wanted. Strangers, relatives, he didn't care. Just so long as he didn't have to go back to prison.

"I'll do whatever it takes," he had promised. ". . . I want to make a deal."[11]

Sheriff's Detective Eric Banducci, who had arrested Coble for grand theft, wrote in his report on the interrogation, "I told Jerry that I suspected he was lying. . . . Every time I asked Jerry about a specific item of inventory or loss, Jerry would again ask about making a deal."[12]

In the Dunn case, Jerry Coble had presented himself on the witness stand as a man who just happened to stumble on a murder in progress, a good citizen who wanted to do the right thing. But Banducci's report showed a very different Jerry Lee Coble, one who kept insisting that he be allowed to deal, that he should be transformed into a witness against someone else so he could avoid his own prison sentence. "What a coincidence," Banducci would observe after Pat Dunn's trial, his voice thick with sarcasm, "that Coble would say all that, then end up a year later with a deal to put Pat Dunn away."[13]

Banducci's report was never given to Pat Dunn or his lawyers, as the law requires.[14] And Banducci, the detective who busted Jerry Coble, never appeared on the lengthy list of witnesses and officers relevant to the Dunn case painstakingly compiled by Laura and her colleagues, because they never heard of him. Prosecutors are legally obliged to reveal all information in a case that might be helpful to a defendant. Even an inadvertent failure to disclose important material can be grounds for a new trial or dismissal of charges. In the Dunn case, though, no one on the defense team knew what they were missing. For his part, Detective Banducci was relieved—and surprised—at not being called as a defense witness in the case.

Had they been given the report, the defense could have called Banducci to the stand and asked him why he had not made a deal with Jerry Lee Coble immediately after Coble's arrest, given that such arrangements are not uncommon in criminal investigations, and Coble seemed more than willing. The detective has since said he would have explained his refusal to deal by pointing out that Coble had been caught in numerous lies during his interrogation and had little credibility at the sheriff's department. Banducci said he would never base a case on the word of such a person as Jerry Coble: "I believed Jerry Coble would say or do anything to avoid going to prison, so he could get back on the street and score more dope."[15]

Such testimony, had the defense known it was available, could have been devastating to Coble's credibility as a witness, as well as the prosecution's entire case, particularly because Banducci could also have shed new light on the unusual manner in which Coble finally got his deal with Detective Soliz and Deputy DA Somers. Contrary to typical practice in such cases, Banducci was kept in the dark about his own suspect and case when the deal was forged. When Soliz returned from his initial meeting with Coble, he knew he had a witness who could be the turning point in the case. Yet Soliz, who knew that Banducci was in charge of the pending case against Coble, did not talk to his colleague. Banducci and Soliz worked in the same office and occupied desks less than ten feet apart, yet Soliz never asked his fellow detective's opinion about Coble's credibility or reliability.[16]

Instead, Detective Soliz decided to keep his new witness in the Dunn case a secret, and never mentioned it to Detective Banducci. Nor did Deputy District Attorney Somers consult with Banducci before dispensing with his grand theft case against Coble as part of the plea bargain that made Jerry Lee a witness against Pat Dunn. Such consultation is normally made when a prosecutor settles a detective's case, but this time, Somers dealt only with Soliz, and therefore presumably had no idea that Banducci thought Coble would make an untrustworthy witness.[17] Banducci would not know anything about Coble's involvement in the Dunn case until Soliz approached him in the office several months later and requested Jerry Coble's driver's license.

Banducci had impounded the license after arresting Coble. This original grand theft case had then dragged on, even after Coble pleaded guilty, because sentencing kept getting delayed to allow Coble medical treatment for epilepsy, the legacy of a head injury sustained many years before—or so Banducci thought. Recently, there had been a new and secret reason for the delays: the Pat Dunn case.

"What do you want Coble's license for?" Banducci asked. "Is he a suspect in something?"

"He needs it back. He's a witness in one of my cases."

"You gotta be kidding," Banducci said, the disbelief in his voice obvious. He waited for Soliz to explain, but the homicide detective offered no additional information. Banducci dug out the license and handed it over.[18] Months later—and then only through news coverage of the Dunn trial—Banducci finally found out just what Coble was testifying about, and that the six-year prison sentence facing him in Banducci's case had been reduced by the Kern County DA to five years' probation.

"You'd think somebody might have mentioned it to me," the detective later complained, "since it was my case."[19]

The DA's failure to pass on information did not end with the Banducci report. Even after eluding punishment in Banducci's case and cutting his deal, Coble could not bring himself to stay out of trouble—but that, too, remained unknown to Pat Dunn's defense team.

Jerry Coble formally entered his new plea agreement and promise to testify against Pat on November 3, 1992, three months after he first called Detective Soliz. In exchange for his anticipated testimony, he got probation with the condition that he refrain from using drugs and committing other crimes. The judge who accepted the plea bargain made it clear that if Coble violated those conditions, he could be sent to prison, yet still have to testify in the Dunn case.[20]

Yet, Jerry Coble continued using heroin before, during

and after that hearing in court. The Dunn defense team knew that, because Coble admitted as much when he took the stand. The DA even suggested to the jury that Coble's willingness to admit such an unflattering detail showed he was being candid and truthful. But Coble also swore he committed no other crimes since cutting his deal. That was why, he said, he could only afford to do heroin five or six times a month after agreeing to testify, instead of his preferred five or six times a week. Had he been committing thefts, he could have afforded more drugs, he claimed. "I wasn't working. I didn't have any money and I wasn't doing any crime," he testified under oath.

This testimony was a lie. And though Detective Soliz and Deputy DA Somers may not have personally known it, other law-enforcement officials in Kern County did.

In late December 1992, a month after his plea bargain—and less than two weeks after he testified in Pat Dunn's preliminary hearing—Jerry Coble was seen in a Bakersfield bar called the Belvedere. A barmaid there remembered Coble distinctly, because he had been a regular there until Thanksgiving, when he had gotten into a fight and stopped coming around. Then he came back one last time late in December.

On the day of Coble's reappearance, five or so blank payroll checks were found missing from the Belvedere. The checks had been kept in an office that was normally off-limits to customers—but which a careful thief could enter if he watched and waited until the bartender went in back to fetch supplies to restock the bar. Two days after the theft, on December 23, a short, bearded man wearing a baseball cap walked into Sherry's, a liquor store in downtown Bakersfield, and identified himself as Richard

Scott Anderson. Sherry's had a lucrative side business cashing paychecks, and Anderson had a payroll check for $944.49 from the Belvedere bar he wanted to cash. He also wanted to wire fifty dollars via Western Union to someone named Aaron Coble, as a Christmas gift.

Anderson produced an American Express corporate card, an insurance card and a photo ID to serve as identification, but the manager at Sherry's felt suspicious. She telephoned the Belvedere to make certain that a Richard Scott Anderson indeed worked there. She was told the bar had no such employee, and that whoever was in her store had a forged and stolen check. While Anderson filled out the Western Union forms, the manager discreetly called the police, then tried to stall the thief until help arrived. Sensing that something was up, Anderson inched toward the door, then suddenly darted outside and began running. The manager got to the door just in time to see the forger climb into an El Camino pickup truck, and she caught the first three digits of the license plate, which she remembered as 4DB. Bakersfield police officers arrived a few minutes later, but too late to find Anderson. All that turned up was a wallet discarded in a nearby parking lot with Anderson's identification in it and a check stub from the Belvedere. The photo identification proved to be phony—whoever Richard Scott Anderson was, he was not the man who tried to cash the check at Sherry's.

After the Christmas holidays had passed, a Bakersfield Police Department detective named J. E. Taylor inherited the case. Taylor contacted the real Richard Scott Anderson by telephone in Alamo, California, where Anderson worked as a real estate broker. It turned out that in January 1992, during a road trip to San Francisco from Los Angeles, Anderson had stopped at a service station and used the restroom. While he was washing up, his wallet and checkbook were stolen from the counter next to him. Since that time, he had received nearly a dozen calls from irate Bakersfield residents who had listed items for sale in the newspaper classified ads, then sold them to someone calling himself Richard Anderson. This Anderson had paid with the stolen checks, using Anderson's identification, but the checks all bounced—since the real Richard Anderson had closed the account. The forger had never been caught.

Then, when Detective Taylor read over the patrol officer's report from Sherry's, he immediately recognized the name Aaron Coble. Having worked several burglary investigations involving the Coble family, Taylor knew that Jerry Lee had a young son named Aaron. A records check told him that Coble owned an El Camino with the license number 4D80212—very close to the partial plate number spotted outside the liquor store. Taylor's next step in the investigation was to go to the Kern County Sheriff's Department, where he obtained a booking photograph of Jerry Lee Coble to show to witnesses at Sherry's and the Belvedere. The day was January 11, 1993, two months before Pat Dunn's trial was to begin. Detective Taylor had just linked Jerry Coble to a new crime and was on the verge of solving the case.

Coble's arrest could have had a dramatic effect on the prosecution of Pat Dunn, for at the time, Coble was on probation for grand theft, thanks to his deal, as well as parole for his previous conviction and two-year prison sentence for receiving stolen property. Even with his arrangement in the Dunn case, another bust would make prison a virtual certainty. And if imprisoned, he almost surely would refuse to testify. What would he have to gain at that point? And without Coble, the whole murder case against Pat could fall to pieces. One alternative, of course, would be for the DA to cut yet another deal with Coble, giving him another free pass, but the result would still leave the prosecution in dire shape—Coble would be revealed as a liar and a scam artist who couldn't stay straight for just a couple of months, even when his entire future was at stake. The DA, in turn, would appear desperate and willing to bend over backward for a dubious witness. Furthermore, the crime Coble was accused of committing—posing as someone else, lying about his identity, forging documents—was uncomfortably close to the sort of trickery and fraud that the Dunn defense team believed he had committed in framing Pat. A habitual criminal who could assume a new identity was undoubtedly capable of collecting enough information to frame another man for murder, they would argue.

Only one thing was certain to preserve the case against Pat Dunn: The new case against Jerry Lee Coble could simply go away. And whether by accident or design, that's exactly what happened.

For reasons unstated in his report on the case, Detective Taylor took no further action on the new Coble case for three months after contacting the Kern County Sheriff's Department—which, of course, was relying on Coble as a star witness. Taylor's reports reveal no attempt to show the photograph of Coble to the manager at Sherry's Liquor, which is why he went to get it from the sheriff's department in the first place. Nor was there any documented investigation of Richard Anderson's statement that his ID and checks had been used to commit a number of other thefts and forgeries throughout Bakersfield over the past year, to see if Coble might be responsible for those as well. And Taylor did not try to contact Coble's parole officer or probation officer, either of whom could have arrested Coble immediately had they known he was passing stolen payroll checks.

It was not until April 5, 1993, that Detective Taylor requested that the Bakersfield police lab process the stolen Belvedere check for fingerprints. Four days later, Coble's prints were identified on the check. The prints made for a cold, irrefutable case against Coble—the kind of hard, objective evidence detectives had searched for so hard in their investigation of Pat Dunn, only to come up empty.

Taylor's request to the police lab was made seven working days after Pat Dunn's trial ended on March 24, 1993, just late enough to be of absolutely no use to the defense.[21] Jerry Lee Coble had been able to take the stand and swear he had committed no crimes since making his deal to testify against Pat. He swore he had received very little in return for his testimony. He portrayed himself as a law-abiding citizen who even went to church shortly after seeing Pat Dunn drag Sandy's body out the door, a man who, despite his long criminal record, just wanted to do the right thing.

Under the circumstances, Jerry Lee Coble sounded quite believable, given that his latest arrest was kept secret.

The delay in handling Coble's case remains unexplained. The significance of this new information could not have been lost on anyone who followed the Dunn trial, which received daily coverage in the Bakersfield news media, including stories about Coble's involvement as a key witness for the prosecution. And Detective Taylor already knew quite a bit about the Dunns on his own, having been acquainted with Sandy years before—Taylor had been the investigating officer in Sandy's embezzlement case against her longtime bookkeeper, Delores Craig. Sandy had talked with Taylor many times and had testified at length against the bookkeeper, who pleaded guilty in 1986 in exchange for a two-year prison sentence. Six years later, early in the Dunn homicide investigation, Sheriff's Detective Soliz and his partner on the case, Dusty Kline, collected information about Taylor's investigation of Craig. Then Detective Taylor, after visiting the sheriff's department in January 1993, delayed his new case against Jerry Coble for three months, even though he had identified Coble as the culprit.

There is no evidence that John Soliz or John Somers had direct knowledge of Coble's new fraud case before Pat Dunn's trial began, so they cannot be faulted personally for failing to disclose its existence to the defense team, as the law would require.[22] Conversely, Taylor had no legal obligation to disclose anything, since he was not involved in the Dunn homicide investigation at all. However, the duty to provide such information extends beyond individuals to whole law-enforcement and prosecutorial agencies, and it's clear that Pat Dunn was denied important, powerful information about his case and the main witness against him.

Inadvertent, coincidental or deliberate, the effect of this remained the same: It benefited the prosecution in the Dunn case and allowed Deputy District Attorney John Somers to stand before a jury and declare that "Mr. Coble was very honest with you. . . . He was credible and he was believable in his testimony."

The new case against Jerry Lee Coble remained buried. And Jerry Lee Coble helped bury Pat Dunn.

• • •

Pat and his defense team were missing another important element of their case besides Jerry Coble's past and present criminal justice history: They were denied the full story behind Kate Rosenlieb's role in Pat's arrest and prosecution. The omission had a profound effect on the course of the trial—once again, to the prosecution's benefit and Pat Dunn's detriment.

Just before the trial commenced, the defense received the packet of notes written by Rosenlieb in the form of a journal, detailing her conversations with Pat and detectives. The last entry contained in this sheaf, dated August 1, 1992, strongly implied that Kate had severed her relationship with Pat and the case long before his arrest in October. In it, Kate states that she had to face the fact that she had lost both Sandy and Pat, and that she just had to get on with life.

But there was more to this journal, and to Kate's role in the case, than was ever disclosed to the defense. The journal's remaining entries—which were not turned over—show that Rosenlieb, far from sitting back and letting the investigation take its course, had actively lobbied for Pat's arrest while organizing a group of Bakersfield movers and shakers to do the same.

Later in August, according to the journal notes not given to the defense, Rosenlieb grew concerned that there had been no progress in the case. She called Detective Soliz and asked, "Is this it? Aren't you going to arrest him?" She became quite angry with him, accusing him and his colleagues of incompetence in the case and of failing to take the most basic steps necessary to put Pat Dunn away. "If I knew it was this easy to kill a spouse," she railed, "I would have killed mine a long time ago."

Soliz bristled at the criticism, wrote Rosenlieb, but in the end told her to keep faith in the system. The case would move forward, he promised.

A few weeks later, on September 16, after Jerry Lee Coble had come forward and the sheriff's department had asked the DA to file charges against Dunn, Rosenlieb again called Soliz to find out what was happening. The detective told her that Somers, another deputy DA and their supervisor were examining the case and would decide whether Pat should be prosecuted.

"If it takes political pressure on the DA's office, I can try that. I know a lot of people who will help," Rosenlieb suggested to the detective. She offered to organize a lobbying effort to persuade the prosecutors, and District Attorney Ed Jagels himself, to go after Pat.

Soliz said no, give it some more time.

Her October 8, 1992, entry finds Soliz in a different mood. When she spoke with him then, Rosenlieb would later recall, he seemed angry and bitter. "I have no respect for Ed Jagels," she remembers Soliz saying. "They have no guts over there at the DA's office." Now Soliz did want Rosenlieb to ready a campaign to get Dunn prosecuted, she wrote in her journal.[23]

An entry dated a week later finds Detective Soliz even more frustrated. According to Rosenlieb, he called her and said, "Now is the time." If she could exert any political pressure on District Attorney Jagels to force him to prosecute Pat Dunn, she should do it now.

With that, Kate Rosenlieb put a two-step plan into motion, a strategy that she had been preparing and rehearsing in her mind for weeks. First, she checked in with Soliz's boss, Sheriff Carl Sparks. Of their conversation, Rosenlieb's notes say, "Carl said the DA is a politician and he plays the percentages. The DA has the highest conviction rate in homicides in the state . . . and he doesn't want to jeopardize his record with a circumstantial case. We believe, like you do, that Pat Dunn's a murderer, but he [Jagels] doesn't want to screw up his prosecution record."

Using this assessment as a prod, Rosenlieb then recruited to her cause three city council members, including two who ultimately testified for the prosecution in the Dunn case, to call Jagels and ask, on behalf of their constituents and themselves, why he was failing to pursue murder charges against Pat Dunn. The goal was to "gently" urge Jagels to do the "right thing." Stan Harper, the Republican consultant, friend and campaign manager for Jagels, also attempted to persuade Jagels to charge Dunn.[24]

Looking back years later, Rosenlieb would recall that Step One, as she called it, failed to get Pat Dunn charged. That, she said, forced her to proceed to Step Two. She called Ed Jagels personally and, dispensing with gentle urging, threatened to go to the press or the grand jury with allegations of cover-up and selective prosecution. As she would tell it, "Jagels said, no murder weapon, no confession, and no one witnessed the crime occur. So I won't prosecute."

To this reasoning, Kate responded, "You had no murder weapon, no confession and no one saw it happen in the Offord Rollins case, either. So if you're poor and black in this town, you go to jail. And if you're rich and white, you get off."

Rosenlieb recalled going on to tell Jagels she would quit her job, make the prosecution of Pat Dunn her full-time work, and make sure everyone in Kern County knew that the district attorney was both racist and willing to let a murderer walk—all unless he prosecuted Pat Dunn. Her memory of this exchange remained quite detailed years later: "Forty-eight hours after all this screaming about Offord Rollins, Pat Dunn was charged. In my mind, if I wasn't the ultimate bitch from day one, nothing would have happened. It just didn't seem important to anyone else."[25]

Upon further reflection, however, Rosenlieb altered her account of this campaign to prosecute Pat Dunn. She didn't actually threaten Jagels directly, she claimed, but left a threatening message on his voice mail. She later changed her recollections again and said she only *contemplated* threatening Jagels, and that Step One, the initial "gentle" lobbying effort by city council members, had worked immediately. Pat Dunn was charged before Rosenlieb had to set Step Two into motion, making it unnecessary for her to carry out her threats to politically "eviscerate" Ed Jagels. She would have happily done so, however, if necessary to see justice done.[26]

Whatever steps Rosenlieb actually carried out, as opposed to actions she merely contemplated, Pat Dunn's defense team knew nothing of this lobbying effort at all. They had no idea that the lead detective on the case, Kate Rosenlieb and other city officials (who were about to be sued by Pat Dunn over the canceled movie-theater project, and who therefore may have had reason to think the worst of him) had all moved behind the scenes to orchestrate a campaign to put Pat in jail—turning a legal decision into a political cause. Rosenlieb and the other witnesses were all presented to the jury at Pat's trial as unbiased individuals who just wanted to tell the truth, but had all of Kate's notes been turned over—or if the

District Attorney and the sheriff's department had revealed the existence of the lobbying efforts, as the law required them to do—the defense could have painted a very different picture.

If all of the information on Kate Rosenlieb had been known to the defense, its impact is impossible to gauge with certainty. John Somers could have told the jury that her efforts mattered not at all, that Kate was simply doing the right thing by coming clean and providing her entire journal, and that she should be admired for making such difficult choices—for doing everything she could to see justice done. The defense team, meanwhile, could have cast her as a woman whose memory was prone to exaggeration and inaccuracy, who had convicted Pat Dunn in her own mind before even speaking with him, who had betrayed a friend's confidences, who had lied to the police, then plotted with them to bolster their case, and whose various accounts since Sandy's disappearance were riddled with contradictions. Finally, the defense could have alleged that Rosenlieb and the other prosecution witnesses she recruited had not remained unbiased, but had instead joined together to conduct a covert campaign to have Pat Dunn jailed at a time when some within the district attorney's office harbored reservations about the case. The defense could, in short, have painted a portrait of a woman and a detective on an unswerving quest to get Pat convicted at all costs—and of a district attorney's office that kept these behind-the-scenes machinations by its own witnesses secret.

And Kate Rosenlieb kept something else to herself that could have aided the defense. As the closest friend of the Dunns to testify for either side in the trial, she could have revealed a statement that Sandy had made to her not long before her murder: that she would never divorce Pat. Years later, Kate would recall suggesting that the Dunns should consider ending their marriage. But Sandy said no way: "They seemed to enjoy making one another miserable," Rosenlieb would say in an interview, long after Pat's trial. "Sandy said she would never divorce Pat."[27]

Rosenlieb might not have known the potential impact of this knowledge, for she did not hear Marie Gates' testimony about Sandy wanting a divorce, one of the key elements in the prosecution's theory of motive. Rosenlieb's information suggested Gates might be wrong, but this would be yet another revelation the jury never heard. Without Rosenlieb to challenge Gates' credible-sounding testimony, jurors felt they had no choice but to believe Pat was about to lose his marriage, and his meal ticket—and therefore had a very good motive for murder.[28]

Kate's failure to mention Sandy's feelings about divorcing Pat did more than merely sustain Marie Gates' credibility. Marie spoke of encountering Sandy Dunn weeks before her death, weeping in the street and complaining about wanting to divorce a husband who had lied about his finances and wanted to spend all her money. While investigating the case, Laura had theorized that Marie was confusing Pat with Sandy's second husband, Leon. But there was no ready way to convey this to the jury. If Kate had made known her information about Sandy's unwillingness to divorce Pat, however, the missing pieces of a puzzle that had eluded Laura and the rest of the defense team would have slipped into place:

It wasn't necessarily Marie Gates who was confused about that day in the street. It was, perhaps, Sandy.

If Sandy Dunn truly were suffering the early onset of Alzheimer's disease, she may have been experiencing an episode of confusion that moment on the street, in which she relived her "mistake in marriage" with Leon as if it were still going on. Were that the case, Marie Gates could have been rendering an accurate account of Sandy's words, without understanding that Sandy had been talking about a husband other than Pat. This would explain how Sandy could tell Marie she wanted a divorce because of a "mistake in marriage"—without ever using Pat's name—while vowing to Kate she would never divorce Pat and telling Kevin Knutson she wanted a living trust to benefit Pat. This theory could have been buttressed further through Ann Kidder's testimony—if the defense pointed out that Sandy, again confused, might have been reliving her marriage to a senile Pat Paola when she babbled about her husband not liking clothes. That comment was a perfect fit not for Pat Dunn, but for Pat Paola, whose habit of stripping and running outside naked was well known.

But with Kate remaining silent on the question of divorce, these pieces never fell into place for the defense. Pat's team was left with no firm repudiation of Marie Gates, leading the jury to feel it had no valid reason to question her credibility.

Even after Pat's conviction, Laura Lawhon and the rest of the defense team remained ignorant of Kate's full knowledge and role in the case. And as much as anyone or anything in the trial, Kate Rosenlieb ensured Pat Dunn would go to prison.

8

THE MONTHS SURROUNDING PAT DUNN'S ARREST AND conviction for murder were interesting times for the justice system in Kern County and the rest of the country as well. If there were official errors and omissions in the Dunn prosecution, they were far from unique. For it was at this time that the problem of withheld evidence and other forms of misconduct in the nation's criminal justice system began receiving serious attention, as complaints about police and prosecutors arose like never before. Major cases in courthouses throughout America started to unravel owing to false or misleading evidence, testimony or argument that had been used to convict people who might otherwise have been found innocent. Other cases crumbled as a result of the chance discovery that the government itself had broken the law, hiding evidence that tended to show innocence. As Laura Lawhon continued digging for some proof that would free Pat Dunn, she saw case after case revealed as a sham.

And nowhere did the problem seem more pronounced than in Kern County, where problem prosecutions surfaced repeatedly in the 1990s. A double murderer named Floyd Gore, for example, was granted a new trial in 1992 because Kern County prosecutors had stacked the jury by excluding minorities—a constitutional violation that

warranted overturning Gore's life sentences, despite overwhelming evidence of his guilt. And though he was tried
and convicted again, this time with a properly constructed jury, the possibility that a murderer could go free
because the government broke the rules created a stir.
(Many Hispanics and African Americans charged with
crimes in Kern County who were not so obviously guilty
as Gore had complained for years about racial problems
in jury selection, Offord Rollins among them.)

In another Kern County case, Sergio Venegas saw his
1992 conviction and sixty-five-year prison sentence for a
brutal rape and assault overturned because the prosecution used erroneous evidence against him. In a precedent-setting decision, the California Supreme Court
ruled that Kern County Deputy District Attorney Lisa
Green (who also prosecuted Offord Rollins) had won the
conviction only because the DNA test she relied upon—
the only hard evidence against Venegas—vastly overstated the likelihood of his guilt. (In fairness to Green, prosecutors and law-enforcement agencies throughout the
nation—from the Justice Department and the FBI on
down—were taken to task throughout most of the
nineties for using inaccurate and overstated DNA evidence to win convictions.)[29]

As in the past, District Attorney Ed Jagels responded
to such rulings not by examining his own office's practices, but by criticizing appellate justices for favoring
criminals' rights over public safety. But the tumult in the
Kern County courts seemed to touch on every sort of
criminal case: The district attorney's office found itself
facing reversals in drug cases, murder cases, rape cases
and car-theft cases because of official misconduct.
Sheriff's deputies had made illegal searches in some

cases, in others coercive interrogations, in which they forced adults to confess much as the children were forced to make molestation accusations in the ring cases. Deputies tried to bolster two drug investigations by targeting defense lawyers through their own clients, leading to more reversals because the deputies violated one of the most elementary of legal principles—that the government may not interrogate a defendant (much less negotiate plea bargains with him, as occurred in one of these cases) once that defendant has been formally charged and is represented by an attorney. Meanwhile, a clearly guilty killer almost went free when an investigator for the DA improperly contacted a juror during the trial, another form of prosecutorial misconduct.

One particularly troubling Kern County case came to light within a year of Pat Dunn's trial—the investigation of a double murder. Two men were found shot to death in an alfalfa field outside the farm town of Delano, an apparent drug deal gone sour. Detective John Soliz, fresh off his victory in the Dunn case, was assigned to find the killers. Early on, witnesses identified three suspects for Soliz, one of them a man named Rosales Meza.

Six months passed with no sign of Meza anywhere in Kern County. Then, while searching a house in Shafter, a police officer found a snapshot of a man who resembled the suspect. When Soliz saw the photo, he agreed it was Rosales Meza, the man wanted for the alfalfa-field murders. Soliz and a group of deputies later returned to the house, burst through the door, and arrested the man in the photo, who they found inside.

The man Soliz booked into the county jail identified himself as a recent Mexican immigrant named Jose Meza Fernandez. Meza Fernandez told the detective he had no

connection to the alfalfa-field killings, and that he had
not even come to the United States until two months
after the murders occurred. He swore he had been home
on his parents' ranch in Mexico, milking cows at the time.
And he insisted he had never gone by the name "Rosales
Meza."

Detective Soliz did not believe him. During their
interview, Soliz repeatedly told the man he was the prime
suspect, that he had been identified as a murderer, that
the authorities knew he was guilty—just as he had done
with Pat Dunn. Later, Soliz made a point of writing down
every inconsistency in the man's statements, knowing
this could be used as evidence of a guilty state of mind—
a lesson from the Pat Dunn case playbook—and he set
about gathering any evidence or statements he could find
to support his case against the suspected killer. What
Soliz didn't do was thoroughly investigate the man's
claim that the detective had arrested the wrong man—
much as his department never attempted to investigate
the Dunn case as a legitimate missing-persons case. "A lot
of these people lie to us," Detective Soliz told a news
reporter by way of explanation. "We don't take their word
at face value."

Soliz did say that he had requested Rosales Meza's fingerprints from the California Department of Motor
Vehicles so that he could compare them to the man he
had just arrested, a matter of routine. But the detective
said he never received the prints from the state and, distracted by other cases, never followed up. It also appears
that neither Soliz nor anyone else thought to put the suspect in a live lineup to see if any of the witnesses in the
murder case could identify him. Jose Meza Fernandez,
then, was booked and jailed on first-degree murder

charges, and the Kern County deputy DA on the case, John Somers, wanted the death penalty.

The defense attorney appointed to represent Meza Fernandez, former Kern County prosecutor Kyle Humphrey, took one look at the case and pronounced it "garbage." He, too, told Somers that the DA had the wrong man. Then, after Meza Fernandez had been in jail more than a month and at Humphrey's insistence, Somers agreed to send for the fingerprints that Soliz had never obtained. After another week passed, the prints arrived and the sheriff's fingerprint expert told Soliz he had, indeed, arrested an innocent man.

Meza Fernandez, set free later that day, announced that he feared staying in Kern County and would return to Mexico. Kern County officials, meanwhile, maintained that nothing untoward had occurred: In the end, they said, the truth had come out, and the justice system had worked.[30]

And they were right, to a degree. But if a less-capable defense attorney had failed to insist on a fingerprint check, an innocent man arrested by John Soliz, who was just as convinced of this suspect's guilt as he had been of Pat Dunn's, could have been sentenced to death for a murder he did not commit.

In another, very different case that also took place in Kern County shortly after Pat Dunn's trial, police misconduct freed four men who seemed very much to deserve prison.

The men, convicted in one of the biggest drug busts in Kern County history, had been sentenced to fifteen to twenty years apiece in prison. But after a review, the California Court of Appeal found itself with no choice but to throw the whole case out, thanks to an illegal search and attempts to cover it up by Kern County officials. Misconduct, in effect, set the guilty free, for the four men were caught red-handed driving vans filled with drums of a dangerous drug—$4 million worth of the potentially deadly hallucinogen PCP.

The problem was, Kern County Sheriff's investigators found the drugs in a warrantless and therefore unlawful search of a rural ranch in an isolated area of the county called Stallion Springs. The authorities suspected that PCP was being manufactured at the ranch, but couldn't prove it. Frustrated after a long and ineffective surveillance, the investigators started nosing around—without first obtaining a warrant, a basic constitutional requirement for such searches of private property that all cops are schooled in. Then, the Court of Appeal found, the officers concealed the existence of this illegal search during their sworn testimony. The district attorney's office, meanwhile, never passed on to the defense a deputy's written report that would have exposed the flaw in the case. This was said to be "inadvertent."

The Kern County judge who oversaw the trial of the four men harshly criticized the two sheriff's deputies involved, but at the strong urging of the prosecutor—who said she had not known of the illegal search until the trial commenced—he stopped short of throwing the case out of court, as the law required. He chose instead to dish out the long prison sentences to the drug dealers, and to criticize the sheriff's deputies for testimony that was "obfuscatory at best, and bordered on absolute lying." The judge also suggested that contempt proceedings against the officers might be considered. Representatives of the district attorney and the sheriff's department publicly praised the offending lawmen instead.

An outraged California Court of Appeal did what the Bakersfield judge would not do, upholding basic constitutional principles by throwing out the convictions and going to the unusual length of reciting in its blistering opinion the famous Sir Walter Scott lines, "Oh what a tangled web we weave, when first we practice to deceive." After reviewing line by line a long list of falsehoods and misleading statements made by sheriff's deputies during their sworn testimonies, the appeals court characterized one deputy as so "inconsistent, misleading and untruthful ... it is difficult to determine what he really knew." As for the other deputy involved—a sergeant in the sheriff's narcotics unit—the appeals court stated, "There really isn't very much left of his testimony that could be considered credible."[31] Such open criticism of lawmen—singled out by name by the appellate justices—is seldom seen in court opinions, even ones like this, which the court withheld from its published compendiums of case law. (Unpublished opinions are often issued in cases of government misconduct, and they cannot be cited in other cases, sparing law-enforcement officials from embarrassment.) This was not the first time this same sheriff's sergeant had come to the attention of the appeals court. Previously, he had been chastised for illegally negotiating a deal with a defendant to set up the defendant's own lawyer—a constitutional violation requiring a new trial and the reversal of an eight-year prison sentence. In another case, a grand-theft conviction and a three-year prison sentence had to be overturned because this sergeant conducted yet another illegal search. Nevertheless, even after the "tangled web" opinion was handed down, the prosecutor on the PCP case maintained that the appeals court was wrong, that she knew the deputies didn't lie, and that, "My confidence in this case and the two officers remains unshaken."[32]

Even as officials defended the Stallion Springs embarrassment, they were besieged on another front when Charles Tomlin, who had been serving life in prison for a 1978 Bakersfield drug killing, also returned to haunt the Kern County courthouse. Tomlin had been in prison for fifteen years by the time Pat's trial concluded, and his case was just coming before the United States Court of Appeals for the Ninth Circuit, in San Francisco, one rung below the Supreme Court. In all probability, this would be his final shot at freedom, as every other court at every level in the Kern County and California justice systems had rejected his claims.

The only problem was, Charles Tomlin was almost certainly innocent. Were he to be retried, everyone involved in the case agreed he would be acquitted with ease. Which is why the Kern County District Attorney adamantly opposed any new trial for Tomlin, and used every procedural and technical ploy at its disposal to keep Tomlin in prison. The case bore startling similarities to Pat Dunn's—a man convicted of murder on the basis of one eyewitness's testimony, with no physical evidence against him and considerable evidence in his favor, and a police investigation that seemed biased against him from the start.

Not that Charles Tomlin didn't create some problems on his own. His nickname since his youth was "Treetop" because, his mother always said, he acted like money grew on trees. It was an attitude that got him into frequent scrapes with the law; early on, he accumulated a record for drugs and theft. His preference for dating white girls brought him trouble as well, given that he was a tall, skinny young black man with long, straightened, shoulder-length hair in Bakersfield circa 1970—a time and place not known for its tolerance or diversity. Certain parts of Kern County—the east-side community of Oildale being particularly notorious at the time—were believed by many to be unsafe for blacks. Cars had been surrounded and stoned, crosses burned on lawns. Treetop was playing with fire—his friends told him so, and so did his enemies.

On December 7, 1978, a small-time white drug dealer from Oildale, twenty-five-year-old Daniel Stewart, was shot to death over nine pounds of marijuana. The dealer's girlfriend, Leticia Mendez, was sitting next to him in his pickup truck when the killer opened the door, sat down and fired a single bullet into Stewart's head. When the police arrived, Mendez described the killer as a short, stocky black man with a bushy Afro—nothing like the lanky, long-haired Treetop Tomlin. But a detective on the case who had had a number of run-ins with Tomlin in the past tracked down a teenager who had helped set up the fatal drug deal. The kid, the detective later testified, was too terrified to speak the killer's name, but instead scrawled "Treetop" on a piece of paper. Bakersfield Police Detective Les Vincent then showed Leticia Mendez a photo lineup that included Tomlin; she picked out Treetop as the shooter. Following his arrest, Tomlin was placed in a live lineup, and, after some hesitation, Leticia identified him as the killer. Though Tomlin had by then retained an attorney who by law should have been present for this, Detective Vincent did not notify the lawyer about the lineup.

At trial, the police claimed that they had lost a central

piece of evidence—the "Treetop" note—and the teenager who supposedly wrote it, charged as an accomplice to murder, did not testify. (He later denied fingering Treetop and said he never wrote a note to detectives.) There were fingerprints in the dead man's truck and on the passenger-side door, none of them Treetop's. Meanwhile, Tomlin brought in multiple alibi witnesses, most of them family members and neighbors, who testified that he was home at the time of the killing. But the prosecution labeled the defense witnesses liars and argued that its own eyewitness had sat right next to the killer, all the proof anyone should need of Tomlin's guilt. Tainted as that evidence was—the lineup had been illegal, and this could have been used to attack and even throw out of court Leticia Mendez's identification of Tomlin as the killer—Tomlin's defense attorney inexplicably failed to pursue this point.[33] Treetop Tomlin was convicted by an all-white jury and sentenced to twenty-eight years to life in prison.

Afterward, Mendez became increasingly concerned that she had helped convict the wrong man. She had been afraid to say so at trial, but she had picked out Tomlin's picture not because she recognized him, but because she had been tipped off by detectives' facial expressions—she could see, as she looked over the photos, what the "right" answer would be. And she recognized Tomlin at the lineup the next day only because she had already seen his photo, and even then she had started to say she couldn't be sure. Then one of the detectives cut her off, telling her any doubts would kill the case, she would later recall. Such pressure would never have been attempted with Tomlin's lawyer present, but alone with the police, Leticia felt she had to come through for her boyfriend's sake. She picked Tomlin and stuck with it, then lived quietly with her guilt.

Six years later, Gerson Horn, a Beverly Hills attorney who took on Tomlin's appeal as a personal crusade, knocked on Leticia Mendez's door, expecting to get it slammed in his face by the woman whose boyfriend had been murdered. Instead, Leticia burst into tears and blurted, "I convicted an innocent man." Together Gerson and Mendez went to court to correct her mistake. In 1986, she told a judge in Kern County everything: Tomlin was innocent. She had been wrong. The detectives had improperly pressured and influenced her. Treetop deserved a new trial.

But the district attorney vehemently fought reopening the case, and the judge—Robert Baca, who would preside over Pat Dunn's case—was unmoved except by his disdain for out-of-town attorneys descending on Kern County to criticize its justice system. "You talk to me like I'm some kind of idiot who doesn't understand the law or the case," Baca railed at Horn. "Just argue the case. Don't argue a lot of propaganda."

At the end of the hearing, Judge Baca ruled that the woman whose word had been sufficient to send Tomlin to prison years before was no longer a credible witness—a common judicial finding whenever prosecution witnesses recant their testimony. Mendez's story of being pressured to identify the wrong man could not be believed, Baca stated. Tomlin would stay in prison. Case closed.

Six more years passed with Tomlin behind bars, as first the state appeals court, and then the California Supreme Court, agreed with Baca's ruling. But his federal habeas corpus appeal caught the attention of the Ninth Circuit Court of Appeals, in San Francisco, where the justices questioned the conduct of the police and prosecution, and found that the authorities had given false information to the defense.[34] However, one of the oddities of appeals in the nation's criminal justice system is the rigorous limits put on them, notwithstanding complaints by Ed Jagels and like-minded critics about endless appeals that undermine finality and common sense in the courts. No matter what might surface during a habeas hearing, the appeals courts can only consider points raised in the original pleadings—and, in Tomlin's case, prosecutorial misconduct was not among those points. Appeals justices also are required to accept as true many of the determinations made by the lower-court judges who preceded them in the case and saw the witnesses face to face, instead of simply reviewing a transcript. Baca found Leticia Mendez's recantation unbelievable, and the appeals justices therefore had to accept this finding even though they thought the opposite to be true, and that, as the court later wrote, "There is a serious risk that Tomlin was, in fact, wrongly identified as the assailant." In other words, the court found ample evidence to show that Tomlin might be innocent, yet evidence of innocence was not sufficient to overturn his conviction. This, too, is a common dilemma faced in the criminal-justice system: After a jury renders its verdict, the only questions that can be raised are strictly "legal" ones—was the trial fair, was there egregious misconduct, did jurors violate their oaths and consider extraneous evidence? "Factual" questions—did he really commit the crime?—are almost always irrelevant.

By the time the Ninth Circuit got the case in 1992, around the time of Pat Dunn's trial, the only legal justification left to free Tomlin was a finding that his original attorney had been so incompetent over the matter of the lineup and identification that, as a result, Treetop did not receive a fair trial. In a 2-1 decision, the Ninth Circuit found just that. The decision was immediately decried by Kern County authorities, who felt the justices simply didn't like the outcome of the trial and had seized on a technicality to free a guilty man. Either way, at age forty-two, with sixteen years in prison behind him, Charles Tomlin walked free, legally innocent. The DA made no attempt to retry him, knowing that, with an eyewitness who recanted, they'd have no chance of winning.

There was one little-known footnote to the Tomlin case. In late 1992, in a completely unrelated trial, an eighteen-year-old man charged as the getaway driver in a robbery and murder at a fast-food restaurant was acquitted despite testimony from a Bakersfield police detective who said the young man had confessed to his part in the crime. After the trial, a juror explained why they had set the defendant free: They had doubts about the detective on the case. The detective was Les Vincent, the same investigator who made—and ultimately lost—the case against Treetop Tomlin.[35]

At the same time Charles Tomlin was winning his freedom, Kern County's vaunted molestation-ring convictions were also coming back to haunt the courts, a process that would span a decade and raise uncomfortable questions about the entire system of justice in Kern County.

The cases had begun unraveling years before, soon after investigative reports in the *Fresno Bee* broke the satanic story—and revealed the provably false allegations at its root. The Kern County Sheriff at the time, Larry Kleier, who fervently believed even the most outlandish devil worship-conspiracy allegations because "children don't lie," ended up at war with District Attorney Ed

Jagels, because the DA's top deputies had refused to lodge molestation and murder charges against eighteen alleged satanists. Kleier considered this a slap in the face, but the only evidence produced by the sheriff's secret satanic task force to support the charges lay in the wild accusations of children. There were no bodies, no forensic evidence, no corroboration that satanic murders and molestations had taken place. Had the DA filed these cases, it would not have been the first time the office had prosecuted Kern County citizens with insufficient evidence or a lack of corroboration of its child witnesses.[36] But the presence of the devil in the mix changed everything; too many of the satanic allegations could be disproved for them to fly, now that word of the secret investigation was out.

These concerns were heightened when news broke of an embarrassing meltdown of a very similar series of cases in Jordan, Minnesota, a small town where a supposed ring of two dozen child molesters had been uncovered in much the same way as the rings in Kern County. Just as in Kern County, children had been interviewed time and again in a suggestive fashion. Just as in Kern County, wild and unsubstantiated allegations were the result, escalating until the children of Jordan began to report witnessing satanic rituals, blood drinking, human sacrifices and baby murders, as well as accusing a police officer and deputy sheriff of being part of the satanic conspiracy. And, just as in Kern County, prosecutors in Jordan kept these satanic allegations secret from defense attorneys while pursuing the more conventional sexual abuse charges in court. When a judge found out about this illegal suppression of evidence and ordered the reports turned over, the Scott County (Minnesota) prosecutor in charge of the case dismissed the charges instead, leading to a media sensation, a public outcry and an investigation by Minnesota Attorney General Hubert Humphrey III into allegations of prosecutorial misconduct. Humphrey eventually issued a report criticizing the prosecutor in Jordan, dismissng the ring case as fantasy, and blaming investigators for coercing false allegations from impressionable children through relentless questioning.[37]

The parallels between Jordan and Kern County were too obvious to miss. Ed Jagels fumed in private that his growing reputation as California's toughest prosecutor, a man who could bring down even Supreme Court justices, would be ruined if the satanic charges were filed and then blown out of court. He'd be a laughingstock throughout the state, his top molestation prosecutor, Andy Gindes, recalled him complaining.[38] It was a concern that slowly began to take hold among many of Jagels' senior prosecutors, who had begun to wonder what went on in that locked room filled with cookies and toys and leading questions, where the child-victims invariably made some of their most sensational and macabre claims. These senior prosecutors, for the first time, began to complain that the sheriff and his satanic task force had brought them incomplete and unprosecutable cases.[39] They wanted more evidence before going forward. The sheriff's investigators, unaccustomed to being challenged, were stunned, and kept trying to go over the heads of prosecutors who rejected the satanic cases.

Finally, Sheriff Kleier angrily demanded a meeting with Jagels. Meanwhile, Kleier's staff, joined by some defectors from the DA's office, embarked on a public-speaking tour to warn Bakersfield of the evils of satanism, and organized a letter-writing campaign to urge Jagels to file charges. When the sheriff arrived at the

DA's office to try to come to terms, Kleier ended up sputtering, "You're all a bunch of ball-less sons of bitches."[40] The meeting came to an abrupt end as Jagels and his office brass stormed out.

A short time later, DA Jagels decided he would not prosecute any of the new satanic charges. In response, Sheriff Kleier called the DA's office "the biggest stumbling block" to justice in Kern County, but Jagels and his lieutenants knew that a full airing of the satanic allegations could end up undoing their prosecutions of the dozens of molestation-ring defendants still awaiting trial—cases in which the child-victims had made wild and disprovable satanic allegations that had been kept secret from the defendants and their lawyers. This secrecy was possible because, even though news of a Kern County satanic investigation had leaked out, the identity of specific suspects and children involved had been carefully safeguarded. Full disclosure, prosecutors knew, would undermine all the remaining ring cases—the same calculation that doomed the prosecutions in Jordan, Minnesota.

By then, officials at the Kern County District Attorney's Office, realizing serious mistakes had been made in these investigations, had quietly gone about changing procedures, usually over the objection of the sheriff's department—limiting the number of interviews with child-victims to the absolute minimum, requiring tape recording of child interviews to help steer clear of leading questions, and barring the once-praised Carol Darling and Velda Murillo from acting as investigators in place of sheriff's detectives, as they had done throughout the ring investigations. But those changes affected only future cases. The existing ring cases were allowed to continue as before, with prosecutors still keeping their explosive satanic aspects under wraps—depriving defendants of information that would undermine the credibility of the witnesses against them.

In the end, though, Kern authorities could not keep a lid on the subject. There were too many suspects, too many yards dug up, too many people party to the secret. After the satanic-abuse allegations were exposed in regional newspapers, the Kern County grand jury, a standing body with broad watchdog powers over local government, stepped in. Spurred on by information about investigative and prosecutorial improprieties supplied by the original ring defendants, the Kniffens, the grand jury began a probe of all of the big child-molestation cases. Their examination produced a highly critical report suggesting that investigators and prosecutors had mishandled the cases and harmed the children—the first official condemnation of the Witch Hunt.[41] The grand jury would have continued investigating officials' conduct in the ring cases but was unexpectedly shut down when a new presiding judge in Bakersfield refused to reappoint any of the existing grand-jury members, normally a matter of routine. That judge was Gary Friedman, who had earlier presided over the notorious Pitts ring case, in which he had made erroneous rulings and refused to rein in Deputy DA Andrew Gindes' misconduct. The new grand jurors whom he appointed included several people with close ties to the sheriff's department and the DA's office, Gindes' wife among them.[42] To no one's surprise, the grand jury's inquiries into ring investigations and law-enforcement misconduct in Kern County abruptly ended.

The old grand-jury panel, however, had already called for a broader investigation by the state attorney general's office. A year later, in September 1986, that office—normally a booster and protector of local district attorneys—lambasted the ring investigation it analyzed (the Nokes case that had metamorphosed into the satanic investigation) as a textbook example of how not to interview children. "The lessons learned from this case extend far beyond Kern County," the report said, in finding Kern County's entire investigation and prosecution of the cases riddled with inconsistencies and improper practices, making it impossible to determine the truth behind the allegations. Every aspect had been contaminated because of the excessive and suggestive questioning of child witnesses by insufficiently trained social workers, therapists and investigators, some of whom suspended all disbelief in accepting even the wildest allegations, the attorney general's report concluded.[43]

Kern County officials, particularly the sheriff, expressed anger and disappointment in the report's conclusions, though even Ed Jagels had admitted to the attorney general's investigators that the satanic allegations were "obviously untrue." Still, he steadfastly defended the ring cases his office prosecuted before the devil-worship allegations surfaced.

The defense attorneys of Kern County, who had so long complained in vain about the Witch Hunt, had every right to gloat as the report was released, but their unofficial spokesman, Stan Simrin, offered one of the more sober and thoughtful reactions of the day: "What has taken place now is equally tragic from both points of view because one cannot really tell whether individual children are telling the truth. Innocent people have been hurt and guilty people may not be successfully prosecuted. Everybody loses."

The portion of the attorney general's report released to the public amid massive publicity made the sheriff and DA look bad enough, but the final blow came when Kern County Superior Court Judge Len McGillivray ordered the release of thousands of pages of previously secret transcripts and interviews collected by the attorney general's investigators. These documents were infinitely more damning, embarrassing and detailed than the attorney general's published report in exposing the massive official incompetence, back-stabbing and misconduct that pervaded the case. Jagels had fought hard to keep these records under seal, still hoping to preserve some of the ring prosecutions. When he lost the secrecy battle and all the information became public, the Witch Hunt era in Bakersfield came to an end.

One after another, then, the ring cases awaiting trial or a charging decision by prosecutors were dropped. Two men accused of being part of the Nokes ring of satan worshipers, once described as Kern County's most dangerous monsters, were allowed to plead guilty to a single count apiece, freed from jail time in exchange for a quick dismissal of hundreds of felony charges that could have put them away for life. Though they protested they were completely innocent, the deal was too good to pass up for men who were drained, emotionally and financially, by their long battle. Their four codefendants were exonerated completely, while fourteen other suspected accomplices, as yet uncharged, were freed from further threat of prosecution. Their children, snatched from their homes by Kern County authorities, some for more than a year, were returned over prosecutors' sullen objections. Freed also was Leroy Stowe, the one Nokes defendant already tried, convicted and sentenced to thirty years—a conviction won while Kern County officials still were keeping secret the children's false satanic allegations about him and the others. The California Court of Appeal overturned his conviction, with one justice calling Stowe's case a "travesty of justice"; he was soon reunited with the eight-year-old son he had once been accused of victimizing. Meanwhile, during a custody hearing involving alleged child-victims in the satanic case, Judge Robert Baca ended the judicial passivity that had characterized the Kern County bench's behavior during the Witch Hunt. Now he flayed the county's social workers for destroying, rather than saving, children by turning them against relatives who had done nothing wrong and leaving them too terrified ever to return home.

"That is the most reprehensible thing that has ever come to my attention . . . You have made the children virtual prisoners, and brainwashed them," the judge raged.[44]

It took years, but eventually attention shifted from pending ring cases contaminated by satanic allegations to the older ones that had never involved the devil and had already ended in convictions. The district attorney tried to argue that any cases that arose before the satanic allegations surfaced should not be called into question, but because the same children and the same investigators asking the same leading questions were involved in both, this argument did not carry much weight. The stunning convictions won in the original ring cases, the victories that had thrust the Kern County District Attorney into the national spotlight, were now being overturned one by one, crumbling in the face of grave questions about the medical evidence, about the way kids were interviewed, and about the conduct of prosecutors. People who had been sentenced to hundreds of years in prison regained their freedom. It was a pattern that repeated itself around the country as well, as other similar cases fueled by hysteria and misconduct self-destructed, a process that bewildered communities that had been taught to believe and fear. Nowhere was this process more dramatic than in Kern County.

In one extraordinary opinion, the California Court of Appeal in 1990 struck down the convictions of seven defendants in the Pitts ring case, rescinding their more than two thousand years in collective prison sentences. The court excoriated both the judge, Gary Friedman, for his numerous errors and proprosecution bias, and the deputy DA, Andrew Gindes, who engaged in acts of prosecutorial misconduct "too numerous to chronicle"— though the court's opinion included nearly a hundred pages citing instances of every type of misconduct imaginable, from providing false information to the jury to introducing Jesus Christ himself as an unsworn witness for the government.

In unusually strong language, the court further wrote of Gindes, "The record is replete with examples of an overzealous prosecutor who, in his blind quest to convict, forgot or ignored his constitutional and ethical duties as representative of the People."[45] Even the indignant Gindes, who denied behaving improperly, called the Pitts opinion "the harshest condemnation of a deputy district attorney in the history of California."

After losing a bid to have the state supreme court reinstate the Pitts case, District Attorney Jagels decided not to retry it, though he denied that he had prosecuted innocent men and women. He suggested instead that it was unfortunate that appeals judges, his favorite targets, had overturned a legitimate jury verdict because of some "minor" problems in the trial. Meanwhile, Deputy DA John Somers, who worked to defend the ring convictions from further appeals when he wasn't prosecuting Pat Dunn, went a step further. He told a news reporter that the appeals court based its decision in the Pitts case solely on prosecutorial misconduct, not a lack of evidence. "This was a solid case with a proper investigation. This was not a case of hysteria with fabrication of charges," Somers proclaimed. "We never had any doubt about their guilt then and we don't have any doubt about their guilt now."[46]

Somers' statement expressed the DA's party line: Once again, rather than look inward, Kern County officials circled their wagons. In this instance, they scapegoated Andrew Gindes, citing him and his performance in the Pitts case as isolated examples of misconduct that had marred otherwise strong, well-investigated cases. This, however, does not square with the record. Gindes may have been unique to the Pitts case, but his presence was all that distinguished it—all of the molestation-ring cases, Pitts included, were dogged by the same claims of bogus medical evidence and suggestive, even abusive, questioning of children. But the appeals court never had to consider the merits of these claims, at least as far as they applied to Pitts, because Gindes' conduct, the first factor that they examined, provided more than enough reason to throw out the convictions.

It would fall to other ring cases to reveal how the errors and misconduct went far beyond one wayward prosecutor, to show they were, indeed, systemic and had been going on long before the excesses of the satanic investigation were exposed. Donna Sue Hubbard's prosecution was one such case. Yet another high-profile ring prosecution from the 1980s, the Hubbard case began

with a single allegation against David Kelly, a self-styled
"big brother" who insinuated himself into families, took
kids on trips to amusement parks, then fondled and
sodomized them. Even after all the reversals and questionable evidence, there seemed to be little doubt about
his guilt.[47]

But the case unfolded during the hysteria of the Witch
Hunt, and the feverish investigation that sprang from solid
evidence of Kelly's alleged abuse of three boys soon led to
less substantial accusations against two others, including
Hubbard, who had reported Kelly to the police in the first
place. She ended up accused of molestation and of selling
her ten-year-old son as a sex slave. The third defendant was
named David A. Duncan. The investigation featured the
usual discredited medical evidence and repeated, high-
pressure interrogations of child-victims, with one investigator accused of verbally and physically abusing children
because they insisted (truthfully, it turned out) that they
had not been molested. The case also produced the familiar laundry list of grotesque allegations—drugged children, kiddie porn, hooks in the ceiling—none of which
could ever be found, let alone proved.[48] Still, all three of
the ring "members" were convicted.

Four years into a sixty-year prison sentence, Duncan
was freed on appeal because he had been illegally interrogated while in jail, despite having invoked his rights
and being represented by a lawyer. The paid undercover
informant who questioned him later testified that
Duncan confessed, which Duncan swore was a lie. In any
case, once his conviction was reversed, the Kern County
DA declined to try Duncan a second time. When he sued
Kern County for civil rights violations, a local judge not
only dismissed the suit as frivolous, he ordered the

impoverished Duncan to pay $123,000 to the county for its time and trouble in fighting his suit. District Attorney Jagels expressed satisfaction with this ruling.

"It is one of the ironies of our system," he told the *Bakersfield Californian*, "that a person who is convicted by a jury of his peers can sue years later after his case is reversed on a technicality in order to try to collect money from everybody who was involved in the case."

As Pat Dunn's trial was wrapping up, the California Court of Appeal reached into Kern County again, this time ruling that the judge and Jagels were wrong—Duncan's suit should not have been thrown out, as he had the same rights as anyone in Kern County to seek redress in court. And, contrary to Jagels' thoughts on the matter, the appeals court did not deem the violations of basic constitutional rights committed in order to falsely convict Duncan a mere "technicality."

Meanwhile, Donna Sue Hubbard, sentenced to one hundred years in prison, remained behind bars. She had no illegal confession in her case,[49] just the by-then standard claims of false medical evidence and coercive questioning of children that Kern County judges and juries routinely rejected. Her son, Richie, had recanted, saying pressure by investigators led him to make false accusations against his mother when only Kelly had molested him. Although many of the ring "victims" in other cases had told similar stories by then, no one in the Kern County justice system would accept the word of Hubbard's son.

Still, she was given one more chance at freedom. Because of irrefutable evidence that false allegations had been made in other ring investigations, the appellate courts ordered Kern County to hold a hearing on

Hubbard's claims. Superior Court Judge Clarence Westra, the same judge who had presided over Hubbard's conviction, held this *habeas corpus* hearing even as Pat Dunn was being tried in the same courthouse basement. Westra heard testimony from Hubbard's son and a variety of experts, including one psychiatrist who called the questioning of children in the case "a virtual catalog of every mistake you can make if you are looking for the truth."

It was Judge Westra who, as a senior prosecutor years earlier, had resisted charging Glenn Fitts in the Dana Butler case. But when it was time to rule on Hubbard's request for a new trial, he showed no such hesitation. His blistering opinion branded her and her son's recantation unbelievable; Hubbard's attorney, Michael Snedeker—a Portland, Oregon, lawyer who had grown unpopular in Kern County by winning appeals in several other ring cases—was called specious. And the judge savaged the expert who challenged the manner in which children were questioned in the case, labeling him biased and elitist for implying that Kern County jurors were too stupid to tell a coerced interrogation from a proper one. Hubbard's trial was fair, Westra decided, as was the investigation of her case. Any other ruling, the judge wrote, "would be an absolute outright attack on the cornerstone of our legal system—the jury system."[50]

District Attorney Ed Jagels pronounced Westra's opinion an extraordinarily fine one. Donna Sue Hubbard would spend two more years in prison before the Court of Appeal in August 1995 told Judge Westra and the Kern County District Attorney that exactly the opposite was true, that the questioning of the children was so tainted by coercion that it could not be believed.[51] Donna Sue Hubbard finally was free.

Jagels launched a war of words with the Court of Appeal's Fifth District after this ruling, accusing it of bias against Kern County. In a press interview, he characterized the inch-thick opinion, with its discussion of fundamental violations of the Constitution, as having "to glom on to one tangential minor point" in order to reverse Hubbard's conviction. He urged the state attorney general—the same office that had years earlier criticized Kern County's ring-investigation practices—to appeal to the California Supreme Court, to try to put Hubbard back in prison. Surprisingly, the attorney general did so, despite objections from some staff members who felt that the office should not defend the Kern County DA in the ring cases, but it mattered little. The supreme court let matters stand: Donna Sue Hubbard would remain free. As in other such cases, Ed Jagels made no attempt to retry her, even as he continued to insist she was guilty.

"The basis for the reversals," he said, "do not, in my opinion, lead to the conclusion that innocent persons were convicted."

"My mother is innocent," Hubbard's son, Richie, said in retort. By the time Hubbard was out of prison, he was twenty-one and had named his newborn daughter after her. "I'll never forgive Kern County for what it did to her. And to me."

The fallout from this string of embarrassments in the ring cases and other short-circuited prosecutions was not obvious to the public, as Ed Jagels, with his thunderous attacks on liberal judges, remained as popular and electable as ever. Beneath the surface, though, everything had changed.

Andrew Gindes, once lauded by Jagels as brilliant, left

the DA's office in disgrace. He began accusing his former boss of improprieties, of burying cases for friends, and of deliberately "throwing" the appeals and retrials of ring cases because he was unwilling to stake his political career further on risky cases. Gindes' legal career was in ruin, and he was forced to take a minimum-wage job as a cashier before finally getting work as a court-appointed attorney in Kern County Juvenile Court—representing the interests of abused kids.[52] Several of the other ring-case prosecutors also left the office a short time later.

Meanwhile, Carol Darling, the sexual-abuse coordinator whose questioning of children had absorbed harsh criticism as the ring cases unraveled, also left the DA's office. Jagels, who once praised Darling for making the molestation prosecutions possible, now opined that she should never have been allowed to interview victims in the first place—a startling indictment of one of the main instigators of the ring prosecutions. During the attorney general's investigation, in fact, he called Darling "the great crack" in the DA's system of investigating cases. (For her part, Darling told investigators for the attorney general that, based upon the children's discredited accusations against a DA, a sheriff's deputy and a social worker, she still believed there was a satanic influence in Kern County law enforcement—but was too fearful to say more.)

Around the same time, her husband, Brad Darling, was transferred to the sheriff's transportation department and away from child-abuse cases for good. Other task-force investigators were transferred out of sex crimes; one, Don Fredenburg, who had been caught on tape coercing accusations from the Kniffen boys, was fired, arrested and sentenced to prison for four years for misappropriation of funds and other improprieties related to his affair with a jail inmate. His boss, Sheriff Larry Kleier, enmeshed in a variety of scandals after staking his career on the satanic-abuse cases, was voted out of office. Within a year of the attorney general's seething report, virtually everyone involved with putting together the massive ring cases and the Satanic Task Force was gone.

The impact of that personnel shift would appear to be dramatic. To this day, no more molestation rings have ever been uncovered in Kern County. Almost immediately, the number of felony molestation prosecutions requested by the Kern County Sheriff's Department dropped by nearly half and became statistically consistent with the Bakersfield Police Department and the police in other communities in Kern County. News coverage of these numbers—in the past so critical of the city police for failing to find any molestation rings—began to suggest that something must have been very wrong at the *sheriff's* department to produce such an abnormal number of cases. The room at the district attorney's office with the toys and crayons, where the child-victims once were interviewed, became a secretaries' lunch room.

In the end, of the fifty-three men and women formally prosecuted in Kern County as members of molestation rings, only six continue to serve their prison sentences. All the rest have had their cases dismissed or overturned, or else they were allowed to plead to crimes requiring no incarceration. Fewer than one out of six ring defendants prosecuted in Kern County were actually guilty of the charges against them. And these figures do not include the twenty-one other cases in which children were removed from families for as long as two years, only to have every allegation against them dropped as well, or the eighty-five other people suspected and traumatized, but never charged.

Yet no one in power in Kern County would admit to making any mistakes when it came to those who still remained in prison, among them the original ring defendants, Scott and Brenda Kniffen, and Alvin and Debbie McCuan. After everything that had come to pass, after all the questions, scandal and dismissals, the Kern County District Attorney still insisted that those four, whose case had started it all, were clearly guilty. Prosecutors—particularly John Somers—insisted that nothing could shake their confidence in those original convictions. The Kniffen boys had recanted and proclaimed their parents innocent, the medical evidence had been shown to be unreliable, and the investigators' credibility and prosecutor Gindes' reputation had been reduced to a shambles. Yet the DA had continued to prevail in the Byzantine world of appeals, writs and *habeas corpus* pleas that Ed Jagels so liked to criticize. Although each ring case involved the same issues, each, for purposes of appeals, required the defense to start from scratch and prove everything, every allegation of misconduct and mistake all over again. Improprieties in one case might lead to freedom, while similar official behavior would be condoned in the next, depending on which judge or panel heard the appeal. The Kniffens and McCuans watched all the other ring prosecutions come unglued, for all the same reasons that they believed their own convictions were flawed, and wondered if their turn might ever come.

By 1993, when Pat Dunn's trial ended and he joined them in prison, they were still waiting.

9

K ERN COUNTY, THOUGH IT SEEMS TO HAVE SENT AN unusual number of innocents to prison, is by no means unique. Just as the county pioneered a national explosion of molestation-ring cases, so did it anticipate a broader trend—a trend of increasing law-enforcement and prosecutorial misconduct. Kern County, it seems, is not an anomaly. It has merely ridden the crest of a wave just now breaking upon the justice system. And no region of the country has been immune.

In March 1993, the same month as Pat Dunn's trial, Walter "Johnny D" McMillian of Monroeville, Alabama— the model for the racially torn town at the center of *To Kill a Mockingbird*—was set free after seven years on death row. Three key prosecution witnesses in the case had lied, and law-enforcement officials knew it and even encouraged it. The misconduct was revealed only after an appeals attorney accidentally received an unedited police tape of one of the witnesses' statements. Unlike earlier versions given to the defense and appeals teams, this one included a portion in which the witness complained that the police wanted him to frame an innocent Johnny D. Even then, the television news show *60 Minutes* had to air a report on the scandal before Alabama authorities finally agreed that the case had been mishandled and decided to reopen it.

By that time, McMillian had already been through four
rounds of failed appeals and was within days of being executed. Once free, he was asked to testify before Congress
about his experience. "I was wrenched from my family,
from my children, from my grandchild, from my friends,
from my work that I loved, and was placed in an isolation
cell the size of a shoe box, with no sunlight, no companionship and no work for nearly six years," he testified.
"Every minute of every day, I knew I was innocent."[53]

Pat Dunn heard about Johnny D on *60 Minutes.*
"Laura," he said, calling her collect from jail. "That's me
on TV."

Nationwide, during the months surrounding Pat
Dunn's legal travails alone, at least seventeen death sentences (seven in 1992, ten in 1993) were reversed because
the men and women convicted were innocent. These
people were not just given new trials; they were simply set
free. Several had come within days, and one within
hours, of execution before last-minute stays rescued
them from wrongful deaths. In addition, at least another
three convicted murderers, who had been sentenced to
life instead of death, also were freed in 1992 and 1993.[54]

Of those twenty capital cases, sixteen—80 percent—
were overturned because of prosecutorial or law-
enforcement misconduct. Most of these reversals owed to
police and prosecutors' failure to turn over evidence that
would have showed defendants' innocence: A high school
principal in Pennsylvania was set free after seventeen years
on death row because a prosecutor hid evidence that
someone else might have killed the teacher and two children who were victims in the case. A man framed and
convicted for murder in New York was released after two

decades in prison, with the appeals court writing that the
only explanation for the moral bankruptcy of the prosecutor in his case was that "The district attorney [failed] to
train or supervise her employees as to such basic norms of
human conduct as the duty not to lie or persecute the
innocent." John Henry Knapp of Phoenix, Arizona, was
sentenced to death for the 1973 arson murder of his two
children, and spent twenty years awaiting execution
despite the prosecution having evidence that fingerprints
on the gas can used to start the fire belonged to someone
else—a fact never revealed to the defense until another
prosecutorial agency took over the case. A Texan who
came within two days of execution, Andrew Lee Mitchell,
was freed after it was learned the sheriff's department had
covered up police reports stating that the victim was seen
alive two hours *after* Mitchell was alleged to have committed murder. A woman in Mississippi, sentenced to
death for killing her nine-month-old baby, was released
from death row after two years because there was no actual
evidence that she had done anything wrong—the police
had responded to her baby's tragic death, most likely from
sudden infant death syndrome, by locking her up after she
frantically brought the child to the hospital for treatment.

The conviction of innocents in the months surrounding Pat Dunn's arrest and trial was not limited to murder
cases.[55] In September 1992, a massive cocaine-smuggling
case against seven men disintegrated when it was
revealed—after trial, convictions and sentencing had
occurred—that the assistant U.S. attorney on the case
had kept hidden a scathing Drug Enforcement
Administration memo about the untrustworthiness of
the star witness. The memo labeled this key witness a frequent liar who had falsely accused others in the past, yet

was rewarded by the U.S. Customs Service with free cars, free run of government offices, phones and safe houses, and other forms of undisclosed payments. The cover-up, with its startling parallels to information about Jerry Lee Coble kept from Pat Dunn's defense, led to the reversal of all seven convictions.

Meanwhile, in Chester County, Pennsylvania, prosecutors fought hard to prevent a man serving a forty-two-year prison sentence for rape from undergoing a DNA test. When the state supreme court finally ordered the test, Dale Brison was proved innocent and released. A few months later, a New York hospital employee convicted of raping a mental patient was also set free after DNA testing proved he had not committed the crime. In that case, prosecutors had disregarded the victim's statements accusing others of the rape, and had not even tried to check out the hospital worker's ironclad alibi.[56]

Around the same time, a former Disney movie actor, Jay Kerr, had drug conspiracy charges against him dismissed in federal court in Montana because of improper evidence and argument by prosecutors. And within a month of that, a federal prosecution in Chicago of sixty-five gang members accused of maintaining a huge drug-running organization—one that bought favors from judges and politicians and whose members were linked to numerous murders—was derailed by prosecutorial misconduct. Convictions were overturned, indictments dismissed and investigations abandoned when it was learned that as reward for their favorable testimony, key witnesses against the notorious El Rukn gang had received beer, money, narcotics and the opportunity to do drugs and have sex in prosecutors' offices—lawbreaking that would have destroyed the witnesses' credibility

(not to mention that of prosecutors), and which therefore was covered up. (Many of the defendants were successfully retried and convicted in untainted proceedings.)

Not long afterward, the deportation of John
Demjanjuk, accused of Nazi war crimes by the United
States Justice Department's Office of Special Investigations, was harshly criticized by the Court of Appeals for
the Sixth Circuit, which found that prosecutors had
"acted with reckless disregard for the truth" and "committed fraud on the court" because, even as it set about
ruining the elderly Demjanjuk's life, it had evidence in
hand of his innocence. The Israeli Supreme Court, not
known for its leniency toward accused Nazis, set
Demjanjuk free because the United States had concealed
evidence proving he was no war criminal at all.

One of the most stinging court decisions on prosecutorial misconduct in recent years involved not a capital
crime, but a relatively minor case in which two people
were convicted of selling $100,000 worth of heroin to an
undercover officer. At trial, Assistant U.S. Attorney Jeffrey
Sinek repeatedly told the jury that a third individual
arrested but not on trial was unavailable to testify
because he had claimed the right to remain silent. Sinek
made this statement to rebut a central defense contention
that the prosecution was keeping this witness under
wraps because the individual in question could help
exonerate the defendants. The prosecutor's more innocuous explanation for the witness's absence helped his
case—but it wasn't true. Federal prosecutors had cut a
deal with that person and so knew that, as the Ninth
Circuit Court of Appeals later put it, this individual
"would sing like a nightingale" if called as a witness. The
resulting testimony could well have benefited the defense,

but the prosecutor and his superiors in the Los Angeles U.S. Attorney's Office kept the information hidden throughout the trial and long after, reluctantly divulging it only when the Ninth Circuit justices forced them to reveal it during appeals arguments. A conservative justice appointed by Ronald Reagan, Alex Kozinski, then wrote a blistering opinion that summed up the temptations and difficulties of prosecutorial misconduct. In it, he noted that, alone among government officials, prosecutors operate with little public scrutiny or accountability in deciding who to prosecute and what evidence to share with defense attorneys—operating on an honor system entirely dependent on each prosecutor's personal integrity—which is why, since the Supreme Court's 1935 ruling in *Berger vs. United States*, it has been a bedrock principle that the prosecution's duty "is not that it shall win a case, but that justice shall be done."[57]

"What we find most troubling about this case is not [the prosecutor's] initial transgression," Justice Kozinski wrote, "but that he seemed to be totally unaware he'd done anything at all wrong and that there was no one in the United States Attorney's Office to set him straight. . . . The overwhelming majority of prosecutors are decent, ethical, honorable lawyers who understand the awesome power they wield, and the responsibility that goes with it. But the temptation is always there: It's the easiest thing in the world for people trained in the adversarial ethic to think a prosecutor's job is simply to win."[58]

Prosecutorial misconduct is handled more gingerly than any other transgression in the justice system (except for judicial misconduct, the most sacred subject of all). Prosecutors are rarely cited by name for misconduct in published court opinions—Justice Kozinski's opinion in the heroin case being an unusual exception. Indeed, the response of the offending prosecutor's supervisor in the Los Angeles U.S. Attorney's Office was not to issue a reprimand, but to petition the court to remove the prosecutor's name from the written opinion to spare him embarrassment.[59] The appeals court eventually agreed to do so.

Appeals courts routinely omit the names of prosecutors accused of misconduct, going so far as to "depublish" lower court opinions to avoid stigmatizing the government lawyers, a consideration never offered individuals charged with a crime—even ones later proved innocent. In one stunning case that occurred in early 1992, one Titus Lee Brown of South Central Los Angeles was released from prison for a murder and robbery conviction in which key evidence against him included jewelry and other items that he had supposedly stolen from the victim. Only the Los Angeles County deputy DA on the case knew—even as she argued otherwise to the jury— that those supposedly stolen items had actually been found by emergency-room workers on the murder victim's body and had been returned to the victim's family. It was a situation remarkably similar to the case against Pat Dunn, in which Deputy DA John Somers insisted that Sandy Dunn always wore expensive jewelry on her predawn walks, despite his own witnesses telling him the opposite. Such misstatements are routinely tolerated. In Titus Brown's case, not only did the state appeals courts deny him a new trial, but the California Supreme Court ordered a lower court's opinion discussing the misconduct "depublished." And then, once again, the Ninth Circuit Court of Appeals had to step in to correct the errors of the California state courts.

"The prosecutor's actions in this case are intolerable,"

the federal justices wrote. "Possessed of knowledge that destroyed her theory of the case, the prosecutor had a duty not to mislead the jury. Instead, she kept the facts secret . . . and then presented testimony in such a way as to suggest the opposite of what she alone knew to be true. . . . Such conduct perverts the adversarial system and endangers its ability to produce just results."[60]

Yet, even as Titus Brown got his new trial and the Los Angeles District Attorney's Office got a black eye because one of its own lied to a jury to win a conviction, the individual prosecutor on the case was spared any public humiliation. The Ninth Circuit opinion, though brutal in its criticism, never mentioned her by name.

There is no agency that tracks prosecutorial misconduct, no outside scrutiny of prosecutors, no mechanism for policing them other than the prosecutors themselves and the chance discoveries of defense lawyers, judges and journalists—which is to say prosecutors are almost never reprimanded for their courtroom misconduct. However, a few measures that do exist suggest that prosecutorial transgressions are on the rise. In 1993, for instance, twenty Justice Department lawyers left their jobs while under investigation for charges of misconduct, a record unmatched since the birth of the nation. Overall, allegations of prosecutorial misconduct that year had climbed 78 percent from the previous year within the Justice Department, the only prosecuting agency in the country that disseminates such statistics for its lawyers. By 1995, that number had soared another 71 percent.

Meanwhile, a 1992 national study of four hundred people wrongfully convicted of death-penalty offenses since the 1940s found 15 to 20 percent of them had been set free because of unethical and illegal conduct by prosecutors. That translates to a total of sixty to eighty innocents sentenced to death because of false or hidden evidence or other government misbehavior over a half century.[61]

A congressional report published in 1993 listed forty-eight men released from death row between 1973 and 1993. All were later found to be innocent; many had been convicted as a result of prosecutorial misconduct.[62]

Nationally, the justice system's reaction to these findings exactly mirrored the reaction in Kern County when its high-profile prosecutions crumbled one by one. The tendency was not to take a hard look at prosecutors and their accountability, or to question the many laws passed in the 1980s and early 1990s that, in an understandable desire to crack down on crime, had shifted power in the justice system from judges to prosecutors. Instead, the solution has been to make it harder for convicts to present new evidence of innocence and to appeal their cases. New federal laws and Supreme Court rulings have sharply limited the number of federal appeals allowed in criminal cases, and the Supreme Court also created a standard that requires near-absolute proof of innocence before a conviction could be overturned for "factual" reasons—not even the strongest of doubts are enough in the absence of "legal" and "procedural" errors in the case.[63] At the same time, many states have imposed strict time limits on the presentation of new evidence. Texas, for example, which leads the nation in executions, set that limit at thirty days. After that period, a man convicted of murder could theoretically discover on day thirty-one a videotape of someone else committing the crime, and still be legally executed—he literally would have no avenue of appeal under Texas law. (This scenario is not fantasy—it was presented by Supreme Court Justice Anthony Kennedy during oral arguments in *Herrera vs. Collins*, a death-penalty case. Kennedy could not have been too concerned, though—he still voted to uphold a law that would allow just such an execution, deciding that it was a matter of states' rights.)[64] Opponents of such strict deadlines argued in vain that the time limits—intended to reduce frivolous appeals in criminal cases and to speed up executions—also give prosecutors an incentive to hide evidence. An unscrupulous prosecutor would know that he or she had to hang on for only a month after conviction before winning by default, no matter what new evidence—or evidence of misconduct—surfaced after that point.

Just such an argument was made in the case of a Virginia coal miner named Roger Keith Coleman, convicted of killing his sister-in-law and scheduled to be executed in May 1992. After his conviction and death sentence, Coleman and his lawyer learned that the police and prosecutors had covered up a host of facts useful to the defense: evidence of forced entry at the victim's house (at trial, they had argued she had known the killer—Coleman—and let him into the house); knowledge that the knife allegedly used by Coleman didn't fit the victim's wounds; and information that a pair of scissors and a blood-soaked sheet had been found in a trash can outside the victim's home by a neighbor. The blood evidence not only had been kept from the defense—it had not even undergone forensics tests. Finally Coleman's team learned that the police hid a time card that they had obtained which would have corroborated Coleman's alibi that he had been at work at the time of the murder.

Meanwhile, the jailhouse informant who was the chief witness in the case, and who had gotten four separate prison sentences reduced to probation for his trouble, had recanted and maintained that Coleman had never confessed to him. On top of all this, new evidence had surfaced linking another man to the crime. That man had lived in the victim's neighborhood, had been accused of raping other women in a similar manner, and had allegedly confessed to one of his rape victims that he had killed Coleman's sister-in-law.

In short, while Coleman did not have a videotape of another man committing the murder, he had assembled a mountain of new evidence that seemed almost as strong, with clear and seemingly irrefutable evidence of prosecutorial misconduct to go with it. Before the Supreme Court, his lawyers argued that prosecutors should not be rewarded, and an innocent man punished, for such misdeeds simply because the prosecutors successfully covered up their conduct long enough to elude a deadline. But the Court not only refused to stop the execution, it wouldn't even consider the new evidence. Coleman's lawyers had blundered and missed a filing deadline of their own—by three days. If the State of Virginia wanted to stick by its deadlines, the federal government would not intercede, Justice Sandra Day O'Connor wrote for the majority.

"This is a case about federalism," O'Connor reasoned. "It concerns the respect that federal courts owe the states."

The State of Virginia appreciated the Supreme Court's deference; prosecutors there used exactly the same sort of "technicality" that they normally accused defense lawyers of exploiting—a deadline missed by seventy-two hours—to deny a hearing to explore Coleman's new evidence. And thus, at 11:00 P.M. on May 20, 1992, Roger Keith Coleman was put to death.[65]

In his dissent in *Herrera vs. Collins*, a subsequent, similar Texas death case, a disgusted Justice Harry Blackmun wrote, "The execution of a person who can show that he is innocent comes perilously close to simple murder."[66] That opinion, however, was in the minority.

10

COMPARED TO THE EVIDENCE DISCOVERED—AND ignored—in Roger Coleman's case, the new evidence unearthed by Laura Lawhon to justify a new trial for Pat Dunn was rather threadbare. Even Laura had to admit that. Try as she might, she just couldn't find the ammunition she desperately sought and hoped for. She never did find out about the missing report from Detective Banducci or the new check forgery charges against Jerry Coble. She could not know of Kate Rosenlieb's full role in the case. Only the district attorney's office and its witnesses could provide that information, and they did not do so.

What Laura did find was this: Jennifer Dunn, Pat's daughter, belatedly recalled that when she had helped gather up Sandy's clothes to donate to charity many months after the murder, there had been several dozen nightgowns, some worn, some unused. To Laura, this suggested that Sandy did not always sleep in the nude, as Deputy DA Somers argued. It was a small point, but a point nevertheless.

Another piece of Laura's case came from Pat's mechanic, who had serviced the Dunns' Chevy Blazer and changed its two front tires the day after Sandy disappeared. Somers had called this evidence of a cover-up, and, Laura knew from her post-trial interviews, the jurors had taken it very seriously. But the mechanic told Laura that it had been his idea, not Pat's, to replace the front tires, which were badly worn and in danger of blowing out. Pat had been out searching for Sandy and gotten worried that the car was shaking so badly, he might not be able to keep looking. The mechanic also recounted to Laura that the oil seals on the wheels were leaking and needed replacement. When he checked them, he saw that the fluid behind them was clean. This would not be the case, the mechanic said, if Pat had recently driven on dirt roads. Thus, the service performed on the Blazer indicated that Pat could not have driven up into the mountains—over rugged dirt roads—to dispose of Sandy's body the day before.

This was somewhat more significant than the nightgowns, but still, the problem with these "new" pieces of evidence was that they weren't really new, for the defense had access to the mechanic and Jennifer before and during the trial. Pat's team simply failed to ask the right questions. The judge would almost certainly reject appeals focusing on the nightgowns and auto repairs out of hand for that reason alone.

There was, however, a new witness. Donald Dean Unsell, a self-described "Dumpster diver," recalled picking "treasures" from trash bins at the College Center mall in July 1992, looking for things to sell at garage sales, his primary source of income. One night while Unsell was at work, a man came by the mall between one and three in the morning, identified himself as Pat Dunn, and asked Unsell if he had seen his wife walking around. While awaiting trial, Pat had recalled such an encounter with an unidentified trash-picker, and the defense team had looked for the man, hoping to use him as a witness at trial to show that Pat really had searched for his missing wife. But they had been unable to find him: Unsell, it seems, had been incarcerated himself, and hadn't been around the mall for many months. He had not heard or read anything about the Dunn case, and so hadn't given another thought to his encounter with a man looking for his wife.

After the trial, Pat's brother Mike renewed the search for the Dumpster diver, posting flyers at the mall asking for information. Unsell spotted one of the flyers, remembered seeing Pat that night about a year earlier, and called. After puzzling over exactly when this had happened and discussing it with his wife, who was also picking trash that night, Unsell decided that the encounter with Pat had been in the early morning hours of July 1— a date he said he remembered because he and his wife had purchased a car the day before, and had taken it to the mall for the first time that night he ran into Pat. The pink slip, which he still had in his possession, had given him the date.

This really was "new evidence" in the legal sense, and the significance of it was twofold. First, it corroborated Pat's account of searching for his wife on the night that she disappeared, and, second, it had him doing it at a time when, according to the prosecution, he was supposed to be burying her corpse sixty miles away, on a tight timetable that left no room for visits to the mall.

The problem here, though, was the somewhat incredible nature of the testimony. Nearly a year after this chance, two-minute meeting in a mall parking lot with Pat Dunn, Donald Unsell claimed to know the exact date of the encounter—even though he hadn't given it a thought since it happened. This seemed unlikely at best.

Indeed, Gary Pohlson had attacked similarly specific recollections by prosecution witnesses who had claimed to
remember minute details of conversations with Pat
Dunn many months after the fact.

"No one's going to believe this guy," Laura told herself
after interviewing Unsell. Yet, even while remaining skeptical, she was satisfied that the man was telling the truth
as he remembered it. Indeed, her initial concern was that
someone might have bribed or cajoled the impoverished
man to come forward. Laura addressed this head-on, asking Unsell flat out if Mike Dunn or anyone else had
offered him money for his testimony. The man's faded
blue eyes lit up at the very suggestion. "No," he said
eagerly. "Should they have?" That flash of unabashed and
unrequited greed convinced Laura that Unsell was the
genuine article.

Convincing anyone else was another matter. When it
came time to hear the new evidence at a hearing on June
14, 1993, the defense team knew that they had a long shot
at best. Judge Baca patiently listened, but the lawyers
could tell where things were headed. They spent most of
their time apologizing to the court, because one of their
main arguments, aside from the new evidence, was that
Judge Baca had committed a grievous error by allowing
the real estate attorney Teri Bjorn to testify, and that this
alone warranted a new trial.

Baca, though, said that he was more certain than
ever that he made the right call on Teri Bjorn. "The
defendant . . . wanted to know how he could go about
getting a power of attorney," the judge stated, once more
misquoting the testimony in the case. Significantly, this
misinterpretation of Bjorn's words affected more than
just the hearing before Baca. It continued to be cited in

appeals briefs and by appeals courts themselves, the error taking on a life of its own as the system dutifully followed its rule of always deferring to lower courts' findings of fact—even when they are wrong. Likewise, other omissions and misstatements of the evidence in the Dunn case were allowed to stand: the information contained in John Somers' big chart of Pat's lies, errors and all, played a major role in future appeals decisions as well.

As for the new witnesses and evidence Laura had uncovered, Somers argued that even if anyone believed them, which he didn't, their appearance in the trial wouldn't have altered the verdict. For instance, Somers stated, if Donald Unsell really did see Pat early that morning, it contradicted nothing—there still would have been ample time for Pat to kill Sandy, bury the body and return to conduct a phony search for his wife. In making this argument, Somers told the court that Jerry Coble had seen Pat dispose of the body at 12:15 A.M.—a clear misstatement of the evidence. Coble actually testified that he last observed the body in the truck at 1:24 A.M., which would not have provided the amount of time Somers needed for his scenario.[67]

Nevertheless, Judge Baca agreed with Somers. And when Pat's lawyers tried to argue that, regardless of the significance of any new evidence, the prosecution case itself was insufficient, that Jerry Coble was unbelievable, and that without Coble, there was no case, Somers replied that there was plenty of evidence to convict Pat Dunn *without* Coble, a position that baffled the defense.[68] Furthermore, Somers explained, the defense team's latest attacks on Jerry Lee Coble's veracity were just going over old ground that had been visited time and again during the trial. The defense had "ample opportunity" to explore Jerry Coble's criminal history, his plea bargain, and his credibility, Somers assured the judge, and nothing new had occurred since then that would justify a new trial.

"All of that was presented to the jury," the prosecutor said. "They had a chance to evaluate it."[69]

Judge Baca agreed once more with every one of Somers' points. He dismissed the Dumpster diver's testimony as incredible and the other new information as minor points that would not have changed the verdict had they been introduced at trial. New evidence warrants a new trial only when it is of sufficient magnitude that a different verdict was probable, Baca said. Clearly, that was not the case here. The defense was wrong about Teri Bjorn, and had nothing new to offer about Jerry Lee Coble.

The conviction would stand.

But, of course, neither Judge Baca nor the jury had heard all the facts, despite what John Somers avowed. Unbeknownst to Baca, by the time this hearing took place, the Kern County District Attorney's Office had filed new charges against Jerry Coble, and, in addition, had information in hand that its star witness in the Dunn case had violated his plea agreement and the conditions of his probation. The DA's office also had information demonstrating that Jerry Coble had given false testimony in the Dunn case, in that he claimed to have been crime free since the preliminary hearing in December, when in fact he had just been charged with attempting to pass a stolen and counterfeit check using stolen and false ID.

When John Somers told the judge that there was nothing new with which to challenge Jerry Coble's credibility, when he argued that there was no real new evidence in the case, that Jerry Coble was a truthful witness, and that the defense and the jury had been able to evaluate all the available information on Coble, his own office had information showing each of these points to be untrue.[70]

J. E. Taylor, the Bakersfield police detective who had identified Coble in January as the offender in the check-forgery case—then reported no activity on the case until after Pat's trial and conviction in March—had finally forwarded the case to the district attorney's office for prosecution on May 11. Though too late to play a role in Pat's trial, this was more than a month before the hearing in which Pat sought a new trial. Then, on May 25, still weeks before Pat's hearing, the DA's office filed a felony complaint against Coble. Despite the new charge, no attempt was made to revoke Coble's probation or plea agreement, though this would normally be routine in such a case. And there is no record of him being arrested, or of a warrant for his arrest being sought by the DA, though this, too, should have been routine. Yet the Kern County court records for May 25 state that, at 9:35 A.M., Jerry Coble was in custody, presumably in the Kern County jail, which is run by the sheriff's department.

Six hours later, at 3:30 P.M., when Coble was supposed to be arraigned on the new charges, no hearing took place; court records indicate: "Defendant not transported to court." The case record on file at the Kern County courthouse ends at that point, without explanation. There was no further attempt to bring Coble to court on the new case, no attempt to revoke his probation, no effort to prosecute or punish him in any way. To this day, the Kern County District Attorney has failed to pursue the forgery case against Jerry Lee Coble, though the case was listed as "open and active" in the court files as late as 1997. The case remained open until July 23, 1997, when the failure of the district attorney to prosecute the case led to its dismissal because Coble had been denied a speedy trial. The DA has never notified Pat Dunn of its existence.[71]

Had the defense known of the new case against Coble—and had they known of Detective Eric Banducci and his report chronicling Coble's desperate attempts to strike a deal to avoid prison—Pat would have had powerful information with which to seek a new trial, to attack Coble's credibility, and to show possible prosecutorial misconduct. Banducci's testimony, had the defense known of its availability, could have gone far beyond simply challenging Jerry Coble's story: It could have undermined the credibility of the entire case against Pat Dunn. The defense could have argued that any investigation that went behind Banducci's back and ignored his and other detectives' concerns about Jerry Coble's veracity ought to be viewed with skepticism on every point.

But the defense had none of this blockbuster information. All it had were some nightgowns, tires and a trash picker. The outcome was never in doubt.

When the arguments were over and the new trial had been denied, Judge Baca began a final ritual before imposing sentence: Pat got his chance to address the court. It was the first and last time he would speak in his own defense, too late to do any good, a rambling ten minutes of fury and stammers.

"I am not what these people pictured me to be," he told the judge, standing at the defense table and breathing hard. The cheap suit was gone; he was wearing jailhouse blues. "I have worked long and hard. Momma and I worked long and hard. Yes, we had a dollar, but it wasn't anything different than you having an education and being a lawyer or a man with a backhoe in his backyard that he can earn a living with."

The words came in a rush, driven by the pressure of months of silence, of sitting in that courtroom watching his life on the dissection table, unable to speak, squirming in his chair, scribbling notes like a madman his only outlet. Now, it seemed, he couldn't stop. "The dollars that we had were to do something with, was to work with. It was nothing but a tool. Mom and I, we ran around in Levi's and a T-shirt and we didn't want anything else. We didn't lack for anything and we didn't want anything, either."

The judge glanced at the clock; he had other cases to deal with that day. He cleared his throat. He tried, a few times, to quiet the man down, but in the end, he let Pat have his say. Baca knew who was going to have the final word.

Meanwhile, Pat rolled on. "And I am not an avaricious person," he declared, "and I didn't kill my wife, and I damn sure didn't kill anybody for money."

He railed against Coble and Soliz and Somers, saying it was all a lie, a terrible lie, a lie that had destroyed him. Then the words finally trickled to a stop, a creek run dry. No one else spoke for a moment. Then the judge filled the silence, businesslike and brief, completing the ritual. He had read all the letters to the court and considered each of them—from Pat's ex-wife, Nancy, swearing he was a kind and good and nonviolent man; from his friends and son Pat Jr. and supporters, all attesting to his good nature; and from Sandy's sister Nanette, seeking retribution. It was a futile exercise. The law permitted only one sentence in this case.

"The court can envision no crime more despicable than murdering somebody for financial gain, regardless of what the gain is, regardless of how big the prize might be." The words sounded tough, but Baca delivered them with little emotion. Everyone in the room, including the judge, seemed tired and ready for the Dunn case to end.

Then Judge Baca sent Pat Dunn to prison for the rest of his life, without possibility of parole, as the law required. As a last gesture, in one of those odd and pointless rituals of the court system, the judge carefully noted that Pat should receive credit for three hundred forty-four days in jail—two hundred thirty of them actual days in custody, the rest "good time" credits. Later, the idea of receiving credit for time served on an infinite sentence almost made Pat Dunn laugh. Almost.

Following sentencing, as Laura Lawhon pointed her car south for that long, slow drive over the Grapevine, she, like Gary Pohlson before her, found herself weeping in anger and frustration, banging the steering wheel and talking to herself. She raced to the freeway, feeling like an escaped prisoner. When a news report on Pat's case suddenly blared from her car radio, she snatched at the off switch so hard she nearly broke it, unable to bear that solemn voice describing Pat as the man who murdered his wife for her millions. *Lies*, she thought to herself. *Lies.* She knew it in her bones. But she couldn't prove it, and could imagine no worse a feeling. She could still hear Pat's angry, rambling remarks to the impatient judge, who did everything but drum his fingers in exasperation. She could still see the pained expressions on the defense lawyers' faces and the pitiful last wave Pat gave her while being led from the courtroom—he looked almost child-like, as if he were shrinking before her eyes.

This place has defeated us, she thought. And now, as she angrily wiped at her eyes, she wanted nothing more than to get back home, to her family and her pets, to other cases in other towns. Pat Dunn's case had taken over her life, with its constant phone calls and letters from jail and endless interviews with witnesses who lied, who changed their stories and who, Laura believed, had helped keep the truth hidden. And now that it was over, she wanted her life back. She pushed down hard on the gas pedal, feeling the Mercedes' big engine struggle with the uphill climb as it blasted by other cars and trucks as if they were hardly moving.

Only when she reached the top of the Grapevine, and she began speeding down the other side of that treeless wall of granite separating Bakersfield from the rest of Southern California, did she begin to feel a palpable sense of relief. The oppressive heat and dust and injustice that she had grappled with in Kern County shrank like a pin-point in her rearview mirror. She rolled down the win-dow and felt cool air rush in, washing over her, carrying with it the scent of things growing. And despite herself, before she even realized what she was doing, Laura found herself thinking of new ways to reopen the case and pry Pat Dunn's cell door open. Maybe she could take another run at Marie Gates. Or Kate Rosenlieb. Maybe she could find out more about Jerry Coble and his family. There had to be something else she could do.

As a blood-red sun dipped below a hillside and the distant galaxy of lights that marked Los Angeles sparked into view before her with the suddenness of a match, Laura found herself speaking these thoughts aloud into the rushing wind: *Maybe*, she said, *just maybe, it's not over yet.*

A few days later, Laura arrived at her office to find an express delivery from the California Department of Motor Vehicles awaiting her. The envelope contained records that she had requested long before but which had never arrived. In her preparation for Pat Dunn's petition for a new trial, she had asked for a computer search for any law-enforcement agencies in Kern County that might have inquired about the license plate number Rex Martin had written down on the day he followed Jerry Coble from Pat's house. Jerry Mitchell, the retired deputy sheriff, had sworn that he passed this number on to Detective Soliz within a day of receiving it from Pat, though Soliz claimed he could recall no such thing. Laura had harbored doubts about the detective's assurances and wondered whether there might be a computer record somewhere showing that Soliz had indeed checked the plates. Only after the trial did Laura learn such a computer check was possible, and she initiated one in the hope that it would reveal something in time for the new-trial motion. But the results had not arrived in time.

Inside the envelope Laura found a printout. It showed the state motor vehicles database had indeed received an inquiry from a Kern County law-enforcement officer about that same license plate—a Pontiac Sunbird owned by Jerry Coble's long-suffering mother. The official police request for information on this car, according to the record, had been made on July 27, 1992—exactly in the time frame Rex Martin claimed to have followed the suspicious car, and when Jerry Mitchell would have communicated the number to John Soliz. Someone in Bakersfield law enforcement—the printout didn't say

who—had run Coble's plate. Just as the defense had
claimed.

It had potential, this new information, but Laura's
excitement at the discovery quickly gave way to frustration. Had it arrived just a few days earlier, it might have
made a difference in the case—perhaps enough to win
Pat a new trial. Now, though, with Pat Dunn's best chance
for acquittal and freedom already behind him, Laura
knew that this document would be little more than a
starting point, a place to start digging for answers that
had continued to elude her.

She put the computer printout down and picked up
the telephone. She had a new trip up the Grapevine to
plan.

PART IV

Epilogue

Justice delayed is not only justice denied—it is also justice circumvented, justice mocked, and the system of justice undermined.
—RICHARD NIXON

Like the Hydra slain by Hercules, prosecutorial misconduct has many heads.
—JUSTICE JOHN PAUL STEVENS

1

WINTER 1998

IN THE FIVE YEARS SINCE PAT DUNN'S CONVICTION AND sentence to life in prison, controversy has continued to shake the justice system of Kern County. The war on crime, fought harder here than most anywhere else, continues to claim innocent casualties.

Few can attest to this more convincingly than Offord Rollins. In August 1995, the California Court of Appeal declared Rollins' trial fundamentally unfair, overturned his conviction, and ordered a new trial. In its opinion, the court lambasted a juror and the prosecutor for misconduct, as well as the defense attorney and judge for numerous errors.[1] Taken alone, any one of these problems might be overlooked. Together, however, these problems made granting Rollins a new trial inevitable.

The clincher for the Court of Appeal was the matter of jury misconduct. The justices could not abide the juror who shared with his colleagues his own inside (and incorrect) knowledge of flies, supposed pesticide spraying near the crime scene, and why there might have been no flies, fly eggs or maggots on the murder victim's body. This brought before the jury improper evidence on a critical issue in the case. Maria Rodriguez, of course, had been found dead and bloody in a patch of desert teeming with insects, yet her corpse showed no sign of fly eggs or maggots. Experts testifying for the defense insisted this meant that Maria had died after dark, since flies cannot see or navigate in darkness, and therefore do not feed and lay eggs once the sun goes down. And Rollins had an alibi beginning five hours *before* sunset that day and continuing through the evening, something even prosecutor Lisa Green conceded.

However, this one juror's "knowledge" gave the rest of the jury an excuse to disregard the expert testimony, clearing the way for conviction. When challenged on the issue during hearings in Kern County, the prosecutor called this and any other such transgressions harmless error, and the trial judge agreed. But the Court of Appeal felt otherwise: In a case already troubled by prosecutorial misconduct and judicial errors, and in which the question of guilt or innocence was so close, the only just outcome would be to declare the trial unfair, erase the conviction, and start over again.[2]

District Attorney Ed Jagels called the appellate court's reasoning "silly." He was already seething over another embarrassing opinion handed down earlier that month from the same court, setting molestation-ring defendant Donna Sue Hubbard free because of coerced child witnesses. As he had done in the Hubbard case, Jagels asked the California Supreme Court to intervene to restore Rollins' conviction. And, as in the Hubbard case, the Supreme Court declined to do so. Offord Rollins, once again presumed innocent, walked out of custody, hoping to salvage what he could of a promising college and athletic career shattered by three years in prison.

Rollins was, however, not quite free. In the spring and summer of 1996, despite pleas from the Bakersfield black community that he be spared a second trial, the district attorney's office pressed forward with Offord Rollins' case before a new judge and jury, with a new and pugnacious defense attorney, and a new prosecutor on board as well—Ed Jagels' second-in-command, Stephen Tauzer. The new judge scrupulously went about policing the second trial for any signs of the misconduct and error that undermined the first. The case now turned squarely on the scientific evidence—blood, fibers, plants and the quality of work performed by the county's aged, contamination-prone crime laboratory—and on Offord's own credibility and inconsistencies. At the heart of the case remained the question of why there were no flies on Maria's body, and what this implied about Offord's guilt or innocence.[3]

Despite the judge's best efforts, the trial became an angry, rancorous affair, marked by ugly confrontations between the defense attorney and the prosecutor. All the anger, resentment and distrust that had festered for years within the Kern County justice system seemed to boil to the surface in the second Rollins trial. There was no room for compromise, no walking in the other man's shoes. This was a war, as cases often are in Kern County, though this one seemed stripped of even the veneer of civility. Shouting, petty bickering and name-calling on both sides constantly mired the proceedings.[4]

At one point, prosecutor Tauzer grew so angry at private investigator Susan Penninger that when the judge and jury cleared the courtroom for a recess, he charged the witness stand, growled an insult, slammed a heavy chart down in front of her, and appeared to physically menace the five-foot-three private investigator. As Penninger, whom Tauzer had known for twenty years, recoiled in shock, thinking she was about to be struck, H. A. Sala, Rollins' dapper defense attorney, interposed himself between the two. Assuming something close to a boxer's stance, he forced Tauzer to take a step back. "You think you're such a big man," Sala hissed, pacing nervously, his face red above his pointed goatee. "Try someone who can defend himself."

Tauzer stalked off, and the strange scene ended as abruptly as it began. The prosecutor later apologized.

Such incidents aside, in the end, the misconduct and error that infected the first trial—including the racial overtones, improper evidence, irrelevant rap poems and sexual innuendo—were generally avoided in the second go-round, in the courtroom and jury room alike. And the result showed just how close the case, on its own merits, was: After four days of exhausting deliberations, the jurors declared themselves hopelessly deadlocked.

Six were certain that Offord was innocent. Six voted guilty. The scientific evidence about flies—and the possibility that crime-lab technicians accidentally planted incriminating evidence from the murder scene in Offord's car—had convinced those jurors voting to acquit. The fibers consistent with Offord's car seat that were found on Maria Rodriguez's body—coupled with Offord's inconsistent statements—convinced those who wanted to convict.

The second trial's hung jury opened the door for a third, but the following month, the DA threw in the towel. A cost-benefits analysis won out in the end: Offord Rollins was fast approaching age twenty-five, and since he had been sentenced as a juvenile, he would have to be released at that age, anyway, even if the DA managed to convict in a third trial. "It would be pointless," District Attorney Jagels explained. "But that does not imply we have any doubts about the evidence against Mr. Rollins."

Rollins' attorney, H. A. Sala, disputed the DA's comments, certain that Jagels would have prosecuted again if he thought conviction possible—if only to make sure that Offord wore the label of murderer for the rest of his life. But the defense would have been even stronger a third time around, Sala believed, because he might have been able to introduce evidence that someone else could have killed Maria—an option that the defense had been denied in the past.[5] Sala had learned that Rodriguez family friend Victor Perez—an alternative potential suspect long favored by the defense—did not have the alibi prosecutors had always claimed he had.

"They didn't want a new trial because they knew they couldn't win," Sala told Offord in a phone call as soon as he learned of the DA's decision. "You're free. That's it. It's over."

Offord hung up the phone, speechless. Five years had passed since his arrest. The teenager had become a man, though he had been robbed of those final years of childhood—of proms, of track meets, of leaving for college, of birthdays with friends and family. He had borne the weight of being the accused murderer, then the convicted murderer, then the appealing murderer for so long that, like a bad back or a broken limb, he no longer knew what it felt like to be without it. Too nervous to eat some days, he had lost ten pounds during the two months of his second trial. He was a quiet and withdrawn man now, unwilling to show any emotion, always fearing that it might be used against him in some future courtroom proceeding. But with exoneration, he was not sure what to do. He was unaccustomed to this feeling of complete freedom, the notion that he could get on a plane and fly anywhere and not be called a fugitive, that he could make plans for the future and not have to worry about whether his room would have bars on it, that he was now officially and legally *innocent*.

As his mother began telephoning everyone she knew with the news, as his supporters planned a party to celebrate, and as his lawyer gave television interviews, Offord Rollins decided what he needed to do next. He excused himself and left the house. He had a class to go to.

In his cell at the California State Prison in Corcoran, Pat Dunn read and reread the article in the newspaper describing Rollins' victory. He was happy for the young man, but envious, too, longing for his own phone call that might, one day, set him free.

As Offord Rollins' trial came to a sputtering conclusion, another case rose from Kern County's past, again to present the specter of innocents wrongfully convicted. Just down the hallway from the Rollins trial, in the same dreary county-courthouse basement with its tired linoleum and hard wooden benches, the first of the convicted molestation-ring defendants, Scott and Brenda Kniffen and Deborah and Alvin McCuan, had at last returned to court after fourteen years of imprisonment. Their *habeas corpus* hearing would, one way or another, put a stamp of finality on the saga of the Kern County Witch Hunt.

Theirs had been the first such prosecution of its kind, a sensational case that launched five years of hysteria in Bakersfield and ignited a national frenzy of similar cases, some of which are still rocking the justice system with allegations of misconduct and wrongful convictions. Now, it seemed, the first ring case to be tried, with its thousand years of imprisonment for the four parents involved, would be among the last to be revisited.

As in other Kern County ring cases, the Kniffens and McCuans had lost their initial round of appeals. Their prosecutor, Andy Gindes, had been flayed for his behavior in other cases, but claims by the Kniffens and McCuans about his conduct in their trial were denied.[6] However, the appellate justices who rejected these appeals made one ruling that gave the four convicted parents hope: The California Court of Appeal would welcome new hearings—to be held at the trial-court level in Kern County—if *new* evidence could be presented to show that key testimony was false or fabricated. It would not be easy, because even though coercion and false testimony had been proven in many other cases, the Kniffens and McCuans had to find new evidence from scratch. According to appellate rules, legally, their convictions were automatically presumed just, their trials fair, the investigations that swept away their children and put them behind bars, unbiased—despite what had been proven in comparable ring cases. Nevertheless, it was a genuine chance, even in the face of the Kern County District Attorney's Office, which was determined to fight their case just as hard as it had the others, mustering all its resources to keep the Kniffens and McCuans behind bars, and acknowledging no doubts about the evidence or official conduct in the case.

By the time of their hearing in the summer of 1996, the Kniffens' lives and families had long been in shambles. In the Corcoran State Prison, north of Bakersfield (where Pat Dunn also was sent), Scott Kniffen had to be placed in protective custody, so reviled are child molesters in the hierarchy of prison life, targets for every sharpened screwdriver and smuggled razor on the yard. Housed with the most notorious inmates in the state, he saw Charles Manson nearly every day and played chess with Sirhan Sirhan, Robert Kennedy's assassin. Meanwhile, Scott's wife, Brenda, dodged lit matches and human waste hurled at her through the bars in her women's prison cellblock. The couple had not seen their children—had barely talked to them—for most of Brian's and Brandon's lives. They had missed the boys' birthdays, their graduations and their first dates; their transformation from boys into young men. Brenda still had the first tooth Brandon, her younger son, lost—she hadn't been there to see it loosen and fall, but the boy's foster parent had taken pity on the imprisoned mother and sent it to her. Brenda would stare at that tooth for hours, a frail woman who had wasted away to seventy pounds by the end of her trial and who fainted at the verdict. Prosecutors at the time complained she was acting.

The Kniffen boys were now twenty and twenty-three. Both maintained that they had never been molested and supported their parents' bids for release. But over the ten years since the charges were first lodged, they had recanted, affirmed and recanted their accusations so many times (depending upon whether Kern County authorities or their parents' defense team was doing the questioning), it was difficult, if not impossible, to determine the truth. It was one of the ironies in the case that the prosecution, which in the past had tried to conceal and ignore contradictions and falsehoods in their child witnesses, now pointed to the very same inconsistencies to argue that Brian and Brandon could not now be believed in their recantations. During the Kniffens' *habeas* hearing, the boys sat in the courthouse hallway with friends and relatives, seething in resentment at this turn of events. As far as they were concerned, it was yet another betrayal by officials who were supposed to protect them, but who in their view had ruined their lives.

Four years earlier, their grandmother—Scott Kniffen's mother, Marilyn—died of a heart attack, suffered at her kitchen table as she wrote a letter to her imprisoned son. She had never doubted his innocence. Nor did Scott's father, Dick, who mortgaged his house and spent his retirement savings on investigators and lawyers, and who died in his sleep a few days after his wife. "They died of a broken heart," Scott would later say, a weary bitterness in his voice and worn face leathery and pale from years of prison food and labor. "As far as I'm concerned, Kern County killed my parents, just as sure as if they had fired a gun into their hearts."

The McCuans had fared no better than the Kniffens. Their marriage had ended. Their daughters still lived with Mary Ann Barbour, the stepgrandmother who had leveled the first allegations of molestation. Jenny and Jane, now adults, had never recanted in their parents' case, though their allegations against others had eventually been disproved or dismissed. The girls still believed wholeheartedly in their memories of molestation, and they wanted nothing to do with their parents, their parents' lawyers or their parents' quest for freedom. The very thought of their parents walking free horrified the young women. When Susan Penninger attempted to interview them at Mary Ann Barbour's home, the door was slammed in her face, after which someone emerged from the house and tried to douse her with a garden hose.

The McCuan-Kniffen appeal hearing began amid a carnival of news crews, lawyers, family members and courtroom voyeurs, the hallway outside transformed into a curious stage for posturing and speeches by various hangers-on mixed with a quiet dignity and anguish shared by those directly involved. Even before it started, several Kern County judges were disqualified from the case, owing to allegations of conflicts of interest, bias and improprieties.[7] The matter finally landed before a newcomer to the Bakersfield bench, Jon E. Steubbe, a studious former law-school dean who had joined the Kern County Superior Court just seven months earlier. A virtual unknown to criminal lawyers, his main experience on the bench to that point was in divorce cases and custody disputes. Observers and prosecutors, as well as the attorneys representing the Kniffens and McCuans, all seemed to assume that the novice Steubbe would adhere to the same pattern every other Bakersfield judge had adopted in the ring cases—they figured he would deny a new trial and let the appeals courts sort it all out.

"I'm always hopeful," appeals attorney Michael Snedeker said on the eve of the hearing. "But let's face it. No Kern County judge has ever overturned one of these cases."

Still, some of the best lawyers in Bakersfield, including Stan Simrin, who had won freedom for many other ring defendants years earlier, assembled to argue the case. They laid before Judge Steubbe a multitude of issues, from the withholding of key evidence to official misconduct. The now-infamous wink test was debunked for Steubbe's benefit, as it had been in other cases, portrayed by a procession of experts as little more than medical quackery rather than a valid indication that a child had been molested, as Kern County prosecutors had labeled it. And the coercive questioning of the children, it was said, made false allegations likely and the truth impossible to know.

As the lawyers made their arguments and the experts gave their testimonies, it was apparent that they were doing so in a profoundly different atmosphere from the one that had prevailed fourteen years earlier at the beginning of the Witch Hunt. Outside the courthouse, there were no protesters this time, no activists demanding thousand-year sentences. The old hysteria had faded, bludgeoned into submission by years of revelations of official errors, overkill and misconduct; in its place was a tired public cynicism about the justice system, a fear that there could never be finality in any big criminal case in Kern County. The DA remained as zealous as ever in other cases, but in this courtroom, there were no prosecutors thundering about God and sin and the devil—only mounting evidence of unfair trials and potential innocence, and, with it, a shift in mood. The guards and bailiffs, who at first watched over the defendants with a stony mixture of fear and contempt, gradually began to relax. Their arms uncrossed and they could be seen smiling and joking with the prisoners; they even removed the defendants' chains and allowed the long-separated Kniffens a brief hug and kiss. Much the same transformation occurred in Brenda Kniffen's cellblock: As her case was made, guards and inmates alike came to believe her innocent. Where once she faced only abuse, now she was cheered and wished luck.

This change in atmosphere was not lost on the district attorney. A decade earlier, Ed Jagels brashly urged the court to allow TV cameras to record the proceedings; now his office felt besieged by "biased" reporting. When a crew from the ABC television newsmagazine *Turning Point* showed up to film the hearing, the defense lawyers readily gave interviews. The district attorney declined.

Yet the DA still expected to win. Deputy District Attorney John Somers, who had so adeptly put Pat Dunn away, led the prosecution team defending the conviction. As he had in the Dunn case, he conceived yet another brilliant strategy, choosing to present almost no evidence and hardly any witnesses to rebut the weeks of seemingly overwhelming evidence and testimony put on by the defense team. To some observers, including the original Kniffen-McCuan prosecutor, Andrew Gindes, it looked as if the DA was rolling over like a beaten dog on this case, preferring to put the controversy to a quick end rather than fight for victory. Others, though, including Stan Simrin, watched the prosecutor in awe while, point by point, he showed how each and every defense argument being presented as new evidence to Judge Steubbe had in fact been hashed out in one form or another during the original trial. It was a canny tactic: if there was no truly *new* evidence, there could be no new trial. Proving innocence, or reproving guilt, was not the point.

With an easy command over thousands of pages of testimony and a roomful of evidence, Somers cited reference after reference where the same ground had been covered thirteen years previously. Perhaps not as well, perhaps not as thoroughly, Somers told the judge, but questions about the interrogations of the children, the medical evidence, the psychiatric problems of the girls' guardian, Mary Ann Barbour—all had been visited before. It was the "been there, done that" argument, and Somers was so convinced of the correctness of his position that he barely cross-examined some of the defense's star witnesses. After all, if he was right, what they said didn't matter.

Somers had boldly sidestepped the defense lawyers'

carefully laid trap. They wanted him to go head to head with their case, for they knew that they could shred any witness who dared suggest that the case had been investigated properly. On those terms, in a battle of experts and evidence, the defense knew it couldn't lose. And so did Somers. But in the peculiar logic of criminal appeals, it didn't matter that, in today's world, the case would never have been investigated in such an improper manner, or that, in all probability, the Kniffens and McCuans would never have been convicted in the first place with today's knowledge and experts. What mattered was the question of whether or not there was new information momentous enough to declare the first trial fundamentally unfair. And if all the issues raised before Judge Steubbe had been confronted and dealt with in the past by judge and jury, even in the most minor and incomplete fashion, then they could not be revisited again, Somers argued.

"There simply is nothing new about any of this," Somers said time and again over the course of the two-week hearing, his small smile and quiet demeanor steadfastly impenetrable and confident. As his simple yet potentially devastating strategy became apparent, the defense team realized that if the judge—or the court of appeal—accepted his argument, the Kniffens and McCuans would die in prison long before becoming eligible for parole.

And Somers did prevail on almost every point of contention. When Judge Steubbe delivered his ruling, moving down the list of ten separate claims by the defense,[8] he agreed with Somers time and again. The questions about Mary Ann Barbour were old news. So were claims of withheld evidence.[9] Even on the issue of bogus medical tests, the judge sided with Somers: It was not new evidence, just a disagreement between experts that had been argued during the original trial. The weight of scientific opinion may be much more in the defendants' favor now, but that was not enough, Steubbe decided, even though he had heard from multiple experts who said there was no evidence of molestation at all.

There was one point, however, on which the judge disagreed with the district attorney, finding there had been new evidence presented. It concerned the interrogation of the children and new research, unknown thirteen years earlier, that helped explain how and when children told the truth—and what might lead them to give false testimony.

Psychologists and child-development experts assembled to testify in the case told the judge how they had been working for years to perfect techniques for police that would ensure unbiased and reliable interviews and interrogations, particularly when children were involved. Open-ended questions, in which the children use their own words rather than simply answering yes or no to pronouncements from adults, were essential, these studies found. Part of this research also involved learning what *not* to do, and in these experiments, it was found that just about anyone—but particularly children eight years old and younger—could be persuaded to make and eventually believe false statements about events they had not witnessed or experienced. Even false memories of painful events could be created, if the questions were sufficiently leading and aggressive, and if they were asked by someone in a position of authority. In one experiment, the judge learned, three out of four children claimed that they saw a school custodian hurt someone, when in fact, they had witnessed him simply mopping the floor.

Another experiment saw three out of four children (and one out of four *adults*) persuaded, through aggressive and leading questions, to remember a past traumatic event (a painful vaccination) that never happened. Weeks and even months later, these false memories persisted.

The high-pressure, suggestive techniques employed to create such false statements, Judge Steubbe learned through the course of the hearing, were the same methods Kern County prosecutors, social workers and investigators used whenever they questioned a child who they believed had been molested. In seeking the truth, investigators had made sure they'd never find it.[10]

With a growing sense of horror, Judge Steubbe realized there was no way to know the truth in the Kniffen case—not now, and not thirteen years ago. The sensational headlines, the apparent mountain of evidence—the entire Witch Hunt—had been built on a foundation of fear, error and coercion. Well-meaning officials—at least, in Steubbe's carefully worded ruling—had become victims of their own preconceptions and biases, questioning children not as potential victims, but as if they were trying to pry confessions from suspects. Maybe the children had been molested, maybe not. Perhaps they had been molested, but not by the individuals on trial. There just was no way to know. Given the manner in which the kids were questioned, anything they said was unreliable. Even the kids couldn't know anymore what was true and what was simply a mixture of fantasy, guilt, remorse and wishful thinking. All Steubbe had to do was hear that tape-recorded interview of Brian and Brandon Kniffen from back when it all began, in which the boys denied everything but were badgered and cajoled into finally accusing their parents. How could that be the road to truth? the judge asked himself. How could men and women be imprisoned on the basis of such information, when the "statements" of the children, the heart and soul of the prosecution's case, had been put into their mouths by the authorities?

"Listen to that tape, your honor. That sets the stage. Listen to those two boys on that tape," Stan Simrin had begged the judge. "That's where it starts. The paranoia and near hysteria that prevailed in parts of this country started here in Kern County in 1982. And we urge you to put a stop to it. Here. In Kern County. Now."

To everyone's surprise, Judge Steubbe did just that. It didn't take years and more rounds of appeals, as the defense lawyers—and prosecutors—had anticipated. It took Steubbe only twelve days to issue a written ruling. Unmindful of the politics and the pressure of the situation, he did what no other judge in Kern County had ever done in a ring case: He found the Kniffens and McCuans wrongfully convicted, because the questioning of their children by the sheriff's department and the district attorney, however well-intentioned it might have been, had hopelessly tainted the case. The trials and guilty verdicts had been fundamentally unfair.

Miles away at the Kern County Jail, Scott Kniffen learned of the ruling hours later, when a sheriff's deputy thrust a crumpled fax into his cell. It was a request from a news reporter for an interview about what it was like to be free. Brenda Kniffen, asleep in her jail bunk, heard around the same time, when other inmates turned up their radios and began banging the bars of their cells and shouting. She lay still as the words echoed through her tiny cell: *You've won. You're free. You're innocent.*

District Attorney Ed Jagels was at the Republican

National Convention in San Diego when the word came down. The news put a damper on Jagels' celebrations, and when reporters tracked him down, he had little to say other than his belief that the case was now "unprosecutable"—meaning it would be impossible at this time to prove that the Kniffens and McCuans had done anything wrong.

Jagels could have appealed Judge Steubbe's decision. Or he could have retried the case and attempted to win a new conviction. But he did neither.

With that, the first of the big ring cases—and the first big trial of Ed Jagels' tenure as Kern County District Attorney—passed into memory. And after fourteen years, four more innocent people finally walked out of prison.

Neither Jagels nor anyone else involved in prosecuting the case has ever backed off their stated belief in the defendants' guilt. Even as Kern County paid the Kniffens a $275,000 settlement in 1998, there were no apologies for the Kniffen or McCuan families. Of Steubbe's decision, John Somers said that, though it was legally sound, "We simply don't agree with his conclusions."

Given such an official position, it is unsurprising that the Witch Hunt's legacy continues to haunt Bakersfield still. It is a legacy that has become increasingly uncomfortable for those in power: In 1998, two of the remaining defendants still in prison on molestation-ring convictions unearthed new evidence of Kern County officials' improprieties.

In January, and over the district attorney's fervent opposition, seventy-four-year-old Harold Weimer was set free after thirteen years behind bars for the alleged molestation of three foster children in his care. He had

484   Edward Humes

been arrested in 1984 shortly after he was proclaimed
Kern County's foster parent of the year, having opened
his and his wife's home to hundreds of neglected and
abused children over the course of twenty-six years. His
arrest had stunned all who knew him and most of the
children he had helped as a foster parent.

The case against him began when a troubled twenty-
seven-year-old woman claimed that Weimer had molested her when she was a foster child in his home about
twenty years earlier. Her recollections came to the attention of authorities after she wrote a letter to the
Bakersfield Californian on the subject. The woman had a
history of drug abuse and of accusing others of molestation; her own mother suspected she hoped to use the
Weimer case to make money through a lawsuit.
Nevertheless, the Kern County Sheriff's Department
immediately removed four foster children then at the
Weimers' home; when they failed to accuse their foster
parent of anything, one of the same deputies who had
interviewed children in the discredited ring cases was
dispatched to interview Weimer's other former foster
children. Two of these former foster children, one of
whom also had a history of leveling false allegations of
abuse, ultimately claimed to have been molested by
Weimer four years earlier, and it was their testimony that
led to his conviction and forty-two-year prison sentence.

More than a decade later, United States District Court
Magistrate Judge Sandra M. Snyder of Fresno found that
Weimer's trial lawyer was incompetent for failing to
inform jurors of the case's questionable origins—the jury
never even heard about the woman whose allegations
sparked the investigation—and for failing to bring out
evidence that would have damaged not only the credibil-

ity of the two girls who did testify, but of the entire investigation. In a ruling that sounded the same points as Judge Steubbe's opinion in the Kniffen case, the magistrate criticized the Kern County Sheriff's Department for its "flawed investigatory techniques," which could have generated false reports of abuse through the sharing of statements of one witness with other witnesses, refusing to accept children's denials of being molested, repeatedly interviewing witnesses, failing to keep proper records of multiple interviews, and "implanting answers in the minds of the children witnesses."[11]

Snyder ordered Weimer released and recommended that his conviction be overturned. Her decision was not final, however, unless the federal judge who oversees the magistrate accepts the recommendation. Kern County is continuing to appeal the case, and officials hope to put the elderly Weimer back in prison.

Ed Jagels called the decision to free Weimer "ludicrous" and "Kafkaesque." He assured the *Bakersfield Californian* that, despite the overturned ring convictions, his office didn't have any higher a reversal rate than other district attorneys in California. Of the previous ring-case reversals, Jagels said, "Obviously we think the court has erred in other cases."[12]

Within a few months, however, new claims of gross prosecutorial misconduct, hiding of key evidence and alleged perjury by Kern County officials surfaced in the case of Jeffrey Modahl, who had been serving a forty-eight-year prison term for supposedly being part of the Cox molestation ring.

The case against Modahl had begun in 1985 during the height of the Witch Hunt, when several children accused brothers Anthony and Leroy Cox, then other members of the family, of molesting them. The evidence against the two Cox brothers was compelling—as it was against their father and three other family members—but the evidence against Modahl was ambiguous at best. In any case, the Cox case remains unique among Kern County molestation rings in that all of its members either remain in prison, have served their sentences completely or died in prison. It was not so much a ring as a large family that preyed on its own children. Even so, as often happened in that era, the accusations took a familiar course, replete with improbable descriptions of mass-molestation scenes, children hanging from hooks in the ceiling, photographic equipment—the same elements described in the other ring cases that, once again, could never be corroborated with physical evidence and which suggested the use of coercive questioning by authorities.

Among the children interviewed during the initial investigation was a cousin to the Coxes, Modahl's ten-year-old daughter, Carla. Although at first she did not accuse her father of any wrongdoing, after repeated sessions with social worker Velda Murillo and Deputy Connie Ericsson, Carla began implicating him. Out of four child victims in the case, she would be the only one who accused Jeffrey Modahl of being part of the "ring"; there was no other substantive evidence of guilt presented at his trial. Nevertheless, he was convicted and sentenced to more time than any of the others.

Though Carla recanted after the trial, the Kern County District Attorney's Office argued she had been pressured by family members into changing her story. Modahl's motion for a new trial was denied in the Kern County Superior Court, and his subsequent appeals over the years failed.

But in late 1997, a previously secret tape recording surfaced and was handed over to Modahl's lawyers by the original trial prosecutor, Deputy DA Craig Phillips. The tape was of the initial interview of Carla's half sister, Teresa Cox, the first victim interviewed in the case. Defense lawyers had repeatedly asked if such a recording existed, and a judge ordered any such tapes turned over to Modahl's attorney, but Phillips never supplied it; he says he only just learned of its existence. Murillo and Ericsson previously had sworn on the witness stand no such tape recording was made. Murillo and Ericsson also swore that they never asked leading questions and never suggested the name of Jeffrey Modahl or any other suspect to the kids—the child victims did that on their own, Murillo and Ericsson said. Ericsson, testifying in the trial of one of Modahl's alleged accomplices, swore he would never do that because "you can lead a person to say anything if you start suggesting."[13]

The newly discovered tape, however, appears to paint a different picture. In that crucial first interview in the case, Murillo and Ericsson do much of the talking, with Murillo telling Teresa that she believes the girl had been abused by numerous relatives, including Jeffrey Modahl—placing the twelve-year-old in the position of having to insist only Leroy and Anthony Cox were the culprits. The tape could have been damaging to the prosecution had it been turned over in time for Modahl's trial, as the defense could have argued it showed the coercive methods used by investigators on the case. Later, at Modahl's 1987 *habeas* hearing, it could have backed up Carla's assertion that she had been coerced by her inquisitors into falsely accusing her father. Keeping the tape secret was illegal, Stan Simrin, Modahl's new attorney, alleges, but it enabled Kern County to convict an innocent man.[14]

The problems with evidence in the case did not stop there, however: Simrin's investigation has revealed that Carla Modahl, before her father's trial, had been taken to Kern County Medical Center for an examination by an expert often used by prosecutors, Dr. Jess Diamond. Like the tape, the results of that exam—and its very existence—were never disclosed to Modahl's trial lawyers. Further, the DA vociferously and successfully opposed all attempts by the defense to have Carla examined by a doctor chosen by the defense, a position it had taken in other ring prosecutions.

Simrin learned in late 1998, however, that Diamond's exam records on Carla Modahl still existed, and that the doctor had found absolutely no evidence that the girl had ever been sexually abused. The exam contradicts early investigative reports in the case detailing Carla's statements to Murillo and Ericsson in which she claims to have been repeatedly and painfully violated with various objects, as well as her father's penis—abuse that should have been corroborated by Diamond's exam. After the exam, Carla's account changed. Her testimony against her father referred only to external sexual touching without penetration—a tailoring of her testimony by Kern County authorities to fit the results of the secret medical examination, Simrin has alleged.[15]

"Egregious misconduct lay at the root of the prosecution's failure to disclose the evidence," Simrin told the Kern County Superior Court judge hearing Modahl's *habeas corpus* plea for a new trial.

The DA has denied these allegations, conceding that failure to disclose the tape was a violation, but calling the omission a harmless error. As for the medical report, Phillips never knew about it because it was handled by Murillo, who then worked for the Kern County welfare department, not the Kern County District Attorney's Office. "If I didn't know about it, I couldn't disclose it," Phillips says. (Simrin accuses the district attorney's office, though not Phillips specifically, of creating a secret and illegal system designed to keep prosecutors—and, therefore, defense attorneys—conveniently in the dark about exams that help the defense, though they always received copies of exam reports that confirmed signs of abuse. Ironically, the source for that accusation is the autobiography of former molestation-ring prosecutor Andrew Gindes.)

Phillips' main legal argument, however, has been to ask the court to disregard the new allegations of government misconduct on procedural grounds, asserting that, as they were not included in Modahl's original *habeas* petition, they should not be the subject of any hearings at all. Phillips has conceded that, if Modahl is allowed to add the new allegations to his case, the office would stand accused of criminal acts and would have to recuse itself from the matter.[16] In the end, however, no recusal was necessary. Kern County Superior Court Judge John Kelly found no deliberate misconduct by prosecutors. Nevertheless, the judge ruled, Modahl's conviction was tainted because evidence in the case had been withheld that would have shown Modahl's daughter was never molested and that Kern County authorities interrogated children in such a way as to likely generate false and unreliable accusations of sex abuse. In May 1999, after fifteen years in prison, Jeffrey Modahl was released, yet another victim of the Witch Hunt freed despite the vigorous opposition of the Kern

County District Attorney. In response to this ruling, the district attorney's office offered its stock response: Prosecutors still believed Modahl was guilty. But they did not back up this assertion by appealing Kelly's ruling, nor would they retry Modahl in order to prove they were right. In short order, prosecutors announced they were dropping the case against Modahl for good.

With the release of Jeffrey Modahl, the Kniffens and McCuans, and Harold Weimer, the number of erroneous or wrongful prosecutions in recent years in Bakersfield reached ninety-two. Ninety-two men and women— arrested and charged with murder, molestation or other serious crimes—have had their cases dismissed or over- turned because of official misconduct or mistakes, hid- den or erroneous evidence or improper interrogations and investigations. The number is particularly extraordi- nary because the American justice system is designed to make such reversals extremely difficult, with laws that favor prosecutors over defendants at virtually every junc- ture once a person is pronounced guilty.

A few of these ninety-two cases involved the clearly guilty, released because of bad searches or improperly obtained evidence. But a majority involved men and women for whom considerable evidence exists to sug- gest—and, in some cases, prove outright—their inno- cence. These were not criminals turned loose on mere technicalities; they were ordinary people who, for the most part, had never been in trouble with the law before they were caught up in something dark and terrible.

This pattern, far from being limited to Bakersfield, has spread to other American communities. Throughout the 1980s and 1990s, official misconduct and the conviction of innocents appears to have risen steadily. All around the country, and despite painful past experience, shockingly similar molestation-ring cases continue to rise up like ghosts from Kern County's past, only to fall apart for the same reasons, the hard-earned lessons of Bakersfield's Witch Hunt lost or ignored. In San Diego, for example, a developmentally disabled man named Dale Akiki watched his careful, quiet life be destroyed in 1991 when he was jailed and charged with the ritual abuse of young children. His trial took seven months; his acquittal by jurors in 1993, who were outraged by what they found to be false charges, took seven hours. The case eventually contributed to the ouster of the once-popular local district attorney, Ed Miller, who had been in office twenty-three years. A highly critical grand jury investigation followed, detailing how a cadre of investigators and therapists promoted community hysteria and false prosecutions with spurious allegations of a widespread satanic conspiracy.[17] In North Carolina, the last of seven alleged ritual abusers from the infamous Little Rascals Day Care Center molestation-ring case was released after gross prosecutorial misconduct was proved.[18] Around the same time, day-care workers imprisoned in the infamous Massachusetts Amirault case were released from lengthy sentences for similar reasons.[19] Each of these sensational cases, and many others like them, followed the lead of the Kern County ring investigations, using the same discredited techniques and interrogations so likely to generate false accusations and wrongful convictions, and stole years of freedom away from several hundred innocent men and women before the cases self-destructed. Some of these men and women remain imprisoned, though the evidence against them has in many cases been discredited.[20]

And it continues still: More than a decade after Kern County's molestation-ring hysteria spent itself, an eerily similar investigation unfolded in the small town of Wenatchee, Washington, a farm community in many ways similar to Bakersfield, surrounded by apple, cherry, peach and apricot groves. In Wenatchee, a lone police detective's aggressive questioning of one girl—whom he took in as his own foster child—blossomed into a series of increasingly grotesque sex-ring allegations against more than one hundred citizens, with forty eventually arrested. Suspected child victims were subjected to the same sort of leading and suggestive questioning that caused such problems in Kern County. As in Kern County, the accused in Wenatchee included people from all ranks of society— ministers, farm workers, even a social worker who knew the girl's troubled history and expressed doubts about the allegations—and the many suspects who were not formally charged nevertheless found themselves ostracized in the small town. In a now-familiar turnabout, the girl at the heart of the case later recanted all of the accusations, claiming that her foster father had coerced and threatened her into fabricating charges—but her revelations came only after fourteen people had plea-bargained their way into prison, choosing to avoid the risk of a trial and potentially far tougher sentences. Virtually all of these fourteen were indigent and had been represented by appointed counsel who recommended the pleas. In contrast, many others—almost all of whom could afford to retain private attorneys who recommended fighting the case—went free. Several who were tried and convicted have since won freedom on appeal, though a civil rights lawsuit against the town failed. As of 1998, Wenatchee remains bitterly divided by the case, with officials still defending their work

and neighbors frightened of one another and the police—
the living legacy of the Bakersfield Witch Hunt.

Aside from the ring cases, in the six years since Pat
Dunn was convicted of murder, literally thousands of
criminal convictions have been called into question
because of official misconduct, and at least three hundred of them reversed or dismissed so far. As in Kern
County, the same players often appear repeatedly. A
forensic expert, Fred Zain, has been accused of giving
false scientific testimony—frequently pivotal evidence in
winning convictions—time and again in West Virginia
and Texas (one hundred thirty convictions have been
reopened so far, with at least twelve men freed from
prison or granted new trials).[21] An entire police precinct
in Philadelphia was charged with the wholesale framing
of defendants, resulting in forty-two charges thrown out
and one hundred sixty more in question. State troopers
in New York state fabricated fingerprint evidence for
years; several hundred cases are being reopened there.
Among federal prosecutors, allegations of professional
misconduct soared another 71 percent between 1993 and
1997, though the Justice Department has taken little, if
any, disciplinary action (in fact, a congressional committee reported that, out of a sample of ten cases in which
federal judges had admonished prosecutors for misconduct, the Justice Department took no disciplinary action
whatsoever). In one extraordinary case in Chicago, the
state prosecutors and local policemen who allegedly
framed a young man named Rolando Cruz for a murder
he didn't commit are now being prosecuted themselves in
an unprecedented assault on prosecutorial immunity.
Before proving his innocence, Cruz had been tried three
times and in each case had been sentenced to die.

By some estimates, allegations of prosecutorial misconduct have nearly tripled since the seventies,[22] in some cases reaching grotesque proportions. In San Francisco, a federal prosecutor brought a witness from the People's Republic of China, Wang Zong Xiao, to appear as the star witness in a massive drug-conspiracy case, then threatened him with deportation back to China when he said that the defendant on trial was innocent. The prosecutor's action was all the more repugnant because U.S. officials knew that Wang had been tortured by Chinese detectives wielding electric cattle prods to get him to implicate—falsely—the defendant on trial in San Francisco. It was also known to federal officials that Wang would almost certainly be executed were he to return to his homeland after refusing to testify against the defendant, making the deportation threat as powerful an inducement to lie as any cattle prod. The huge drug-conspiracy prosecution—the "Goldfish Case," as it was known—was eventually dismissed when this chain of events was exposed, and the courts saved Wang from deportation and death. "The facts show such clear, flagrant and shameful constitutional violations that they shock the conscience of the court," U.S. District Court Judge William Orrick of San Francisco declared as he threw the case out in 1993.

Still, the U.S. government appealed Orrick's ruling, so intent was it on deporting Wang Zong Xiao. In 1996, federal prosecutors lost their appeal and Xiao received asylum.[23]

A few months later in March 1997, in Rhode Island, a massive racketeering and corruption case against a former governor, Edward D. DiPrete, and his son—the most sensational case in the state in years—was dismissed on account of outrageous prosecutorial misconduct and hiding of evidence that reached the highest levels of the state attorney general's office. The same prosecutors were already under investigation for improperly using informants and arresting dozens of innocents in drug cases. The lead prosecutor accused of misconduct in the governor's case, Michael F. Burns, committed suicide in the midst of the controversy. (The Rhode Island Supreme Court, while agreeing that the attorney general committed egregious misconduct, reinstated the charges in May 1998, concluding that judges lack the power to punish wayward prosecutors by throwing out cases before trial.)[24]

In Lancaster County, Pennsylvania, meanwhile, a young woman named Lisa Michelle Lambert, sentenced to life in prison in 1992 for murdering a romantic rival, was set free in April 1997, after a federal judge declared her innocent, then wrote a riveting opinion saying prosecutors had obstructed justice, knowingly used perjured testimony, suppressed evidence of Lambert's innocence and manufactured evidence of her guilt—all while allowing the real killer, Lambert's boyfriend, Lawrence Yunkin, to escape with a light sentence as a mere accomplice in exchange for his testimony against Lambert. Of the justice system in Lancaster County, U.S. District Court Judge Stewart Dalzell wrote, "It lost its soul and almost executed an innocent, abused woman. Its legal edifice now in ashes, we can only hope for a barn raising of the temple of justice."

The Lambert case garnered unusually extensive publicity—prosecutorial misconduct cases mostly just die quietly—and struck a nerve like no other before it. The fallout from the decision was enormous, angry and stretched across the nation. But the target of this anger was not the police and prosecutors of Lancaster County, who vehemently denied any misconduct to the press (though in

Dalzell's courtroom, they previously had admitted mishandling the case). The target was Judge Dalzell.

A drive to impeach him was launched. Prosecutorial
agencies around the country filed "friends of the court"
appeals briefs demanding the decision be overturned, on
grounds that it suggested judges still held too much power
over prosecutors. Legislation was immediately proposed
in the U.S. Senate to limit the power of federal judges to
proclaim prisoners innocent. Victims'-advocacy groups
wielded their considerable clout and demanded "reforms"
that would eliminate the possibility of release for others
like Lisa Lambert. A conservative lobbying organization,
the Free Congress Foundation, condemned Dalzell in a
fund-raising video as yet another liberal judicial activist
appointed by the Clinton administration (ignoring the
fact that Dalzell, long known as a conservative, law-and-
order jurist, was appointed to the bench by George Bush).

At no time, however, could the critics refute Dalzell's
actual findings—that Lambert had been framed and that
government officials had committed misconduct in the
process. Even so, seven months later, the U.S. Court of
Appeals for the Third Circuit in Philadelphia overturned
his ruling and returned Lambert to prison, where she
remains. The reversal came not because the appellate justices disagreed with Dalzell's factual findings, but because
of a procedural technicality cited by prosecutors. The
appeals court ruled that Lambert, who had filed her own
handwritten appeal to Dalzell after she had been raped by
a prison guard, had not completely exhausted all her possible state appeals before turning to the federal courts. In
effect, the appeals court noted that whether Lisa Lambert
was innocent or not, or whether there had been massive
misconduct or not, simply didn't matter. She had not fol-

lowed the proper procedure in filing her desperate appeal. In the face of the law, innocence was irrelevant. Back in the Lancaster County courts, before the same judge who convicted her in the first place, Lambert's appeal and Judge Dalzell's findings were dismissed out of hand in a hearing in August 1998. Any improprieties by police or prosecutors were harmless errors, Lancaster County Judge Lawrence Stengel ruled.[25]

Indeed, the Lambert and DiPrete cases are the general rule when misconduct occurs—judges declare "no harm, no foul." Although there have been an increasing number of reversed convictions that have been upheld in recent years, more often, convictions won after prosecutors lied, hid evidence, coerced false testimony or made wildly improper argument have been allowed to stand, with no relief for the convicted or consequences for the government officials who broke the rules. Legislators and courts have effectively worked in concert to enhance police and prosecutors' powers at the expense of suspects, defendants and the convicted—innocent and guilty alike. Many states, as well as the federal government, have adopted legislation making it harder to file, much less win, appeals to criminal convictions, even in cases where evidence of innocence appears to exist. Tough Texas laws designed to give prosecutors enormous and unfettered powers left Kevin Byrd no alternative when, after twelve years in prison for a rape he did not commit, new DNA tests proved his innocence beyond any doubt: the law literally left him no legal appeal. His only option was to seek a pardon from Texas governor George W. Bush— who denied it, declaring that it wasn't his job to be a judge. (Bush relented some months later and issued the pardon.) Meanwhile, in Idaho, the courts approved the police practices of lying to obtain search warrants and intimidating witnesses who might otherwise help the defense. Such transgressions were harmless error, it was opined. And in Kentucky, Charles Howard West, sentenced to twenty-two years in prison for murder in a case with slim evidence, was subjected to "a barrage of vilification, misleading innuendo and outright deception" by the prosecutor, the Kentucky Supreme Court found. Yet, much as the federal appeals court had in Lisa Lambert's case, the Kentucky court still upheld West's conviction because his lawyer neglected to follow proper procedure by seeking a mistrial while the prosecutor was carrying on in open court. Federal appeals courts have upheld this ruling as a matter of states' rights.

Perhaps the surest indication that the trend toward false convictions and prosecutorial misconduct represents a national phenomenon rather than one limited to a few distinct communities like Kern County may be found on death rows around the country. Thirty-two death sentences have been overturned since 1993, when Pat Dunn was convicted. These cases involved some of the highest-profile criminal prosecutions in the country, in which public scrutiny and expectations were great, and major resources were expended to achieve justice. Yet twenty-eight of these condemned men and women were not only granted new trials, they were exonerated and set free, innocents who were found to have been wrongly convicted and sentenced to death—more often than not because of misconduct by police or prosecutors. Further, the rate at which these innocents have been found on death row has accelerated as well—nearly double what it was between 1973, when the Supreme Court restored the death penalty in America, and 1993.[26] The release of men and women wrongly convicted of murder came to be an almost weekly event in the United States by the end of the century. In New York, a man named John Duval walked out of prison after twenty-six years when it was finally shown that the only eyewitness to the crime had initially told police he saw nothing—a story he changed after being held in jail for seven months as a material witness. The police report that documented this shifting story was never given to the defense, judge or jury, making it appear that this witness told the same, consistent account from the start. Two days later, in Oklahoma, Ronald Keith Williamson, who spent twelve years on death row and whose loved ones had to make funeral arrangements when they were told his execution was imminent, was proven innocent of a brutal rape and murder and set free. Williamson was lucky—his appeals had been exhausted, but his supposed accomplice, a high-school teacher named Dennis Fritz, was able to convince a judge to order DNA testing of hairs left behind by the killer. Prosecutors opposed this testing as a waste of time and money. But not only did DNA analysis exonerate both men, it proved prosecutors had relied on bogus scientific examinations in the first place to falsely link those same hairs to Fritz and Williamson. Further tests showed DNA traces at the crime scene actually matched the prosecution's chief witness in the case, a criminal who had been given leniency in exchange for his convenient but false testimony. It seems prosecutors may have cut a deal with a killer in order to prosecute two innocent men.

In Florida, meanwhile, the state Supreme Court, after reversing seven death sentences in recent years because of prosecutorial misconduct, issued an unprecedented warning to state prosecutors that it was fed up with ethical lapses in such high-profile, high-stakes cases. In freeing a Tampa man, Walter Ruiz, from a death sentence in April 1999, the high court wrote that "this trial was permeated by egregious and inexcusable prosecutorial misconduct," railing against the prosecutors on the case for trying to tilt the playing field in their favor through misstatements of the law, insulting the defendant, attempting to generate sympathy among jurors for their own personal tragedies, and introducing improper evidence. The high court said such transgressions had been occurring with "unacceptable frequency" in other death cases throughout Florida, and that something had to be done to protect the innocent from wrongful conviction—and execution.

Yet, even as such concerns mount and the number of innocents discovered on death row has increased, so has the pace at which executions in general are carried out. This will only continue, as new laws designed to reduce the number and scope of appeals take effect. The justice system must have finality, it is said. Victims must have closure. It has always been assumed that only a tiny fraction of death sentences are unjust, and that prosecutorial misconduct is a small problem in such cases. But this turns out not to be true: Of the approximately six thousand death sentences imposed between 1973 and 1997, a total of eighty have been reversed,[27] with a third involving substantial allegations of police and prosecutorial misconduct. Most of these sixty-nine men and women, in fact, have been fully exonerated and released, when previously they had been scheduled to die.

That means one out of every eighty people sentenced to death in the United States since 1973 has turned out to be innocent. And the pace is quickening.[28]

2

PAT DUNN LIVES AT CORCORAN STATE PRISON NOW, A home built of concrete and concertina wire surrounded by mile after mile of farmland that occupies the drained and dry bed of ancient Tulare Lake. A mere hour from Bakersfield, the prison is most notable for the unusually high number of inmates shot to death by guards under questionable circumstances.

These days, Pat spends his time working in the prison library and administrative offices. In his cell on his own time, he carefully reads the *Bakersfield Californian,* tearing out any articles that even hint at some injustice in the Kern County courts. He has a notebook full of them, a chronology of wrongful convictions: the releases of the Kniffens and McCuans, Offord Rollins, Charles Tomlin. Each overturned conviction, for a time, gives Pat new hope, but it is followed by the crushing realization that no one seems to be interested in his case anymore. If these other people could be imprisoned because of errors or lies, Pat asks anyone who will listen, is it so hard to believe he could have suffered a similar fate? The other cons just stare at him, appalled at his naiveté.

It has been a frustrating time for Pat, and he has withdrawn even further into himself, closing off his emotions from view even more than when he was free. He describes

himself as viewing his days in prison as if through a telescope. That's how he pictures himself when he allows
himself to consider his fate—as if he is outside his own
body, on some distant hilltop, watching Pat Dunn trudge
from cell to mess hall to showers, to yard and back to cell
again. The imaginary telescope is his personal trick;
everyone on the yard has a trick, whether they admit it or
not. It is his trick to stay sane as the time creeps by, days
without end, the rest of his life consigned to a gray place
of bars and cinder blocks. He has no friends, no visitors.
Not even his family comes to see him, except his older
brother Jay, who stops by for an occasional hour or two.
His older son, Pat Jr., lives too far away, and Pat has not
seen his other son, Danny, in years. His daughter,
Jennifer, still in Bakersfield, bursts into tears at the
thought of visiting. "Too painful," she says.

There is little left of his old life. Everything he
owned—money, furniture, cars, house, books, even his
dogs—is gone. He cannot say where. He watches from
afar as his former sister-in-law, Nanette Petrillo, with the
paralegal assistance of City Councilwoman Pat DeMond,
disposes of one piece of Sandy's estate after another, millions of dollars' worth of real estate. By law, DeMond is
required to send Pat written notice of the sales in
advance, but somehow the letters always get addressed
incorrectly and never arrive on time. Even the Columbus
Avenue property, where Pat and Sandy had wanted to
erect a movie theater complex, has been sold. The same
city council that stymied the Dunns' plans to build there
has allowed the new owner to develop the property without a hitch. And someone else has constructed a new
movie-theater complex a short distance from where the
Dunns wanted theirs, no problem.

As he has watched this last chapter in his life unfold, Pat has become a pale and nervous old man, beset by rashes and bowed by the strict routines of prison life. He has the shuffling walk so common on the prison yard, the over-the-shoulder glances, the ceaseless hoarding of every little possession to protect against thieving inmates. His manner is dominated by the need to keep one's eyes to oneself, to avoid giving offense in a world where there is little reason to live and therefore little reason not to lash out and kill—a world where men forget that, in other times and places, it is considered polite to look a man in the eye. Still, he is left alone for the most part, too old to be recruited into gangs or lusted after for sex or harassed by guards. He is respected for his intelligence, his quiet dignity and his status as a murderer, for murder sits at the top of the penitentiary pecking order, even for old men. Thieves, burglars, crackheads—they all come from the same world, the bottom feeders of the prison food chain, Pat has observed. But murderers come from all walks of life, a true cross-section of society, from gangsters to millionaires. "I'm a member of the elite," Pat likes to say with a bitter laugh. Sometimes, he can say it without his voice cracking.

His appeals and writ of *habeas corpus* did not go well. The DA won on every point, as happens with the vast majority of appeals. The one major issue raised in his appeal was whether Pat's real estate lawyer, Teri Bjorn, should have been required to testify at his trial about their discussion of power of attorney. Pat's appeals attorney, Richard Schwartzberg, attempted to argue that Kern County Superior Court Judge Robert Baca incorrectly interpreted the law and therefore violated Pat's attorney-client privilege of confidentiality when Baca ordered

Bjorn to testify. The Court of Appeal found this argument without merit, affirming that the law had been applied correctly. If Pat sought Bjorn's help in obtaining a power of attorney over Sandy's money, the court ruled, it would have been a violation of the law, and Pat could not use attorney-client privilege as a shield.

The problem, though, was not in Baca's interpretation of the law, but in his interpretation of the *facts*. Judge Baca and prosecutor John Somers had repeatedly stated during the trial that Pat sought a power of attorney—which would, indeed, have been illegal. But their statements were not true: Teri Bjorn, the sole witness to these events other than Pat, made it clear that Pat did not know what a power of attorney was, and merely asked *about* it, with no attempt to get Bjorn to do anything illegal. But this critical distinction was never clear to the appeals court. The misstatements of Bjorn's testimony were never corrected by Pat's attorney, or anyone else, to this day.

Likewise, Pat's appeals attorney did not raise the issue of the numerous errors and false statements made by the prosecutor during the trial and in closing arguments— the lies he attributed to Pat Dunn that were not lies, the incorrect statements he made about Sandy's jewelry and glasses. Nor did the appeals attorney raise the question of possible incompetence by the defense attorney, Gary Pohlson, for neglecting to object to the prosecutor's misstatements, or for the defense attorney's failure to point out the many inconsistencies of crucial witnesses in the case, including Marie Gates, Kate Rosenlieb, John Soliz and other detectives on the case, and Pat's housekeeper, Cindy Montes. And, of course, there was no mention of the crucial evidence that was never given to Pat, because his defense and appeal teams remained in the dark—

there was no way for them to know about it, and no way for the appeals court to consider it.

Pat's *habeas* petition, in which he was permitted to present new evidence, fared no better. His plea for a new trial relied primarily upon the new information Laura Lawhon had turned up from the state Department of Motor Vehicles. The DMV computer printout showed Jerry Lee Coble's license plate had been queried by local authorities right around the time Pat and Rex Martin had seen him skulking around the house—and when Pat's friend Jerry Mitchell recalled passing on the number to Detective Soliz to check out. Laura and Pat's lawyers had hoped they could use this information to prove that Jerry Coble and Kern County authorities had framed Pat Dunn.

In the end, though, the motor vehicle information turned out to be a tantalizing clue that seemed to prove nothing definitively. The request for information on Coble's car did not originate from computers at the Kern County Sheriff's Department, where Sandy's murder was being investigated, but from the Bakersfield Police Department, which at that time had nothing to do with Coble or the murder investigation. The defense team could find no way to connect it up, no way to identify what police officer made the request or why. Prosecutors wrote it off as a meaningless coincidence, probably a mere traffic stop. Laura felt the timing was too suspicious to be mere coincidence, but she had no proof. The argument was shot down by the appeals courts.

Meanwhile, the hidden information on Jerry Coble, Kate Rosenlieb and other witnesses remained hidden, even as the government fought to have Pat's conviction upheld by claiming there was no new evidence to consider. Had the information been revealed, Pat's bid for an overturned conviction and new trial would have been a strong one, far stronger even than Offord Rollins' already successful appeal. But without this information, the court of appeal had no choice but to reject Pat's last, anemic bid for freedom. The state supreme court declined to review the case as well. Eighteen months after a jury pronounced him guilty, Pat's appeals died.

After that, nothing happened in Pat's case for years. His lawyers moved on to other cases. He had no money to finance any further legal efforts, anyway. As a convicted murderer, he could inherit nothing from Sandy—everything went to Sandy's sister, Nanette, except for some small trust funds that passed on to Pat Paola's relatives. Pat's brother Mike, who had financed the trial defense, became mired in his own financial problems and declared bankruptcy. Several bills from the defense attorneys and investigators remained unpaid.

Only Laura Lawhon stayed in contact with Pat, though she had little time to devote to him or his case. She had parted company with her employer not long after the Dunn trial, and with several other colleagues formed her own firm, which quickly became one of the preeminent private investigation firms in Orange County. Later, she began splitting her time between California and her old hometown in Connecticut, where she had inherited a profitable gravel quarry after her father passed away. Yet with all that going on in her life, and despite no longer officially working on Pat's case, she still kept in touch with him, certain of his innocence, still angry and disappointed at herself for not winning his freedom. The same woman who penned postcards to her convicted former clients while vacationing in Hong Kong still accepted Pat's regular collect phone calls, and she still read his

voluminous letters scrawled on yellow legal tablets filled
with outrage and pain, piling up quickly enough to fill an
entire file drawer in less than a year. In her spare time, she
tried to chase down some new leads Pat had developed
through fellow inmates—tips about Jerry Coble, mostly,
which never panned out. Laura suspected the other
inmates were using Pat, conning him for one reason or
another—profit or sport, she figured. In any case, the
pattern became depressing: Pat would get his hopes up,
then Laura would have to crush him with bad news. A
year passed in this way before it suddenly hit Pat—as if it
hadn't occurred to him before—that he might never get
out of prison. "I'm going to die here, aren't I, Laura?" he
asked her one day.

"I don't know, Pat," she said quietly. "I hope not." The
lack of conviction in her voice scared both of them.

It was around then, in early 1995, that Laura mentioned the case of *The People of the County of Kern vs.
Patrick O. Dunn* to this author. In short order, she produced three boxes of files—everything she had on the
case—and handed them over with this comment: "Judge
for yourself."

It was in the course of researching this book that the
errors, hidden evidence and new information about the
murder of Sandy Dunn came to light. As often happens
when a criminal case is prosecuted unfairly, the justice
system of Kern County and the State of California simply
failed to detect, or at least acknowledge, any problems on
its own. No one had noticed that the DA had failed to disclose to Pat's lawyers, as the law required, a wealth of evidence that could have helped prove his innocence. The
defense remained in the dark about the lobbying efforts
by Kate Rosenlieb and other city officials to have Pat pros-

ecuted; they never heard about statements made by the Dunns' housecleaner that Sandy never wore her jewelry on her predawn walks, a critical point in the prosecution case. Most dramatically, the defense never knew that there were new charges against Jerry Lee Coble, or that the police and the DA neglected to pursue this new case against the star witness despite overwhelming evidence of his guilt. Pat and his lawyers never knew that, even as the DA vowed there was no new information in the Dunn case and urged the court to get on with Pat's sentencing, Coble had been allowed to elude arrest despite a plea bargain requiring him to maintain a crime-free existence.

Nor did anyone seem to notice that Pat Dunn's defense team never received a critical police report about Coble that detailed how the man who claimed to have accidentally witnessed Pat Dunn commit murder had previously begged to be allowed to make a deal, any kind of deal, vowing he'd do whatever it took to stay out of prison. Without that report, the defense had no way of knowing about Detective Eric Banducci, who arrested Coble but who was left out of the loop when Deputy DA John Somers and Sheriff's Detective John Soliz cut their deal with the career criminal—though Banducci sits less than ten feet away from Soliz. The defense had no way of knowing that Banducci, along with several other fellow detectives, considered Coble a chronic liar and a completely unreliable witness, and would have said so under oath as witnesses in Pat Dunn's defense. Locked within the files of the district attorney's office was a police report that could have destroyed Jerry Coble as a witness and seriously eroded the credibility of the entire case against Pat Dunn—except for the fact that Dunn and his lawyers never saw that report.

At this writing, as the millennium draws to a close, the Kern County District Attorney has yet to provide an explanation for such oversights, though one had been promised by John Somers for more than a year. District Attorney Ed Jagels declined requests for an interview with the author, saying such matters either are or will be the subject of litigation, and that he was barred from discussing them by the county's legal counsel.

Once the first edition of *Mean Justice* appeared in February 1999, however, Jagels broke his silence, launching a series of television and newspaper interviews in which he angrily denied any wrongdoing by his office in the Dunn case or any other. The legal reasons for his previous unwillingness to comment apparently forgotten, Jagels opined that the evidence of wrongful prosecution contained in *Mean Justice* was "fantasy" and "sheer, unadulterated bull." He offered few specific rebuttals, preferring instead to make sweeping condemnations, such as his view that the book showed "contempt for the victims' movement, contempt for . . . a law-enforcement–oriented community like ours . . . [and] a sneering L.A. view of Kern County."[29]

The district attorney got specific in one interview, however, when he assured the citizens of Kern County that his office would never rely on an informant like Jerry Lee Coble unless prosecutors were certain he was being truthful. "We don't use an informant or make a deal with him," Jagels vowed, "unless he saw something, unless his statement is something that he could not have known unless he was actually there and is actually telling the truth."[30]

If this is the practice of the Kern County District Attorney when dealing with informants, it would be a model policy, one that would greatly reduce instances of propitious lying by informants anxious to barter testimony for freedom. But, notwithstanding Jagels' assurances, no such policy was in evidence in the Dunn case. Sheriff's reports and trial testimony show that Jerry Coble's account of inadvertently witnessing Pat dispose of Sandy's body contained no such corroborating information—there were none of the telling details Jagels promised, none of those "he had to have been there" hallmarks of a truthful witness, none of the proof the DA said he required before cutting a deal with a crook. Indeed, Coble's account contained errors and omissions that should *not* have been there had he actually been present to see Pat hurling his wife's body into the back of a pickup truck, yet Jagels' office still bargained away a prison sentence in exchange for Coble's testimony.

A few months later, Jagels hired a private polling firm, which reported that the DA remained very popular in Kern County despite the publication of *Mean Justice*. The poll purported to show that most voters did not believe wrongful prosecutions were a problem. One of the poll respondents later contacted the local newspaper to assert that the pollster's questions were biased and slanted to produce results favorable to the district attorney.

Finally, in July 1999, five months after the initial publication of *Mean Justice* and more than two years after Jagels was first asked to respond to questions raised during the course of research for the book, the Kern County District Attorney issued a 154-page report titled "Junk Journalism." The report purported to correct "factual errors and distortions" in *Mean Justice*, but it consisted primarily of a rehash of the prosecution's original case in *People vs. Dunn* and failed to respond directly to most key issues raised in the book.

While the DA spoke out, Gary Pohlson, Pat Dunn's former trial lawyer, found in the initial publication of *Mean Justice* the ammunition he needed to launch a last-ditch round of appeals. With the help of law clerk Mike Turrell, Pohlson—who was not being paid by his penniless client but who still believed in his innocence—filed a new writ of *habeas corpus* in March 1999. The writ demanded that the murder conviction be overturned, alleging that the trial had been infected by official misconduct, the hiding of evidence favorable to the defense and damaging to the prosecution, false testimony by Jerry Coble, and other problems that rendered the verdict unfair.

The case landed back on the desk of Judge Robert Baca, who had presided over the trial six years earlier, retired now but still hearing cases from time to time. Baca ordered both the DA and the Kern County Sheriff to respond to the allegations of misconduct, setting in motion a long and uncertain process that could lead to Pat Dunn's freedom, or seal his fate for good—while leaving him to wonder just how much life might be left to him should he succeed in prying open his cell door.

There are no guarantees that day will ever come, he knows. As had been the case with so many others in his position, proof suggestive of innocence may not be enough to set him free. It is fairness, not innocence, that is at issue: He must prove that the authorities behaved so badly in his case that justice can be served only by wiping his conviction from the books. And this is something the Kern County DA simply cannot abide. Ed Jagels has fought such findings long and hard in all the other cases of wrongful prosecution and conviction that have emanated from his county. He has never admitted a seri-

ous error in those cases, even when they were overturned
or led to severe criticism of his office.

Such is the power of prosecutors that it would be a
simple matter for the Kern County District Attorney to
engineer Pat Dunn's freedom, or at least grant him a new
trial. With Jagels' assent—and an admission of mistakes
in the Dunn case—this could be accomplished in a matter of days, without the protracted litigation that otherwise would be required. But the district attorney has
opposed overturning the Dunn case with the same trademark ferocity he has always relied upon, using all his considerable power, credibility, and ability to persuade the
people of Bakersfield, who have so long trusted him as
their guardian of public safety.

As Pat Dunn prepared to launch one last bid for freedom,
police officers were called to investigate a disturbance at
an apartment building in Bakersfield. They found a man,
cut, bruised, and disoriented, standing in his underwear
on his second-story porch. He was thirty-seven years old
but he looked older to the officers, aged by a troubled life
of minor crimes, mental illness, problem drinking, and
drug abuse. "What's your name?" one of the cops called
out as the man swayed and shuffled at his porch rail.

"Danny," he yelled back, his speech slurred. "Danny
Dunn."

Here was Pat Dunn's long-estranged son, still spiraling
downward, sick and in trouble again, seemingly drunk.
The officers didn't know he had been in a bicycle accident
half a day earlier. They didn't know he had suffered a concussion, confirmed by head scans, but that he had fled the
hospital before he could be treated. With his wobbly gait,
slurred words and confused behavior, Danny Dunn

appeared intoxicated to the officers (though blood tests would later disprove this—he apparently was disoriented from his head injury). Fearing for his safety as he stood unsteadily on his upstairs porch, the policemen decided to make a misdemeanor public intoxication arrest.

After letting him get dressed, the officers brought Danny Dunn to the county jail, which is run by the Kern County Sheriff, so that he could "sleep it off." Because he was said to have both AIDS and hepatitis, the detention officers at the jail were wary of touching him, wearing gloves whenever they were forced to have contact with him. Jail records make it clear they viewed him with distaste; though the Bakersfield city police officers who made the arrest reported him to be quiet and cooperative, the sheriff's department would report that he was combative and abusive, requiring physical restraints and imprisonment in an isolation cell. He was also observed to be delusional.

Shortly after one in the morning on February 19, 1999, two detention officers at the jail went to the isolation cell because, they would later report, Danny Dunn was yelling and banging on the door. When the officers opened the cell, however, they found their prisoner lying quietly on the floor. When he tried to get up, one of the officers pushed him back down with his boot. A struggle ensued. More detention officers came. They used pepper spray and "carotid holds" that block blood flow to the brain through pressure to blood vessels in the neck. Then the unruly inmate was dragged out into the cellblock hallway and placed in leg irons. When it was over, Danny Dunn was dead. His last words, screamed after he was doused with a searing shot of pepper spray to the face that brought him to his knees, were, "It burns, it burns!"

Afterward, jail officers denied striking Danny during their struggle, saying they only used "pressure" to restrain him as he writhed and aimed wild kicks at them. None of the jail officers was injured. An autopsy would report that the thin, pale son of Pat and Nancy Dunn died of massive internal bleeding from "compressive trauma to abdomen." He had a broken rib, a bruised torso, and a badly lacerated liver—the cause of the bleeding. A lifetime of excessive drinking may have made the liver particularly vulnerable to injury, it was reported. The coroner's office—part of the sheriff's department—determined the fatal injuries occurred during the struggle with officers, but that the death itself was accidental.[31]

It is a finding that has left Danny's family, particularly his mother, Nancy Dunn, livid. She does not understand why her injured and delusional son was jailed instead of given medical treatment. She does not understand how a man in an isolation cell, designed to muffle noise and prevent him from harming himself or others, could have made such a racket that he had to be restrained by three deputies using their leather boots, caustic spray, and choke holds. She finds it hard to accept the notion that a mere accident could have injured her son's liver so badly that it was nearly cut in half by the force of the trauma he suffered. She knows that X-rays taken after his bicycle accident showed no broken ribs, but that his autopsy showed one rib had been shattered—and that the break was located in a position that could have caused his liver injury.[32] She fears Danny might have been targeted for revenge and abuse in the jail, either because of the publication of *Mean Justice* and the ensuing publicity, in which the Dunn name figured prominently, or because Danny exposed deputies to AIDS, or simply because he mouthed off too much, which even she concedes would not be unusual for Danny. She wants—needs—to know the truth of this. If the tragedy unfolded as the sheriff's department claims and the detention officers are blameless, Nancy Dunn says, let that be determined by an outside, independent investigation. Nothing else will satisfy the family.

But there has been no outside investigation of the circumstances surrounding Danny Dunn's demise, and none is likely, unless his mother decides to sue and launches her own investigation, a daunting prospect on her high school counselor's salary. Only one agency has examined what happened at the jail that night: The Kern County Sheriff's Department. The same sheriff's department that investigated Pat Dunn for murder and that had custody and control of Danny Dunn when he died also investigated the younger Dunn's death, then cleared itself of any wrongdoing.

In April 1999, as prosecutors drew up legal briefs opposing Pat Dunn's bid for freedom, his friend and former business partner, Rex Martin, received an unexpected telephone call. The caller offered something that had eluded the defense team for six years. He provided seemingly irrefutable corroboration of the central theme of Pat Dunn's defense—that he had been framed by a convict desperate to avoid his own prison sentence.

At the trial, Rex Martin had been a key witness on this point, claiming to have witnessed Jerry Lee Coble casing Pat's house in the weeks after Sandy's murder. Rex swore he followed Coble, memorized his description, and wrote down his license plate number some three of four weeks after Sandy vanished to give to the sheriff's department.

The defense had argued this occasion marked the first time Coble ever visited the Dunns' neighborhood, a reconnaissance mission that enabled the informant to construct a phony eyewitness account, which he then used as leverage to negotiate his plea bargain. But Coble swore the only time he passed by the Dunn house was on the night of the murder. Detective Soliz denied being told about the license number. And Deputy District Attorney John Somers stood up before the jury and branded Rex Martin a liar with a financial motive to concoct a cover story for his friend. The jury went with Somers' version of events; Rex left the courtroom livid, his faith in law enforcement shattered.

Six years later, his voice still shook with the memory of it as his lifelong friend, Bob Patterson, spoke to him on the phone and asked him to recall the events surrounding the trial. Patterson had just finished reading *Mean Justice*, he told Rex. One passage in particular caught his attention: the one about a curious defense discovery that went nowhere, the Department of Motor Vehicles printout on Coble's license number, created at the Bakersfield Police Department right around the time Coble was seen outside Pat's house.

"You know who ran that license number, don't you?" Patterson asked his friend. And when Rex, puzzled by the question, had no answer, Patterson said, "It was me."

At the time of the Dunn murder and trial, Bob Patterson was Bakersfield's chief of police, one of the most respected figures in law enforcement in his community. He had since retired. "Don't you remember?" he continued. "You wanted to know if that might be an unmarked police car hanging around outside Dunn's house, so you asked me to check it out."

And with that, Rex did remember. He had forgotten all about it, mostly because it seemed so insignificant at the time, and because another friend, a retired sheriff's deputy, had promised to pursue the matter—something that was explored in-depth at the trial. The occasion was easy to forget because Rex had never heard back from Patterson. The former chief explained he had never said anything about it at the time because the mysterious green car Rex followed came back registered to an ordinary citizen—Coble's mother. The chief dismissed it at the time as not worth mentioning to Rex, and he, too, had forgotten all about it. After all, Coble's role in the case would not be known to Pat or anyone else for months. Patterson's city police department had nothing to do with the investigation of Sandy's murder—that was a county sheriff's case, completely separate. By the time Pat's trial rolled around, Rex and Patterson forgot all about their inquiry into the car registration—until the book jogged Patterson's memory.

"I have no doubt whatsoever that Rex was telling the truth when he testified he saw Coble," Patterson says now. "Because he told me all about it at the time."[33]

Patterson's recollection puts the defense case in an entirely new light. Bob Patterson is not only a veteran investigator and police chief, with an impeccable record—he's a friend of District Attorney Ed Jagels. Prosecutors could never brand him a liar as they did with Rex Martin, nor could they challenge his recollection of the date in question, because the computer printout he requested is dated: July 27, nearly four weeks after Sandy disappeared, exactly when Rex recalled following Coble. Deputy DA Somers and Detective Soliz, who had argued that the motor vehicle printout was meaningless, were mistaken.

Unless the ex–police chief is lying, too, there is no way the incident outside Pat's house could have been concocted, as Somers exhorted jurors to conclude in convicting Pat Dunn. Jerry Coble *did* stalk Pat Dunn. Then he denied it in court.

With that one phone call, the defense had been given tangible proof to back up their theory that Pat Dunn had been framed.

Nothing, it seems, is ever final in the case of *The People vs. Patrick O. Dunn*. Marie Gates, the kindly older woman who swore at Pat Dunn's trial that Sandy announced she wanted a divorce, thereby providing motive for an otherwise senseless crime, now says Sandy was not planning to divorce Pat after all. Marie was really the one who brought up the subject of divorce in their last conversation together, not Sandy, Gates now maintains. "Tell him to take a hike," Marie recalls urging, when Sandy complained about Pat's vile temper when he was drunk. But, as Marie now tells it, Sandy said no, she did not want to divorce Pat. "When he's not drinking, he's very nice," Marie recalls Sandy saying. "I'm going to talk to him about it. See if he'll change."[34]

This is far different from her damning trial testimony, and it would diminish the web of circumstantial evidence spun by John Somers. It also matches a similar statement that Kate Rosenlieb recalls Sandy making—though Kate never shared this particular recollection during Pat's trial. It is impossible to know which version of Marie Gates' story to believe; she now also claims Pat Dunn confessed outright to the murder in her presence, something she never mentioned before in any statement, in or out of court. "I heard Pat Dunn say to his own mother that he killed Sandy," Gates says. "He just said it right out, that he killed her, and that his mother should keep her dang mouth shut. He didn't know I was there, but I heard it."[35]

This completely contradicts her statements to detectives and testimony at trial, where she said nothing about a confession, and recalled Pat telling *both* his mother and her to keep their dang mouths shut about Sandy being missing. This new revelation does, however, fit the pattern Marie displayed before Pat's trial. Her consistent altering of her account, with each change more damning of Pat, suggests that Marie Gates, though well-meaning, is not a credible witness and never was. She has told so many conflicting versions of the same events that the truth can no longer be determined. The Kern County authorities, of course, were happy to overlook inconsistencies in witnesses when they helped convict Pat, and the defense never brought these matters to the jury's attention. Both sides, it seemed, were focused on strategy, on winning, on building a case—for this is how our adversarial justice system is expected to work—and yet, somehow, this vaunted process, this crucible of truth our courtrooms are said to be, ended up masking, rather than uncovering, the truth. The jury was allowed to believe that Marie Gates was an utterly credible and consistent witness. And they voted to convict accordingly. It is as telling as anything in this case that such questions do not even merit mention in Pat's appeal. For all their power to harm in the real world, they are but harmless error under the law.

In the spring of 1998, as Pat Dunn began his sixth year in prison, another Kern County murder case with remarkable parallels to his own came to an abrupt and very different end.

Marie Haven, a prison guard in Kern County, had been arrested for murdering her ex-husband with the help of a fellow guard named George Curtis. Both were charged with capital crimes.

As in the Dunn case, financial gain was supposed to be the motive: this time, in the form of a half-million dollars in retirement benefits and life insurance proceeds. Like Pat, Marie Haven was said to have behaved in a most peculiar way immediately after the murder. Detectives decided that she seemed more interested in a quick ten-thousand-dollar disbursement from the insurance company than in grieving for her former husband. And, as they had with Pat, detectives disregarded a reasonable explanation for this behavior: The financially strapped Haven family needed that insurance money to cover funeral costs.

As in the Dunn case, there was no physical evidence linking either Haven or Curtis to the crime. And, as in the Dunn case, investigators attempted to overcome this lack of tangible evidence by relying on an informant as their star witness—an informant who, like Jerry Coble, had a checkered past, dubious credibility and a possible motive to lie. (The informant was Curtis's ex-girlfriend, and the breakup had not been amicable.) Yet detectives and prosecutors pressed ahead with their case, even after this woman admitted to lying about critical evidence in the case. She also confessed to destroying evidence in a 1991 welfare-fraud case and to inventing a twin sister to hide the fact that she had been a prostitute.

There was one big difference between Pat Dunn's prosecution and this case, however: The key informant's credibility problems were not kept hidden, but were exposed in open court. Defense attorneys grilled her on the witness stand during a preliminary hearing, forcing her to admit her lies and past misconduct. In the course of her testimony, she claimed her right to remain silent and asserted her Fifth Amendment right against self-incrimination five separate times. When the hearing ended, the judge reluctantly agreed that the minimal evidence needed to bring the pair of prison guards to trial had been presented by the prosecution. But he made it clear there was no way they could ever be convicted with such testimony.

After Haven and Curtis had spent one hundred days in jail, the Kern County District Attorney's Office apparently came to the same conclusion. The authorities dismissed all charges and the two walked free. During that one-hundred-day period, they had lost their jobs, Curtis lost his home, and Haven watched members of her own family turn against her, even though, under the law, she and Curtis were innocent and always had been.

Later, in the comfort of her home, Marie Haven found herself wondering why the detective on the case was so convinced of her guilt and dismissive of her version of events, while at the same time so willing, even eager, to take the word of a witness with questionable motives and credibility. And in this lies one final common thread linking Haven and Curtis to Pat Dunn, the one that caught Pat's eye and had him sitting bolt upright in his cell as he read about the case in the newspaper. The detective on the now-discredited Haven murder case was one Pat Dunn knew very well: Kern County Sheriff's Detective John Soliz.

There is one other curious aspect to Pat Dunn's case and, oddly enough, it has to do with flies—the same sort of evidence so critical to young Offord Rollins.

It came out in Pat's trial, when John Somers launched an odd series of questions to the medical examiner who autopsied Sandy's badly decomposed body. Somers wanted to know about the maggots and fly eggs found on portions of the corpse that had been buried. Through his questioning, he established that the insects could have gotten there only if those parts of the body were exposed to the elements for some length of time *before* burial. Otherwise, there would be no flies or maggots.

Somers dropped the subject then, and it played no further role in the case or in the jury's deliberations. Yet the very same questions had been crucial in the Rollins trial, just a few months earlier. Somers had nothing to do with that case, but he knew that the testimony had been critical. That's why, he later explained, he brought it up in the Dunn trial, just in case he needed it later. Indeed, because of the Rollins case, the Kern County District Attorney's Office, as well as the county's medical examiners, knew all about flies and their habits. They knew that flies lay eggs above ground only. And they also knew something else: that flies lay eggs in daylight only. Entomologists have long known that flies, blind in the dark and unable to navigate without light, neither feed nor lay eggs at night. That's why the defense in the Rollins case was so sure the murder had happened after dark: There were no flies or eggs on Maria Rodriguez's body in a desert teeming with them by day.

Yet John Somers, when he argued his theory of the Dunn case to the jury, said that Pat Dunn killed his wife in the evening, dragged her body to his truck at one in the morning, drove ninety minutes into the desert to bury her, then returned home before sunrise in order to receive a five o'clock call from his housekeeper, who remembered him being out of breath and the sound of water running in the background.

It was the theory that convicted Pat Dunn, so tidy, so neat, seeming to fit together like all of John Somers' puzzle-piece cases. But how can it be true? When, in that nighttime scenario of murder and covert burial, did Sandy's body lie exposed to the daylight so the flies could lay their eggs?

At times I think I will explode, Pat Dunn says. *I spend too much time thinking about the lies and the mistakes and the injustice that put me here. I probably say this too much— Laura can tell you that—but I am sixty-one years old now, and I repeat myself. It is hard to think about anything else.*

His voice is hoarse, his stare unfocused. Physically, he is in the prison visiting room. Mentally, he is on the hilltop with his telescope, far away, where it is bearable to speak of such things.

I used to be such a believer. We learned it all in social studies in grade school. Hell, I taught it to my own students: If you need help, call the men in blue. They're your friends. I always believed that, right up until the day they marched me in here. I even guess I still believe it. I think the system works most of the time the way we want it to. But more often than anyone wants to admit, it fails. When officers of the court violate their oaths and lie—or turn their heads from other people's lies—the system fails. And the guilty go free. Or the innocent are imprisoned.

Sometimes, though, I can clear my head for a while and think about other things. I think about riding fence with Mom, and looking at the land, talking about our plans for it. I can still see the excitement on her face when we'd make a decision and know it was good, and I knew it was like looking in a mirror, because I had the same expression on my face, too.

It was a good partnership that we had. I know people lied on me and said Mom and I always fought, but it's just not true, and least of all when it came to money. We agreed early on that we both would always try to make good decisions, and that neither would ever use the word fault. We kept that agreement to the very end.

I'll swear here and now and to anyone who cares to listen that I did not kill Mom. But I must confess that at this moment, I sure do miss her.

PROLOGUE: BEGINNINGS AND ENDINGS

1. From the tape-recorded and transcribed telephone call by Patrick Dunn to the Kern County Sheriff's Department on July 1, 1992, in Kern County Sheriff's Missing Persons Case KC92-14851, entered in evidence in the case of *People of Kern County vs. Patrick O. Dunn,* Kern County Superior Court Case No. 52347.

2. Ibid.

3. Ibid.

4. Ibid.

5. The preceding account of the defense team's preparations and the trial's concluding moments is based upon the author's interviews with Laura Lawhon, Pat Dunn and Dunn's lead trial attorney, Gary Pohlson.

PART I: PAT AND SANDY

1. Cynthia H. Craft, "Rogers Plans Talk to Group Termed Racist," *Los Angeles Times,* April 27, 1994; Cynthia H. Craft, "Sen. Don Rogers Finds Favor with Militia Movement," *Los Angeles Times,* April 30, 1995; "Lawmaker Used Race in Tax Ploy," Associated Press, April 12, 1996. According to the "tax ploy" article, State Senator Don Rogers owed the IRS $150,000 in back taxes and penalties when in October 1992 he filed a signed and notarized document that argued he was not a U.S. citizen, that the Constitution's Fourteenth Amendment applied only to citizenship of freed slaves, and that, as a white citizen, he had no tax or other obligations to the United States. The document was not discovered by newspaper reporters for four years because it was filed in

Sonoma County, in the California wine country, hundreds of miles from Rogers' own district in Kern County.

2. Chris Brewer, "Stringin' 'em up," *Bakersfield Californian*, Centennial Edition, 1998.

3. Kern County Grand Jury report on Ku Klux Klan activities in the County of Kern, C. A. Melcher, chairman, filed with Kern County Superior Court Judge T. N. Harvey on May 19, 1922; and "Klan Report High Lights," *Bakersfield Californian*, May 20, 1922.

4. According to Jennifer Dunn, in an interview with the author, her father's drinking was a principal cause of the family's problems and the divorce. While many friends and acquaintances of the Dunns' described Pat as a problem drinker and believed him to be alcohol dependent, he denies this and asserts that he and his first wife simply drifted apart.

5. Letter and attached reports to Stan Simrin, from private investigator Roger Ruby, November 21, 1992. According to Ruby's report, Larry Cox, the attorney who drafted the will, recalled that Sandy wanted it, not Pat, that he saw no evidence whatsoever that Pat had pressured her in any way, and that Sandy was alone with the attorney when the will was drafted.

6. Kate Rosenlieb described the incident in an interview with the author. She recalled that, when she arrived, it seemed to her Pat was acting strangely, babbling about politics and what a great governor Kate would make—things that seemed to make no sense. She assumed Sandy was asleep. Pat would later say he had been rattled and upset by Sandy's behavior.

7. Kern County Sheriff's Department Report KC-8925184, October 20, 1989; and the author's interview with Pat Dunn.

8. Financial Planner Kevin Knutson relayed this account on a number of occasions, first to Kern County Sheriff's detectives in a report dated July 7, 1992, in Kern County Sheriff's Department Case KC-14851 (the Alexandra Dunn missing persons case); in a second report dated August 17, 1992, in Case MO92-00633 (the Dunn homicide case); in his testimony in *People vs. Patrick Dunn;* and in interviews with the author. Although the Kern County authorities investigating Sandy's murder theorized that Pat was after her money, Knutson was adamant that the trust was entirely Sandy's idea. It would put Pat in charge were she to become disabled and, in the event of her death, it provided an economical way

of bypassing probate courts and estate taxes, while also eliminating the possibility of other relatives challenging Pat as sole heir—something that easily could happen under a simple will. According to Knutson, Sandy expressed specific wishes that her estranged sister should receive nothing in the event of her death.

9. Planning Commissioner Marino's account is contained in his sworn testimony in *People vs. Dunn*, and in a report to attorney Gary Pohlson detailing his March 9, 1993, interview with Laura Lawhon. Although the question of Sandy's mental state was raised from the first day of the sheriff's investigation into her disappearance, detectives never spoke with Marino.

10. The account of Kevin Knutson's June 30 meeting with Pat and Sandy is based upon Knutson's testimony in *People vs. Dunn*; his statements as reported in Kern County Sheriff's Department Case KC-14851 and Case MO92-00633; his January 15, 1993, interview with defense investigator David Sandberg as reported by Sandberg in an undated memorandum to attorney Gary Pohlson; and in interviews with the author.

11. Michael Trihey, "Feuding in court: Prosecutors rap judges in articles," *Bakersfield Californian*, November 8, 1981. The article details the fallout from a series of four articles on Kern County judges published October 20–October 27, 1981, in the *Los Angeles Daily Journal*, a newspaper devoted to covering California legal issues. The Foster Farms reference was to Kern County Superior Court Judge William A. Stone, a highly regarded jurist who later rose to the Fifth District panel of the California Court of Appeal that Jagels so despised. The article reports that Stone learned from other Kern County prosecutors that Jagels was the unnamed source and, as a result, he disqualified himself from a death penalty case Jagels was trying. Another *Journal* article again quoted an unnamed prosecutor—the Kern County bench once more suspected Jagels—as harshly criticizing Judge Marvin Ferguson for presiding over "Department 352." This was a derogatory reference not to Ferguson's courtroom number, but to the California evidence code section under which a judge may exclude evidence he deems confusing or prejudicial. It is a code section most often used to the benefit of defendants who want to toss out incriminating evidence. The unnamed source for the article claimed this judge used Section 352 more than any other in Kern County. "It's death

to take a case in there," the unnamed prosecutor said, "because he'll emasculate it." Ferguson was so incensed by the article that he called then DA Al Leddy down to his chambers, screamed at him about his inability to control his arrogant young prosecutors and told him he should punish and possibly fire the culprits. When Leddy declined, Ferguson announced he would run for district attorney, so he could take over the office and banish Ed Jagels to a distant and undesirable branch court deep in the wastelands of the Mojave Desert, where he would spend his days prosecuting traffic violations. The threat, Jagels would later say, provided additional motivation for his own ultimately successful run for the office of district attorney.

12. Michael Trihey, "Murder charges dropped," *Bakersfield Californian*, August 12, 1983. The *Californian* reported that murder charges against Neil Shewcraft, a Kern County rancher, were dismissed by Jagels' office in the wake of a California Supreme Court decision limiting a sweeping "Victims' Bill of Rights" voter initiative. The initiative had been championed by Jagels, and was designed to allow prosecutors to use any relevant evidence, even if it was illegally obtained through unlawful searches or coercive interrogations. Shewcraft's attorney presented compelling evidence that the rancher had been coerced into incriminating himself by Kern County Sheriff's deputies who persisted in interrogating him despite his repeated statements that he wished to remain silent, and even threatened to sue the man's elderly father if he didn't confess. The rancher later insisted that he was innocent and had been forced by threats to tell detectives what they wanted to hear. Decades earlier, Bakersfield's most prominent but least appreciated figure, U.S. Supreme Court Justice Earl Warren, had ruled that evidence obtained in this manner had to be excluded to protect the innocent from false charges and established the famous "exclusionary rule" that the Victims' Bill of Rights sought to eliminate. When the California Supreme Court ruled that the Victims' Bill of Rights did not apply in Shewcraft's case, the confession had to be tossed out, leaving the prosecution with no evidence. This sent Jagels into a fury, and he advocated the recall of six of the seven justices on the high court. The California Supreme Court justices "simply do not care about public safety," he ranted. "They don't care to balance the defendant's rights with the victim's. They

sit up there, in San Francisco, surrounded by state policemen and wring their hands about what's going to happen to criminals." Stan Simrin, the president of the Kern County Bar Association, who represented Shewcraft, and who would later represent Pat Dunn for a time, labeled Jagels' comments as "contemptuous of the Supreme Court, the rule of law and common decency," and declared that "To even suggest that six respectable justices would deliberately oppose the promoting of public safety is not only incredible, but extremely dangerous."

13. The incident involving the release of juvenile records during the 1982 district attorney's race was investigated by the Kern County Grand Jury, the results of which are contained in a document entitled "A Special Interim Report of the 1982-1983 Kern County Grand Jury," dated July 5, 1983, Bill N. Johnson, foreman. The grand jury was assisted by a lawyer and an investigator from the state attorney general's office because of possible conflicts with the local district attorney's office, which normally assists the grand jury. The report details what it calls the "unethical" and "unlawful" release of confidential juvenile files for "political purposes," pinning blame on Colleen Ryan and tracing the files' path from her to a representative of Jagels' campaign consultant, Stan Harper, and from there to Jill Haddad and the embarrassing confrontation with Jagels' opponent. The resulting controversy was subsequently reported in articles in the *Bakersfield Californian* July 6, 1983, September 2, 1983, and September 7, 1983, reflecting an initial denial by Jagels that Ryan had done anything wrong, followed by calls from grand jurors for disciplinary action against Ryan, and by Jagels' concession that confidentiality policies should be changed and enforced to prevent similar incidents in the future.

14. *People vs. Tony Galindo Perez,* Opinion of the California Court of Appeal, Fifth Appellate District, No. 4381, dated May 18, 1981. As is typical when appellate courts criticize prosecutors, the official opinion was designated "not to be published in official reports," sparing Jagels from having the account of his conduct available to attorneys and law libraries throughout the state.

15. This notion is advanced in Bennett Gershman's annual *Prosecutorial Misconduct* (Deerfield, Ill.: Clark Boardman Callaghan), the seminal legal work on its title subject. In his introduction, Gershman, a Pace University Law School professor and

former prosecutor in the Manhattan District Attorney's Office, writes:

> First, it becomes inescapably clear that the prosecutor, for good or ill, is the most powerful figure in the criminal justice system. To be sure, the judge exercises considerable power, but only after the prosecutor has made the crucial decisions about whom to charge, whom to punish and how severely. And this power to charge, plea bargain, grant immunity, and coerce evidence is largely uncontrolled. Second, acts of misconduct by prosecutors are recurrent, pervasive, and very serious. Case reports do not adequately describe the extent of such misconduct because so much of the prosecutor's work is conducted secretly and without supervision. . . .
>
> Restraints on prosecutorial misconduct are either meaningless or nonexistent. Relatively few judicial or constitutional sanctions exist to penalize or deter misconduct; the available sanctions are sparingly used and even when used have not proved effective. Misconduct is commonly met with judicial passivity and bar association hypocrisy. This judicial and professional default is not easily explained. Perhaps the prosecutor's standing, prestige, political power, and close affiliation with the bar may account for the lethargic responses. Another explanation may be the confusion between disciplining prosecutors and freeing guilty defendants. Some courts believe that reversal of a conviction because of prosecutorial misconduct may punish the prosecutor but exact too great a toll on society. Whatever the reasons, the absence of significant external controls requires prosecutors to be self-regulating. With so much at stake, however, and the potential for abuse so great, self-regulation is not an acceptable safeguard.

16. In a landmark case, *Berger vs. United States*, 295 U.S. 78 (1935) the United States Supreme Court outlined the duties and

responsibilities of prosecutors and the consequences of prosecutorial misconduct. The case involved a conspiracy to produce and sell counterfeit money. The evidence against one of the four defendants, Berger, was weak and contradictory, with ample evidence to suggest his innocence. Berger, however, was convicted anyway. In his appeal, the catalogue of criticism recited by the high court bore a striking resemblance to the criticisms leveled against Jagels in the Perez case, and focused on the fact that the federal prosecutor "overstepped the bounds of that propriety and fairness which should characterize the conduct of such an officer." In order to bolster his case against Berger, the federal prosecutor "was guilty of misstating the facts in his cross-examination of witnesses; of putting into the mouths of such witnesses things which they had not said; of suggesting by his questions that statements had been made to him personally out of court, in respect of which no proof was offered; of pretending to understand that a witness had said something which he had not said and persistently cross-examining the witness upon that basis; of conducting himself in a thoroughly indecorous and improper manner." Had the case been overwhelming, it might be possible to sustain the guilty verdict against Berger, the justices opined, but in a close case, "the evil influence" of the misconduct could not be overlooked. Berger's conviction was overturned and a new trial granted.

In a passage that is still widely quoted in court opinions sixty years later (including in the California case law cited in the discussion of Jagels' misconduct in the Perez case), the court explained why the conduct of prosecutors is so crucial to justice:

> The United States Attorney is the representative not of an ordinary party to a controversy, but of a sovereignty whose obligation to govern impartially is as compelling as its obligation to govern at all; and whose interest, therefore, in a criminal prosecution is not that it shall win a case, but that justice shall be done. As such, he is in a peculiar and very definite sense the servant of the law, the twofold aim of which is that guilt shall not escape or innocence suffer. He may prosecute with earnestness and vigor—indeed, he should do so. But, while he may

strike hard blows, he is not at liberty to strike foul ones. It is as much his duty to refrain from improper methods calculated to produce a wrongful conviction as it is to use every legitimate means to bring about a just one.

17. "Jagels' attacks draw criticism," *Bakersfield Californian*, May 27, 1982. Jagels was quoted by the *Californian* as saying he did not regret his behavior in the Perez trial, and that Perez might have been acquitted had he not acted accordingly. Jagels pinned the blame for problems in the case on opposing counsel's misbehavior and the trial judge's passivity. "It became obvious after a very short time that the judge was not going to control the defense attorney," Jagels said. "If I had not done something to control defense counsel myself, there is no telling what would have happened in that case." The appeals court opinion in the case refutes Jagels on these points, painting the prosecutor as the primary malefactor and stating that nothing the defense attorney did warranted Jagels' misbehavior or could have led to an acquittal in the case. Jagels, however, remained adamant, and was quoted in the *Californian* as saying such advocacy as he displayed in the Perez case is required of a dedicated prosecutor. The appeals judges, on the other hand, were "the most extreme pro-criminal judiciary in the country," he complained. Ironically, the defense attorney in the Perez case with whom Jagels found so much fault would go on to become a judge of the Kern County Municipal Court, where he regularly hears criminal cases brought by Jagels' office.

18. From the author's interviews with *Bakersfield Californian* photographer John Harte, and confirmed by other Kern County journalists. District Attorney Ed Jagels declined the author's requests for an interview.

19. William Vogeler, "Kern County Prosecutor Attacked as Overzealous," *Daily Journal* (San Francisco), July 6, 1989. According to this legal newspaper's research, nineteen cases alleging prosecutorial misconduct against the Kern County District Attorney had reached the appellate level in the first six years of Jagels' term in office—triple the number in the preceding twelve years. (Further research by the author indicates that number was actually twenty-three cases. At least eight of these cases involving

twenty-one defendants eventually were reversed, though misconduct provided the decisive grounds for reversal in only three of them, affecting a total of nine defendants.)

20. Ibid. Justice George A. Brown of the Fifth District panel of the California Court of Appeal, now retired, made these comments in open court during oral arguments in the appeal of the 1986 first-degree murder conviction and life sentence of Jerry William Blackman of Bakersfield. Blackman's attorney, Mark Christiansen, complained that Kern County prosecutors had failed to reveal the existence of a jailhouse informant in the case until trial, a form of misconduct. Christiansen asserted that the case fit into a "pattern of misconduct" among Kern County prosecutors, and that judges in Kern County had grown concerned. Another justice, James Ardaiz, followed up Brown's comments by saying, "Trying every case to the edge and expecting the appellate court to keep you from falling over the edge is inappropriate." Brown then suggested the state attorney general should look into the matter and "do something about it." A representative of the attorney general subsequently telephoned Jagels' office in response to Brown's suggestion, but no formal action or inquiry was made. Notwithstanding the extraordinary public criticism—rarely made in the staid atmosphere of appellate oral arguments—the Blackman conviction was unanimously upheld, and the court's opinion made no comment on the misconduct allegations. (The reason for Justice Brown's apparent ire at Jagels and his office became clear a few months later, when the same appeals court overturned a massive criminal case involving seven defendants sentenced to thousands of years in prison. The seven men and women convicted in an enormous molestation-ring case had to be set free because of massive prosecutorial misconduct, the appeals court found. The opinion in the case was being written at the time of the Blackman hearing.)

21. Pat's recollections about Sandy's odd behavior are not considered credible by Kern County authorities. They say that because Pat did not describe this driving incident in initial interviews with detectives, it probably did not happen, and Pat most likely manufactured the tale to bolster his story about Sandy developing Alzheimer's disease and wandering off. Pat counters by saying he was distraught and simply forgot to mention the incident in

initial interviews with detectives, though he did describe other occasions on which Sandy seemed overly forgetful. It should be noted that Pat failed to mention several instances of Sandy's forgetfulness that were witnessed by others, including James Marino.

22. Pat Dunn and Jim Weins, interviews with the author.

23. The account of Kate Rosenlieb's discussions and meetings with Pat Dunn and Detective Kline, and her reasoning for suspecting Pat of killing Sandy, is based primarily on Rosenlieb's recollections, as related in Kline's July 5, 1992, report on his initial interview with Rosenlieb, filed in Kern County Sheriff's Department Case KC92-14851; Rosenlieb's personal journal, portions of which were contained in the legal discovery file in *People vs. Pat Dunn* and portions of which were never disclosed until Rosenlieb provided copies to the author; and the author's interviews with Rosenlieb. Kline, in an interview with the author, provided some additional details.

24. The account of Detective Kline's meeting with Pat Dunn is based on Kline's July 5, 1992, report in Kern County Sheriff's Case KC92-14851; and the author's interviews with Kline and Dunn.

25. The account of Jerry Coble's interrogation by Detective Banducci is based upon Banducci's report, in Kern County Sheriff's Department Case KC91-06787, and the author's interview with Banducci and his partner, Sheriff's Detective Jeff Niccoli, who was witness to Coble's arrest and interrogation. Coble, in an interview with the author, called Banducci a liar, and denied any connection between his desire to strike a deal after his arrest in the theft case and his eventual plea bargain and agreement to testify against Pat Dunn.

26. The request was an unusual one, under the circumstances: Most polygraph experts believe that creating surprising or tense circumstances for a lie-detector test can blur or invalidate the results—the test, had Pat taken it, would in all likelihood have been worthless. Still, the net effect was that relations between Pat and the department sank rapidly downhill from there. The detectives accused Pat of failing to cooperate in their investigation. Pat, in turn, accused the detectives of being more interested in questioning people about him than in searching for his missing wife.

27. The warrant authorizing a search of the Dunn home at 1700 Crestmont Drive was signed by Bakersfield Municipal Court

Judge John Fielder on July 23, 1992, at 8:57 P.M., and served on Pat Dunn fifty-seven minutes later. It was filed in the municipal court under Case KC92-14851. The sworn affidavit filed by Detective John Soliz in order to obtain the search warrant is supposed to show probable cause that Pat Dunn committed murder. Instead, it contains information from Kate Rosenlieb describing the Dunns' alleged drinking and fighting, as well as Rosenlieb's various misstatements concerning Sandy's walking habits and jewelry; it describes Pat's 1989 arrest for spousal abuse (but does not mention that the case was dismissed and never proved); it quotes several individuals who claimed Sandy had no memory problems while failing to mention individuals who did detect such problems; it mentions the fact that Pat canceled a housecleaning appointment, supposedly on the day Sandy disappeared, and that he was out of breath with water running in the background when he and the housecleaner spoke on the phone; it asserts a previous voluntary search by detectives at the Dunn home was performed in "a hostile environment" and "done under pressure from Pat Dunn"; it says Pat's foreclosure business was losing money and in turmoil before he shut it down (without mentioning the fact that this was due to his surgery and convalescence); it describes how Pat failed to tell some people that his wife was missing; and, finally, it explains how a body found in the desert was eventually identified as Sandy's. No witnesses, no physical evidence and no circumstantial evidence were provided in the search warrant request to link Pat to the place where the body was found, to any sort of murder weapon, or to any sort of recent threat against Sandy. Indeed, there is nothing cited in the warrant application that can be described as evidence of criminal activity of any kind by Pat Dunn. Nevertheless, Bakersfield Municipal Court Judge John Fielder, based upon Soliz's affidavit, found probable cause that a crime had been committed and authorized the search. Dunn's attorney, Gary Pohlson, later said that had the search turned up anything incriminating, it might well have been tossed out of court because of the lack of probable cause in the affidavit. However, because nothing at all was found—suggesting Pat's innocence—the defense never challenged the search warrant's validity.

28. There are no clear-cut rules on when to take notes or to record statements during a police investigation; practices vary

from detective to detective, agency to agency. Many investigators jot notes contemporaneously, but others, like Soliz, prefer to write up notes after an interview, to avoid distracting themselves or their suspects. Many police agencies decline to tape-record interviews as well, though this practice varies greatly, even within Kern County, where certain types of interviews—particularly those involving child victims of sexual abuse—are now routinely taped because of past controversies. The stated reason for not tape-recording is the belief that a suspect or witness is less likely to relax and open up during an interview if he or she is aware of being taped. Another reason put forth by defense attorneys is that the actual dialogue of tape-recorded statements is often more ambiguous than it appears to be in a summary written up in police reports, and therefore less favorable to the prosecution. Furthermore, the reluctance to tape-record initial interviews of suspects may arise from official concerns that hardball interrogation tactics (which legally can include using lies to trick a suspect into confessing) would be captured on tape as well, and could become an issue once the case is before a jury. Recent concerns about false and coerced confessions have led many police agencies to rethink their posture on taping, with over 2,400 of them adopting a policy of recording all interrogations and some witness interviews, according to a U.S. Department of Justice Study described in "Police Refine Methods So Potent, Even the Innocent Have Confessed," Jan Hoffman (*The New York Times*, March 30, 1998).

29. The account of Rex Martin's relationship with Pat Dunn and their trip to Paris-Lorraine is based upon Martin's statements to detectives on July 21, 1992, contained in Kern County Sheriff's Department Case KC92-14851, and on July 27, 1992, in Case MO92-00633; his statements to private investigator Laura Lawhon on February 24, 1993, contained in an undated report by Lawhon to attorney Gary Pohlson; Martin's testimony in *People vs. Patrick Dunn;* and the author's interviews with Martin and Dunn.

30. Kate Rosenlieb's pivotal role in the identification of Sandy's body, and her communications with Detective Kline on the subject, were related to the author during his interviews with Rosenlieb and Kline.

31. Detective Vernon "Dusty" Kline, interview with the author. As is typical (and lawful) in criminal investigations, these

hardball interrogation tactics were not documented in official crime reports in the case, and thus were never put before any judge or jury as the case was litigated and decided. However, in an interview with the author, Kline readily and even proudly described his method of interrogating Pat Dunn as a deliberate attempt to "get under his skin" in order to provoke an incriminating statement or outright confession. It should be noted that the courts have long approved such tactics—and other, more powerful psychological warfare tactics—as acceptable law-enforcement tools.

32. In "The Social Psychology of Police Interrogations: The Theory and Classification of True and False Confessions" (*Studies in Law, Politics and Society* 16 [1997]) and "The Consequences of False Confessions: Deprivations of Liberty and Miscarriages of Justice in the Age of Psychological Interrogation" (*Journal of Criminal Law and Criminology,* 1998), Professors Richard A. Leo and Richard J. Ofshe detail at least sixty proven cases of false confessions occurring since the 1966 *Miranda* decision, finding that, even in the face of overwhelming evidence of innocence, false confessions still lead to convictions. The authors opine that, despite an end to overt physical brutality against suspects in order to "wring confessions" from them—a practice now believed to have generated many false confessions during the first half of this century—"contemporary American psychological interrogation practices continue to induce false confessions, as did earlier Third Degree methods."

Meanwhile, Jan Hoffman, in "Police Refine Methods So Potent, Even the Innocent Have Confessed" (*The New York Times,* March 30, 1998) points out, "Although the number of false confessions is in dispute, their prevalence is shaking the confidence of both prosecutors and juries in the reliability of confessions. . . . [such that] at least 2,400 sheriff's and police departments around the country are audiotaping and even videotaping not just confessions, but often interrogations as well." Kern County has not joined this trend, and at least two murder cases and numerous other felonies there have been dismissed or overturned after questions were raised about the coercive manner in which the sheriff's department extracted confessions and witness statements.

According to "The Psychology of Confession Evidence" *American Psychologist* 52, no. 3 (1997), a study by psychologist Saul

Kassin of Williams College showed the remarkable ease with which false confessions can be extracted by authority figures. A majority of university students in Kassin's experiment were persuaded to confess to pushing a forbidden button and thereby causing a computer to crash, when in fact they had not done so, and the consequence of confessing was receiving an angry phone call from their professor. The reactions of different groups were gauged; some subjects were merely accused, others were told that there had been eyewitnesses. When it was claimed that a witness had seen the subject push the forbidden button—much as police interrogators sometimes fabricate eyewitnesses—nine out of ten students in the study signed a false confession, and 65 percent actually came to believe their own false confession to be true.

33. It is true that many guilty suspects keep talking well past the point where silence would be in their self-interest, a tendency that helps police and prosecutors secure criminal convictions on a daily basis. But research by social scientists and psychologists suggests that this tendency is by no means an absolute sign of guilt: Innocents under suspicion seldom clam up, either, because they essentially trust the police and feel that cooperating by answering all questions will help set things straight.

34. The account of the interrogation of Pat Dunn is based upon Detective Soliz's written report on the July 23, 1992, search and interview at the Dunns' home; on Soliz's testimony in *People vs. Dunn;* and on the author's interviews with Detective Kline and Pat Dunn.

35. The account of Soliz's initial theories about Sandy's call to Ann Kidder and Kidder's value as a witness are drawn from a report by Soliz dated July 27, 1992, filed in Kern County Sheriff's Department Case KC92-14851 (the report discusses statements by Kidder and her employer, accountant Rick Williams); from the author's interviews with Detectives Soliz and Kline; from statements by Ann Kidder on February 23, 1993, as contained in an undated memorandum by private investigator David Sandberg to attorney Gary Pohlson, and from the testimony of Ann Kidder in *People vs. Patrick Dunn.*

36. The description of Detective Soliz's first encounter with Jerry Lee Coble is drawn from Soliz's September 21, 1992, report on his interview of Coble filed in Kern County Sheriff's Department Case KC92-14851; Soliz's testimony in *People vs.*

Patrick Dunn; Coble's testimony in *People vs. Dunn;* and the author's interviews with Soliz, Coble, Detective Eric Banducci and Kern County Deputy District Attorney John Somers.

PART II: LAURA

1. Jerry Lee Coble's complete criminal record at the time of Pat Dunn's arrest shows a remarkable talent for eluding punishment, even in notoriously tough-on-crime Kern County. His crimes include the following:

- November 3, 1992: Coble received probation for grand theft in Kern County Superior Court Case 47620, reduced from multiple counts of grand theft and conspiracy after Coble agreed to testify against Pat Dunn. He had been on parole for prior offenses at the time of his arrest on April 4, 1991, yet was not required to serve out the prior prison term.
- December 12, 1989: Coble received two years in prison after his arrest for burglary, receiving stolen property and other felonies is reduced to a single count of receiving stolen property through a plea bargain in Kern County Superior Court Case 39768. Coble was paroled September 27, 1990, and was still on parole for this offense at the time of his next arrest.
- March 18, 1987: Sentenced to three years in prison for burglary after six counts are reduced to one through a plea bargain in Kern County Superior Court Case 32800. He was paroled June 20, 1988.
- August 26, 1982: Sentenced to three years for grand theft after nine counts are reduced to one through a plea bargain in Kern County Superior Court Case 24075.
- February 5, 1981: Sentenced to time served for aggravated assault in Marietta, Georgia, where he previously lived.

Additional arrests—in which cases were handled as misdemeanors, citations or were dismissed outright—include multiple drug possession charges, assault, battery, obstructing police, driving under the influence of alcohol or drugs, armed robbery, check fraud, theft and petty theft.

Source: Kern County Superior Court records; Kern County Municipal Court records; Kern County Sheriff's Department reports; testimony of Jerry Coble in *People vs. Dunn*.

2. Though Kern County has a population one sixth the size of the City of Los Angeles, its sheriff and police departments have in some years been responsible for as many shootings as their counterparts to the south. During one eight-month stretch in 1995, the problem became especially pronounced: There were seventeen shootings by law-enforcement officers in Kern County, a majority of them by the sheriff's department. Five were fatal and several involved unarmed suspects attempting to flee. The most notorious involved a Los Angeles woman named Suzannah Cody, the distraught twenty-six-year-old wife of a Los Angeles cop, who led police—and a live television audience—on a freeway chase and hour-long standoff on a lonely Kern County road. Surrounded by police but still armed, Cody was killed by a sheriff's sharpshooter after she made what officials later described as an "ambiguous" move with her pistol. (Video of the incident suggests she may have been scratching her back at the time the fatal shot was fired.) All seventeen of the shootings were eventually deemed justified by Kern County authorities. See "Trigger Happy in Kern County," *California Lawyer*, October 1995; Lucille Renwick, "Woman Killed After Chase Is Identified," *Los Angeles Times*, July 7, 1995; "Slayings by Kern Deputies Prompt Internal Review," Associated Press, July 7, 1995.

3. Judge Milton Elconin, presiding judge of the West Kern Municipal Court, based in Bakersfield, was also known for feuding with some of his fellow judges, for treating female attorneys in a fashion designed to make them cry, and for his courtroom attacks on the former police chief of the small Kern County town of Shafter, Gene Kaplan. Kaplan, himself a controversial figure, sued the judge for libel (and later settled for one third of the judge's estate, about $7,500) after Elconin publicly branded him "a painful abscess in the side of law enforcement throughout the county" and a "posturing, paranoid, pusillanimous pissant" who had earned the "disrespect of all legitimate law enforcement lead-

ers in this county." Elconin had never met or spoken to Kaplan prior to issuing this denunciation, though he was close to several of Kaplan's detractors and political opponents. Many who had appeared in Elconin's courtroom—defendants and lawyers both—felt his diatribe more aptly described Elconin himself than anyone else, though he was recalled in his May 14, 1981, *Bakersfield Californian* obituary in glowing terms as "one of the last remnants of frontier justice . . . (who) believed people had not only the right to be stupid but also to say what they believed." It was in retaliation against Kaplan's allegedly brutal treatment of offenders—allegations never proved—that Elconin dismissed charges against a courtroom filled with fifteen criminal defendants. Prosecutors in Kern County subsequently branded this action illegal. Sources: W. J. McCance, "His comments livened courtroom," *Bakersfield Californian*, May 14, 1981; Steve E. Swenson, "Charges further split feuding judges," *Bakersfield Californian*, December 18, 1979; Steve E. Swenson, "Late judge's estate settles libel case," *Bakersfield Californian*, February 12, 1982; letter dated March 12, 1980, from Shafter Police Chief Gene Kaplan to West Kern Municipal Court Presiding Judge James G. Bowles; letter dated March 17, 1980, from Judge Milton Elconin to Kaplan; Michael Trihey, "Judge threatens FBI probe," *Bakersfield Californian*, March 20, 1980; complaint letter dated April 1, 1980, from the City of Shafter to the California Commission on Judicial Performance; Michael Trihey, "Gripe Against Kaplan Rings False," *Bakersfield Californian*, April 24, 1980; and the author's interviews with attorneys in practice in Kern County during Elconin's tenure.

4. Kern County Superior Court Judge Gary T. Friedman was reprimanded in 1993 by the state Commission on Judicial Performance for willful misconduct for the 1987 rattlesnake incident. Source: Associated Press, "Judge reprimanded for snake trick," June 22, 1993.

5. Bakersfield Municipal Court Judge Alan E. Klein, who left office after fifteen years on the bench amid the controversy, was prosecuted and acquitted of soliciting a bribe from stripper Lashay Munoz. The state Commission on Judicial Performance agreed to drop separate civil charges of willful misconduct and lying to investigators in exchange for his resignation. Sources: Tamara

Koehler, "State panel admonishes Kern judge," *Bakersfield Californian*, January 23, 1997; Editorial, "Public's trust damaged," *Bakersfield Californian*, January 19, 1996; Tamara Koehler, "Judge Klein resigns Municipal Court post," *Bakersfield Californian*, March 12, 1996; and the author's interview with attorney Stan Simrin, who represented Klein.

6. This account is based on transcripts, reports and testimony in Kern County Superior Court Case HC-5092, "In re Scott and Brenda Kniffen, on Habeas Corpus." The record in the case is undisputed in showing that the alleged child-victims were repeatedly interrogated and asked leading and suggestive questions throughout the case. Kern County authorities maintain that they acted with the best of intentions and solely with the welfare of the children in mind, and they dispute to this day the contention that their techniques led to false accusations and charges. Attorneys representing the defendants and others, including independent grand jurors who examined the investigation and a variety of judges who have reviewed the case and listened to the taped interrogation of Brandon and Brian Kniffen, have asserted otherwise, questioning both the results and the motives of Kern County social workers, prosecutors and investigators.

7. The evolution of the boy's story about money and other key aspects of his alleged molestation was documented in police reports and trial transcripts in the case and lay buried in the public record for years. It remained unknown to the general public until it was graphically illustrated in a groundbreaking series of stories entitled "Stolen Innocence: A Case in Review," published April 13-15, 1986, by Michael Trihey, then a *Bakersfield Californian* reporter. Trihey's lengthy inquiry into the Kniffen-McCuan case raised grave questions about a whole series of similar molestation-ring investigations in Bakersfield that had led to dozens of prosecutions and convictions. Trihey's reporting left him an unpopular figure with Kern County law enforcement (the then-sheriff of Kern County vowed never to speak to him again), as his stories reversed what had been to that point the newspaper's unquestioning acceptance of official representations in the case.

8. Michelle Smith and Lawrence Pazder, *Michelle Remembers* (New York: Congdon and Lattes, 1980). An examination of the book's factual problems was undertaken by Denna Allen and Janet

Midwinter in "The Debunking of a Myth: Why the original 'ritual abuse' victim may have suffered only from her childhood fantasies," *London* (England) *Sunday Mail,* September 30, 1990. Furthermore, a Vatican-sponsored investigation concluded that the events in the book never occurred, and Pazder himself has since suggested that the book may not be historically accurate, admitting that he knew only that Michelle *believed* her memories of ritual abuse, though he could not say for certain they had occurred.

9. The author has employed pseudonyms for the first names of the Nokes children.

10. Jay Smith, Susan Penninger and Stan Simrin, interviews with the author.

11. Unlike the federal government and most states, which rely on secret grand juries dominated by prosecutors to make charging and probable-cause determinations, California grants every criminal defendant the right to a preliminary hearing, in which a judge reviews the state's case to determine whether there is probable cause to proceed to trial.

12. The description of events leading up to and following the preliminary hearing in *People vs. Dunn* is based on investigative notes and reports filed by Detective John Soliz on his contacts with Mike Dunn and Rex Martin in Kern County Sheriff's Case KC92-14851; and the author's interviews with Deputy DA John Somers, Stan Simrin, Gary Pohlson, Jennifer Dunn and Pat Dunn. Mike Dunn did not respond to requests for interviews with the author.

13. The account of Laura Lawhon's interview with Marie Gates is based upon the investigation report by Lawhon detailing her February 5, 1993, interview with Gates and Lillian Dunn; the transcripts of tape-recorded interviews of Gates by Lawhon on February 18, 1993, and April 20, 1993; and the author's interviews with Lawhon and Gates.

14. Marie Gates' tips were recorded in "Secret Witness" reports filed at the Kern County Sheriff's Department on July 26, 1992, and August 13, 1992, under the code name "Taylor 1," and in an August 20, 1992, report by Detective Kline detailing his first interview with Marie Gates, filed under Kern County Sheriff's Department Case MO92-00633.

15. Gates, interview with Kline, August 20, 1992, Kern County

Sheriff's Department Case MO92-00633; and the author's interviews with Gates and Kline.

16. The evolution in Marie Gates' story is documented in Kern County Sheriff's reports on the Dunn case dated August 20, 1992, September 21, 1992, and October 15, 1992; Gates' statements to Laura Lawhon recorded in written reports and tape transcriptions; Gates' testimony in *People vs. Dunn;* and several interviews with the author in which Gates' account continued to shift.

17. Rosenlieb first mentioned the cut shin in her July 4 interview with Detective Kline. Rosenlieb did not question Sandy about the cut, and so couldn't say whether Sandy meant Pat had caused the cut by accident or on purpose. The incident occurred about four months before Sandy died. Pat Dunn recalls Sandy tripping and cutting herself on the edge of a metal sliding door leading to their patio around that time.

18. Marie Gates, interviews with Laura Lawhon.

19. The author's interviews with Marie Gates and Laura Lawhon.

20. The author's interview with Detective John Soliz.

21. There are numerous examples of this phenomenon, and they all involve instances in which the authorities targeted a suspect, then sought evidence to support their theories: Gary Nelson was sentenced to death in Chatham County, Georgia, for the 1978 rape and murder of a six-year-old. He remained on death row until 1991, when it was shown that Nelson, who had always asserted his innocence, had been prosecuted even though the police had a credible confession from another man, which they had kept secret during Nelson's trial. Perjured testimony by the police, the hiding of potential alibi witnesses and false forensic evidence all contributed to Nelson's conviction—a body of evidence created and manipulated to fit the initial theory in the case, that Nelson was the culprit. He was finally freed by the Georgia Supreme Court (which overruled a lower court's finding that this gross misconduct was "harmless error") after eleven years on death row.

In another case, four young men from Tucson were subjected to marathon interrogations over three days, after which they confessed to nine vicious murders at a Buddhist temple in Phoenix—a sensational, headline-grabbing case. After the "Tucson Four" were charged with the murders, two teenagers who had nothing to do with the four suspects were found in possession of the murder weapons. These two soon confessed to the temple murders, in doing so providing key details that only the killers could know and swearing that the other four had nothing to do with the crime. Despite this, and the fact that the information contained in the Tucson Four's confessions did not match any of the crime-scene evidence, the authorities in Phoenix still sought to prosecute them. The county prosecutor refused, however. The men who made the false confessions later explained that they would have done or said anything to put a halt to the nonstop interrogations.

In a notorious Chicago case, Rolando Cruz was convicted and sentenced to death for murdering eight-year-old Jeanine Nicarico in 1985. However, it was eventually proved that authorities had manufactured evidence against Cruz and ignored a confession from a convicted sex offender who had already pleaded guilty to two rapes and murders (and whose DNA was linked to Nicarico's body). Cruz was exonerated and released in 1995 and a codefendant was released from an eighty-year prison sentence. Meanwhile, three prosecutors and four law-enforcement officers have since been indicted for obstruction of justice in the case.

The outcome is seldom so favorable for defendants, however. In the spring of 1993, for example, as Pat Dunn awaited his trial, evidence was presented in Texas that Leonel Herrera, convicted and sentenced to death for killing a police officer, was actually innocent. The new evidence included an eyewitness to the crime who exonerated Herrera, as well a former Texas state judge who implicated someone else—a man who had, in fact, confessed to the crime. Herrera also passed a polygraph test. None of this evidence was available during Herrera's trial. But the U.S. Supreme Court, in a strictly procedural ruling that did not consider this new evidence, found that Herrera was not entitled to a federal hearing on the question of his innocence because the State of Texas had imposed strict time limits on the presentation of new evidence. The high court recommended that he seek a highly unlikely commutation from the governor of Texas, who declined to intervene. Herrera was executed in May 1993, without further hearing on his new evidence. Since the Herrera ruling, at least two other men have been executed after being denied hearings on new evidence of innocence. Sources: Laura Frank, "Convicted on False Evidence? False science often sways juries," *USA Today*, July 19,

1994; Russ Kimball and Laura Greenberg, "False Confessions," *Phoenix* magazine, November 1993; Ken Armstrong, "Indictments Tear at Prosecutorial Teflon; Misconduct Allegations Almost Unprecedented," *Chicago Tribune,* December 13, 1996; Jeffrey Bills, and Maurice Possley, "Judge Rules Cruz Innocent," *Chicago Tribune,* November 4, 1995; Janan Hanna, and Stacey Singer, "Cruz Judge Lambastes State Case," *Chicago Tribune,* November 4, 1995; Maurice Possley, "The Nicarico Nightmare: Admitted Lie Sinks Cruz Case," *Chicago Tribune,* November 5, 1995; Michael Kroll, "Killing Justice: Government Misconduct and the Death Penalty," March 1992, Death Penalty Information Center (Washington, D.C.); "Innocence and the Death Penalty: Assessing the Danger of Mistaken Executions," Staff Report by the Subcommittee on Civil and Constitutional Rights, Committee on the Judiciary, U.S. House of Representatives, October 21, 1993; "Innocence and the Death Penalty: The Increasing Danger of Executing the Innocent," Death Penalty Information Center, July 1997; and *Herrera vs. Collins,* 113 S.Ct. 853 (1993).

22. The evolution in official perceptions of Ann Kidder's contribution to *People vs. Patrick Dunn*—and the timing of that evolution—can be charted in reports of the Kern County Sheriff's Department in KC92-14851, dated July 7 and July 27, 1992 (before Jerry Lee Coble's involvement in the case, when Kidder was considered an invaluable prosecution witness and a major reason for suspecting Pat Dunn of foul play), and October 14, 1992 (after Coble's appearance in the casee, when Kidder became a liability to the prosecution case). By the time he made closing arguments in *People vs. Dunn,* Deputy Districy Attorney John Somers had settled on a description of Kidder as essentially honest, but mistaken and confused about the telephone call from Sandy. Kidder herself describes this same evolution in her February 23, 1993, interview with private investigator David Sandberg, reported in an undated memorandum to Gary Pohlson.

23. The conviction was reversed by a 4–2 vote of the California Supreme Court in *People vs. Carl David Hogan,* 31Cal.3d 815, decided July 1, 1982, in an opinion authored by Chief Justice Rose Bird, whom Kern County DA Ed Jagels campaigned to oust several years later. In analyzing the interrogation of Hogan by Kern County Sheriff's investigators, Bird concluded that

interrogators had taken a sobbing, wailing, vomiting shell of a man who insisted he was innocent and convinced him that he did not remember killing anyone because he was insane, that there were witnesses and physical evidence that absolutely proved he was guilty, and that if he would only admit the crime, they could get him treatment for his mental illness. The police also enlisted Hogan's wife to help them, after convincing her that they had conclusive evidence of Hogan's guilt—though there was no such evidence. In her opinion, Bird wrote for the majority:

> While no physical abuse of appellant [Hogan] occurred, coercion also includes the brainwashing that comes from repeated suggestion and prolonged interrogation. . . . It is a truism of the modern world that when sufficient pressures are applied most persons will confess. . . . It was repeatedly suggested to appellant that he was unquestionably guilty and that he suffered from mental illness. The certainty of his guilt was suggested by deceptive references to nonexistent eyewitnesses and proof of rape. These came not only from the interrogating officers, but also from appellant's wife. . . . The statements were involuntary due to implied promises of leniency [and] . . . there is evidence of other forms of psychological coercion that raises a strong doubt as to whether appellant's statements were truly volitional.

In a concurring opinion, one justice pointed out that Hogan's confession was clearly unreliable because it did not match the facts of the crime, and because the interrogators, not Hogan, suggested key elements for Hogan to confess to, such as an alleged motive for the crime—the theft of forty dollars. "The record clearly shows that during these sessions the police firmly planted in his mind the suspicion that he was 'crazy.' . . . This confession . . . is more like a series of emotional outbursts than a coherent description," Bird's colleague wrote.

24. This point was hotly disputed at Rollins' trials. Others at the scene reported from the outset that the blood spots and pud-

dles they examined appeared hard and dry. One detective revised his opinion, initially describing the blood as fresh, but later said it was baked dry. Sources: Testimony in *The People of Kern County vs. Offord Rollins IV*, Kern County Superior Court Case 47815; the unpublished opinion of the California Court of Appeal, Fifth Appellate District, in *People vs. Rollins*, Case No. F18547; and the author's interviews with attorneys H. A. Sala and Jim Fahey.

25. Testimony of Dale Knox, Detective Randy Raymond and Deputy Paul Hussey in *People vs. Rollins*; and Raymond's August 5, 1991, report in Kern County Sheriff's Department Case BW91-00538.

26. The account of the initial investigation of Maria Rodriguez's death, including the exchange between Detective Raymond, Miriam Rodriguez and Victor Perez, is drawn from reports by Raymond and Deputy Paul Hussey in Kern County Sheriff's Department Case BW91-00538; the testimony in *People vs. Rollins* of the civilian and law-enforcement witnesses who were present at the crime scene; and Appellant's Opening Brief to the California Court of Appeal in *People vs. Rollins*.

27. Much later, Offord's father, in an interview with the author, would assert that an attorney had prompted the young suspect to claim he had met Maria on Thursday in order to explain away the evidence, when in fact he had not. At the second trial, evidence was presented that Maria often showed up unexpectedly at Offord's house, and may have simply leaned against or even sat inside the car while waiting for Offord to show up on the Friday she died.

28. To address these shortcomings, Kern County has since built a new crime lab under the control of the district attorney.

29. Testimony of Deputy Hussey, *People vs. Rollins*.

30. Dale Knox would testify in *People vs. Rollins* that he had tried to be as consistent as he could in his recollections and that, though he admitted using the phrase "dumb Mexican," he said this was more a comment on the erratic nature in which the maroon car was being driven than an accurate observation of the driver's ethnicity. He testified he was never certain of the driver's race.

31. Statements and testimony of Maria Rodriguez's friend Alma Gonzalez in *People vs. Rollins*; and the author's interview with Susan Penninger.

32. The statements and testimony of Maria Rodriguez's neighbor and friend Juan Escalante in *People vs. Rollins*.

33. In reviewing the case, the California Court of Appeal rejected claims that the black jurors were dismissed improperly for racial reasons, finding that the prosecution justified excluding those jurors for other reasons, such as bias or a relationship with parties involved in the case. Allegations that minorities have routinely been excluded from jury service in Kern County were common throughout the eighties and early nineties, and led to several complaints and successful appeals. In June 1992, for example, Kern County Superior Court Judge Lewis E. King disqualified himself from the trial of a black murder defendant because he felt himself unable to remain impartial after a prosecutor excused black jurors in the case. The defendant, Jimmie Lee Pollard, was being prosecuted for a second time; an earlier trial ended in a hung jury, with an 11–1 vote in favor of acquittal.

34. Jim Fahey, appellant's opening brief in *People vs. Rollins*, in which Fahey points out Green's attempt to make the "sexual savage" argument and relates it to long-standing racial stereotypes; and the opinion of the Fifth District Court of Appeal, in its unanimous May 11, 1995, unpublished opinion in the case. The court found no support for Fahey's complaints of racial animus, which Deputy DA Lisa Green adamantly denied. The appeals court did, however, agree that Green improperly questioned Rollins and other black witnesses about their sexual activities. The opinion is unclear as to whether Green's improper questions constituted prosecutorial misconduct. She may have committed misconduct in asking some of them, the opinion states, but the fault might instead lie with the trial judge for erroneously authorizing and even encouraging those improper inquiries.

35. Deputy DA Green questioned Andre Harrison, a friend of Rollins, about his allegedly watching Rollins have sex with Maria Rodriguez, something Harrison had denied in early testimony during a preliminary hearing in the case. As the Court of Appeal wrote, it is prosecutorial misconduct to ask such a loaded question knowing the answer would be no. The court also found the whole line of sexual questions to Rollins and others to have been improper. In its analysis of the case, the appeals court wrote, "Once again, whether this is deemed prosecutorial misconduct or trial court

error because it was sanctioned by the court's ruling, the jury heard evidence it should not have."

36. This account is based on the author's interviews with H. A. Sala, who represented Rollins at his retrial, and a review of pleadings in *People vs. Rollins*. The district attorney's office does not dispute the sequence of events, but argues that no harm was done to Rollins in the process, noting that Rollins almost certainly would have been transferred to adult court on the basis of the murder charge alone. In addition, while the district attorney's office had information in hand showing the sodomy allegation to be incorrect, the individual prosecutor handling the juvenile-court hearing apparently did not personally receive that information until later.

37. California Court of Appeal opinion in *People vs. Rollins*. After the prosecutor asked Offord's seventeen-year-old steady girlfriend about their sexual relationship, and the girl answered, "It wasn't limited to kissing but it wasn't sex," the trial judge, Len M. McGillivray, decided to pose a question of his own: "Did that sexual activity from kissing on up, if you will, involve any acts of penetration of any kind?" Later, the judge explained that he wanted to ask the follow-up question because the girl's reply "left things up the air."

Rollins' attorney during his first trial, Timothy Lemucchi, then considered one of Bakersfield's top criminal-defense lawyers, objected occasionally but remained silent throughout other portions of this bizarre episode. The Court of Appeal would later find he could have—and should have—objected more frequently than he did. The appellate justices added, however, that the defense lawyer could reasonably have concluded from the trial judge's rulings (and questions to witnesses), that many potential objections to prosecutorial improprieties would have been futile. In any case, the trial seemed to take on the aspect of a lurid soap opera, in which Offord Rollins was cast as some sort of sexual predator equipped with, as Lisa Green suggested again without evidence, "a drawer full of condoms." Jim Fahey, Rollins' appeals attorney, would later say in an interview with the author that such questions had a devastating impact on the case: "That trial became an old-fashioned morality play, a classic battle of good versus evil. Such a thing could not have occurred anywhere but Kern County, where the right to a fair trial is often treated as though it were a mere technicality. . . . It was a travesty, from start to finish."

38. Dean Wayne, "Shock Over the Evil Poetry of Offord Rollins," *Bakersfield Bi-Weekly Report*, October 3, 1991. The article detailed several of the rap poems, claimed one of them described the murder (something even the DA never asserted at trial) and appeared to be based on documents supplied by the sheriff's department, as well as an interview with Detective Randy Raymond.

39. The gun testimony came from Maria's sister, Marisol, who recalled she had seen Offord and his friend Andre Harrison together a few months before the murder, and one of them mentioned having had a gun at the house. Since Offord denied ever having access to a gun, this was key, but the vague nature of the testimony, and the fact that Marisol could not remember exactly who said what, made it inadmissible as proof that there was a gun. There was a limited use for such evidence—to "impeach" Harrison's testimony that neither he nor Offord ever said such a thing—but the prosecution attempted to use the evidence as firm proof that there was a gun in Offord's possession. This was improper, the Court of Appeal later decided, even though the defense attorney failed to object, and the trial judge failed to address the matter as well at the time.

40. From the Court of Appeal opinion in *People vs. Rollins* (5th Cir. 1995). Piceno denied the "damn lie" comment, but admitted that he had made mention of his familiarity with the area and the possibility that pesticides accounted for the absence of flies.

41. Judge McGillivray also discounted testimony from two customers of a bank in which one of the jurors worked as a teller. These two witnesses claimed that the juror expressed opinions about Offord's guilt and discussed the case with them before the trial ended, again in violation of the juror's oath. (The juror denied the allegations.) Any juror misconduct that might have occurred, the judge decided, was so minor that it had no impact on the case. The Court of Appeal was, by law, bound to accept McGillivray's assessment of the bank customers' credibility and that of alternate juror Peggy Traylor. But because Piceno and some of the other jurors acknowledged having the pesticides discussion, the appeals court still found sufficient information to make a finding of prejudicial jury misconduct, since Piceno's comments revolved around a key point of evidence that may have had a

direct impact on the verdict. Source: The unpublished opinion of the California Court of Appeal in *People vs. Rollins;* defense motion for new trial in *People vs. Rollins;* Steve E. Swenson, "Rollins jurors violated orders, alternate says," *Bakersfield Californian,* June 6, 1992; Steve E. Swenson, "Jury made trial 'a mockery,' alternate says," *Bakersfield Californian,* June 9, 1992; Steve E. Swenson, "Rollins' plea for new trial dashed," *Bakersfield Californian,* September 2, 1992.

42. The Kern County DA complained bitterly about this sentence, but was helpless to do anything about it: This was one of the few areas of the law in which judges retained full authority to do as they saw fit, although legislators have since curtailed judges' discretion in such matters, leaving the question of fitness for the juvenile system more up to prosecutors to decide. After the Rollins case was reversed on appeal, the prosecutor assigned to try it a second time, Stephen Tauzer, decried the fact that the defendant could not receive a punishment that fit the crime and called sentencing laws that barred a more severe penalty should Offord again be convicted an outdated legacy of former Supreme Court Justice Rose Bird, whom Ed Jagels helped oust years before. But the reason for this law limiting sentences on retrial is a simple one: to curb prosecutorial and judicial abuses. Without it, convicts—even innocent ones—might be reluctant to pursue valid appeals, fearing that they could be punished with a tougher sentence later on. Rollins, for example, no matter how great a case for innocence he might build, would have been foolish to ask for a new trial in which his release by age twenty-five could be replaced by life in an adult prison. Hypothetically, without the sentencing safeguards, unscrupulous prosecutors and judges could keep their own misconduct hidden by threatening the wrongfully convicted with longer sentences should they pursue appeals.

Some in Kern County's legal community wondered if McGillivray's unexpectedly lenient sentence had been the judge's way of expressing, if only tacitly, some measure of doubt about the case against Rollins. It has long been the unspoken prerogative of judges to impose light sentences in close or questionable cases, rather than run the risk of dismissing a case outright, because sentences, unlike convictions and dismissals, are rarely subject to appeals in state court. (This has changed somewhat since the Rollins trial—recent laws limiting judges' options in sentencing in both federal and state justice systems has led to more sentencing appeals, many of them by prosecutors urging lengthier prison terms for convicts.) The lenient sentence for Offord Rollins had been doubly surprising because it came after a blistering evaluation of him from the California Youth Authority's own psychiatrist who, after ninety days of observation, declared Rollins a dangerous and potentially violent offender unworthy of treatment as a juvenile. Judges normally give such opinions great deference. However, a respected psychologist hired by Offord's family testified at the sentencing hearing that the only justification for this negative opinion was the fact that Offord still insisted he was innocent and therefore showed no "remorse" for killing Maria Rodriguez. This was deemed unacceptable by the Youth Authority, which considers offenders hopeless in terms of rehabilitation unless they confess and express regret. Given his pending appeals—and the fact that he feared any such admission of remorse could be used against him if he ever won a new trial—it would be unfair to hold this supposed lack of remorse against Offord, the Rollins-family psychologist said. In every other respect, she stated, Offord had shown himself to be an ideal candidate for juvenile treatment rather than adult prison, in his behavior, attitude, acceptance of authority and desire to better himself while incarcerated. The judge agreed.

In prison, juvenile authorities kept up the pressure on Offord to confess, and he claimed it accelerated as his appeal moved through the system and it became increasingly clear that he might be released. He was transferred out of a facility where he had been able to attend college, and placed in another institution where his education came to a standstill. His lack of remorse for murder was cited as the reason. "They're trying to break me down," he told his father during one visit. Yet he never wavered in his insistence that he was innocent, and when he was finally released, the Youth Authority could not pass on any information to the Kern County District Attorney that might have been used against him in court. Source: Sentencing memoranda, reports and testimony in *People vs. Rollins*; Steve E. Swenson, "Rollins sentenced to CYA," *Bakersfield Californian*, September 26, 1992; Steve E. Swenson, "Psychiatric evaluation calls Rollins 'dangerous,'" *Bakersfield*

Californian, August 26, 1992; testimony of Adrienne Davis, psychologist and witness for the defense in *People vs. Rollins;* and the author's interviews with Susan Penninger, H. A. Sala, Offord Rollins III and Offord Rollins IV.

43. The account of events surrounding Gary Coble's decision to testify against his brother Jerry is based upon the author's interviews with Gary Pohlson and Laura Lawhon; and Gary coble's testimony in *People vs. Dunn.* Gary Coble did not respond to requests by the author for an interview. (Jerry Coble and Elvin Coble, in interviews with the author, asserted that Gary made up his story and had accepted a bribe to do so. They offered no evidence to support this bribery allegation, however, and Kern County authorities have never leveled such an accusation, though records show they did investigate Gary Coble once it was disclosed that he would be testifying for the defense in *People vs. Dunn.*)

44. This description of Norwood's statements and objections to Detective John Soliz's account of them is drawn from Soliz's undated report on his and Detective Kline's interview with Charles Roger Norwood on August 5, 1992, in Kern County Sheriff's Department Case MO92-00633; an undated memorandum from Laura Lawhon to Gary Pohlson regarding her February 26, 1993, interview with Norwood; and Norwood's testimony in *People vs. Dunn.*

45. The broker Sandy worked with during her first year of marriage to Pat Dunn, Ed Wilkerson, was interviewed by Detective Soliz on August 4, 1992, as reported by Soliz in Kern County Sheriff's Department Case MO92-00633. In that interview, and in his subsequent testimony in *People vs. Dunn,* Wilkerson said he recalled Sandy instructing him to keep her investment information secret from Pat. This occurred well before Roger Norwood took over the brokerage accounts in 1988. Some of Soliz's confusion over who said what on this subject could have stemmed from the fact that Wilkerson also relayed in his interview with the detective a considerable amount of secondhand information he had garnered from conversations with Norwood when the two brokers chatted about Sandy's disappearance. Furthermore, this secondhand information, as reported by Soliz, was garbled in such a way as to make Pat look more suspicious than the facts warranted. For example, Wilkerson is quoted in Soliz's report as suggesting Kevin Knutson's visit to the Dunn home to discuss a living trust was Pat's

idea, when in truth it was Sandy's. In Wilkerson's secondhand and incorrect rendition, Sandy "blew her cool" over the subject of a living trust when she realized it was simply a ploy of Pat's to get at her money. "It was at that time that Pat Dunn realized he would never see a single penny until after Alexandra Dunn was dead," Soliz's report quotes Wilkerson as saying. The implication of this allegation is clear—such a falling-out could have provided a meaningful motive for Pat to kill—except for the fact that the witness who was actually present to observe these events firsthand, Kevin Knutson, swore it never happened. Wilkerson, according to Soliz's report, also incorrectly relayed something Norwood had told him about Pat calling him up and trying to obtain some of Sandy's funds after the disappearance. Wilkerson's statement to Soliz portrayed Pat as trying to loot Sandy's accounts as soon as she disappeared, but the firsthand source of the information, Norwood, said there was nothing untoward or suspicious about Pat's request for funds because it was simply a follow-up to a withdrawal Sandy had requested shortly before she vanished. Yet, despite the shortcomings inherent in Wilkerson's account, when the time came for Kern County authorities to argue the case against Pat in court, they relied upon Wilkerson's statements rather than the firsthand information that contradicted him.

46. This discrepancy in statements by Cindy Montes is reflected in a July 27, 1992, report by Detective Soliz in Kern County Sheriff's Department Case KC92-14851, documenting his July 8, 1992, interview with Montes; in an undated memorandum from David Sandberg to Gary Pohlson, documenting his February 2, 1993, interview with Montes; and in Montes' testimony in *People vs. Dunn,* in which she again stated the day of the crucial early-morning phone conversation with Pat was Tuesday, June 30 (as she initially told Sandberg). She subsequently changed her testimony to Wednesday when prompted by Deputy DA John Somers.

47. Although their true names are matters of public record, the first names of the McCuan girls have been changed here.

48. Defense attorneys would later argue that Mary Ann Barbour's repeated examinations of the girls' genitals, rather than molestation, could have caused this condition. Source: Testimony and argument, "In re Scott and Brenda Kniffen, on Habeas Corpus," Kern County Superior Court Case HC 5092.

49. Although most of the research in this area has been done in the years since those interrogations, concerns had already been raised in law-enforcement circles in the late 1970s and early 1980s about the use of suggestive interviewing with children. Since then, a variety of studies have definitively shown that suggestive interviewing techniques can lead to false allegations by children, and most federal, state and local law-enforcement standards recommend open-ended questioning that allows children to use their own words rather than parrot adult comments. During her testimony in the Kniffen habeas hearing in Kern County Superior Court in July 1996, McGill University psychologist Maggie Bruck described her research on child suggestibility. In one of Bruck's studies, a group of young children were asked leading questions about whether they had witnessed a school janitor's abusive behavior. Though they had not witnessed any such behavior, more than half of the children claimed to have done so after being asked in a suggestive and leading manner. Bruck and other researchers have conducted many similar experiments and observed like results.

50. Sources: Testimony of Murillo and Bruck and arguments of Michael Snedeker and Stan Simrin in the Kniffen and McCuan habeas hearing; Debbie Nathan and Michael Snedeker, *Satan's Silence*, (New York: Basic Books, 1995) pages 56, 146; and Tamara Koehler, "Sex acts were described to children," *Bakersfield Californian*, July 19, 1996.

51. Police reports and medical records filed in the Kniffen habeas corpus action and described by Nathan and Snedeker in *Satan's Silence* state that, prior to her hospitalization, an insomniac Mary Ann Barbour lost twenty pounds in the space of a month, was plagued by nightmares when she could sleep, and had hidden a gun in her car so she could be safe when "they" came to get her, "they" being representatives of some nameless conspiracy she believed was persecuting her. On January 15, 1980, after she threatened to stab her husband, Gene, and herself, Gene dialed 911. The sheriff's deputy who responded to the call found Gene pinning Mary Ann to a kitchen counter. Shoeless and unkempt, her hair wild, she yelled at her husband, "I hate you. I'll kill you! I hate you." The deputy promptly took her to the county hospital's psychiatric unit, where she was placed on a seventy-two-hour hold as a danger to herself and others. It was her second time as a mental-health

patient, having been treated five years earlier for a suicide attempt and depression. The social worker assigned to her case at that time wrote, "Patient has much anger, a passive aggression that comes out in fear and distrust of others, a need to belittle others and Sgt.-like control of her children." This time, she babbled endlessly about her granddaughter's molestation and the fact that she believed Rod Phelps had killed people, displaying a condition that psychiatrists call "pressure of speech" (excessive, fast talking often associated with mania). She was diagnosed as delusional and obsessive, and was treated with the powerful antipsychotic drug Thorazine. Then she was transferred to another hospital, where different doctors did not consider her condition so serious. Six days later, she was sent home as an outpatient with only sleeping pills for medication.

52. Mary Ann Barbour had turned for help to Jill Haddad, the child-abuse crusader and Ed Jagels' campaign supporter. At the time, the vocal Haddad led a local chapter of an anti-molestation organization, S.L.A.M. (Stronger Legislation Against Molesters), which had been spawned by the murder of young Dana Butler and the failure to prosecute her suspected killer, Glenn Fitts, three years earlier. Haddad, who believed—correctly—that child molestation was woefully underreported and lackadasically prosecuted in that era, also believed in the existence of large-scale, secret conspiracies of molesters who communicated with one another, sharing information, photographs and even victims. Haddad also maintained a special relationship with the Kern County District Attorney that ensured her views would be taken seriously. She recommended that the social worker Carol Darling get the job as the DA's child-abuse coordinator, making Darling a key figure in the Witch Hunt cases to come. Haddad, moreover, was the person who stood up during a pivotal campaign debate and publicly confronted Ed Jagels' opponent in the DA's race with confidential juvenile records (an event in which Darling also played a role in helping to retrieve those same records). Haddad was given access to all sex-crime arrest reports in Kern County, and the district attorney's office began consulting with her on which cases to prosecute. This extraordinary arrangement with a civilian expanded further when the DA began using Haddad in the courtroom as an expert witness in molestation cases. Among other things, Haddad testified in favor of removing Jenny and Jane McCuan from their parents' care and

turning them over to Mary Ann Barbour. Sources: Nathan and Snedeker, *Satan's Silence*, pages 57, 58; "Why adults molest the young," *Bakersfield Californian*, April 10, 1982; Kern County Grand Jury, "A Special Interim Report," July 5, 1983; Michael Tribey, "Adult's Obsession Blamed in Children's Charges," *Bakersfield Californian*, April 13, 1986; and deposition of Mary Ann Boucher, *McCuan vs. Kern*, Kern County Superior Court case 181864, October 9, 1985.

53. Sources: Kniffen habeas petition—Exhibit 22 (records from the Shalimar child protective home regarding Jenny and Jane McCuan), Exhibit 23 (notes of social worker Dana Maciewitz) and Exhibit 28 (April 26, 1982, report of Deputy Betty Shaneyfelt in Kern County Sheriff's Department Case KC81-41195); and Nathan and Snedeker, *Satan's Silence*, pages 58-59.

54. One veteran social worker who worked with the McCuan and Kniffen children, Georgia Herald, recalled raising such questions. Herald had been concerned that every time the girls added a new suspect or allegation to their account, they were rewarded with praise, trips to the park, ice cream, and the like. In essence, the girls were given an incentive to make up increasingly sordid stories. No matter that their new stories contradicted their old ones, Herald said. The new stuff was hotter, bigger, capable of generating more indictments, more headlines, more juice come election time. "I don't want to be alone with those girls," Herald recalls telling Carol Darling, the child-sexual abuse coordinator for the district attorney's office, Velda Murillo's coworker and a former childwelfare colleague of Herald's. "They accuse everyone around them sooner or later."

Darling had been handpicked by Jill Haddad to work in the district attorney's office with the child victims of the molestation rings, interviewing them, supervising their care, forging a bond with them. She was an ardent Ed Jagels supporter during his first campaign for office, a member of the group that trooped to the courthouse one weekend and uncovered the embarrassing records that helped defeat his opponent. Darling's curly blond hair and easy way with children almost, but not quite, masked the steely resolve of a prosecutorial zealot—a "true believer," Herald called her, one who seemed to see a victim in almost every child she encountered. "You've got nothing to worry about, Georgia," Herald recalls Darling replying. "Those girls would never accuse you of anything—as long as you don't do anything to them."

Herald perceived an unspoken warning: Whatever the girls said, no matter how outlandish, would be believed, no matter who they accused. The only time they were disbelieved was when they asserted someone's innocence. Then they would be questioned relentlessly until they accused once again. Herald eventually resigned because of this case, and, years later, her testimony would help free innocents from prison. Sources: Georgia Herald, interview with the author; Kniffen habeas petition, Exhibit 85 (the September 29, 1993, sworn declaration of Georgia Herald); testimony of Georgia Herald at the Kniffen-McCuan habeas hearing in July 1996.

55. Only the third female prosecutor ever hired by the Kern County District Attorney ("You're not some fuzzy-haired feminist, are you?" one of the attorneys conducting her job interview had asked), Grady was a proponent of a new, aggressive trend in prosecuting crimes against children. Instead of bundling all of the allegations into a single charge of molestation as was traditionally done, Grady took each separate sex act mentioned by the kids and charged it as a separate count—an approach that turned a misdemeanor case with an inevitable probation sentence into a major felony prosecution with a potential sentence of dozens of years in prison. This was a novel approach at the time, and though it is now standard, Grady was treading in uncertain waters, especially considering that she had little experience with major crimes to guide her and faced a great deal of head-shaking in her office. Source: Medalyian Grady, interview with the author.

56. Although no verbatim record exists of Velda Murillo's conversations with the girls, Medalyian Grady recalls tape-recording most of her conversations with Jenny and Jane. The tapes could have shown how much or how little pressure Grady put on the girls to continue their accusations of molestation—after those first interviews with Velda and sheriff's detectives—and whether the later questioning was open-ended or leading. Grady says she applied no pressure herself. But the tapes that could have verified this have mysteriously vanished. Grady recalls turning them over to one of her successors on the case, but their whereabouts are now unknown. The district attorney never turned them over to defense

attorneys, despite court orders requiring them to do so. Source: Medalyian Grady, interview with the author.

57. Sources: the sworn affidavits and testimony of Brian and Brandon Kniffen in the July 1996 Kniffen habeas hearing; the testimony of Velda Murillo in that same hearing, regarding the suggestive nature of her interviews with children; and the April 13, 1982, tape-recorded sessions between the Kniffen boys and Kern County Sheriff's Sergeant Don Fredenburg and Deputy DA Don McGillivray, introduced as evidence in the habeas hearing as Exhibits 79 and 80. The tactics used to overcome the boys' denials of molestation, including separating the terrified children from one another, telling them that the authorities "knew" they had been molested and sold as sexual slaves, and telling each of them, falsely, that the other had admitted to being molested. *Your brother is telling us all about being molested,* the inquisitors would say. *Won't you tell us, too?* The boys also recall being told they could go home to their parents if only they would tell police the allegations were true—which was, of course, false.

58. Medalyian Grady, interview with the author.

59. This sort of unflagging faith in the credibility of the children was not limited to prosecutors. It was also adopted by the Kern County judge who ruled there was sufficient evidence to bring the McCuans and Kniffens to trial—Municipal Court Judge Alan Klein, who would later preside unremarkably over pretrial matters in the Dunn case, then become embroiled in scandal for consorting with a stripper on trial in his court. In *People vs. Kniffen, et al.* West Kern Municipal Court Cases 33610, 33614 and 33624, Klein made the odd finding that Jenny's recantation of accusations against her uncle and other inconsistencies in the children's testimony made them *more*, rather than less, credible. Judge Klein also concluded that the similarities in the four children's stories, and the fact that they had so many seemingly sophisticated sexual details in common, proved they were telling the truth. Kids don't fantasize such things, the judge ruled—unaware, as was Grady before him, that in dozens of interviews, social workers, detectives and DA staffers had supplied every imaginable sexual detail to the kids, requiring them only to say, "Yes, that's what Mommy and Daddy did to me." Sources: Transcript of August 10, 1992, conclusion of the preliminary hearing in *People vs. Kniffen, et*

al; and Kathy Freeman, "Testimony isn't child's play," *Bakersfield Californian*, December 5, 1982.

60. Nothing seemed to sway the authorities in their steadfast belief that the children had been molested. They were not interested in the parents' denials, and barely bothered to question them when they failed to confess. Later, the authorities showed no interest in the fact that the Kniffens passed lie-detector tests administered by ex-law-enforcement officials, nor would the DA agree to have law-enforcement experts from the California Department of Justice administer additional polygraph examinations, ones that could not be dismissed as bought and paid for by the defense.

61. Scott Kniffen's father, Dick, who was well known in the community and a partner in one of Bakersfield's largest accounting firms, mortgaged his and his wife's house to pay for private investigators and to have an engineer rip out the ceiling in his son's house, revealing virgin plaster and beams, with no signs of hooks, holes or repairs. The authorities' response was to claim publicly—without any evidence—that the elder Kniffens were in on the plot as well. Dick Kniffen was accused (but never charged) of destroying evidence of child pornography, and Marilyn was alleged to have pressured the boys into recanting, though she, too, was never formally charged. (Both passed privately administered polygraph tests refuting these allegations.) Once the elder Kniffens sided with Scott and Brenda, prosecutors and child-protection workers—in an unprecedented joining of forces—did everything they could to limit contact between the Kniffen children and their grandparents, even if it meant violating a judge's orders allowing them visitations. Later, the boys' aunt, Pamela Kniffen, tried to gain temporary custody. A real estate appraiser in Montana, she and her husband had adopted several troubled children there, after a thorough investigation by Montana officials deemed their home safe, wholesome and loving. Kern County authorities, however, vehemently opposed allowing the boys to live there, and accused Pamela of child molestation even though no such evidence existed. Sources: Author's interviews with private investigator Denver Dunn (no relation to Pat Dunn), attorney Michael Snedeker and Pamela Kniffen; a 181-page analysis of the Kniffen-McCuan prosecution and related cases completed in January 1995 by private investigator Denver Dunn; Michael Trihey, "Molestation inquiry tactics

questioned," *Bakersfield Californian,* April 13, 1986; and Trihey, "Detective uses mannequins to re-enact crimes," *Bakersfield Californian,* April 15, 1985.

62. Kern County authorities were so confident in Woodling that his results would be used to prosecute many subsequent cases, including some in which the child victims denied being molested even after many interrogations. According to an affidavit filed in the Kniffen and McCuan habeas corpus action, one eleven-year-old girl, now grown, recalls Woodling announcing he *knew* she had been molested, despite her pleas that nothing had happened. "This test will show who's right and who's wrong," she swore he told her. Then he examined the girl, using his wink test as well as placing various glass tubes inside her rectum and vagina—an experience she later likened to being "violated against my will." In an interview with the author, Dr. Woodling, who now runs a children's program in the Palm Springs, California, area and who still testifies in abuse cases there, said he could no longer recall the specifics of this case. However, he said he would never have made such statements to a child nor would he have examined any child against his or her will. Sources: In Re Scott and Brenda Kniffen, Exhibits 84A (interview of Tricia McCuan) and 84B (declaration of Tricia McCuan); and author's interview with Bruce Woodling.

63. Woodling, in an interview with the author, conceded that there had been no scientific studies performed to validate his opinions about the Wink Test, which he said were based solely on his own experience examining abused children. Woodling said he had made this distinction clear in his testimony, though the defense argued strenuously that jurors were led to believe Woodling's tests provided decisive proof of molestation. The scientific studies have since been performed, however, and they decisively show that Woodling's wink test is useless in proving or disproving molestation. Woodling says he no longer uses the wink test in evaluating suspected abuse in children. Woodling's work was the subject of extensive testing and argument in the 1996 Kniffen habeas hearings.

64. These conflicts arose continually as the number of molestation-ring cases grew. In one subsequent case, a single deputy DA simultaneously prosecuted parents accused of being part of the Nokes molestation ring, fought in juvenile court to keep

the children away from their other relatives, and expressed a personal interest in adopting one of the victims—a profound conflict of interest and ethical lapse no one at the time even questioned.

"When it came to deciding what was best for children, there was God, and then there was the Kern County District Attorney," the social worker Georgia Herald would later recall in an interview with the author. "Not necessarily in that order."

65. Gindes won the conviction of a man named Robert Valdez for murdering another man outside a wedding reception. Having secured a lengthy prison sentence against Valdez, Gindes fought hard to minimize and undermine new evidence and discredit witnesses who surfaced after the trial to suggest he had prosecuted the wrong man. Gindes was adamant that the new witnesses must be lying, and a law clerk under his supervision was dispatched to impersonate a news reporter in order to interview one witness who did not want to talk to the DA—a move which was roundly criticized. Valdez's conviction was later overturned on appeal because of new evidence. A new trial, with the new witnesses, led to his acquittal. He had spent three years behind bars. Sources: Jim Foley, "Posing as a reporter stirs DA criticism," *Fresno Bee*, May 9, 1978; Miles Shuper, "Robert Valdez looks around—after three years behind bars," *Visalia Times-Delta*, May 30, 1979.

66. Gindes has consistently denied ever pressuring the Kniffens or any other child victims, and says his only concern when prosecuting alleged molesters was protecting children and seeing justice done. If there was any coercion in the Kniffen-McCuan case, he never witnessed it, Gindes has said. He stated that he does not believe any such coercion occurred, but he cannot completely rule it out either, because he came to the Kniffen case many months after charges were originally filed, and after the many initial interviews—later said to have been suggestive and coercive—had already been performed. Source: Andrew Gindes, interview with the author; and Gindes, interview on ABC's *Turning Point*, November 14, 1996.

67. In persuading the judge, Gindes argued that Barbour's psychiatric hospitalization and obsession with molestation were irrelevant, even though she was the initial interrogator of the children and the primary conduit of information to the authorities. The judge assigned to hear the *People vs. Kniffen and McCuan* was

none other than Judge Marvin Ferguson, who had just lost the DA's election to Ed Jagels after being tarred as soft on molesters. Ferguson agreed with Gindes—he ruled that defense lawyers could not use or even see Mary Ann Barbour's psychiatric records.

68. Palko later sued Jagels for slander for calling him guilty. The suit was dismissed, though not because it was factually inadequate. Rather, Jagels had the law on his side: Although an ordinary citizen could be sued for such statements, district attorneys are immune from liability, even if they slander someone, so long as they do it in their "official capacity."

69. In the ring cases, this fundamental lapse in basic investigating procedures was explained away by asserting that corroboration was unnecessary because of the since disproven axiom that children do not "lie" about such things. One senior sheriff's investigator, Dan Fredenburg, even cited in court the extensive research conducted by an expert favored by prosecutors, Roland Summit, who originated the concept of "Child Sexual Abuse Accommodation Syndrome," which purports to explain how children who denied being molested were actually lying in order to protect their parents. The sheriff's investigator testified that Summit's research proved that, once a child got past this syndrome and admitted to being molested, only a negligible fraction of the resulting molestation allegations were ever found to be fabricated. There is no doubt this investigator, along with most of his colleagues in Kern County, genuinely believed these "research" findings to be true. The only problem was, no such research had ever been conducted—not by Summit, nor by anyone else. Roland Summit, by his own admission in a deposition in *State of Florida vs. Bob Fijnje*, Dade County Circuit Court Case No: 89-43952 (filed as Exhibit 64 to In Re Kniffen), had never even treated child victims of sexual abuse. It is true that some children deny being molested out of shame or fear or because they don't want a loved one—even an abusive loved one—harmed or jailed. Common sense and experience, not research, attests to that. But it is also indisputable that the vast majority of genuine research on the subject shows that children *do* tell untruths about a great many things, including molestation—particularly when asked leading, suggestive questions that telegraph to the child what the questioner wants to hear. In study after study (see, among many exam-

ples, Stephen J. Ceci and Maggie Bruck, *Jeopardy in the Courtroom: A Scientific Analysis of Children's Testimony* [New York: American Psychological Association, 1995]), false allegations, and even false memories, have been produced in children through exactly the sort of questioning used by social workers, sheriff's detectives and DAs in the ring cases of Kern County. When leading questions are used with young children, it can be impossible to weed out truth from fiction, these studies show. Indeed, young children may not be able to distinguish fact from fiction once subjected to such questioning, and though they may be trying earnestly to tell the truth, they may still deliver factually false testimony. The authorities prosecuting the molestation rings in Kern County (and in other communities where such cases have and continue to crop up) remained curiously unaware of such studies, or, when forced to acknowledge their existence in court, have dismissed them as defense-attorney propaganda, rebutting them with Summit's phantom research. The notorious McMartin Preschool ring case in Los Angeles was undone in this same way, when proof of the suggestive questioning of children was finally brought before jurors.

The lack of evidence to corroborate the children's stories was not the only striking absence in the ring cases. Another was that no other police agency in Kern County ever found any signs of molestation rings operating in their jurisdictions; only the Kern County Sheriff's Department could find them. As it turned out, the sheriff's department was also the only police agency that permitted social workers and the DA's abuse coordinators, Carol Darling and Velda Murillo, to participate in and sometimes run the initial interviews with suspected victims (a practice later criticized by Ed Jagels, though at the time he praised Carol Darling and received regular briefings from her). This unusual partnership evolved in part because none of the sheriff's personnel had been adequately trained in the art of investigating child-molestation cases, not even the sheriff's sergeant in charge, Brad Darling—husband to Carol Darling. Source: Attorney General John Van de Kamp, "Report on the Kern County Child Abuse Investigation," September 1986; Andrew Gindes, *Crimes Against Children*, (1996), self-published; Nathan and Snedeker, *Satan's Silence*; and the author's interviews with Snedeker and Gindes.

By contrast, the Bakersfield Police Department, serving just as large and diverse a population as the sheriff's adjacent jurisdiction, conducted its own independent investigations in every suspected molestation case, without relying on Carol Darling or Velda Murillo. In their investigation, the city police force (long considered the premiere police agency in the county in terms of pay, experience and skills) turned up plenty of one-adult, one-child molestation cases. But not one of these cases ever metamorphosed into a large-scale molestation ring, as so many sheriff's department cases seemed to. Neither did cases in the police departments serving the smaller towns and cities of Kern County. In 1984, the Bakersfield Police Department's requests to the district attorney to prosecute child-molestation cases were less than half the total of those brought by sheriff's department—a statistical improbability that should have been a glaring red flag to indicate that something was wrong, given the similar size and demographics of the neighboring populations patrolled by the two departments. Why should molestation rings only operate in the unincorporated areas of Kern County? The anomaly *was* duly noted, but not as evidence something might be out of kilter at the sheriff's department. The *Bakersfield Californian*—quoting unnamed prosecutors, social workers and sheriff's deputies involved in the ring cases—chalked the disparity up to the inadequacies and lack of aggressiveness of the *city* police, suggesting that if only the rest of the cops in town would get on board with the sheriff's practices, even more molestation rings could be busted. Source: Steve E. Swenson and Michael Trihey, "Sex Abuse Statistics Contrast," *Bakersfield Californian*, February 3, 1985.

70. Source: Stan Simrin. Similar examples of the destructive nature of the investigation abound. The head of the local postal workers' union was fingered by one child; though he was never charged, he lost his position, as well as custody of his daughter for several months. The preacher of a local church was also accused after accompanying an accused parishioner to court, though he, too, was never charged. Fearing his own children might be taken, the preacher moved away, forfeiting his job and his congregation. Another man became a suspect simply because his wife went to court to provide moral support to a friend charged in one ring case. A child victim, scanning the courtroom at the behest of a

social worker who warned that "they" might be anywhere, picked the woman out of the audience and said, "She's one of them. Her and her husband, the man with the ponytail." The woman was promptly arrested, as was her husband, who did not wear his hair in a ponytail and never had. Yet another man—who had fully cooperated with authorities when his daughter accused neighbors of running a molestation ring—lost his daughter and son after he began to express doubts about the case. (This girl, Brooke, played a prominent role in the satanic cases. See note 71.) As soon as he started questioning the authorities about the fact that some of his daughter's statements couldn't be true, he became the enemy. His children were isolated in Kern County custody, and the inevitable accusations of molestation followed. It took a year of hearings and agony for that man and his family, but, finally, his children were returned to him by none other than Judge Marvin Ferguson, the failed DA candidate who had presided over the Kniffen-McCuan trial. Ferguson by then had his own doubts about molestation prosecutions in Kern County. "The evidence is overwhelming these parents did not molest the child," the judge ruled. "Her story . . . is fraught with inconsistencies. More than that, it was unbelievable." His ruling was too late to save the devastated family, however. The young girl who had made the allegations had been taught to fear her parents and wanted to stay with the social workers who "saved" her.

71. What came to be known in Kern County as the satanic case began on March 15, 1985, with one child, Brooke—a girl later determined to be unbelievable by Judge Marvin Ferguson, who returned her to her family. Brooke first was questioned after a child victim in a ring case named her as a fellow victim. Once interviewed, she initially accused two men of abusing her. One of them was her neighbor, Reverend Willard Thomas, pastor of a small Kern County nondenominational church. Brooke described Thomas as a short and stout black man—though Thomas actually was tall and thin—and, when asked to identify him, she picked out the wrong photo from a lineup put together by a sheriff's deputy. It seemed then the case would go nowhere. But then the deputy on the case left Brooke alone with a social worker named Cory Taylor, another adherent of the leading-question school of child interviewing. When the deputy returned, Brooke picked

Thomas out of the lineup without hesitation, and had changed her description of her abuser to tall and skinny. The deputy knew something wasn't right, but said nothing. This, and the information about the suspicious photo lineup was kept secret, so Thomas's defense attorney could not use its obvious implications to assert that the minister had been framed. The deputy would later say that she knew what had happened was wrong, that the case was "tainted from the very beginning," but that she could not bring herself to speak out; to do so would have been both difficult and dangerous. Her fears were common in Kern County law enforcement at the time, as former cops and prosecutors would admit much later: You were either a true believer, or you kept your mouth shut. Ironically, as the investigation later spiraled out of control, at least one child "victim" accused Cory Taylor of being a molester and devil worshiper. (Source: John K. Van de Kamp, California Attorney General, "Report on the Kern County Child Abuse Investigation," September 1986, including supplementary reports and data; and Michael Trihey, "Agencies' infighting, procedural errors triggered collapse of molestation case," *Bakersfield Californian*, January 25, 1987.)

The satanic allegations arose almost a year after the questionable lineup. When Brooke's father began to express doubts about the case and its new, bizarre direction, investigators decided that, though he had always been cooperative with authorities, he, too, must be part of the conspiracy. As detectives and social workers arrived to take Brooke away, she tried to hit the police with her shoes to stop them from carting her off. It took fifteen days and repeated contacts with Kern County officials before she finally accused her parents. Within a month, she announced she was too fearful of her own family to have even an officially supervised visit with them.

72. In keeping with the past practice of interviewing children over and over as allegations multiplied, the nineteen most talkative children in the satanic case were interviewed a total of one hundred thirty-four times. Such repetition is almost guaranteed to generate false information, according to the testimony of psychologist Maggie Bruck and other evidence presented in the 1996 Kniffen habeas hearing. One kid was interrogated a total of thirty-five times, and rarely told the same story twice—yet he became the

star witness in the satanic case. Source: Van de Kamp, "Report on the Kern County Child Abuse Investigation."

73. Los Angeles County Sheriff's Sergeant W. Gleason, "Satanic Related Child Abuse Investigations in Kern County-Lamont Area," a May 21, 1985, report to the McMartin task force; Michael Trihey, "'High elements' in society linked to satanic acts," *Bakersfield Californian*, April 17, 1986; Jim Boren, "Child abuse investigator speaks out," *Fresno Bee*, April 17, 1986; Steve E. Swenson, "Speech on Satanism was 'exaggerated,'" *Bakersfield Californian*, May 28, 1986.

74. There were other double standards at that time in Kern County. One case that arose in this era stood out and proceeded quite differently from the others, not because the evidence was any stronger or weaker against this particular "ring," but because, in this case, police and prosecutors decided to do nothing. No charges, no arrests, not even credible attempts at investigation were made. Alone among the many children identified—and misidentified—as sex-abuse victims in Kern County during the Witch Hunt years, young Robert Mistriel was deemed unworthy of saving.

Mistriel entered the Kern County justice system through its juvenile court, a victim of neglect and abuse. An older brother molested him, while his alcoholic mother provided a perpetually squalid series of hovels and motel rooms to call home. Juvenile court did little to help. By age twelve, Mistriel was prostituting himself to older gay men. Around this time, his probation reports started talking about his sociopathic tendencies. At thirteen, Mistriel was implicated but never charged in the murder of one of his older lovers, a well-known, middle-aged hairdresser named Tommy Tarver, whose Bakersfield shop was frequented by Kern County's elite. Tarver was found bludgeoned, comatose and dying on the floor of his salon early one morning in 1978; he died a few days later. Mistriel had been dropped off at Tarver's place by a cab driver a short while before the attack, and later was found with Tarver's car in addition to stolen goods from the salon. But the Kern County District Attorney chose to prosecute him only for burglary, pinning the murder on an out-of-town university student who was promptly acquitted.

Following the Tarver episode, Mistriel was placed in a series of Kern County foster homes, from which he ran off regularly, and was allowed, with other delinquents, to work for a prominent local businessman who also used the juveniles as his sexual playthings. At the same time, Mistriel, still a teenage county ward, prowled the men's rooms of Beach Park, a notorious Bakersfield rendezvous for casual gay sex, where he forged relationships with a number of men prominent in the community. By age sixteen, Mistriel could be seen around town driving expensive cars belonging to some of these men, and he boasted openly to friends about the money, drugs and privileges he earned by sexually servicing some of Kern County's most powerful.

This was an open secret: Kern County authorities were aware of these relationships. A probation officer assigned to Mistriel's case would later swear that she confirmed these relationships, but took no action other than counseling the boy about them. Yet then, as now, any sexual relationship with a minor—particularly one who was a ward of the juvenile court—was a crime for the adults involved. If the relationships as Mistriel described them occurred, the same laws were broken that were tenaciously being enforced in all the ring cases. But Mistriel's probation officer explained that she felt that Mistriel, though only sixteen, was the one taking advantage of the older men, manipulating them for monetary gain.

Another factor influencing the lack of action on Mistriel's case may have been who Mistriel was sleeping with: Edwin Buck, the personnel manager of Kern County, one of the local government's most senior and powerful administrators, had a long-standing affair with Mistriel, whom he met in Beach Park. Buck was widely respected, a pillar of the community, a wily politician with enormous clout. He had been personnel director since 1955, in charge of hiring, firing and dispensing all county patronage jobs. Local vice officers had repeatedly warned the fifty-five-year-old Buck and several of his cronies about their brazen solicitations at Beach Park and assignations with minors, but no official action was taken. Nor was anything done to protect, help or even punish Robert Mistriel with regard to his liaisons with the rich and powerful.

Then, in July 1981, Buck's body was found nearly cremated in the back of his burned-out car. He had been bludgeoned to death with a hammer—the same weapon suspected in the murder of Tommy Tarver three years earlier—before his body was set ablaze. The trail quickly led to Mistriel and a friend, Roy Matthew

Camenisch, he had recruited to rob and murder Buck. By then seventeen, Mistriel was transferred from juvenile to adult court. His trial—moved to another county so an unbiased jury could be picked—brought some startling testimony about the men he worked for, lived with and slept with in Bakersfield. (He had previously shared this information with Bakersfield police, who did nothing.) Mistriel—and his probation officer—took the stand and named as the boy's long-term gay lovers Ted Fritts, the publisher of the *Bakersfield Californian* newspaper, the city's only daily paper, and another man, a powerful political consultant who had worked for numerous politicians in Kern County, including District Attorney Ed Jagels. Mistriel was said to have lived with this man, while Fritts (who had received and ignored the same warnings from vice cops as Ed Buck, and who since has died of AIDS) loaned his luxury car to the veteran delinquent, sent him on errands out of town and put him to work at the newspaper. This unrebutted testimony garnered two paragraphs near the bottom of two articles in the local newspaper, and was forgotten.

Such testimony, however shocking, could not overcome the overwhelming evidence of Mistriel's guilt in the murder of Edwin Buck, even though it suggested Kern County authorities could have prevented the murder by doing something about Mistriel's prior conduct—and the men who used him sexually. Mistriel received a sentence of thirty-two years to life in prison, which, as of July 1998, he is still serving. None of Mistriel's or the probation officer's testimony about the publisher or the political power broker or any of the others Mistriel identified as having sex with minors was ever disputed, in court or out. But no official action was ever taken, even though this testimony came to light just as the first ring case, Kniffen-McCuan, was coming to trial, and Kern County authorities were in the midst of their fervent pursuit of other molestation-ring cases. Sources: *People vs. Robert Glenn Mistriel*, record on appeal archived with the California Court of Appeal, Fourth District, Division Two, Case No. E000323 (appeal from Riverside County Superior Court, Case CR-19638); testimony of Deputy Probation Officer Sally Rockholt and defendant Robert Mistriel, and argument of Deputy District Attorney Clarence Westra and defense attorney David A. Huffman, in *People vs. Mistriel;* Detective W. D. Vines, homicide investigation report dated July 28, 1981, Bakersfield Police Department Case 81-18080; Michael Trihey, "Mistriel admits planning murder," *Bakersfield Californian*, June 30, 1983.

75. Even then, the authorities did not stop investigating the satanism allegations, still hoping to find more witnesses or just one bit of physical evidence, one sign of a ritual, one animal sacrifice. The sheriff's department, from then-Sheriff Larry Kleier on down, was convinced the stories were true. Kleier—already under fire for allegedly rigging the auction of a stolen gun he wanted for his own collection (despite the real owner being a phone call away) and for the manner in which his daughter's drunken-driving arrest vanished from the court system—had staked his reputation on the satanic case. He declared that he maintained "absolute faith" in the children's stories, even as the cases unraveled. "Children don't lie," he stated, though he later denied making the remark when it became clear that his child witnesses had, indeed, made false allegations.

76. Kern County's experience with molestation conspiracies presaged a national phenomenon in the 1980s. After the first Bakersfield ring cases broke, there came the more prominent McMartin Preschool investigation in Los Angeles, destined to become the nation's most notorious example of discredited molestation ring charges ever. Like the Kniffen-McCuan case, McMartin began with one woman with a history of mental illness who was certain her children had been molested, and with officials who felt the best way to question children was to put words in their mouths. There followed a wave of similar cases in almost every state, many of them involving day-care centers, with particularly notable ones occurring in New York, Nevada, New Jersey, Massachusetts, Minnesota, Illinois, North Carolina, Florida, Oregon and throughout California—as many as a thousand defendants accused of molesting hundreds of children, according to the estimates of Carol Hopkins's National Justice Committee. (Hopkins was formerly foreperson of the San Diego County Grand Jury, which exposed several unjust molestation prosecutions in its jurisdiction.) All the ring cases were accompanied by massive media coverage, which was often sensationalistic and riddled with errors, and the testimony of "survivors" and self-proclaimed experts. Many of the cases seemed remarkably similar in the sug-

gestive way in which children were interrogated, the types of questionable medical evidence cited, and the manner in which any evidence that undermined the prosecution somehow got lost, forgotten or covered up in the rush to convict. Kern County was by no means unique in this regard—just first.

77. *Satan's Underground* (Eugene, Ore.: Harvest House Publishers, 1988) garnered enormous publicity when it was published. The author, whose true name is Lauren Wilson, appeared on the television shows *Oprah, Geraldo,* and *The 700 Club,* among others, where she claimed to have been repeatedly raped, to have been forced into satanic rituals and to have given birth to babies which were ritually sacrificed. The Chicago-based Christian magazine *Cornerstone* published in December 1989 (*Cornerstone,* Vol. 18, Issue 99, page 24) a detailed refutation of most of the key dates, events, places and facts in the book, locating the author's mother (said to be dead in the book), her sister (said not to exist in the book), and other friends and relatives, who all refuted most of the book's claims. Harvest House later withdrew the book.

78. John Soliz, reports dated July 27, 1992, and July 30, 1992, in Kern County Sheriff's Department Case MO92-00633. The July 27 report documents a July 8, 1992, telephone conversation between Soliz and Nanette Petrillo, stating: "Pat Dunn told her Alexandra Dunn had consumed two glasses of wine that same evening prior to her disappearance . . . Petrillo said she did not know Alexandra to drink alcoholic beverages."

Three days later, in the July 30 report, Soliz documents his July 27 visit with Petrillo and her husband, stating: "Nanette described Alexandra as being both verbally and physically abusive to her mother when she was alive. She said she recalled of a time when Alexandra slapped her mother on the face. Nanette said Alexandra was also verbally and possibly physically abusive to Pat Paola when Alexandra and Paola were married. Both Nanette and Douglas Petrillo said they also thought that Alexandra was an alcoholic."

79. Rob Walters, "Woman cites husband of sister for 'undue influence' on will," *Bakersfield Californian,* October 18, 1992.

80. Rob Walters, "Elderly woman manipulated, family claims: Allegations similar to Patrick Dunn case," *Bakersfield Californian,* October 29, 1992. The article, which was published as a companion story to additional accounts detailing Pat's arrest for murder,

began: "The sister of murder suspect Patrick O'Dale Dunn used 'undue influence' to get an elderly lady to make her trustee and beneficiary of a living trust worth about $1.2 million, the woman's family alleges."

81. The correction was a small paragraph entitled "For the Record," published in the *Bakersfield Californian* on October 31, 1992, stating in its entirety: "Dianne Dunn-Gonzalez is not related to murder suspect Patrick O. Dunn. Because of source error, a story in Thursday Local section was incorrect." Though the source for the erroneous information was not specified in either the initial story or the correction, the author has learned from sources at the *Californian* that the story tip came from a high-ranking sheriff's official who was intimately involved in the Dunn homicide investigation.

82. Author's interviews with Jerry Lee Coble, Marie Gates, Gary Pohlson, Jay Dunn and Pat Dunn.

83. The defense team was concerned that the prosecution would use some version of this incident with Coble as evidence against Pat, but though the district attorney's office was aware of Coble's bribery allegations, it took no action and the matter was not brought up during the trial. Coble maintained that Mike Dunn offered him $10,000 to leave the county and not testify; according to the Dunn family, Jerry Coble offered to sell photographs of Pat's house to Mike Dunn. These photographs were supposed to be ones Coble had taken while casing the house, and that he had developed at the photomat where Rex Martin followed him that day in late July. The Dunns allege that Mike paid several hundred dollars, but never saw the photos in question. Coble denies that they ever existed. Source: Author's interviews with Gary Pohlson, Deputy District Attorney John Somers, Jerry Lee Coble, Pat Dunn and Jay Dunn.

84. While Teri Bjorn has said that she recalls telling Kate Rosenlieb about Sandy being missing, the timing of the call—a critical matter—is unclear. Further, Bjorn's partner, Kevin Knutson, specifically recalls Bjorn telling him that she learned about Sandy's disappearance *from* Kate, which would mean that Rosenlieb's first story, about getting the news about Sandy from Pat, would be the correct version. Source: Testimony of Teri Bjorn and Kate Rosenlieb, in *People vs. Dunn*; and the author's interviews with Rosenlieb and Kevin Knutson.

85. Rosenlieb, interview with the author.

86. Ibid., and John Somers, interview with the author.

87. In interviews with the author, Deputy DA Somers stated that he turned over all of Rosenlieb's notes in his possession; if he had the additional entries, the law would have required him to turn them over to Pat Dunn's lawyers as well.

PART III: TRIAL AND ERROR

1. Somers countered this testimony by calling to the witness stand Ed Wilkerson, a broker, who did recall Sandy wanting her accounts kept confidential, even from Pat. But this broker had stopped working for Sandy in 1988, during her first year of marriage to Pat and while she was still getting over her second marriage and its ugly battles over money (*People vs. Dunn,* testimony of Ed Wilkerson).

2. The defense neither objected to Somers' mischaracterization of Montes' testimony, nor did it return to the matter on cross-examination in an attempt to prove the more favorable time line. Gary Pohlson later conceded this was an error on his part (*People vs. Dunn;* and Gary Pohlson, interview with the author).

3. From *People vs. Jesse Dewayne Jacobs,* 31F.3d 1319, 1322, n. 6(CA5 1994), and *People vs. Bobbie Hogan,* (Ibid.) two Texas prosecutions discussed in a dissent by Supreme Court Justice John Paul Stevens, in *Jacobs vs. Scott,* 115.S.ct.711(1996), Jacobs got death; Hogan was sentenced to ten years in prison. "In my opinion, it is fundamentally unfair for the State of Texas to go forward with the execution of Jesse Dewayne Jacobs," Stevens wrote in January 1995. "The principal evidence supporting his conviction was a confession that was expressly and unequivocally disavowed at a subsequent trial, by the same prosecutor who presented the case against Jacobs. . . . The injustice, in my view, is self-evident." Only one other justice, Ruth Bader Ginsburg, agreed, however. The majority declined to review the case.

4. John Somers, interview with the author.

5. Rosenlieb, in an interview with the author, said she had not observed memory or mental impairment in Sandy, though she had found her to be "eccentric" and "child-like."

6. At least four other witnesses could have attested to

Sandy's developing memory problems, but they were not called to testify.

7. Although she was not asked about it on the witness stand, Bjorn and her colleagues at her law firm had combed their files in search of anything that might document this conversation with Pat. Bjorn found a short memo she had written to herself about the conversation that says, in part, "Sandy missing since last nite. filed missing pers report? bills due—check with Rex Martin re amount." On the top line of the memo are two notations: "tk Pat Dunn" (an abbreviation that indicates she needs to call Pat) and a date, July 1. When Bjorn saw the date, she concluded that it meant that July 1 was the day on which the conversation with Pat took place, rather than an indication of when Sandy disappeared. But other documents in the law office, including the message slips kept by the secretaries at Bjorn's law firm—indicate that Pat called and left a message for Bjorn on the morning of July 2, not July 1. Meanwhile, Kevin Knutson, who lived with Bjorn, recalled her coming home from work on a Thursday or Friday (July 2 or July 3) and telling him of hearing that day that Sandy was missing—again suggesting that Pat's call to his real estate attorney came after he reported Sandy missing.

Finally, there is the initial police report by Detective Vernon Kline on Kate Rosenlieb's statements about her conversation with Pat after Sandy vanished (Kern County Sheriff's Department Case KC92-14851), in which she puts the day Sandy disappeared at July 2, two days off. Rosenlieb would later recall that Teri Bjorn called her two days after Sandy disappeared, which, by her first statement, would have been July 4. She later revised her account to correct the date, but the confusion over times and dates makes it virtually impossible to know when, precisely, Pat talked to his real estate attorney: It could have been anywhere from twelve hours after Sandy disappeared to seventy hours.

Even so, a point made by Somers and Judge Baca remains valid: Whether it took place on July 1, July 2 or July 3, this conversation still came awfully early in the game, at a time when most people would expect Pat to be more concerned about finding Sandy than dealing with money matters, even if it had been Bjorn who first raised the subject. If innocent, he could not have known Sandy would not return imminently and straighten out the money prob-

ENDNOTES 577

lems herself. In interviews with the author, Pat has insisted he did not talk to Teri Bjorn until July 7, which is not nearly so unseemly as July 1—but which flies in the face of all the other evidence and testimony. He also says the paying of bills for Morning Star was critical and had to be done immediately—and that Sandy would have wanted him to attend to it.

8. Laura Lawhon, "Investigation Report: Post Verdict Juror Interviews," April 1, 1993, memorandum to Gary Pohlson.

9. Ibid.

10. Ibid.

11. Detective Eric Banducci, Kern County Sheriff's Department Supplemental Report, Case No. KC91-06787, April 5, 1991.

12. Ibid.

13. Banducci, interview with the author.

14. Laura Lawhon and Gary Pohlson, interviews with the author. Neither Deputy District Attorney John Somers nor District Attorney Edward Jagels responded to the author's written request for an explanation of this apparent disclosure violation, though Somers promised a response.

15. Banducci, interview with the author.

16. Certainly, there was no shortage of opinions available on Coble. Several other detectives at the Kern County Sheriff's Department knew of Coble and considered him an unlikely figure on whom to base a criminal prosecution, including Senior Deputy Jeff Niccoli, who helped Banducci bust Coble. "The Coble family is well known in Kern County law enforcement," the recently retired, highly regarded Bakersfield chief of police, Bob Patterson, observed in an interview with the author. "There's no way I would ever allow Jerry Coble to be a witness in any case unless he passed a polygraph test first." The lie detector is sometimes used by the sheriff's department—Soliz considered Pat Dunn's refusal to take one highly suspicious—but no thought was ever given to asking Coble to submit to the same test.

17. Banducci, interview with the author.

18. Ibid.

19. Detective Soliz's dealings with informants had occasioned at least one controversy in the past. Six years before the Dunn case, when he was working narcotics, Soliz took on another small-time drug offender, Lloyd Mason, as an informant. Mason was supposed

to provide information on drug dealers in order to "work off" his own legal problems. But Mason and his wife, Joy, later were arrested by another police agency in Kern County for a host of drug charges, including conspiracy to sell and manufacture methamphetamine. Mason claimed he had been creating a cover to further his work as a snitch. But Soliz denied this, saying that he never gave Mason permission to own the equipment and drug-related chemicals found in his house, and that, in any case, Mason was a lousy informant, having never produced any usable information. When cross-examined on this point during the Masons' trial, Soliz was confronted with two sworn affidavits for search warrants executed in other drug cases. The search warrants were obtained on the word of a confidential informant—who was none other than Lloyd Mason—and stated that the informant had given information in the past that led to arrests and the seizure of narcotics. Mason, it seemed, may have provided usable information after all. Nevertheless, Mason was convicted and sentenced to six years in prison due to the overwhelming evidence against him, though enough questions had been raised to lead jurors to acquit his wife. Sources: Opinion (unpublished portions) of the California Court of Appeal, Fifth Appellate District, *The People vs. Lloyd Mason,* Case F008097, May 6, 1988 (Kern County Superior Court Case 31585 [1986]); and Greg Mitts (defense attorney for Joy Mason), interview with the author.

20. This was not the only break dealt Coble by the district attorney's office. He should have been in prison at the time he allegedly spotted Pat Dunn dumping Sandy's body. He had been on parole for an earlier theft when Banducci arrested him, and that parole had been revoked. Coble had been sent back to state prison while the new case made its way through the system. But an apparent mistake by the DA's office produced a written request that prison officials bring him back to Kern County so he could stand trial—months before his case was due in court. He bailed out of the county jail two days after returning to Kern County, and had been free ever since—free to do heroin several times a week while simultaneously receiving methadone treatments, and free to cruise through Pat Dunn's neighborhood. Source: *The People vs. Jerry Lee Coble,* Kern County Superior Court Case No. 47620A (1991), including the following documents: "Agreement

Regarding Testimony," November 3, 1992; transcript of hearing before Superior Court Judge Arthur E. Wallace, November 3, 1992; October 18, 1991, minute entry documenting a trial date setting of December 20, 1991; request from the Kern County District Attorney to the state Department of Corrections on October 25, 1991, that Coble be transported forthwith to Kern County for trial; minute entry documenting the November 4, 1991, arrival of Coble at the Kern County Jail; and minute entry showing Coble's release on bail on November 6, 1991, at 2:15 P.M.

21. The account of the stolen-check case and the ensuing investigation is drawn from Detective J. E. Taylor's reports, and other Bakersfield Police Department reports, contained in Bakersfield Municipal Court Case BF066673.

22. In an interview with the author, Somers said he and the investigators on the Dunn case had no knowledge of the new case against Coble until the author brought it to his attention.

23. This account of communications between Kate Rosenlieb and John Soliz is based upon the author's interviews with Rosenlieb, and her journal notes, which she supplied to the author.

Rosenlieb's journal entry for October 8, 1992, reads:

> John Soliz called and said the DA's office was being
> unreasonable. John Somers has been fantastic but
> that Sara Ryals [a deputy district attorney] has been
> a major obstacle. Both John and Sara report to Dan
> Sparks [a supervising DA]. He [Soliz] said Dan and
> Sara were spineless and were afraid that this case
> will generate lots of publicity and that Patrick could
> hire the best attorney in the nation. He said Sara
> was asking for the impossible, like a confession, a
> witness to the actual murder and a murder weapon.
> He said not to release any political pressure yet, but
> to get ready. He said every time they meet with the
> DA, a new list of items the DA wants comes out of
> it. He said it had gotten to the point of being ridicu-
> lous and they were actually threatening each other.
> He said the sheriff's department had threatened to
> arrest Patrick without indictment but only on
> probable cause.

24. The author's interviews with Kate Rosenlieb and Stan Harper. Harper recalled that the effort to persuade Jagels to prosecute Pat Dunn included officials at the highest levels of municipal government. However, Harper, a close friend of Jagels', said he believed Jagels was resistant to such political pressures. Harper recalls bringing up the subject, only to have the DA tell him he did not wish to discuss pending criminal investigations, and that his office based its charging decisions on legal, not political, factors.

25. The author's interviews with Kate Rosenlieb.

26. Ibid. Rosenlieb explained her contradictory accounts by asserting that much time had passed since the events at issue.

27. Ibid.

28. The prosecution, of course, could argue that Sandy's statements to Rosenlieb about divorce were months old, and that Sandy could well have changed her mind by the time she spoke to Marie Gates. However, Rosenlieb's testimony would still have added greatly to the defense, especially when considered with Kevin Knutson's testimony about Sandy—on the day she disappeared—acting in a loving way toward Pat, saying she wanted to take care of him financially and give him more control over her money.

29. *People vs. Sergio Venegas* 98 C.D.O.S. 3561. Resolving a long-simmering dispute over the reliability of DNA matching in criminal cases, the California Supreme Court authorized its general use throughout California, even as it rejected the specific way it was used in the Venegas case. The court ruled that prosecutors must employ a more conservative statistical analysis than the one used in Kern County to measure the likelihood that a particular DNA sample comes from a particular individual. In securing Venegas' conviction, Deputy DA Green introduced evidence that the DNA traces recovered from the rape victim—who could not identify her assailant—had only a 1-in-65,000 chance of coming from someone other than the defendant. But the more conservative calculations deemed reliable by the Supreme Court (and previously endorsed in an authoritative and widely accepted study by the National Research Council) reduce those odds to as little as 1 in 378—a less than overwhelming match in a case with little corroborating evidence.

30. John Soliz, reports filed in Kern County Sheriff's Department, Case DE94-00151; and Steve E. Swenson, "Suspect

falsely ID'd released from jail," *Bakersfield Californian*, October 25, 1994.

31. *People vs. Abelardo Gamboa et al.*, California Court of Appeal, Fifth Appellate District, Case F017155, an unpublished opinion in the appeal of Kern County Superior Court Case 45981.

32. The account of the Stallion Springs case and official reaction to the appellate ruling overturning the convictions is drawn from: the unpublished Court of Appeal opinion in *People vs. Gamboa et al.*; Steve E. Swenson, "Cops hid evidence, judge says," *Bakersfield Californian*, December 12, 1991; and Steve E. Swenson, "Huge PCP conviction overruled," *Bakersfield Californian*, June 16, 1993. The erasure of PCP manufacturing convictions due to the illegal search meant Abelardo Gamboa was freed from a prison sentence of twenty years; Abel Bernard Medina, nineteen years; Benjamin Tiburico Torres, seventeen years; and Manuel Chavez, fifteen years. Because the critical evidence—the $4 million worth of PCP and everything related to it—had to be suppressed because of the government's constitutional violations, there was no way to retry the four.

33. The defense lawyer, Thomas P. "Skip" Daly, a veteran of 175 murder trials, even brought up the subject of the lineup before the jury—something the prosecution had been barred from doing. The prosecutor then pounced on this mistaken "opening of the door," using it as an excuse to bring in evidence about the lineup and repeatedly arguing that it had been "fair," when in fact it had been illegal. Source: Mark Arax, "A Long, Bitter Wait for Freedom Ends," *Los Angeles Times*, October 30, 1994; "Conviction Overturned," *Bakersfield Californian*, July 29, 1994; and *Tomlin vs. Myers*, 30 F. 3d 1235 (9th Cir. 1994).

34. Commenting on the conduct of police and prosecutor in the case, Justice Alex Kozinski wrote for the 2-to-1 majority, "We're quite troubled by the prosecutor's actions. . . . The government's behavior here, in the face of its own initial culpability in conducting an illegal line-up, and doing nothing to later correct the error, pushes hard on the limits of acceptable [argument]." Kozinski also noted that Tomlin's original defense attorney was led by the prosecution to believe that the teenaged middleman to the fateful drug deal—the person who supposedly wrote the Treetop note—would testify against Tomlin if the attorney successfully challenged Leticia

Mendez's identification. This turned out to be false. Source: *Tomlin vs. Myers.*

35. Steve E. Swenson, "Jury finds man innocent of murder," *Bakersfield Californian*, May 15, 1993.

36. Jagels' second in command, Stephen Tauzer, told a news reporter that his office had filed charges against people without sufficient evidence, hoping that the pressure of being prosecuted would lead to confessions or other breaks in the case—a practice universally recognized as an abuse of power. The senior prosecutor also lamented the fact that this practice had come to an end because of the flap over the satanic cases. "We're just not going to file the charges if we can't prosecute it. As bad as it sounds, the philosophy now is we don't file charges if we can't go all the way in the courtroom." Source: Michael Trihey, "Molestation filings decline," *Bakersfield Californian*, September 29, 1986.

37. Hubert Humphrey III, "Report on Scott County Investigations," Minnesota Attorney General's Office, February 1985.

38. Author's interview with Andrew Gindes; and Gindes, *Crimes Against Children.*

39. One of these senior prosecutors, Sara Ryals, who years later was said (by Kate Rosenlieb, at least) to be hesitant about charging Pat Dunn, wrote a memo to DA Ed Jagels complaining that colleagues in the office were guilty of "indiscriminate, uninvestigated filing of charges." She also stated she would never have a child alone in her office again because of the risks of false accusations from the "ring" children. Ryals was one of the law-enforcement officials eventually accused by one of the Nokes ring victims. Source: John K. Van de Kamp, California Attorney General, "Report on the Kern County Child Abuse Investigation," September 1996, supplementary reports and data (May 7, 1986, interview of Deputy DA Sara Ryals by Special Agent Jack Richards and Special Agent Michiel Hyder, California Department of Justice).

40. John K. Van de Kamp, California Attorney General, "Report on the Kern County Child Abuse Investigation," September 1986, supplementary reports and data (April 22, 1986, interview of Supervising Deputy DA T. Daniel Sparks and Supervising Deputy DA Stephen Tauzer by Special Agent Jack

Richards and Special Agent Michiel Hyder, California Department of Justice).

41. Final Report of the 1985–1986 Kern County Grand Jury, Carleen A. Radanovich, foreman, released July 2, 1986. The report condemned a "presumption of guilt" assumed by county officials in their pursuit of molestation-ring suspects, and found that, instead of relying upon legally acceptable evidence, social workers and investigators were removing children from homes, denying family visitations, and arresting parents based on nothing more than "gut feeling." The report also alleged that "guilt by association was sufficient to bring charges against individuals," even while investigators and prosecutors ignored medical evidence that some of the victims had not been sexually abused. The grand jury also reported that judges in Kern County had abdicated their responsibility to make an independent review of files and evidence in the ring cases, and had instead blindly followed the recommendations of social workers and prosecutors when deciding whether to remove children from their homes and where children should be placed when in foster care,

The grand jury's concerns had been a matter of public record for many months before the final report was issued. In an August 1, 1985, letter to California Attorney General John Van de Kamp, the grand jury requested an immediate investigation of the handling of child molestation and satanic cult allegations in Kern County. "Our prime concern is the obvious mishandling of the children involved," the grand jury foreman wrote. " . . . In addition, the arbitrary arrest and release of accused parents, with no charges filed, have become prevalent." The attorney general's review was nearly complete by the time the grand jury report was issued. Official reaction to the grand jury report was less than favorable. Sheriff Larry Kleier, who was singled out for criticism by the grand jury, scoffed at the detailed report signed by the panel's nineteen members. He characterized it as the result of a grudge against the sheriff's department held by the grand jury foreman over an incident in which a sheriff's department dog allegedly bit the foreman's daughter. (Jim Steinberg, "Children 'in limbo,' report says: Kern grand jury criticizes molest case," *Fresno Bee*, July 3, 1986.)

42. Cynthia Cheski, "Grand jury gets 19 all-new members: Outgoing forewoman assails judge for not retaining current pan-

elists," *Bakersfield Californian*, July 3, 1986; and Michael Trihey, "Ex-grand jurors fear muzzling of new panel," *Bakersfield Californian*, July 6, 1986. The departing grand jury foreman, Carleen Radanovich, reacted to the decision by Judge Friedman not to retain some hold-overs on the new grand jury panel, a past tradition intended to provide continuity, by alleging, "Government doesn't want government checked out. Citizens do." Judge Friedman said he merely wanted to bring "more diversity" to the grand jury by appointing, in addition to Gindes' wife, the retired former chief investigator for the district attorney's office, the mother of a deputy sheriff, and, for the panel's foreman, a retired police captain.

43. Van de Kamp, "Report on the Kern County Child Abuse Investigation."

44. "In the matter of [Kevin] Nokes, a minor," Kern County Superior Court Case 58875, transcript of proceedings before Judge Robert Baca, July 1, 1986.

45. *People vs. Pitts*, 223 Cal. App 3d 606 (1990). Unlike most court opinions that criticize prosecutors for misconduct, this decision was certified for publication—and took the almost unheard-of step of naming the offending prosecutors in the opinion, a public "shaming" that can have devastating effects on lawyers' careers. In the opinion, both Gindes and his co-prosecutor at trial, Michael Vendrasco, were faulted for misconduct by the appeals court. But Vendrasco's improprieties were termed "fairly isolated," while the court wrote that "Gindes' behavior . . . can only be termed gross misconduct." Of the two prosecutors, only Gindes was reported by the court to the state bar association for further investigation and possible discipline for his misconduct. (The presiding judge of the appeals court recommended disbarment, but no disciplinary action was ever taken by the bar against Gindes.) The court also wrote: "Interspersed throughout trial, to an extent this court has never before seen, were comments by one or both prosecutors which disparaged defense counsel; questioned their tactics, competence, and/or ethics; accused them of wasting time; etc. We have reviewed the entire record and have identified instances too numerous to chronicle where misconduct clearly or arguably occurred. Thus, the examples we set forth herein, while necessitating extensive quotes from the record, should not be viewed as iso-

lated conduct, but as representative samples of what occurred. To set forth all of the misconduct would literally take many hundreds of pages."

It should be noted that prosecutorial misconduct in the courtroom was only one of many grounds of appeal cited by the Pitts defendants. Other grounds cited included the coercive and suggestive questioning of children by the authorities; the use of improper and false medical evidence; the withholding of evidence that would prove the defendants' innocence; and Gindes' successful argument to prevent defense experts from examining the child victims because more exams would be too traumatic—an argument he advanced even as his office secretly arranged re-examinations by a prosecution expert. The appeals court never considered these other grounds, however. Once the courtroom misconduct was found to have occurred and to have rendered the Pitts trial unfair, the court did not examine the other grounds—the case was over.

Gindes, who left the district attorney's office after the opinion in the Pitts case, has always denied committing misconduct. He said in an interview with the author that his only interest had been protecting children and punishing molesters, and he asserted that he behaved in exactly the same fashion during the trial of the Kniffens and McCuans in Kern County's first ring case. In reviewing that case, a different panel of judges on the California Court of Appeal found no misconduct on his part (though improprieties in the investigation of that case ultimately were proved). Gindes also suggests he was vindicated when he prevailed in a civil rights suit filed by the Pitts defendants in Kern County Superior Court.

46. Miles Corwin, *Los Angeles Times,* September 10, 1990. "Court Ruling Forces New Look at Sex Abuse Case," "Defendants say they were victims of overzealous investigators and hysteria in Bakersfield area at the time. Prosecutors are confident that convictions will be upheld if a new trial is ordered," read the *Times*'s subtitle. Such confident predictions aside, the Kern County District Attorney later decided not to retry the case, and dismissed all charges.

47. Kelly remains in prison, his appeals denied, serving a sixty-one-year term for seventeen felonies.

48. Hubbard's son, Richie, was interviewed numerous times

over the course of six weeks. During that time, he never mentioned any involvement by his mother, who had been fully cooperating with the investigation and had initially called the police because she had heard that Kelly was under investigation and he had spent time with her son. The sheriff's investigator who finally coaxed Richie into accusing his mother was later accused himself of browbeating and threatening children who failed to confirm his belief that they had been molested—allegedly shouting at them in near-hysterical outbursts, threatening them, and allegedly striking one girl in the mouth. (He denied any such misconduct.)

49. The very same informant used to generate the illegal—and almost certainly fabricated—confession against Duncan also gave birth to the charges against Hubbard. This informant was the first to suggest to sheriff's investigators that Hubbard was involved in the molestations, claiming Duncan had implicated her during one of his "confessions." This was the tip that led investigators to repeatedly ask Richie and the other two child victims whether Hubbard was involved. As in other ring cases, their initial denials were ignored, and the kids eventually agreed with insistent investigators that Hubbard had molested them. But, unlike Duncan, the informant did not testify against Hubbard, leaving her no illegal confession to complain about, despite the information that launched the case being every bit as unreliable.

50. Judge Clarence Westra, "In the Matter of Donna Sue Hubbard, writ of habeas corpus," ruling in the order to show cause from the court of appeals, Kern County Superior Court Case No. 5.5-2738, January 18, 1994.

51. Tom Kertscher, "Molestation hysteria left sad legacy in overzealous Kern County," *Fresno Bee*, September 10, 1995.

52. Author's interview with Andrew Gindes.

53. "Innocence and the Death Penalty: Assessing the Danger of Mistaken Executions," Staff Report of the Subcommittee on Civil and Constitutional Rights, House Judiciary Committee, October 21, 1993; "Justice Revisited: An innocent man is finally freed from Alabama's death row," *Time*, March 15, 1993; "U.S. High Court rejects Alabama sheriff liability," Reuters, June 2, 1997; and "A grant for their thoughts: 2 MacArthur winners have ties to Atlanta," *Atlanta Journal and Constitution*, June 13, 1995. The reaction to the outcome of the case was instructive. McMillian's deter-

mined appeals attorney, Bryan Stevenson, executive director of the Alabama Capital Representation Center, which represents the poor in death cases, received a MacArthur Foundation "genius" grant of $230,000. Around the same time, Congress cut funds to centers like his around the country, making it much harder for indigent defendants like McMillian to prove their innocence. And the Supreme Court dismissed a lawsuit in the case, deciding that county sheriffs were not legally liable in such cases, even when the misconduct is undisputed and extreme, as in McMillian's case. Courts and lawmakers often respond to allegations of prosecutorial misconduct not by placing greater supervision on prosecutors, but by making it harder for defendants to prevail on appeal when they have been victims of misconduct.

54. These cases are: 1992: Sabrina Butler, Mississippi; Jay Smith, Pennsylvania; Federico Macias, Texas; Sonia Jacobs, Florida; John Henry Knapp, Arizona; Muneer Deeb, Texas; Herbert Bassette, Virginia (death sentence commuted to life).
1993: Walter McMillian, Alabama; Gregory Wilhoit, Oklahoma; Thomas R. Merrill, California; Kirk Bloodworth, Maryland; Clarence Smith, Texas; Andrew Lee Mitchell, Texas; Kerry Max Cook, Texas; Andrew Golden, Florida; Gary Gauger, Illinois; Clarence Chance and Benny Powell, California (freed from life sentences); John Demjanjuk (freed from life sentence in Israel because of U.S. prosecutorial misconduct).

See also Appendix B.

55. There is no reliable or complete source of data on the total number of individuals released from prosecution or prison due to official misconduct. Primarily through press reports and reported federal appellate decisions, the author has been able to identify more than one hundred major felony cases around the country that were undone by prosecutorial misconduct between the time of Sandy Dunn's disappearance and Pat Dunn's sentencing, a twelve-month period (July 1992-June 1993). Of course, this represents only a tiny fraction of the nation's felony convictions in this period, most of which were untainted and fairly won, with the attendant prison sentences richly deserved and sometimes all too short. Still, the magnitude of the problem is greater than many in the justice system wish to admit. More than a hundred defendants in a year released from wrongful convictions because of govern-

ment malfeasance is a significant number. These cases represent only a sampling, for they did not include other instances of misconduct litigated solely in state courts, where most appeals die, or those cases in which misconduct may have occurred, but—because they were resolved by guilty pleas—were never appealed at all. There simply are no comprehensive statistics on such cases, and no way to know the magnitude of the problem.

There is no agency that polices or keeps track of prosecutorial misconduct. In many cases, state attorneys general are the only agencies in any position to monitor the conduct of individual district attorneys. But since the role of most states' attorneys general is to litigate appeals on behalf of the DAs—in essence, defending the DAs' work while fighting to uphold criminal convictions—the AGs have a vested interest in minimizing or denying outright the existence of prosecutorial misconduct (hence, a common argument in appeals is that, either the misconduct didn't happen, or if it did happen, it was harmless error). Indeed, when one senior assistant attorney general in California suggested that his office stop defending the molestation-ring convictions in Kern County because of the official conduct in those cases, he was chastised and instructed that the appeals process would continue unabated. Even though the California Attorney General's investigative staff previously had issued a harshly critical report of the Kern County molestation investigation methods, its appellate staff continues to this day to defend the few remaining convictions against any and all appeals, keeping people in prison on the basis of interrogations and testimony deemed unreliable by the attorney general's own investigators.

56. From *Convicted by Juries, Exonerated by Science* (Washington, D.C.: National Institute of Justice, June 1996). According to the report, the advent of DNA testing has, since 1992, led to the reversal of at least twenty-eight wrongful rape convictions, in which men served an average of seven years in prison for crimes they did not commit. Of these twenty-eight cases, a majority involved erroneous eyewitness identification; eight—29 percent—involved misconduct by police or prosecutors.

57. *U.S. vs. Kojayan*, 8 F. 3d 1315 (9th Cir. 1993). Among other cases quoted, Kozinski turned to the late Justice William O. Douglas, known for his vigorous dissents, who wrote in *Donnelly*

vs. DeChristoforo (1974): "The function of the prosecutor under the Federal Constitution is not to tack as many skins of victims as possible to the wall. His function is to vindicate the right of people as expressed in the laws and give those accused of crime a fair trial."

58. Ibid. Nora Manella, the U.S. Attorney for Los Angeles who assumed office after the Kojayan case concluded, took issue with the court's ruling in the case and argued that an error had been blown out of proportion by Kozinski, whom she described as a legal scholar with great insight into the law, but relatively little experience in the practical matters of trying a case in court. She said the prosecutor on the case had been undeservedly vilified and had been devastated by the justice's assault on his professional reputation.

59. At the time, Sinek's boss was acting U.S. Attorney Terry Bower, who left office to prosecute war crimes in the Hague.

60. *Brown vs. Borg*, 951 F.2d 1011 (9th Cir. 1991).

61. Dan Weikel, "When the Prosecutor Is Guilty," *Los Angeles Times*, May 13, 1994; and Michael L. Radelet, Hugo Adam Bedau, and Constance E. Putnam, *In Spite of Innocence: The Ordeal of 400 Americans Wrongly Convicted of Crimes Punishable by Death* (Boston, Mass.: Northeastern University Press, 1992).

62. "Innocence and the Death Penalty: Assessing the Danger of Mistaken Executions."

63. *Herrera vs. Collins*, slip op. No 91-7328 (January 25, 1993).

64. Ibid.

65. *Coleman vs. Thompson*, 504 U.S. 188 (1992); No A-877 (91-8336). "Innocence and the Death Penalty: The Increasing Danger of Executing the Innocent," Death Penalty Information Center, July 1997; "New Clues Fuel a Race with Electrocutioner's Clock," *The New York Times*, May 8, 1992.

66. *Herrera vs. Collins* (1993).

67. *People vs. Dunn*, transcript of proceedings, June 14, 1993. Alternatively, Somers also suggested that even if Unsell was right and there had not been ample time to bury Sandy during the early morning hours of July 1, Pat could simply have stashed the body somewhere else and buried Sandy at a later date. Though this contradicted the theory of the case presented to jurors, it still fit the evidence, the prosecutor argued. However, it raises new questions. Had Somers suggested this theory at trial, the defense could have

poked numerous holes in it. Given Pat's documented activities on the morning after Sandy disappeared, as well as the difficulty in handling a dead body in broad daylight, he would have to have buried her sometime *after* he reported Sandy missing to the sheriff's department. This would have been a needlessly risky venture—why, for instance, didn't he dispose of the body once and for all that first time?

68. In an interview with the author, Somers said he seriously considered trying the case without calling Coble as a witness at all, but then decided to go with him, out of an abundance of caution, fearing that jurors—or the judge—might find insufficient evidence to convict without Coble's eyewitness testimony, however flawed it might be.

69. *People vs. Dunn,* transcript of proceedings, June 14, 1993.

70. Even if Somers did not personally know about the new charges against Coble, as he has since said, the law requires that prosecutors set up procedures for ensuring that law-enforcement officials pass on all relevant information in a criminal case. Claiming prosecutorial ignorance is no defense when favorable evidence is suppressed.

71. *People vs. Coble,* Bakersfield Municipal Court Case BF066673, May 24, 1993. Years later, when asked by the author to explain the case, which was discovered during research for the book, John Somers would say that he had no personal knowledge of it. He said that his inquiries at the DA's office suggested that the report in the court file of Coble being in custody was erroneous, that Coble actually was never arrested, and the arrest warrant request that should have been issued by the DA's office was for some reason never issued. These were innocent mistakes, Somers maintained, though he agreed that, "It does look bad." Somers said these mistakes could create the appearance that Jerry Coble received additional secret consideration in exchange for his testimony, though the prosecutor asserted this was not the case. (Somers, interview with the author.)

PART IV: EPILOGUE

1. *People vs. Rollins,* California Court of Appeal, Fifth Appellate District, unpublished opinion in Case FO18547.

Offord Rollins' appellate attorney, Jim Fahey, a veteran of Kern County appeals though he lives hundreds of miles north in the small town of Arcata, filed a brief detailing a virtual laundry list of prosecutorial misconduct, jury misconduct and judicial error, much of which was adopted as true by the Court of Appeal. The brief accused the prosecutor, Deputy DA Lisa Green, of misconduct for her use of racist stereotypes, improper inquiry into the sex lives of Rollins and other defense witnesses in an effort to attack their characters, inflammatory comments and arguments unsubstantiated by evidence, and inadmissible and irrelevant—but highly prejudicial—information before the jury (such as hearsay testimony from Maria's sister that "someone" said Offord might have had a gun in his car at one time, or the suggestion, without evidence, that Offord demeaned Maria by letting others watch him use her sexually). Fahey also criticized the judge on the case, Len McGillivray, for condoning and even joining in the prosecutor's excesses by asking embarrassing sexual questions of his own that were irrelevant to the case. In addition, Fahey's brief cited numerous occasions on which Rollins' trial attorney failed to object to possible instances of prosecutorial misconduct and evidentiary errors, even blatant and egregious ones. Finally, Fahey alleged numerous examples of jury misconduct; some of the jurors who found Offord guilty after two days of deliberations were said to have discussed the case outside of court, asked the opinions of others about the case, read news coverage, made up their minds in advance that Offord was guilty, and considered information that was not presented as evidence in the case—all in violation of their oaths as jurors. While agreeing with most of Fahey's points, the appeals court rejected his argument about racist stereotypes, and suggested some improper conduct by the prosecutor may have been the trial judge's fault for permitting the introduction of irrelevant and inflammatory evidence and argument.

2. The appeal in the Rollins case differs in this respect from another improper Kern County murder conviction, the Charles Tomlin case, in which a federal appeals court was bound by the factual determinations of the trial judge who found a key witness's recantation unbelievable. The trial court's determination in the Rollins case that the jury misconduct was harmless did not carry

such weight, because the question was not whether the misconduct occurred—the juror admitted it—but whether it rendered Rollins' trial and conviction unfair. This is a legal, not *factual* question, and thus subject to full review on appeal. At the same time, the appeals court was unable to consider other allegations of jury misconduct, because the Kern County trial judge made a *factual* determination that such misconduct did not occur and that the alternate juror who alleged that it had was not credible. Had the one juror who discussed his knowledge of pesticides with fellow jurors failed to admit it, the trial judge could have declared that it never happened, and Rollins' conviction could well have stood up on appeal because of the rigid rules prosecutors use to protect convictions during the appeals process.

3. The defense testimony on this point seemed more irrefutable than ever, with numerous experts—who normally testified for prosecutors—lined up to argue in favor of Rollins. But, to counter them, Deputy DA Stephen Tauzer shocked the courtroom by announcing that he had newly discovered evidence of pesticide spraying in the area of Maria's murder, something Kern County officials always insisted had never occurred. Now Tauzer claimed to have found a helicopter pilot who recalled spraying pesticides in that area just before the murder—just as the juror in the first trial had claimed. Defense attorney H. A. Sala complained that this late revelation was a fabrication and an example of prosecutorial misconduct, remarks the prosecutor called slanderous. In the end, though, the pilot proved so contradictory, inconsistent, and in conflict with official county records of pesticide use that Tauzer never called him to the stand. The jury heard none of this. It was also revealed that the pesticide supposedly used, Lorsban, affected mosquitoes, not flies—the witness's information was meaningless.

4. For the second trial, the Rollins family hired H. A. Sala, a combative young attorney with a growing reputation as one of Bakersfield's top defense lawyers, which he was not shy about pointing out to journalists. "This is gonna be a war," Sala declared gleefully, as he hobnobbed with the TV and print reporters milling about outside court during the first day of the trial. "We're taking no prisoners. In Kern County, when you've got an innocent client, there's no other way to try a case."

Sala's opponent, Stephen Tauzer, was a cagey, white-haired veteran of the DA's office, Ed Jagels' second in command, who often stepped in to handle politically sensitive cases. Tauzer had been Jagels' roommate for a time after the DA's divorce years earlier, and he was known to be fiercely devoted to his boss, to the point of harshly criticizing others in the office for anything remotely resembling disloyalty. Tauzer also had a reputation as one of the most able trial lawyers in the office, and for that he had been assigned to attempt to preserve the satanic-molestation cases before they self-destructed years before. (He had fought to keep secret the thousands of pages of investigative reports from the state attorney general documenting the errors and abuses of the ring investigations; when he lost this battle, he began cutting deals and with Jagels' blessing, dismissing charges.) With his laid-back, soothing demeanor and easy, jowly grin, Tauzer provided a perfect foil to Sala's hyperactive, hyperaggressive courtroom truculence. Tauzer had a rumpled, relaxed, country-boy persona that seemed to lull entire courtrooms as he continually poked fun at his own supposed failings, laughing aloud at his inability to find the right piece of paper in the stack of files at the prosecution table, or at his failure to master new courtroom technologies—in particular, the compact video disk player used to present evidence photos. Throughout the long trial, Tauzer always seemed to be hitting the wrong button on the machine's remote control, though every time he did, somehow the same image invariably materialized in front of the jury: a coroner's photo of Maria's bloody, battered corpse. Tauzer's apparent discomfort with the new machine, on at least four different occasions, ended up putting in front of the jury that same gruesome photo of a young woman senselessly murdered, an image that would make anyone with a heart anxious to punish the offender. Sala never quite decided if this was an accident or not.

On virtually every other point, however, the two lawyers fought constantly and bitterly, hurling accusations of misconduct, concealing evidence, or putting perjuring witnesses on the stand. Sometimes their attacks degenerated into name-calling ("Liar" and "ethically challenged" were two favorites).

5. Information about a possible alternative suspect developed along an unusual and twisting trail. Before the second trial, while Rollins waited out his appeal, the NBC television news show

Dateline brought new controversy to the case, with a February 15, 1995, report questioning Offord's guilt and featuring an interview with a new witness, an incarcerated car thief named Esther Jean Smith. Smith told *Dateline* she had been a friend of Maria Rodriguez and that they were together on August 2, 1991—the day of Maria's murder—until about 4:30 that afternoon. At that time, according to Smith, as the two young women talked in a park, a light-skinned man—not Offord Rollins—pulled up, got out of a car and dragged Maria by the arm and by her hair into his car. That was the last time she saw Maria alive, Smith said. She had remained silent about this incident for years out of fear that she would be killed as well, she explained to *Dateline*.

Smith's story, if true, meant the prosecution theory of the case—that Offord killed Maria between 1:00 and 2:30 on the afternoon of August 2—was wrong. Given Offord's alibi witnesses, who swore they could account for his movements after 2:30, Esther Smith's new information suggested Offord was innocent, the *Dateline* report asserted.

But Esther Smith's story contained a fatal error. One day after the broadcast, District Attorney Ed Jagels held a press conference and gleefully produced records placing Smith in the Kern County jail on the day that Maria Rodriguez died, awaiting trial on charges of possession of stolen property and passing a bad check. Jagels's own in-house investigators had talked to Smith and learned she was sure only that she had talked to Maria on "the second of the month"—she was not sure *which* month that had been. She had been heavily abusing cocaine at the time, Jagels explained to reporters, and could have had memory problems as a result. He did not suggest she was lying outright. Instead, Jagels theorized that the incident Esther Smith recalled, in which Maria was dragged into a car by the arm and her hair, might have occurred on July 2, an entire month before the murder. (Source: Marc Benjamin and Rob Walters, "NBC stands by story, despite new facts," *Bakersfield Californian*, February 18, 1995.)

The district attorney took great delight in skewering the national news show for failing to check on Esther Smith's whereabouts at the time of Maria's murder. And *Dateline* presented an easy target: Two years before the Rollins/Smith story, the show had suffered credibility problems over a report in which it charged that the fuel tanks on certain General Motors trucks exploded during crashes. *Dateline* had illustrated the problem by planting incendiary devices on the trucks to make them explode on cue, but allowed viewers to assume these explosions were spontaneous. *Dateline*'s anchor later apologized on air to the automaker, and NBC paid $2 million in damages. "It would appear . . . this television news show learned relatively little from its General Motors experience," Jagels dryly observed at his press conference.

The Smith debacle effectively destroyed the credibility of every other point raised in the *Dateline* piece, even the completely valid ones, such as the insistence of the young man who discovered Maria's body that the blood at the scene was wet. Wet blood would have been impossible had Maria died in the sunny, hot early afternoon, as the prosecution insisted.

More interesting, though, was what *Dateline* failed to report: Esther Jean Smith knew the first name of the man whom she saw drag Maria away. She said it was "Victor." This was potentially stunning new evidence. A man named Victor Perez had lived with the Rodriguez family and, moreover, had a history of domesticviolence allegations involving Maria's sister. Maria feared him, too, according to a friend and a teacher, and it was Victor Perez who had provided police with the incorrect information about Offord Rollins that had first made him a suspect. At the first trial, even without Esther Jean Smith's information, Rollins' original attorney had wanted to offer Perez up as an alternative suspect in the case, but had been barred from doing so. Yet when the *Dateline* story appeared, the Kern County district attorney put a new spin on questions about Perez. It was reported that the DA had "explored" him as a potential suspect, but rejected the possibility because he had an alibi.

This was, however, not true: Kern County authorities never investigated Victor as a potential suspect in Maria Rodriguez's murder. Indeed, during Offord Rollins' trial, the DA fought hard to keep Perez from even being named by the defense as a potential suspect, claiming that he was with Maria's mother at the time of the murder, and therefore had an ironclad alibi. But this was not true, either. Maria's mother, Miriam Rodriguez would swear during the second trial that she was out searching the streets for her missing daughter—alone. She could not provide any alibi for Perez.

The press and Rollins' lawyers seemed to miss the true significance of Esther Smith's recollections, so preoccupied was everyone with the fact that she had been wrong about the date of her last day with Maria. No matter what day the incident happened, Esther Smith remained adamant that the rest of her story was true, and Ed Jagels conceded as much. Whether it happened a few days before Maria died, or a month before, Esther Smith could provide eyewitness testimony to a violent confrontation between Maria and someone with first name Victor not long before the murder. In the hands of Rollins' defense lawyer, this information could be used to suggest that Kern County pursued the wrong suspect from the very beginning. But Rollins' second attorney, H. A. Sala, was unaware of this chain of events. As soon as Rollins' conviction was overturned on appeal and a second trial granted, Sala rejected any defense that attempted to implicate someone else in the murder of Maria Rodriguez. Apparently Sala believed the DA's assertion that Victor Perez had an alibi for the time of the murder. When Offord's family asked him about this avenue of defense, Sala said, "Ain't no way anyone's going to believe the murder victim's mother would lie to protect thue killer." And that was the end of it. He never considered the possibility that the DA had simply been wrong about the alibi. After the second trial and hung jury, Sala realized from Miriam Rodriguez's testimony that there was no alibi, and was prepared to retool the defense to go after an alternative suspect had a third trial been pursued.

6. The appeal in *People vs. Pitts* ring case that led to reversal because of prosecutorial misconduct by Deputy DA Andrew Gindes was decided by a different three-man panel of justices at the California Court of Appeal's Fifth District than the group of judges who denied the initial Kniffen-McCuan appeal two months later.

7. The original trial judge, Marvin Ferguson, who normally would have conducted the hearing, had died, and the defense feared the case was being sent deliberately to the most hostile judges in Bakersfield. First it went to Gary Friedman, the judge who was excoriated by the California Court of Appeal in the Pitts molestation-ring case for allowing rampant prosecutorial misconduct and for his biased and incorrect rulings. Friedman recused himself from the case. Next, Judge Len McGillivray, in the midst of the Offord Rollins retrial, was assigned to hear the

matter, but he stepped down because of his history as a former prosecutor, and because his brother was the assistant DA who could be heard on the now-notorious taped interviews of Brian and Brandon Kniffen that the defense deemed coercive. Following McGillivray, the case went to Judge Kenneth Twisselman, who had earlier refused to hold a hearing in the case despite the Court of Appeal ruling authorizing one. Twisselman left the case in a fury after defense lawyers accused him of bias and of making rulings both ignorant of the law and the case—criticisms he denied and termed "impertinent, scandalous, insulting and contemptuous." That, he said, left him too outraged to be fair to the defense.

8. The Kniffen-McCuan petition for habeas corpus listed ten separate issues that the defense believed warranted granting a new trial:

1. The failure of the original trial court to unseal Mary Ann Barbour's mental-health records, which the defense sought in order to prove that Barbour fantasized the molestation allegations and pressured Jenny and Jane McCuan into repeating them. (The same records were released to other ring defendants, whose cases subsequently were dismissed.)

2. Failure to provide exculpatory evidence, including information contained in hidden tapes or destroyed tapes of child interviews, and inaccurate police reports that masked the coercive questioning methods used with the child victims.

3. Failure of the Kern County District Attorney's Office to recuse itself because of bias and because the DA had taken legal custody of the children at one point, creating a conflict of interest.

4. Intimidation of defense witnesses.

5. Appointment of attorneys to represent the children who were agents of the prosecution rather than independent representatives of the children's best interest (one such attorney wrote letters to relatives of the Kniffens containing thinly veiled suggestions that they should commit suicide for their "crimes").

6. The DA's failure to disclose evidence that the McCuan girls had made satanic allegations.
7. The fact that investigators and DA employees were improperly trained to investigate sex crimes involving children.
8. False medical evidence.
9. Coercive and suggestive interviews of child witnesses.
10. The use of confabulated testimony from the children.

9. The defense failed to prove that the DA had hidden or destroyed tape-recorded interviews with the children, the judge ruled, marking yet another victory for the prosecution. Neither Steubbe—nor the defense team—heard from the original Kniffen prosecutor, Medalyian Grady. In an interview with the author, however, Grady recalled taping virtually every significant conversation with Jenny and Jane McCuan. The tapes were never turned over to the defense, as required by law—apparent proof that evidence had indeed been withheld in the case. (Later, in 1998, evidence surfaced that yet another crucial tape that would have aided a defendant in the Cox molestation ring had been kept secret—and that Kern County officials allegedly perjured themselves about its existence.)

10. "These interviewers had one hypothesis, it seems—that these children had been abused," Professor Maggie Bruck, a pioneering researcher in the field of the reliability of children's testimony, swore during the habeas hearing. "There was no chance for these children to deny being abused. . . . Through the use of bribes . . . threats . . . playing one child off the other . . . you can get children to make statements of things that never happened. And those statements can be quite damaging."

Bruck is an associate professor of pediatrics at McGill University in Montreal, and the coauthor of *Jeopardy in the Courtroom* (New York: American Psychological Association, 1995). Judge Steubbe, in an interview with the author, called her one of the most impressive witnesses in the case, citing her catalog of research proving that the prosecutors and investigators had pursued their case in exactly the wrong way. It wasn't that Bruck could prove that the children had lied about everything—if she had said that, Steubbe likely would have considered her biased and disregarded virtually everything she said. Instead, Bruck merely said that the testimony of the children was unreliable, that no one could know truth from fiction in it. And she knew this to be so because she could take virtually any group of normal children and, over the course of one or more interviews, persuade them that they had been harmed by someone they had never met.

11. Sandra M. Snyder, United States Magistrate, "Finding and Recommendation," *Howard Weimer vs. William Duncan*, United States District Court for the Eastern District of California Case CV-F 95-5411. The case was yet another victory in Kern County for the Portland, Oregon, attorney Michael Snedeker, who represented the Kniffens, Donna Sue Hubbard and the Pitts defendants on appeal, and who coauthored the book *Satan's Silence* to chronicle similar such cases.

12. Jonathan Nelson, "Ex-foster dad leaves prison," *Bakersfield Californian*, January 7, 1998.

13. Stanley Simrin, "Points and Authorities in Support of Motion to Add Claim of Governmental Misconduct," and attached transcripts, In re Jeffrey B. Modahl on Habeas Corpus, Kern County Superior Court Case HC5752; and the author's interviews with Stan Simrin and Deputy DA Craig Phillips.

14. Ibid; and the author's interview with Stan Simrin.

15. Ibid.

16. Author's interview with Craig Phillips. Phillips, in the interview with the author, said that he acted ethically in the Modahl case, provided the tape recording to the defense as soon as he learned of its existence from Deputy Connie Ericsson, and still believes Carla's testimony at trial. He described her reluctance to testify against her father in the 1986 trial—not because the accusations were untrue, but because the girl felt bad about causing her father to be in trouble. In the end, she testified only because her grandmother—Modahl's mother—told her to go in and tell the truth, no matter what happened, Phillips recalled. He also pointed out that he had nothing to do with any of the discredited and successfully appealed molestation-ring prosecutions in Kern County, and that alone among the ring cases, his is the only one to hold up over the years. Indeed, two defendants who successfully appealed

their convictions and won the right to new trials—Richard Alan Cox and Ruth Ann Taylor—subsequently pleaded guilty anyway, albeit to lesser sentences (twelve and six years apiece, respectively). Phillips said he does not know personally if improprieties occurred in other Kern County ring cases, and he offered no opinion on the rationale employed by appeals courts to reverse them. "I had nothing to do with those cases," he said. "I was one of the outsiders back then. I only know what I did in this case."

17. Laura Mecoy, "Backlash Builds Over Abuse Claims," *San Jose Mercury News*, June 13, 1994; Ofra Bikel, "Innocence Lost: The Plea," *Frontline*, broadcast May 27, 1997, and its internet edition, "Other Well-Known Cases," at www.pbs.org/wgbh/pages/frontline/shows/innocence/etc/other.html; and San Diego County Grand Jury for 1991–92, "Child Sexual Abuse, Assault, and Molest Issues."

18. Bikel, "Innocence Lost: The Plea," Nathan and Snedeker, "Satan's Silence," Editorial, "'The Little Rascals Case,'" *The Washington Post*, May 24, 1997; Estes Thompson, "'Rascals' scandal ends," *Philadelphia Daily News*, May 24, 1997.

19. Alison Fitzgerald, "Verdicts voided in another child molestation case," *The Philadelphia Inquirer*, June 13, 1998; Dorothy Rabinowitz, "A Darkness in Massachusetts II," *The Wall Street Journal*, January 30, 1995; Rabinowitz, "A Darkness in Massachusetts II," *The Wall Street Journal*, March 14, 1995; Ruling granting a new trial, *Commonwealth of Massachusetts vs. Cheryl Amirault Lefave*, Middlesex ss., Criminal Action 85-63 and related cases, Judge Isaac Borenstein, June 12, 1998.

20. Kenneth Lanning, head of the FBI's Behavior Sciences Unit, conducted an extensive study of allegations of satanic abuse and satanic conspiracies that were alleged in communities around the country, including Kern County's hysteria in the mid-eighties. He turned up no evidence to support any of the allegations, and much to disprove them. Among other things, he found that epidemics of satanic-abuse allegations would often follow conferences at which social workers and therapists were exposed to a "survivor" or other speaker on the subject. Such was the case in Kern County, San Diego and numerous other communities where similar cases erupted in the mid-eighties and early nineties. (Kenneth V. Lanning, "Investigator's Guide to Allegations of 'Ritual' Child

Abuse," Behavioral Sciences Unit, National Center for the Analysis of Violent Crime, Federal Bureau of Investigation, Quantico, VA [1992].)

21. According to a U.S. Justice Department report on innocent men and women convicted wrongfully then later freed from prison through DNA testing ("Convicted by Juries, Exonerated by Science," June 1996), Zain posed a remarkable menace to the justice system:

> A special commission convened by order of the West Virginia Supreme Court of Appeals investigated Zain and the West Virginia State Police Crime Laboratory. As a result of this investigation, the State Supreme Court ruled that none of the testimony given by Zain in more than 130 cases was credible. The court further ordered that Zain be indicted for perjury. It is sobering to reflect that but for the adventitious appearance of DNA typing.... Fred Zain might still be sending innocent persons to prison.

The West Virginia court also concluded that Zain's "supervisors may have ignored or concealed complaints of his misconduct." Zain was tried for perjury in West Virginia but acquitted. He described himself as a "scapegoat" and his attorney said that Zain had been ruined by a "witch hunt." However, a county in Texas where Zain's work also led to allegations of perjury had to pay an $850,000 settlement to two wrongfully convicted men, while West Virginia has paid more than $2 million in such settlements.

22. Dan Weikel, "When the Prosecutor Is Guilty," *Los Angeles Times*, May 13, 1994.

23. *Wang Zong Xiao vs. Reno*, 81 F.3d 808 (9th Cir. 1996). The U.S. Court of Appeals for the Ninth Circuit affirmed the district court's decision that "United States officials and prosecutors engaged in an extraordinary pattern of misconduct that violated the Fifth Amendment due-process rights of Wang Zong Xiao, a prosecution witness brought to the United States to testify falsely. ... The government's actions forced Wang to make a Hobson's

choice: whether to abide by his oath in the American court to tell the truth on the witness stand, and thereby face near certain execution in the PRC [People's Republic of China], or to lie under oath in the American court and receive leniency in the PRC." The court also found gross prosecutorial misconduct because the U.S. Attorney knew Wang's statements had been coerced through torture, and were therefore possessed of little credibility, yet did not inform the defense in the Goldfish case, as required by law. The appeals court also expressed disgust with the "callous" technical argument advanced by the U.S. government in its attempt to overturn Judge Orrick's decison to dismiss the case. Prosecutors did not challenge the judge's conclusion that they acted with gross negligence and deliberate indifference to Wang's rights and well-being, but that the government "has no constitutional duty to protect a witness from harm stemming from his or her testimony that may occur after the witness is released from the government's custody." The appeals court ridiculed this position, finding that federal prosecutors had a duty to protect their witness once "the government placed Wang in danger of violating his own conscience and the federal perjury statute, or of facing torture and possible execution in China."

24. Mike Stanton, "DiPrete Charge Dismissed," *Providence Journal-Bulletin*, March 12, 1997, and Tracy Breton, "Justices Explain DiPrete Decision," *Providence Journal-Bulletin*, May 2, 1998.

25. Lancaster County Judge Lawrence Stengel, who convicted Lambert in 1992 in a court trial without a jury, found no reason to overturn the conviction when presented with the same evidence Judge Dalzell had found so horrendous. That evidence included the fact that one of the key pieces of testimony used against Lambert—a supposed dying declaration from the murder victim, sixteen-year-old Laurie Snow, that "Michelle did it"—was probably false because Snow's throat and vocal cords had been slashed too badly by her assailant. The medical expert who had reached that opinion before Lambert's trial had been intimidated into changing his views when prosecutors threatened to cut off lucrative county contracts the expert had been receiving, Dalzell found. Lambert's motive for murder was said to be her jealousy of Snow, who had dated Lambert's boyfriend, Lawrence Yunkin.

26. "Innocence and the Death Penalty: The Increasing Danger of Executing the Innocent," Death Penalty Information Center, Washington, D.C., July 1997 (with February 24, 1998, update). See also Appendix B for a list of cases.

27. Ibid.

28. Ibid. The report states:

> The danger that innocent people will be executed because of errors in the criminal justice system is getting worse. . . . The average time spent on death row before release [because of innocence] is about seven years. This length of time is important because both state and federal legislation in recent years will shorten the length of time death-row inmates have before their execution. Currently, the average time between sentencing and execution is eight years. If that time is cut in half, then the typical innocent defendant on death row will be executed before it is discovered that a fatal mistake has been made.

The report also calculates that between 1973 and 1993, there was an average of 2.5 people released from death row every year because they were found innocent. From 1993 through July 1998, that rate nearly doubled to 4.8 a year.

29. *News at Sunrise*, Channel 17-TV, Bakersfield, March 4, 1999. Jagels' response to *Mean Justice* consisted mostly of generalized comments and personal attacks; a number of his statements were inaccurate. In this interview and others, for example, Jagels repeatedly—and incorrectly—denounced the author for being from Los Angeles, suggesting that a journalist from the nation's second largest city could never understand or accept the wholesome and conservative values Jagels claimed to champion in his community. (For the record, the author lives, not in Los Angeles, but in a Southern California town much smaller than Bakersfield.) The District Attorney also told reporters he was surprised by the points raised in the book, when in fact he and others in his office had been notified by letter of those points more than a year before publication and had declined to respond. He also asserted—

incorrectly—that his office had evidence in hand that corroborated the details of Jerry Coble's testimony before agreeing to offer him a plea bargain.

30. *News at Five,* Channel 17-TV, Bakersfield, March 4, 1999.

31. Danny Dunn was arrested on February 18, 1999, and died the following morning—the official publication date of *Mean Justice.* The Bakersfield print and broadcast media had extensively reported on the book and the surrounding controversy during the previous five days. The account of Danny Dunn's arrest, incarceration, struggle with jail officers and death is drawn from the following documents: "Public Intoxication Arrest," Bakersfield Police Department Report 99-06720, February 18, 1999; "Special News Release," April 1999, Kern County Sheriff's Department; "Report of Autopsy," Case C-0310-99, Decedent: Daniel Anthony Dunn, by Dr. Donna L. Brown, forensic pathologist for the Kern County Sheriff-Coroner; and "Supplemental Report," Kern County Sheriff's Case SR99-04717, February 22, 1999, by Detective J. C. Plank, reviewed by Sheriff's Sergeant Glenn Johnson, with attached reports by the jail officers involved in Danny Dunn's death.

32. From the author's interviews with Nancy Dunn and her attorney, James L. Faulkner, who obtained the X-rays and had radiologists compare the two. It is unclear how and when the rib was broken—sheriff's reports quote one witness who believed Danny fell down the stairs before the police arrived. It is possible the rib was broken then, rather than in the jail; however, the severe liver laceration, which caused Danny Dunn to bleed to death in a matter of minutes, had to have occurred during the struggle in the jail.

33. From the author's interviews with Rex Martin and former Bakersfield Police Chief Robert Patterson.

34. Marie Gates, interviews with the author.

35. Ibid.

Wrongful Prosecutions in Kern County

Case	Suspected[1]	Charged	Convicted	Upheld	Remain in Prison	Comments
Molestations Rings						
Kniffen-McCuan April 1982–August 1996	10	10	4	0	0	The first of the molestation "ring" cases that swept the nation in the eighties; virtually all were based on incredible, sometimes disprovable allegations generally unsupported by physical evidence. Denials and recantations by "victims" were ignored and disbelieved, but the wildest allegations were accepted as fact by the police and prosecutors. After fourteen years, all four defendants were exonerated and set free because prosecutors, police, and social workers coerced children into making false accusations. Case also relied on discredited medical testimony. One of several Kern County cases to become models of how *not* to investigate child abuse.
Hubbard February 1984–August 1995	3	3	3	1	1	One defendant freed after four years because of illegal interrogations by the sheriff, another

Case	Suspected[1]	Charged	Convicted	Upheld	Remain in Prison	Comments
						after ten years because authorities coerced children into making false accusations. The third defendant—a lone molester who had nothing to do with any ring—remains in prison.
Nokes June 1984–January 1987	10–20	7	3[2]	0	0	First molestation-ring case to produce satanic-ritual abuse allegations. Prosecutors hid evidence, coerced witnesses, refused to allow medical exams of victims. After defendants spend two years in jail, five hundred charges dismissed in wake of report on investigative and prosecutorial errors.
Satanic case 1984–1986	85–150	18[3]	0	0	0	Year-long probe into ritual abuse created hysteria despite no evidence and much to disprove case. Children coerced, crucial information kept hidden by prosecutors, and Kern County ended up excoriated by grand jury, and state attorney general. Case became another example of how not to investigate child abuse.
Pitts June 1984–September 1990	9	9	7	0	0	Massive prison sentences overturned after five years because of gross prosecutorial misconduct.

Case	Suspected[1]	Charged	Convicted	Upheld	Remain in Prison	Comments
Stoll June 1984– July 1998 (ongoing)	4	4	4	2	2	Two in "ring" granted new trials because favorable psychological testimony was barred from first trials. Kern County declined to retry them, as same concerns about coerced testimony, bogus medical evidence infect this case. Other two defendants failed to preserve appeal, remain in prison; habeas hearing pending for one.
Wong August 1984– July 1985	5	5	3[4]	0	0	Coerced testimony and disprovable satanic allegations lead to dismissals.
Cox October 1984– July 1998 (ongoing)	8	8	7	5	4	Some charges dismissed, two defendants set free. Most of "ring" remain in prison despite recantations of victims and concerns about coercion and erroneous medical evidence. Habeas hearing pending on government perjury and hidden evidence.
Forsythe January 1985–1986	8	8	7[5]	0	0	Allegations of ring that preyed on sixteen children dismissed in wake of other ring-case revelations about coercion.

Case	Suspected[1]	Charged	Convicted	Upheld	Remain in Prison	Comments
Other ring-era molestation cases, 1983–1986	32	12	2	0	0	Twenty-one children removed from parents. Allegations later disproven.
Ring totals:	174–249	84[6]	39[7]	8[8]	7	
Other Cases						
Stallion Springs (drug) 1991–1992	4	4	4	0	0	Illegal search by Kern County Sheriff led to dismissal of case.
Offord Rollins (murder) 1992–1996	1	1	1	0	0	Track star's murder conviction overturned because of jury misconduct, prosecutorial misconduct, and judicial errors.
Flody Gore (murder) 1992–1994	1	1	1	0	1	Double murderer given new trial because prosecutor exluded Hispanic jurors. Retried and convicted.
Sergio Venegas (rape) 1992–1998	1	1	1	0	0	Rape conviction and sixty-five-year sentence overturned because prosecution DNA evidence overstated likelihood of guilt.
Charles Tomlin (murder) 1978–1994	1	1	1	0	0	Freed after sixteen years because of defense attorney incompetence and prosecutor's reliance on faulty and illegal eyewitness identification.

Case	Suspected[1]	Charged	Convicted	Upheld	Remain in Prison	Comments
Encarnacion Barrientos (murder) 1995–July 1998 (ongoing)	1	1	1	0	1	Prosecutor introduces improper hearsay testimony that impugns defendant, requiring new trial.
Rosales Meza (murder) 1993–1994	1	1	0	0	0	Detective (John Soliz, investigated Pat Dunn) arrests wrong man, neglects to check fingerprint evidence.
Christopher Ridge (auto theft) 1995	1	1	1	0	0	Conviction overturned because prosecution relied upon evidence from illegal search.
Carl Hogan (murder) 1978–1994	1	1	1	0[9]	—	Double-murder conviction reversed because sheriff's detectives coerced a confession. Retried and convicted again. Died in prison with new appeal planned.
Michael Denney (murder) 1980–1986	1	1	1	0	1	Robbery-murder conviction overturned because confession obtained by sheriff's department through threats, coercion, and after ignoring suspect's demands for attorney.

Case	Suspected[1]	Charged	Convicted	Upheld	Remain in Prison	Comments
Melvin Hayes (drug) 1984–1988	1	1	1	0	0	Eight-year prison term overturned when sheriff's department improperly attempts to use defendant to bust his own attorney, then reneges on deal when defendant can't deliver.
Calvin Howard (grand theft) 1983–1984	1	1	1	0	0	Four-year prison term overturned because prosecutors introduced evidence obtained through illegal search.
Jarnail Singh Jaspal (murder) 1984–1991	1	1	1	0	0	Life sentence overturned because prosecutor and judge introduced improper evidence suggesting that the defendant's decision to exercise his right to remain silent at an extradition hearing proved his "consciousness of guilt."
Marie Haven/ George Curtis (murder) 1998	2	2	0	0	0	In a case investigated by Sheriff's Detective John Soliz, the principal investigator in the Dunn case, two prison guards, Marie Haven and George Curtis, are charged with the murder of Haven's ex-husband for insurance money. As in the Dunn case, this prosecution relied upon an informant with severe credibility problems (witness, for example, admitted on the stand

Case	Suspected[1]	Charged	Convicted	Upheld	Remain in Prison	Comments
Pat Dunn (murder) 1992–July 1998 (ongoing)	1	1	1	1	1	that she lied in this and other cases). In another parallel to the Dunn case, Soliz said that he suspected Haven because she began asking about insurance money shortly after the murder, trying to get $10,000. Soliz disregarded the fact that the family needed the money to pay for the funeral. After 100 days in jail, both defendants were released with all charges dropped for lack of evidence, their jobs and homes lost. Evidence that would discredit key witness never given to defense; other crucial information never disclosed. Initial appeals lost, new habeas plea pending.
Total nonring cases:	19	19	16	1	3	
GRAND TOTAL	193–269	103	55	9	10	

1. Suspects include individuals who were actively investigated and/or arrested.
2. Two of these pleaded guilty to a single count in exchange for the dismissal of over a hundred felonies and no jail time.

3. Referred by sheriff's department to district attorney for prosecution, but never formally indicted.
4. Defendants allowed to plead to greatly reduced charges.
5. Defendants allowed to plead to greatly reduced charges.
6. Includes ten parents who were accused of molestation in civil proceedings that led to removal of their children, but not criminal prosecution.
7. Twelve of these defendants were convicted of minor charges resulting in no incarceration after they agreed to plead guilty in exchange for the dismissal of hundreds of counts against them.
8. Does not include minor charges that led to no jail time and therefore were never appealed.
9. Granted new trial; retried and convicted.

APPENDIX B

THE TOLL OF MISCONDUCT

What follows is a sampling of major felony cases arising since 1900 in which prosecutorial and investigative misconduct or negligence led to unjust prosecution, false arrest or wrongful conviction. (Bakersfield and Kern County cases are excluded.) Culled from news articles, appellate opinions and reports of the Justice Department, Congress and the Death Penalty Information Center in Washington, D.C., they represent only a small fraction of such cases. A comprehensive accounting of wrongful convictions linked to official misconduct is not possible, as there is no agency in the country (or at any state level) that monitors ethical and legal violations by prosecutors and police. News articles detail only the most sensational cases, and appellate opinions do not include the vast majority of cases that are never appealed—such as those that end in pleas or dismissals. The extent of the problem, then, is not known. What is known, however, is that during that nine-year span, thirty-eight men and women who had been sentenced to death were found to have been convicted as a result of some sort of official misconduct. Of those thirty-eight, thirty-five were subsequently exonerated and released—innocents nearly executed for crimes they did not commit. Some came within hours of execution.

1990

Clarence Brandley is released after a decade on Texas' death row. Official misconduct in his case occurred at every level, from police officers who threatened witnesses who could attest to Brandley's innocence, to a trial judge and prosecutor who held secret meetings to rehearse objections and rulings, to prosecutors who destroyed evidence proving Brandley's innocence, to a state attorney general who lied about results of a critical witness's lie-detector test. The only reason for Brandley's arrest: the victim of murder and rape had been a white schoolgirl and the likely perpetrator was one of the five janitors at her school, only one of whom—Brandley—was black. The detective who arrested Brandley told him, "Since you're the nigger, you're elected." He came within days of being executed before a last-ditch appeals ruling saved him. All charges were subsequently dropped. A federal judge who examined the case later wrote: "In the thirty years this court has presided over matters in the judicial system, no case has presented a more shocking scenario of the effects of racial prejudice, perjured testimony, witness intimidation, an investigation the outcome of which was predetermined, and public officials who, for whatever motives, lost sight of what is right and just."

Charges in a much-publicized federal effort in Hollywood to crack down on payola in the music industry are dismissed against Joseph Isgro, once the nation's largest independent record promoter. The federal judge making the ruling criticized prosecutors for withholding evidence of Isgro's innocence and lying about it in court. The Justice Department, while admitting the misconduct and reprimanding the prosecutor, nevertheless appealed the dismissal based on a legal technicality and won. The charges were thus reinstated, not because of an absence of serious misconduct, but because the U.S. Supreme Court created new limits on the ability of judges to dismiss cases as punishment of prosecutors for misdeeds. Six years later, after government prosecutors spent another $10 million going after Isgro and he was ruined by legal bills, the charges were dismissed for good because the government had violated his right to a speedy trial.

In one of many rulings that deem grave instances of prosecutorial misconduct "harmless error," murder convictions against Norman Wayne Willhoite and Philip James Syzemore of Sacramento, California, are upheld even though a prosecutor misrepresented the generous plea bargain he gave to an alleged accomplice in the case in order to gain his crucial cooperation. Jurors who decided to believe this witness never knew he had been promised freedom in exchange for his damning testimony. A concurring opinion in the federal appeals-court case—which upheld the conviction—stated, "The prosecutor wanted to deprive the jury and the defendants of information to which they would ordinarily be entitled, i.e., information reflecting on the credibility of a key prosecution witness . . . .This is inconsistent with a system of justice that expects integrity from prosecutors, not cheap tricks designed to skirt clear responsibilities." Nevertheless, the convictions stand, a demonstration of prosecutorial power and the reluctance of the justice system to overturn guilty verdicts, even when tainted by official misconduct.

The headline-grabbing corruption prosecution and conviction of former San Diego Mayor Roger Hedgecock is thrown out when it is revealed that the bailiff in the 1985 trial had assured jurors Hedgecock was guilty, plied them with liquor during deliberations, talked over the evidence with them, partied with them during and after deliberations, and told them that a previous hung jury had failed to do its job by focusing on meaningless details raised by the defense. The bailiff and jurors admitted this gross misconduct to state law-enforcement officials shortly after Hedgecock's conviction. There is no question this misbehavior tainted the case and automatically entitled Hedgecock to a new trial, but prosecutors in San Diego kept this information secret for five years. When the improprieties finally came to light—only after the California Supreme Court compelled prosecutors to divulge the information they had guarded so long—Hedgecock was exonerated. In exchange for his plea to a single misdemeanor, numerous felonies were dismissed. He is now a radio talk-show host.

Dale Johnston, sentenced to death for the murder of his stepdaughter and her fiancé in Ohio, is freed after six years because prosecutors hid evidence that tended to show his innocence. Once he was released, the state dropped charges against him rather than bring him to trial a second time.

The Staff of the Breezy Point Day Care Center in Bucks County, Pennsylvania, was cleared of a massive number of molestation and ritual-abuse allegations because the district attorney for the area, Alan Rubenstein, took the unusual step of reinvestigating the case brought to him for prosecution by a local police department. (Most prosecutorial agencies involved with molestation "ring" cases never conducted an independent investigation.) The insular, suburban community had been consumed by hysteria over the case, which, in startling parallel to Kern County's Witch Hunt, included allegations that three- and four-year-old children had been beaten, locked in cages, forced to eat feces and urine and watch animals being slaughtered while the teacher held the animals' beating hearts. Investigators claimed the children were forced to have sex, cut and stabbed by their abusers, and photographed naked. The original purpose of the district attorney's reinvestigation was to find corroborating evidence for the case, which initially was based entirely on the testimony of children. The children had been subjected to a repeated barrage of suggestive interviews, during which a single allegation from one parent blossomed into hundreds more—a familiar pattern of misconduct in the many molestation-ring cases that have been discredited since they first appeared in the early 1980s. However, rather than finding evidence to support a prosecution, the DA found just the opposite: no evidence of cages (the children, it turned out, were referring to a metal jungle gym in which they played "zoo"); no secret room at Breezy Point, where the children said the ritual abuse had occurred; no remains of sacrificed animals where they were supposed to have been buried; no scars from cuts or stabs on any children; no child pornography; and no medical evidence of molestation. Finally, the expert who in the initial police investigation confirmed that the children had been abused by a pedophile turned out to have no expertise in this field: He was an unemployed plumber. After a year, Rubenstein announced that the charges were baseless and would not be prosecuted further. "We proved that none of this ever happened," he later said. "This wasn't a question of maybe it happened and we just can't prove it. This was conjured up by the hysteria of the parents who bought into this. It never happened."

The infamous McMartin Preschool molestation case against three Manhattan Beach, California, day-care operators ended with the dismissal of all remaining charges, drawing to a close a case that caused a national sensation, panicked hundreds of parents, and ruined the lives of seven men and women who would ultimately be found innocent. The saga began in 1983, when the mentally ill mother of one child at the day-care center leveled accusations of molestation against the son of the center's owner, and the local police department followed up with a "confidential" letter to two hundred parents accusing McMartin of being a hotbed of sex abuse. The letter created predictable hysteria. Coercive and suggestive interviews and counseling sessions with hundreds of children who had attended the day-care center followed, the goal of which was not to find out what happened, but to persuade the children to say they had been molested. Children were rewarded if they agreed there had been abuse, chided for denying it. Pressured and prodded for weeks, the children eventually spoke of torture, child pornography, the mutilation and killing of animals, satanic rituals that included murdering infants and drinking their blood, being buried alive, jumping out of airplanes, digging up bodies at cemeteries and being taken into tunnels and underground rooms at the center to be abused. The children also claimed the owner's son was a witch who could fly and disappear. No evidence to support any of this could ever be found. Though medical evidence of molestation was absent, a doctor hired by the prosecution still concluded 120 kids had been sexually abused. The center was razed in an effort to find the tunnels—there were none. Of the original seven people charged, five had all counts dismissed before trial. Then, after a thirty-three-month, $15 million trial—the longest and costliest in U.S. history—the owner, Peggy McMartin Buckey, was acquitted on all counts, and her son, Ray Buckey, was acquitted on most, with the jury hanging on the rest (all were ultimately dismissed, after Buckey had spent five years in jail). The case was rife with evidence of prosecutorial and investigative misconduct and, though preceded by the Bakersfield ring cases, was the first to come to widespread national attention, stoking hysteria over organized rings of child-abusing devil worshipers. After the trial, jurors said they believed that some of the children might have been molested by someone at the center, but that the suggestive interviews of the victims made it impossible to determine what really happened. Later, a wrongful-arrest lawsuit filed by the Buckeys and others charged in the case was dismissed, not because their allegations of official wrongdoing were disproved, but because California law gives prosecutors, child-protective workers and others involved with the case absolute immunity, even if they are negligent.

Ray Girdler of Prescott, Arizona, wins a new trial in the arson deaths of his wife and child in a home fire. He originally was convicted with false scientific evidence provided by a prosecution expert who found indications of a flammable liquid as the catalyst for the fire at the Girdler home. These indicators were later shown to have been caused by a natural physical effect called "flashover" that has nothing to do with flammable liquids or deliberate arson. In recent years, many other arson convictions have been reopened and overturned because flashover had been erroneously labeled arson by prosecution experts.

The Los Angeles County Grand Jury details a jailhouse "snitch" scandal, in which dozens of criminal convictions are called into question because prosecutors at the Los Angeles County District Attorney's Office relied for years on perjured testimony from informants who fabricated testimony in order to elude their own criminal charges.

A Los Angeles County deputy district attorney resigns rather than face firing for destroying evidence that might have made jurors in a murder case more sympathetic to the defendant.

Prosecutor Christine Gosney, while trying to imprison college student Edward Vasquez in the fatal shooting of a security guard, found a photo of a young child inside a critical piece of evidence in the case—the jacket Vasquez said he was wearing at the time of the murder. Gosney later admitted destroying the picture, inscribed "to my cousin Eddie," because "I did not want the jury to be swayed by sentiment because of some little boy that obviously loved his cousin." Vasquez was acquitted nevertheless because another piece of critical evidence was found stuffed in another pocket of the jacket as jurors were about to deliberate: a moldering burrito. Vasquez claimed all along that, at the time of the 1988 shooting, he was standing some distance away, buying a burrito, a claim that Gosney had disputed.

1991

Jeffrey Jenkins' conviction and prison sentence for possessing an illegal sawed-off shotgun is overturned because prosecutors knowingly used against him a confession that had been obtained through death threats and beatings by police.

Jimmy Lee Horton, sentenced to death for a burglary-murder, receives a new trial because a Georgia prosecutor had systematically kept blacks off the jury (in Horton's and numerous other since-overturned murder cases) and had gone so far as to issue a memo instructing clerks on how to keep blacks and women off juries without getting caught. (Such misconduct is not unique: hundreds of cases around the country have been reversed in recent years because of racially biased jury selection. In 1997, for example, the district attorney's office in Philadelphia was struck by a similar scandal with the public release of a training video instructing prosecutors on how to keep minorities, women and other "undesirables" off juries.)

The conviction of Edward Westerdahl for armed bank robbery is overturned because, an appeals court ruled, prosecutors "distorted the fact-finding process." Federal prosecutors promised immunity to two of Westerdahl's accomplices if they would implicate Westerdahl, but they threatened to prosecute another accomplice in the robbery who told them that Westerdahl was innocent. Fearing for his own liberty, the man then refused to testify on Westerdahl's behalf.

In a highly publicized, high-pressure case, four young men from Tucson, Arizona, are interrogated virtually nonstop for three days by Phoenix authorities until they confess—falsely—to nine murders at a local Buddhist temple. Later, two teenagers unrelated to the four suspects are found in possession of the murder weapons and confess (with little prompting) to carrying out the killings on their own. Although this second pair of confessions is consistent with the facts of the case, while the four initial coerced confessions were not, the Phoenix authorities continue to try to prosecute their original four suspects. Months pass before charges against the "Tucson Four" are finally thrown out. At around the same time, several studies are published that suggest current psychological-warfare techniques used by police interrogators may have increased the frequency of false confessions by innocent men and women.

Gary Nelson is freed after eleven years on death row for the 1978 rape and murder of a six-year-old in Chatham County, Georgia, after it is revealed that his conviction was based on official lies, knowing use of false testimony, the suppression of evidence supporting his claims of innocence, and the hiding of information implicating another man in the crime. There had been no eyewitness or fingerprints linking Nelson to the crime, and a search of his home turned up nothing. To combat these shortcomings, the prosecution manufactured phony scientific evidence linking Nelson to a hair found on the victim's body. The director of the Savannah crime lab said the hair came from Nelson when, in fact, his lab never examined it. Additionally, a police detective swore falsely that Nelson's brother had linked the suspect to the murder weapon. The jury based its conviction largely on this information. Years later, the defense discovered an FBI report finding no link between Nelson and the hair, along with a tape recording of the brother being interviewed by police in which he consistently denied knowing anything about the murder weapon. It was also shown that police covered up an alibi that could have exonerated Nelson. Despite all this, Nelson lost his first two appeals—the misconduct was deemed "harmless error." The Georgia Supreme Court finally granted him a new trial, and a newly elected Chatham County District Attorney refused to prosecute Nelson a second time, saying, "There is no material element of the state's case in the original trial which has not subsequently been determined to be impeached or contradicted."

Titus Lee Brown is freed from his 1984 murder conviction and life prison sentence when it is revealed that the Los Angeles assistant district attorney on his case knowingly introduced false evidence linking Brown to a murder-robbery. Contrary to what she told the defense, judge and jury, the prosecutor knew that the property allegedly stolen by Brown actually had been found on the victim's body by the coroner, who returned it to the victim's family. The case shows just how hard it can be to win a new trial, even when such prosecutorial misconduct occurs: The California Court of Appeal upheld the conviction, though it condemned the prosecutor's actions; the state supreme court not only refused to take Brown's side, it ordered the lower court's opinion "depublished," so as to spare the prosecutor any embarrassment. The case had to go all the way up to the U.S. Ninth Circuit Court of Appeals—one rung below the Supreme Court—before Brown received a new trial. The appeals court wrote: "The prosecutor's actions in this case are intolerable. Possessed of knowledge that destroyed her theory of the case, the prosecutor had a duty not to mislead the jury. Instead, she kept the facts secret . . . and then presented testimony in such a way as to suggest the opposite of what she alone knew to be true. . . . Such conduct perverts the adversarial system and endangers its ability to produce just results."

The conviction of Thomas R. Merrill for a double murder committed during a coin-shop robbery in Orange County, California, is thrown out because a prosecutor hid a witness statement that exonerated Merrill.

1992

Kerry Kotler is freed after eleven years in prison for rape, burglary and robbery in Suffolk County, New York. Long before his release, Kotler had proved that he was the victim of prosecutorial misconduct, police perjury, and concealment of evidence (the victim in the case originally failed to identify Kotler as the rapist). But this was deemed harmless error, and Kotler lost all his appeals. In 1990, however, DNA testing showed conclusively that Kotler could not have committed the crime. The Suffolk County District Attorney continued to fight the case for two more years before Kotler finally was declared innocent and released.

Sabrina Butler walks off death row after her 1990 conviction for murdering her nine-month-old child is overturned. The Mississippi Supreme Court finds that prosecutors insisted the young mother had killed her baby when the evidence suggested that Sudden Infant Death Syndrome was actually the cause.

High school principal Jay Smith, sentenced to death for three killings in Upper Merion, Pennsylvania, is released by the state supreme court because of egregious prosecutorial misconduct and the withholding of evidence that would have helped Smith's defense. The case was the subject of a television miniseries and a book.

Citing prosecutorial misconduct, a federal appeals court in San Diego throws out the convictions of four Mexicans and three Bolivians who supposedly ran a massive cocaine importation ring called the "Corporation." Federal prosecutors hid from the defense a memo that detailed their chief witness's many lies, his lack of credibility and the false allegations he had made in the past. Federal authorities also kept secret the fact that this informant was given free run of government offices, telephones, undercover sports cars, undercover houses and other perks in exchange for testimony favorable to the prosecution. By keeping this information secret, prosecutors were able to suggest to the jury their witness was a trustworthy fellow with no incentive to lie.

In the case of the "Prime Time Rapist" in Tucson, Arizona, in which an innocent man was wrongfully arrested, kept incommunicado, relentlessly interrogated by police, then publicly named even as investigators realized they had the wrong man, the U.S. Ninth Circuit Court of Appeals decides that the normal immunity from liability that protects law-enforcement officials does not apply. The court decides that Michael Cooper, falsely accused of being the culprit, should be allowed to sue officials for their misconduct, as the violations of his constitutional rights were simply too premeditated, systematic and egregious. Tucson had been beset by a serial rapist from 1984 to 1986, one who struck in the early evening by brazenly striding into the homes of his victims as they watched television—thus, "Prime Time Rapist." Police and sheriff's officials created an arrest plan that they put into motion when Cooper was picked up after his fingerprints were mistakenly matched to one of the rape scenes. According to the plan, they ignored Cooper's pleas to see a lawyer, refused to allow him to remain silent, and pushed him to confess for hours on end. In essence, the plan called for violating every one of his constitutional rights, lying to him about evidence and witnesses, and subjecting him to as much stress and pressure as possible, so he would "crack." Later, when the fingerprint error was discovered, Cooper was released, but it took two months for the police to publicly clear him. (The real rapist eventually was caught.) The appeals court was so outraged by the conduct of officials in Tucson that they began their opinion with the following statement: "It is an abiding truth that nothing can destroy a government more quickly than its failure to observe its own laws, or worse, its disregard for the charter of its own existence."

Jay Kerr, a former Disney movie actor, is freed from his drug-conspiracy conviction because of prosecutorial misconduct, after an appeals court concludes that a federal prosecutor in Montana improperly vouched for the reliability of an informant in the case.

Federico M. Macias is freed from his death sentence in Texas after coming within two days of execution. An appeals court found that Macias had received a grossly incompetent, government-paid defense attorney who did virtually nothing in the case, while the prosecution ignored substantial evidence of Macias's innocence in order to secure his conviction. Once the conviction was overturned, the grand jury refused to indict him a second time—normally a rubber-stamp process for the prosecution—because there literally was no legitimate evidence of his guilt.

In *United States vs. Yizar,* the U.S. Court of Appeals for the Eleventh Circuit in Atlanta overturns an arson conviction because the prosecutor failed to reveal that an accomplice in the case said the defendant was innocent.

In the case of *Jacobs vs. Singletary,* a convicted murderer receives a new trial from the U.S. Court of Appeals for the Eleventh Circuit when it is learned prosecutors kept secret a key witness's original statement that he did not know who fired the fatal shot—exactly the opposite of his testimony at trial.

A series of major federal drug convictions in New York City are reversed because prosecutors concealed the highly pertinent fact that the group of drug agents involved in the cases had developed a pattern of committing perjury and were themselves under criminal investigation.

In *Walker vs. City of New York,* a convicted murderer won his freedom after two decades when it was finally proven that prosecutors had pursued the defendant's conviction and continued imprisonment even though they were aware of his probable innocence, and lied and concealed evidence in the process. The U.S. Court of Appeals for the Second Circuit, in New York, in freeing the man, criticized the entire chain of command at the local district attorney's office, finding the agency had failed to train trial attorneys "in such basic norms of human conduct as the duty not to lie or persecute the innocent."

Coal miner Roger Keith Coleman is executed in Virginia despite substantial new evidence of innocence in the murder of a young woman. His appeal failed not because the new evidence was lacking, but because his lawyers were three days late in filing it. Coleman produced uncontroverted evidence that police and prosecutors had favorable information and witnesses while concealing the existence of another suspect. The U.S. Supreme Court declined to intervene, however, calling Virginia's decision to deny Coleman a new hearing because of the three-day filing delay a matter of "states' rights."

Sonia Jacobs is freed from death row in Florida, where she had been sentenced for the 1976 murders of two policemen at a highway rest stop. Prosecutors kept secret the fact that their star witness in the case—an alleged accomplice in the crime—had failed a lie-detector test. After being granted a new trial, Jacobs pleaded no contest in exchange for a sentence of time served. Her codefendant, Jesse Tafero, did not fare so well: his execution had already been carried out in 1990, before evidence of prosecutorial misconduct surfaced.

John Henry Knapp is freed from further prosecution after coming within three days of execution for the 1973 arson death of his baby in Arizona. Shortly after the fatal fire, Knapp confessed to the crime, but then recanted within minutes, saying he was only trying to protect his wife, who had fled the state. He maintained his innocence from then on, but was convicted anyway. At trial, the gas can that started the fire was introduced, and Maricopa County prosecutors presented evidence that the prints on it were smudged and unidentifiable. But the prosecution knew this to be a lie: there were usable prints, none of them Knapp's. When the state attorney general took over the case on appeal, it learned that the prints on the can belonged to Knapp's wife, who had been given immunity but was never called to testify. The prosecution had also kept hidden a secret tape recording of Knapp's phone call to his wife moments after his confession—in which he confided in her he was innocent but had confessed in order to protect her. When Knapp asked her to come home, she responded, "They'll have to come and get me." Knapp's defense would eventually allege that the prosecution ignored and kept secret more than a hundred witness interviews that would have helped prove his innocence. When he was finally granted a new trial, Knapp agreed to plead no contest to a lesser charge in exchange for his immediate freedom.

1993

A thirty-six-year-old developmentally disabled Navy supply worker and church volunteer named Dale Akiki is freed after spending thirty months in jail on charges of molestation and satanic ritual abuse. After a seven-month trial, Akiki's jury acquitted him in just a few hours, then harshly criticized the San Diego County District Attorney for filing the case at all. The investigation mirrored many of the discredited molestation-ring cases in Bakersfield and elsewhere, like them featuring extremely suggestive interviews of children, no physical evidence and increasingly wild and disprovable allegations by young children that included the ritual sacrifice of elephants, giraffes and the hanging of children upside down during molestation, all of which supposedly occurred during a series of ninety-minute Sunday-school classes where Akiki was a volunteer baby-sitter. The case was handled by therapists, investigators and prosecutors who had become convinced that San Diego was a hotbed of satanic child abusers, and their questioning of the children reflected that bias, a subsequent county grand-jury investigation concluded. There was no evidence to support that belief beyond simple hysteria, the grand jury reported after consulting with experts from the FBI. The grand-jury report detailed an entire series of such false prosecutions in the San Diego area and chastised the gullibility, bias and hysteria of a local task force—since disbanded—linked to most of the problems. The district attorney in office at the time, who had been reelected more often than any other prosecutor in the state, lost his subsequent bid to serve another term in office.

Margaret Kelly Michaels, in prison since 1988, is freed from her conviction on 115 counts of child abuse stemming from allegations that she had sexually assaulted twenty young students at the Wee Care Day Nursery in Maplewood, New

Jersey, where she worked part-time while saving up for acting school. The twenty-five-year-old woman was accused of forcing the children to have sex with her, lick peanut butter off her genitals, and insert objects into her anus. She was also accused of sodomizing them with knives and forks, and forcing them to eat feces and urine. Moreover, the children spoke of Michaels being able to levitate cars and trees, assaulting them with swords, and amputating little boys' penises. All of the abuse allegedly took place in the day-care center when other teachers, as well as parents and children, were present in the building. No medical evidence confirmed the abuse. During Michaels' appeal, forty-five psychologists and child-development experts filed a brief attesting to the fact that the children had been subjected to a veritable brainwashing by police and prosecution, in which adult interrogators convinced children that they knew Michaels had done bad things and that the authorities needed the help of the children to keep her locked up. Kids who gave the "right" answers were rewarded with police badges and other gifts; those who gave the "wrong" answers about abuse at Wee Care were denied food or humiliated. The appeals court that granted Michaels a new trial deplored the prosecution's interrogation of the children, saying it denied Michaels a fair trial. The following tape-recorded exchange between interrogator and child was typical:

SOCIAL WORKER	Do you think that Kelly was not good when she was hurting you all?
CHILD:	Wasn't hurting me. I like her.
SOCIAL WORKER:	I can't hear you, you got to look at me when you talk to me. Now when Kelly was bothering kids in the music room . . .
CHILD:	I got socks off.
SOCIAL WORKER:	Did she make anybody else take their clothes off in the music room?
CHILD:	No.
SOCIAL WORKER:	Yes.
CHILD:	No.

(After the conviction was reversed and she was freed, another year and a half passed before prosecutors in New Jersey finally decided not to retry Michaels, and she was fully exonerated.)

Sixty-five-year-old Columbus, Ohio, businessman Bill Garland, who had been convicted of interstate fraud in federal court, has his conviction overturned on appeal because prosecutors had charged him without fully investigating the case, and in so doing, prosecuted a fraud where the victim said there was no crime (Garland had paid him back) and ignored evidence of his innocence. Prosecutors told the jury that Garland was involved with a gold-trading fraud, though there was no evidence to support this allegation.

Walter "Johnny D" McMillian of Monroeville, Alabama, is freed from his 1986 death sentence and declared innocent. The three main witnesses against him later revealed how they were coerced and pressured by police into incriminating McMillian (a tape of one such session, long kept secret by the police, was inadvertently handed over to one of McMillian's defense attorneys, corroborating the witnesses' claims). The pressure to convict McMillian was so great that he was actually held on death row *before* he went to trial. Though he had many alibi witnesses, no criminal record, and there was no physical evidence linking him to the murder of a young employee of a dry-cleaning shop, McMillian did not see his case reopened until *60 Minutes* did a report on his pending execution. Prosecutors eventually admitted to mishandling the case, and McMillian went on to testify before Congress about the plight of an innocent man on death row: "I was wrenched from my family, from my children, from my grandchildren, from my friends, from my work that I loved, and was placed in an isolation cell, the size of a shoe box, with no sunlight, no companionship, and no work for nearly six years. Every minute of every day, I knew I was innocent."

Gregory R. Wilhoit is acquitted of murdering his estranged wife as she slept. He had been sent to Oklahoma's death row because the prosecution presented expert testimony falsely linking him to a bite mark on his wife's body; afterwards, eleven forensic experts swore the bite mark was not his, leading to a new trial. Jurors found him innocent the second time around.

In *People vs. Todd A. Brecht*, the United States Supreme Court establishes a new rule that makes it far harder for defendants—even potentially innocent ones—to win new trials because of prosecutorial misconduct. The ruling puts previously unacceptable forms of misconduct by prosecutors into the category of "harmless error." In this particular case, Brecht lived in Alma, Wisconsin, where he was most unpopular, known to be a drunk and a paroled thief, and where he eventually was arrested for murdering his brother-in-law. At trial, Brecht said the fatal shooting had been an accident, but the prosecutor derided this claim, suggesting to the jury that Brecht's decision to remain silent after he was arrested and read his rights proved he was lying. An innocent man would have spoken up immediately, the prosecutor argued. The jury agreed, and Brecht got a life sentence. It was misconduct for the prosecutor to suggest that Brecht's exercising his constitutional right to remain silent proved guilt, since many innocents exercise this same right out of distrust of the police. The legal test approved by the Supreme Court for examining prosecutorial misconduct of such constitutional dimensions at the time Brecht was arrested required that his conviction be overturned unless the misconduct could be said to be "harmless beyond a reasonable doubt"—a standard that favored granting new trials in close cases where the misconduct might have influenced the verdict. But in Brecht's case, the high court decided to scrap that test in favor of a new standard: New trials would be granted in the future only if the misconduct could be said to have had a "substantial and injurious effect" on the jury's verdict. This new standard results in far fewer overturned convictions, even in cases of serious misconduct. Brecht remains in prison for life.

The execution of Leonel Herrera, convicted of killing a police officer, takes place in Texas as scheduled, despite new witnesses, including an eyewitness and a former Texas state judge, who implicated someone else in the crime. Additionally, another suspect confessed, and Herrera passed a polygraph test attesting to his own innocence. But the United States Supreme Court ruled that Herrera was not entitled to a federal hearing on the case, not because the evidence was lacking or disprovable, but because of the strictly technical limits Texas places on the introduction of new evidence in an effort to speed up executions. The high court suggested Herrera seek a commutation from the governor of Texas, George W. Bush; Bush denied the plea, as he has done with every condemned prisoner who has sought a pardon. In dissent, Justice Harry Blackmun wrote of the Herrera case: "Just as an execution without adequate safeguards is unacceptable, so too is an execution when the condemned prisoner can prove that he is innocent. The execution of a person who can show that he is innocent comes perilously close to simple murder."

Federal prosecutors in Chicago are accused of massive and long-standing misconduct in their legal assault on the infamous El Rukn drug-trafficking, terrorist and murder-for-hire organization. Pending cases against sixty-five members of the El Rukn gang are threatened because of the scandal and at least fifteen convictions of El Rukn "generals" are thrown out when federal judges find that prosecutors suppressed evidence and may have provided bizarre and criminal forms of payment to prosecution informants. Key witnesses were allegedly allowed to use cocaine and heroin regularly inside government facilities, while others were permitted to conduct sexual liaisons inside prosecutors' offices. Furthermore, drug-test results on several witnesses were withheld from defense attorneys. One federal paralegal allegedly smuggled contraband into jail for one witness and engaged in sexually explicit phone calls with others. In this case, justice was ultimately achieved despite the allegations of official misconduct: The fifteen were later retried and convicted—there being little question about their guilt—and a total of fifty-seven El Rukn members were sent to jail over the course of several years. The lead prosecutor was fired after a lengthy Justice Department investigation, but later ordered reinstated when an arbitrator determined that the informants exaggerated or fabricated their tales of favors and misconduct, and that there was no evidence the lead prosecutor knew about the withheld drug-test results.

A series of extortion convictions out of Chicago's Chinatown are thrown out when it is revealed that federal prosecutors withheld evidence that a key informant lied, and that they knowingly used his perjured testimony at trial. On the eve of a hearing in which two assistant U.S. attorneys were to testify about their conduct in the case, their office dismissed charges against Thomas Woo and Chen Li. A third defendant in the case was acquitted.

In the case of *People vs. Kojayan,* the United States Court of Appeals for the Ninth Circuit uses a rather ordinary drug case to restate the burdens and responsibilities of prosecutors— foremost of which is to put "doing justice" over winning convictions. The court overturns the convictions of a Lebanese man and woman accused of selling $100,000 worth of heroin to an undercover drug agent in a deal that had been set up by a paid government informant. In a scathing opinion aimed at the U.S. Attorney's Office in Los Angeles, one of the premier prosecutorial agencies in the nation, three conservative appeals judges, led by Reagan appointee Alex Kozinski, found that the federal prosecutor on the case committed misconduct, and that his supervisors made matters worse by minimizing and denying the transgression until forced to admit it during oral arguments before the appellate court. The misconduct occurred when the prosecutor told jurors not to worry about the fact that a crucial informant had not appeared on the witness stand to clear up some grave questions in the case, because the man had the right to remain silent anyway, and would not have said anything if called. (The defense had suggested the informant would have hurt the prosecution's case.) In fact, the prosecutor knew that the informant had struck a secret agreement with the government in which he promised to testify—the prosecutor's statement to the jury was completely false. "What we find most troubling about this case," Kozinski wrote, "is not [the prosecutor's] initial transgression, but that he seemed to be totally unaware he'd done anything at all wrong, and that there was no one in the United States Attorney's Office to set him straight." According to Kozinski's opinion, the prosecutor and his office continued to misrepresent the facts of the case, even during appeals, and seemed more concerned about sparing the prosecutor embarrassment than doing justice:

> As Justice Douglas once warned, "The function of the prosecutor under the Federal Constitution is not to tack as many skins of victims as possible to the wall. His function is to vindicate the right of people as expressed in the laws and give those accused of crime a fair trial." The government has strayed from this responsibility. . . . Much of what the U.S. Attorney's Office does isn't open to public scrutiny or judicial review. . . . It is therefore particularly important that the government discharge its responsibilities fairly, consistent with due process. The overwhelming majority of prosecutors are decent, ethical, honorable lawyers who understand the awesome power they wield, and the responsibility that goes with it. But the temptation is always there: It's the easiest thing in the world for people trained in the adversarial ethic to think a prosecutor's job is simply to win.

After initially denying any wrongdoing, the response of the U.S. Attorney was to admit a mistake had been made, and to ask the court of appeals to remove the prosecutor's name from the published opinion to spare him further embarrassment. The appeals court did so.

The United States Court of Appeals for the Sixth Circuit concludes that the Justice Department's vaunted Office of Special Investigations "acted with reckless disregard for the truth," and committed "fraud on the court," and is guilty of prosecutorial misconduct in the prosecution and deportation of John

Demjanjuk, accused of being the Nazi war criminal "Ivan the Terrible." After being charged with capital crimes in Israel, where he was sent by American authorities, the Israeli Supreme Court ordered Demjanjuk released when it was revealed that U.S. prosecutors had withheld substantial evidence of his innocence.

In *United States vs. Udechukwu*, a new trial is granted to a woman convicted of smuggling heroin at the San Juan, Puerto Rico, airport. Upon her arrest, the woman begged to cooperate with authorities and said she had been forced to smuggle by a sinister drug merchant based in Aruba. Federal investigators confirmed the existence of this Aruban drug trafficker and discovered that he was the target of an investigation himself. Yet this information was never given to Udechukwu's defense, and when she came to trial and told her story of coercion, the federal prosecutor falsely suggested to jurors that the Aruba drug dealer was a mere concoction created by the defendant to bolster a phony story.

Kirk Bloodworth is released from prison in Maryland after DNA testing proves that he had nothing to do with the rape and murder of a nine-year-old girl. Tried twice in the case, Bloodworth was initially sentenced to death in 1984, but the conviction was overturned because the prosecution withheld evidence of his possible innocence and the involvement of another suspect. At a second trial, he was convicted again, but sentenced to life. Years later, the DNA test proved his claims of innocence had been true all along. Maryland state bars the introduction of new evidence of innocence after one year, which could have kept Bloodworth in prison, but the prosecutor on his case, aghast at the injustice, joined a petition calling for Bloodworth's pardon, which he finally received.

Clarence Chance and Benny Powell are freed after seventeen years in prison for a murder they did not commit. Reverend Jim McCloskey of Centurion Ministries, a Princeton, New Jersey-based organization that specializes in revealing unjust convictions, uncovered misconduct by Los Angeles police and prosecutors that had effectively framed Powell and Chance. The city later paid the men $7 million to settle their wrongful-imprisonment lawsuits.

Muneer Deeb is acquitted of murder in Texas. Deeb had been sentenced to death in 1985 for allegedly hiring three hit men to kill his girlfriend, but his conviction was reversed and a new trial granted by the state court of criminal appeals because prosecutors relied upon improper evidence. The chief informant in the case was revealed to have lied repeatedly, and Deeb had been ruled out as a suspect by one police department before the detective on his case transferred to another department and targeted Deeb once again. One alleged accomplice pleaded guilty in exchange for mercy and testified against Deeb, but his testimony was riddled with lies and mistakes. The alleged shooter, David Wayne Spence, convicted on the same evidence originally used against Deeb, was executed in April 1997, even as Deeb was acquitted of hiring him.

In a case with macabre connections to Muneer Deeb's and David Wayne Spence's, Sidney Williams is released from a life sentence for the rape and murder in Waco, Texas, of Juanita White, Spence's mother, because the prosecution and investigator on the case—the same as in Deeb's and Spence's—relied upon questionable informant testimony to win convictions. Before her death, White had received a letter from an inmate who had testified against her son; in it, the inmate confessed to perjury and begged for forgiveness. Forty-eight hours after a police memo about the letter was issued, White was murdered—though investigators never checked out a possible connection between the letter and White's death. At Williams' trial, fifteen Waco police officers testified for the *defense,* saying the informants in the case could not be trusted. One of those officers had been threatened with indictment when she tried to get the county grand jury to investigate official conduct in the case. Once he was released, prosecutors declined to attempt a retrial of Williams. His alleged accomplice, Calvin Washington, convicted on exactly the same evidence, remains in prison for life.

Andrew Lee Mitchell is released from a 1981 death sentence after it is revealed that the sheriff who arrested him suppressed statements of police officers who saw the murder victim alive two hours after the murder supposedly took place—at a time when Mitchell had an alibi. A key witness also recanted in the case, and even the prosecutor filed an affidavit saying Mitchell had not received a fair trial. He came within two days of being executed.

Kerry Max Cook, sentenced to death for a 1977 mutilation-murder in Tyler, Texas, has his sentence overturned because of systematic government misconduct and the hiding of evidence in his favor. The same Smith County District Attorney's Office that prosecuted Andrew Mitchell also prosecuted Cook. (Cook was tried and convicted again, but, in 1996, he was granted yet another new trial, again because the appeals courts found "prosecutorial and police misconduct has tainted this entire matter from the outset." Cook was subsequently released on bail while authorities decide whether to try him yet again, after spending twenty of his forty-one years on death row.)

Andrew L. Golden, a high school teacher in Florida, had his 1991 murder conviction and death sentence for allegedly killing his wife reversed by the Florida Supreme Court, which found that prosecutors won their case without ever proving the death was anything other than an accident. (Golden was fully exonerated and released from further charges a year later.)

Mark Bravo, a Los Angeles mental-hospital worker sentenced to eight years for the 1990 rape of a patient, is released after DNA testing proves his innocence. Misconduct had infected this case, ensuring his wrongful conviction: The victim had recanted and accused others in the rape during interviews with police, though this information was kept secret, and the government refused to investigate what was later shown to be Bravo's ironclad alibi.

The California Court of Appeals overturns the drunken driving conviction of Rafael Garcia Garcia, a San Diego-area car salesman, after finding that both the San Diego County District Attorney and the California Attorney General hid evidence that the prosecution's accident-reconstruction expert was unreliable. Ninety-one others convicted because of this same expert's testimony had to be contacted and offered the opportunity to reopen their cases as well, while a deputy attorney general sued his employer, claiming to have been demoted, ridiculed and harassed because he expressed concerns early on about official misconduct in the Garcia case.

1994

The Justice Department reports that twenty of its prosecutors around the nation resigned in the 1993–94 fiscal year while they were under investigation for misconduct. During that same period, allegations of prosecutorial misconduct in the department rise 78 percent compared to the previous fiscal year. (The U.S. Justice Department is the only prosecutorial agency out of thousands in the country that tracks and publicly reports on allegations of misconduct by its lawyers.)

Edward Honaker is released after serving ten years in prison for a Nelson County, Virginia, rape he could not have committed. Evidence of prosecutorial misconduct in the case included the fact, kept secret by prosecutors, that two key witnesses had been induced hypnotically to recall details of the events in question, which greatly reduced their credibility; the hiding of the fact that the victim's initial description of her attacker did not match Honaker, but changed once she was shown a picture of him; and the fact that prosecutors never told their forensic expert that Honaker had a vasectomy years before the rape, which meant he could not have left the sperm found in an examination of the victim. Another prosecution expert claimed a hair found on the victim was unlikely to match anyone other than Honaker—patently false testimony, as no test exists that can positively match a hair to an individual. When DNA tests, unavailable at the time of the rape, were finally performed, Honaker was completely exonerated, because the sperm sample matched neither Honaker nor the victim's two sex partners, which meant that it had to have come from another, unidentified rapist. Honaker still could not win his freedom, however: Tough state laws in Virginia allow only twenty-one days from the time of conviction for the introduction of new evidence, a deadline long since lapsed. Evidence of prosecutorial misconduct did not come to light for years, but Virginia law makes no allowances for a delay in the presentation of new evidence of innocence, even when it is the fault of government neglect or malfeasance that it was not available sooner. Honaker had to petition the governor and beg for a pardon, his only chance to escape wrongful imprisonment, and his plea was finally heeded when prosecutors joined the request and admitted to convicting the wrong man. The case demonstrates that prosecutors, not judges, are often the final arbiters of justice under current laws, and that, in many cases, only their personal integrity and willingness to admit embarrassing conduct can save innocent men and women from false imprisonment.

Ronnie Bullock, convicted of the 1983 rape of a nine-year-old girl on the basis of a composite sketch produced with the help of the victim, is released after eleven years in prison. DNA testing, unavailable at the time of his trial, revealed that he could not have committed the crime, as he tried all along to convince unsympathetic police and prosecutors. The testing could have been accomplished years earlier, but the authorities had misplaced the key piece of evidence. The prosecution later admitted to imprisoning the wrong man.

Gary Ramona wins a $475,000 lawsuit against his daughter's therapist after presenting evidence that his daughter's "recovered memory" of molestation was false and the result of suggestive and improper counseling techniques.

John Spencer is released from a fifty-years-to-life sentence when state police in New York admit to planting his fingerprints at the scene of a double murder. (Three state-police troopers were later convicted of falsifying fingerprints in a scandal that affected more than one hundred cases.)

Gilbert Alejandro, convicted of rape in 1990 in Uvalde County, Texas, is freed because his conviction rested on false testimony from a forensics expert, Fred Zain, later prosecuted for perjury and obstruction of justice. (The same expert's false evidence brought one hundred thirty other criminal cases into question.) Charges were dropped and Alejandro was awarded a $250,000 settlement; Zain was acquitted.

Joseph Burrows is released from death row in Illinois after five years when the two main witnesses against him recant, one saying police coerced him into accusing Burrows and the other confessing to the murder himself. There was never any physical evidence linking Burrows to the crime. Yet the district attorney appealed the trial court's decision to free Burrows, trying to keep him on death row despite the crumbling of the prosecution's case. The state appeals courts have upheld the decision freeing Burrows.

In *United States vs. Robinson*, the United States Court of Appeals for the Tenth Circuit in Denver reverses a drug conviction because a prosecutor, who had interviewed a key witness, told the defense that the witness could not say who retrieved the drugs at issue in the case. In fact, the witness had provided identifying information that clearly did not fit the defendant. Had that witness's information been given to the jury, the appeals court determined, the defendant could easily have been acquitted.

Adolph Munson is freed from an Oklahoma death sentence after nine years because prosecutors withheld evidence that supported his claims of innocence. The prosecution's case was further undermined when the prosecution forensic expert who testified against Munson, Ralph Erdman, was subsequently convicted of seven felonies for misrepresenting facts in other cases. (Munson was acquitted in 1995 when retried for murder, though he remained in prison on other charges.)

Ricardo Aldape Guerra, sentenced to death in 1982 for the murder of a Houston police officer, is freed after fourteen years on death row when a federal judge finds that Guerra was the victim of an outrageous misconduct. The judge calls police "merchants of chaos" bent on revenge and on threatening witnesses into lying. The court also accused prosecutors of manipulating evidence to falsely convict Aldape, when all the physical evidence pointed to another man killed in a shootout with police. Rather than retry Aldape, the authorities ultimately dropped the case. The judge wrote, "But for the conduct of the police officers and the prosecutors, either [Aldape] would not have been charged with this offense or the trial would have resulted in an acquittal." Prosecutorial misconduct cited by the judge included threatening and intimidating witnesses, most of whom were children, and hiding evidence of Aldape's innocence while lying in closing arguments about evidence of his guilt. The court asserted that the prosecutors' "misconduct was designed to obtain a conviction and another 'notch in their guns' despite the overwhelming evidence that [another man] was the killer."

Bruce Turner is freed from his 1991 conviction and ten-year prison sentence for assault and battery because a Middlesex County, Massachusetts, prosecutor threatened two defense witnesses who would have attested to Turner's innocence, preventing them from testifying and depriving Turner of a defense.

In Will County, Illinois, felony misconduct charges against Wilmington Police Chief Frank Lyons and his police officer son are dismissed because of prosecutorial misconduct—the use of improper evidence in obtaining a grand jury indictment. Charles Bretz, the prosecutor responsible—the top prosecutor in his county—was forced to resign when it was revealed that he maintained a private law practice that may have conflicted with his public prosecutorial duties. Several murder convictions were called into question when it was later revealed that Bretz maintained a hidden relationship with the trial judge on the case. The same judge and prosecutor also were accused in a federal civil rights suit of misusing the court system to deprive a father of his parental rights.

1995

Jesse DeWayne Jacobs is executed in Texas for the murder of a suburban Houston woman in an abandoned house. Even though a prosecutor said Jacobs did not commit the crime, it was not enough to induce the U.S. Supreme Court to halt the execution. Prosecutors originally had won the death sentence by convincing a jury that Jacobs pulled the trigger in the crime, though he claimed his sister had done it. Later, at the trial of the sister, the same prosecutor who convicted Jacobs announced that the sister had indeed pulled the trigger, and that Jacobs had no idea what his sister planned to do at the time she committed the crime. She received a ten-year prison sentence. In a six-to-three vote, the U.S. Supreme Court said it was perfectly permissible for the same prosecutor to argue mutually exclusive theories in separate trials and to proceed with the execution of Jacobs. Justice John Paul Stevens dissented, saying that one of the prosecution's versions of the case had to be a lie, raising "a serious question of prosecutorial misconduct." Stevens further wrote, "In my opinion, it would be fundamentally unfair to execute a person on the basis of a factual determination that the state has formally disavowed."

A police corruption scandal in Philadelphia's Thirty-ninth Police District explodes with allegations of innocent men and women framed, evidence planted and witnesses coerced on a massive scale. More than 1,000 criminal convictions have to be reviewed; at least 116 are overturned. Another 150 pending charges are dismissed. Six officers are eventually prosecuted and imprisoned, with many more fired, demoted or transferred.

Rolando Cruz of DuPage County, Illinois, twice convicted and sentenced to death for the 1983 murder of ten-year-old Jeanine Nicarico, is exonerated amid evidence of massive police and prosecutorial misconduct, phony confessions, withheld evidence, lying witnesses and a refusal to accept the confession of a convicted child rapist and killer who admitted to the Nicarico murder (and whose semen was found at the crime scene). Granted a third trial, Cruz was acquitted by a judge who harshly criticized the authorities in the case. Ultimately, three DuPage County prosecutors (one of whom had gone on to become a judge) and four former sheriff's deputies were indicted for allegedly concealing evidence that could have exonerated Cruz and for allegedly cooking up other evidence in their quest for a conviction in the high-pressure and sensational case.

Alejandro Hernandez of DuPage County, Illinois, having been sentenced to death, retried and resentenced to eighty years in prison for the murder of ten-year-old Jeanine Nicarico, is exonerated along with Rolando Cruz, again because of official misconduct. The man who confessed to the crime and whose DNA has been linked to the victim's body has never been charged.

Lloyd Schlup, a Missouri convict, was freed from his 1985 death sentence for a murder inside prison. The government had kept hidden a videotape and statements from twenty other witnesses, which all indicated that Schlup was in another part of the prison when the murder occurred. An appeals judge found that no reasonable juror in possession of these facts would have convicted Schlup. After the evidence of his innocence surfaced, Missouri state prosecutors still fought to have Schlup executed, invoking a 1996 law that limits prisoners to a single federal appeal and one writ of habeas corpus. This law enables prosecutors to exploit a legal technicality empowering them to disregard even irrefutable proof of innocence and to proceed with executions. The U.S. Supreme Court, however, granted Schlup a hearing despite the new law, declining to apply it retroactively to Schlup's case, and the new evidence led to his overturned conviction. Had he been convicted in 1996, however, Schlup would have had no recourse and could have been legally executed despite his innocence.

In a landmark case, the U.S. Supreme Court reverses the murder conviction and death sentence of Curtis Kyles because Louisiana prosecutors hid several pieces of critical evidence that would have helped the defense, including information about a paid informant in the case who implicated himself in the murder—evidence that the high court felt could well have altered the verdict had jurors heard about it. The Court told prosecutors that when there is any doubt about whether information is helpful to a defendant, it must be disclosed.

"This is as it should be," the Court wrote. "Such disclosure will serve to justify trust in the prosecutor as the representative of a sovereignty whose interest in a criminal prosecution is not that it shall win a case, but that justice shall be done. And it will tend to preserve the criminal trial, as distinct from the prosecutor's private deliberations, as the chosen form for ascertaining the truth about criminal accusations." (Later, with all the evidence fully aired in the fatal carjacking case, two retrials of Kyles led to hung juries, with a majority of jurors voting for acquittal. Charges eventually were dropped and Kyles went free.)

In *United States vs. Alzate*, the United States Court of Appeals for the Eleventh Circuit overturns a cocaine-smuggling conviction when it is revealed that the prosecution kept secret key information that would have reinforced the defendant's claims of innocence. The accused smuggler, arrested as he stepped off a plane from Colombia, claimed that he had been forced by death threats into smuggling a kilogram of cocaine, and that he knew little about smuggling himself. At one point in the trial, the defendant testified that a remark he had made about the value of cocaine—which the prosecutor seized upon as evidence of the defendant's drug expertise—did not concern his own smuggling, but was an innocent reference to another arrest and drug seizure that took place in the Miami International Airport Customs Service office as he sat there in custody. The prosecution derided this claim, labeling it all part of a fabricated excuse. The prosecutor assured jurors that there had been no other seizure that day, which was false. There had been one, just as the defendant described.

In *Smith vs. New Mexico Department of Corrections*, the United States Court of Appeals for the Tenth Circuit reverses a double-murder conviction because information that would have cast doubt on the testimony of the government's key witnesses was never turned over to the defense by law-enforcement officials who investigated the crime. The fact that the prosecutor on the case did not possess the information was no excuse, the court ruled: It was the duty of prosecutors to make sure that police turn over all relevant information, particularly when it is as potentially explosive as this evidence, which undermined the entire prosecution theory of the crime.

In *Banks vs. Reynolds,* the Tenth Circuit Court of Appeals reverses a death sentence and orders a new trial because prosecutors failed to reveal that another person had been initially arrested for the murder in question and that eyewitnesses had identified other suspects. Lower courts had ruled this devastating omission "harmless error."

Robert Charles Cruz is acquitted of murder in Phoenix, Arizona. His original conviction and death sentence for a 1980 double murder were reversed because prosecutors illegally stripped his jury of Hispanics; later, questions were raised about immunity granted the main witness in the case.

In a case that shows just how difficult winning freedom for convicted innocents can be, an Oregon judge declines to set aside the murder convictions of a man and a woman even though the prosecutors who convicted them said they were innocent—and despite the fact another man confessed to the crime and provided evidence that proved him the true culprit. Sixty-two-year-old Laverne Pavlinac had falsely confessed to the murder of a young woman in Portland and implicated her forty-one-year-old boyfriend, John Sosnovske, in order to escape from their abusive relationship. She later recanted, but both were convicted anyway and sentenced to life in prison. Later, Keith Hunter Jesperson, a serial murderer known as the "Happy Face Killer," confessed and provided details of the crime that only the killer could know (and that Pavlinac had gotten wrong). In prosecuting Pavlinac and Sosnovske, authorities ignored the fact that Pavlinac had tried a year earlier to implicate Sosnovske in a bank robbery he didn't commit. When prosecutors realized Jesperson was the true killer and that they had made a terrible mistake, they petitioned the court for a belated acquittal. However, tough new Oregon laws limit the time for presenting new evidence to five days after sentencing, a rule intended to preserve the integrity and finality of jury verdicts, but which implicitly assumes that new evidence of innocence is always bogus. In this case, there was no legal route of appeal, and Pavlinac and Sosnovske languished in prison for another two months after everyone involved agreed they were innocent. Finally, the judge in the case decided that the solution was to declare Sosnovske's civil rights had been violated by Pavlinac's false accusations, thereby erasing his conviction on constitutional grounds. Angered by Pavlinac's lies, the judges refused to erase her conviction, but ordered her released on the grounds that it would be cruel and unusual punishment for her to serve a prison sentence for a crime she did not commit. Whether or not his ruling ultimately met the letter of the law was irrelevant, as the prosecution made clear it had no intention of appealing their release. The case is an example of justice achieved in spite of tough new laws, not because of them.

1996
All charges against Methodist minister Nathaniel Grady and four other men convicted of sexually abusing children at daycare centers in the Bronx, New York, are dismissed, and all are exonerated after a variety of appeals lead to reversal of their 1984 convictions. High-pressure interrogations of children and prosecutorial misconduct, including hiding evidence of innocence, brought about the reversal of these molestation-ring convictions and lengthy sentences. Once new trials are granted, a new prosecutor assigned to the case quickly determines that there is no evidence worth pursuing.

The conspiracy and fraud conviction of a Washington, D.C., aerospace engineer and retired Marine lieutenant is overturned because of "severe" prosecutorial misconduct and the "troubling" bias of the federal judge on the case. Prosecutors had attempted to excuse it, but the misconduct and bias is clearly demonstrated in the trial transcripts, the U.S. Court of Appeals for the District of Columbia Circuit decides. In the case, Patricia Donato was accused of arranging the theft of her leased sports car so she could rid herself of the burdensome vehicle payments and collect the insurance. Just before trial, prosecutors plea-bargained an arrangement with the man who physi-

cally stole the car, who then claimed to have been hired by
Donato. During closing arguments, the prosecutor provided
jurors with a false motive for the crime—that returning the car
she had come to hate before the lease expired would cost
Donato a fortune, leaving fraud as her only way out. In fact,
turning the car in early would have posed a break-even proposition for Donato and imposed no out-of-pocket costs, while
the fraud would have earned her very little in return for the
enormous risk of being discovered. The truth was that there
was no reasonable motive for Donato to have entered into this
conspiracy. Compouding this prosecutorial misconduct, the
judge presiding over the trial—who severely reprimanded and
derided both Donato and her defense lawyer throughout the
case while helping the prosecutor at every possible turn—
refused to correct the misstatement of the evidence. The
appeals court found the conduct of both prosecutor and judge
inexcusable and ordered the case returned to a different courtroom for retrial.

Gary Gauger is freed from his Illinois death sentence for killing
his parents after it is determined that the authorities had no
evidence or cause to arrest him, and therefore no reason to subject him to twenty-one hours of intensive interrogation, which
supposedly produced incriminating statements.

A massive bank fraud case initially touted by the government as
a blow against white-collar crime is thrown out by a federal
judge because of prosecutorial misconduct. Ten Houston,
Texas, investment bankers are exonerated. The judge said there
was a complete lack of evidence that any laws had been broken
by anyone except two federal prosecutors on the case. In acquit-
ting the ten men, U.S. District Court Judge Kenneth Hoyt
accused the prosecutors of hiding evidence that suggested the
defendants' innocence, and found that the prospect of a fair
trial had been "snared on the branches of strange and subverted
truth" because of the government's misconduct. The prosecution had sought to prove that the bank owners had hidden the
financial problems of their troubled banks from federal regula-
tors so that they would not be shut down, but the defense

presented evidence that the ten men had actually come up with an innovative and legal plan for keeping the banks afloat.

A biker named Joseph Spaziano is released from death row in Florida after twenty years because his conviction for the murder of a young woman was based solely on the testimony of a drug-addicted teenager who, after hypnosis (known to lead to false memories) thought he recalled Spaziano implicating himself in the murder. The witness later recanted his testimony as unreliable and false, a revelation made public by *Miami Herald* reporter Laurie Rozsa, at which time the case was reopened.

A developmentally disabled man named Donald Gunsby is released from his seven-year-old death sentence and granted a new trial after it is learned that the prosecution withheld crucial evidence in the case, while, in addition, his defense lawyer had been out of law school but one year before being assigned to try the capital case.

The death sentence (but not the actual conviction) of robber-murderer Kevin Shelby Malone is reversed by the California Supreme Court because the chief informant in the case had gotten leniency in exchange for his testimony, though this fact was never disclosed. On the witness stand, the informant denied receiving any deal from the prosecution, which was not true. Prosecutors allowed this perjured testimony to stand. The high court reasoned that because another culprit got lenient treatment, the jury might have reconsidered imposing the death penalty on Malone.

Denying an appeal from the Justice Department, the U.S. Court of Appeals for the Ninth Circuit upholds a lower-court finding of an "extraordinary pattern of misconduct" in the wrongful prosecution of Wang Zong Xiao. Wang was a witness brought to San Francisco from China in 1989 to testify in the "Goldfish Conspiracy," an international heroin-trafficking case. During the trial, Wang revealed that he had been brutally tortured by Chinese authorities until he implicated—falsely—the three Goldfish conspirators targeted for prosecution in the United

States. Once tortured into submission, he had been handed over to the U.S. authorities. In San Francisco, federal prosecutors responded to his story of torture by threatening to deport him back to China unless he testified as they wished against the three suspects, even though Wang would face certain torture and execution there (whereas he had been promised leniency by Chinese authorities if he falsely implicated the Goldfish defendants). When Wang still refused to testify falsely in the case and made his plight known to the court, an ensuing investigation revealed that the prosecution had kept secret a memorandum from Hong Kong authorities documenting their belief that Wang had been tortured—which is why the Hong Kong government refused to prosecute the case there. The judge on the case in San Francisco then enjoined the government from deporting Wang and later excoriated the Justice Department for "outrageous lies," prosecutorial misconduct and a "policy of willful ignorance" when it came to substantive allegations of torture by Chinese authorities.

Verneal Jimerson, sentenced to death for a 1978 double murder and rape in Cook County, Illinois, is freed when a group of journalism students on a class assignment reinvestigate his case and learn that police pressured a key witness, prosecutors allowed the same witness to perjure herself, and authorities failed to investigate more likely suspects in the case. Jimerson was one of four defendants—a group dubbed the "Ford Heights Four" in the press—singled out by this witness, a developmentally disabled woman who named none of the four in her initial police interviews. Later, she fingered them, only to recant her identifications, saying that she had been pressured by police into lying. The charges were dismissed, but the case was refiled seven years later when the witness changed her story yet again to implicate the four—after which her own fifty-year prison sentence was reduced to two years' probation. The witness then was allowed to perjure herself about this deal during the Ford Heights Four trial. Thanks to the college students' investigation of misconduct in the case, DNA tests were ordered by the court. The tests proved conclusively that Jimerson and the rest of the Ford Heights Four were innocent. Other suspects have since been charged, and the Cook

County State's Attorney publicly apologized to all four men, who spent nearly half their lives behind bars.

Dennis Williams, another member of the Ford Heights Four, is released from a death sentence won through official misconduct, his innocence proven by DNA testing. He had been incarcerated for eighteen years for crimes that he did not commit.

Willie Rainge, the third member of the Ford Heights Four, is exonerated and released from a wrongful life sentence.

Kenneth Adams, the last member of the Ford Heights Four, is exonerated and released from a seventy-five-year sentence.

The City of Philadelphia pays $1.9 million to Neil Ferber, who had been sentenced to death for a double murder based on the perjured testimony of a prosecution informant. The judge overseeing his ensuing civil suit described Ferber's experience as "a Kafkaesque nightmare . . . a malevolent charade . . . the so-called justice system of a totalitarian state."

George Franklin Sr. is set free after six years behind bars in a notorious "recovered memory" case. Franklin's daughter claimed to recall him murdering a childhood friend twenty-one years after the fact, a memory she supposedly had long suppressed. The case fell apart when it was learned that a key prosecution witness had been hypnotized to enhance her recollections. Use of hypnosis in prosecutions is illegal in California, because of the danger that it may implant false memories. Also, the daughter, Eileen Franklin-Lipsker, had told investigators about other crimes committed by her father and another man that she had suddenly recalled after many years. These recovered "memories" were later proven to be false, raising questions of credibility. Finally, the prosecution used improper evidence against Franklin, sending his daughter as their agent into a jail visit to elicit his confession, then attempting to suggest his ensuing silence was tantamount to a confession. One of many "recovered memory" cases in the late 1980s and early 1990s, this case, like the others, has been challenged as evidence has surfaced that certain therapists were inadvertently leading psychologically vulnerable individuals to mistake fantasies and therapists' own suggestive questions for actual memories. The sensational Franklin case led to two books and a TV movie long before the verdict was overturned.

U.S. District Court Judge Saundra Brown Armstrong, in San Jose, California, dismisses charges and bars further prosecution of four men accused of plotting an escape from the Dublin Federal Detention Center in Northern California. The plot, which allegedly included murdering guards, blasting through a window and using a helicopter to rendezvous with a ship at sea, was never carried out. The key witness was an informant named Joseph Calabrese, an ex-Las Vegas cop who was in jail for stealing $7 million in a phony investment scheme. Facing a lengthy prison term, Calabrese came forward with his story of a planned jailbreak in exchange for leniency. During the trial of the four men, Calabrese took the stand and denied cutting a deal with prosecutors, and, though it was his duty to do so, the federal prosecutor on the case did not correct this lie. The prosecutor also prodded his informant to give inadmissible evidence to the jury, and then suggested that one defendant's decision not to testify showed his guilt, two more instances of prosecutorial misconduct that Armstrong found intolerable. While agreeing that the case had unraveled with the star witness's lies and that it should be dismissed, the U.S. Attorney for the region, Michael J. Yamaguchi, responded chiefly to the judge's findings by begging her to remove the prosecutor's name from her written opinion so as to spare him embarrassment.

1997
A massive racketeering and corruption case against a former governor of Rhode Island and his son—the most sensational case in the state in years—is dismissed because of outrageous prosecutorial misconduct and concealment of evidence that reached the highest levels of the state attorney general's office. The Providence judge who threw out all charges against former governor Edward DiPrete and his son, Dennis, accused of solic-

iting $294,000 in kickbacks on state contracts, said he was compelled to do so because prosecutors had attempted to deceive the defense and the court, and that top officials in the attorney general's office knew that evidence that would help the defense was being kept secret. The judge opined that such misconduct, if allowed to stand, would erode the public's confidence in the justice system. Prosecutors, angry at the ruling, said it was the judge's decision that would have that effect. (The lead prosecutor accused of misconduct in the governor's case committed suicide after the controversy erupted, while the same prosecutors also came under investigation for improperly using informants in drug cases.) In May 1998, the Rhode Island Supreme Court reinstated the DiPrete case. In a bitterly divided 3-2 ruling, the court agreed that the state attorney general's office had committed egregious misconduct in hiding evidence and misrepresenting it to the trial court. But the majority ruled that trial court judges lack the power to punish wayward prosecutors by dismissing their cases. The high court imposed no sanctions; the two dissenters suggested the attorney general had committed a fraud on the court that could be considered criminal.

A federal prosecutor in Fort Myers, Florida, accused of misconduct, burglary and criminal trespass, is removed from the multimillion-dollar fraud case she had been prosecuting, the highest-profile case in the region. The prosecutor admitted to ordering an IRS agent to break into a locked storage unit belonging to Richard P. Hamric, accused of a massive mortgage-fraud scheme, and to take and copy confidential documents belonging to Hamric's defense attorney. The prosecutor, under investigation by the Justice Department for her misconduct, died of heart problems before the investigation could be completed. Hamric was allowed to plead guilty to reduced charges and was sentenced to seven years in prison.

The rape conviction of Charles Demars of Hampden County, Massachusetts, is overturned because of a pattern of severe prosecutorial misconduct. Demars, sixty-three, was accused of raping and photographing in the nude a fifteen-year-old girl who had agreed to go home with him to be photographed so she could earn money for college tuition. Demars, while denying the rape, admitted to the photos, but said he believed the girl to be eighteen at the time. Absent any physical evidence or eyewitnesses, the case came down to the credibility of the victim and Demars. A Massachusetts appeals court decided that the prosecutor had tipped the scales in the victim's favor by repeatedly asking improper questions, insinuating that damning evidence existed when it did not, and introducing inadmissible evidence to the jury. On appeal, the government agreed that the prosecutor had acted improperly, but insisted the errors were harmless. The appeals court felt otherwise, reasoning, "The prosecutor's conduct of this case was a wholesale violation. . . . She sought to cause the jury to loathe the defendant. That she may have succeeded was the substantial risk of a miscarriage of justice." In a concurring opinion, one justice went further still, suggesting that wayward prosecutors should be penalized financially for such misconduct:

> The Commonwealth's conduct here was not merely unprofessional, it was outrageous. This was not a momentary misstep but a persistent course of conduct designed to prejudice the defendant. This old refrain needs to be repeated: "If prosecutors do not see the light, they must be made to feel the heat." It is still my hope that ultimately a prosecutor whose misconduct is flagrant will be required personally to reimburse the Commonwealth for the costs of any resultant retrial.

In a stunning repudiation of the hysteria over satanism and child-molestation rings that began in Bakersfield and spread nationwide in the early and mid-1980s, a federal grand jury in Houston indicts two psychiatrists, a psychologist, a social worker and a hospital administrator for allegedly collecting millions of dollars in fraudulent insurance payments by convincing patients that they had been involved in nonexistent acts of ritual abuse. The false memories allegedly implanted in the patients through brainwashing, hypnosis, solitary confinement and unnecessary restraints at the hospital often led to criminal investigations and child-custody actions against the supposed abusers. One of the patients, who came to realize that her recovered memories were false, successfully sued the hospital and therapists and won nearly $6 million because her false memories of abuse and molestation destroyed her family and her career.

The last two of seven defendants charged with hundreds of counts of molestation and ritual abuse in the Little Rascals Day Care Center case in Edenton, North Carolina, are freed after prosecutors decline to retry them. Their convictions and life sentences had been overturned for a variety of reasons, including gross prosecutorial misconduct. In the pattern typical in such cases, coercive interrogations of children produced fantastic and disprovable allegations that were conveniently ignored, such as the children's contention that they were forced to swim with sharks, take trips to outer space, and that babies had been killed in their presence. (The authorities subsequently lost or destroyed documentation and tape recordings of these interviews.) The allegations in the case first arose shortly after Edenton police officers attended a seminar on satanic ritual abuse, another common pattern in such cases. Initial denials by the children that they had been molested were disregarded, but by the time questioners were through, ninety children had accused twenty adults, including the mayor and sheriff (who were never charged). A San Diego County Grand Jury report on false charges of ritual abuse around the nation included this startling information from the Little Rascals case and the hysteria that gripped the entire small town of Edenton:

> Eighty-five percent of the children received therapy with three therapists in the town; all of these children eventually reported satanic abuse. Fifteen percent of the children were treated by different therapists in a neighboring city; none of these children reported abuse of any kind after the same period of time in therapy.

The California Court of Appeal upholds the felony stalking conviction of George F. Falck, a mentally ill army veteran and

MBA from Alameda County, despite finding the case rife with "inexcusable prosecutorial misconduct." The misconduct included exhorting the jury to convict Falck even if he was innocent, for the sake of the victim and stalking victims everywhere. The appeals court found the misconduct to be "harmless error" because, even without the prosecutor's wayward arguments, the jury would almost certainly have convicted Falck anyway.

Operation Lost Trust, a massive federal investigation of corruption among South Carolina legislators, collapses when a federal judge dismisses charges against five former lawmakers because of egregious prosecutorial misconduct. The legislators had been videotaped accepting bundles of cash during a secret sting operation. Prosecutors called these payments bribes, while the defense said they were lawful campaign contributions. The truth will remain unknown because of the government's misconduct; U.S. District Court Judge Falcon Hawkins wrote in his blistering opinion on the case that federal prosecutors were guilty of hiding evidence, lying in court and allowing perjurious testimony in order to win wrongful convictions. He wrote:

> An investigation and subsequent prosecution of what might have started out with the altruistic motive of ridding the State Legislature of drugs and political corruption became a political bombshell that backfired. Overzealousness and political pressure upon those in positions of authority appear to be the detours that led the government to rush to trial . . . ; to withhold volumes of exculpatory evidence; to allow perjured testimony to stand uncorrected on more than one occasion; to allow its primary cooperating witness . . . to take an unusual amount of control of the sting operation; to go outside of its own regulations to target certain legislators; and to mislead this court to such an extent as to perpetrate a fraud upon the court.

Criminal cases against five defendants are dismissed, with more to come, when it is alleged that two Boston detectives had used their badges and positions to launch a five-year crime spree that included extortion, conspiracy, theft of a quarter million dollars' worth of cash, drugs and guns, the dropping of charges in exchange for money, and the framing of other people for the detectives' fifty-six separate alleged crimes. The pair was also said to have carried out hundreds of illegal searches of people's homes with bogus warrants. The detectives were found out and indicted only after a federal probe that was triggered by an investigation by the *Boston Globe*.

Twenty highly publicized organized-crime convictions are brought under review because the FBI failed to disclose the existence of mob informers to defense attorneys, while also keeping in the dark judges who were issuing wiretap orders—placing the constitutionality of the convictions in grave question. The FBI went so far as to protect from arrest and identification one informer, James "Whitey" Bulger, even while he ran a loanshark and drug business in league with men who murdered four people.

Susie Mowbray is released after nine years in Texas state prison when she proves—thanks to her son's dogged amateur investigation—that evidence used to convict her of her husband's shotgun murder was invalid. Prosecutors covered up a more-detailed forensic report that found the victim, a prominent Brownsville, Texas, car dealer, probably killed himself while in bed—something Mowbray had claimed all along. (There had been a previous suicide attempt, and the victim was deeply depressed because his Cadillac dealership was under investigation by the IRS.) The prosecution had won a life sentence against Mowbray with bogus evidence of microscopic blood spatters on her nightgown; a report showing that there were no such blood spatters was kept hidden. Mowbray was eventually fully exonerated.

Thomas Thompson, convicted of the 1983 rape and murder of a Laguna Beach, California, woman, is spared thirty-six hours before execution by a divided Ninth Circuit Court of Appeals, which finds that the prosecution withheld evidence in the case and argued inconsistent versions of the crime at a codefendant's trial. The U.S. Supreme Court later restored Thompson's sentence in a strictly procedural ruling, finding that the appeals court had no standing to act in the case.

Tennessee Judge David W. Lanier flees to Mexico after being freed by an appeals court that ruled his federal conviction for civil rights offenses for raping five women in his chambers had to be overturned because there was "no general constitutional right to be free of sexual assaults." Justices on the Sixth Circuit Court of Appeals who decided the case joked about it during oral arguments, wondering aloud if they, too, could be charged with crimes for doing various things while wearing their judicial robes. The ruling was a veritable endorsement of prosecutorial and judicial misconduct, as the Tennessee authorities who would normally be responsible for prosecuting the sexual-assault charges had refused to rein in the serial-rapist judge—he was the brother of the local district attorney, who unsurprisingly declined to prosecute. In desperation, a little-used Civil War-era civil rights law had been employed to launch a federal prosecution, but the appeals court decided that being raped did not amount to a civil rights violation, even when done in chambers by a judge in the midst of litigating the victims' cases, and when local authorities knew about the judge's conduct and tolerated it. Apparently shocked by the appeals court's ruling, a unanimous U.S. Supreme Court reinstated the conviction and Lanier was eventually found hiding out in Mexico. He was returned to serve a twenty-five-year prison sentence.

Robert Lee Miller, sentenced to death in Oklahoma for the rape and murder of two elderly women in 1988, has charges against him dismissed by a judge who finds no evidence to justify Miller's incarceration. DNA evidence exonerated Miller and implicated another defendant already imprisoned for a similar crime—yet prosecutors sought to keep him in prison anyway and appealed the judge's ruling. (After another year of incarceration, prosecutors finally gave up and Miller was freed.)

Paris Carriger, after nineteen years on Arizona's death row for allegedly beating a man with a skillet and strangling him with a necktie during a jewelry-store robbery, is granted a new trial after evidence of prosecutorial misconduct and probable innocence arises. The prosecution kept secret extremely damaging information to their case, namely that their star witness was a habitual felon who had in the past tried to pin his crimes on others and who had been caught in numerous lies to the police. Prosecutors also hid the fact that this witness had boasted about framing Carriger and gloated over his ability to frame others, and that he told his stepson how gruesome it was to see someone's head crushed with a skillet—revealing details of the crime that only the killer could have known. During arguments at trial, the prosecutor vouched for the witness's credibility and nonviolent nature, though the government knew him to be both a liar and an extremely violent individual. (This same witness eventually confessed to the murder himself.) Carriger remained imprisoned while the State of Arizona appealed this ruling to the U.S. Supreme Court, arguing that it should still be able to execute Carriger and that any misconduct in the case was "harmless error." (In 1999, Carriger accepted a plea offer from prosecutors that set him free in exchange for pleading guilty to second-degree murder.)

In a case that drew national attention, Lisa Michelle Lambert is declared innocent by a federal judge after being sentenced in state court to life in prison for the throat-slashing murder of a sixteen-year-old romantic rival in Lancaster County, Pennsylvania. U.S. District Court Judge Stewart Dalzell, a Bush appointee known as a conservative, law-and-order jurist, proclaimed that Lambert was "the victim of wholesale prosecutorial misconduct," with all the key evidence against her either perjured, altered or fabricated. Dalzell, who looked into the case after Lambert's handwritten appeal landed on his desk, wrote that the misconduct that led to her conviction included "obstruction of justice, perjured police testimony, the wholesale suppression of exculpatory evidence and the fabrication of inculpatory evidence." Key to Lambert's conviction was testimony that the victim said "Michelle did it" as she died—which experts later said was impossible because of the damage to the victim's throat, nerves and arteries. Dalzell found that a detective on the case, who went on to become a local judge, fabricated evidence, witnesses' statements and a statement by Lambert, and that the county's senior prosecutor sought to have Lambert executed while he "knowingly used perjured testimony and presided over dozens of violations, may have committed perjury, and unquestionably violated the rules of professional conduct before our very eyes." (The reaction to the ruling was outrage—but against Dalzell, not the authorities in Lancaster County. Legislation was introduced in Washington to bar federal judges from dismissing cases like Lambert's in the future, an impeachment campaign was launched against Dalzell, a conservative group in Washington published a video falsely labeling Dalzell as a liberal activist appointee of President Clinton, and Lancaster County successfully appealed the ruling on a legal technicality—citing a law stating that a state court, rather than Dalzell, should have heard the allegations of misconduct. Lambert was returned to prison and forced to replead her evidence of misconduct before a lower court.)

A veteran gang prosecutor in San Diego is fired for acting unethically in handling confidential informants in a murder case and a conspiracy case, both of which had been reversed because of prosecutorial misconduct. Jemal Kasim had been convicted of hiring two men to injure a rival gang member, but was freed after it was learned that the prosecutor had secretly worked for leniency on behalf of a key witness while telling jurors that he planned to prosecute. A judge holding hearings on the matter concluded that the prosecutor had not been truthful on the witness stand about his actions in the case, and even the prosecutor's own boss accused him of withholding evidence from the defense. Another man, Jerauld Harrell, convicted of stabbing a rival gang member to death, was granted a new trial when it was revealed that, during a closed hearing with the judge on the case, the prosecutor proposed that witnesses deny under oath that one of them was an informant. A subsequent San Diego County Grand Jury report criticized the entire gang-prosecution unit for mishandling informants and thereby jeopardizing a host of criminal cases and convictions.

After nearly fourteen years in Alabama state prison, two brothers, Dale and Ronnie Mahan, are released and granted new trials after DNA tests show they had been wrongfully convicted of a 1983 rape and kidnapping. The prosecution's main witness— the rape victim—had lied about the source of semen found on her clothing after the rape. It belonged to a boyfriend she had never mentioned because she was married to another man at the time. The boyfriend, who defense attorneys now believe was the rapist, was subsequently killed in an unrelated confrontation with police in Mississippi. Despite the DNA tests and the victim's lies, prosecutors in Alabama announced that they intended to prosecute the Mahan brothers again in an attempt to return them to prison.

In Philadelphia, where nearly three hundred felony convictions were overturned because of police corruption, a new revelation threatens to overturn even more cases: a training video for young district attorneys, instructing them how to lie and how to keep minorities off juries. The tape was made by a prosecutor running for the post of district attorney. "You don't want those people on your jury," prosecutor Jack McMahon says on the video, describing his belief that young blacks are less likely to convict criminals. "The only way you're going to do your best is to get jurors that are unfair and more likely to convict than anybody else in that room." (McMahon lost the election.)

Because of misconduct by the Los Angeles County District Attorney's Office, former Black Panther Party leader Elmer "Geronimo" Pratt is released after spending twenty-five years in prison for a wrongful murder conviction. Prosecutors had concealed the fact that the key witness in the case was a government informant who was given money and allowed to carry guns even though he was a convicted felon. Prosecutors then let their witness lie about his role as an informant while testifying against Pratt. Other evidence surfaced, through the testimony of a retired FBI agent, that the FBI knew Pratt was in another city at the time of the murder, but kept silent because they were "at war" with the Black Panthers. The Los Angeles County District Attorney decided not to retry Pratt.

Texas Governor George W. Bush refuses to grant a pardon to Kevin James Byrd of Houston, who spent twelve years in prison for a rape that DNA testing later proved he could not have committed. Bush, who aspires to the presidency and relishes his tough-on-crime reputation, rejected the unanimous recommendation of the state board of pardons, as well as pleas from the judge who presided over Byrd's case and the prosecutors who convicted him, all of whom now say that Byrd is innocent. The victim in the case, who was raped while eight months pregnant, had originally told police that her assailant was white, but though Byrd is black, he was still convicted. Texas law does not allow new evidence to overturn convictions after more than thirty days, leaving a governor's pardon as Byrd's only way out. (Bush eventually relented and pardoned Byrd.)

The practice of police officers perjuring themselves in order to secure wrongful convictions in criminal cases—"testilying"— becomes so rampant in Boston that the chief judge for the Superior Court of Suffolk County creates a reporting system to refer all such cases for prosecution as they arise. The judge's move came after an embarrassing series of stories appeared in the *Boston Globe* that demonstrated the sometimes impossible testimony by police officers used to win convictions, often with prosecutors' acquiescence or active participation, along with the burying of evidence that could prove innocence. Even when caught testilying, officers were not disciplined or prosecuted in the past; one was even promoted. One man who spent six years in prison for attempting to murder a police officer, Christopher Harding, receives a new trial after his case is publicized in the *Globe* series; the judge hearing the case finds the Boston police "perpetrated a fraud on the court" by concealing the whereabouts of a police officer who could have exonerated Harding.

1998

After nearly a decade on death row, Shawn Hill of Los Angeles is freed from his conviction and death sentence, because of the gross misconduct of Los Angeles Deputy District Attorney Rosalie Morton, a seventy-four-year-old career prosecutor with a storied history punctuated with repeated allegations of prosecutorial misconduct. The California Supreme Court took the unusual step of naming Morton in its published opinion, accused her of conducting a "pervasive campaign to mislead the jury" during Hill's trial in a 1986 drug-robbery-and-murder case and of perpetrating "a mountain of deceit" in order to win. "Morton's actions, at times childish and unprofessional and at other times outrageous and unethical, betrayed her trust as a public prosecutor," the court wrote. "Her methods were deceptive and reprehensible." Morton was said to have misstated and mischaracterized evidence, told the jury information that was not in evidence, misstated the law and told "outright falsehoods." The court found that Morton's misconduct helped win Hill's conviction despite the testimony by two of three eyewitnesses who said Hill had not committed the murder. Morton had been cited for misconduct in three other criminal cases in the seventies and eighties, and a federal magistrate in 1989 had recommended she be disbarred for unethical conduct, though a judge rejected the recommendation. In addition, a 1977 opinion cited her for twenty transgressions during a robbery trial, including threatening to kick the defense lawyer in the ankle and hit him in the face. That conviction was upheld, however, and Morton was reported to have bragged about her performance in the case. Despite this history, Morton was not removed from prosecuting cases for her office until after the Hill decision was made public.

In the same week that it frees Shawn Hill, the California Supreme Court—known as a conservative body that upholds almost every capital conviction—reverses another death sentence, this time ordering a new trial for John Brown, convicted of killing a policeman in Garden Grove, California, in 1980, again because of prosecutorial misconduct. The prosecution failed to disclose a lab report that would have lent support to Brown's defense of diminished capacity. The supreme court ordered Brown to be retried or to have his conviction reduced to the non-capital offense of second-degree murder.

In the small town of Linden, Alabama (population 2,500), Goodloe Sutton, the editor of the *Democrat Reporter* newspaper, withstands death threats, advertising losses, subscription cancellations and other repercussions when he documents extortion, petty theft, drug trafficking, framing of innocents and other misconduct by the most powerful politician in the county, Sheriff Roger Davis. The case demonstrates the difficulty in reining in misconduct by law-enforcement officials. Sutton had complained for years to Alabama authorities, who ignored both his stories and the blatant corruption displayed by Davis's department, which enjoyed the support of powerful politicians throughout the state. Finally, federal authorities stepped in and prosecuted the sheriff and two of his men, including the county's chief drug-enforcement officer. Davis received a twenty-seven-year prison sentence after pleading guilty to extortion.

Five New York City police officers are indicted under federal civil rights statutes in a case that sparked national outrage—the alleged torture and sexual assault in a police station of Haitian immigrant Abner Louima, who was arrested outside a Brooklyn nightclub where a brawl had taken place. Louima was never charged with any offense. However, he required four operations to repair his ruptured bladder and colon from when the policemen sodomized him with a nightstick. A supervisor was indicted for allegedly lying under oath about the incident.

A study of the quality of government-appointed defense attorneys reveals that minimum-wage employees at McDonald's often make more money per hour of work than some states pay defense attorneys for the poor in murder cases. According to a study by the Southern Center for Human Rights in Atlanta, the maximum indigent-defense fee in Virginia, for example, is $265 for investigating, litigating and defending a felony charge that carries a punishment of twenty years or less; the fee rises to a maximum of $575 if the potential sentence exceeds twenty years. (By comparison, a top-flight criminal-defense attorney hired privately would earn more than that in one hour of trial in a murder case.) According to the study, an Alabama lawyer who spends five hundred hours preparing for a death-penalty trial will make $4 an hour. The study is replete with case histories of underpaid lawyers who slept through key portions of trials, appeared in court drunk or unprepared, or displayed complete ignorance of the law—and resulting convictions that were allowed to stand.

In Washington, Benjamin Harris is freed from his conviction and death sentence for the 1984 murder of Jimmie Turner. Harris maintained all along that he had been framed, but his attorney, in preparing for the capital case, only talked to his client for a mere two hours and interviewed but three of thirty-two witnesses. On appeal, Harris was granted a new trial because of his incompetent defense. (A codefendant, more ably represented, had been acquitted.) Prosecutors chose not to retry him, but, unwilling to give up, instead attempted to have him confined as insane despite previously arguing that he was sane enough to be tried for the murder. A jury heard the matter and ordered his release from a mental hospital.

Robert Hayes, convicted in Florida and sentenced to death for the rape and murder of a coworker, is exonerated at a second trial. He had been convicted on the basis of faulty DNA evidence presented by the prosecution, but was granted a new trial by the Florida Supreme Court. Prosecutors continued to press charges even though the victim was found clutching the hairs of her presumed attacker—which came from a white person. Hayes is black.

New York City police burst through the door of the home of Ellis Elliott of the Bronx, dragging him naked from bed into the hallway of his apartment building and then force him to sit there for an hour before finally bringing him women's clothing to wear to the police station. "You're nothing but an animal, nigger. You don't deserve any clothes," he recalls one officer telling him. The police had a warrant to search for drugs, and though they find none, Elliott is still hauled to jail and locked up overnight. Only then did the police realize that they had gone to the wrong apartment and arrested and humiliated an innocent man by mistake. They sent him home, still in women's clothes, where he found his apartment, minus a front door, filled with police officers watching television and helping themselves to the contents of his refrigerator. Another team of NYPD officers that same day did the same thing in a search for drugs at the apartment of Shaunsia Patterson, who was eight months pregnant and at home with her two young children and teenaged sister when police broke the door down. Once again, they had targeted the wrong apartment in the wrong building. The officers screamed obscenities and abuse at the pregnant woman, who was so terrified by the invading wave that she wet herself. Furniture was destroyed, flooring removed, the refrigerator was broken and Patterson was kept handcuffed in her soiled clothes for several hours. *New York Times* columnist Bob Herbert, who documented both incidents in successive newspaper columns, wrote, "It is difficult to overstate the terror that is provoked by these inherently dangerous commando-like raids on the premises of innocent people. It is the sort of thing you would expect from a totalitarian state, not the municipal government of a city like New York." The city has yet to offer an apology or compensation in either case.

The FBI reaches a $1 million settlement with whistleblower Frederic Whitehurst, who claimed to have been harassed and mistreated for revealing misconduct and shoddy work at the once-vaunted FBI crime laboratory. Under the terms of the settlement, Whitehurst will be given FBI reports and will set up a review panel to examine potential government misconduct in thousands of criminal cases in which the lab's work and analyses were critical tools for prosecutors. The cases range from mundane drug convictions to murders to the Oklahoma City bombing investigation.

Forty-four law-enforcement officers from five police agencies in and around Cleveland, Ohio, are charged with taking money to protect cocaine traffickers, hiring themselves out as security guards for criminals, trafficking in drugs themselves, covering up crimes, framing others for their own criminal acts, and other acts of corruption. Dozens of criminal cases handled by the officers were immediately called into question, raising fears of innocents wrongly convicted. The Cleveland case represents the latest in a series of police-corruption cases from around the nation, in which 509 officers in forty-seven cities have been convicted in federal courts in the past three years.

Murder charges are dropped for good against Earl Rhoney, convicted of a burglary-murder based solely on bloodhound evidence and an experimental "scent-machine," which was supposed to have extracted the killer's scent from the murder victim's clothing. The Orange County, California, judge who overturned Rhoney's conviction—and then left office to become district attorney—found that the bias of the bloodhound's handler more than likely led the dog to choose Rhoney, and subsequent rulings have called into question the reliability of the scent machine. Nineteen at the time of his arrest and conviction, Rhoney spent two years imprisoned before being released.

At age fifty-two, Marilynn Malcom, owner of the Rainbow Christian Day Care Center in Vancouver, Washington, remains in prison despite overwhelming evidence that the massive 1986 ritual-abuse case against her was false. The children questioned by authorities denied being molested, but as has happened so often in similar cases, relentless interrogation led to tales of ritual abuse. The prosecutor on the case ignored the bizarre and disprovable allegations and used only the more conventional allegations of sex abuse as evidence, winning his case. The medical evidence introduced at trial to show the children had been sexually penetrated has since been shown to be false. Yet, so far, Malcom has lost all her appeals.

In Wenatchee, Washington, where claims that a ring of forty-three adults abused sixty children have torn the town and led to sweeping allegations of official and investigative misconduct, two of the key convictions in the case are reversed on appeal, freeing Mark and Carol Doggett from eleven-year prison sentences. The Doggetts had sought help from child-protection officials when they learned that their adolescent son and daughter had been having consensual sex. Questioning the teens in the midst of the town's high-pressure molestation-ring investigation, therapists soon elicited accusations that the teens' parents were molesters. The appeals court that overturned the convictions criticized the now-familiar technique of using suggestive and coercive questioning to produce allegations of abuse from children. The chief detective on the case used his own foster daughter to build many of the cases; she later recanted and accused him of coercing her. Throughout the massive Wenatchee case, allegations have surfaced describing coercion, threats from the police detectives and threats against any officials who failed to support the investigation. Indigent defendants were persuaded to plead guilty; those who could afford private lawyers—twenty-six—have been exonerated. Numerous lawsuits are pending and other convictions have been overturned or charges dismissed.

In another notorious molestation-ring case, Cheryl Amirault LeFave, convicted a decade earlier with her brother and mother in the Fells Acres Daycare Center case in Cambridge, Massachusetts, is granted a new trial and freed by Middlesex County Judge Isaac Borenstein, who found that investigators used such improper and suggestive techniques to interview children that the testimony was "forever tainted." Secret rooms, magic clowns and other preposterous tales peppered the children's accounts, while repeated denials of molestation were ignored during the initial investigation. Those children who said nothing happened were simply labeled "Not ready to disclose," so certain were investigators that abuse had taken place. The investigation began when a child told an uncle that Gerald "Tooky" Amirault, LeFave's brother, pulled the child's pants down. Assuming that molestation had occurred, no one bothered to question the child further as to why Amirault had done that. (It turns out, as the boy said much later, that Amirault simply was changing the boy's diaper after he had wet himself during nap time.) Medical evidence of abuse was introduced to prove vaginal and anal penetration; this evidence has since been proven false. While LeFave was released, her brother remains in prison on a thirty-year sentence, though the evidence against him is identically flawed. Their mother, Violet Amirault, imprisoned for eight years before being released on appeal, died at age seventy-four before she could be cleared. The judge who released LeFave exonerated Violet Amirault posthumously.

Because of an illegal search by government investigators, an otherwise valid fraud case against a Los Angeles–area defense contractor accused of selling shoddy electrical parts for fighters, missiles, the space shuttle and the as-yet unfinished International Space Station is dismissed by a federal judge. Because of the misconduct involved—defense department investigators read privileged memos between attorneys and clients outlining defense trial strategy and evidence—U.S. District Court Judge Robert M. Takasugi of Los Angeles rules that the charges cannot be re-filed against Solid State Devices, Inc., of La Mirada.

When two boys, ages seven and eight, were arrested in Chicago for the brutal murder of eleven-year-old Ryan Harris—supposedly so the boys could take her bicycle—a national uproar ensued, in which lawmakers, pundits and many members of the general public expressed revulsion at the fact that children so young could not be tried as adults and sentenced to life in prison for even the most heinous crimes. Lawmakers in Illinois and in other states rushed to introduce legislation to allow adult punishments for the very young because of the Harris murder. The boys were said to have confessed, and the case against them was characterized as ironclad. A month later, however, the Chicago police are forced to admit that, because of the discovery of semen on the victim's clothes, a culprit older than the prepubescent pair must have committed the crime. Amid admissions that investigators turned a blind eye to several other pieces of evidence that suggested the crime was committed by an adult sex offender, the boys are released. Their confessions, taken outside the presence of the boys' family, social workers or lawyers had, apparently, been coerced—along with their supposed waivers of their Miranda rights. The department also reveals that the same interrogating officer involved in the Harris confessions had four years earlier coaxed a strikingly similar confession from an eleven-year-old boy accused of murder—an alleged confession that led to his conviction despite the fact that a bloody palm print and footprint at the murder scene were not his. (That case is now the subject of a civil rights lawsuit.) In the end, the primary fallout from the mistaken arrest has been growing support for a requirement that the police videotape all such confessions in the future—something the Chicago Police Department has long resisted.

After a mere five hours of deliberation, V. James Landano is acquitted of murdering a Newark police officer twenty-two years ago. Originally convicted of the crime and sentenced to life in prison in 1977, he spent twelve years behind bars before he was granted a new trial because the prosecutor hid evidence of two witnesses to the crime who said Landano did not look like the killer.

In July, the United States Court of Appeals for the 10th Circuit in Denver sends shock waves through the justice system by declaring plea bargains in which leniency is traded for testimony to be a form of bribery. The decision outlaws a prosecutorial practice observed on a nearly daily basis for decades—one that appears in both mundane cases such as Pat Dunn's and some of the most high-profile cases in the country, from the prosecution of major Mafia figures to the conviction of former Panamanian President Manual Noriega to the failed impeachment case brought by Kenneth Starr against President Clinton. The court found that offering immunity or release from prison in exchange for testimony violates the federal bribery law—on the books for many years but long ignored. The law states that "whoever" offers "anything of value to any person" for testimony commits a crime—seemingly unambiguous wording that sounds as if it should apply to anyone, even government officials. Were a defense attorney to offer, for example, free legal services in exchange for favorable testimony, that lawyer would be guilty of bribery—and the resulting testimony would be untrustworthy. The appeals court, for the first time, said the same standard must apply to prosecutors, and that buying witnesses with freedom from prison led to suspect results. Choosing a mundane drug case to make its point, the court wrote, "The judicial process is tainted and justice cheapened when factual testimony is purchased, whether with leniency or money." The Justice Department immediately objected, saying the ruling would make criminals out of every federal prosecutor in the country. The far-reaching decision, issued by a three-judge panel of the appeals court, was later rescinded and nullified by the full twelve-member court within a matter of days.

Two Reno, Nevada, men serving life sentences since 1990 for child molestation are exonerated and released after their alleged victim told a judge that he had been forced to fabricate his testimony against them by his mother. He said his mother had locked him up and starved him until he agreed to implicate his own father and another man. The testimony by the then-nine-year-old boy had always sounded incredible—allegations that his father and a coworker sexually assaulted him fifty times a night, and that he had been taken to satanic rituals in an underground cavern near the Mustang Ranch, a legal brothel. But, as in so many other such cases, the obvious problems with his testimony were not taken into consideration until the boy, now seventeen, recanted. A judge then overturned the convictions and prosecutors agreed to drop charges rather than seek a retrial.

1999

Anthony Porter, imprisoned on death row for sixteen years for the double murder of a Chicago couple in 1982, is freed and exonerated when another man is implicated in the crime. Northwestern University Professor David Protess and his journalism class investigated the case, found key prosecution witnesses who recanted their testimony—one of whom claimed to have been pressured by authorities to incriminate Porter—and produced a videotape of a new suspect confessing to the crime (while maintaining he killed in self-defense). The new suspect has since been charged with the murders. Porter, who has an IQ of 51, came within two days of being executed, but was spared because a judge questioned his mental competence (raising the possibility that, had he been of normal intelligence, Porter would have been executed before Protess and his class uncovered the new evidence in the case). Porter is the sixth convict to be freed from death row and declared innocent through the work of Protess and his class.

Steven Smith, convicted and sentenced to death for the 1985 murder of an assistant prison warden outside a Chicago tavern, is freed when the Illinois Supreme Court found prosecutors had won their conviction despite having insufficient evidence that Smith was the actual killer. "When the state cannot meet its burden of proof, the defendant must go free," the court ruled. The ruling was somewhat unusual in that appeals focusing on the sufficiency of the evidence in a case, rather than on legal flaws in trial, rarely succeed.

Shareef Cousin, sentenced to death at age sixteen in Louisiana, is exonerated of the murder charge against him because prosecutors used improper evidence to win his conviction. Prosecutors subsequently dropped the case against Cousin, whose basketball coach had provided an alibi for the time of the murder.

Twenty-six criminal cases against black and Hispanic motorists, all investigated by the same two New Jersey state troopers, grind to a halt when a state probe produces evidence that the troopers had planted and falsified evidence in a number of the cases.

The Florida Supreme Court issues an unprecedented warning to state prosecutors, calling for a halt to the prosecutorial misconduct it was seeing with "unacceptable frequency" in capital cases. If prosecutors fail to observe ethical and legal restraints in the future, despite repeated admonitions from the high court, new laws might have to be carved out by the court to punish prosecutors in future cases, the state justices warned. In freeing a Tampa man, Walter Ruiz, from a death sentence for a 1995 murder, the high court wrote that his trial was "permeated by egregious and inexcusable prosecutorial misconduct." The court listed six other cases it was forced to reverse in recent years because of the misbehavior of prosecutors.

New Orleans District Attorney Harry Connick calls for a grand jury investigation of his own office after revelations that critical evidence of innocence involving a man scheduled to be executed in two weeks had been hidden by his own deputy prosecutors for years. John Thompson had been convicted in two separate trials, first for armed robbery, then for murder. The armed robbery conviction had been used by prosecutors to win the death penalty in the murder case. Newly disclosed blood evidence—known to prosecutors for fourteen years—points to a different suspect in the armed robbery.

In New York, John Duval is released from prison after twenty-six years for an armed robbery and murder in which a key eyewitness—kept jailed for seven months until he testified against Duval—had originally said he never saw Duval at the crime scene. The police report detailing the witness's original story was kept hidden from defense, judge and jury.

Two days after John Duval was freed, two men in Oklahoma, Dennis Fritz and Ronald Williamson, are released and exonerated after twelve years for a rape and murder case that had devastated their small town of Ada, Oklahoma, in 1982. The case had gone unsolved for five years before prosecutors used bogus scientific analyses to link the two men—a junior high-school science teacher and a minor-league ball player—to hair samples found at the crime scene and on the body of the twenty-one-year-old murder victim. The men were also convicted with the help of a jailhouse informant, who received leniency in exchange for his testimony against the two men. In a bizarre twist, DNA testing done this year not only exonerated Fritz and Williamson but implicated the prosecution informant as the actual rapist and murderer. The testing was done at the urging of lawyers representing Fritz, who was serving a life sentence. Testing was opposed by prosecutors as a waste of time. Williamson got lucky—his appeals had been exhausted and, at one point, he was five days away from execution. His sister had been called and told to make funeral arrangements.

On April 19, the "Citizen's Protection Act" becomes law—legislation cosponsored by a conservative Republican congressman concerned about prosecutorial misconduct and wrongful convictions at the federal level. The act, vigorously opposed by the U.S. Justice Department, requires federal prosecutors to follow the local ethical rules in the states in which they practice—just as every other lawyer must. Justice Department officials and their legislative allies—including the powerful Judiciary Committee chairman, Senator Orrin Hatch of Utah—fought the legislation, saying the seemingly commonsense notion that prosecutors, like other lawyers, must adhere to ethical regulations, would hamstring the war on crime. They succeeded in killing many of the bill's original provisions, but its core requirement on ethics passed as a rider to a budget bill. An unprecedented attempt to reign in prosecutorial misconduct, the law nevertheless had limited impact in that it affects only federal prosecutors. The majority of criminal prosecutions—and prosecutorial misconduct—occurs at the state and local level, where the Citizen Protection Act has no authority.

Allegations of misconduct, improper leaks and abuse of power are raised against Whitewater Special Prosecutor Kenneth Starr during his epic confrontation with President Bill Clinton. The nation's best-known prosecutor and investigator of high-level wrongdoing, Starr himself comes under investigation for allegedly leaking secret grand jury information to the press, and for secret payments allegedly made to a witness who offered testimony against the president. Starr's tactics also come under attack in the prosecution of presidential friend Susan McDougal and defense witness Julie Steele, both of whom accused Starr of using his power to attempt to persuade them to lie, then prosecuting them when they refused. (McDougal was subsequently acquitted of criminal contempt, and Steele's jury could not reach a verdict.) Starr was also criticized when he subpoenaed presidential aide Sidney Blumenthal before the grand jury to question him about his comments to the press about two of Starr's assistants (the comments concerned past allegations of prosecutorial misconduct lodged against the assistants). Starr asserted that Blumenthal—and anyone else who publicly criticizes the special prosecutor in a fashion Starr considers inaccurate—could be guilty of obstruction of justice, a notion many journalistic and legal observers condemn. Ken Starr, more than any public figure or criminal case has ever done in the past, has made the general public aware of the sweeping power prosecutors possess in contemporary America: how a prosecutor often answers to no authority but his own conscience and sense of duty; how he may remain unbowed even before the President of the United States; and how the grand juries he convenes have become his tools rather than the checks and balances envisioned by the Founding Fathers. What is not as abundantly clear to the public is the fact that Starr's extraordinary powers and absence of accountability are in large part shared by every local, county, state and federal prosecutor in America.